SEMANTICS OF NATURAL LANGUAGE

W9-BUB-882

SYNTHESE LIBRARY

MONOGRAPHS ON EPISTEMOLOGY,

LOGIC, METHODOLOGY, PHILOSOPHY OF SCIENCE,

SOCIOLOGY OF SCIENCE AND OF KNOWLEDGE,

AND ON THE MATHEMATICAL METHODS OF

SOCIAL AND BEHAVIORAL SCIENCES

Editors:

DONALD DAVIDSON, *The Rockefeller University and Princeton University*

JAAKKO HINTIKKA, *Academy of Finland and Stanford University*

GABRIËL NUCHELMANS, *University of Leyden*

WESLEY C. SALMON, *Indiana University*

SEMANTICS OF
NATURAL LANGUAGE

Edited by

DONALD DAVIDSON

The Rockefeller University and Princeton University

and

GILBERT HARMAN

Princeton University

SECOND EDITION

D. REIDEL PUBLISHING COMPANY

DORDRECHT-HOLLAND/BOSTON-U.S.A.

Library of Congress Catalog Card Number 73–76427

ISBN 90 277 0310 8

Published by D. Reidel Publishing Company,
P.O. Box 17, Dordrecht, Holland

Sold and distributed in the U.S.A., Canada, and Mexico
by D. Reidel Publishing Company, Inc.
306 Dartmouth Street, Boston
Mass. 02116, U.S.A.

Printed in The Netherlands by D. Reidel, Dordrecht

PREFACE

The idea that prompted the conference for which many of these papers were written, and that inspired this book, is stated in the Editorial Introduction reprinted below from Volume **21** of *Synthese*.

The present volume contains the articles in *Synthese* **21**, Numbers 3–4 and *Synthese* **22**, Numbers 1–2. In addition, it includes new papers by Saul Kripke, James McCawley, John R. Ross, and Paul Ziff, and reprints 'Grammar and Philosophy' by P. F. Strawson. Strawson's article first appeared in the *Proceedings of the Aristotelian Society*, Volume **70**, and is reprinted with the kind permission of the author and the Aristotelian Society. We also repeat our thanks to the Olivetti Company and Edizione di Comunità of Milan for permission to include the paper by Dana Scott; it also appeared in *Synthese* **21**.

DONALD DAVIDSON

GILBERT HARMAN

EDITORIAL INTRODUCTION

The success of linguistics in treating natural languages as formal syntactic systems has aroused the interest of a number of linguists in a parallel or related development of semantics. For the most part quite independently, many philosophers and logicians have recently been applying formal semantic methods to structures increasingly like natural languages. While differences in training, method and vocabulary tend to veil the fact, philosophers and linguists are converging, it seems, on a common set of interrelated problems.

Since philosophers and linguists are working on the same, or very similar, problems, it would obviously be instructive to compare notes. Inspired by this thought, we organized a small working conference on the semantics of natural language in August of 1969. The conference was sponsored by the Council for Philosophical Studies, and supported by the Council and the National Science Foundation. The Center for Advanced Study in the Behavioral Sciences in Stanford, California supplied a noble setting for our talks, and lent its efficient and friendly help in other ways.

A number of the papers in this volume spring from talks given at that summer conference, or were written by people who were there; the rest are by people we wish could have been there. The purpose of the volume is the same as that of the conference: to encourage the active exchange of ideas among logicians, philosophers and linguists who are working on semantics for natural languages. We trust it will be agreed that there is more to this than the usual business of rubbing two or more disciplines together in the expectation of heat and the hope of light. In the present case, a common enterprise already exists; our aim is to make it a cooperative one.

DONALD DAVIDSON

GILBERT HARMAN

TABLE OF CONTENTS

CHARLES J. FILLMORE

SUBJECTS, SPEAKERS, AND ROLES

1. This report is a record of issues in the semantics of natural languages that have concerned me in the past few years, some of the things I have had to say about them, and some of the things that others have had to say about them. There is nothing new in these pages, and there is much that is borrowed. I use numbered paragraphs mostly to create favorable associations – but also to make it obvious that I do not expect the reader to perceive here any structure beyond that of sheer sequence.

2. The traditional first task of sentence analysis has been that of understanding and recognizing the highest-level division in a sentence, that between its *subject* and its *predicate*. On the traditional account, the subject of a sentence is that portion of it which indicates 'the person or thing about whom or which a statement is made or a question asked', and its predicate is that portion of the sentence which contains 'the statement or the question asked'.

3. In formal grammars of the type first discussed by Chomsky, the subject/ predicate distinction is captured in terms of *labeled co-constituents* of sentences. The two major co-constituents of a sentence are a nounphrase (NP) and a verbphrase (VP). A NP that is an immediate constituent of a sentence is defined as its subject; a VP that is an immediate constituent of a sentence is its predicate.[1] We may refer to this as the *configurational* definition of subjects and predicates.

4. In theories of grammar that derive from the work of Chomsky, a distinction is made between the *deep structure* of a sentence and its *surface structure*. Since both the deep structure and the surface structure are capable of having major co-constituents of the same types, and since the entities so identified may be different in the deep and surface representations of the same sentence, it is necessary to speak of both deep structure and surface structure subjects and predicates.

Davidson and Harman (eds.), Semantics of Natural Language, 1–24. All rights reserved
Copyright © 1972 by D. Reidel Publishing Company, Dordrecht-Holland

5. It is of concern, therefore, whether the traditional account of the subject/predicate distinction applies to the distinction as it is defined for the surface structure or the deep structure level. Something akin to the traditional distinction is apparent in the surface structure of some sentences. On the interpretation that the passive transformation in English is meaning-preserving, it can be said that sentences (5-a) and (5-b) differ only in the identification of one or another NP as subject.

    (5-a)   Pianists play pianos.
    (5-b)   Pianos are played by pianists.

There are arguments for saying, however, that while (5-a) is 'analytic', (5-b) is 'synthetic'. Such claims might be made for the interpretation that (5-a) is a general statement *about pianists* and that (5-b) is a general statement *about pianos*.

6. It might be argued that either of the sentences in (5) can in fact be interpreted in either of the two mentioned ways. If that is so, then it follows that the traditional account of the semantic relevance of the subject/predicate distinction cannot be captured by the configurational definition at all, on either the deep or the surface structure level, unless grammatical description is a good deal more subtle and abstract than grammarians have thought.

7. The transformations which link deep structures with surface structures are taken, in the standard theory, to have in themselves no semantic import. It has therefore been assumed that the semantic relevance of the subject/predicate distinction should be sought only in the deep structure.

8. However, the semantic role of deep-structure subjects appears not to be univocal, at least when we look for the role of this entity in the most straightforward way. The involvement of the entity named by the subject NP in the event or situation described by the sentences given below appears to be quite different in each case.

    (8-a)   The boy slapped the girl.
    (8-b)   The boy fell down.
    (8-c)   The boy received a blow.

(8-d)   The boy has a toothache.
(8-e)   The boy has blue eyes.
(8-f)   The boy [=his appearance] shocked me.

In order for a semantic theory to relate THE BOY to the predicate expression found in each of these sentences, reference must of course be made to the 'subject' NP; but there appears to be no common notional property of 'subjectness' which semantic descriptions of these sentences can exploit.

9. A commitment to the view that 'subjects' defined in the configurational way must be relevant to semantic descriptions has led to two varieties of re-analysis. The first is mentioned in Sections (10)–(14), the second, briefly, in (15).

10. Though it may not be possible to find a single semantic contribution for the subject role with all types of predicate expressions, it may at least be possible to find a unique subject role for each predicate word, or, better, for each type of predicate word. There is a group of verbs in English which have both transitive and intransitive uses and which show the same NP role with respect to the subject in their intransitive uses as they do with respect to the direct object in their transitive uses. Typical examples can be constructed with movement-verbs like ROTATE or change-of-state verbs like BREAK.

(10-a)   The cylinder rotated.
(10-b)   Fred rotated the cylinder.
(10-c)   The lens broke.
(10-d)   Fred broke the lens.

11. According to one attractive and popular proposal for capturing facts of the sort exhibited by the sentences in (10), the transitive sentences contain, in their deep structures, the intransitive sentences embedded to the verb CAUSE.[2] In each case the subject of the underlying verb CAUSE is the subject of the transitive sentence; the analysis interprets the sentence as representing the proposition that the entity identified by the subject NP of CAUSE is causer of an event characterized by the intransitive sentence. The sentences (10-b) and (10-d) can be thought of as having in their deep structure something of the sort suggested by (11-a) and (11-b) below:

(11-a)   Fred cause (the cylinder rotate).
(11-b)   Fred cause (the lens break).

[I ignore here the problem of tenses.] On this analysis, the relation between the verb (ROTATE or BREAK) and its *underlying subject* is the same in both its (surface) transitive and intransitive uses. The appearance of these underlyingly intransitive verbs in transitive-verb positions is a matter of surface detail.

12. The cases presented in (11) show a reconstruction that gives a unique subject/verb relationship for different 'uses' of the *same* verb. By allowing the relation between deep and surface structures to be more abstract still, it is possible to show semantic relations between two *different* verbs in a way that will reveal their underlying semantic commonalities; and, in particular for our purposes, will show that, for the given verb pairs, the role of the deep-structure subject is the same in both cases. Thus the deep structures of (12-a) and (12-c) are something like what is suggested by (12-b) and (12-d) respectively.

(12-a)   Peter killed the cat.
(12-b)   Peter cause (the cat die).
(12-c)   Peter put the beer in the icebox.
(12-d)   Peter cause (the beer be in the icebox).

The replacement of CAUSE TO DIE by KILL and CAUSE TO BE by PUT is, again, a matter of surface detail.

13. One might object to the semantic equivalence of (12-a) and (12-b) on the grounds that (13-a) and (13-b) are not exact paraphrases.

(13-a)   Peter killed the cat in the attic.
(13-b)   Peter caused the cat to die in the attic.

This objection is not critical, because it is quite possible to constrain the replacement by KILL of CAUSE TO DIE to only those situations in which the interior sentence has no adverbial modification. The locative phrase IN THE ATTIC, in (13-a), can only refer to the place where the causing took place.

14. Apparent difficulties of the sort mentioned in (13) are counter-

balanced by the advantages that this reanalysis offers in sentences like
(14-a) below:

(14-a)   Peter put the beer in the icebox for three hours.

The complex sentence analysis makes intelligible the occurrence in this
sentence of an adverbial of time duration (FOR THREE HOURS), an adverb
which cannot be construed as qualifying the action which Peter performed,
but only the situation of the beer's being in the icebox. Efforts which
consider semantically complex verbs as inserted pretransformationally
are required to say of verbs like PUT that they are used in referring to
actions which have resulting *states* and that they tolerate adverbial
modification of either the preceding action or the resulting state, but
not (presumably) both. Observe (14-b).

(14-b)   *Peter instantly put the beer in the icebox for three hours.

15. Certain researchers continue to seek a univocal interpretation to the
deep structure NP for all cases in which it occurs. These workers are
required to assign the agentive or causing role to the deep structure
subject, and then to interpret all sentences which fail to contain a NP
that has this semantic role as sentences which have no deep structure
subject whatever.[3] I will not say more of this approach, since I do not
consider it distinct – with respect to the agent' role – from an approach
which assigns 'roles' to NPs explicitly.

16. The second grammatical function of NPs which is defined configura-
tionally within the standard theory is that of the direct object. On the
traditional account, the role of the direct object in a sentence is that of
'patient' of the action referred to by the verb of the sentence, though
deviations from this have long been understood and classified. By its
configurational definition, the object NP is identified as that NP which
is an immediate constituent of the main VP of the sentence. That the
direct object relation is not semantically univocal can be seen in the
following sentences:

(16-a)   I smashed the pumpkin.
(16-b)   I grew the pumpkin.
(16-c)   I like the pumpkin.

(16-d)   I imagined the pumpkin.

(16-e)   I made the pumpkin into a mask.

(16-f)   I made a mask out of the pumpkin.

17. Defenses of the underlying univocality of the semantic role of the direct object can be pursued in the same style as those dealing with sentence subjects.

18. It would seem, however, that linguistic theory ought to provide some way of distinguishing (i) the semantic roles which NPs have with respect to their predicate words, from (ii) facts about their positions in syntactic configurations, on either deep or surface structure levels. In some of my work I have tried to show how this could be done.

19. Certain verbs and adjectives seem to require inherently a given number of NPs in the sentences in which they take part. Another way of saying this is that certain verbs and adjectives seem quite naturally to be reconstructible as n-place predicates in formulations within the predicate calculus. In descriptions of logical n-place predicates, there is no special status by which one or another of the arguments can be isolated from the rest, a status that would correspond to the role of subject or object. The relation between unstructured (but, of course, ordered) n-place predicate expressions and syntactic configurations appears to require the positing of certain mechanical correspondence rules which will make use of the left-to-right position of the arguments in the predicate expression.

20. For example, the verb REMIND – as seen in that sense of (20-a)

(20-a)   Harriet reminded Fred of Charlotte

according to which Fred, on encountering Harriet, thought of Charlotte – can be viewed at the semantic level as a three-place predicate, representable [ignoring tenses again] as (20-b)

(20-b)   remind [Harriet, Fred, Charlotte],

a representation which is subject to the following syntactic configuration rules; the NP which identifies the first argument assumes the subject position; the NP which identifies the second argument assumes the direct object position; and (a special rule) the NP which identifies the third argument becomes part of a preposition-phrase which begins with OF.

21. Assuming that the underlying semantic predicates have their argument slots arranged in a fixed order, one can define *converse* relations between predicates in terms of their underlying expressions. Thus, the pair LIKE/PLEASE will be defined as 1-2 converses; the pair SELL/BUY will be defined as 1-3 converses; the pair ROB/STEAL will be defined as 2-3 converses.

(21-a) John likes roses;
(21-b) roses please John;
(21-c) like $[a, b] =_{df}$ please $[b, a]$;
(21-d) John sells roses to schoolgirls;
(21-e) schoolgirls buy roses from John;
(21-f) sell $[a, b, c] =_{df}$ buy $[c, b, a]$;
(21-g) Harvey robs John of roses;
(21-h) Harvey steals roses from John;
(21-i) rob $[a, b, c] =_{df}$ steal $[a, c, b]$.

22. Unfortunately, the method just proposed requires that each converse pair be separately identified, for each language, by some defining expression like (21-c), (21-f), or (21-i). It is assuredly reasonable to demand of a semantic theory that observed converse relations among predicate words in natural languages be *explainable* from their meanings and their syntactic properties, not that they need to be stated by a set of *definitions*. For two expressions to be converses of each other is a surface syntactic fact; the description of this situation should not depend on prior definitions made on underlying semantic representations.

23. One type of theory that would allow such explanations would require that all surface converse pairs have the same ordering of arguments in their underlying representation, and that special rules for subjectivalization and objectivalization be defined for one member of each such pair. The 'explanation' of the relation is that one member of the pair represents an irregularity in the grammar with respect to the subjectivalization and objectivalization rules.

24. A second approach is one which presents, with each underlying

predicate expression, an unordered set of argument slots, each of which is labeled according to its semantic role (or 'case' relationship) with the predicate word. It is this last position that I have taken.[4]

25. One finds that a decision to speak of predicates, arguments and role types, rather than predicates, arguments and positions, makes it possible to provide a sharp separation between what I take to be purely syntactic phenomena – the left-to-right positioning of elements in the flow of speech – and facts about semantic interpretation. Two phonologically distinct predicate words may be interpreted as being semantically identical, having the same number of arguments in the same roles, but differing solely in the processes which arrange their elements into syntactic configurations. Each member of such pairs as BUY/SELL, TEACH/LEARN, SEND/RECEIVE, etc., 'take' essentially the same argument types, in the same roles, but they differ as to the role identification of the argument whose name or description becomes its *subject*.

26. Such an explanation is not in itself fully satisfactory, however. It is quite frequently the case that differences in subject selection properties (independently of the formation of passive sentences) are correlated with other kinds of facts about predicate words. Two semantically similar predicate words may differ, for example, in the optionality of the surface manifestations of certain of their arguments. In expressions containing SELL, for example, it is not necessary to include a NP that mentions the 'customer'; thus (26-a) is a syntactically complete sentence.

 (26-a) Harvey sells shoes.

In expressions containing BUY, it is not necessary to include a NP that mentions the 'merchant'; thus (26-b) is a syntactically complete sentence.

 (26-b) The girl bought some shoes.

Similarly, expressions containing ROB may lack overt mention of the 'loot', just as expressions containing STEAL may lack overt mention of the 'victim', as is seen in the syntactically complete sentences (26-c) and (26-d)

 (26-c) the boy robbed a bank;
 (26-d) the girl stole some shoes.

27. The view which recognized labeled roles for the arguments of a predicate expression makes it possible, furthermore, to speak of the relatedness of predicates having different numbers of terms. Two verbs can differ in that one manifests an n-place predicate and the other manifests an m-place predicate, the roles of the arguments that are present in the one and absent in the other accounting for the differences in the semantic interpretation of the sentences which contain them. This way of speaking provides a fairly natural way of speaking of the relationship between KILL and DIE, or that between PERSUADE and BELIEVE. The role by which KILL differs from DIE, and that by which PERSUADE differs from BELIEVE is that of the individual that is 'agentively' involved in the events named by these verbs. Apart from this difference, we are dealing here with pairs of synonyms.

28. (It has been maintained that the relation between words like these is more revealingly captured by the paraphrases with CAUSE like those mentioned in (10)–(14) above. The question is whether this reformulation is indeed significantly closer to the underlying conceptual reality to justify claims that have been made about the non-distinctness of semantic representations and deep structures of sentences. The word CAUSE itself seems to have a substructure: to say that John caused the cat to die is to say that John engaged in some activity and that activity directly resulted in the death of the cat.)

29. Anyway, the view which separates semantic roles from grammatical functions as sharply as this proposed role-structure analysis does, makes it possible to explore, as a *separate* type of inquiry, the function of the subject/predicate division. There might be some difference between reasons for choosing the verb BUY as opposed to the verb SELL, independently of the optional omissions mentioned in (26).

30. The verbs BUY and SELL refer to institutionalized interpersonal activities involving two participating parties, a sum of money, and goods or services that are to be provided for one of the participants by the other. There are no situations that can in themselves be distinguished as buying situations or selling situations; but the choice of one or another of these verbs seems to make it possible to speak of a buying/selling transaction

from one of the participant's point of view. One of the reasons for providing this distinction is to make it possible to determine the scope of modification of certain kinds of adverbs added to the sentence. I refer to the difference we sense, with regard to the scope of SKILLFULLY, in (30-a) and (30-b).

(30-a)   He sells apples skillfully.
(30-b)   She buys apples skillfully.

31. It even appears that there is a difference between the processes for determining the scope of adverbial modification and the processes which determine the deep-structure subject as distinct from the surface-structure subject. This can be seen by comparing sentences (31-a) and (31-b), where VICIOUSLY in both cases related to Harvey's participation in the act, with sentences (31-c) and (31-d), where WILLINGLY in both cases relates to the participation in the act of the individual indicated by the surface subject NP.

(31-a)   Harvey viciously took advantage of Melissa.
(31-b)   Melissa was viciously taken advantage of by Harvey.
(31-c)   Harvey willingly took advantage of Melissa.
(31-d)   Melissa was willingly taken advantage of by Harvey.

32. The proposal hinted at in (31) suggests that there is some validity to the notion deep-structure subject; but the facts are not really that decisive. It may appear instead that certain adverbs may be introduced into a sentence as ways of qualifying one participant's role in the activity, the identity of that individual being recognized by the associated role type (Experiencer, Agent, etc.). Thus, Manner adverbs of the type VICIOUSLY may appear only in sentences having underlying Agents, the scope of the adverb being unaffected by the ultimate choice of surface subject. Postal has noticed that the adverb PERSONALLY occurs only in sentences with subjective experience verbs and in connection with the NP identified as the Experiencer – again independently of whether this NP is or is not the sentence subject.[5] Examples like his are given below:

(32-a)   personally, I don't like roses;
(32-b) ˙ your proposal doesn't interest me, personally;
(32-c)   *personally, you hit me;
(32-d)   *personally, ontogeny recapitulates phylogeny.

33. A theory which separates information about grammatical configurations from information about the nature of the underlying semantic relations must find some way of dealing with the so-called symmetric predicates. It should be possible, at some level, one might think, to say of verbs like MEET, COINCIDE, AGREE, etc., that they require expressions referring to two or more entities, but such expressions may appear in any of the several ways provided by English grammar: as plural subjects, as in (33-a); as conjoined subjects, as in (33-b); or as paired NPs arranged in different (depending on the verb) syntactic configurations, as in (33-c), and (33-d).

(33-a)   The boys met/agreed.
(33-b)   John and Fred met/agreed.
(33-c)   John met Fred.
(33-d)   John agreed with Fred.

It must be agreed that no theory of grammar should be constrained in such a way that it has to recognize two different verbs MEET, two different verbs AGREE, etc., in order to distinguish the intransitive from the non-intransitive use of these forms.

34. This means recognizing, for some *n*-place predicates, that they 'take' two or more NPs in *identical* roles; but the main insights that have come from 'case grammar' or the theory of semantic role structure have depended on the assumption that no simple sentence requires the occurrence of more than one NP in a given role.

35. There do seem to be some differences in the conjoined subject as opposed to the distributed NP versions of symmetric predicate sentences, but for many of these the difference does not need to be seen as basic. We may consider again the effect of adverbial modification, once again taking the adverb WILLINGLY.

(35-a)   John and Fred willingly agree.
(35-b)   John willingly agrees with Fred [not a paraphrase of (35-a)].
(35-c)   John and Fred fought with heated mud.
(35-d)   John fought Fred with heated mud[not a paraphrase of (35-c)].

36. For the examples in (35), the answer seems to bear on the procedure

by which adverbs of various kinds are to be introduced into sentences. It may be the case that in the symmetric-predicate sentence itself, there is no necessary semantic difference that accompanies one subject choice or the other. Once a choice has been made, however, the sentence is limited as to the embedding context which will welcome it. Thus, sentence (36-a) requires the 'transitive' form of MEET in its embedded sentence, but only because the verb ENJOY requires an identity between its subject and the subject of its object sentence; and the subject of ENJOY is JOHN and not JOHN and MARY.

(36-a)   John enjoyed meeting Mary.
(36-b)   John enjoyed (John meet Mary).

The point is that analogous interpretations are possible for sentences with the adverb WILLINGLY, and with Instrumental WITH-phrases. It is required merely that the adverb WILLINGLY be analyzed as a disguised embedding verb, as suggested by (36-d)

(36-c)   John willingly met Mary;
(36-d)   John was willing (John met Mary),

and that WITH-phrases be associated with paraphrases containing the verb USE, as suggested already by Lakoff.[6,7]

37. It is frequently the case, however, that apparent symmetric predicates are not properly symmetric after all. Sentences of the form (37-a)

(37-a)   NP resembles NP.

are extensionally symmetric if both NPs are definite referring expressions, but otherwise (as in (37-b)) not.

(37-b)   Your brother resembles a horse.

My interpretation of the Similarity Predicates is that one of the terms has the role Stimulus (or what I would call Instrument, but with the notion of 'implement' abstracted away), the other has the role Theme (or what I have called Object in my earlier writings), and the sentence is an expression of a 3-place predicate in which the third and phonetically absent argument is the Experiencer, which is understood, when unexpressed, to be identified with the speaker of the sentence. The Stimulus must be expressed as a referring expression, but the Theme need not. The sentence means roughly that your brother as stimulus evokes in me memories of horses. [Incidentally, the verb REMIND, mentioned earlier, has a very similar structure, except that with it an NP representing the Experiencer must be present in the surface sentence.]

38. For many other so-called symmetric predicates there are arguments that the associated NPs do not serve in absolutely identical roles. It is difficult to capture such information in the face of the wide range of facts accounted for in the conjoined-subject source analysis of Lakoff and Peters,[8] but such a reanalysis may prove to be necessary after all. And this is to say nothing of the problem of dealing with the Asymmetric Joint Action Predicates of the type discussed by one of the members of this Conference [under an alias] and illustrated by sentences of the form:

(38-a)   Fred and Sheila were blanking;
(38-b)   Fred was blanking Sheila;
(38-c)   *Sheila was blanking Fred[9].

39. The occurrence of quantifying expressions of various types seems to be constrained in fairly mysterious ways according to the surface arrangements of the NPs in a sentence. Lakoff's 'derivational constraints'[10] fail, as far as I can tell, to account for the particular set of mysteries I have in mind. In general, DEVELOP INTO and DEVELOP OUT OF are 1-2 converses (although they also have a use as 2-3 converses of 3-place predicates); but there is a skewness in the pattern of quantification compatible with these expressions, as can be seen by comparing the paraphrasibility facts shown below:

(39-a)   every acorn developed into an oak;
(39-b)   an oak developed out of every acorn [a paraphrase of (39-a)];
(39-c)   every oak developed out of an acorn;
(39-d)   *an acorn developed into every oak [not a paraphrase of (39-c)].

[Jeffrey Gruber first drew my attention to sentences (39-a, b, c, d).] Similarly, MAKE INTO and MAKE OUT OF are 2-3 converses of 3-term predicates, and the patterns seen above are repeated, only this time between the direct object and the object of a preposition.

(39-e)   I made every log into a canoe.
(39-f)   I made a canoe out of every log [a paraphrase of (39-e)].
(39-g)   I made every canoe out of a log.
(39-h)   *I made a log into every canoe [not a paraphrase of (39-g)].

40. Lest the data of (39) be thought of as involving exceptional properties of 'verbs of physical transformation', we can show here that verbs which are themselves converses of each other (FOLLOW and PRECEDE) exhibit similar patterns with their own passive counterparts.

(40-a)   A Sunday follows every Saturday.
(40-b)   Every Saturday is followed by a Sunday [a paraphrase of (40-a)].
(40-c)   Every Sunday follows a Saturday.
(40-d)   *A Saturday is followed by every Sunday [not a paraphrase of (40-c)].
(40-e)   A Saturday precedes every Sunday.
(40-f)   Every Sunday is preceded by a Saturday [a paraphrase of (40-e)].
(40-g)   Every Saturday precedes a Sunday.
(40-h)   *A Sunday is preceded by every Saturday [not a paraphrase of (40-g)].

I suspect that the data offered in sections (39) and (40) are ultimately explainable in terms of 'derivational constraints' of the kind discussed by Lakoff. A reason for bringing them up in this report is that they show restrictions of a fairly interesting sort that relate both to the formation of deep-structure subjects (put differently, to the choice of particular members of a converse pair) and to the formation of surface-structure subjects.

41. In my proposals on 'case grammar' I have assumed that the role types which one can refer to in describing the semantic structure of predicates make up a universally valid and reasonably well-specified set of concepts. I have assumed, too, that the role types are themselves unanalyzables, corresponding to elementary perceptions on the part of human beings concerning such matters as who did it, who experienced it, where it happened, what the result was, where a thing that moved

ended up, where it started out, what moved, and a few others. I have convinced myself that certain role notions recur across widely variant languages, namely those for which one finds useful the terms Agent, Instrument, Location, Object, Patient, etc. I have found that many valid assertions about languages can be made by describing the structure of their sentences in these terms. The most serious difficulties have had to do with specifying exactly what this small set of role types consisted of, and determining whether or not it would turn out to be necessary, at least for some verbs, to interpret certain arguments as serving two role functions simultaneously.

42. This last difficulty is that of seeing the relationship between the case functions that seem to be involved in almost every sentence – such as, for example, those I named in the last section – and the sort of role structure that is involved in the description of particular kinds of institutionalized transactions for which a 'field' of vocabulary may exist in a language. I have in mind the roles of customer, merchant, goods, and instrument of exchange in the vocabulary field that includes BUY, SELL, PAY, DICKER, etc.; and those of defendant, judger, deed, victim, etc., in the field that includes verbs like ACCUSE, CRITICIZE, FORGIVE, APOLOGIZE, CONFESS, CONCEDE, JUSTIFY, EXCUSE, etc. I am at the moment ready to assume that it may be necessary to treat the semantic roles of arguments on two 'levels'. I mean that I may want to be able to say that in expressions with BUY there is one argument which has Customer function on one 'level', Agent function on another, whereas in expressions with SELL, the argument which has Agent function is the Merchant, not the Customer. In what follows I leave open the possibility that the roles associated with a predicate word may not bear a one-to-one correspondence with the arguments associated with it.

43. A great deal of attention has been given in the last year or two, in linguistic circles, to the fact that the semantic description of expressions containing particular predicate words needs to distinguish what the speaker of the sentence might be saying (or 'doing in saying') explicitly from what he is said to presuppose about the situations concerning which he is speaking. The apparatus for formulating the presuppositions will need to refer to the entities which serve particular role functions with respect to the event or situation identified by the predicate.

44. In my description of verbs of judging,[11] for example, I have pointed out that for sentence (44-a)

(44-a)   Harvey accused Fred of writing the letter

the utterer of the sentence presupposes (that Harvey presupposes?) that someone's having written the letter in question was bad, and what he is declaring, in uttering (44-a), is that Harvey claimed that Fred is the one who did it. On the other hand, for sentence (44-b)

(44-b)   Harvey criticized Fred for writing the letter

the speaker of the sentence presupposes (that Harvey presupposes?) that Fred was the one who wrote the letter, and is declaring, in uttering (44-b), that Harvey claimed that for Fred to have written the letter was bad. The force of Harvey's utterance in (44-a) is what is presupposed in (44-b), and vice versa.

45. Paralleling the pair of words offered in (44) is the pair CREDIT and COMMEND. These differ in that where ACCUSE and CRITICIZE carry the idea of blameworthiness, CREDIT and COMMEND carry the idea of goodness. That is, in (45-a) someone's having written the letter is judged in advance as being good, and what is communicated is that Harvey claimed Fred did it; in (45-b) Fred's responsibility is presupposed, and what is communicated is that Harvey claimed that what Fred did was good.

(45-a)   Harvey credited Fred with writing the letter.
(45-b)   Harvey commended Fred for writing the letter.

46. The distinctions seen here are analogous to those which J. L. Austin recognized in an ambiguity of BLAME and in the pair of words EXCUSE and JUSTIFY.

47. Some of the verbs of judging are illocutionary verbs, as are, for those I have mentioned, ACCUSE and COMMEND. What this means is that, for those verbs of judging which are capable of serving as 'explicit performatives' or 'illocutionary force indicating devices', a presuppositional analysis of them comes to show certain resemblances to, say, Searle's analysis of promising and other illocutionary verbs. The analysis of

illocutionary acts along the line developed by Searle[12] is a special case of the analysis of the type I have in mind (especially as it concerns pre-suppositions), being special only in that what is presupposed of the subject of the verb must be true of the speaker of the utterance, and that a performance of the utterance under the first-person-present-tense conditions appropriate to performatives 'counts as' the performance of an act which has extralinguistic validity.

48. Searle's type of analysis can easily be extended, working in the other direction, to the description of non-linguistic-act verbs. Thus the 'pre-paratory condition' for a valid utterance of (48-a)

(48-a)   Sheila borrowed five dollars from Fred

is that Fred had five dollars; the 'sincerity condition' is that Sheila intends to give Fred five dollars at some time in the future; the 'essential condition' – which here, however, cannot be matched with a rule which governs the use of an operative linguistic expression – is that Sheila has undertaken an obligation to return Fred his five dollars some day.

49. (This is not to say that one can accept all of what Searle has to say about promising. His account fails, as far as I can tell, in one or two respects. For example, he claims that in performing a valid promising act one has taken on an obligation to perform in a particular way in the future. If this is so, then the utterances, on a mother's part, of the re-assuring words (49-a) or (49-b) must be defective as acts of promising.

(49-a)   I promise you that your father will come back
(49-b)   I promise you that the sun will come up again tomorrow.

If it were seen, however, that in making a promise one provides a personal guarantee of the (future) truth of a statement, such promising acts would not need to be described as defective. Promising of the type Searle has in mind must be understood in terms of guarantees of the (future) truth of statements whose propositional content contains descriptions of acts to be performed by the maker of the promise. (That is, in which an expression referring to the maker of the promise is in the Agent role.))

50. (A second quibble might be raised in connection with Searle's hint

that THREATEN is the unfavorable-consequence counterpart of PROMISE. This is wrong because (i) threatening acts do not need to be (accompanied by) linguistic acts, and because (ii) in threatening somebody, one does not take on an obligation to do anything. You can succeed thoroughly in threatening me by merely saying that you might consider beating my brains out. It may be, however, that I am confused by an ambiguity in THREATEN between an illocutionary and a perlocutionary sense. I know, for example, that one can declare that threatening words are ineffective either by saying (50-a) or (50-b).

(50-a)   You can't threaten me [perlocutionary].
(50-b)   Your threats don't bother me [illocutionary].

51. We have thus seen that the semantic analysis of ordinary language sentences, in order to incorporate observations and rules about illocutionary force, must include in its scope ways of dealing with the participants in the speech act itself. The traditional term for dealing with matters of this sort is *deixis*. One speaks of *person deixis* (references to the speaker and the addressee), *place deixis* (references to the locations of the speaker and the addressee), *time deixis* (references to the time of the speech act), as well as references to portions of the utterance itself (*discourse deixis*), and references to the relative social statuses of the speech act participants (*honorific systems*, etc.).

52. In the description of certain predicate words, there is a necessary reference to deictic features, especially in the description of the presuppositions or 'preparatory conditions'. The prime example of this for English is the verb COME.[13] In sentences of the form given in (52-a)

(52-a) O (object) comes to P (place) at T (time)

it is presupposed of P that it is either

(i)   where the speaker of the sentence is at the time of utterance; or
(ii)   where the addressee of the sentence is at the time of utterance; or
(iii)   where the speaker of the sentence is/was/will be at T; or
(iv)   where the addressee of the sentence is/was/will be at T.

53. Sentences containing no other deictic references permit all four pre-suppositional possibilities, as in (53-a)

(53-a)   Fred will come to the office tomorrow.

But others are limited because of presuppositions associated with other deictic parts of the sentence. Thus, (53-b) presupposes either that you are there now or that you will be there tomorrow, but not that I am there now nor that I will be there tomorrow at the time I arrive; and (53-c) presupposes that I will be there tomorrow at the time of your arrival, or that you are there now while I am speaking.

(53-b)   I will come there tomorrow.
(53-c)   You will come there tomorrow.

54. (A full semantic theory of a language must additionally take into account the fact that there is an extended or displaced use of deictic features corresponding to the ways in which the speaker of a third-person narrative 'identifies' with one or another of the characters in his narrative. If one of the *basic* functions of deictic categories is to express directly the speaker's role or viewpoint with respect to his subject matter, in the 'displaced' use the speaker performs some kind of psychological 'identifi-cation' with one of the parties in his narrative. It seems that instances of 'displaced ego' can be seen in sentences like (54-a), where the author is interpreted as viewing the situation from Harry's point of view, rather than from Fred's or Bill's.

(54-a)   Fred came to where Harry was, and then Harry went to where Bill was.

In (54-b) the author is aloof; sentence (54-c) is unacceptable.

(54-b)   Fred went to where Harry was, and then Harry went to where Bill was.
(54-c)   *Fred came to where Harry was, and then Harry came to where Bill was.

The phenomenon is quite analogous to the distinction provided by some (e.g., Algonquian) languages between 'proximative' and 'obviative' third persons. It has been noted that the proximative forms are only associated with one individual in a third person narrative at a time, and that the switch in the application of the form from one individual to another corresponds to a shift of point of view in the development of the narrative.)

55. As stated earlier, it is the inclusion of reference to speech act participants in semantic descriptions which makes possible the incorporation of matters of 'illocutionary act potential' in the description of sentences. An attractive view is that the illocutionary force of a sentence is represented in the deep structure of that sentence, or at least that what one might call the 'straightforward illocutionary act potential' of a sentence should be so represented. Evidence that maybe *all* conversational sentences should be provided with this sort of superstructure at their 'deepest' representation has been offered by Ross. For sentences whose utterances have the illocutionary force of asserting or informing ('declaring'), there are reasons for believing that there is, in the deep structure, a silent illocutionary verb of declaring having a first-person Agent NP, a second-person Dative NP, and having the non-silent part of the sentence as its direct object.[14]

56. The occurrence of adverbs like PERSONALLY is now permitted a consistent accounting. The adverb occurs in sentences with 'psychological' verbs and in which the Experiencer NP is coreferential with the Agent NP of the immediately commanding linguistic-act verb. Where the upper linguistic-act verb is apparent in the surface structure, this observation accounts for the acceptability of (56-a) as opposed to (56-b).

(56-a)   Fred said that he personally dislikes roses.
(56-b)   *Fred said that Martha personally dislikes roses.

By assuming a first person declarative supersentence above all declarative sentences, one can account, in Ross's fashion, for the acceptability of (56-c) as opposed to (56-d).

(56-c)   Personally, I dislike roses.
(56-d)   *Personally, Fred dislikes roses.

57. Analogously, the pleading-word PLEASE occurs only in sentences immediately commanded by verbs of ordering or requesting. The requirement is that the Agent NP of the interior sentence be coreferential to the Dative NP of the ordering or requesting verb. Where the ordering or

requesting verb is present in the surface sentence, this accounts for the acceptability of (57-a) as opposed to (57-b).

(57-a)   I told Fred to please leave the room.
(57-b)   *I predict that you will please leave the room.

Assuming that imperative sentences are contained in silent performative structures of ordering allows one to explain, by the same principle, the acceptability of (57-c) as opposed to (57-d).

(57-c)   Please leave the room.
(57-d)   *Fred please left the room.

58. One question about the presuppositional structure of sentences that I have not discussed is that of *who does the presupposing*. Presupposing may be thought of as an act performed by the speaker in his production of the utterance, or as an act imputed by the speaker to one or more of the individuals whose properties or actions are described by the utterance in question. I assume that there will be much more to say about such matters after one has seen the results of Lakoff's explorations into the logic of 'world-creating verbs'.

59. The view of semantic interpretation that I have been assuming is roughly this: I believe that, given a full grammatical description of a sentence, with complete semantic descriptions of the lexical items it contains, it should be possible to 'compute' the full semantic description of the sentence, including, of course, information about what its utterers must presuppose to be true, including its utterers' imputations of presuppositions to individuals described or referred to in the sentence. This 'computation' will involve many types of grammatical facts and a great many subtle properties of lexical items. The view is representative of what is called *interpretive semantics*, but it is one which involves operations which are quite distinct from those proposed in the earliest presentations of interpretive semantics. Operations involving selection restrictions are here replaced by an understanding of presuppositions; this has the effect of dissolving the problem of discovering the boundary between the semantic properties of words (e.g., nouns) and the physical properties of the things to which the words could be correctly applied. Interpretive

semantics is one which welcomes lexical items that contain in their definitions variables not found in the expressions that contain them. These variables are relevant to the semantic interpretation of sentences, because there are situations in which predications involving these variables are more essential parts of the communication than anything else. To use a familiar example: to say of Fred, literally, that he is a bastard, is to say of his mother that she was not married on the day he was born. And that is to 'refer' to someone not mentioned in the original assertion.

60. The alternative view, within what has come to be called 'generative semantics',[15] has it, if I understand correctly what is going on, that all of the information relevant to the semantic interpretation of a sentence must be present in a representation of the deep structure of that sentence, and that, in fact, there is no level of 'deep structure' that is distinct from the level of semantic representation. If in the end the 'generative semantics' view turns out to be more valid – and I don't know what I am revealing about myself to admit that I find the arguments favoring generative semantics overwhelming but somehow not coercive – then descriptions of the type I am capable of coming up with through my work will fall in place, within the correct theory, on the level of lexicology. I believe, that is, that the observations about the meanings of lexical items, the relations which must be described in characterizing the semantic structure of expressions containing specific lexical items, and the format for expressing these facts, can be exactly the same under either view.

61. It is the apparatus for dealing with presuppositions that makes me retain faith in the interpretive-semantics position. It is frequently possible to state the presuppositions of a sentence in the form of a schema which operates on the grammatical description (in fact, often enough, the surface grammatical description). If we take, for example, the presuppositional effect of 'contrastive stress', it generally seems to be the case that a sentence of the form suggested by (61-a)

(61-a) $X \underline{Y} Z$ [where underlining represents emphasis]

is associated with the presupposition suggested by (61-b)

(61-b)   it has been suggested that $X Y' Z$ [where $Y' \neq Y$].

Given this formula, we can figure out in what contexts one might say
(61-c)

(61-c)   It's an essay in *descriptive* metaphysics.

by imagining what different type of metaphysics somebody might have
alluded to in the utterances that preceded (61-c). If it is impossible for
us to do this – because, say, we know nothing whatever about how the
word METAPHYSICS is used – we cannot understand the presuppositional
content of (61-c), but we know something about how to acquire this
understanding.

62. Perhaps the main reason I cling to views of interpretive semantics
is that I am unconsciously guilty of the much-discussed sin of confusing
the linguistic technical term 'generate' with the psychologically more
immediately understandable notion 'produce' (as in 'produce utterances').
I so frequently find myself speaking without any understanding of what
I am saying that I quite naturally think of the ability to produce a sentence
as involving essentially different principles from those that are employed
in figuring out what if anything its utterer intended.

Ohio State University

REFERENCES

[1] See Noam Chomsky, *Aspects of the Theory of Syntax*, M.I.T. Press, Cambridge,
Mass., 1965, Chapter 2.
[2] See, e.g., James D. McCawley, 'Lexical Insertion in a Transformational Grammar
Without Deep Structure' in *Papers from the Fourth Regional Meeting of the Chicago
Linguistics Society* (ed. by C.-J. Bailey, B. J. Darden, and A. Davison), Chicago, Ill., 1969,
pp. 71–80.
[3] For examples of this approach see Barbara Hall, *Subject and Object in English*, M.I.T
doctoral dissertation, 1965, and P. Gregory Lee, 'Subjects and Agents', *Ohio State
University Working Papers in Linguistics* 3 (1969) 36–113.
[4] See, e.g., my 'The Case for Case' in *Universals in Linguistic Theory* (ed. by E. Bach
and R. Harms), Holt, Rinehart, and Winston, New York 1968, pp. 1–88, and 'Lexical
Entries for Verbs', *Foundations of Language* 4 (1968) 373–393.
[5] Paul M. Postal, 'Cross-Over Phenomena' in *Specification and Utilization of a Transformational Grammar* (Scientific Report No. 3), IBM Research Center, Yorktown
Heights, New York, 1968.
[6] See George Lakoff, 'Instrumental Adverbs and the Concept of Deep Structure',
Foundations of Language 4 (1968) 4–29.
[7] For further discussion of the matters taken up in Sections 19–36, see my 'Types of

Lexical Information', *Ohio State University Working Papers in Linguistics* **2** (1968) 65–103 (to appear in *Semantics: An Interdisciplinary Reader in Philosophy, Linguistics, Anthropology and Psychology* (ed. by Leon Jakobovits and Danny Steinberg), Cambridge University Press, Cambridge, 1970.

[8] George Lakoff and Stanley Peters, 'Phrasal Conjunction and Symmetric Predicates' in *Modern Studies in English* (ed. by David Reibel and Sanford Schane), Prentice-Hall, Englewood Cliffs, N.J., 1969, pp. 113–142.

[9] Quang Phuc Dong, 'A Note on Conjoined Noun Phrases', *PEGS* (1968), unpublished.

[10] George Lakoff, 'On Derivational Constraints' in *Papers from the Fifth Regional Meeting of the Chicago Linguistics Society*, Chicago, Ill., 1969, pp. 117–139.

[11] For a somewhat more detailed discussion, see my 'Verbs of Judging: An Exercise in Semantic Description', *Papers in Linguistics* **1** (1969) 91–117 (Florida State University).

[12] John R. Searle, *Speech Acts: An Essay in the Philosophy of Language*, Cambridge University Press, Cambridge, 1969.

[13] See my 'Deictic Categories in the Semantics of "Come"', *Foundations of Language* **2** (1966) 219–226.

[14] For a persuasive statement of this analysis, see John R. Ross, 'On Declarative Sentences' in *Readings in English Transformational Grammar* (ed. by Roderick Jacobs and Peter S. Rosenbaum), Blaisdell, Boston, 1970.

[15] See, for a survey of the literature on and the arguments for generative semantics, George Lakoff's 'Generative Semantics' in *Semantics: An Interdisciplinary Reader in Philosophy, Linguistics, Anthropology and Psychology* (ed. by Danny Steinberg and Leon Jakobovits), Cambridge University Press, Cambridge, 1971.

GILBERT HARMAN

DEEP STRUCTURE AS LOGICAL FORM*

I

A *transformational derivation* of a sentence is a sequence of labeled phrase structure trees. The last tree in the sequence represents the *surface structure* of the sentence. The first tree represents the *deep structure* of the sentence.[1] Each later tree is derived from its predecessor via the application of exactly one transformational rule. The surface structure tree represents that syntactic structure relevant to the way in which the sentence is pronounced. It will be assumed here that the deep structure tree is a full semantic representation of the sentence.[2]

Until recently, transformational grammarians assumed that deep structures took the form *subject phrase followed by predicate phrase*. But considerable simplification results if deep structure takes the form *predicate followed by one or more arguments*. If auxiliary verb is ignored (as it will be throughout this paper), the difference is given in Figure 1.

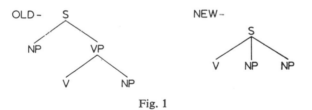

Fig. 1

On the new analysis, transformations such as passive, indirect-object inversion, and extraposition can move around the NPs that follow the V. Later, the first NP that ends up following the V is moved in front of the V and raised into a higher S. The result of such *subject raising* is shown in Figure 2.

This sort of surface structure is just like what one had on the old analysis, except that the node that was labeled VP on the old analysis is labeled S on the new.

This points to one advantage the new analysis has over the old. It had
been known that verb phrases in surface structure have the properties of
embedded sentences. The relabeling permits a simplified statement of the
relevant facts. A good example is *backwards pronominalization*, where a

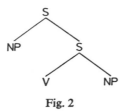

Fig. 2

pronoun precedes its antecedent. In many dialects this can occur when the
pronoun is in either a subordinate clause, or a verb phrase, that does not
also contain its antecedent. In my dialect, there can be backwards pronominalization in (1) and (2) but not in (3).

(1)   When she smiled, Bob kissed Mabel.
(2)   Bob kissed her, when Mabel smiled.
(3)   *She kissed Bob, when Mabel smiled.

There is backwards pronominalization into a subordinate clause in (1)
and into a verb phrase in (2). There can be no backwards pronominalization in (3) because the pronoun is in neither a subordinate clause nor a
verb phrase. When verb phrases are labeled S, they become subordinate
clauses in surface structure. Instead of saying that backwards pronominalization can occur in either of two circumstances, into subordinate clauses
and also into verb phrases, we can simplify the rule: backwards pronominalization can occur into subordinate clauses.

More importantly, various transformations are simpler on the new
analysis than they were on the old. For example, on the old analysis, the

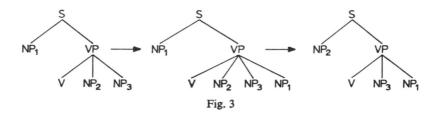

Fig. 3

passive transformation moved the subject of the sentence to the end of the verb phrase and then put the object where the subject used to be. (This way of putting things assumes that all NPs contain prepositions that may later get deleted. The subject contains the preposition *by*, the object *of*, the indirect object *to*, etc.) (Figure 3).

A problem for the old analysis arose from the assumption that transformations can be rather simply represented. Passive might have been written like this:

$$NP_1 - V - NP_2 - X \rightarrow NP_2 - V - X - NP_1$$

(Introduction of the verb *to be* is here ignored as are other considerations involving the auxiliary verb.) Given the accepted limitations imposed on the statement of transformations, it was not clear why the original subject should end up inside the VP rather than following it and attached directly to S, as shown in Figure 4.

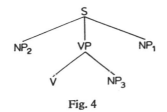

Fig. 4

Eventually, a rather *ad hoc* solution to this problem was adopted. It was assumed that the deep structure of a passive sentence was different from that of its corresponding active version in that it contained within the VP a constituent labeled 'PASSIVE' (Figure 5).

The passive transformation applied only to structures containing that special constituent. The subject NP would then be substituted for PASSIVE, and this was to explain how it ended up in the VP.[3]

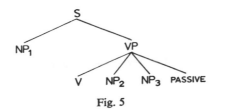

Fig. 5

The new view avoids this *ad hoc* treatment of passive. The passive transformation occurs before subject raising and moves NPs so that they remain within the same clause. After subject raising, this clause represents the verb phrase and contains what would have been the subject had passive not been used (Figure 6).

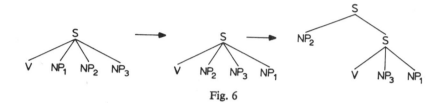

Fig. 6

A further advantage of the new analysis is that passive is no longer represented as two operations – moving subject, then moving object – but as one – moving first argument to the end of the clause.

But the full power of the new analysis does not really emerge until other transformations are considered. Extraposition is a good example. Extraposition yields sentences like

(4)   It had surprised him that Bob was sick.

from a structure that could also yield

(5)   That Bob was sick had surprised him.

Notice that *him* can refer to Bob in (5) but not in (4). To account for the impossibility of backwards pronominalization in (4), it must be supposed that the extraposed sentence 'that Bob was sick' occurs within the verb phrase. On the old analysis, extraposition would have to move the extraposed sentence from subject position outside the verb phrase into predicate position within the verb phrase. That raises the same problem for the old analysis that its treatment of passive does. And the new analysis permits the same sort of simplification. Extraposition moves the extraposed sentence to the end of the clause, leaving an 'it' behind. That 'it' may later be raised into subject position (Figure 7).

Infinitival clause separation is a kind of extraposition appropriate to infinitive clauses. It leaves behind, not 'it', but whatever was in subject position. For example,

(6)   Bob is believed by her to love Mary.

comes from a structure that could also have yielded

(7)   *(For) Bob to love Mary is believed by her.

except that (7) is not well formed, for reasons not relevant to this discussion. The impossibility of backwards pronominalization in (6) shows that the phrase 'to love Mary' is contained within the verb phrase. There-

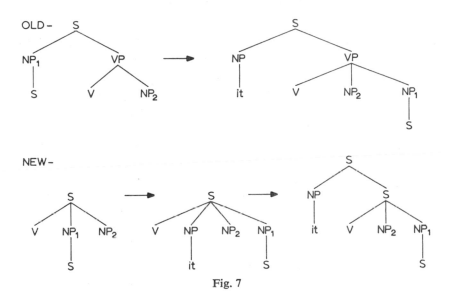

Fig. 7

fore, infinitival clause separation raises the same problem for the old analysis that passive or extraposition does; and the new analysis offers a similar simplification.

Actually, the simplification afforded is much greater than so far indicated. Both extraposition and infinitival clause separation can apply when the clause to be extraposed or separated does not appear in subject position. That means the old analysis will have to provide two quite different statements of these transformations, whereas only one statement of each is needed on the new analysis.

For example, infinitival clause separation must be used to obtain

(8)   I believe myself to be honest.

For this sort of reflexive pronominalization (yielding 'myself') is possible only if the item thus pronominalized is separated out of the embedded sentence. Compare

(9)   *I believe that myself am honest.

Furthermore, infinitival clause separation applies after passive, since (10) but not (11) is well formed.

(10)   Bob is believed by me to be honest.
(11)   *Bob is believed to be honest by me.

If passive could apply after infinitival clause separation, (11) would be well formed. Therefore, on the old analysis, infinitival clause separation must sometimes apply to clauses in subject position, in order to get (10), and sometimes to clauses not in subject position, in order to get (8). And that means there will have to be two different statements of infinitival clause separation on the old analysis.

A similar duplication must arise on the old analysis of extraposition, since a clause not in subject position may be extraposed. Compare

(12)   I know it well.
(13)   I know well that Bob is honest.

All such duplication is avoided on the new analysis. Extraposition and infinitival clause separation apply possibly after passive and before subject raising to move something to the end of the clause.

Many years ago philosophers went beyond an Aristotelian subject-predicate logic to develop a logic of relations. The distinction between subject and predicate was seen to be a matter of surface form, of no logical importance. For logic, the important distinction became that between a predicate and its arguments. It is interesting to observe that what holds for logic holds for deep structure as well. Here is a first example of benefits to be derived through the identification of deep structure with logical form.

II

For philosophers, the logical form of a sentence is given by a paraphrase into quantification theory. This leads one to wonder whether anything in deep structure corresponds to the quantifiers of logic. Work by the linguist James McCawley and by the philosopher John Wallace suggests the following answer.

Quantifiers in deep structure differ from the familiar quantifiers of modern logic in their variety of type and in the restrictions they carry with them. First, there are many more kinds of quantifier than the simple universal and existential quantifiers mentioned in discussions of quantification theory. Types of quantifiers are roughly indicated by what linguists sometimes call the *determiners* of noun phrases, words such as *any, every, all, each, a, the, some, few, a few, several, many, much, most, one, seven,* etc. Second, the quantifiers in a natural language have a varying range whereas quantifiers used in logic are usually associated with a fixed range: the universe of discourse. Occasionally, a logician will let certain quantifiers range over one universe while others range over other universes, depending on the style of variable employed. In that case, a small number of different sorts of quantifier are envisioned with fixed ranges. On the other hand, the quantifiers in a natural language have a varying range, where this is determined by a restricting phrase that follows the word indicating quantifier type. For example, the quantifier represented by the noun phrase 'many arrows' ranges over arrows and not over all things in the universe of discourse. How many count as many depends on that restricting phrase. If there are not many green arrows, then many of the green arrows will not be many of the arrows: many of the green arrows can hit the target without many of the arrows hitting the target.

Consider

(14)   Many arrows didn't hit the target.
(15)   The target wasn't hit by many arrows.

On the old analysis, (14) and (15) are corresponding active and passive. Since (14) does not mean what (15) means, at least in some dialects, the old analysis must permit transformations to change meaning. If quantifiers are represented in deep structure, (14) and (15) can be assigned different deep structures. For example, (14) might be assigned a deep structure as shown in Figure 8 whereas (15) might be assigned a deep structure as given in Figure 9.

The relative scopes of *many arrows* and *not* are different in (14) and (15). These scopes are determined by the deep structure: the scope of a constituent in deep structure includes whatever is dominated by the constituent immediately dominating it.

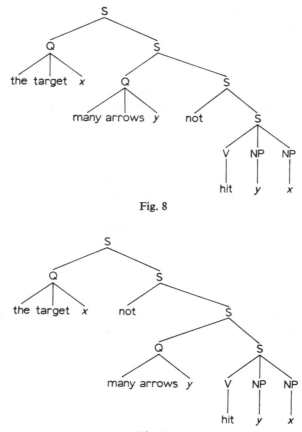

Fig. 8

Fig. 9

(14) is derived from its deep structure by the following transformations in this order: subject raising, not-placement (changing *hit* to *didn't hit*), NP-placement (substituting *many arrows* for *y*), and another NP-placement (substituting *the target* for *x*). The order of these operations is determined by the *cyclic nature of transformational rules* which are to apply

to more deeply embedded sentences before they apply to less deeply embedded sentences. Similarly, (15) is derived from its deep structure by passive, subject raising, NP-placement, not-placement, and a final NP-placement.

(14) and (15) cannot be derived from each other's deep structure because of some general constraints on derivations that have been discussed by George Lakoff. In particular, for many operators, including certain quantifiers and negation, if in deep structure the scope of one includes a second, then in later stages of the derivation the first must precede the second whenever the second *commands* the first. (X commands Y if all S's dominating Y also dominate X.) This constraints would be violated with respect to *not* and *many* if (14) or (15) were derived from the other's deep structure.[4]

Quantifiers are variable binding operators. Sometimes a variable bound by a quantifier is replaced by the relevant noun phrase. Bound variables in deep structure that do not get replaced with noun phrases become pronouns:

(16)   If any arrow is green, it will hit the target.
(17)   If it is green, any arrow will hit the target.

(17) can be read as an instance of backwards pronominalization, in which case it is equivalent to (16). On the old view, pronominalization occurred when a noun phrase was 'identical' with its antecedent. (18) was supposed to have come from (19):

(18)   If this arrow is green, it will hit the target.
(19)   If this arrow is green, this arrow will hit the target.

(16) or (17) would have come from

(20)   If any arrow is green, any arrow will hit the target.

Since (20) does not mean what (16) or (17) means, this provides another instance in which transformations do not preserve meaning on the old analysis.

A series of difficulties eventually undermined the old theory. One was that it could not account for the fact that

(21)   Everyone loves everyone.

does not reduce via obligatory reflexive pronominalization to

(22)　　　Everyone loves himself.

Another was that the theory sometimes seemed to lead to infinite regress.

(23)　　　A boy who was fooling her kissed a girl that loved him.

According to the old theory, both *her* and *him* represent full NPs that are identical with their antecedents. (23) might come from

(24)　　　A boy who was fooling a girl that loved him kissed a girl that loved a boy who was fooling her.

Even apart from the fact that (24) is not equivalent to (23), there is the added problem that it contains pronouns which – according to the old theory – represent full noun phrases identical with their antecedents. Obviously an infinite regress results. The old theory cannot account at all for sentences like (23).[5]

When semantic considerations are brought in, it becomes clear how linguistic theory benefits from the introduction of quantifiers and variables into deep structure. The *they* in

(25)　　　If any arrows are green, they will hit the target.

cannot be the result of identical NP pronominalization, since (25) is not equivalent to

(26)　　　If any arrows are green, any arrows will hit the target.

But *they* in (25) is easily taken as the trace of a variable:

(27)　　　(Any arrows x) (if x are green, x will hit target).

Furthermore, when quantifiers appear in deep structure, ambiguity of scope becomes a form of syntactic ambiguity. The sentence

(28)　　　Jones believes someone to be a spy.

may mean that there is someone in particular that Jones believes is a spy or it may mean that Jones believes there is at least one spy. On the new theory, this difference is reflected in there being two possible deep structures for (28): Roughly

(29)　　　(Someone x) (Jones believes (x is a spy)).
(30)　　　(Jones believes (Someone x) (x is a spy)).

Notice that in

(31)   Someone is believed by Jones to be a spy.

the scope of *someone* cannot be read as confined to the embedded sentence, although it can be read that way in (28). We can account for this difference between (31) and (28) by supposing that the infinitival clause separation transformation can move only variables and sentences. For then (31) could be derived only from (29) and not from (30). Infinitival clause separation could not apply if *someone* has already been substituted for the relevant variable by NP-placement. Only a variable could be separated out from the rest of the infinitival clause. If *someone* has narrow scope, NP-placement will have to apply before infinitival clause separation can, this preventing the latter operation. If *someone* has wide scope, infinitival clause separation can apply before NP placement. Therefore, (31) can only be read with *someone* having wide scope, although (28) can be read either way.[6]

III

Improved grammars result from the identification of deep structure with logical form. Two points have been mentioned so far, the replacement of the subject-predicate form with predicate plus arguments and the introduction of quantifiers and variables. But mention of sentences like (28) and (31) suggests a problem about the analysis of *statements of propositional attitude*. Can the deep structure of such sentences be identified with their logical form?

Here are two sentences of propositional attitude:

(32)   Jones believes that Ortcutt is a spy.
(33)   Sam wants Ortcutt to be a spy.

Deep structures usually cited for such sentences contain as an embedded sentence, expanded in the usual way:

(34)   Ortcutt is a spy.

But the most familiar philosophical analyses of the logical form of (32) or (33) suppose that (34) cannot appear as an embedded sentence in (32) or (33).

The problem is this. (34) and

(35)   Ortcutt is the president of the local bank.

logically entail

(36)   The president of the local bank is a spy.

But (32) and (35) do not logically entail

(37)   Jones believes that the president of the local bank is a spy.

And (33) and (35) do not logically entail

(38)   Sam wants the president of the local bank to be a spy.

(36) follows from (34) and (35) by the *substitutivity of identity*. The problem is to explain why contexts of propositional attitude block the substitutivity of identity.

One philosophical answer supposes that in (32) and (33) the word 'Ortcutt' does not refer to the same thing it refers to in (34). According to Frege, words that appear in a context of propositional attitude do not have the same meaning and reference they have outside that context. In (34) the word 'Ortcutt' refers to Ortcutt. In (32) and (33) it refers not to Ortcutt but to something else, e.g. to itself, or to the usual meaning of the word 'Ortcutt', or perhaps to the mental word 'Ortcutt'. What corresponds to (34) in (32) and (33) does not function semantically as a sentence but rather serves to refer to a sentence, a proposition, or a propositional attitude. Substitutivity of identity permits one to substitute one reference to a thing for another reference to the same thing. Given (35), 'Ortcutt' and 'the president of the local bank' refer to the same thing, but only in ordinary contexts. In a context of propositional attitude these phrases do not refer to the same thing, since e.g. they refer to the meaning of 'Ortcutt' and the meaning of 'the president of the local bank' respectively; so the substitutivity of identity does not authorize the replacement of one with the other.

An alternative answer, due to Donald Davidson, permits Ortcutt to have its usual reference in (32) and (33). But (32) and (33) are not taken to be sentences that contain (34) embedded within them. What corresponds to (34) in (32) and (33) is not taken to be part of the original sentence at all. Instead it accompanies the original sentence as an example or illustration referred to by that sentence. More perspicuously written, (32) and (33) would look like this:

(39)   Jones believes that. Ortcutt is a spy.
(40)   Sam wants (that). Ortcutt (is) to be a spy.

When someone asserts (39) or (40), he asserts the first sentence, not the second. In uttering the second sentence he produces an example of the sort of thing referred to in his first sentence. Similarly in (32) or (33). In uttering the words 'Ortcutt is a spy' or 'Ortcutt to be a spy', one gives an example of what one's assertion refers to. These words are not part of what one says when one utters (32) or (33) but are rather part of what one is talking about. In one's example, the word 'Ortcutt' does refer to Ortcutt; but substitutivity of identity cannot be applied to (32) or (33) with respect to 'Ortcutt' since that word does not occur in these sentences. It only occurs in something that accompanies them and to which they refer.

Neither of these philosophical answers to the problem of failure of substitutivity in these contexts fits in with the idea that deep structure is logical form. Deep structure is supposed to provide a full semantic representation of a sentence. There seems to be no syntactic alternative to the assumption that the deep structure of (34) appears embedded in the deep structures of (32) and (33). These philosophical answers would have us suppose that something that must function syntactically in deep structure as an embedded sentence does not function semantically as an embedded sentence. And that seems to violate at least the spirit of the idea that deep structure is full semantic representation. Thus, on Davidson's analysis, a structure that behaves syntactically as an embedded sentence in deep structure is semantically a sentence but is not semantically embedded. On Frege's analysis, that structure is semantically embedded but it is not semantically a sentence, although it behaves syntactically as a sentence. So both analyses conflict with the idea that at the deepest level syntactic and semantic structure coincide.

However, there is a way to account for the failure of substitutivity of identity in sentences such as (32) and (33) without supposing that syntactic and semantic structure diverge at the level of deep structure. The analysis of noun phrases and quantification already sketched above will do the trick. On that analysis all noun phrases come from quantifiers and therefore have a certain scope in deep structure. If the principle of the substitutivity of identity is stated so as to apply only when the noun phrase in question has wide scope, it will automatically fail to apply in contexts of propositional attitude.

If (32) is understood like this

(41)   Jones believes ((Ortcutt x) (x is a spy)).

then from (32) and (35) one cannot infer (37), because 'Ortcutt' does not have wide scope in (32). On the other hand, (32) can be understood like this

(42)   (Ortcutt x) (Jones believes (x is a spy)).

In that case (32) and (35) do entail (37) because 'Ortcutt' has wide scope and substitutivity of identity applies.

Philosophers sometimes argue that an adequate analysis of logical form must permit a truth characterization. So it is important that a truth characterization of sentences of propositional attitude can be given if deep structure is identified with logical form. Into a Tarski-type theory of truth one might add principles for the denotation of names. Then one might take the representation of the object of a propositional attitude – which includes in deep structure an embedded S plus something more – to denote the embedded S itself or alternatively the proposition S expresses. The embedded S and its constituents retain their usual meaning. What is syntactically an embedded sentence is semantically an embedded sentence.[7]

IV

Finally, it is useful to consider what sort of theory results if deep structure is identified with logical form in the analysis of action sentences and causal sentences. Here there are competing philosophical theories of logical form as well as competing syntactic theories about the proper deep structures. Furthermore, all these theories are in a state of flux and development. The subject is too complex for detailed consideration here. All that can be done is to present a rather crude version of a theory of logical form that is being developed by Donald Davidson and then to compare that theory with standard grammatical analyses involving embedded sentences.

Consider these sentences:

(43)   Jack opened the door with the key at ten o'clock.

(44)   Fear caused Jack to open the door with the key at ten o'clock.

A semantic analysis of such sentences must account for the fact that (43) entails

(45)   Jack opened the door with the key.

(46)   Jack opened the door at ten o'clock.

(47)   Jack opened the door.

One must also account for the fact that (44) and the following sentences can be understood so that (44) entails them.

(48)   Fear caused Jack to open the door with the key.

(49)   Fear caused Jack to open the door at ten o'clock.

(50)   Fear caused Jack to open the door.

The problem is made more difficult by the fact that an indefinite number of adverbial phrases can occur in the verb phrase of (43). So it does not seem that one can account for the first set of entailments by supposing that e.g. (47) is a reduced form of

(51)   Jack opened the door with something at some time ...

One might attempt to account for the second set of entailments in terms of the first set along with the principle that, if P entails Q, then X causes P entails X causes Q. But there is a difficulty here.

(52)   A house that Jack built burned down.

entails

(53)   Jack built a house that burned down.

but

(54)   A short circuit caused a house that Jack built to burn down.

does not entail

(55)   A short circuit caused Jack to build a house that burned down.

This does not refute the principle in question, since a defender of that principle can replay that the scopes of the noun phrases in (54) and (55) are wide, so that (52) and (53) do not actually occur in (54) and (55). But then the problem becomes that of explaining why (54) and (55) cannot be understood in such a way that the relevant noun phrases have narrow scope and (52) and (53) do occur in them.

Davidson analyzes all these sentences as containing implicit quantification over events or actions. There is talk of Jack's opening of the door, where that is a particular event related in various ways to Jack, the door, the key, and ten o'clock. That event is caused by fear. In order to get a rough idea of the structure of his analysis, consider the following abbreviations:

(Ex) for *there is an event x such that*
Ox for *x is an opening (of something by someone)*
Bxy for *x is done by y* or *y is the agent of x.*
Fxy for *x is of (or done to) y* or *y is the object of x*
Wxy for *x is (done) with y* or *y is the instrument used in doing x*
Axy for *x is (done) at the time y*
Cxy for *x causes y*
j for *John*
d for *the door*
k for *the key*
t for *ten o'clock*
f for *fear*

Then Davidson's analyses of (43)–(50) are respectively

(56) $(Ex)(Ox \ \& \ Bxj \ \& \ Fxd \ \& \ Wxk \ \& \ Axt).$
(57) $(Ex)(Ox \ \& \ Bxj \ \& \ Fxd \ \& \ Wxk \ \& \ Axt \ \& \ Cfx).$
(58) $(Ex)(Ox \ \& \ Bxj \ \& \ Fxd \ \& \ Wxk).$
(59) $(Ex)(Ox \ \& \ Bxj \ \& \ Fxd \ \& \ Axt).$
(60) $(Ex)(Ox \ \& \ Bxj \ \& \ Fxd).$
(61) $(Ex)(Ox \ \& \ Bxj \ \& \ Fxd \ \& \ Wxk \ \& \ Cfx).$
(62) $(Ex)(Ox \ \& \ Bxj \ \& \ Fxd \ \& \ Axt \ \& \ Cfx).$
(63) $(Ex)(Ox \ \& \ Bxj \ \& \ Fxd \ \& \ Cfx).$

On these analyses, the fact that (43) entails (45), (46), and (47) is represented by the fact that (56) entails (58), (59), and (60) in elementary quantification theory. The fact that (44) entails (48) (49) and (50) is represented by the fact that (57) entails (61), (62), and (63). If with Davidson one treats these sentences as involving implicit quantification over events, one can give a perfectly straightforward account of the relevant entailments.

However, if Davidson's analyses are accepted, the semantic representation of (44) cannot contain embedded within it the semantic representation of (43). The semantic materials out of which (43) is constructed are also used in the construction of (44) but these materials are put together differently, so that (43) itself is not used in the construction of (44). The point stands out if the relevant materials are underlined when (56) is compared with (57):

(56) $(Ex)(Ox \,\&\, Bxj \,\&\, Fxd \,\&\, Wxk \,\&\, Axt)$.

(57) $(Ex)(Ox \,\&\, Bxj \,\&\, Fxd \,\&\, Wxk \,\&\, Axt \,\&\, Cfx)$.

What corresponds to (56) in (57) is not quite a sentence: it lacks a left parenthesis – or, perhaps, it contains a gap right before its left parenthesis. That lack or gap is enough to keep (56) from appearing in (57). So, if Davidson's analysis is accepted and if deep structure is identified with logical form, one cannot say that the deep structure of (43) is embedded in that of (44) and the usual syntactic analyses of these sentences must be rejected.

As noted already, the situation is complicated by the existence of alternatives to Davidson's analysis and to the usual syntactic analyses. All analyses, including Davidson's, are in the process of being developed, elaborated, and modified. It is not possible to say at this time what the end result will be. It is to be expected that that result will be compatible with the identification of deep structure with logical form.

APPENDIX: PRONOMINALIZATION PROBLEMS

How is one to analyze (23)?

(23)   A boy who was fooling her kissed a girl that loved him.

It is true that in some sense (23) is equivalent to

(64)   (A boy x) ((a girl y) (x was fooling y and x kissed y and y loved x)).

But the quantifiers in (64) range over all boys and all girls respectively, while that does not seem true in (23). Karttunen makes an analogous point by considering the presuppositions of a sentence like

(65)   The boy who was fooling her kissed the girl who loved him.

This sentence presupposes that there is exactly one pair consisting of a boy and a girl and such that he was fooling her and she loved him. Such presuppositions ought to be reflected in restrictions on appropriate quantifiers. This would not be so if (65) were analyzed as

(66)   (The boy x) ((the girl y) (x was fooling y and x kissed y and y loved x)).

One needs something like

(67)   (The boy x such that x was fooling y) ((the girl y such that y loved x) (x kissed y)).

But (67) is not correct since the first occurrence of y is not bound by the relevant quantifier.

The same problem emerges in clearer form in

(68)   A boy who was fooling them kissed many girls who loved him.

Since *many* here must be associated with a narrower scope than that associated with the *a* of *a boy*, one is tempted to try:

(69)   (A boy x such that x was fooling y) ((many girls y such that y loved x) (x kissed y)).

Again the first occurrence of y has not been bound by the relevant quantifier. Since the major quantifier ranges over boys who are fooling many girls who love them, one is tempted to try this:

(70)   (A boy x: (many girls y: y loved x) ((x was fooling y)) (x kissed y).

[Here the colon is used for 'such that' introducing the restriction on a quantifier.] But now the final occurrence of y remains unbound by the relevant quantifier. If all occurrences of y are to be bound by a single quantifier, that quantifier will have to have wider scope. But, if *many* is given wide scope, the wrong meaning results; for then one is quantifying over girls who love some boy or other, not necessarily the same one.

One might consider a mixed analysis. For example, one might suppose that (68) comes from

(71)   A boy who was fooling many girls who loved him kissed many girls who loved him

via identical NP pronominalization, whereas the pronouns in (71) are traces of bound variables. But this conflicts with the point noted in the main body of this paper, namely that identical NP pronominalization does not in general preserve meaning. Thus (68) and (71) are not equivalent. A boy who was fooling many girls who loved him might kiss many other girls who loved him. In that case (71) would be true but (68) could be false.

Indeed, it is not very clear what the logical form of (68) could be. It seems at least roughly equivalent to

(72) A boy who was fooling many girls who loved him kissed and was fooling many girls who loved him.

That suggests a deep structure roughly like this:

(73) (A boy x: (many girls y: y loved x) (x was fooling y)) ((many girls z: z loved x) (x was fooling z and x kissed z)).

But it is not at all obvious what transformations would be used to get (68) from (73).

An example that raises a similar problem is due to Geach:

(74) Almost every man who borrows a book from a friend eventually returns it to him.

A possible deep structure for (74) might be this:

(75) (Almost every man x: (a book y) ((a z: z is a friend of x) (x borrows y from z))) ((a book w: (a u: u is a friend of z) (x borrows w from u)) ((a v: v is a friend of x and x borrows w from v) (x eventually returns w to v))).

This would be to treat (74) as somehow a reduced form of

(76) Almost every man who borrows a book from a friend eventually returns a book that he has borrowed from a friend to a friend from whom he has borrowed it.

Again it is not clear that this gets the meaning right nor is it easy to see what transformations should be postulated to get (74) from (75). That suggests these analyses are wrong; but it is unclear what an alternative would be.

Here is an apparently similar problem which does seem to have a plausible solution. Recall that the *they* in

(25)   If any arrows are green, they will hit the target.

represents the trace of a variable in

(27)   (Any arrows x) (if x are green, x will hit the target).

Notice that

(77)   If some arrows are green, they will hit the target.

can be read as equivalent to (25). Here too *they* cannot be the result of identical NP pronominalization, since (77) is not equivalent to

(78)   If some arrows are green, some arrows will hit the target.

Furthermore, there seems to be no way to analyze *they* as the trace of a variable bound by *some arrows*. Thus

(79)   (Some arrows x) (if x are green, x will hit the target).

gives a reading of (77) but not the intended reading on which (77) is equivalent to (25). Nor can we simply confine the scope of *some arrows* to the antecedent of the conditional, for then the *they* in the consequent would not fall under its scope:

(80)   If (some arrows x) (x are green), x will hit the target.

A similar problem arises if *some* in (77) is replaced with *several, many, a few, two, seven*, etc.

One might try to argue that a third kind of pronominalization is at work here. (77) is equivalent with

(81)   If some arrows are green, those arrows will hit the target.

Furthermore, one might take (81) as transformationally derived from

(82)   If some arrows are green, those arrows that are green will hit
         the target.

by deleting *that are green*.

However, the problem with this solution is that the phrase *those arrows* in (81) would seem itself to be more a kind of pronoun, a variant of *they*, than a reduced version of *those arrows that are green*. Compare (81) with

(83)   If some arrows are such that those arrows are green, those arrows will hit the target.

The phrase *those arrows* seems to have the same function in (81) and in both of its occurrences in (83). But (83) cannot be read as

(84)   If some arrows are such that those arrows that are green are green, those arrows that are green will hit the target.

So it is doubtful that in (81) *those arrows* represents a reduced form of *those arrows that are green*.

Similarly, consider

(85)   Any arrows are such that, if those arrows are green, those arrows will hit the target.

Here *they* may replace *those arrows* on each of its occurrences without change of meaning. Furthermore, *those arrows* has the same function on each of its occurrences, and its occurrence in the antecedent is obviously not a reduced version of *those arrows that are green*. One can best account for these cases by assuming that bound variables that are not replaced by the NP of the quantifier binding them can become, not only pronouns, but also NPs of the form *the, these,* or *those Fs*, where *F* is a possibly reduced form of the restriction on the relevant quantifier.[8]

How then is one to account for the pronominalization in (77)? One plausible solution is to suppose that the deep structure quantifier in (77) is not *some arrows* but is rather *any arrows*. This is to suggest that both (25) and (77) have the same analysis:

(25)   If any arrows are green, they will hit the target.
(77)   If some arrows are green, they will hit the target.
(27)   (Any arrows x) (if x are green, x will hit the target).

One must also suppose that *any* can sometimes be changed to *some* during NP-placement. This can only happen when an NP is placed into certain contexts, e.g. the antecedent of a conditional; however, it is not clear how one might give a general characterization of the relevant contexts.

This theory explains the otherwise puzzling difference between (77) and

(86)   If they are green, some arrows will hit the target.

If *they* is treated as (cross) referring to the relevant arrows, (77) is ambiguous in a way that (86) is not. In (77) *some arrows* can be read as coming from an underlying *some arrows*, with wide scope, or from *any arrows*. In (86), since *some arrows* appears in the consequent, it can come only from an underlying *some arrows*, and not from *any arrows*.

This suggestion can be extended to examples in which *some* in (77) is replaced by *several, many, a few, two, seven*, etc. For example,

(87)   (Any seven arrows *x*) (if *x* are green, *x* will hit the target).

can become any of the following:

(88)   If any seven arrows are green, they will hit the target.
(89)   If some seven arrows are green, they will hit the target.
(90)   If seven arrows are green, they will hit the target.

So, the second problem seems solvable in a completely satisfactory way. Whether an analogous trick will take care of the first problem remains unclear.

Princeton University

BIBLIOGRAPHY

Bach, Emmon, 'Nouns and Noun Phrases' in *Universals in Linguistic Theory* (ed. by E. Bach and R. Harms), Holt, Rinehart, and Winston, New York, 1968, pp. 90–122.
Chomsky, Noam, 'Deep Structure, Surface Structure, and Semantic Interpretation' in *Semantics: An Interdisciplinary Reader in Philosophy, Linguistics, Anthropology and Psychology* (ed. by Leon Jakobovits and Danny Steinberg), Cambridge University Press, Cambridge, 1970 (to appear).
Davidson, Donald, 'Causal Relations', *The Journal of Philosophy* 64 (1967) 691–703.
Davidson, Donald, 'The Logical Form of Action Sentences' in *The Logic of Decision and Action* (ed. by Nicholas Rescher), University of Pittsburgh Press, Pittsburgh, Penn., 1968.
Fillmore, Charles J., 'The Case for Case' in *Universals in Linguistic Theory* (ed. by E. Bach and R. Harms), Holt, Rinehart, and Winston, New York, 1968.
Geach, P. T., 'Quine's Syntactical Insights', *Synthese* 19 (1968–69) 118–129.
Karttunen, Lauri, *Problems of Reference in Syntax*, Indiana University doctoral dissertation, 1969.
Lakoff, George, 'On Generative Semantics' in *Semantics: An Interdisciplinary Reader in Philosophy, Linguistics, Anthropology and Psychology* (ed. by Leon Jakobovits and Danny Steinberg), Cambridge University Press, Cambridge, 1970 (to appear).
McCawley, James D., 'Where Do Noun Phrases Come From' in *Readings in English Transformational Grammar* (ed. by Roderick Jacobs and Peter S. Rosenbaum), Blaisdell, Boston, 1970.

McCawley, James D., 'English as a VSO Language', *Language* **46** (1970), 286–299.
Postal, Paul M., 'Cross-Over Phenomena', in *Specification and Utilization of a Transformational Grammar* (Scientific Report No. 3), IBM Research Center, Yorktown Heights, New York, 1968.
Ross, John R., *Constraints on Variables in Syntax*, M.I.T. doctoral dissertation, 1967.
Quine, W. V., *Word and Object*, M.I.T. Press, Cambridge, Mass., 1960.
Seuren, Pieter A. M., *Operators and Nucleus*, Cambridge University Press, Cambridge, 1969.
Smullyan, A. F., 'Modality and Description', *Journal of Symbolic Logic* **13** (1948) 31–37.
Smullyan, Raymond M., 'On Languages in Which Self Reference Is Possible', *Journal of Symbolic Logic* **22** (1955) 55–67.
Wallace, John, *Philosophical Grammar*, Stanford University doctoral dissertation, 1964.

REFERENCES

* Work reported here was supported in part by the National Science Foundation.
[1] The notion 'deep structure' is sometimes defined differently.
[2] This assumption is accepted by James McCawley, Paul Postal, Emmon Bach, Charles Fillmore, John Ross, George Lakoff, and Pieter A. M. Seuren. The presentation here is (selectively) based on their work, especially McCawley's. Noam Chomsky defends a theory not discussed here in which deep structure trees are not full semantic representations.
[3] PASSIVE appeared in the VP because it was taken to be a form of manner adverbial which appears in the VP. Thus, many manner adverbial phrases contain the preposition *by* which the subject is assigned when put into passive position. And verbs that take passive also take manner adverbial – and vice versa.
[4] Lakoff points out that these constraints are weak and vary from person to person, so (14) or (15) or both may be ambiguous for some readers.
[5] Not that such sentences are easy to handle on any theory. For more discussion, see the Appendix.
[6] Generalizing the movement constraint here placed on infinitival clause separation may shed light on movement constraints discussed by Ross and by Postal; but this point cannot be pursued here.
[7] The preceding paragraphs generalize points made by Smullyan. I am indebted here to John Wallace.
[8] Quine makes roughly this point.

TROUBLES ABOUT ACTIONS*

In a recent, important series of papers,[1] Prof. Donald Davidson has proposed and illustrated a theory about theories of meaning. The theory, to put it very much more crudely than Davidson does, is simply that a theory of meaning for the (natural) language L ought to take the form of a truth definition for L. That is, such a theory ought to recursively associate each truth-valuable sentence of L with a representation of its truth conditions. Davidson says "what we require of a theory of meaning for a language L is that without appeal to any (further) semantical notions it place enough restrictions on the predicate 'is *T*' to entail all sentences got from schema [1] when '*s*' is replaced by a structural description of a sentence of L and '*p*' by that sentence." (T & M 309)

(1)   *s* is *T* if and only if *p*

Davidson has a number of interesting things to say about the project of framing a truth definition for a natural language, two of which I want to mention here. The first is that a proposed truth definition for L amounts to an *empirical* theory of (an aspect of) the structure of L. "Like any theory, it may be tested by comparing some of its consequences with the facts ... we only need to ask, in selected cases, whether what the theory avers to be the truth conditions for a sentence really are" (T & M 311). I assume Davidson would want to add that other sorts of constraints upon the adequacy of empirical theories of language would also operate here: simplicity, naturalness, and so on.

Second, a truth definition for L amounts to an empirical theory of an aspect of the *structure* of L. In particular, such a theory must contribute to an account of the learnability of L by showing how the truth conditions upon the infinitely many sentences of L can be finitely represented. This latter consideration is important, for it blocks certain philosophical moves which are both easy and unilluminating. For example, Davidson points out, it is allright for the English sentence 'Bardot is good' to have, as its representation in a correct truth theory, the formula 'Bardot is good' (i.e.,

Davidson and Harman (eds.), Semantics of Natural Language, 48–69. All rights reserved
Copyright © 1972 by D. Reidel Publishing Company, Dordrecht-Holland

it is allright for that sentence to be represented by a formula consisting of a primitive predicate together with a name). But " 'Bardot is a good actress' is another matter. The point is not that the translation of the sentence is not in the metalanguage – let us suppose it is. The problem is to frame a truth definition such that 'Bardot is a good actress' is true if and only if Bardot is a good actress – and all other sentences like it – are consequences. We might think of taking 'is a good actress' as an unanalyzed predicate. This would obliterate all connection between 'is a good actress' and 'is a good mother'. And it would give us no excuse to think of 'good' in this use as a word or semantic element. But worse, it would bar us from framing a truth definition at all, for there is no end to the predicates we would have to take as logically simple (and hence accommodate in separate clauses in the definition of satisfaction.)" (T & M 317).

To put it briefly, then, what Davidson wants is a theory which pairs each (declarative) sentence in a language with a representation of its truth conditions and which does so in a way that reveals whatever semantically significant structure the sentence contains. A theory does the first if and only if it entails all formulae of the form '*p*' *is true iff p*. A theory does the second if and only if it (a) pairs each sentence with a formula which formally determines the entailments of the sentence and (b) effects the pairing by reference to whatever productive structures the sentence contains. Davidson appears to believe (what seems to me to be far from obvious) that a theory which entails all formulae of the form '*p*' *is true iff p* cannot help but reveal the semantically significant structure of the sentences which it describes; that is, Davidson appears to believe that there is no trivial way of satisfying the constraints upon a truth definition.

Actually it remains to be shown that a truth definition must, *ipso facto*, reveal logical form. Say *S* is a syntax of *L* iff S recursively enumerates all and only the well-formed formulae (the grammatical sentences) of L. Every sentence in the range of S will be identifiable with an ordered sequence of markers (say, for the sake of simplicity, words) and every such sequence will, presumably, be of finite length. It is trivial, given a well formed formula $F(= w_1, w_2 \ldots w_n)$ to define a function which maps that formula onto a formula of the form " '$w_1, w_2, \ldots w_n$' is true iff $w_1, w_2, \ldots w_n$". If we now want a theory which entails all formulae of this latter form, we need only adopt the postulate that every well formed formula of that form is an axiom.

It will be objected (a) that this is a finite representation of the desired set of formulae, but not a finite axiomatization of that set and (b) that a theory so constructed will certainly prove to be inconsistent. But (a) though the fact that languages can be learned presumably proves that they can be finitely represented, it does not prove that they can be finitely axiomatized, and (b) the reasons for thinking that a theory constructed in the proposed manner would be inconsistent are just the reasons for supposing that *any* truth definition for natural language L would be inconsistent (e.g., the semantic paradoxes.) As Davidson says "... I think we are justified in carrying on without having disinfected this particular source of conceptual anxiety ... most of the problems of general philosophical interest arise within a fragment of the relevant natural language that may be conceived as containing very little set theory" (T & M 314). To put it succinctly, for that wide portion of the language for which there is reason to believe that we *can* construct a consistent truth definition, it is unclear why the quite vacuous truth definition suggested above won't do.

Nevertheless, Davidson is onto something. What we need as part of a theory of language is a mechanical procedure for pairing a sentence with a representation of its logical form; that is, with a formula which formally determines the entailments of the sentence. Moreover, if this procedure is to provide an account of how we (do?, can?) understand sentences, it had better compute the semantic representation of a sentence as a function of the (syntactic) structure of the sentence together with its lexical content. That is, linguistic objects which are, in the syntactic sense, complex must not, in general, be represented as primitive in the metalanguage (idioms, etc. being the tiresome exceptions that prove the rule.) In what follows, I will assume, with Davidson, that a truth definition is, perforce, a theory of logical form. If this turns out not to be the case (if, for example, the theory of logical form turns out to be the theory of a nontruth functional relationship) then what I shall be saying about the representation of action sentences in truth theories applies, *mutatis mutandis*, to their representation in whatever kind of theory the theory of logical form turns out to be.

If we wish to devise a theory which provides representations of the logical form of the sentences of L, and if we wish to test that theory against the facts about the sentences of L, we had better have some cases in which we know, pretheoretically, what the logical form of sentences in

L is. Davidson is well aware of this and has recently been investigating several types of English sentences and proposing accounts of the representations of truth conditions that we might wish a truth definition for English to assign them. In the present paper, I want to take a close look at what Davidson says about the logical form of action sentences – both with an eye to determining whether what Davidson says will do, and with an eye to asking what the logical behavior of action sentences has to tell us about the general character of the theory of logical form.

Actions are, presumably, a proper subclass of events. Sentences which report upon the properties of actions may thus be treated as consisting of (a) expressions referring to events (or variables whose values are designated by such expressions) and (b) predicates over such expressions. This is the fundamental insight upon which Davidson's account of action sentences turns. "The basic idea is that verbs of action ... should be construed as containing a place for singular terms or variables, that they do not appear to. For example, we would normally suppose that 'Shem kicked Shaun' consisted in two names and a two place predicate. I suggest, though, that we think of 'kicked' as a *three* place predicate, and that the sentence be given in this form: $(\exists x)$ (kicked (Shem, Shaun, x)). If we try for an English sentence that directly represents this form, we run into difficulties. 'There is an event x such that x is a hitting of Shem by Shaun' is about the best I can do ..." (LFAS 92).

The most important point about this analysis is that it provides for a straight-forward account of sentences which *prima facie* express modified statements about actions (or, for that matter, modified statements about other kinds of events. The distinction between actions and other events is not really either exploited or explained in Davidson's theory). For example, a sentence like 'Shem kicked Shaun at two o'clock' goes over into $(\exists x)$ (kicked (Shem, Shaun, x)) & (x at two o'clock). Davidsonian paraphrases (as I shall call them) thus provide a normal form for the semantic treatment of adverbial modifiers on action sentences. Adverbs in action sentences report properties of events, and the logical form of an action sentence containing adverbial modifiers is a conjunction.

Now, this is a testable hypothesis, just as it ought to be. What we must ask, if we are to test it, is whether it is true that the logic of adverbial modification is, in the relevant respects, like the logic of conjunction;

whether we can, in general, represent the logical force of an action sentence containing adverbial modifiers by pairing it with conjunctions of sentences which do not contain adverbial modifiers. In particular, we want to know whether we get a natural treatment of adverbial modification if we adopt a policy of representing sentences containing such modifiers by conjunctions of sentences containing predicates over event variables. I shall argue, presently, that this policy runs into considerable trouble, and that the kind of trouble it runs into is, in a variety of ways, illuminating. First, however, I want to digress long enough to try and undermine one of the arguments Davidson gives in favor of adopting this policy.

Davidson thinks that there are structural facts about the behavior of pro-forms in English sentences which argue for the existence of covert event variables in the logical representations of sentences with action verbs. "It is something like 'there is a house such that I brought it, it is downtown, it has four bedrooms' ... and so forth. We can tack on a new clause at will because the iterated relative pronoun [sic] will carry the reference back to the same entity as often as desired .... Much of our talk of action suggests the same idea: that there are such *things* as actions, and that a sentence like (2) describes the action in a number of ways. 'Jones did it with a knife.'

(2)   Jones buttered the toast in the bathroom with a knife at midnight.

'Please tell me more about it.' The 'it' here doesn't refer to Jones or the knife, but to what Jones did – or so it seems." (LFAS, 84).

Now, it is true that the Davidsonian paraphrase of (2) contains a style of variable whose behavior corresponds closely to that of the anaphoric form in (3). Thus, (2) presumably goes over into something like (4), and

(3)   Jones buttered the toast, and it was with a knife, and it was in the bathroom and it was at midnight.
(4) $(\exists x)$ (butter (the toast, Jones, x)) & (x with a knife) & (x in the bathroom) & (x at midnight)

the parallelism between the 'it' in (3) and the 'x' in (4) is self-evident. It is, however, pretty clearly also artifactual. Consider (5). The 'it' in (5)

(5)   John hit Mary on the head and then Bill did it to Sally.

can be paraphrased 'what John did', just as the 'it' in (3) can be paraphrased as 'what Jones did'. That is, just as (3) has the paraphrase: 'Jones buttered the toast and what Jones did, Jones did with a knife, in the bathroom, etc.', so (5) can be paraphrased as 'John hit Mary on the head, and what John did to Mary, Bill then did to Sally'.

Yet the differences between the 'it' of (3) and the 'it' of (5) are more important than the similarities. That is, nothing much follows from the fact that both can be paraphrased 'what John (Jones) did'. Note, in the first place, the syntactic difference. In (3), 'it' replaces a sentence, but in (5) the anaphoric reference is to a verb (namely, 'hit'). That is, in (3), 'it' is paraphrased by 'what Jones did' because it is a pro-form for the sentence 'Jones buttered the toast' and what Jones did, according to (3), was butter the toast. But in (5), 'it' paraphrases 'what John did' because 'it' is a pro-form for the verb 'hit' and, according to (5), what John did is hit (Mary). That is, though the two 'its' paraphrase the same way, they do so for quite different reasons and are quite differently related to the sentences in which they occur. And this shows up in their formal representations. Thus, as we have noted, (4) contains a style of variable that behaves similarly to the anaphoric element in (3). But now consider (6), the presumed Davidsonian paraphrase of (5). Clearly, (6) contains no variable

(6) $(\exists x)\,(\exists y)\,(\text{hit (John, Mary, } x) \,\&\, (\text{hit (Bill, Sally, } y)))$

whose behavior is comparable to that of the anaphoric element in (5). Roughly speaking, the event variables in Davidsonian paraphrases act like place holders for sentences (strictly speaking, we must replace them by nominalized sentences like 'Jones' buttering the toast' or 'John's hitting Mary' if the resultant from is to be syntactically coherent). So, not surprisingly, Davidson's event variables will correspond to English anaphoric elements only when the latter happen to be engaged in sentential anaphora.

The moral would seem to be that there is no particular comfort to be gleaned for Davidson's analysis from the behavior of 'it' in English sentences like (3). Probably we should think of anaphoric elements as literally syntactic devices, i.e., as transformationally introduced replacements for iterated parts of sentences. If this is correct, then the natural further assumption is that the function which takes us from sentences to representations of logical form should operate only *after* the work of

these transformations has been undone (that is, after anaphoric elements
have been replaced by copies of the strings to which they refer). This
amounts to suggesting (a) that there are no anaphoric elements in deep
structure and (b) that semantic representations are computed as a function of deep structure (as well as? rather than?) surface structure.[2] On this
kind of view, it is, at any event, no particular desideratum that the representation of logical form for a sentence should contain styles of
variables that correspond to the anaphoric elements in the sentence. The
behavior of such elements reflects only the superficial syntactic organization of the sentence.

I want now to turn to what seems to me to be a serious problem for
Davidson's account of sentences containing action verbs. To see what this
problem is, consider the difference between sentences like (7) and sentences like (8)/(9).[3]

(7)   John spoke clearly.
(8)   John spoke, clearly.
(9)   Clearly, John spoke.

It is presumably unnecessary to argue for the claim that (7) is logically
independent of (8)/(9), and, *a fortiori*, not logically equivalent to or synonymous with (8)/(9). What does need an argument is that a theory of the
logical form of sentences containing action verbs ought to provide an
account of the distinctions between, and the relations among, sentences
like (7) and (8)/(9). I shall try to show the following things in the following
order: (a) that a theory of the logical form of sentences containing action
verbs ought to provide such an account; (b) that it is at least not obvious
that Davidson's theory can provide such an account; and (c) that the fact
that (b) is interesting.

(a). There are two kinds of cases in which a theory of the logical form of
action sentences can properly decline to provide an account of the relation
between prima facie related sentences which contain action verbs and
modifiers. The first kind of case is the one where it is plausible to construe
the modifier as modifying (not the action but) either the agent or the
recipient of the action. So, a theory of the logical form of action sentences
might properly decline to provide an analysis of the relation between, say,
'John kicked a girl who lived in Chicago' and 'John kicked a girl' on the

grounds that 'who lived in Chicago' modifies the recipient of the action rather than the action *per se*. Analogously, such a theory might decline to provide an analysis of sentences like (10) on the grounds that though (10) *appears* to contain a modifier of an action (vide the paraphrase 'John's kicking his mother was careless') it in fact contains a modifier on 'John' (vide

(10)   John carelessly kicked his mother

the paraphrase 'it was careless *of John* to kick his mother' or, marginally, 'John was careless to kick his mother').

I don't want to try and decide here whether a theory of action sentences would be well advised to opt out of (10) on the grounds just cited.[4] It seems to me that the decision whether a modifier is on an action or on its agent/recipient is often intuitively quite unclear. My present point is just that in neither (7) nor (8)/(9) could 'clearly' conceivably be considered a modifier of 'John'. So, even if there are grounds for a theory of the logical form of action sentences opting out of (10), there could not conceivably be *those* grounds for its opting out of (7), (8)/(9).

The second case where a theory of the logical form of action sentences might properly fail to provide a construal of the relation between *prima facie* related action sentences is the case where it turns out on analysis that there is no such relation to construe. In the present case, it might be argued that, while (7) and (8)/(9) *appear* to be structurally related sentences, they in fact are not; i.e., that they are no more closely related than, say, 'John bit' and 'John scratched'; i.e., that (7) is of the form '*Fa*' and (8)/(9) is of the form '*Ga*', $F \neq G$ i.e., that 'clearly' is ambiguous.

In fact, however, it seems implausible to say that the difference between (7) and (8)/(9) is one that it would be proper to represent by representing 'clearly' as ambiguous. Notice that, in order to exhibit the difference between (7) and (8)/(9), we need not paraphrase 'clearly' out of the sentences. Rather, we can paraphrase in ways that make explicit the differences between the syntactic relation 'clearly' bears to the rest of the sentence in each case. So (7) paraphrases as, perhaps, 'John's manner of speaking was clear', while (8)/(9) paraphrases as, perhaps, 'It is clear that John spoke'. Again, 'clearly' shows up in both paraphrases, but it shows up in different syntactic relations to the embedded sentence 'John spoke', and this seems to me strongly to indicate that the difference between (7) and (8)/(9) is a matter of their structure rather than their vocabulary.

It is, for once, pretty obvious what's going on here. English acknowledges (at least) two kinds of relations between an adverbial phrase and the other structures in a sentence which contains it. The adverbial phrase may modify the *entire* sentence, or it may modify (just) the verb phrase of the sentence.[5] (8)/(9) would seem to be a case of the first kind of relation and (7) to be a case of the second. That is, in (8)/(9) we have a sentence whose (underlying) bracketing is something like (11), while, in (7), we have a sentence whose underlying bracketing is something like (12).[6]

(11)   (Clearly (S))$_S$
(12)   ((John)$_{NP}$ ((spoke$_V$)$_{VP}$ clearly$_D$)$_{VP}$)$_S$

That there *are* these two kinds of syntactic relations between English adverbs and the structures they modify is suggested by a number of considerations. First, there are sentences which are quite naturally treated as being ambiguous between the two. Consider (13), where the difference between the two meanings appears to be correctly represented by the difference between (14) and (15); and (16) which can be either (17) or (18). (If the ambiguity of (16) is not immediately evident, contrast the most natural reading of 'John cooked the meal slowly' with that of the cookbook injunction 'Cook the meal slowly'. Clearly, what is enjoined in the latter case is that you make the meal cook slowly, not that you slowly make the meal cook).

(13)   John will do the job in a minute.
(14)   In a minute (John will do the job).
(15)   John (((will) (do))$_{VP}$ (in a minute)$_D$) the job.
(16)   John cooked the meal slowly.
(17)   (Slowly (John cooked the meal)).
(18)   John ((cooked) slowly) the meal).

I have been arguing that differences like that between (7) and (8)/(9) should be explained by postulating the existence of two distinct classes of adverbial phrases: sentence modifiers and constitutent modifiers. I suggested that the existence of ambiguities like (13) and (17) provides independent motivation for the assumption that there in fact exist modifiers of these two kinds. It may now be remarked that there seems to be a difference in the sentential positions that the putative two types of modifiers can occupy. Thus, we have (19) but not (20) for what appear to be true verb phrase modifiers, but both (21) and (22) for what appear to be true sentence modifiers.

(19)   John made the model boat by hand.
(20)   *By hand, John made the model boat.
(21)   John made the model boat by the river.
(22)   By the river, John made the model boat.

To summarize the argument so far: structures like (7) and (8)/(9) fall within the purview of a theory of action sentences first because, in both sentences, we are dealing with modifiers on actions (rather than on the agents or recipients of actions) and, second, because the differences between (7) and (8)/(9) appear to turn on facts about their structure rather than on idiosyncracies of the syntactic behavior, or of the lexical content, of 'clearly'. We may therefore proceed to ask how Davidson's theory fares with distinctions between sentences like (7) and (8)/(9).

(b). I now want to argue that Davidson's theory of action sentences provides no natural account of distinctions like the one between (7) and (8)/(9); in particular, that Davidson's theory provides for no natural treatment of those adverbs which are constituent modifiers rather than sentence modifiers.

It will be remembered that Davidson's canonical form for a simple action sentence containing an adverbial modifier and what would normally be taken to be an n-place relation is (23). In the case where $n=2$, this formula has as its schematic English translation

(23) $(\exists x)\,(V(p_1, p_2, ...p_n, x))\,\&\,(Dx)$
(24)   (There is an event x such that x is a Verbing of p_2 by p_1 and (Dx)).

something like (24). It's extremely important to keep clear on how the variables are being handled here. Presumably, though this is not critical to the argument, the values of $p_1 ...p_m$ $(m<n)$ are persons, and the values of $p_{m+1} ... p_n$ are either persons, things, or events (vide 'John bit Mary', 'Russell and Whitehead wrote *Principia*', 'De Gaulle brought about the

end of the Algerian war', etc.) But (and this *is* critical) the values of '*x*' are explicitly constrained to be events. E.g., possible substitutions for '*x*' in well-formed sentences are 'John's speaking', 'Shem's kicking Shaun', 'the sun's rising', etc. but not 'the sun', 'John', 'Shem', 'Shaun', 'kicking', 'rising', 'speaking', etc. As we remarked above, the formulae which substitute for '*x*' are (a certain kind of) nominalized sentence.

All this amounts to saying that, while Davidsonian paraphrases provide for a natural way of paraphrasing sentences like (8)/(9), there is going to be trouble with sentences like (7). To put it succinctly, instantiations of (Dx) in a Davidsonian paraphrase are most naturally read as having the syntactic analysis (adverb (nominalized sentence)). But in (7) we have a modifier *not on a sentence but on a non-sentential phrase*. In particular, (25) is arguably an analysis of (8)/(9), but as an analysis of (7) it would appear to be a non-starter.

(25) $(\exists x)$ (spoke (John, x) & (clearly (x)))

That this kind of trouble is going to be a serious one for Davidson can be seen even from some of Davidson's proprietary examples. Davidson says that the logical form of 'I flew my spaceship to the Morning Star' is (26).

(26) $(\exists x)$ (Flew (I, my spaceship, x)) & To (The Morning Star, x)

But it is possible to doubt that (26) is so much as well formed. For, what 'to the Morning Star' designates is not a property of *events* (no more than to the Morning Star is a property of prime numbers or of the Morning Star). Possible properties of events are designated by: 'occurring on the fifth of July', 'occurring on the Morning Star', 'being dreaded by Mary', 'being over too soon', 'being the third of its kind this month', etc. But not, surely, being 'to the Morning Star'. (Vide the literal ungrammaticality of 'my flying my spaceship was to the Morning Star'.) What has gone wrong is that Davidson wants to express the force and structure of: 'I ((fly) to the Morning Star) my spaceship'. But his notation permits him only: '((I fly my spaceship) to the Morning Star)'.

It should be emphasized that one's hesitancy about (26) is not merely a matter of an over-scrupulous regard for category restrictions. For, even if we accept that (26) represents the logical form of 'I flew my spaceship to the Morning Star', we run into what appear to be very serious difficulties with other, structurally analogous sentences.

Consider (27). (27) is ambiguous in a way that is (roughly) indicated by saying that on one reading it answers such questions as 'What did John aim his gun at?'. And, on the other reading, it answers questions like 'Where did John do his gun aiming?' or 'What happened at the target?' Syntactically, we have the familiar pattern of contrast between a sentential adverb and a verb phrase adverb. So, in the case where (27) answers 'Where did John do his gun aiming?' the structure is, presumably, (28). In the sense in which the sense in which (27) answers 'What did John aim his gun at?' the structure is presumably (29). As one would expect, (30) is unambiguous and has the structure (28).

(27)   John aimed his gun at the target
(28)   At the target (John aimed his gun)
(29)   John ((aimed) at the target) his gun
(30)   At the target, John aimed his gun

Now, the point is that Davidson's theory provides for only one kind of paraphrase of (27), namely, one modeled on (26). Presumably, this would be something like (31). For present purposes, it doesn't much matter which reading of (27) we say that (31) represents. I should have thought that (31) is at best

(31) $(\exists x)$ (Aimed (John, his gun, x)) & (x at the target)

a paraphrase of the reading (27) has under the structural analysis (28). I suspect that Davidson thinks that things like (31) paraphrase sentences like (27) under structural analyses like (29). In any event, it is clear that (31) cannot paraphrase *both* (28) *and* (29) since (28) and (29) are not so much as logically equivalent. The upshot appears to be that Davidson's theory is at best insufficiently rich to account for the full range of types of relations that English allows between events and their modifiers. (Example (27) courtesy of Barbara Hall Partee, to whom I am also indebted for noticing a mistake in an earlier version.)[7]

(c). It is not necessarily interesting that there is a kind of action sentence that Davidson's notation does not capture. Better a theory of the logical form of some action sentences than no theory of the logical form of any action sentences. What I want to show now is that Davidson's problem is a special case of a quite general problem, and that the general problem *is* interesting. I hope it will be understood that I think it enormously to Davidson's credit that he has provided a theory that is clear enough so that general problems can be raised about it.

I have been saying that English acknowledges both adverbs that modify sentences and adverbs that modify verb phrases. This latter phenomenon, of modifiers on non-sentential constituents, is, in fact, quite general in natural languages and tends to pose a problem wherever it occurs. For example, everyone knows that there is a problem about the difference between (32), which translates into the conjunction 'John is nice' and 'John is young' and

(32)   John is a nice young man.
(33)   John owns a typical Georgian house.

'John is a man', and (33), which, egregiously, does *not* translate into 'John owns a house and it is typical and it is Georgian'. The problem here is quite analogous to the problem about constituent adverbs. What we have, in both cases, are modifiers whose heads are something other than sentences. Sometimes, sentences containing such modifiers happen to be logically equivalent to conjunctions of sentences that do not. Not only (32), but also (15) can be handled in this way, since (15) is, presumably, logically equivalent to (34), (If John does the job in a minute, then John's doing the job takes a minute). But, often enough, there is no such conjunctive equivalent at hand (vide (7), (29)) and then we are in the soup.

(34) $(\exists x)$ (Do (John, the job, x)) & (x take a minute)

There are two ways of putting the general problem. One can put it as a problem about truth theories, and one can put it as a problem about differences between the syntax of natural language and the syntax of the standard logical formalisms. Since I don't know for sure which is the right way of putting it, I shall try both.

A truth theory explicates linguistic structure in two ways. In the case of linguistic objects which it takes to be 'simple', it states (i.e. lists) satisfaction conditions. In the case of linguistic objects which it takes to be complex, it shows how their truth conditions are inherited from the truth conditions upon simple objects. But, in the present case, we have to do with complex linguistic structures (including some adjectival structures and some adverbial structures) which, *prima facie*, are *not* built out of sentences with their modifiers, but out of nonsentential phrases with *their* modifiers. Such structures fall into interstices which the standard mechanisms for constructing truth theories fail to illuminate. We do not want to state satisfaction conditions for such objects because they are complex, they exhibit productive structure, there are characteristically infinitely many of them. But, on the other hand, we cannot characterize them by showing how they inherit their truth conditions from the truth conditions upon their parts because their parts, being phrases rather than sentences, *are not the kind of things that have truth conditions.*

It is an indication of our dilemma that when we teach baby logic, we teach our students to fudge. Given a structure containing a modified constituent, we teach them to find a logically equivalent conjunction if there happens to be one, otherwise to invent an unanalyzed predicate. In the first case, we pair the sentence with the kind of object truth theories are built to handle: a complex linguistic object whose parts are sentences. In the second case, 'typical Georgian house' goes over into (x is typical-Georgian & x is a house) thereby loosing structure – and inferences – that we do not know how to represent. It is notable that the bits of this problem inter-connect. For example, attributive adjectives are a kind of constituent modifiers which do not translate into conjunctions. For many such, there are corresponding sentences with adverbial constituent modifiers, so that 'John is a good baker' corresponds to 'John bakes well' both in that they are at least close to synonymous and in that we have a theory for the logical form of neither.

The other way of putting the point is that there are a number of important differences between the syntax of natural languages and the syntax of the standard logical formalisms. Among these is the fact that natural languages acknowledge modifiers both on sentences and on constituents, whereas the standard formalisms acknowledge only the former. There are cases in which we can make do by finding conjunctions of formulae that are logically equivalent to natural language sentences containing modified constituents. But there are also cases in which, apparently, we cannot – i.e., because there does not happen to be any such conjunction. That is, we have no *a priori* guarantee that it is *possible* to model a language containing constituent modification and sentence modification and sentence conjunction in a language which contains only the last two; not, at least, if we wish our theory to represent all the significant structure there is to represent, to stick to smooth translation algorithms, and to respect reasonable ontological scruples.

One further example of a case in which the existence of constituent modification in natural languages presents problems for the standard formalisms.

One of the modifiers that can apply to a constituent in natural languages is negation. Thus, we have not only (35), but also (36), (37), etc. Now,

(35)   It is not the case that John left his house.

(36)   It was not John who left his house.

(37)   It was not his house that John left.

it is arguable that (35)–(37) are logically equivalent, but it is pretty clear that they differ in their presuppositions. (Thus (36), unlike (35) and (37), presupposes that someone left his house; (37), unlike (35) and (36), presupposes that John left some (thing?) (where?) etc.) If, however, we allow the semantic theory to associate (35)–(37) with the standard paraphrase (neg (John left his house)), we lose precisely the structure we need to keep these distinctions of presupposition clear. Here again, when we try to model a language which contains constituent modifiers in a language which does not, we lose something that we would much rather keep. One feels inclined to say, with Wittgenstein, that what we get is either a primitive model of a language or a model of a primitive language; not, in either case, what we had set out to get, which is a sophisticated model of English.[8]

I have argued that sentences like (7) present a serious problem for Davidson's account of action, and that this is a special case of a general problem about how we are to represent the force of constituent modification in languages which, like the standard logical systems, do not permit it. It may be worth the while, as an exercise, to see how much trouble we get into if we insist on a conjunctive paraphrase for sentences like (7).

We might, for example, consider, as a representation of (7), something like (38).

(38) $(\exists x, y)$ (Spoke (John, x)) & (y is a manner) & (y is John's) & (y is clearly)

That there are very serious objections to this formulation is pretty evident. First, it abandons all hope of ontological parsimony, since we are now committed to quantifying, not just over events, but also over manners. It might be argued, indeed, that (38) is not merely ontologically unparsimonious but also ontologically disreputable. What are the identity conditions for manners?

Second, (38) strains the genitive, perhaps beyond bearing, in the third conjunct. Can a manner have the property of being John's? In the way that a nose can? In the way that a house can? In what way?

Third, something has gone wrong in conjunct four. Notice that it is strictly ungrammatical as read, since what stands as predicate to a manner must be an adjective rather than an adverb. That is, the fourth conjunct ought to read 'y is clear', not 'y is clearly'. The shift in its grammatical category suggests that 'clear(ly)' is playing a different role in (38) than in (7), and this turns out to be true. What (7) says is clear is John's speaking. But what (38) says is clear is John's manner.

Finally, and I think decisively, (38) fails to say what (7) certainly does say, namely that the manner in question is John's manner *of speaking* and, in particular, that it is John's manner of speaking on the occasion of those events which are values of x. (38) would, for example, be true if ((there is an event on which John spoke) & (John writes clearly)).

We can patch things up a bit by changing (38) to (39). But notice

(39) $(\exists x, y)$ (speak (John, x) & (y is a manner of speaking) & (y is John's) & (y is clear)

that (39) still attributes clarity to John's manner, not to his speaking. What's worse (what is, in fact, fatal), the second conjunct now contains the unanalyzed complex predicate 'is a manner of speaking' (vide such contrasting formulae as 'is a manner of losing/winning/writing/flying to the Evening Star/etc.') and, predictably, it is a predicate whose natural-language counterpart contains a constituent modifier. Thus, 'y is John's manner of speaking' is, syntactically, 'John ((speak) in a manner which is y)'.

Notice, too, that (39), like (38) fails to say that y is John's manner of speaking on the occasion of some event x. That is, nothing in (39) says that the value(s) of y which make the second through fourth conjuncts true are properties of the event(s) which make the first conjunct true. It might be thought that, since conjunct two says that y is a manner of speaking, it must follow that y designates a property of speech events. This *does* follow if we say it does (i.e. if we adopt a special postulate to that effect.) But it is not determined by the form of (39) since, in (39), 'is a manner of speaking' is an unanalyzed predicate in which the terms 'manner' and 'speaking' do not, of course, occur.[9]

One might try to remedy the last-mentioned defect of (39) by adopting something like (40). 'R' is here taken to designate a primitive relation

(40) $(\exists x, y)$ (spoke (John, x)) & $(R(y, x))$ & (y is clear)

between a manner y and an event x, such that $(R(y, x))$ iff (x is an action and y is the manner in which the agent of the action performed the action). I assume that Davidson would not stand for this for a minute, and rightly so. (40) does not solve the problem of expressing the force of constituent modifiers in a language which contains no such modifiers. Rather, it abandons the program of translating meaning into structure by assuming (what is simultaneously implausible and unilluminating) that sentences like (7) express a primitive relation between a manner and an event. If, moreover, we ask *which* relation this primitive relation is, we are forced, in the meta-meta language, to resort to constituent modification all over again: i.e. to say that "it is a relation which obtains iff a certain agent ((performs) in a certain way) a certain action".

Indeed, if we are going to permit (40), we might as well think of *speak* as a relation between an event, a person, and a manner (and a time, and a place, and ... etc.) Davidson (plausibly) disallows this last sort of solution because we would then have no way of telling how many places a given relation is supposed to have. But, given that we allow formulae like (40), we have the precisely analogous problem that there is no way of telling how many primitive relations between events and persons, places, manners, motives, times etc. the semantic theory may be forced to recognize. Or how many rules of inference the theory will need to mediate the logical relations between them.

I close this lugubrious section by remarking that, even if we were able to discover an adequate conjunctive analysis for (7), there is no particular reason to suppose that it would provide so much as a clue to how to deal with the inadequacies of (26) or the ambiguities of (27).

What, then, is to be done? The previous discussion does not *prove* that it is impossible to amend Davidson's proposal in a way that permits us to represent the force of adverbial constituent modification in the notation of the standard logical formalisms. But it provides what I think is a reasonably strong prima facie case for that conclusion. If it is not misleading in that respect, then it looks as though we have two options.

We might try distinguishing sharply between the theory of meaning and the theory of truth (more precisely, between the theory of meaning and the theory of logical form). In particular, we might try saying that what phrases like 'speak clearly' or 'fly to the Evening Star' inherit from their constituents is not their truth conditions but their meanings. If we have a theory of how the meaning of a complex predicate derives from the meanings of its constituents, then there is no reason why we cannot acknowledge infinitely many predicates which receive no analysis *within the theory of truth*. On this view, a theory of meaning is a device for providing an infinite lexicon (one which defines, by list, a finite number of words and recursively defines an infinite number of non-sentential phrases). From the point of view of the theory of truth, on this analysis, 'John spoke clearly' has the form 'F (John)' and 'John spoke well' has the form 'G (John)' and $F \neq G$. The truth conditions upon each are established by some such satisfaction rule as " 'P(John)' iff the individual designated by 'John' has the property designated by 'P.' " If, however, we want to know what property 'P' in fact designates, or what the logical consequences of having the property designated by 'P' may be, in infinitely many cases where 'P' is constructed from a non-sentential constituent with its modifiers we shall have to resort to the (recursive component of the) dictionary. This *seems* to be the kind of thing that, e.g., Katz and Fodor (1964) had in mind,[10] but I wouldn't bet on it.

The other alternative is to assume that the meta-language, in which the truth conditions on natural language sentences are to be represented, has a syntax very much more like the syntax of English than has usually been supposed. In particular, perhaps we ought to assume that the meta-language too contains constituent modification. If we choose this tack, then what needs to be worked on is the formalization of whatever inference rules govern modified constituents. This proposal perhaps deserves a moment's consideration.

The project of translating sentences which contain modifiers into conjunctions of sentences which do not, receives its impetus almost entirely from the fact that we know what the inference rules governing sentence conjunction are like. Clearly, we want a theory of meaning to provide representations of sentences which formally determine their entailments. That is, we want such a theory to provide, for each sentence, a representation which has the property that whether a given rule of inference applies to that representation is mechanically determinable. We want, in short, to formalize natural languages. Now, systems of representation which permit sentence conjunction, but not constituent modification, have, to that extent, got the desired property. And systems which permit constituent modification to that extent do not. But this is as much a comment on our *de facto* inability to formulate the relevant rules of inference as it is a comment upon the nature of such systems. Analytic philosophers have been rather generally inclined to assume that the theory of meaning is a complicated algorithm which takes natural language sentences into formulae which exhibit a simple syntax and behave according to simple and general rules of inference.[11] It is possible to imagine, however, that the theory of meaning is a relatively simple algorithm which takes sentences of natural languages into formulae which have a complicated syntax and which behave in accordance with rules of inference no one has yet been able to state. At the end of this road, one glimpses the possibility that such rules apply directly to (syntactically analyzed) English sentences; i.e., that there is no theory of meaning in the classical sense of that notion. That is a route which I, for one, will travel only under compulsion.[12]

REFERENCES

* Thanks are due, *inter alia*, to Janet Dean Fodor, Prof. Judith Thomson, Prof. Helen Cartwright and Prof. Richard Cartwright, all of whom helped with the hard bits. But none of the preceding is guilty of any of the following.

[1] I shall be referring to 'T & M' and 'LFAS'. The former is cryptic for Donald Davidson, 'Truth and Meaning', *Synthese* 17 (1967) 304–323; the latter for Donald Davidson, 'The Logical Form of Action Sentences' in *The Logic of Decision and Action* (ed. by N. Rescher), University of Pittsburgh Press, Pittsburgh, Pa., 1967, pp. 81–95.

[2] It should be mentioned, however, that there are plenty of troubles with this (or any other known) view of anaphora. See, *inter alia*, Chapter III of David Reibel and Sanford Schane (eds.), *Modern Studies in English*, Prentice Hall, Englewood Cliffs, N.J., 1969. For discussion of proforms for verbs, see J. A. Fodor, 'Three Reasons for Not Deriving "Kill" from "Cause to Die"', *Linguistic Inquiry* 1 (1970).

[3] Davidson explicitly excludes adverbs like 'clearly' from his discussion on two grounds. First, they function similarly to comparatives (John spoke clearly for a man with his mouth full of marbles, but unclearly for a Yale man) and the logical form of compar-

atives is, in general, unknown territory. Second, unlike such adverbs as 'at twelve noon' or 'in New York', 'clearly' introduces no "new entity" into sentences like (8/9).

However, neither of these peculiarities of 'clearly' is the one on which our discussion of (8/9) will turn; and we will see presently that some sentences which have neither of these properties are nevertheless counterexamples to Davidson's analysis.

4 In fact, I think the right account is that (10) is ambiguous in the same way as (27) below.

5 This point has been widely recognized in the linguistic literature. For an extended analysis, see Noam Chomsky, *Aspects of the Theory of Syntax*, M.I.T. Press, Cambridge, Mass., 1965.

6 'S' for 'sentence', 'NP' for 'noun phrase', 'V' for 'verb', 'VP' for 'verb phrase', and 'D', indiscriminately, for 'adverb' or 'adverbial phrase'.

7 That this case is not isolated, and not restricted to verbs which govern opaque contexts, can be seen from the existence of rather subtle ambiguities like 'John left the train at the station'. On the most obvious reading (where 'left' has the force of 'disembarked from' the Davidsonian paraphrase is the natural one since the presumed deep structure is (at the station (John left the train)), i.e. 'at the station' functions as a sentence modifier. But consider the alternative reading where the train is a toy train and John left it, say, at the station baggage counter. Here 'John left the train at the station' does *not* entail 'John disembarked from the train', nor can we paraphrase this reading by 'At the station, John left the train' (cf. the patent ungrammaticality of 'At the station, John left his umbrella'). On this second reading, the presumed deep structure is (John ((left) at the station) the train) or, possibly, John ((left the train) at the station); in any event, a constituent modifier rather than a sentence modifier seems to be at issue. The point is, of course, that the two readings are not equivalent, so that $(\exists x)$ (leave (John, the train, x)) & At (the station, x) can represent at most one of them.

There may be some temptation to suppose that 'leave' is lexically ambiguous, but I think the temptation should be resisted. 'John left his friend at the station' has the same ambiguity as 'John left the train at the station', but here neither reading can be captured by rendering 'left' as 'disembarked from'. Indeed, in this case the relevant difference between (at the station (John left his friend)) and (John ((left) at the station) his friend) is just that the former entails that both John and his friend were at the station when they parted, while the latter would be true if, say, John drove his friend to the station and then drove off.

8 It should be added, however, that the problem of modeling the presuppositions of negative sentences in a language which contains no constituent negation is not *quite* so worrying as the problems about adjectival and adverbial constituent modification. This is because, if we assume the mechanisms of set theory, and in particular a complement operator, we can get something of the force of constituent negation. At, by the way, a corresponding sacrifice of naturalness in the mapping from English into the canonical language. (It is important to remember that this mapping is, *ex hypothesi*, to be accomplished by a *mechanical* procedure. It is thus a rule of thumb that the more structural dis-similarity we permit between natural language expressions and their meta-linguistic translations, the more trouble we are likely to have in characterizing the mechanism that performs the translation). For discussion of the relations between constituent negation and presupposition, see Noam Chomsky, 'Deep Structure, Surface Structure, and Semantic Interpretation' in *Semantics: An Interdisciplinary Reader in Philosophy, Linguistics, Anthropology and Psychology* (ed. by Leon Jakobovits and Danny Steinberg), Cambridge University Press, Cambridge 1971.

⁹ It is worth mentioning the existence of a reading of (7) which attributes to John not a *performance* but, roughly, a *trait*. This is, in fact, a kind of ambiguity that is exhibited quite pervasively by past tense action sentences. (Cf. 'John was greedy', 'John was self-sacrificing', 'John spoke Latin', etc.) I have ignored this reading of sentences like (7) because there is not a prayer of capturing it with Davidsonian paraphrases. In particular, 'there are one or more events which consist of John's speaking clearly' surely does not entail 'John (chronically) speaks clearly' though it is, perhaps, entailed by it.
¹⁰ Jerrold J. Katz and Jerry A. Fodor, 'The Structure of a Semantic Theory', *Language* 39 (1963) 170–210.
¹¹ One price they have paid for this assumption is an unresolved problem about how to draw the distinction between inferences mediated by structure (for which the assumption might be true) and inferences mediated by (lexical) content (for which it quite certainly is not).
¹² It is worth suggesting how this sort of approach might hope to handle entailment relations which turn upon the presence of adverbial phrases.

Clearly, we shall need both rules which introduce adverbial phrases and rules for their elimination (i.e., rules which, respectively, determine when a sentence which does not contain a certain adverbial entails a sentence which does; and rules which determine when a sentence which does contain a certain adverbial entails a sentence which does not).

The general character of the latter sort of rule is fairly clear. Roughly, given a sentence S whose deep structure contains a verb phrase with its m adverbial modifiers, this sentence will entail any sentence S' which is identical to S except for the deletion of the $m-1th$ adverbial phrase. (I assume that the adverbs are ordered in deep structure and that the order is left-to-right by increasing scope. If this assumption is false, minor modifications will have to be made in the rule.) This rule explains why 'John spoke clearly' entails 'John spoke', etc. On the other hand, it does *not* permit the (invalid) inference from 'Probably John spoke' to 'John spoke' since it does not apply to sentence operators.

Two remarks may be made about this rule for 'peeling off' adverbial phrases. First, it applies to *syntactically analyzed* sentences (presumably, to deep structures). For example, the rule must 'know' that 'except Sunday' is not an independent adverbial in 'John and Mary make love every day except Sunday'; otherwise it will allow us to infer from that sentence to 'John and Mary make love every day'. I am assuming that the aspects of structural descriptions that may be mentioned in characterizing the domain of such rules may be quite abstract and are, in fact, precisely the sorts of syntactic properties of sentences that are investigated in modern grammars.

Second, it is worth noting that the rule for peeling off adverbial phrases is strikingly analogous to the rule of simplification which allows us to infer P, Q from $P \& Q$. (For example, both rules fail in the scope of opaque verbs, in the scope of negation, etc.) The primary difference is that since the peeling off rule operates on phrases, it allows us to capture the entailments of sentences containing adverbials without first translating them into conjunctions à la Davidson.

The general character of the rule for shortening sentences by peeling off adverbial phrases seems to be fairly clear. What is more complicated is the rule which allows us to lengthen sentences by adding such phrases. Roughly, the following rule of addition would seem plausible. Assume, as Davidson does, that verbs have fixed numbers of argument places and that a verb may appear in well-formed sentences in which some of its places are unfilled. Suppose, in particular, that we have a verb

V of α places appearing in a sentence S where only $\beta < \alpha$ of its places are filled. Then the rule of addition allows us to infer any well-formed sentence S' which differs from S only by the addition of a 'dummy' phrase ('sometime', 'somewhere', 'in some manner', etc.) in the position of the appropriate unfilled place of V. Thus, the rule of addition lets us infer from 'John bit Mary' to 'John bit Mary sometime', 'John bit Mary somewhere' (in both senses), etc.

Two points about the rule of addition. First, it is, as stated, grossly informal. But formalizing it would be quite straightforward given: a canonical form for representing base structures of sentences containing verbs with their argument positions, an enumeration of the lexical sequences that are to count as dummy phrases, and an enumeration of the well-formed sentences. There would appear to be no principled reason for believing that these conditions cannot be met.

More serious is the following worry. The rule of addition assumes that certain adverbials (together, for that matter, with direct objects, indirect objects, etc.) appear as fillers for the argument positions of verbs, and this returns us to the problem of how we are to determine which and how many arguments a given verb should be assigned. For example, we presumably want the theory to allow us to infer from 'John pointed the stick' to 'John pointed the stick at something' but we do not want it to let us infer from 'John waved the stick' to 'John waved the stick at something'. Clearly, the rule of addition will block the latter inference while permitting the former only if we assume that the phrase for what is pointed at occupies an argument position of 'point' but the phrase for what is waved at does not occupy an argument position of 'wave'. This amounts to saying that the criterion for whether a phrase should be treated as occupying an argument position of a verb is simply whether the rule of addition applies. In particular, assume that an adverbial phrase occupies an argument position of the verb V if and only if a sentence whose verb phrase contains just V entails a sentence which differs only in that its verb phrase contains a dummy for the adverbial as well.

JOHN ROBERT ROSS

ACT

o

In this paper, I will present evidence that every verb of action is embedded in the object complement of a two-place predicate whose subject is identical to the subject of the action verb, and whose phonological realization in English is *do*. That is, such sentences as (1) will be derived from such structures as that shown in (2) by some rule such as that shown in (3).[1]

(1)   Frogs produce croaks.

(2)

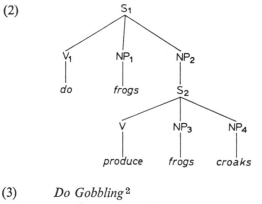

(3)   *Do Gobbling*[2]
$$X - [_s do - NP - [_s V - Y]_s]_s - Z$$
$$\text{OBL}$$

1	2	3	4	5	6 ⇒
1	4	3	0	5	6

In Section 1 below, I will present ten arguments that (2) underlies (1), and that (3), or some rule with the same effect, must therefore be in the grammar of English. In Section 2, I will give arguments against an initially plausible alternative analysis, one which would make use of an

Davidson and Harman (eds.), Semantics of Natural Language, 70–126. All rights reserved
Copyright © 1972 by John Robert Ross

inverse of the rule of *Do Gobbling*. In Section 3, I will discuss a number
of problems for, and implications of, this analysis.

I

I.1.   As a first piece of evidence for the correctness of (2), note that any
grammar of English will have to contain a lexical item *do* which will
require an animate NP as subject, and an abstract NP as object, so that
the sentences in (4) can be generated.

(4a)

$$
\text{Jack did}
\begin{cases}
\text{a study of bat guano} \\
\text{a report on marshmallows} \\
\text{research on hedonism} \\
\text{a dive from the south bulwark} \\
\text{some (snark-) hunting}
\end{cases}.
$$

(4b)

$$
\text{Jack did}
\begin{cases}
\text{*knowledge of karate} \\
\text{*some meaning (that he was ill)} \\
\text{some hunting} \begin{cases} \text{for} \\ \text{*\_\_} \end{cases} \text{snark}
\end{cases}.
$$

(4c)   **This article does a report on marshmallows.

(4d)   This article reports on marshmallows.

The contrast between (4c) and (4d) supports the claim that this verb *do*
requires animate subjects, for *report* can occur as an object of *do*, as
(4a) shows. The contrast between (4a) and (4b) shows that only abstract
nouns denoting activities can appear as the object of *do*, and furthermore,
that non-prepositional phrase objects of these abstract nouns will produce ungrammatical sentences unless they are incorporated into the
noun.[3]
    Thus since such a lexical item as this *do* must be assumed to exist on
independent grounds, its appearance in S_1 of (2), a clause which has an
animate subject and an abstract object whose main verb denotes an
activity, will engender no problems in remote structure. Hence, the
sentences of (4a) provide some indirect support for the correctness of
(2): V_1 in (2) is not a verb that must be created *ad hoc*.

I.2 In Lakoff and Ross (1966), it was proposed that the pro-VP *do so* of such sentences as those in (5) be introduced via some such rule as that in (6).

(5a)   You've bungled a lot of hands, Goren, but fortunately Jacoby has done so too.

(5b)   I'll take the curare off of my toothpicks if you do so first.

(6) $$X - \left[\left[\begin{smallmatrix}+V\\-\text{Stat}\end{smallmatrix}\right]^4 - Y\right]_{VP} - Z - \left[\left[\begin{smallmatrix}+V\\-\text{Stat}\end{smallmatrix}\right] - W\right]_{VP} - R \quad \text{OPT}$$

$$1 \qquad 2 \qquad 3 \qquad 4 \qquad 5 \quad 6 \qquad\qquad 7 \quad \Rightarrow$$

$$1 \qquad {}_1\left\{\begin{smallmatrix}2 & & 3\\ & do\ so &\end{smallmatrix}\right\}_1 \quad 4 \quad {}_1\left\{\begin{smallmatrix} & do\ so &\\5 & & 6\end{smallmatrix}\right\}_1 \qquad 7$$

Condition: 2 3 = 5 6

It is obvious that this rule is not even minimally adequate. Later rules must treat the *do's* introduced by (6) as verbs, so that affixes (like the *-en* of (5a)) can be permuted around them (cf. *has done so*). Thus (6) would have to be restated in such a way that the *do's* were daughter-adjoined to the feature bundles in 2 and 5 of the rule and were verbs in derived structure.

But aside from this relatively minor technical failing of (6), this rule makes the implicit claim that the content of the terms substituted for the deleted VP's in its structural change is a matter of no importance; that it is an accident that it is the two morphemes *do* and *so*, in that order, which show up when a verb phrase is pronominalized. The rule would be no more highly valued if it introduced these morphemes in the reverse order, or only one of them, or some random string of them, or some other random morphemes, like *hootchie cootchie*, as exemplified in (7).

(7a)   *You're bungling the play on this hand, Blackwood, but you're soing do cleverly.

(7b)   *I took the curare off my toothpicks, because I sincerely believed that my roomie was soing.

(7c)   *Drop that heater, Derringer! You're a dead man if you haven't done do do do so do so so do do do by the time I count to three.

(7d)   *The House has already drafted a bill, and the Senate is at this moment hootchying cootchie.

Lakoff and I would now reject the analysis we proposed in Lakoff and Ross (1966), in favor of one embodying the analysis of (2) and rule (3). Under such a reanalysis, it is possible to explain why the pro-VP *do so* contains the pro-sentence *so*, as well as explaining why it contains the morpheme *do*, why both are necessary, and why they appear in that order. The *do* is the *do* of (4a). Since this *do* requires that its underlying objects be abstract NP's denoting activities, the feature [−Stative] need not be mentioned in the rule which replaces its sentential object, S_2 in (2), with *so*. Furthermore, since the grammar must contain in any case a rule of *So Insertion*, stated roughly as in (8), no new rule of VP pronominalization will be required.

(8)   *So Insertion*[5]
$$X - S - Y - S - Z$$

$$\text{OPT}$$
$$1 \quad 2 \quad 3 \quad 4 \quad 5 \Rightarrow$$

$$1 \quad _1\left\{ \begin{matrix} 2 \\ so \end{matrix} \right\}_1 \quad 3 \quad _1\left\{ \begin{matrix} so \\ 4 \end{matrix} \right\}_1 \quad 5$$

Condition: 2=4

This rule will cause (9a) to be converted to (9b),[6] yielding ultimately (9c), and in an exactly parallel manner, it will cause (10a) to be converted to (10b), which will eventually yield (10c).

(9a)

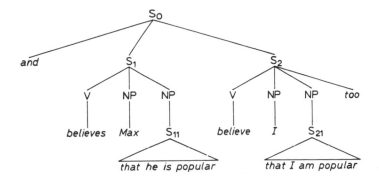

(9b)

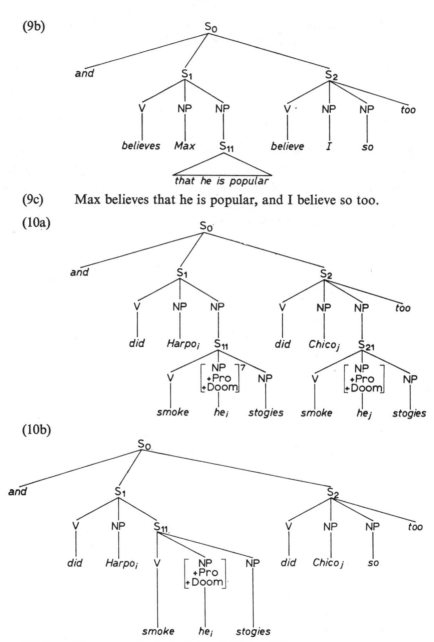

(9c)   Max believes that he is popular, and I believe so too.

(10a)

(10b)

(10c)   Harpo smoked stogies and Chico did so too.

There exists, however, a serious problem for this analysis or for any analysis which attempts to provide an explanation for the occurrence of the morpheme *so* in (5): it appears, namely, that in all cases involving what are normally called true verbs, *so* can only replace complement sentences which have finite main verbs. Verbs which may only appear in surface structure with infinitival objects (such as *manage, tend, condescend, dare*, etc.), gerundive objects (such as *avoid, keep, finish, stop*, etc.) and tenseless *that*-clauses (such as *desire, require, stipulate, command*, etc.) can never be followed by *so*: thus *I managed so, *They kept so, *I desire so* are all impossible.

It might be thought that this difficulty could be circumvented by merely allowing S_2 in (2) to be a tensed clause. This escape route appears unusable, however, for two reasons: (a) if McCawley is correct, as he appears to be, in his conjecture that tenses are higher stative verbs (cf. McCawley, 1971), then the next verb above each activity verb would be a stative verb, and only above this stative verb would *do* appear. To prevent other undesirable configurations of verbs above activity verbs would require constraints involving three adjacent verbs, an *ad hoc* and counterintuitive extension to an otherwise fairly well established theory of types of possible selection. (b) *do* is a verb which requires that its subject and the subject of its complement be identical.[8] That is, no well-formed surface structure can result from the ill-formed underlying structure shown in (11).

(11)

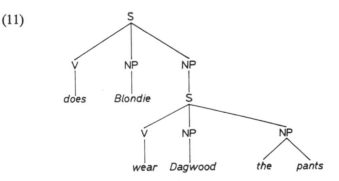

No other English verb with this property (i.e., such verbs as *try, manage, condescend, avoid, begin*, etc.) ever shows up in any sentence with a tensed object clause. Thus to assume that *do* is followed by a tensed clause is

incompatible with the assumption that the underlying subject of this
tensed clause must be identical to the subject of *do*.

The only way out of this difficulty that I see at present is provided by
such sentences as those in (12).

(12)

They say Jack { was there, and so he was
has guts, and so he has
is working, and so he is
has goofed, and so he has
can belch, and so he can }.

There is a considerable body of evidence, some of it discussed in Ross
(1969, 1971)[9], which indicates that auxiliaries must be analyzed as main
verbs, albeit verbs with many idiosyncratic properties, not as some
English-particular morphemes, as different from verbs as from *of*, which
is the claim implicitly made in Chomsky's classic analysis of the English
auxiliary.[10] If the reanalysis suggested is correct, and such auxiliary
elements as *be*, *have*, *can*, etc., are main verbs, then it would appear that
rule (8), or possibly a second rule for inserting *so*, can apply to replace
the objects of these verbs with *so*. That is, I would argue that some transformational rule of pronominalization must convert (13a) to (13b), which
will ultimately yield (13c).

(13a)

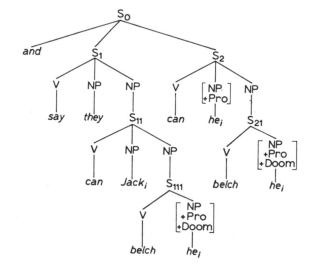

(13b)

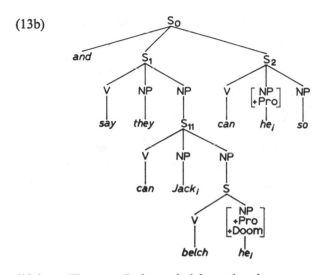

(13c)   They say Jack can belch, and so he can.

If my conjecture that (13a) underlies (13c), and that it is converted to (13b) by transformational rule, is correct, then it might also be this rule that converts (10a) to (10b), even though it might not be possible to identify this rule with the one which converts (9a) to (9b). If, however, my reanalysis of English auxiliaries is wrong, and such structures as (13a) need not be postulated, then what will follow is that there is no explanation for why *so* appears in the pro-VP *do so*. Some *ad hoc* rule, an amended version of the one proposed in Lakoff and Ross (1966), will replace the object of *do* by *so*, and no explanation will be available as to why this morpheme is inserted, instead of, say, *cootchie*. But even in this glum state of affairs, which, it should not be necessary to emphasize, is not improved upon by any analysis which merely inserts *so* by some *ad hoc* rule, the fact that the verb *do* appears in the pro-form *do so* can be explained, given the analysis implicit in (2) and rule (3). Thus even in the worst circumstances, this analysis can be used to explain one facet of *do so* pronominalization.

I.3.   Let us now turn to happier phenomena. In addition to *do so* pronominalization, activity verb phrases can be replaced by the proform *do it*, as in (14).

(14a)   Herb Fuller washed his cars before I could do it.
(14b)   Men who can do it sleep late.

Again, *do it* is restricted to replacing VP's whose main verb is [−Stative]: (15) is ungrammatical.

(15)   *The plot involves drug addiction, but it didn't use to do it.

This fact, and the fact that VP's are replaced by the sequence of morphemes *do* and *it*, in that order, can be explained, on the basis of the independently necessary rule of *S Deletion*,[11] which I have stated in (16).

(16)   *S Deletion*

$$X - [S]_{NP} - Y - [S]_{NP} - Z$$
$$\qquad\qquad\qquad\qquad\qquad\qquad\text{OPT}$$
$$1 \quad\quad 2 \quad\quad 3 \quad\quad 4 \quad\quad 5 \Rightarrow$$

$$1\left\{\begin{matrix}2\\\left[\begin{matrix}2\\+\text{Pro}\end{matrix}\right]_1\end{matrix}\right\}_1 3 \left\{\begin{matrix}\left[\begin{matrix}4\\+\text{Pro}\end{matrix}\right]\\2\end{matrix}\right\}_1 5$$

Condition: 2=4

This rule converts sentences like (17a) into (17b), which will eventually become (17c).

(17a)   The fuzz believe $_{NP}[$ $_S[$ that Max is a junkie $]_S$ $]_{NP}$, but I don't believe $_{NP}[$ $_S[$ that Max is a junkie $]_S$ $]_{NP}$.
(17b)   The fuzz believe $_{NP}[$ $_S[$ that Max is a junkie $]_S$ $]_{NP}$, but I don't believe $_{NP}[$ $[^S_{+\text{Pro}}]$ $]_{NP}$.
(17c)   The fuzz believe that Max is a junkie, but I don't believe it.

If (2) underlies (1), the fact that *do it* is a pro-VP is an automatic consequence of the independently necessary rule (16). Thus this rule will convert (18a) into (18b), for S_5 and S_6 are identical in (18a). Later rules will transform (18b) into (14b).

Thus the analysis implicit in (2) can be seen to explain the fact that *do it* can function as a pro-VP, in the sense that extra restrictions would be necessary to *prevent* (18a) from being converted to (18b), and ultimately to (14b). Given (2), and the general rule of *S Deletion,* we expect that

(18a)

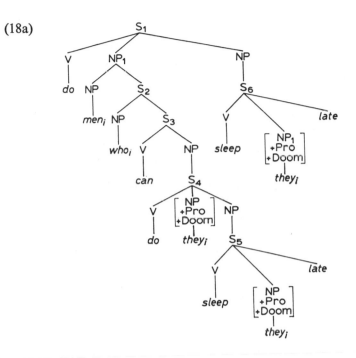

(18b)

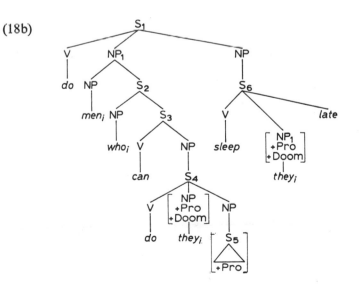

such pro-forms as those in (14) will arise, and that *do* will precede *it*, and not conversely; and that *it* will appear, not some random morpheme like *hoc*. The perfect parallelism of (17) and (18) constitutes evidence of the strongest kind for rule (3), *Do Gobbling*.[12]

I.4. Let us now turn our attention to appositive clauses, such as the subordinate clause of (19).

(19)   Little Bo Peep, who also lost her cool, soon regained it.

As far as I know, it is generally agreed upon that such clauses are to be derived from conjoined sentences. Since arguments to this effect have appeared elsewhere[13], I will not reiterate them here. I know of no counterevidence to the proposed analysis.

Such sentences as (19) would arise by a two-step process. First, a rule of *Swooping*, which is formulated in (20), Chomsky-adjoins a conjoined clause to a NP in a following conjunct, subject to the condition that the swooped clause contain an occurrence of the identical NP.

(20)   Swooping
$$[_s \; and - [_s X - NP - Y_s]_s] - S'' - [_s \; and - [_s W - NP - Z_s]_s]$$

1	2	3	4	5	6	7	8	9	OPT
0	0	0	0	5	6	7 8 # [1234] 9			$\Rightarrow$

Condition: $3 = 8$

This rule would thus convert (21a) to (21b).

(21a)

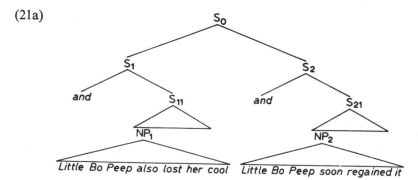

(21b)

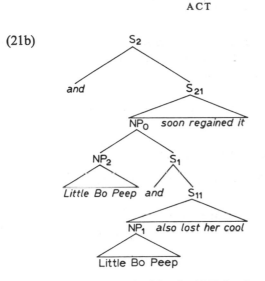

Following *Swooping*, the identical NP in the swooped clause is fronted by the rule of *Relative Clause Formation*, presumably the same rule that applies in the case of restrictive relative clauses.

(22)   *Relative Clause Formation*

$$W - {}_{NP}[NP - {}_s[X - NP - Y]_s]_{NP} - Z$$

$$\quad 1 \qquad 2 \qquad 3 \qquad 4 \qquad 5 \qquad 6 \quad \overset{\text{OPT}}{\Rightarrow}$$

$$\quad 1 \qquad 2 \begin{bmatrix} 4 \\ +\text{Pro} \end{bmatrix} \#\ {}_s[\ 3 \ \ 0 \ \ 5 \ ]_s \ \ 6$$

Condition: $2 = 4$

With various refinements, and later rules, which I will not go into here,[14] rule (22) will convert (21b) into (23), which is approximately the correct derived structure for (19).

(23)

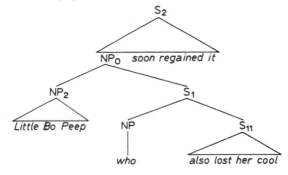

Now observe that if (2) underlies (1), the same two rules of *Swooping* and *Relative Clause Formation*, without any change whatsoever, will generate such sentences as those in (24).

(24a)   That Bob resigned, which I think I should do, was a good idea.

(24b)   Ted left, which he shouldn't have done.

(24c)   Curling, which is difficult to do, is also boring.

The structure of (24a) prior to *Swooping* would be (25a). *Swooping* and *Relative Clause Formation* (and other rules) will convert (25a) to (25b) and then to (25c).

(25a)

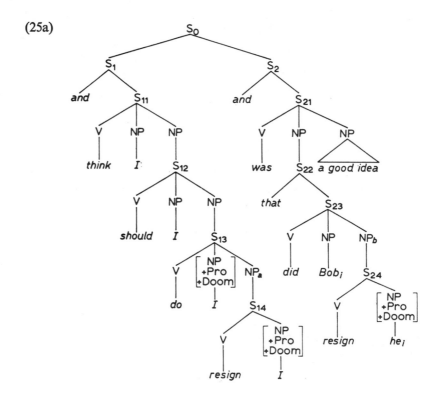

(25b)

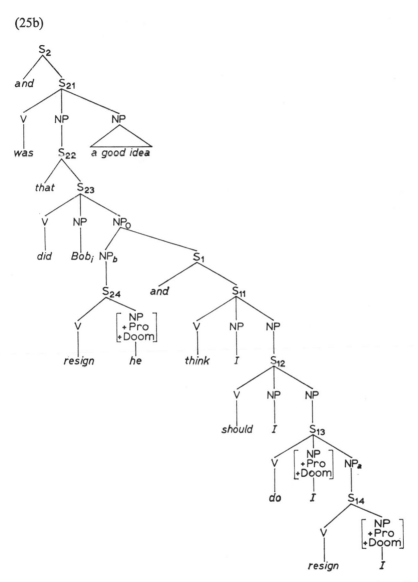

Swooping can apply to (25a) because S_1 and S_2 contain two sloppily identical NP's: NP_a and NP_b, respectively. After S_1 has been Chomsky-adjoined to NP_b, the node NP_0 in (25b) meets the structural description for *Relative Clause Formation*. The head NP of NP_0, namely NP_b, is

(25c)

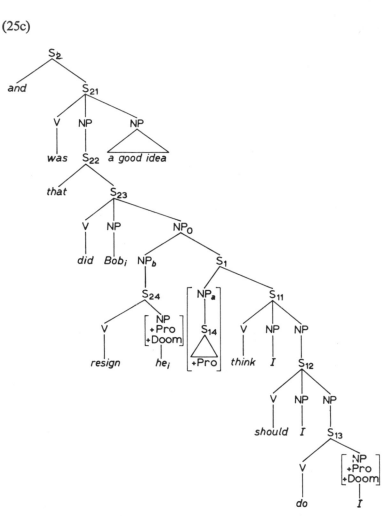

identical to NP_a in the swooped clause, so NP_a can be fronted and pronominalized, eventually becoming *which*. The only other rules that have
to apply to (25c) to produce (24a) are the rules which delete doomed
pronouns (cf. Postal (1970b)); the general rule which obliterates the *and*
which starts S_3; *Do Gobbling*, which will substitute *resign* in S_{24} for *did*
in S_{23}, yielding *resigned*;[15] and *Verb Subject Inversion*, which will permute
V and the immediately following NP in S_{21}, S_{23}, S_{11}, and S_{12}.

It is important to note that all the rules needed in the derivation of

(24a), and of the other sentences of (24), are needed independently, with the exception of *Do Gobbling*. None of the rules need to be changed in the slightest respect to generate these sentences, if (2) is assumed to underlie (1), and if the grammar contains *Do Gobbling*. This rule can thus be said to *explain* the grammaticality of the sentences of (24) (and, of course, of (5), (10c), and (14) above.) Thus such sentences strongly argue for the correctness of the claim that (1) derives from (2).

I.5.   Consider next equative sentences, such as those in (26).

   (26a)   Jack is unbeaten: no one even dares to challenge him.
   (26b)   Rudolf gave many things to Greta: he gave lox and bagels to her.
   (26c)   You do one thing right now: you apologize right now.

I have no idea what such equative sentences are to be derived from. Their clauses seem to be semantically linked in some way (thus all the sentences in (26) would become deviant if either of their clauses were replaced by *Tiny Tim is a knockout*). Possibly the requirement is that the clauses of such sentences share the same topic. Be that as it may, if they share syntactic, as well as semantic, material, they may be abbreviated, by a rule which seems intuitively to be very close to *Sluicing*[16] – the rule of *Equative Deletion*.

   (27)   *Equative Deletion*[17]

$$_s[X-\underset{-Def}{[NP]}-Y]_s : {}_s[X-NP-Y]_s \qquad \text{OPT}$$

1	2	3	4	5	6	7	⇒
1	2	3	4	0	6	0	

   Conditions: 1 = 5
                     3 = 7

Since the clauses of (26b) are identical, except for the fact that the first clause has the NP *many things* where the second has the NP *lox and bagels*, *Equative Deletion* can operate upon this structure, deleting *Rudolf gave* and *to Greta*, producing (28).

   (28)   Rudolf gave many things to Greta: lox and bagels.

The clauses of (26c) do not appear, in surface structure, to meet the structural description of *Equative Deletion*, for they do not both admit of a parsing into $[X-NP-Y]_S$. Yet an abbreviation of (26c) is possible: (29).

(29)   You do one thing right now: apologize.

Thus if the deep structure of the second clause is anything like (30),

(30)

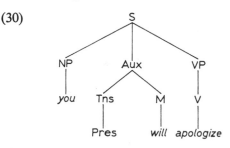

it will be impossible to derive (29) from (26c) by the general rule given in (27). However, if *Do Gobbling* is in the grammar, and if the underlying structure of (26c) parallels (2), as in (31), then *Equative Deletion*, in the general formulation given for this rule in (27) can apply, in the manner indicated by the dotted lines in (31), and (29) will result.

(31)

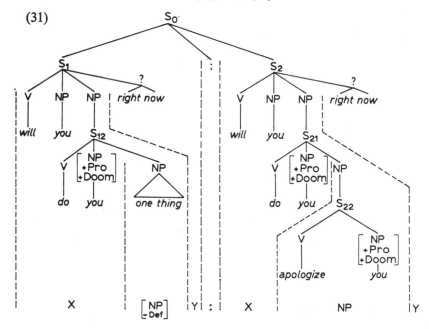

Of course, *Equative Deletion* is an optional rule, and it need not apply to (31). If it does not apply, the rule of *Do Gobbling* will obligatorily substitute *apologize* for the *do* of S_{21}, and sentence (26c) will result.

Thus the fact that (26c) and (29) are optional variants, paralleling (26b) and (28), also argues that (2) underlies (1), and that *Do Gobbling* must appear in the grammar of English.

I.6.   As we saw in the immediately preceding section, the generalization concerning abbreviated equative sentences was that only NP's could follow the colon in such sentences. Some examples appear in (32).

(32a)   He built [something fantastic]$_{NP}$: [a golden igloo]$_{NP}$.

(32b)   He said [something absurd]$_{NP}$: [that curling was moribund]$_{NP}$.[18]

(32c)   Angel wanted [only one thing]$_{NP}$: [to dance with Betty Grable]$_{NP}$.[18]

(32d)   Dan left the truck [where I thought I'd never find it]$_{NP}$: [behind the books]$_{NP}$.[19]

(32e)   She is [what her brother never was]$_{NP}$: [fearless]$_{NP}$.[20]

(32f)   Mike did [what I wanted to do]$_{NP}$: [tickle Henrietta]$_{NP}$.

Above, I argued that the analysis implicit in (2) should be adopted, so that (32f) could be subsumed under this generalization.

Now note that exactly the same class of constituents is possible after *other than* and *but* (suggesting, incidentally, that these forms be treated as variants), as (33) indicates.

(33a)   He built nothing $\left\{\begin{array}{l}\text{other than}\\ \text{but}\end{array}\right\}$ [a golden igloo]$_{NP}$.

(33b)   He said everything $\left\{\begin{array}{l}\text{other than}\\ \text{but}\end{array}\right\}$ [that curling is moribund]$_{NP}$.

(33c)   Angel wanted nothing $\left\{\begin{array}{l}\text{other than}\\ \text{but}\end{array}\right\}$ [to dance with Betty Grable]$_{NP}$.

(33d)   Dan leaves trucks everywhere $\begin{Bmatrix} \text{other than} \\ \text{but} \end{Bmatrix}$ [in the toy box]$_{\text{NP}}$.

(33e)   I am anything $\begin{Bmatrix} \text{other than} \\ \text{but} \end{Bmatrix}$ [eager to volunteer]$_{\text{NP}}$.

(33f)   Hortense did everything $\begin{Bmatrix} \text{other than} \\ \text{but} \end{Bmatrix}$ [whistle Dixie]$_{\text{NP}}$.

While the syntax of *other* is, if anything, even less clear than the syntax of equative sentences, if the analysis implicit in (2) is adopted, it will at least be possible to give a general characterization of the phrases which can follow *other than* and *but*: only noun phrases can.[21] Thus I take such sentences as those in (33) to constitute at least weak confirming evidence for the correctness of the claim that (2) underlies (1).

I.7.   Consider now pseudo-cleft sentences, such as (34).

(34)   What I like to angle for is killer whales.

Again, the basic generalization seems to be that what follows the copula in such sentences must be a NP – cf. the sentences in (35).

(35a)   What he said was [that he couldn't understand the Early Bird]$_{\text{NP}}$.
(35b)   What Betty wanted was [to stay out of Angel's reach]$_{\text{NP}}$.
(35c)   Where Dan likes to put pencils is [into the plastic horse]$_{\text{NP}}$.
(35d)   What I have never been is [prudent]$_{\text{NP}}$.
(35e)   What Mortimer must not do is [juggle with live grenades]$_{\text{NP}}$.

Thus these sentences also suggest that the analysis implicit in (2) is correct, for with this analysis, a general characterization of those constituents that can follow the copula in pseudo-clefts can be given.

However, with this construction, as opposed to those involving equative sentences and sentences containing *other than* and *but*, I think it is possible to make somewhat more specific claims as to the nature of the syntactic processes involved in the derivation of such sentences as those in (34) and (35). While a full justification of this analysis is beyond the scope of the present paper[22], I believe that it can be maintained that such sentences as (34) should be derived from a structure containing two embedded clauses, such as (36).

(36)

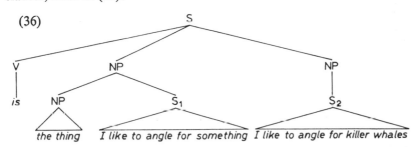

As can be seen, the two embedded clauses are identical, except for the two NP's *something* and *killer whales*. The following rule, which is again very reminiscent of *Sluicing*, deletes those parts of S_2 which are identical to parts of S_1.

(37)　　*Pseudo-cleft Formation*

$$be - [NP - [X - NP - Y]_S]_{NP} - [X - NP - Y]_S$$
$$\;1\quad\;\;2\quad\;\;3\quad\,4\quad\,5\qquad\;\;6\quad\,7\quad\;\,8$$
$$\Rightarrow$$
$$\;1\quad\;\;2\quad\;\;3\quad\,4\quad\,5\qquad\;\;0\quad\,7\quad\;\,0$$

Conditions: $3 = 6$
$5 = 8$

One argument for the correctness of this analysis is the fact that in colloquial speech, the rule is optional for many speakers, and S_2 can appear in surface structure, as in (38).

(38)　　What I like to angle for is I like to angle for killer whales.

Almost all speakers can optionally not apply the rule when the NP in term 4 is the object of *do*. That is, most speakers have the sentences in (39) in free variation with one another.

(39a)　　What I did then was $\begin{Bmatrix} \text{call the grocer} \\ \text{I called the grocer} \end{Bmatrix}$.
(39b)

Although there are many serious flaws in this analysis, I know of no competing analysis which can avoid them, so let us provisionally assume the correctness of (36) and (37), for the purposes of discussion.[23] (37) is the simplest formulation of the rule which will derive the least problematic of pseudo-cleft sentences – namely, sentences like (34). Observe now that if (2) underlies (1), such sentences as (35e) and (39a) will result automatically. The deep structure of (39) is (40), which can be partitioned in such a way as to meet the structural description of rule (37), as shown by the dotted lines.

(40)

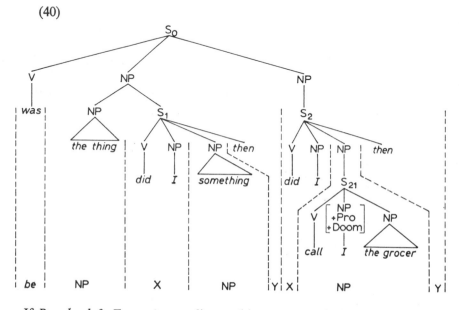

If *Pseudo-cleft Formation* applies to this proper analysis, deleting *did I* and *then* in S_2, sentence (39a) will result. If these terms are not deleted, then *Do Gobbling* will obligatorily apply in S_2, substituting *call* under *did*, producing *called*. *Verb Subject Inversion* in S_0, S_1, and S_2 will then yield (39b).

While the details of this analysis of pseudo-cleft sentences have not been gone into here, one salient point should have emerged: if the analysis implicit in (2) is adopted, such sentences as (35e) and (39) will be generated by the most general formulation of the rule of *Pseudo-cleft Formation*. This fact constitutes strong evidence for the analysis in (2).

I.8.   Let us now examine the syntax of such sentences as those in (41).

(41a)   That girl I wouldn't touch with a fork.

(41b)   That ice cream contained calories I hadn't known.

(41c)   Proud of her I don't think he ever was.

The rule which produces such sentences I have referred to as *Topicalization* (cf. Ross, 1967).[24] While not all NP's can be topicalized[25], it appears that only NP's can be. Thus while not all speakers accept sentence (42), for those dialects in which it is grammatical, it supports the derivation of (1) from (2).

(42)   Waxing the floors I've always hated to do.

For those dialects in which (42) is unacceptable, it will presumably be excluded by whatever constraint is responsible for prohibiting sentence (b) in footnote 25.

   I conclude, therefore, that since (42) would most naturally be derived from a source like (43),

(43)   *I've always hated to do [waxing the floors]$_{NP}$.

to which *Do Gobbling* would obligatorily apply to produce (44),

(44)   I've always hated to wax the floors.

The grammaticality of (42) in some dialects supports the claim that (1) derives from (2).

I.9.   William Cantrall has called to my attention the fact that *Tough Movement* can be used to make the same point as *Topicalization*. The former rule converts such sentences as those in (45) to the corresponding ones in (46).[26]

(45a)   It is impossible to solve English crossword puzzles.

(45b)   It is easy to see that we're not wanted here.

(45c)   It will be tough for Fiorello to agree to try cooking without garlic.

(46a)   English crossword puzzles are impossible to solve.

(46b)   That we're not wanted here is easy to see.

(46c)   Cooking without garlic will be tough for Fiorello to agree to try.

Thus, since all subjects of *Tough-Movement* predicates (except *it*) arise through the application of this rule, we must presume that the source for (47) is the ungrammatical (48).

(47)   Solving English crossword puzzles is impossible to do.

(48)   *It is impossible to do [$_{NP}$ solving English crossword puzzles]$_{NP}$.

But *Do Gobbling* would convert this ungrammatical string to the grammatical (45a). Thus the incorporation of this rule into the grammar of English allows *Tough Movement*, too, to retain its maximally general form. Without *Do Gobbling*, the formulation of *Tough Movement*, like the formulation of *Topicalization*, would have to be complicated.

I.10   The strongest argument for the correctness of the analysis in (2) was discovered by Paul Postal. He observed[27] that such sentences as (49)

(49)   Kissing gorillas just isn't done (by debutantes).

can only be derived by the most general formulation of the rule of *Passive* if such structures as (2) are assumed to exist.[28] And since a structure like (50) must be assumed to underlie (49),

(50)   *Debutantes just don't do [kissing gorillas]$_{NP}$.

a rule like *Do Gobbling* must be postulated to convert (50) into the grammatical (51).

(51)   Debutantes just don't kiss gorillas.

I.11.   To recapitulate, I have argued above that the postulation of a remote structure like (2) for (1), where the highest verb of (2) is deleted by the rule of *Do Gobbling*, makes possible an explanation of the fact that *do* is the morpheme that shows up in two kinds of pro-VP, as well as explaining why the morpheme *it* can appear as a part of a pro-VP. While I have no entirely satisfying answer to the question as to why the object of *do* should be convertible into *so* by rule (8) (or possibly by the rule which converts (13a) into (13b)), if *do* has a sentential object in deep structure, at least a partial explanation of the presence of the morpheme *so* can be attempted. In Sections 1.4–1.8, I argued that the rules governing the formation of appositive clauses, equative sentences, sentences containing *other than*, pseudo-cleft sentences, topicalized sentences, and sentences involving *Tough Movement*, when formulated in such a way that they would account only for the simplest sentences (e.g., for *Swooping*, clauses in apposition to non-complement NP's), would automatically extend to generate such sentences as (24), (29), (35e), (39), (42) and (47), if remote structures like (2) were assumed. Finally, I argued that the existence of such passive sentences as the main clause of (a) in footnote 12 could be explained on the basis of the analysis implicit in (2), but not on any analysis paralleling that in Lakoff and Ross (1966), and that *no* analysis other than (2) seemed to provide a plausible source for Postal's sentence, (49).

One further claim which I made in Section 0, namely that all activity verbs in remote structure appear as complements of a higher verb *do* in such sentences as (4a), (5), (14), (24), (29), (35e), (39), (42), (47) and (49), where this *do* leaves a phonological reflex, they do not suffice to show that this *do* is necessary in *all* remote structures, over *every* activity verb.[29]

There is a simple answer to such a position: the existence of the above-mentioned sentences constitutes evidence not only for the existence of such deep structures as (2), but for the existence of some rule like (3) as well. Therefore, if some structure such as (52) were postulated as a possible underlying source for (1),

(52)

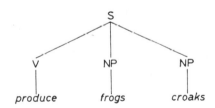

the claim would be made that (1) was structurally ambiguous – it would be derivable from either (52) or from (2). That it would be derivable from (2) follows from the fact that (2) must be assumed to be a well-formed remote structure, in order for the abovementioned list of sentences to be derivable, and from the fact that (3) is a rule of English, and could apply to (2), converting it into (52). However, (1) is not ambiguous, so if both (52) and (2) are well-formed remote structures, semantic rules must be devised which would map them onto the same semantic object. There is reason to believe that (2) more nearly represents the meaning of (1) than (52),[30] so a semantic rule would have to be postulated which would have essentially the opposite effect of *Do Gobbling*, in that it would map (52) onto some *semantic* representation resembling (2). Hence if (52) is a well-formed remote structure, an otherwise unnecessary semantic rule, which performs an operation which is the inverse of *Do Gobbling*, will have to be added to the grammar. That is, not only is there not the slightest evidence for assuming that (52) is a well-formed remote structure, but this assumption actually engenders a complication in the grammar. I conclude that (52) is not well-formed; that is, that no remote structure containing an activity verb not embedded in the object of *do* is well-formed.

II

The ten arguments above seem to me to demonstrate conclusively that remote structures like (2) must be inferred to exist, and therefore, that some rule like *Do Gobbling* must appear in the grammar of English. It might be thought, however, that an analysis which 'went in the other direction' would be feasible. In such an analysis, it might be maintained that some rule of *Do Insertion* could be formulated which would not entail the postulation of remote structures like (2). Though no published analysis along these lines exists, it does have some plausibility on first glance, so I think it is worthwhile detailing some of the disadvantages that such an insertion analysis would encounter, difficulties which are avoidable under the gobbling analysis proposed above.

II.1.   First, though this is not a difficulty with an insertion analysis *per se*, the possible claim that the rule of *Do Insertion* which would be necessary could be identified with the rule which inserts the 'empty' *do* of the auxiliary analysis of *Syntactic Structures* seems to me to be mistaken. In the first place, some sentences exhibit *both do*'s.

(53)   What they didn't do is lock the door.

The *do* in *didn't* is the 'empty' *do*, while the second *do* is the one deleted by *Do Gobbling*. It is difficult for me to imagine how a reasonable, non-disjunctive environment for any rule of *Do Insertion* could be given which would allow an insertionist to claim that his theory allowed one to dispense with what might be claimed to be, under the competing theory, an extra rule – the rule of *Do Gobbling*. Thus I see no way for the claim to be substantiated that any insertion analysis is a rule simpler than the gobbling analysis.

II.2.   Secondly, while it might be claimed that an insertion analysis would allow certain rules, such as *Topicalization, Pseudo-Cleft Formation, Tough Movement*, etc. to be 'generalized' in such a way that they would apply not only to NP's, but also to non-stative VP's (thus *Topicalization* would be formulated as in (54), with a later rule inserting *do* in the place left by yanking out the VP),

(54)   *'Generalized' Topicalization*

$$X - \left\{ \begin{array}{c} NP \\ \left[\begin{array}{c} VP \\ -\text{Stative} \end{array} \right] \end{array} \right\} - Y \qquad \text{OPT}$$

$$\begin{array}{ccc} 1 & 2 & 3 \quad \Rightarrow \\ 2 \neq_s [1 & 0 & 3]_s \end{array}$$

I must confess that in my opinion, exactly the reverse is the case. That is, despite the fact that (54) would apply to more nodes than would (55), which is what I would regard as basically the correct formulation of *Topicalization*,

(55)   *Topicalization*

$$X - NP - Y \qquad \text{OPT}$$

$$\begin{array}{ccc} 1 & 2 & 3 \quad \Rightarrow \\ 2 \#_s [1 & 0 & 3]_s \end{array}$$

it seems to me that under every standard use of the term 'general' in linguistics, (54) would have to be regarded as less general than (55). For instance, I believe that almost all phonologists would agree that the rule (56a) is more general than the rule in (56b).

(56a) $s \rightarrow [+\text{voiced}]/V - V$

(56b) $\left\{ \begin{array}{c} s \\ p \end{array} \right\} \rightarrow [+\text{voiced}]/V - V$

While it is probably necessary to concede that rules may generalize (e.g., diachronically) by the disjunctive addition of new *environments* for the application of the rule, it seems to me that it is never the case that rules

can be shown to generalize by the disjunctive addition of unrelated segments to the part of the rule which specifies what segments are to be
changed. We would, of course, admit that rule (57a) is a generalization
of (56a),

$$(57a) \quad \begin{Bmatrix} f \\ s \\ x \end{Bmatrix} \rightarrow [+\text{voiced}]/V - V$$

$$(57b) \quad \begin{Bmatrix} +\text{obs} \\ -\text{cnt} \end{Bmatrix} \rightarrow [+\text{voiced}]/V - V$$

$$(57c) \quad \begin{Bmatrix} +\text{obs} \\ -\text{cnt} \\ +\text{cor} \end{Bmatrix} \rightarrow [+\text{voiced}]/V - V$$

but that is precisely because the new members of the change part of
(57a) are *related* to the previous member. In feature terms, (57a) is more
general than (56a), because the former can be expressed with fewer
features than the latter, as is shown by the contrast between (57b) and
(57c).

Note that no analogous move can be justified in the matter of the
decision between (54) and (55). That is, it would be pointless and *ad
hoc* to propose a feature analysis of syntactic node types, in such a way
that NP would be analyzed as $\begin{bmatrix} +\text{Movable} \\ +\text{Object-like} \end{bmatrix}$, whereas the disjunction

of $\begin{Bmatrix} \text{NP} \\ \begin{bmatrix} \text{VP} \\ -\text{Stative} \end{bmatrix} \end{Bmatrix}$ would be analyzed as $[+\text{Movable}]$. Not that such a fea-

ture analysis of constituent types is *a priori* wrong or self-contradictory,
of course – it is merely that without independent justification of such
putative features as $[+\text{Movable}]$ and $[\pm\text{Object-like}]$, justification of
the sort that can readily be provided for each of the phonological
features in (57b) and (57c), the thrust of my argument to the effect that
(54) is less general than (55) cannot be avoided.

Most importantly, note that if (54) were to be countenanced as a valid
reanalysis of the facts of (41) and (42), then we would also have to consider (59) to constitute a valid counterproposal to the traditional analysis

of reflexives and imperatives that is expressed in the two rules of (58)[31].

(58a) *Reflexive*

$$X - NP - Y - NP - Z$$

$$\text{OBL}$$

$$\begin{array}{ccccc} 1 & 2 & 3 & 4 & 5 & \Rightarrow \end{array}$$

$$\begin{array}{ccccc} 1 & 2 & 3 & \left[\begin{array}{c} 4 \\ +\text{Refl.} \end{array}\right] & 5 \end{array}$$

Conditions: (i) 2=4

(ii) 2 and 4 are clausemates[32].

(58b) *Imperative*

$$\text{Imp(Neg)} - you - will - X$$

$$\text{OBL}$$

$$\begin{array}{cccc} 1 & 2 & 3 & 4 & \Rightarrow \end{array}$$

$$\begin{array}{cccc} 1 & 0 & 0 & 4 \end{array}$$

(59) *Impflexive*

$$\left\{\begin{array}{c} X - NP - Y - NP \\ \# - V - Y - you \end{array}\right\} - Z$$

$$\text{OBL}$$

$$\begin{array}{ccccc} 1 & 2 & 3 & 4 & 5 & \Rightarrow \end{array}$$

$$\begin{array}{ccccc} 1 & 2 & 3 & \left[\begin{array}{c} 4 \\ +\text{Refl.} \end{array}\right] & 5 \end{array}$$

Conditions: (i) If 2=NP, then 2=4

(ii) 2 and 4 are clausemates.

If the analysis of (59) is adopted, no rule like (58b) need appear in the grammar – imperative sentences can be generated without subjects in deep structure.

Of course, to ensure that only imperatives like the *a*-sentences in (60)–(62) will be generated, it will also be necessary to restate disjunctively the rules by which the morpheme *own* is transformationally (?) introduced, the rules which copy the subject NP in idiomatic expressions like *to crane one's neck*, *to watch one's step*, etc., and the rules which govern the formation of tag sentences.

(60a) Buy your own lid.

(60b) *Buy Ralph's own lid.

(61a) Crane your neck.

(61b) *Crane our necks.

(62a)   Give us a ring, won't you?
(62b)   *Give us a ring, won't I?

Formally, such disjunctive reformulations are trivial to construct.

In an exactly similar fashion, if the analysis in (2) is not adopted, it will be necessary to reformulate not only (55) disjunctively, as was done in (54), but also the rules of *Swooping, Relative Clause Formation, Equative Deletion, Pseudo-cleft Formation, Tough Movement,* and whatever rules can be devised to·account for sentences containing *other than.*

What is wrong with such 'reanalyses'? The answer is simple: they miss generalizations. Put otherwise, they repeat the same fact many times. In the case of the imperative 'reanalysis', the repetition would show up as special branches on many rules like *Impflexive*; where these special branches all mentioned the pronoun *you.* In the case of the analysis implicit in (2), what would be repeated many times would be the unnatural line in (54). But any theory containing such repetitions is a wrong theory. Realizing this, transformational grammarians have postulated an underlying *you* subject in imperatives, and a rule like (58b) to delete it, rejecting such disjunctive rules as *Impflexive.* In my view, exactly parallel reasoning should lead one to postulate an underlying *do* in activity sentences, and a rule like (3) to delete it. And just as it has been said that rule (58b) *explains* the presence of *you* in imperatives like those in (60a), (61a), and (62a), so I think it can fairly be said that rule (3) explains the presence of *do* in sentences like (5), (14), (24), (29), (35e), (39), (42), (47) and (49).

At present, I can see no logical distinction between the reasoning underlying the traditional imperative analysis and the reasoning underlying the analysis in (2). Therefore, until such time as a real reanalysis of the facts in Section I has been worked out, it seems to me that one can only accept the former [33] if one also accepts the latter.

II.3.   A third difficulty with *Do Insertion* is that while it might be possible to 'generalize', with the above *caveat*, the rules for insertion of *so* and *it*, so that they applied to $\left\{ \begin{array}{c} S \\ VP \end{array} \right\}$, thus allowing (63a) to become (63b),

(63a)   Jack has often [sung off-key] and he will probably [sing off-key] again.

(63b) *Jack has often sung off-key, and he will probably $\left\{ \begin{array}{c} it \\ so \end{array} \right\}$ again.

it would then be necessary to rescue (63b) from ungrammaticality by requiring the rule of *Do Insertion* to stuff in *do before* the pro-forms *so* and *it*. Thus one fact about *Do Insertion* – that *do* would precede *so* and *it* – would be accidental. That is, as was pointed out in Section I.2 above, in criticism of Lakoff and Ross (1966), only the gobbling analysis can link the fact that *so* and *it* follow *believe*, *say*, and other true verbs, with the fact that they also follow *do*.

II.4. Fourthly, and most damagingly, how can any insertion analysis preserve the rule of *Passive* in any reasonable form, and yet generate (49)?

It may be, of course, that I, as a gobbler, am too blinded by the beauty of my analysis to be able to conjure up an insertionist who is clever enough to counter these four problems. Only time will tell. In the meantime, it seems to me that the above are strong reasons for assuming the correctness of the gobbling analysis.

III

There are a number of serious difficulties with the gobbling analysis, however. I will review them here, in the hope that highlighting them will aid future researchers in getting around them.

III.1. Possibly the most serious problem has to do with a restricted class of sentences that was pointed out to me by Edward Klima. Some examples are shown in (64).

(64a)

$$\left\{ \begin{array}{l} \text{All} \\ \text{The only thing} \\ \text{*What} \end{array} \right\} \text{the samples} \left\{ \begin{array}{l} \text{need} \\ \text{have to} \\ \text{must} \\ \text{*can} \\ \text{*are required to} \\ \text{*will} \end{array} \right\} \text{do is}$$

contain protein molecules, and we're sunk.

(64b)   All that it is $\begin{Bmatrix} ?\text{necessary} \\ *\text{possible} \\ *\text{odd} \\ *\text{expected} \end{Bmatrix}$ for Jack to do is to resemble

Granny, and he'll win the prize.

(64c)   If the oatmeal contains strontium, which it will probably do, let's send it back to Quaker Oats.

The problem is, where do the *do's* in these sentences come from? The verbs *contain* and *resemble* are [+Stative], so the *do* which figures in the examples of Section 1, which requires a [-Stative] verb in its complement, cannot be the source. I have no idea what this source could be.

For what it is worth, there are a number of highly restrictive and idiosyncratic features of this construction. First, to the best of my knowledge, of all the sentence types cited in Section 1 as providing support for *Do Gobbling*, the only two which allow contamination by this vexatious *do* with a stative complement are pseudo-clefts and appositive clauses. All the other constructions seem to exclude this *do*, as (65) shows.

(65a)   ?My samples *did* contain PH385, and yours will have to do $\begin{Bmatrix} \text{it} \\ \text{so} \end{Bmatrix}$ too, if you want to wrest the Chem Cup from me.

(65b)   *If you want to get a fellowship, your proposal will have to do something pretty unusual for you: make sense.

(65c)   ?*The soup has to do nothing but smack of bay leaf, and the coveted Golden Spatula will be yours.

(65d)   *Smacking of lard I'm afraid your peanut butter will have to do, or I won't touch it.

(65e)   *Involving anything but drugs and perversion is hard for a successful Broadway play to do, these days.

(65f)   *Resembling fairy queens just isn't done by today's debutantes.

Also, as the distribution of asterisks within the curly brackets around the verbs in (64a) and (64b) indicates, this construction seems to be possible only when in the complement of some verb which expresses necessity. And another semantic fact of interest is the fact that the construction can only occur in an *if*-clause, or in its semantic equivalent. Thus note that the *and*-clauses of (64a) and (64b) are semantically equivalent to *then*-clauses of conditionals. The grammatical sentences of (64a) and (64b) could be roughly paraphrased as (66a) and (66b), respectively.

(66a)   If (it turns out that) these samples contain protein, then we're sunk.

(66b)   If Jack resembles Granny, then he'll win the prize.

As we would expect of conditional sentences, the sentences in (66) would become sentence fragments if their *then*-clauses were not present. And in precisely the same way, the sentences in (64a) and (64b) would become ungrammatical if their *and*-clauses were removed – a fact which sets these *and*-clauses off from other *and*-clauses, which are normally not required constituents. This fact suggests that these *and*-clauses are derived from *then*-clauses,[34] and again emphasizes the weird general character of this whole construction.

Two final quirks deserve mention. First, as the asterisk before *what* in (64a) shows, this construction has the honor of being the only pseudo-cleft-like sentence type of my acquaintance which allows *all* but not *what*. To my ear, (64a) does not sound totally impossible if *the only thing* replaces *all*, a fact which may indicate that the former is the source of the latter.[35] Second, negatives and factives with negative presuppositions, as well as certain other verbs, are excluded from the subject clauses of this construction, but not from the corresponding clauses of less hair-raising, more normal, pseudo-clefts, as the contrast between (67) and (68) shows.

(67a)   *All this milk doesn't have to do is contain DDT and I'll buy a pint.

(67b)

All I $\left\{ \begin{array}{l} \text{think} \\ \text{*doubt} \\ \text{*am surprised} \\ \text{*regret} \\ \text{*fear} \end{array} \right\}$ that this sample has to do is fit into

that triangular hole and this case is solved, King.

(68a)   All we didn't photograph was *La Victoire de Samothrace.*

(68b)

$$\text{All I} \begin{cases} \text{think} \\ \text{doubt} \\ \text{am surprised} \\ \text{regret} \\ \text{fear} \end{cases} \text{that he would wear is his sealskin}$$

bloomers.

All these horrors must be accounted for by whatever analysis would aspire to unlock the riddles posed by facts like those of (64) and (67). I would like to emphasize, however, that sentences like these do not directly *contradict* the gobbling analysis, even though they show that its coverage is not complete. That is, ideally, one would like to be able to account for the distribution of non-'empty' *do* by one mechanism, one set of rules. I cannot do this at present. Two conclusions are possible; (i) it is accidental that *do* shows up both in (64) and in the examples of Section I – the two *do*'s are distinct, and are inserted (or deleted) by separate processes; or (ii) my analysis is too limited, and must be extended in some at present unguessable way, so that both areas will fall under its purview. The many idiosyncrasies of the sentences of (64) which I have cited might succor one who would wish to defend (2), but I am a dis-believer in such accidents. While the sentences may not contradict the gobbling analyses, they certainly should not let gobblers sleep easy.

III.2. A more serious problem, which probably invalidates the identifi-cation, attempted in Section I.1 above, of the *do* of *do homework* with the *do* of *do so, do it*, and the other constructions discussed in Sections I.2–I.10, was also noted by Anderson. This problem arises in connection with such sentences as those in (69).

(69a)   Mel sometimes does his homework, but often he doesn't do so until too late.

(69b)   Sounds like Maggie doing some more of her exercises. I wish she wouldn't do $\begin{cases} \text{them} \\ \text{it} \end{cases}$ so late at night.

(69c)   What I've got to do this weekend is
         i. do some tiger-strangling
         ii. some tiger-strangling

What these sentences suggest is that another *do* is necessary. That is, since intuitively, the *so* of (69a) does not replace *his homework*, but rather *do his homework*, the structure of the second clause of (69a) would have to be roughly as shown in (70).

(70)

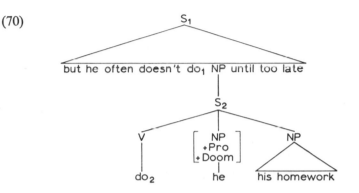

Similarly, in the case of (69b), while the occurrence of the pronoun *them*, anaphoric with *exercises*, occasions no difficulties, the occurrence of *it* is another matter, for this pronoun must refer to the phrase *do some more of her exercises*. Again, to account for such a sentence, a structure like (70) would be necessary. Finally, the gobbling analysis predicts that the two sentences in (69c) should not be synonymous – underlying the subject clause in (69ci) would be (71a), and underlying the subject clause of (69cii) would be (71b).

(71a) (71b) (see following page)

The do_2 that appears in (70) and (71b) is the *do* that appears before remote structure constituents which are realized as abstract nouns denoting activities (e.g., *dish-washing, homework, exercises, tiger-strangling*, etc.), while the do_1 of those diagrams is the *do* which shows up in the constructions discussed in Sections I.2–I.10. Thus presumably, since the structure underlying (69cii) contains one more clause than does the structure underlying (69ci), they should not be synonymous, unless some *ad hoc* rule which would put them into the same semantic equivalence class were to be postulated.

I am not sure that this is a bad result – there may be a slight difference in meaning, or focus, between the sentences of (69c). It would be one

(71a)

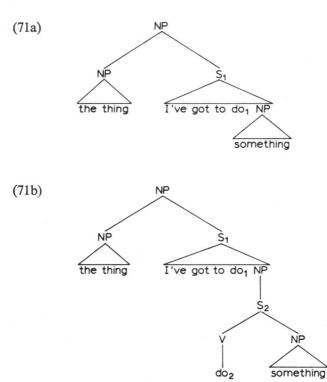

(71b)

roughly on the order of the differences in meaning which exist between the pairs of sentences in (72).

(72a)   I tried (to try) to be serious.
(72b)   They think (that they think) that there are 11 planets.
(72c)   I want (to want) to be respected.

There are clear differences here, but the sentences with the parenthesized elements included are weird, in some at present uncharacterizable way. It may be that this weirdness is what causes it to be so difficult to ascertain whether the sentences in (69c) do truly differ in meaning. I will leave this problem to those with a finer ear for semantic differences than I have.

Whether the sentences in (69c) are synonymous or not, it is discouraging for a gobbler to have to postulate the existence of two verbs with almost identical semantic and syntactic properties – the verbs do_1 and do_2 if (70) and (71b)[36]. Again, as was the case with the sentences of (64), these facts are not inconsistent with the gobbling analysis, and one could cite putatively parallel examples, such as the oft-noted fact that there are closely related, but not identical *persuade*'s, *remind*'s, *tell*'s, etc., but they do show that no unified account of all occurrences of *do* can now be achieved.

III.3.   What are the consequences of the analysis in (2) for semantics? Donald Davidson reviews a number of philosophical investigations of the logical form of actions in Davidson (1967). For reasons pertaining purely to semantics (e.g., so that the set of correct entailments of an action sentence will be deducible from its logical form, or so that it will be possible to refer to an action by a singular term, so that it can be described in a number of different ways, etc.), Davidson comes to the conclusion that the logical form of an action sentence whose agent is denoted by x should be something like (73),

(73)   It was intentional of x that p

where p is a proposition describing an event in which x is involved. Obviously, there is a close convergence between the analyses in (2) and (73), although these were motivated by totally different considerations. Davidson suggests that the logical form of action sentences must contain a two-place predicate ('intentional') relating an agent and an event. In the syntactic analysis I have argued for, *do* is the English realization of this semantic predicate.

Although I have used only English examples in the present paper, arguments similar or identical to those in Section 1 can be found in all languages with which I am familiar, the major differences being the particular phonological shape that the underlying predicate of intentionality assumes (*faire* in French, *göra* in Swedish, *tun* or *machen* in German, *suru* in Japanese, etc.). I would thus expect that if (2) can be maintained for English, it will provide a universal analysis of action sentences. However, whether or not this exceedingly strong claim can be maintained must await future research. At present, let me merely say that I know of no semantic arguments *against* the analysis of activity verbs implicit in (2).

One further question pertaining to semantics suggests itself: could Fillmore's notion of *Agent* (cf. Fillmore, 1968) be replaced by the notion 'possible subject of *do* in (2)'? And similarly, can all (or at least some)

of the other types of actants whose syntactic behavior Fillmore investi-
gates similarly be replaced by deriving them from parts of higher clauses?
At present, I am afraid that the answer to the first question must be 'no'.
The second question is far more complex than the first, so complex as
to preclude even a fragmentary discussion here.[37] The reason that it now
seems impossible to replace *Agent* by 'subject of *do*' is that there are
sentences which contain the *do* of (2) but which have a (presumably)
non-agentive subject of *do*. Some examples appear in (74).

(74a)   What the rolling boulders did is crush my petunias to
         smithereens.

(74b)   ?The plank broke, but it wouldn't have done $\left\{ \begin{matrix} so \\ it \end{matrix} \right\}$ if you
         hadn't bounced on it.

(74c)   ?The wind knocked down the fence, which I thought it might do.

It is not clear to me exactly what case function is played by such NP's
as *the rolling boulders* in (74a). Agents are usually described as animate
beings, acting volitionally. But do we ascribe volition to the subjects of
crush, break, and *knock down* in (74)? It seems to me that we do not, a
fact which thus casts the identification of the analyses of (2) and (73)
into doubt.[38]

Let us suppose, however, that for at least some action sentences, in
particular, those with animate subjects, the parallelism between (2) and
(73) can be maintained. What conclusions can be drawn from such a
parallelism for the theory of grammar?

It seems to me that the analysis implicit in (2), if correct, is but one of
many analyses in generative grammar which conform with the principle
stated in (75).

(75)   *The Principle of Semantic Relevance*
        Where syntactic evidence supports the postulation of elements
        in underlying structure which are not phonetically manifested,
        such elements tend to be relevant semantically.[39]

By 'syntactic evidence', I will mean evidence which pertains only to the
distribution of formal syntactic elements – grammatical morphemes.
Thus syntactic evidence, in this sense, would be the only evidence admissible in establishing *syntactic rules*, which would specify which strings

of morphemes are well-formed and which are not.[40] Thus evidence pertaining to ambiguities, semantic anomalies, paraphrases, etc. is not syntactic evidence, in this sense.

A famous instance which supports (75) is the imperative analysis, which was discussed in Section 2. There is abundant syntactic evidence which justifies the establishment of an underlying *you* subject in imperatives, an element which is of course necessary for semantic purposes. Other equally well-known cases which support (75) are the sentences in (76).

(76a)   The fat boys spurned the higher-priced spread.

(76b)   Somebody wants my toothbrush.

(76c)   Ed wins at poker more frequently than Jeff.

(76d)   I promise you ____ to anoint myself with Mazola.

(76e)   I tried to write a novel, and Fred ____ a play.

For each of the underlinings in (76), syntactic evidence exists which supports the postulation of elements in underlying structure which are not present in surface structure: a clause *who were fat* in (76a), a clause *which I have* in (76b), a clause *Jeff wins at poker (with some frequency)* in (76c), a subject NP *I* in (76d), and a clause *Fred tried to write a play* in (76e). I will not reiterate the syntactic arguments here, for I am only interested in pointing out that these missing elements conform to the Principle of Semantic Relevance. To me, it appears self-evident that any adequate semantic analyses of the sentences in (76) must contain semantic elements which correspond to the clauses and NP's which syntactic evidence suggests have been deleted in the derivations of the sentences in (76). Of course, if the analysis in (2) is correct, and if Davidson's analysis of the logical form of actions is correct, then a partial parallelism between (2) and (73) can be maintained, a result which would also conform with the Principle of Semantic Relevance.

The question is, why should so many syntactic analyses conform to this principle?[41] It is obvious that there is no logical reason for it to be true (thus nothing prevents there from being syntactic evidence galore that imperative sentences derive from structures with *you* subjects, where imperatives, nonetheless, are *interpreted* as if they had first person subjects, or as if their semantic subjects always referred to Aunt Jemima.

Since such alternative states of affairs are conceivable, it must be asked whether Chomsky's Extended Standard Theory (hereafter EST)[42] can explain the truth of (75).

It seems to me that it cannot. If we examine the conditions placed on deletions in Chomsky (1964), we find that deletion is possible under all of the following situations:

(77a)   Elements of a syntactic structure which are identical to other elements can be deleted.

(77b)   Members of a set of designated elements (e.g., *someone, something, sometime*, etc.) can be deleted.

(77c)   Elements can be deleted if they are mentioned in the structural description of a transformation (i.e., *you* and *will* in (58b), *who* (or *which*) *is* in *Whiz Deletion*, the rule which reduces relative clauses, forming the subject NP of (76a), etc.)

It is immediately clear that (77c) is far too permissive, for it would designate a rule like (78) as a possible rule.

(78)   Imp(Neg) $-$ *cleavage* $-$ *will* $-$ X

				OBL
1	2	3	4	$\Rightarrow$
1	0	0	4	

This impossible rule could of course be excluded by restricting (77c) so that only grammatical morphemes could be deleted, but such a restriction would still not be sufficient to rule out (79).

(79)   *Imperative*
Imp(Neg) $-$ *I* $-$ *will* $-$ X

				OBL
1	2	3	4	$\Rightarrow$
1	0	0	4	

Assume that imperatives were only interpreted, semantically, as having second-person subjects, but that syntactic evidence could be found for deleting *I* (i.e., imperatives could only contain *myself, my own, crane my neck*, etc.). As far as I can see, the EST does not say that such an absurd situation could not exist. But I contend that it could not exist, any more than a language with no vowels could exist, or a language which passivized by reversing word order could exist. If the standard theory countenances rule (58b) as a possible rule of grammar, it must, as far as I can see, also countenance (79). Thus it must fail as a theory of language.

I think, however, that the theory of Generative Semantics can suggest an explanation for the Principle of Semantic Relevance.[43] This theory asserts that the mapping which links surface structures and semantic representations is effected by one type of rule: derivational constraints, which have as a subcase grammatical transformations, essentially as these are defined in the standard theory. Since derivational constraints map trees onto trees, it follows that semantic representations, within the theory of Generative Semantics, are also essentially in the form of trees. The theory postulates no level of representation which would correspond to the deep structures of the EST, but if syntactic evidence could be found which suggested the existence of such a level, the theory could accommodate it,[44] for the basic claim of the theory of Generative Semantics is that there is only one kind of mapping linking surface structure and semantic representation.

If this basic claim is correct, the Principle of Semantic Relevance follows as a consequence. For the theory of Generative Semantics asserts, essentially, that surface structure trees are only distorted versions of semantic trees. Every time a transformation applies to a semantic tree it deforms that tree (by deletion or reordering) into a tree which more nearly resembles a surface tree. Viewed alternatively, every time syntactic evidence can be found which supports increasing the syntactic 'distance' of an intermediate form from the surface tree this form will be realized as, this increase in syntactic 'distance' will give rise to a decrease in semantic 'distance', where 'distance' is measured by the number of motivated operations it is necessary to perform upon this intermediate form to convert it to surface structure, or to semantic representation. Since in the EST there is no necessary connection between the distance from an intermediate form to surface structure and its distance to semantic representation, there is no reason why the Principle of Semantic Relevance should hold. It could be the case than an increase in syntactic distance occasioned a corresponding increase in semantic distance. That is, to the extent that the Principle of Semantic Relevance is correct, the EST is disconfirmed and Generative Semantics is supported.

III.4.   One final point deserves mention, in regard to the theory of Generative Semantics. Within this theory, lexical items can be inserted after the application of certain transformations,[45] an aspect of the theory which renders it incompatible with the EST, which requires all lexical items to have been inserted before any transformation can apply. One widely discussed pre-lexical rule is McCawley's rule of *Predicate Raising*, a rule which rips out the embedded predicate of certain complement-taking verbs and Chomsky-adjoins it to the left of the complement-taking verb. A rough formulation of the rule is given in (80).

(80)   *Predicate Raising*
$$[_sV-(NP)-[_sV-Y]_s]_s$$

				OPT
1	2	3	4	⇒
3+1	2	0	4	

This rule does not, in English, produced derived verbs that are bimorphemic on inspection. Some well-know outputs of this rule are *kill* (from CAUSE (COME ABOUT (NOT(ALIVE)))) (cf. McCawley, 1968), *remind* (from *strike-similar* (cf. Postal, 1970b)), and *bring* (from CAUSE-*come* (cf. Binnick, 1971)). None of these is bimorphemic in the way one might expect an output of (80) to be. Possibly it is this lack of an immediately apparent superficial analysis which has led some linguists to take issue with (80).

Therefore, in support of (80), it should be noted that there are languages in which just such a superficial analysis is available. One such language is Japanese: there is an indefinitely extendable class of compound verbs, such as *tabehazimeru* ('begin to eat' [lit. eat-begin]), *yomihazimeru* ('begin to read') *wakarihazimeru* ('begin to understand'), etc.; *tabetuzukeru* (continue to eat'), *kaituzukeru* ('continue to buy'), etc.; *tabeoeru* ('finish eating'), *yomioeru* ('finish reading'), *nomioeru* ('finish drinking'), etc.[46] Thus the rule is not only a formally possible transformation, but an actually attested one.

Further, it should be noted that even if counterarguments to the claim that *Predicate Raising* is a syntactic rule of English can be found (I know of none, at present), it must not be supposed that the content of this rule could be omitted from the theory of grammar.'For what it in effect states is that it is only possible to decompose a lexical verb into two *semantically adjacent* predicates. That is, it specifies that a semantic representation such as (81) can only surface as (82) or (83) (or possibly as (84), if (80) applies twice) – but never as (85) or (86).

(81)

(82)

(83)

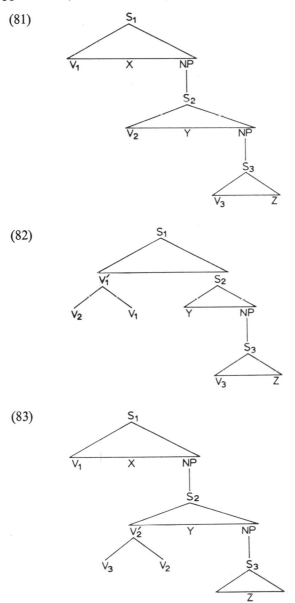

(84)

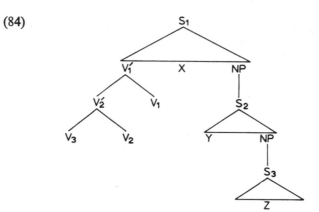

(85)

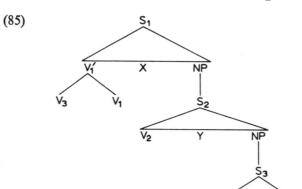

(86)

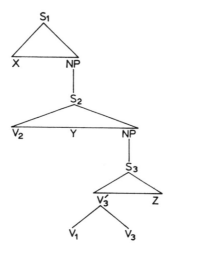

That is, to take a concrete example, presumably the relevant semantic structure of *Fritz looked for entertainment* is roughly as shown in (87).

(87)

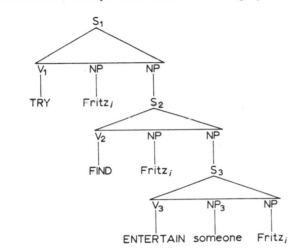

Postulating *Predicate Raising* as a universal rule (and thus, as a rule available for the construction of a grammar for English, or for Japanese) entails predicting that a tree like (87) could be realized as (88a) (without *Predicate Raising*) or as (88b) (with V_2 adjoined to the left of V_1, giving a derived structure like (82)), but never as (88c), which would parallel the impossible (85) [in (88c), *smish* would mean 'try-entertain'].

(88a)   Fritz tried to find entertainment.

(88b)   Fritz looked for entertainment.

(88c)   *Fritz $\begin{Bmatrix} \text{trentertained} \\ \text{smished} \end{Bmatrix}$ to find ([$_{NP3}$ someone]$_{NP3}$)

That is, whether or not McCawley is right, as I believe him to be, in postulating (80) to be a syntactic transformation of English, it is clear that something cognate to (80) must appear as a constraint on possible lexical entries. Thus even an interpretivist who might wish to exclude such transformations as (80) from the grammar of English, possibly on the grounds that the evidence for its existence in English is inferential, would have to state essentially the same rule in his theory of possible lexical items – in this case, of possible compound verbs. Thus there can be no simplicity argument directed at the inclusion of *Predicate Raising* in the grammar of English.

The consequence for the gobbling analysis of the assumption that (80) is a rule of English is that there is probably no need to postulate a special rule like (3) – *Predicate Raising* can do the job.[47] That is, if we allow *Predicate Raising* to apply to (2), it will output (89).[48]

(89)

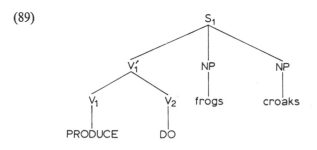

Now that the predicate DO (which I assume is identical with Davidson's 'intentional' (cf. (73) above)) and the complex semantic entity which I have symbolized by the word PRODUCE have been grouped together under one node by the operation of rule (80), it remains to insert some lexical item into the tree, so that the tree in footnote 2 will result, with (1) being the final result. I propose that the lexical insertion rule which inserts the English word *produce* for V_1' in (89) be stated in such a way that it can operate either to insert *produce* for the semantic entity abbreviated by PRODUCE and that abbreviated by DO, when they are sisters under the same V node, or to replace PRODUCE by *produce* when no DO precedes.

In other words, the lexical entries for *produce* and for all other activity verbs will contain an optional element, in a way suggested by the rule in (90).

(90)   [PRODUCE (DO)]$_V$

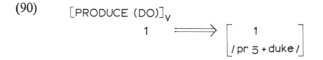

The interpretation of parentheses in (90) is parallel to the way they are interpreted in generative phonology (cf. e.g. Chomsky and Halle, 1968): if the phonological matrix to the right of the arrow can be associated with either a node for [PRODUCE DO]$_V$ or for just [PRODUCE]$_V$, then the longer option must be taken. This will ensure that while V'_1 will be associated with /prō+duke/ in (89) [and subsequently in (1)], it will still be possible to associate this phonological matrix with occurrences of PRODUCE which do not precede DO, as is the case with V_2 in (91).

(91)

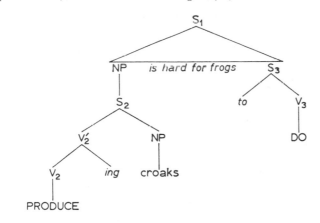

What will be necessary, in addition to this type of disjunctive lexical insertion, is a restriction that PRODUCE, and all other activity predicates, can only appear in a well-formed semantic representation if embedded immediately below DO. The necessity for including such 'upward selection' in syntactic theory is argued for on independent grounds in Ross (1971). Without such upward selection, nothing would prevent some stative verb such as *abhor* from appearing for V_2 in (91), which would produce an ungrammatical string like (92).

(92)   *Abhorring croaks is hard for frogs to do.

Note that this device of upward selection is cognate with the type of restriction Lakoff and Ross (1966) used to restrict the rule which inserted *do so* so that it would only replace [-Stative] VP's with this pro-form. Thus it could not be argued to be superfluous merely on the grounds of simplicity – every analysis of do_1 must somewhere make mention of the link between constructions manifesting this verb and stativity.

In other words, the analysis implicit in (2) does not necessitate the addition of any grammatical machinery which is not independently needed, under the theory of Generative Semantics, with the exception of allowing lexical insertion rules like (90) to contain parenthesized elements in the part of the tree which is becoming lexicalized, a theoretical device for which I know of no independent support at present, but one which does not strike me as unnatural. Of course, until other cases can be found which argue for such a device, it must provisionally be regarded as *ad hoc*. However, I doubt that it will remain *ad hoc* for long. Whether my faith in the naturalness of this device is justified must await further empirical research into the formal properties of lexical insertion rules, however.

The fact that Generative Semantics obviates a rule necessary in gobbling analyses which are stated in other theories constitutes evidence for the correctness of Generative Semantics. The facts of Section I argue conclusively, to my mind, that some gobbling analysis is necessary – that *all* activity verbs must be 'factored' syntactically into do_1 and some other predicate. If this do_1 must appear in underlying structures, then some means must be provided to 'dispose of the body', as it were – to get rid of this do_1 when it immediately precedes its complement. In any theory other than Generative Semantics, this body-disposal must, as far as I can see, be effected by some *ad hoc* rule like my rule of *Do Gobbling*, or the equivalent rules in Anderson (*op. cit.*) and Lee (*op. cit.*). Thus, viewed from this new perspective, the facts in Section I constitute strong evidence for the existence of a rule of *Predicate Raising*, and for the correctness of the theory of Generative Semantics, for it is only within this theory that lexical insertion can follow the application of transformational rules.[49]

III.5.   In conclusion, I have argued in Section I that the underlying structure of all propositions describing activities contains a higher predicate of intentionality, whose phonological realization in English is *do*, in those environments in which rule (80), *Predicate Raising*, cannot operate. In Section II, I presented a number of arguments which argue against the possible claim that this *do* does not appear in remote structure, but is inserted transformationally. Finally, in Section III, after calling attention to the fact that a number of difficulties are still inherent in my analysis of *do*, I pointed out that this analysis supports the theory of Generative Semantics in two ways. First, only within this theory does the analysis of (2) not entail the addition of extra grammatical machinery (except for parentheses in lexical insertion rules); and second, in conforming to the Principle of Semantic Relevance, this analysis, viewed pragmatically, suggests a heuristic for doing research into the nature of semantic representation: do syntax.

Language Research Foundation and
Massachusetts Institute of Technology

REFERENCES

*This research was supported in part by a grant from the National Institute of Mental Health (Grant No. 5-P01-13390-04) and by a grant from the National Science Foundation (Grant No. GS-3202). A version of this paper was presented at the 1970 summer meeting of the Linguistic Society of America, at the Ohio State University.

The analysis argued for here was arrived at independently by Stephen Anderson, on the basis of a number of the same arguments. The reader should consult the paper by him which is listed in the references. I am grateful to him for his comments on an earlier draft of this paper.

I also wish to thank George Lakoff and Paul Postal for the many criticisms of these ideas they have made and for their many insights, both of which have played a significant role in the final shape of the paper. Such errors as don't remain they caused me to get rid of. The others are on me.

[1] For arguments supporting the claim that English is a VSO language in remote structure (this term is due to Postal (cf. Postal, 1970a)), cf. McCawley (1970), and Ross (to appear). In (2), and elsewhere in this paper, I have drastically oversimplified the syntactic representations shown in diagrams, as long as these simplifications do not affect the point at issue. The abstract VSO structures McCawley has shown to be necessary in very abstract representations will be converted to the more recognizable SVO surface order by a late post-cyclical rule of *Verb Subject Inversion*, which will prepose to the left of the verb the first NP following the verb of a clause, in an environment which is the complement of the environment of the more familiar rule of *Subject Verb Inversion*. Thus in the VSO analysis, *Verb Subject Inversion* replaces *Subject Verb Inversion*.

[2] I have chosen this absurd name for the process formally described in (3) as a reminder that the details of the process by which the *do* which I will try to show must appear in the underlying structure of acts is deleted are not known. The rule in (3) and the rule of *Equi*, which deletes NP_3 under identity with NP_1 (cf. Postal, 1970b for an extensive discussion of this rule), coupled with some such convention(s) of tree-pruning as I argued for in Ross (1967), Ch. 3, will convert (2) into the structure below,

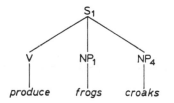

which *Verb Subject Inversion* will convert into (1).

Actually, I believe it to be possible to dispense with *Do Gobbling* altogether, in favor of the rule of *Predicate Raising*. Cf. below, Section 3.4 for further discussion.

[3] Thus **some hunting snark = some snark-hunting*, via a presumably universal rule of *Object Incorporation*. For some discussion of the operation of this rule in Mohawk, cf. Postal (1964).

[4] The feature [-Stative], which for the purposes of this paper we can take to be identical to the semantic notion of activity, is discussed in G. Lakoff (1966). It is necessary to restrict (6) to VP's denoting activities, because of the impossibility of such sentences as **I meant that there was no room and the sergeant did so too, This plot smacks of communism, and* The Realist *does so too*, etc., etc.

[5] This rule appears to be governed, despite the fact that it makes crucial use of a variable in term 3. Thus while *think so, guess so, expect so, hope so, say so*, etc. are grammatical, *anticipate so, regret so, mutter so*, etc. are not. This fact poses a serious problem for the theory of exceptions, for by and large, if a rule makes crucial use of variables, it has no lexical exceptions: its applicability is determined on the basis of what phrase-structure configurations are input to it. But there are not known to be any configurational differences whatsoever separating such verbs as *say* and *mutter*, so rule (8) presents an impasse for the moment. For a discussion of the theory of exceptions, cf. G. Lakoff (1970) and R. Lakoff (1968).

[6] Note that although S_{11} and S_{21} in (9a) are not strictly identical, for their subjects are not coreferential, this formal difference is of precisely that kind that can be disregarded: S_{11} and S_{21} are 'sloppily identical'. Exactly the same remarks apply to S_{11} and S_{21} in (10). For some discussion of the notion of sloppy identity, cf. Ross (1969b), Section 3.2.

[7] For discussion of the feature [+Doom], cf. Postal (1970b).

[8] Cf. Perlmutter (in press) for a discussion of this remote structure constraint.

[9] Revised versions of these papers will appear in Lakoff and Ross (in preparation).

[10] Cf. Chomsky (1957).

[11] One interesting argument that (16) must be a rule of English has to do with the following sentences.

(a)   My hubby is a dear. But nobody believes that he's a dear.
(b)   My hubby is a dear. But nobody believes it.

Since (a) and (b) can be synonymous, we see that sentential *it* must be able to refer to clauses outside of its own sentence. This is not always the case, however. For many speakers, myself included, the *it* of (c) cannot refer back to the first clause of (c).

(c)   *Like father, like son. But nobody believes it.

This fact can be explained if rule (16) is in the grammar, for the sentence which would have to underlie the second clause of (c) would be (d), which many speakers (again, myself included) find ungrammatical.

(d)   *(But) nobody believes (that) like father, like son.

If the same speakers who find ungrammatical such sentences as (d), in which asyntactic sentential idioms like *like father, like son* have been embedded, also find that a sentential *it* cannot refer back to a preceding sentence which consists of this idiom (some preliminary questioning has more or less supported this hypothesis), then this fact can be explained, if occurrences of sentential *it* are derived by pronominalization of embedded clauses. Since (d) must be excluded in any case, its ungrammaticality can be used to predict the impossibility of anaphora in (c), if *S Deletion* is a rule of English.

[12] As a further piece of evidence that (2) is a correct deep structure, note that *do it* can be passivized, as in (a) below.

(a)   If you can apologize, it should be done immediately.

This, of course, is in line with what we would expect, given (2) as a deep structure: since *do* is a transitive verb, we should expect it to passivize (even stronger evidence that *do* must be able to passivize will be given in Section I.10 below).

Note that in any analysis which treats *do it* in a way parallel to the way *do so* was analyzed in Lakoff and Ross (1966) – that is, in any analysis in which *do it* is inserted transformationally for an activity VP, by some such rule as (6) above – the fact that *do it* can be passivized can only be accounted for by allowing a transformation to convert (b) into (c).

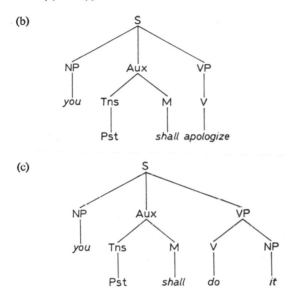

(b)

(c)

Note that such a transformation must introduce not only the morphemes *do* and *it*, but also a new node – the NP object of *do* in (c) – so that the rule of *Passive* will be able to convert (c) into the second clause of (a). But a mapping from (b) to (c) is a kind of formal operation which transformations have previously been prohibited from effecting. Thus any solution parallelling the Lakoff-Ross (1966) analysis would be forced to extend the theory of elementary transformations in an *ad hoc* way, in order to account for sentence (a).

It may be, of course, that such an extension can be independently motivated, but such justification is at present not available. Chomsky's suggestions regarding the rule of *There Insertion* (cf. Chomsky, 1970) are not cogent arguments for allowing transformations to build nodes; the considerations about *There Insertion* which McCawley (cf. McCawley, 1970) brings to bear point toward a more adequate analysis, and one which does not necessitate node-building. I feel, however, that the rule of *There Insertion* will remain a mystery until it can be explained why it is the morpheme *there*, a locative pronoun, that shows up in existential sentences in English, rather than some random morpheme like *hurray*. There are too many parallels between locatives and existentials in other languages (cf. Lyons, 1967) for the presence of *there* in English existentials to be an accident.

I consider, therefore, that the question as to whether or not structure-building elementaries are to be countenanced in the theory of grammar is still open. Notice, however, that even if this question could be answered in the affirmative, a Lakoff-Ross (1966) type of rule which converted (b) to (c) would not have *explained* why such sentences as (a) exist. For any rule which can introduce in (c) an *it* which is dominated by NP could just as well have introduced it dominated by V or S or VP, or by some other node which would not allow for subsequent passivization. Thus any analysis which picks (c), instead of any of the other possible trees which (b) could have been converted into, has no explanatory power. The analysis implicit in (2), however, which is independently motivated by the many other arguments in Section I, does provide an explanation for (a), in that special restrictions would have to be imposed to prevent (a). Thus the analysis implicit in (2) is clearly superior to any analysis which makes use of some rule of insertion to convert (b) into (c).

[13] Cf. Grinder (1970), and Ross (1967), pp. 434–5.

[14] For instance, the rules must be formulated in such a way as to generate intermediate forms in which the shared NP is not preposed (*Caspar Milquetoast, und I'm sure you all remember him, was not a stud.*), as well as forms in which the preposed NP has not been converted into a WH-word (*Caspar Milquetoast, and him I'm sure you all remember, was not a stud.*).

[15] Note that *Do Gobbling* violates no constraints on variables in moving *resign* out from under NP$_b$ in (25c), because *Do Gobbling* does not make crucial use of variables, and thus will not be subject to the constraints on reordering transformations (Cf. Ross (1967), esp. § 6.3).

[16] The operation of this rule is discussed in Ross (1969b).

[17] I have included the colon ':' in the structural description of this rule in my ignorance of any better way than by including such intonation markers to constrain its operation. Thus (27) should be looked upon as a highly provisional formulation of the process of *Equative Deletion*.

[18] For arguments that *that*-clauses and certain infinitival complements are to be analyzed as NP's, cf. Rosenbaum (1967).

[19] For arguments that prepositional phrases are to be analyzed as NP's, cf. Postal (1971) and Ross (1967), especially § 4.3.

[20] For arguments that adjective phrases must be dominated by NP at some level of structure, cf. Ross (1969c).

[21] This is a slight oversimplification, for there are contexts in which *other than* (though not *but*) can be followed by full clauses, as in (a).

(a)   He writes poems in other ways than he writes books.

There is a widespread parallelism between *other than* and comparatives, both with respect to the fact that both exclude negative elements (compare (b) and (b')),

(b)   He writes poems in other ways than $\left\{ I \left\{ \begin{matrix} \text{do} \\ \text{*don't} \\ \text{*nobody does} \end{matrix} \right\} \right\}$

(b′)   He writes poems in more ways than $\begin{Bmatrix} I \begin{Bmatrix} do \\ *don't \end{Bmatrix} \\ *nobody\ does \end{Bmatrix}$

and both exhibit the same peculiar patterns of deletions (cf. (c) and (c′)).

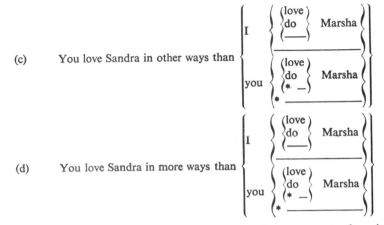

(c)   You love Sandra in other ways than

(d)   You love Sandra in more ways than

These facts, in addition to the morphological resemblances, suggest a deep similarity between comparatives and *other*, but I have not as yet been able to find a unified analysis which would link the two. Nor is it at all clear to me how such sentences as (a), (b), and (c) are to be related to those in (33).

[22] Cf. Faraci (1970), and Lakoff and Ross (in preparation) for this justification.

[23] For more discussion of this analysis, and for more arguments which support it, cf. Bach and Peters (1968).

[24] In Postal (1971), the ethnolinguistically more felicitous term *Y Movement* is proposed.

[25] In particular, most prepositional phrases, and most non-finite complement NP's cannot, as is shown by the sentences in (a) and (b), respectively.

(a)?   *Into his pocket I think he's going to put a gat.
(b)   **To have even half a blintz I don't want.

[26] For a justification of the claim that sentences such as those in (46) must be derived by way of a movement rule, and not by deletion, cf. Postal and Ross (1971).

[27] Personal communication.

[28] Note that not all structures of the form of (2) can undergo *Passive:* (a) is ungrammatical.

(a)   *Kissing that gorilla hasn't been done by Frank Buck.

By and large, such sentences as (45) are only possible if they have a generic meaning, although I have not studied this sentence type enough to say with certainty that this is always the case. Whatever restriction turns out to be necessary can be stated on the rule of *Passive*. The fact that such restrictions do exist in no way invalidates Postal's argument, however: some sentences of the form of (45) must be generated, and they are obviously passives. Thus they must be assumed to derive from a structure like (2).

[29] I must confess that I regard this man, even though made of straw, as bizarre. Would

one who wishes to maintain this position not also wish to argue that the rule deleting *you*-subjects in imperatives was operative in the derivations of such sentences as those in (a), where this *you* 'leaves traces', but not in (b)?

(a)   i. Protect yourself.
          ii. Make your own voodoo doll.
          iii. Don't blow your stack.
(b)   i. Protect Mike.
          ii. Make a voodoo doll.
          iii. Don't blow on my soufflé.

I cannot imagine any advantages that could derive from either of the above positions, so I will shelve the matter, until someone wishes to advance either one seriously.

[30] This topic will be discussed in Section 3.3 below.

[31] Cf. Postal (1969) for the basic arguments which support the analysis of (58).

[32] Cf. Postal (1971) for a definition of this term. Rule (58a) is essentially identical to the rule proposed by Lees and Klima (1963).

[33] Of course, I do not mean to imply that there is any special connection between the analysis in (2) and the imperative analysis. As far as I can tell, the logic underlying all standard analyses – namely, in essence, that repetition of the same fact can never be tolerated – is the same as that underlying the imperative analysis. Thus any standard analysis could have been chosen for comparison with the analysis in (2).

[34] One is of course reminded of the *and*-clauses in pseudo-imperatives (*Inherit a million beans and everyone's your friend*), which it will hopefully one day be possible to demonstrate also derive from *then*-clauses.

[35] As Ray Jackendoff has pointed out to me, the presence of *all* in pseudo-cleft sentences is something of a mystery, given the general impossibility of other quantifiers in this position. Thus note the sentences in (a).

(a)
$$\left\{\begin{array}{l} \text{All (*the things)} \\ \text{*Both} \\ \text{*Each} \\ \text{*Everything} \\ \text{*Several (things)} \\ \text{*Much} \end{array}\right\} \text{that I want is to go home.}$$

Thus if the otherwise baffling sentences of Klima's can be used to clear up this problem, they can, I suppose, be looked upon as a (slight) blessing in disguise.

[36] Another fact which differentiates these two *do*'s is the following. While do_2 is only possible with animate subjects, as (4c) shows, do_1 allows *picture* noun subjects, as the sentences below show:

(a)   What this paper will do is demonstrate the impossibility of flight.
(b)   My report took up the problem of missing funds, but his did not do so.
(c)?   All these articles do the same thing: overlook the great natural beauty of the proposed pipeline.

[37] This topic is taken up in Lakoff and Ross (in preparation.)

[38] This same unhappy conclusion is reached in Lee (1969), a paper which independently arrives at essentially the analysis of (2), coupled with the additional interesting claim that *do* and *occur* are essentially transitive and intransitive alloforms of the same underlying predicate, parallel to the two verbs *begin* (cf. Perlmutter (in press)).

39 The following discussion essentially recapitulates the section of Postal (1970a) which deals with what Postal refers to as 'the directionality of abstractness'. It is, as Postal observes, generally true that the input of a transformational rule is closer to its semantic structure than its output is. However, for many cases of reordering rules (e.g. *Extraposition, Extraposition from NP, Complex NP Shift, Adverb Preposing*, etc. [for some discussion of these rules, cf. Ross, 1967]) it would seem that Postal's claim is too strong. That is, I see no reason to claim that either input or output of e.g. *Extraposition from NP* is closer to semantics. There are some cases of deletion, too, which cannot be claimed to proceed from 'more nearly semantic' to 'less nearly semantic' – one clear case is the rule which deletes the complementizer *that*, in some environments. Clearly, we cannot maintain both that the rule that inserts complementizers and that the rule that deletes them are exhibiting the same directionality of abstractness. Another case is the rule that deletes prepositions after verbs (i.e. **blame on Max for the snafu → blame Max for the snafu*), since it is unlikely that these prepositions can be argued to have appeared in remote structure. Rather, it is probable that underlying NP's become PP's during the course of a derivation, by the transformational insertion of a preposition.

However, it does seem that it is largely the case that only semantically relevant nodes can be deleted, which is the basis for the tendency expressed in (75).

40 Let us assume, counter to my present beliefs, that the facts of string well-formedness are clear and well-defined. The claim that the set of all strings of morphemes can be partitioned into two disjoint sets, one well-formed, the other ill-formed, is a theoretical claim which must be justified. It is clearly the case for arithmetical expressions that the set of all possible strings of arithmetical elements (e.g. '=', '(', '2', '+', '÷', etc.) admits of such a partitioning, but it is not clear that the set of all strings of morphemes in any natural language does admit of one. In fact, I believe this not to be the case. This matter is discussed in Lakoff and Ross (in preparation).

41 I say 'so many', because there are interesting exceptions to (75), in addition to the sentences in (74) and those cases discussed in footnote 39 above. Two of them I am responsible for: the analysis of adjectives in Ross (1969c) [for a slight revision, cf. Ross, 1971], under which the underlying structure of *Brigitte is callipygous* would be as in (a),

(a)

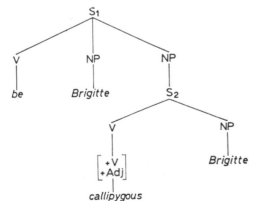

and the analysis of pseudo-cleft sentences exemplified in (36). Obviously, S_1 in (a) contributes nothing of semantic relevance, and it is highly dubious to me that S_2 in (36) contributes anything, either. Thus if either of these two analyses is correct, (75) cannot be stated as a law, but only as a tendency. Of course, this fact does not render (75) any less interesting, or any less in need of an explanation. In fact, I would conjecture that it is precisely because (75) is true in such a large number of cases that research in generative grammar has aroused such a lively interest in other disciplines, notably, philosophy and psychology. The statistical truth of the Principle of Semantic Relevance gives syntacticians a way of inferring a (probable) structure of verbal thought. If it were not for this principle, transformational grammar would probably interest researchers in neighboring fields as little as did the oligosynthetic theories of Nikolai Yakovlivich Marr.

[42] For an exposition of this term, cf. Chomsky (1970).

[43] For expositions of this theory, cf. McCawley (1968), G. Lakoff (1969), and Postal (1970a).

[44] In fact, however, there is a growing body of evidence incompatible with the postulation of any such level. In Postal (1970a), one extremely telling argument to this effect is presented.

[45] This facet of the theory is discussed and motivated in McCawley (1968) and Postal (1970a), among other places.

[46] These facts are presented more fully in Nakau (1971), Ch. 7.

[47] Rules exactly like *Do Gobbling* appear in the abovementioned works by Anderson and Lee. The possibility of replacing *Do Gobbling* by *Predicate Raising* was suggested to me by Steve Anderson.

[48] In (89), as in various places above, I have used the device of capital letters to designate what we can, for our present purposes, regard as semantic primes. To be sure, a fuller analysis of (PRODUCE, X, Y) would doubtless yield some more fine-grained structure such as (CAUSE X, (COME ABOUT (EXIST Y))), but such refinements are not germane to this discussion.

[49] Needless to say, the fact that *Do Gobbling* can be dispensed with in favor of *Predicate Raising* and conditions on lexical insertion rules counts as a further simplicity argument against the insertionist theories discussed in Section II.

BIBLIOGRAPHY

Anderson, S. R., 'Pro-Sentential Forms and Their Implications for English Sentence Structure', NSF-20 p. VI-1-43, 1968.

Bach, E. and Harms, R., *Universals in Linguistic Theory*, Holt, Rinehart and Winston, New York, 1968.

Bach, E. and Peters, S., 'Pseudo-cleft Sentences', unpublished University of Texas ditto, 1968.

Chomsky, N., *Syntactic Structures*, Mouton, The Hague, 1957.

Chomsky, N., 'Current Issues in Linguistic Theory', in *The Structure of Language, Readings in the Philosophy of Language* (ed. by J. Fodor and J. Katz), Prentice-Hall, Englewood Cliffs, N.Y. (1964), p. 50–118.

Chomsky, N., 'Remarks on Nominalizations', in *Readings in Transformational Grammar* (ed. by R. Jacobs and P. S. Rosenbaum), Blaisdell, Waltham, Mass., 1970, p. 184–221.

Chomsky, N. and Halle, M., *The Sound Pattern of English*, Harper and Row, New York, 1968.

Davidson, D., 'The Logical Form of Action Sentences', in *The Logic of Decision and Action* (ed. by N. Rescher), University of Pittsburgh Press, Pittsburgh, Pa. (1967), p. 81–120.

Faraci, R., 'On the Deep Question of Pseudo-clefts', unpublished MIT ditto, 1970.

Fillmore, C., 'The Case for Case', in Bach and Harms, (1968), p. 1–88.

Fillmore, C. and Langendoen, D. T., *Studies in Linguistic Semantics*, Holt, Rinehart and Winston, New York, 1971.

Fodor, J. and Katz, J. J., *The Structure of Language: Readings in the Philosophy of Language*, Prentice Hall, Englewood Cliffs, N.J., 1964.

Grinder, J., 'On the Derivation of Non-Restrictive Relative Clauses', unpublished paper, 1970.

Lakoff, G., 'Stative Verbs and Adjectives', in *Mathematical Linguistics and Machine Translation, Report NSF-17*, the Computation Laboratory of Harvard University, Cambridge, Mass., 1966.

Lakoff, G., 'On Derivational Constraints', in *Papers from the Fifth Regional Meeting, Chicago Linguistic Society*, University of Chicago, Department of Linguistics, Chicago, Ill., 1969.

Lakoff, G., *Irregularity in Syntax*, Holt, Rinehart, and Winston, New York, 1970.

Lakoff, G. and Ross, J. R., 'A Criterion for Verb Phrase Constituency', in *Mathematical Linguistics and Machine Translation, Report NSF-17*, the Computation Laboratory of Harvard University, Cambridge, Mass., 1966.

Lakoff, G. and Ross, J. R., *Abstract Syntax* (in preparation).

Lakoff, R., *Abstract Syntax and Latin Complementation*, MIT Press, Cambridge, Mass., 1968.

Lee, P. G., '*Do* from *Occur*', Working-Papers in Linguistics No. 3, pp. 1–21, Technical Report No. 69-4 to the National Science Foundation from the Computer and Information Science Research Center, The Ohio State University, Columbus, Ohio, 1969.

Lees, R. and Klima, E., 'Rules for English Pronominalization', *Language* 34 (1963), 17–29.

Lyons, J., 'A Note on Possessive, Existential, and Locative Sentences', *Foundations of Language* 3 (1967), p. 390–6.

McCawley, J., 'The Role of Semantics in Grammar', in Bach and Harms, 1968.

McCawley, J., 'English as a VSO Language', *Language* 46 (1970), 286–99.

McCawley, J., 'Tense and Time Reference in English', in Fillmore and Langendoen, p. 97–113, 1971.

Nakau, M., *Sentential Complementation in Japanese*, unpublished Doctoral dissertation, MIT, 1971.

Perlmutter, D. (in press), *Deep and Surface Structure Constraints in Syntax*, Holt, Rinehart and Winston, New York.

Postal, P., 'Limitations of Phrase Structure Grammars', in Fodor and Katz, 1964.

Postal, P., 'Underlying and Superficial Constituent Structure', in *Modern Studies in English* (ed. by D. Reibel and S. Shane), Prentice-Hall, Englewood Cliffs, N.Y., 1969.

Postal, P., 'On the Surface Verb *Remind*', *Linguistic Inquiry* 1, 1, 1970a.

Postal, P., 'On Coreferential Complement Subject Deletion', *Linguistic Inquiry* 1. 4, 1970b.

Postal, P., *Crossover Phenomena*, Holt, Rinehart, and Winston, New York, 1971.

Postal, P. and Ross, J. R., '*Tough·Movement* si, *Tough Deletion* no!', to appear in *Linguistic Inquiry* **2**. 4, 1971.

Reibel, D. and Schane, S., *Modern Studies in English*, Prentice-Hall, Englewood Cliffs, N.Y., 1969.

Rosenbaum, P., *The Grammar of English Predicate Complement Constructions*, MIT Press, Cambridge, Mass., 1967.

Ross, J. R., *Constraints on Variables in Syntax*, unpublished Doctoral dissertation, MIT., 1967.

Ross, J. R., 'Auxiliaries as Main Verbs', in *Studies in Philosophical Linguistics* (ed. by W. Todd), Series One, Great Expectations Press, Carbondale, Ill., 1969a.

Ross, J. R., 'Guess Who?' in *Papers from the Fifth Regional Meeting, Chicago Linguistic Society*, University of Chicago, Department of Linguistics, Chicago, Ill., 1969b.

Ross, J. R., 'Adjectives as Noun Phrases', in Reibel and Schane, 1969c.

Ross, J. R., 'Doubl-ing'. to appear in *Linguistic Inquiry*, 1971.

Ross, J. R., 'Mirror Image Rules and VSO order'. to appear in *Linguistic Inquiry* **2**. 4, 1971.

TERENCE PARSONS

SOME PROBLEMS CONCERNING THE LOGIC OF GRAMMATICAL MODIFIERS

ABSTRACT. This paper consists principally of selections from a much longer work on the semantics of English. It discusses some problems concerning how to represent grammatical modifiers (e.g. 'slowly' in 'x drives slowly') in a logically perspicuous notation. A proposal of Reichenbach's is given and criticized; then a 'new' theory (apparently discovered independently by myself, Romain Clark, and Richard Montague and Hans Kamp) is given, in which grammatical modifiers are represented by operators added to a first-order predicate calculus. Finally some problems concerning applications of adjectives to that-clauses and gerundive-clauses are discussed.

0. INTRODUCTION

This paper is a rephrasal of portions of a much longer essay on English semantics.[1] That essay is an attempt to develop an approach to the semantics of natural languages by combining the insights and results of two previously disjoint fields: the study of intensional logic based on formal or artificial languages, and the study of natural language grammar in empirical linguistics. In particular, it is an attempt to associate a semantics with English by first developing the semantics in a formal manner, along the lines of recent work in intensional logic, and then associating the resulting semantics with English sentences via an explicit translation procedure from English into the formal system. The translation procedure (although not the original semantics) exploits a system of English syntax developed by recent work in transformational grammar.[2]

I will not discuss the translation procedure here; instead I will concentrate on certain problems which arise in formulating the semantics – in particular, certain problems concerning grammatical modifiers: adverbs, adjectives, and prepositions. I will assume that we already have a modicum of ability to see how to 'translate' English sentences into the formal system, this ability stemming from a long tradition of such translation embodied in elementary logic texts. My discussion will by no means exhaust the various problems concerning grammatical modifiers.[3]

Davidson and Harman (eds.), Semantics of Natural Language, 127–141. All rights reserved
Copyright © 1972 by D. Reidel Publishing Company, Dordrecht-Holland

1. SOME PROBLEMS

How are we going to analyse phrases like '*x* drives slowly'? We cannot refuse to analyse this into parts, for the parts contribute to its logical form, and they should ultimately figure in an analysis of inferences like: *x* drives slowly / ∴ *x* drives. And we cannot write such a phrase as a conjunction, say as '*x* drives & *x* slowlys'. For, even ignoring the puzzle about how to interpret '*x* slowlys', we can show that this analysis would sanction false inferences. Suppose it were true that people smoked only while driving. From this ('If *x* smokes then *x* drives') together with the supposition that *x* smokes slowly ('*x* smokes & *x* slowlys') we could infer that *x* drives slowly ('*x* drives & *x* slowlys') – which should not follow.[4]

A new treatment is needed. In the next section I will examine a proposal of Reichenbach's. It too is faulty, but its examination will help bring out some of the problems involving modifiers, and it will set the stage for a more adequate approach.

2. REICHENBACH'S ACCOUNT[5]

2.1. *Adverbs*

Reichenbach's account of adverbs is the key to his treatment of other modifiers. The account involves expressing adverbial phrases within the *higher*-order predicate calculus. The initial step in this approach is to construe all verbs as complex predicates defined in terms of properties of properties. To use Reichenbach's example[6]: to say that something moves is to say that it has one of a number of specific motion-properties. In other words, '*x* moves' means 'there is a motion-property which *x* has', or, in notation:

$$(1) \qquad m(x) =_{df} (\exists f)\, [f(x)\ \&\ \mu(f)]$$

where '$m(x)$' means '*x* moves', '$(\exists f)$' is a quantifier over properties, '$f(x)$' means '*x* has the property f', and 'μ' means 'is a motion-property'. This provides a schema for writing all intransitive verbs: let 'm' stand for vhe verb in question, and 'μ' for the range of specific properties which the terb picks out. For example, if the verb is 'dances', 'μ' stands for 'is a kind of dancing'. We now introduce adverbs as predicates which express properties of these verb-properties (like f), and we apply them to the bound variable in (1) above. Thus, 'x moves slowly' is analysed as 'there is a specific motion-property which x has and which is slow', i.e.:

$$(2) \qquad msl(x) =_{df} (\exists f)\,[f(x) \,\&\, \mu(f) \,\&\, \sigma(f)]$$

where 'σ' is the second-order property corresponding to 'slowly'. In general, Reichenbach's account amounts to putting all adverbial modifications into a schema like (2), where 'μ' replaces the modified verb, and where 'σ' replaces the modifying adverb.[7]

2.2. *Adjectives*

Suppose A is an adjective and N a common noun. A is said to be in *attributive* position in a phrase of the form 'x is an A N', and in *predicative* position in the corresponding phrase "x is A & x is an N'. A significant distinction among adjectives is between those whose appearances in attributive positions can be analysed in terms of corresponding appearances in predicative positions, and those which cannot. For example, the phrase 'x is a red book', which contains an attributive occurrence of 'red', can be analysed in terms of the phrase 'x is red and x is a book', which contains 'red' only in predicative position. The attributive occurrence of 'small' in 'x is a small elephant', however, cannot be so analysed. For if it could, we could infer 'x is a small animal' from 'x is a small elephant & x is an animal', which is fallacious.

I will call adjectives of the former kind 'predicative', since they can be treated as if they always occupy predicative positions (and since we will analyse them as logical predicates). Examples of predicative adjectives are 'red', 'scarlet', 'likable', 'hollow', 'edible'; examples of nonpredicative adjectives are 'small', 'impure', 'apparent'.

Reichenbach gives no analysis of non-predicative adjectives. However, there is a perfectly straightforward treatment totally within the spirit of his enterprise. That is to treat non-predicative adjectives on a par with adverbs. For example, 'x is a small elephant' can be analysed according to schema (2), now letting 'm' stand for 'is an elephant', and 'sl' for 'small'. Reichenbach already assimilates common nouns to verbs, and the reason that 'small' cannot be treated predicatively exactly parallels the reasons that 'slowly' cannot be treated like an independent predicate. So I assume that this is the analysis that he would give.

2.3. *Prepositions*

Reichenbach treats uses of prepositions in two different ways. Some, as in '*x* is between *y* and *z*' are amalgamated to the predicate in which they occur. Thus '*x* is between *y* and *z*' is to be treated as a single unanalysed predicate.[8] Other uses of prepositions modify already existing predicates, as in '*x* stabbed *y* with *z*'. Here '*x* stabbed *y*' is a two-placed predicate, and 'with *z*' modifies it. In this case the phrase 'with *z*' is to be treated just like an adverb,[9] and analysed as in schema (2) above. On this line the only difference between adverbs and prepositions is that prepositions carry a term-place along with them, and adverbs do not. The preposition schema for intransitive verbs would look like:

$$(2')   \qquad vp\,(x, y) =_{\mathrm{df}} (\exists f)\, [f(x, y)\; \&\; v(f)\; \&\; \pi(f, y)]$$

where v is expressed by 'v' (the verb) and π by 'p' (the preposition).[10]

2.4. *Criticisms*

There are two crucial gaps in Reichenbach's account.

Objection 1: Among non-predicative adjectives, and some adverbs, there are modifiers which have a peculiar trait. This is that a complex predicate containing one of them modifying a noun or verb can be true of things which the noun or verb alone is not true of. For example, there are *toy guns* which aren't *guns*; *apparent heirs* which aren't *heirs*; and it can be true of someone that he *supposedly stole* the gems without his having *stolen* the gems. Let us call these words, 'toy', 'apparent', 'supposedly' *non-standard* modifiers. Specifically, we define a *standard* modifier as a modifier, A, which obeys the following law:

For adjectives:

> '*x* is an *A N*' logically implies '*x* is an *N*'

and for adverbs:

> '*x V*'s A*ly*' logically implies '*x V*'s'.

Modifiers like 'toy', 'apparent', 'supposedly' do not obey these laws, and are thus non-standard.

Non-standard modifiers cannot be written in Reichenbach's symbolism in the manner discussed above; i.e., where the verb (or noun) is represented by 'μ', the modifier by 'σ', and the modifier-verb (or modifier-noun) complex by schema (2):

$$(\exists f)\,[f(x)\ \&\ \mu(f)\ \&\ \sigma(f)].$$

For whenever anything is written in the form of schema (2), a formula in the form of schema (1) follows logically from it, i.e., something of the form:

$$(\exists f)\,[f(x)\ \&\ \mu(f)]$$

follows. But this is precisely the inference which *fails* in the case of non-standard modifiers; non-standard modifiers are just *defined* as the class of modifiers for which that inference fails. So Reichenbach has not offered a means of symbolizing claims containing non-standard modifiers; nor do I see any way to take account of these locutions within the spirit of his analysis.

Objection 2: Reichenbach doesn't discuss how to handle phrases which contain more than one modifier. Let me make a case for the inability of his symbolism to handle this phenomenon. Consider the following three sentences:

(a)   John painstakingly wrote illegibly.
(b)   John wrote painstakingly and illegibly.
(c)   John wrote painstakingly and John wrote illegibly.

There is at least one way to construc these sentences so that they represent three different claims. (a) differs from (b) and (c) in that the latter two sentences do not require that the illegibility of the writing was at least one of the things John was taking pains to do. And (b) differs from (c) in that (c) can be true when (b) is false. In particular, if there were two separate past occasions on which John wrote, on one of which he wrote painstakingly, and on the other of which he wrote illegibly, but no past occasion on which he did both at once, then (c) would be true, but (b) would (in the sense intended) be false. (Also if on one and the same occasion he wrote painstakingly with one hand and illegibly with the other.)

Now how are we to write these three claims in Reichenbach's notation? Let us represent 'wrote' by 'w'; 'x wrote' is then to be analysed in Reichenbach's manner as:

(3) $w(x) =_{\mathrm{df}} (\exists f)\,[f(x)\ \&\ \omega(f)].$

And let us represent 'painstakingly' and 'illegibly' by the second-order property letters 'π', and 'ι' respectively.

I think it is clear that there are only two combinations of these symbols that might have anything to do with (a)–(c). They are (letting '*j*' stand for 'John'):

(4) $(\exists f)\,[f(j)\ \&\ \omega(f)\ \&\ \pi(f)]\ \&\ (\exists f)\,[f(j)\ \&\ \omega(f)\ \&\ \iota(f)]$
(5) $(\exists f)\,[f(j)\ \&\ \omega(f)\ \&\ \pi(f)\ \&\ \iota(f)]$

Now (4) is obviously the correct canonical notation for claim (c), and I am reasonably sure that (5) is the notation for (b). And since (a) is different from (b) and (c), it is not represented by either (4) or (5). But (4) and (5) are the only plausible candidates, so long as adverbs are being represented as properties of first-order properties. So Reichenbach's account offers no means of representing (a).

This illustrates a general point. Whenever we have reiterated modification of phrases which is not reducible to forms like (4) or (5), we will be unable to mirror these locutions in accordance with Reichenbach's theory. And the examples of such reiteration are countless.[11] Reichenbach's account, as it stands, then, is inadequate. Of course, the higher order predicate calculus is so rich that *some* modification or extension of Reichenbach's approach, achieved by appeal to higher and higher levels, would be adequate. However, the only workable modification I know of within the higher-order predicate calculus simply mirrors the more austere approach discussed below.

3. THE NEW APPROACH

The approach which I believe best avoids the difficulties sketched above is this: we represent adverbs as operators added to an ordinary *first*-order predicate calculus.[12] Syntactically these operators precede well-formed formulas (frequently atomic), forming more complex well-formed formulas; semantically they can be construed as functions (I'll call them 'operations') which map the properties expressed by the formulas they modify onto new properties. For example, '*x* drives slowly' would be written '*S*(*Dx*)'; this is a formula formed by preceding the formula '*Dx*' ('*x* drives') by the operator '*S*' ('slowly'). Semantically it expresses the property of driving slowly; the operation that '*S*' represents maps the property of driving onto this property.

Reiterated modification now comes quite naturally. The phrase '*x* painstakingly wrote illegibly' is simply written '$P(I(Wx))$', where 'pain-stakingly' modifies the phrase 'wrote illegibly'. Non-predicative adjectives are also written as operators; e.g., 'x is a fake gun' becomes '$F(Gx)$'. We can also resolve ambiguity in certain adjective strings; e.g., the phrase 'x is a small four-footed animal' has two representations:

$$S(Fx \ \& \ Ax) \quad \text{and} \quad S(Ax) \ \& \ Fx.$$

The former signifies that x is small relative to the class of four-footed animals, and the latter signifies that x is small relative to the class of animals, and is also four-footed. These say quite different things; if we are stringent enough in our standards of size we might want to deny that the latter was true of anything at all (on the grounds that all really small animals are many-footed or no-footed), while consistently maintaining that the former was true of baby shrews.

As with Reichenbach, we treat prepositions like adverbs (or like non-predicative adjectives); they are operators which add a term-place to the formula they modify.[13]

The above is just an account of the simplest and most usual constructions; in this brief account I will ignore complications like higher-order modifiers (e.g., 'very' in 'very good wine') conjunctions of modifiers ('painstakingly and illegibly' in (b) of Section 2.4), etc.

Our use of terms like 'property' above suggests that we are treating adverbial modification as creating non-extensional contexts. This is not a contribution of the approach, it is forced upon us by the linguistic data. Our arguments that adverbial phrases cannot be treated as conjunctions, and that some adjectives are non-predicative, simply mimic arguments that they create non-extensional contexts. That is, logical predicates (nouns and verbs) with the same extensions cannot be substituted for one another within modified contexts without a possible change in the extension of the complex phrase. This is not to deny that *some* analysis of these contexts is possible which does not itself employ non-extensional contexts (see discussion below) – only, such analyses must pay for extensionality by quantifying over entities like properties, propositions, etc. In any event, intensional contexts are not so bad, even within a scientific analysis of language. In particular, the semantic theory sketched above can be filled in in a way typical of recent work in intensional logic,[14] rules can be given, and a completeness theorem proved.[15]

4. HIGHER-ORDER ENTITIES: PROPOSITIONS AND ACTIONS

At first glance, that-clauses, gerundive clauses, infinitival clauses, etc, seem to function in English much on a par with names or definite descriptions. In particular, they typically occur in contexts where names or definite descriptions otherwise occur. After 'John knows' we can write either 'the one thing that Bill doesn't know' or 'that Yosemite is in California'; before 'surprised Mary' we can write either 'What John did' or 'John's striking Bill', etc. Recent work in grammar confirms this, *in the sense that* it turns out to be syntactically simplest to generate that-clauses, gerundive clauses, etc., as noun phrases. It is natural, then, to try to develop a theory of logic and semantics which treats such phrases as referring expressions, where 'that John struck Bill' names a proposition, 'John's striking of Bill' an action, and so on.

This can be done in a relatively straight-forward manner for that-clauses, by generating structural descriptions of the propositions expressed by the sentence within the that-clause. To do this we introduce, for each predicate, operation symbol, connective, and quantifier of the unenriched language a predicate true of the property or operation which it expresses. Thus we will add predicates meaning 'is wisdom', 'is redness', 'is the slowly-operation', 'is the existential quantification operation', etc. For perspicuity of notation, I will symbolize these new predicates by means of the old symbols with bars over them. Thus '$\bar{S}$' stands for 'is the slowly-operation', '$\bar{R}$' for 'is redness' etc. We also need a predicate expressing the relation that a complex property or proposition bears to its immediate constituents; let us use '$Rxyz$' for 'x is the result of operating on y by z'. The propositional name that we use to symbolize a that-clause is now a complex definite description which describes the one and only proposition expressed by the original sentence. For example, corresponding to the clause 'that there are men' we have:

$$(\iota x)\,(Ey)\,(\bar{M}y\ \&\ (Ez)\,(\bar{\exists}z\ \&\ Rxyz))$$

where '$\bar{M}$' reads 'is the property, manhood', and '$\bar{\exists}$' reads 'is the existential quantification operation'. The description then reads, roughly, 'the proposition which results from operating on manhood by the existential quantification operation'.

Analogously, 'that someone drives slowly' becomes:

$$(\imath x) \, (Ey) \, (\bar{D}y \, \& \, (Ez) \, (\bar{S}z \, \& \, (Eu) \, (Ruyz \, \& \, (Ev) \, (\bar{\exists}v \, \& \, Rxuv))))$$

or, 'the result of operating with the existential operation on the result of operating on the property of driving with the slowly-operation'. I see no objection to abbreviating the former description as 'the proposition, that there are men' or, more simply, as 'that there are men', and the latter as 'that someone drives slowly'. Since that-clauses already seem to function as designators of propositions, the only innovation here is to provide an overt analysis of the mechanism by which they do so – showing how each part of the contained sentence contributes to the description of the designated proposition.[16]

Actions require a slightly more complicated treatment. We seem to designate actions by jointly designating both the agent of the action and the kind of action that is done. For example, 'John's playing the piano' identifies an action by identifying both John and the property, playing the piano.[17] The idea suggested here is to mirror gerundive names of actions by descriptions of the form:

$$(\imath x) \, (x \text{ is an action of kind } k \, \& \, a \text{ does (performs) } x)$$

Here we introduce two new primitives, 'does' (or 'performs') and '— is of kind —', plus the notion of a kind of action. This latter notion, of a *kind of action*, can simply be taken to hold of our already-employed properties expressed by action-verb phrases. For example, the property, running (i.e., $(\imath x) \, \bar{R}x$), the property of running slowly, the property of carefully writing illegibly, will each be an action-kind. Let us take running as a simple example, and let us use 'Dxy' for 'x does y' and 'Kxy' for 'x is of kind y'. Then the action-name 'John's running' will be written:

$$(\imath x) \, (Ey) \, (\bar{R}y \, \& \, Kxy \, \& \, Djx)$$

where 'j' is a name for John. Typically action-kinds will be more complex than just 'running'; here our earlier terminology lets us construct their descriptions.[18]

5. DISCOURSE ABOUT HIGHER-ORDER ENTITIES

One of the philosophical advantages of the constructions of the last section is that they allow us to formulate our philosophical theories in extensional rather than non-extensional language. All we need to do is to introduce a predicate of propositions 'T' meaning 'is true', and replace every sentence S with our formulation of 'that S is true'. For example, the non-extensional 'Supposedly there are unicorns' ('$S(\exists x)\ Ux$') becomes the extensional 'That supposedly there are unicorns is true' ('$T(\imath x)\ (\exists(y\ (\bar{U}y\ \&\ (\exists z)\ (\bar{\exists}z\ \&\ (\exists u)\ (Ruyz\ \&\ (\exists v)\ (\bar{S}v\ \&\ Rxuv))))$'). That we can do this in general, that we can replace a blatantly non-extensional symbolism with a purely extensional one without loss of expressive power, should not be particularly surprising;[19] for we buy extensionality at the price of quantifying over 'intensional' entities.[20] It's not clear that there is any ultimate advantage in doing this, but it may have short-term heuristic benefits. Certainly many philosophers do seem to have strong predilections for expressing their most careful views in extensional terminology, even when it requires quantification over properties, propositions, and the like.[21] This is probably due to a strong feeling that the background logic of our theories ought to be familiar and trust-worthy; until recently, this has amounted to the requirement that our language be extensional. The requirement has not been unreasonable, at least when construed as an ideal; analyses that looked good in the past have been found to have concealed important difficulties and to have begged important questions due to the use of non-extensional language.[22] And, at least sometimes, turning to extensional formulations has helped clarify issues.[23]

But moving to higher-order discourse does not *guarantee* extensionality. In the remainder of the paper I will discuss one case in which we probably do not have extensionality, even at the higher level of discourse.

Once we have names of propositions and actions we can form sentences which seem to ascribe new properties to them. Of special interest here are adjectives which arise from the occurrence of adverbs at a lower level. 'Necessarily, S' gives rise to 'That S is necessary'; 'John drove slowly' to 'John's driving was slow'; 'John intentionally hit Bill' to 'John's hitting of Bill was intentional'. I will confine my discussion to sentences containing descriptions of actions; similar points can be made concerning descriptions of propositions.[24]

Suppose Adj is an adjective of actions which has an adverbial form, Adj-ly. What is the relation between the meanings of these two forms? It is natural to suppose that a necessary and sufficient condition of an adjective's applying to an action is that the sentence from which the action-name is derived, supplemented by the corresponding adverb, is true; i.e., that something like the following holds:

(6) x's ϕing is Adj if and only if x ϕ's Adj-ly

which in our terminology is just:

(7)   Adj$(\imath y)$ $(\exists z)$ $(\bar{\phi} z$ & Kyz & $Dxy)$[25] if and only if Adj-ly(ϕx)

(6) is, of course, vague, and probably violates some sorts of grammatical restrictions. But it should be clear enough for our purposes. It is intended at least to yield cases like 'John's driving was slow if and only if John drove slowly'.

So far our new idiom is just a new way of saying old things. But now trouble arises in the form of claims about the identity-conditions of actions. Davidson[26] has argued persuasively that in a large number of cases we wish to identify actions which are described in different ways. For example, we may wish to identify Jones' pouring of poison into the well with Jones' poisoning of the populace in a nearby community. But suppose that Jones poured the poison rapidly. Then by (6), his pouring of the poison was rapid. But his pouring of the poison was his poisoning the populace. Thus his poisoning of the populace was also rapid, and, reading (6) backwards, we get that he rapidly poisoned the populace. Which isn't true.[27] John Wallace[28] has pointed out that the number of cases of this sort is enormous, encompassing not just ordinary adverbs, but adverbial prepositional phrases as well. My playing of the piano might be the same action as my distressing you, but although I played the piano with my left hand I did not distress you with my left hand. My administering the medicine may be through a tube, but I do not cure the patient through a tube, even though my administering the medicine is my curing the patient. And so on.[29]

One move that might be made here is to insist, in opposition to Davidson, on individuating actions via their correlated sentences. On this line, my administering the medicine would *not* be my curing the patient (even though 'the action which I most liked doing on Tuesday morning' might still refer to either of these – i.e., this is not a complete rejection of the view that we can have different descriptions of the same actions, it only rules out alternate *gerundive* descriptions of the same action). I think that this won't work, not so much because we can't have a notion of 'action' like this, nor because it diverges from ordinary usage (it does this some, but so does the other), but rather because we do also have a notion of 'action' of the Davidson type, and here is where the problems arise. I see only two plausible reactions:

First, we might want to weaken (6) to a mere conditional:

(8)   If x ϕ's Adj-ly then x's ϕing is Adj.

This would let us infer, for example, that x's pouring of the poison, and thus x's poisoning of the populace, were both rapid, while failing to conclude from this that x poisoned the populace rapidly. I think we are often motivated to take such a line; here we predicate an adjective of an action if the corresponding adverb appears as part of *one* way of viewing the action. The result, if we are to be consistent, is that many actions will now be both rapid and slow (because he poured the poison rapidly and poisoned the populace slowly), both careless and careful, both knowing and unknowing, etc.

Faced with such peculiarities, there is a motivation to move to another analysis, wherein one speaks of 'action under descriptions'. This device allows one to identify actions in the desired way, but makes attribution of adjectives to actions relative to their descriptions. I.e., schema (6) is replaced by something like

(9) x's ϕing is Adj under description 'ψ' if and only if x ψ's Adj-ly

This is usually urged for treatment of adjectives like 'intentionally', but it is equally appropriate for locutions like 'slowly'.

What I want to suggest is that we do not need the metalinguistic reference to descriptions here, nor do we need to treat the phenomenon under discussion as a special case, utilizing a new primitive notion 'is — under ...' not needed in other areas of discourse. The idea of making the attribution of an adjective to things depend on how those things are described is already apparent in the analysis of non-predicative adjectives. Whether desirable or not, usage of adjectives in higher-order discourse is already non-predicative usage, and we *can* analyse such adjectives simply as special cases of non-predicative adjectives. The advantage of (9) over such an analysis is that (9) is extensional, and has whatever philosophical benefits accompany extensionality. But our move to higher-order discourse was motivated primarily by an attempt to get a natural natural-language semantics. While philosophers may prefer (9) to the treatment below for their special interests, these interests may not coincide completely with those of linguistic analysis.

It's easy to treat higher-order adjectives as non-predicative; what we *also* want to do is to specify their relations with their corresponding adverbs. In attributive position the account is easy:

(10) x is an Adj ϕing if and only if x is a (ϕ Adj-ly)ing

i.e.

(11) $\text{Adj}((\exists y)\,(\overline{\phi}y\ \&\ Kxy))$ if and only if $(\exists z)\,(\overline{\phi\ \text{Adj-ly}}\ z\ \&\ Kxz)$

Non-attributive occurrences of these adjectives are analysed just like non-attributive occurrences of ordinary non-predicative adjectives; they are elliptical for attributive uses.

Just as 'John's pet is small' is elliptical for 'John's pet is a small A', where 'A' will typically, but not always, be 'pet', 'x's ϕing is Adj' will be elliptical for 'x's ϕing is an Adj ψing', again, where 'ψ' will often, but not always be 'ϕ'. (In cases where 'ψ' = 'ϕ', we are just maintaining (6), which was our original proposal.)

Chicago Circle, February 1970

BIBLIOGRAPHY

[1] Rudolf Carnap, *The Logical Syntax of Language*, Harcourt, Brace, New York, and K. Paul, Trench, Trubner, London, 1937.
[2] Roderick M. Chisholm, *Perceiving: A Philosophical Study*, Cornell University Press, Ithaca, N.Y., 1961.
[3] Noam Chomsky, *Syntactic Structures*, Mouton, The Hague, 1957.
[4] Noam Chomsky, *Aspects of the Theory of Syntax*, M.I.T. Press, Cambridge, Mass., 1965.
[5] Romaine Clark, 'Concerning the Logic of Predicate Modifiers', *Nous* 4 (1970).
[6] Donald Davidson, 'The Logical Form of Action Sentences' in *The Logic of Decision and Action* (ed. by Nicholas Rescher), University of Pittsburgh Press, Pittsburgh, Pennsylvania, 1967, pp. 81–95.
[7] R. M. Hare, *The Language of Morals*, Clarendon Press, Oxford, 1952.
[8] Richard C. Jeffrey, *The Logic of Decision*, McGraw-Hill Book Company, New York, 1965.
[9] Anthony Kenny, *Action, Emotion and Will*, Routledge and Kegan Paul, London, 1963.
[10] George Lakoff, 'Repartee, or a Reply to *Negation, Conjunction and Quantifiers*', *Foundations of Language* 6 (1970).

[11] James D. McCawley, 'Meaning and the Description of Languages', *Kotoba no uchū* **2**, nos. 9, 10, 11.

[12] Richard Montague, 'English as a Formal Language' in *Linguaggi nella società e nella technica*, Edizione di Comunità, Milan, 1970.

[13] Richard Montague, 'Pragmatics and Intensional Logic', *Synthese* **22** (1970).

[14] G. E. Moore, *Principia Ethica*, Cambridge University Press, Cambridge, 1903.

[15] Terence Parsons, 'On a General Theory of Modifiers' (dittograph).

[16] Terence Parsons, *A Semantics for English* (mimeograph).

[17] C. S. Peirce, 'The Fixation of Belief', *Popular Science Monthly*, 1877.

[18] H. Reichenbach, *Elements of Symbolic Logic*, Macmillan, London and New York, 1947.

[19] Dana Scott, 'Formalizing Intensional Notions' (dittograph).

[20] John Wallace, 'On What's Happening' (dittograph).

[21] John Wallace, 'On What Happened' (dittograph).

REFERENCES

[1] Parsons [16]. Research was partially supported by NSF GS 2087.

[2] The system of transformational grammar employed is the 'classical' sort, outlined in Chomsky [3], [4]; this is the hardest way to do it, but the grammar is well known.

Recent work by other linguists, e.g. Lakoff [10], McCawley [11], in which something like the classical predicate calculus actually appears within the base component of the syntax should make endeavors of this sort easier.

[3] For more discussion concerning these see Clark [5], Davidson [6], Kenny [9], Ch. VII, Montague [12], Wallace [20], [21].

[4] Throughout this paper I have ignored problems about tenses; I believe that none of my examples fail because of this.

[5] From Reichenbach [18], esp. Section 53. Actually, Reichenbach has two accounts; for discussion of his other account, see Davidson [6].

[6] *Op. cit.*, pp. 301–307.

[7] He makes adverbs of tense and modal adverbs exceptions to this. Schema (2) only works for intransitive verbs; a transitive verb, m, would require the analysis:

$$msl(x, y) =_{df} (Ef) [f(x, y) \& \mu(f) \& \sigma(f)].$$

[8] *Op. cit.*, p. 252.

[9] *Op. cit.*, p. 325.

[10] This is my interpretation of his terse remarks on p. 325. The schema for transitive verbs would be correspondingly more complex.

[11] For some problem constructions even more complex than reiterated modification, and also troublesome for Reichenbach, see Wallace [20], [21].

[12] This idea was apparently discovered independently by Clark [5], J. Kamp (see discussion in Montague [12]), and myself [15], [16]. The present discussion ignores some important distinctions, particularly that between what Montague calls 'ad-verbs' and 'ad-formulas'. See discussion in Montague [12] and Parsons [15], [16] Section 4.2.

[13] Exceptions to this are a large class of prepositions which originate in grammatical transformations; e.g. 'of' in 'the tolling of the bell'.

[14] As in Montague [13] and Scott [19].

[15] See Parsons [16] Section 3.

[16] This is described precisely in Parsons [16] Section 5.1.

[17] Frequently specifying both agent and action-kind will not uniquely specify a single

action; this is a common characteristic of all definite descriptions. In such cases the action-kind must be given in greater detail, perhaps supplemented with time and place specifications, etc. Also, some gerundive clauses (in some uses) seem to refer not to actions, but to activities; consider: 'John's teaching got worse during 1969'. I will ignore such uses of gerundives in the present paper.

[18] For details see Parsons [16] Sections 5.1, 5.5.

[19] But it may not be entirely uncontroversial; if true it seems to falsify Chisholm's version of Brentano's Thesis, in Chapter 11 of Chisholm [2].

[20] This is similar to the device of formulating claims in a metalanguage rather than the object-language (cf. Carnap [1]), except (i) it is not metalinguistic, both in the sense that it does not refer to language, and in the sense that we are discussing constructions which are a common part of our object-language, English, and (ii) previous accounts did not show how the transition to the metalanguage could work with modifiers like adverbs.

[21] Cf. Jeffrey's discussion of propositions in Jeffrey [8].

[22] E.g., Peirce's use of subjunctive conditionals in analysing validity in Peirce [17].

[23] Moore's rephrasal of 'x is good' into 'x has the property goodness' (see Moore [14]) made explicit presuppositions that were previously concealed – that 'good' is a predicative adjective – a presupposition that has since been denied by many philosophers. Cf. Hare [7].

[24] See Reference 29.

[25] I use '$\bar{\phi}$' for the predicate which is true of the property expressed by 'ϕ', even when '$\bar{\phi}$' is complex; in this case the predicate is a complex one; cf. Parsons [16] Section 5.1.

[26] In Davidson [6].

[27] Davidson is aware of this, but considers it a special case, where the adjective form of the word is non-predicative. If Wallace is right, most prepositional phrases cause trouble here too.

[28] Wallace [20].

[29] The comparable problem about propositions is this: if we identity propositions whenever they are logically equivalent, then if 'x believes that S' is true, and if 'S' is logically equivalent to 'T', then 'x believes that T' is also true. But this seems wrong – take 'S' to be 'For every number there is a greater number', and 'T' to be 'There is no greatest number', and let x be someone who doesn't see that they are equivalent.

All of the moves discussed below for actions have analogues for propositions. In addition, it may be more plausible, in the case of propositions, to require tighter identity conditions than logical equivalence.

RICHARD MONTAGUE*

PRAGMATICS AND INTENSIONAL LOGIC

The word 'pragmatics' was used in Morris [1] for that branch of philosophy of language which involves, besides linguistic expressions and the objects to which they refer, also the users of the expressions and the possible contexts of use. The other two branches, syntax and semantics, dealing respectively with expressions alone and expressions together with their reference, had already been extensively developed by the time at which Morris wrote, the former by a number of authors and the latter in Tarski [1].

Morris' conception of pragmatics, however, was programmatic and indefinite. A step towards precision was taken by Bar-Hillel, who suggested in Bar-Hillel [1] that pragmatics concern itself with what C. S. Peirce had in the last century called *indexical expressions*.[1] An indexical word or sentence is one of which the reference cannot be determined without knowledge of the context of use; an example is the first person pronoun 'I'. Indexical sentences can be produced in various ways, for instance, by using tenses. Consider 'Caesar will die'. This sentence cannot be considered either true or false independently of the context of use; before a truth value can be determined, the time of utterance, which is one aspect of the context of use, must be specified.

Though Bar-Hillel suggested that pragmatics concern itself with indexical expressions, he was not wholly explicit as to the form this concern should take. It seemed to me desirable that pragmatics should at least initially follow the lead of semantics – or its modern version, model theory[2] – which is primarily concerned with the notions of truth and satisfaction (in a model, or under an interpretation). Pragmatics, then, should employ similar notions, though here we should speak about truth and satisfaction with respect not only to an interpretation but also to a context of use.

These notions I analyzed some years ago in connection with a number of special cases, for instance, those involving personal pronouns, demonstratives, modal operators, tenses, probability operators, contextual ambiguity, and direct self-reference.[3] An important feature of many of these analyses was a treatment of quantifiers due largely to my student Prof. Nino Cocchiarella, and persisting in the general development below.[4]

In each special case, however, truth and satisfaction had to be defined anew; in particular, no unified treatment of operators was seen. Intuitive similarities existed; but full formal unity was not achieved until 1965, and then it came about through joint work of Dr. Charles Howard and myself.

Let me sketch the general treatment. By a *pragmatic language* is understood a language of which the symbols (atomic expressions) are drawn from the following categories:

(1) the logical constants $\neg$, $\wedge$, $\vee$, $\rightarrow$, $\leftrightarrow$, $\wedge$, $\vee$, $=$, E (read respectively 'it is not the case that', 'and', 'or', 'if ... then', 'if and only if', 'for all', 'for some', 'is identical with', 'exists'),

(2) parentheses, brackets, and commas,

(3) the individual variables $v_0, ..., v_k, ...,$

(4) individual constants,

(5) n-place predicate constants, for each natural number (that is, nonnegative integer) n, and

(6) operators.

(The individuals to which such a language refers will be regarded as possible objects; accordingly, the symbol E will occur in such contexts as $E[x]$, which is read 'x exists' or 'x is actual'. I consider under (6) only what might be called 1-*place operators*. These are symbols which, like the negation sign, generate a sentence when placed before another sentence; examples are the modal operators 'necessarily' and 'possibly', as well as the expressions 'it will be the case that', 'usually', and 'it is probable to at least the degree one-half that'. Purely for simplicity I have disallowed operation symbols, descriptive phrases, and many-place operators; but an extension of the present treatment to accommodate such expressions would be completely routine. Indeed, many-place operators can be expressed in both extended pragmatics and intensional logic, which are considered below; and a partial theory of descriptive phrases occurs within intensional logic.)

The *formulas* of a pragmatic language L are built up exactly as one would expect. To be explicit, the set of formulas of L is the smallest set Γ such that (1) Γ contains all expressions

$$\mathsf{E}\,[\zeta],$$
$$\zeta = \eta,$$
$$P\,[\zeta_0, \ldots, \zeta_{n-1}],$$

where each of ζ, η, $\zeta_0, \ldots, \zeta_{n-1}$ is an individual constant of L or an individual variable and P is an n-place predicate constant of L, (2) Γ is closed under the application of sentential connectives, (3) $\bigwedge u\phi$ and $\bigvee u\phi$ are in Γ whenever u is an individual variable and ϕ is in Γ, and (4) $N\phi$ is in Γ whenever N is an operator of L and ϕ is in Γ.

To interpret a pragmatic language L we must specify several things. In the first place, we must determine the set of all possible contexts of use – or rather, of all complexes of relevant aspects of possible contexts of use; we may call such complexes *indices*, or to borrow Dana Scott's term, *points of reference*. For example, if the only indexical features of L were the presence of tense operators and the first person pronoun 'I', then a point of reference might be an ordered pair consisting of a person and a real number, understood respectively as the utterer and the moment of utterance.

In the second place, we should have to specify, for each point of reference i, the set A_i of objects present or existing with respect to i. For example, if the points of reference were moments of time, A_i would be understood as the set of objects existing at i.

In the third place, we should have to specify the meaning or *intension* of each predicate and individual constant of L. To do this for a constant c, we should have to determine, for each point of reference i, the denotation or *extension* of c with respect to i. For example, if the points of reference were moments of time and c were the predicate constant 'is green', we should have to specify for each moment i the set of objects to be regarded as green at i. If, on the other hand, c were an individual constant, say 'the Pope', we should have to specify, for each moment i, the person regarded as Pope at i.

The fourth thing we must provide is an interpretation of the operators of L. To do this we associate with each operator of L a relation between points of reference and sets of points of reference. The role played by such relations, as well as the intuitive reasons for regarding them as interpreting operators, can best be discussed later.

In order to be a bit more precise about interpretations, let us introduce a few auxiliary notions. Understand by a $\langle U_0, ..., U_{n-1} \rangle$-*relation* a subset of $U_0 \times \cdots \times U_{n-1}$ (by which we intend the Cartesian product $\prod_{i<n} U_i$ of the sets $U_0, ..., U_{n-1}$), and by an $\langle I, U_0, ..., U_{n-1} \rangle$-*predicate* a function from the set I into the set of all $\langle U_0, ..., U_{n-1} \rangle$-relations. (I use the word 'relation' for a possible candidate for the extension of a predicate constant, while 'predicate' is reserved for the intension of such a constant. Consider the special case in which $n=1$. Then the $\langle U_0 \rangle$-relations will coincide with the sets of elements of U_0, the $\langle I, U_0 \rangle$-predicates are what we might regard as *properties* (indexed by I) of elements of U_0, and both will correspond to 1-place predicate constants. In case $n=0$, we should speak of Λ-relations (where Λ is the empty sequence, that is, the empty set); and these are the subsets of the empty Cartesian product, which is of course $\{\Lambda\}$. Thus the only Λ-relations will be the empty set Λ and its unit set $\{\Lambda\}$; let us think of these two objects as the truth-values F and T respectively. The corresponding predicates are $\langle I \rangle$-predicates; and they will be functions from the set I to truth-values, that is, what we might regard as *propositions*[5] indexed by I.)

By a *k-place relation among members* of a set U and by a *k-place I-predicate of members of* U are understood a $\langle U_0, ..., U_{k-1} \rangle$-relation and an $\langle I, U_0, ..., U_{k-1} \rangle$-predicate respectively, where each U_p (for $p < k$) is U.

DEFINITION I. A *possible interpretation for a pragmatic language* L is a triple $\langle A, F, R \rangle$ such that (1) A is a function, (2) for each i in the domain of A, A_i is a set (I use the notations 'A_i' and '$A(i)$' indiscriminately for function value), (3) F is a function whose domain is the set of predicate and individual constants of L, (4) whenever c is an individual constant of L, F_c is a function whose domain is the domain of A and such that, for all j in the domain of A, $F_c(j)$ is a member of the union of the sets A_i for i in the domain of A, (5) whenever P is an n-place predicate constant of L, F_P is an n-place $\mathbf{D}A$-predicate of members of the union of the sets A_i (for $i \in \mathbf{D}A$), where $\mathbf{D}A$ is the domain of A, (6) R is a function whose domain is the set of operators of L, and (7) whenever N is in the domain of R, R_N is a $\langle \mathbf{D}A, \mathbf{SD}A \rangle$-relation, where $\mathbf{SD}A$ is the power set (set of all subsets) of $\mathbf{D}A$.

A few remarks are perhaps in order in connection with this definition.

Let $\mathfrak{A}$ be a possible interpretation for a pragmatic language L, and let $\mathfrak{A}$ have the form $\langle A, F, R \rangle$. We understand the domain of the function A to be the set of all points of reference according to $\mathfrak{A}$. If i is a point of reference, A_i is understood as the set of objects existing with respect to i (according to $\mathfrak{A}$). The union of the sets A_i for i in $\mathbf{D}A$ is thus what we might regard as the set of all possible individuals (according to $\mathfrak{A}$). By the definition above, an individual constant denotes a *possible* individual, and a 1-place predicate constant a set of *possible* individuals, with respect to a given point of reference. To see that it would be overly restrictive to demand that the respective denotations be an individual that exists with respect to the given point of reference or a set of such individuals, suppose that the points of reference are instants of time, and consider the individual constant 'the previous Pope' and the predicate constant 'is remembered by someone'. A similar point can be made in connection with predicate constants of more than one place. Consider, for instance, the 2-place predicate constant 'thinks of' (as in 'Jones thinks of Jove'). Under a standard interpretation of which the points of reference are possible worlds, the extension of this constant with respect to a given world would be a relation between individuals existing in that world and possible individuals (that is, objects existing in some world).[6]

The notions central to pragmatics, those of *truth* and *satisfaction*, are expressed by the phrases 'the sentence (that is, formula without free variables) ϕ is true with respect to the point of reference i under the interpretation $\mathfrak{A}$' and 'the possible individual x satisfies the formula ϕ with respect to the point of reference i under the interpretation $\mathfrak{A}$', which we may abbreviate by 'ϕ is true$_{i,\mathfrak{A}}$' and 'x sat$_{i,\mathfrak{A}} \phi$' respectively. The following clauses do not constitute definitions of truth and satisfaction, but are rather to be regarded as true assertions exhibiting the salient features of those notions; the full definitions will be given later.

CRITERIA OF PRAGMATIC TRUTH AND SATISFACTION. Let $\mathfrak{A}$ be a possible interpretation, having the form $\langle A, F, R \rangle$, for a pragmatic language L; let $i \in \mathbf{D}A$; let x be a member of the union of the sets A_j (for $j \in \mathbf{D}A$); let P be a 2-place predicate constant of L; and let u be an individual variable. Then:

(1) $P[c, d]$ is true$_{i,\mathfrak{A}}$ if and only if $\langle F_c(i), F_d(i) \rangle \in F_P(i)$;

(2) x sat$_{i,\mathfrak{A}} P[c, u]$ if and only if $\langle F_c(i), x \rangle \in F_P(i)$;

(3) x sat$_{i,\mathfrak{A}} c = u$ if and only if $F_c(i)$ is identical with x;

(4) x sat$_{i,\mathfrak{A}}$ E $[u]$ if and only if $x \in A_i$;

(5) if ϕ is a sentence of L, then $\neg \phi$ is true$_{i,\mathfrak{A}}$ if and only if ϕ is not true$_{i,\mathfrak{A}}$;

(6) if ϕ, ψ are sentences of L, then $(\phi \wedge \psi)$ is true$_{i,\mathfrak{A}}$ if and only if both ϕ and ψ are true$_{i,\mathfrak{A}}$;

(7) if ϕ is a formula of L of which the only free variable is u, then $\vee u \phi$ is true$_{i,\mathfrak{A}}$ if and only if there is an object y in the union of the sets A_j (for $j \in \mathbf{D}A$) such that y sat$_{i,\mathfrak{A}}$ ϕ;

(8) if ϕ is a sentence of L and N an operator of L, then $N\phi$ is true$_{i,\mathfrak{A}}$ if and only if $\langle i, \{j : j \in \mathbf{D}A$ and ϕ is true$_{j,\mathfrak{A}}\}\rangle \in R_N$.

According to (8), $N\phi$ is true at i (under $\mathfrak{A}$) if and only if i bears the relation R_N to the set of points of reference at which ϕ is true (under $\mathfrak{A}$). To see that (8) comprehends the proper treatment of, for example, the past tense operator, consider an interpretation $\mathfrak{A}$ in which $\mathbf{D}A$ is the set of real numbers (that is, instants of time) and R_N is the set of pairs $\langle i, J \rangle$ such that $i \in \mathbf{D}A$, $J \subseteq \mathbf{D}A$, and there exists $j \in J$ such that $j < i$. Then, by (8), $N\phi$ will be true at i (under $\mathfrak{A}$) if and only if there exists $j < i$ such that ϕ is true at j (under $\mathfrak{A}$); and therefore N will correctly express 'it has been the case that'. It is clear that the future tense, as well as the modal operators (interpreted by relevance relations) of Kripke [1], can be similarly accommodated. These examples, however, could all be treated within a simpler framework, in which R_N is always a relation between two points of reference (rather than having as its second relatum a *set* of points of reference). To see the necessity of the more general approach, we could consider probability operators, conditional necessity, or, to invoke an especially perspicuous example of Dana Scott, the present progressive tense. To elaborate on the last, let the interpretation $\mathfrak{A}$ again have the real numbers as its points of reference; and let R_N be the set of pairs $\langle i, J \rangle$ such that $i \in \mathbf{D}A$, $J \subseteq \mathbf{D}A$, and J is a neighborhood of i (that is, J includes an open interval of which i is a member). Then, by (8), $N\phi$ will be true at i (under $\mathfrak{A}$) if and only if there is an open interval containing i throughout which ϕ is true (under $\mathfrak{A}$). Thus N might receive the awkward reading 'it is being the case that', in the sense in which 'it is being the case that Jones leaves' is synonymous with 'Jones is leaving'.

According to (7), quantification is over *possible* (and not merely *actual*) individuals. The desirability of this can be seen by considering, within the special case of tense logic, the sentence 'there was a man whom no one remembers'. One can of course express quantification over actual individuals by combining quantifiers with the symbol E of existence.

To be quite precise, the desiderata (1)–(8) can be achieved by the following sequence of definitions; that is to say, (1)–(8) are simple consequences of Definitions II–V below. We assume for these that $\mathfrak{A}$ is a possible interpretation for a pragmatic language L, $\mathfrak{A} = \langle A, F, R \rangle$, U is the union of the sets A_j for $j \in DA$, U^ω is the set of all infinite sequences (of type ω) of members of U, $i \in DA$, and n is a natural number.

DEFINITION II. If ζ is an individual variable or individual constant of L, then by $\text{Ext}_{i,\mathfrak{A}}(\zeta)$, or the *extension* of ζ at i (with respect to $\mathfrak{A}$) is understood that function H with domain U^ω which is determined as follows:

(1) if ζ is the variable v_n and $x \in U^\omega$, then $H(x) = x_n$;

(2) if ζ is an individual constant and $x \in U^\omega$, then $H(x) = F_\zeta(i)$.

The *extension* of a *formula* of L at a point of reference (and with respect to $\mathfrak{A}$) is introduced by the following recursive definition.

DEFINITION III. (1) If ζ is an individual constant of L or an individual variable, then $\text{Ext}_{i,\mathfrak{A}}(\text{E}\,[\zeta])$ is $\{x : x \in U^\omega \text{ and } (\text{Ext}_{i,\mathfrak{A}}(\zeta))\,(x) \in A_i\}$.

(2) If each of ζ, η is either an individual constant of L or an individual variable, then $\text{Ext}_{i,\mathfrak{A}}(\zeta = \eta)$ is $\{x : x \in U^\omega \text{ and } (\text{Ext}_{i,\mathfrak{A}}(\zeta))\,(x)$ is identical with $(\text{Ext}_{i,\mathfrak{A}}(\eta))\,(x)\}$.

(3) If P is an n-place predicate constant of L and each of $\zeta_0, \ldots, \zeta_{n-1}$ is an individual constant of L or an individual variable, then $\text{Ext}_{i,\mathfrak{A}}$ $(P[\zeta_0, \ldots, \zeta_{n-1}])$ is $\{x : x \in U^\omega \text{ and } \langle(\text{Ext}_{i,\mathfrak{A}}(\zeta_0))\,(x), \ldots, (\text{Ext}_{i,\mathfrak{A}}(\zeta_{n-1}))\,(x)\rangle \in F_P(i)\}$.

(4) If ϕ, ψ are formulas of L, then $\text{Ext}_{i,\mathfrak{A}}(\neg\phi)$ is $U^\omega - \text{Ext}_{i,\mathfrak{A}}(\phi)$, $\text{Ext}_{i,\mathfrak{A}}((\phi \wedge \psi))$ is $\text{Ext}_{i,\mathfrak{A}}(\phi) \cap \text{Ext}_{i,\mathfrak{A}}(\psi)$, and similarly for the other sentential connectives.

(5) If ϕ is a formula of L, then $\text{Ext}_{i,\mathfrak{A}}(\bigvee v_n \phi)$ is $\{x : x \in U^\omega \text{ and, for some } y \in U$, the sequence $\langle x_0, \ldots, x_{n-1}, y, x_{n+1}, \ldots \rangle \in \text{Ext}_{i,\mathfrak{A}}(\phi)\}$, and similarly for $\bigwedge v_n \phi$.

(6) If ϕ is a formula of L and N an operator of L, then $\text{Ext}_{i,\mathfrak{A}}(N\phi)$ is $\{x : x \in U^\omega \text{ and } \langle i, \{j : j \in DA \text{ and } x \in \text{Ext}_{j,\mathfrak{A}}(\phi)\}\rangle \in R_N\}$.

DEFINITION IV. If ϕ is a sentence of L, then ϕ is $\text{true}_{i,\mathfrak{A}}$ if and only if $\text{Ext}_{i,\mathfrak{A}}(\phi) = U^\omega$.

DEFINITION V. If ϕ is a formula of L of which the only free variable is v_n, then $y \text{ sat}_{i,\mathfrak{A}}\phi$ if and only if there exists $x \in \text{Ext}_{i,\mathfrak{A}}(\phi)$ such that $x_n = y$.

It is seen from the definitions above that the extension of a formula (at a point of reference) is a set of sequences (indeed, the set of sequences 'satisfying' that formula at that point of reference, in the sense in which sequences, rather than individuals satisfy) and that the extension of an individual constant or variable (again, at a given point of reference) is a function assigning a possible individual to each sequence in U^{ω}. How does this construction accord with the fundamental discussion in Frege [1]? It should be remembered that Frege considered explicitly the extensions only of expressions without free variables – thus, as far as our present language is concerned, only of sentences and individual constants. For Frege the extension (or *ordinary extension*) of a sentence was a truth value; but it is easily seen that according to Definition III the extension of a sentence of L will always be either U^{ω} or the empty set, which in this context can be appropriately identified with truth and falsehood respectively. For Frege the extension (or *ordinary extension*) of an individual constant was the object it denotes, while for us the extension is the constant function with that object as value (and with U^{ω} as domain). Apart from set-theoretic manipulations, then, Frege's extensions agree with ours in all common cases.

I introduce for the sake of later discussion the *intensions* of certain expressions with respect to $\mathfrak{A}$, as well as the notions of *logical consequence*, *logical truth*, and *logical equivalence* appropriate to pragmatics.

DEFINITION VI. If ϕ is an individual constant of L, a formula of L, or an individual variable, then $\mathrm{Int}_{\mathfrak{A}}(\phi)$ is that function H with domain $\mathbf{D}A$ such that, for each $i \in \mathbf{D}A$, $H(i) = \mathrm{Ext}_{i,\mathfrak{A}}(\phi)$.

DEFINITION VII. A sentence ϕ is a *logical consequence* (in the sense of pragmatics) of a set Γ of sentences if and only if for every pragmatic language L and all $\mathfrak{A}$, A, F, R, i, if $\mathfrak{A} = \langle A, F, R \rangle$, $\mathfrak{A}$ is a possible interpretation for L, $i \in \mathbf{D}A$, $\Gamma \cup \{\phi\}$ is a set of sentences of L, and for every $\psi \in \Gamma$, ψ is true$_{i,\mathfrak{A}}$, then ϕ is true$_{i,\mathfrak{A}}$. A sentence is *logically true* if and only if it is a logical consequence of the empty set. A sentence ϕ is *logically equivalent* to a sentence ψ if and only if the sentence $(\phi \leftrightarrow \psi)$ is logically true.[7]

If we understand the extension of a predicate constant P (at i and with respect to $\mathfrak{A}$) to be $F_P(i)$, then inspection of Definition III will show that Frege's functionality principle applies fully to our notion of extension: the extension of a formula is a function of the extensions (ordinary extensions) of those of its parts not standing within indirect contexts (that is, for the present language, not standing within the scope of an operator), together with the intensions (what Frege also called *indirect extensions*) of those parts that do stand within indirect contexts. It is clause (6) of Definition III which creates the dependence of certain extensions on intensions, and which consequently makes it impossible to regard Definition III as a simple recursion on the length of formulas. Instead, the recursion is on a well-founded relation S between ordered pairs, characterized as follows: $\langle\langle j, \psi\rangle, \langle i, \phi\rangle\rangle \in S$ if and only if $i, j \in \mathbf{D}A$, ϕ, ψ are formulas of L, and ψ is a proper part of ϕ.[8]

On the other hand, we could have adopted another order, introducing intensions first and defining extensions explicitly in terms of them. In that case, as is easily seen, we could have introduced intensions by a simple recursion on the length of formulas; in other words, the intension of a complex expression is a function purely of the intensions of its components. (We thus answer negatively, for pragmatic languages at least, a question raised by Frege, whether we need to consider *indirect intensions* as well as ordinary extensions and ordinary intensions. The answer remains negative even for the richer languages considered below.)

The general treatment of operators, embodied in clause (6) of Definition III and due to Charles Howard and me, has the advantage of comprehending all known special cases but the drawback of a seemingly *ad hoc* and unintuitive character. This semblance can be removed, and at the same time a theoretical reduction accomplished, by the consideration of *intensional logic*. Attempts to construct intensional languages suitable for handling belief contexts and the like have been made previously, but without complete success; I report now my own efforts in this direction.

By an *intensional language* is understood a language of which the symbols are drawn from the following categories:

(1) the logical constants of pragmatic languages,

(2) parentheses, brackets, and commas,

(3) the individual variables $v_0, ..., v_n, ...,$

(4) individual constants,

(5) the *n*-place predicate variables $G_{0,n}, ..., G_{k,n}, ...,$ for each natural number n,

(6) predicate constants of type s, for each finite sequence s of integers $\geqslant -1$,

(7) the operator $\Box$ (read 'necessarily'),

(8) the descriptive symbol T (read 'the unique ... such that' and regarded, along with the symbols under (1) and (7), as a logical constant).

Under (6) we admit predicate constants taking predicate variables, as well as individual symbols, as arguments. The type of such a constant indicates the grammatical categories of a suitable sequence of arguments, -1 indicating an individual symbol and a nonnegative integer n indicating an n-place predicate variable. Thus our previous n-place predicate constants are comprehended, and can be identified with predicate constants of type $\langle s_0, ..., s_{n-1} \rangle$, where each s_i (for $i < n$) is -1. The descriptive symbol will be applied only to predicate variables; this is because it will be needed only in such contexts and because its use in connection with individual variables would require some small but extraneous attention to the choice of a 'null entity'.[9] The descriptive phrases we admit will be completely eliminable, and are introduced solely to facilitate certain later examples.

The set of *formulas* of an *intensional* language L is the smallest set Γ such that (1) Γ contains the expressions

$$E[\zeta],$$
$$\zeta = \eta,$$
$$G[\zeta_0, ..., \zeta_{n-1}],$$

where each of $\zeta, \eta, \zeta_0, ..., \zeta_{n-1}$ is an individual constant of L or an individual variable and G is an n-place predicate variable of L, as well as all expressions

$$P[\zeta_0, ..., \zeta_{n-1}],$$

where P is a predicate constant of L having type $\langle s_0, ..., s_{n-1} \rangle$ and, for each $i < n$, either $s_i \geqslant 0$ and ζ_i is an s_i-place predicate variable, or $s_i = -1$ and ζ_i is an individual constant of L or an individual variable, (2) Γ is closed under the application of sentential connectives, (3) $\wedge u\phi$ and $\vee u\phi$ are in Γ whenever ϕ is in Γ and u is either an individual variable or a predicate variable, (4) $\Box\phi$ is in Γ whenever ϕ is in Γ, and (5) whenever ϕ, ψ are in Γ, and G is a predicate variable, then Γ also contains the result of replacing in ϕ all occurrences of G which do not immediately follow $\wedge$, $\vee$, or T by $TG\psi$.

By a *term* of L is understood either an individual constant of L, a variable, or an expression $TG\phi$, where G is a predicate variable and ϕ a formula of L.

DEFINITION VIII. A *possible interpretation for an intensional language* L is a pair $\langle A, F \rangle$ such that clauses (1)–(4) of Definition I hold, and in addition (5′) whenever P is a predicate constant of L having type $\langle s_0, ..., s_{n-1} \rangle$, F_P is a $\langle DA, U_0, ..., U_{n-1} \rangle$-predicate, where, for each $i < n$, either $s_i = -1$ and U_i is the union of the sets A_i for $i \in DA$, or $s_i \geqslant 0$ and U_i is the set of all s_i-place DA-predicates of members of the union of the sets A_i for $i \in DA$.

Clause (5) of Definition I is a special case of the present (5′), taking $s_0 = ... = s_{n-1} = -1$.

Again we shall be primarily interested in notions of truth and satisfaction, expressed by the phrases 'the sentence ϕ is true with respect to the point of reference i under the interpretation $\mathfrak{A}$', and 'x satisfies the formula ϕ with respect to the point of reference i under the interpretation $\mathfrak{A}$'. Since, however, our formulas may now contain free predicate variables as well as free individual variables, we must understand 'x' to refer either to a possible individual or to a predicate of individuals. The intuitions underlying the present development will become clear upon consideration of the following criteria.

CRITERIA OF INTENSIONAL TRUTH AND SATISFACTION. Let $\mathfrak{A}$ be a possible interpretation, having the form $\langle A, F \rangle$, for an intensional language L; let $i \in DA$; let U be the union of the sets A_j (for $j \in DA$); let $x \in U$; let P be a predicate constant of L of type $\langle -1, -1 \rangle$; let c, d be individual constants of L; and let u be an individual variable. Then:

(1)–(7) of the criteria of pragmatic truth and satisfaction.

(8′) If ϕ is a formula of L of which the only free variable is the n-place predicate variable G, then $\bigvee G\phi$ is true$_{i, \mathfrak{A}}$ if and only if there is an n-place DA-predicate X of members of U such that X sat$_{i, \mathfrak{A}}\phi$.

(9′) If G is an n-place predicate variable, $\mathscr{P}$ a predicate constant of L of type $\langle n \rangle$, and X an n-place DA-predicate of members of U, then X sat$_{i, \mathfrak{A}} \mathscr{P}[G]$ if and only if $\langle X \rangle \in F_{\mathscr{P}}(i)$.

(10′) If ϕ is a sentence of L, then $\square\phi$ is true$_{i, \mathfrak{A}}$ if and only if ϕ is true$_{j, \mathfrak{A}}$ for all $j \in DA$.

(11′) If G is an n-place predicate variable, $\mathscr{P}$ a predicate constant of L of type $\langle n \rangle$, and ϕ a formula of L of which the only free variable is G, then $\mathscr{P}[TG\phi]$ is true$_{i,\mathfrak{A}}$ if and only if either there is exactly one n-place **D**A-predicate X of members of U such that X sat$_{i,\mathfrak{A}}$ ϕ, and that predicate is in $F_{\mathscr{P}}(i)$; or it is not the case that there is exactly one such predicate, and the empty predicate (that is, **D**$A \times \{\Lambda\}$) is in $F_{\mathscr{P}}(i)$.

(12′) If G is a 0-place predicate variable and X a $\langle$**D**$A\rangle$-predicate, then X sat$_{i,\mathfrak{A}}$ $G[\,]$ if and only if the empty sequence is a member of $X(i)$ (hence, if and only if $X(i) = \{\Lambda\}$).

In view of (8′), predicate variables range over predicates of possible individuals. In view of (10′), $\square$ should be regarded as the *standard* necessity operator. In view of (8′) and earlier remarks, 0-place predicate variables range over propositions; accordingly, we may, by (12′), read $G[\,]$ as 'the proposition G is true'.

Quantification over individual concepts and over relations (in the extensional sense) is lacking, but its effect can nevertheless be achieved. Let $\langle A, F\rangle$ be a possible interpretation for an intensional language, and let U be the union of the sets A_i for $i \in$ **D**A. By an *individual concept* of $\langle A, F\rangle$ is understood a function from **D**A into U. But individual concepts of $\langle A, F\rangle$ can be identified with $\langle$**D**$A, U\rangle$-predicates satisfying the formula

$$\square \vee u \wedge v(G[v] \leftrightarrow v = u).$$

Further, as J. A. W. Kamp has observed, $\langle U, U\rangle$-relations can be identified with $\langle$**D**$A, U, U\rangle$-predicates satisfying the formula

$$\wedge u \wedge v(\square G[u, v] \vee \square \neg G[u, v]);$$

and a similar identification can be performed for relations of more or fewer places.

Let us now introduce precise definitions having Criteria (1)–(12′) as consequences. We assume that $\mathfrak{A}$ is a possible interpretation for an intensional language L, $\mathfrak{A} = \langle A, F,\rangle$, U is the union of the sets A_j for $j \in$ **D**A, and $i \in$ **D**A. We can no longer regard simple infinite sequences as assigning values to variables; the presence of variables of various sorts requires the consideration of *double* sequences in which one of the indices determines the sort of variable in question. In particular, let us understand by a *system* associated with $\mathfrak{A}$ a function x having as its domain the set of pairs $\langle n, k\rangle$ for which n is a natural number and k an integer

$\geqslant -1$, and such that whenever $\langle n, k \rangle$ is such a pair, either $k = -1$ and $x(\langle n, k \rangle) \in U$, or $k \geqslant 0$ and $x(\langle n, k \rangle)$ is a k-place **D**A-predicate of members of U. We assume that S is the set of all systems associated with $\mathfrak{A}$; as is customary, we shall understand by $x_{n,k}$ the function value $x(\langle n, k \rangle)$. In addition, we assume that n, k are natural numbers; and if x is a function, we understand by x_b^a the function obtained from x by substituting b for the original value of x for the argument a, that is, the function $(x - \{\langle a, x(a) \rangle\}) \cup \{\langle a, b \rangle\}$.

The *extension* of a *term* or *formula* is introduced by a single recursion.

DEFINITION IX. (1) If c is an individual constant of L, then $\text{Ext}_{i,\mathfrak{A}}(c)$ is that function H with domain S such that, for all $x \in S$, $H(x) = F_c(i)$.

(2) $\text{Ext}_{i,\mathfrak{A}}(v_n)$ is that function H with domain S such that, for all $x \in S$, $H(x) = x_{n,-1}$.

(3) $\text{Ext}_{i,\mathfrak{A}}(G_{n,k})$ is that function H with domain S such that, for all $x \in S$, $H(x) = x_{n,k}$.

(4) If ϕ is a formula of L, then $\text{Ext}_{i,\mathfrak{A}}(TG_{n,k}\phi)$ is that function H with domain S such that, for all $x \in S$, either $\{H(x)\} = \{Y : x_Y^{\langle n,k \rangle} \in \text{Ext}_{i,\mathfrak{A}}(\phi)\}$, or there is no Z for which $\{Z\} = \{Y : x_Y^{\langle n,k \rangle} \in \text{Ext}_{i,\mathfrak{A}}(\phi)\}$, and $H(x)$ is $\mathbf{D}A \times \{A\}$.

(5) If ζ is an individual constant of L or an individual variable, then $\text{Ext}_{i,\mathfrak{A}}(\mathsf{E}[\zeta])$ is $\{x : x \in S \text{ and } (\text{Ext}_{i,\mathfrak{A}}(\zeta))(x) \in A_i\}$.

(6) If each of ζ, η is either an individual constant of L or an individual variable, then $\text{Ext}_{i,\mathfrak{A}}(\zeta = \eta)$ is $\{x : x \in S \text{ and } (\text{Ext}_{i,\mathfrak{A}}(\zeta))(x) \text{ is identical with } (\text{Ext}_{i,\mathfrak{A}}(\eta))(x)\}$.

(7) If η is an n-place predicate variable or a term $TG\phi$ (with G an n-place predicate variable), and each of $\zeta_0, ..., \zeta_{n-1}$ is an individual constant of L or an individual variable, then $\text{Ext}_{i,\mathfrak{A}}(\eta[\zeta_0, ..., \zeta_{n-1}])$ is $\{x : x \in S \text{ and } \langle (\text{Ext}_{i,\mathfrak{A}}(\zeta_0))(x), ..., (\text{Ext}_{i,\mathfrak{A}}(\zeta_{n-1}))(x) \rangle \in (\text{Ext}_{i,\mathfrak{A}}(\eta))(x)(i)\}$.

(8) If P is a predicate constant of L of type $\langle s_0, ..., s_{n-1} \rangle$ and, for each $i < n$, either $s_i \geqslant 0$ and ζ_i is either an s_i-place predicate variable or a term $TG\phi$ in which G is an s_i-place predicate variable and ϕ a formula of L, or $s_i = -1$ and ζ_i is an individual constant of L or an individual variable, then $\text{Ext}_{i,\mathfrak{A}}(P[\zeta_0, ..., \zeta_{n-1}])$ is $\{x : x \in S \text{ and } \langle (\text{Ext}_{i,\mathfrak{A}}(\zeta_0))(x), ..., (\text{Ext}_{i,\mathfrak{A}}(\zeta_{n-1}))(x) \rangle \in F_P(i)\}$.

(9) If ϕ, ψ are formulas of L, then $\text{Ext}_{i,\mathfrak{A}}(\neg\phi)$ is $S - \text{Ext}_{i,\mathfrak{A}}(\phi)$, and similarly for the other sentential connectives.

(10) If ϕ is a formula of L, then $\text{Ext}_{i,\,\mathfrak{A}}(\bigvee v_n \phi)$ is $\{x : x \in S$ and, for some $y \in U$, the system $x^{\langle n,\,-1 \rangle}_{y} \in \text{Ext}_{i,\,\mathfrak{A}}(\phi)\}$, and similarly for $\bigwedge v_n \phi$.

(11) If ϕ is a formula of L, then $\text{Ext}_{i,\,\mathfrak{A}}(\bigvee G_{n,\,k}\phi)$ is $\{x : x \in S$ and, for some k-place $\mathbf{D}A$-predicate Y of members of U, the system $x^{\langle n,k \rangle}_{Y} \in \text{Ext}_{i,\,\mathfrak{A}}$ $(\phi)\}$, and similarly for $\bigwedge G_{n,\,k}\phi$.

(12) If ϕ is a formula of L, then $\text{Ext}_{i,\,\mathfrak{A}}(\square\phi)$ is $\{x : x \in S$ and, for all $j \in \mathbf{D}A$, $x \in \text{Ext}_{j,\,\mathfrak{A}}(\phi)\}$.

DEFINITION X. If ϕ is a sentence of L, then ϕ is $\text{true}_{i,\,\mathfrak{A}}$ if and only if $\text{Ext}_{i,\,\mathfrak{A}}(\phi) = S$.

DEFINITION XI. If ϕ is a formula of L with exactly one free variable, then y $\text{sat}_{i,\,\mathfrak{A}}\phi$ if and only if either there is a natural number n such that the free variable of ϕ is v_n and there exists $x \in \text{Ext}_{i,\,\mathfrak{A}}(\phi)$ such that $x_{n,\,-1} = y$, or there are natural numbers n, k such that the free variable of ϕ is $G_{n,\,k}$ and there exists $x \in \text{Ext}_{i,\,\mathfrak{A}}(\phi)$ such that $x_{n,\,k} = y$.

DEFINITION XII. If ϕ is a term or formula of L, then $\text{Int}_{\mathfrak{A}}(\phi)$, or the *intension* of ϕ with respect to $\mathfrak{A}$, is that function H with domain $\mathbf{D}A$ such that, for each $i \in \mathbf{D}A$, $H(i) = \text{Ext}_{i,\,\mathfrak{A}}(\phi)$.

DEFINITION XIII. A sentence ϕ is a *logical consequence* (in the sense of intensional logic) of a set Γ of sentences if and only if for every intensional language L and all $\mathfrak{A}$, A, F, i, if $\mathfrak{A} = \langle A, F \rangle$, $\mathfrak{A}$ is a possible interpretation for L, $i \in \mathbf{D}A$, $\Gamma \cup \{\phi\}$ is a set of sentences of L, and for every $\psi \in \Gamma$, ψ is $\text{true}_{i,\,\mathfrak{A}}$, then ϕ is $\text{true}_{i,\,\mathfrak{A}}$. A sentence is *logically true* if and only if it is a logical consequence of the empty set. A sentence ϕ is *logically equivalent* to a sentence ψ if and only if the sentence $(\phi \leftrightarrow \psi)$ is logically true.

The remarks about extensions and intensions made in connection with pragmatic languages continue to apply here, with infinite sequences everywhere replaced by systems. Further, Criteria (1)–(12′) are immediate consequences of Definitions IX–XI.

It was said earlier that descriptive phrases of the sort we admit, that is, descriptive phrases involving predicate variables, are eliminable. We can now make a more precise statement: if ϕ is any sentence of an intensional language L, then there is a sentence of L without descriptive phrases that is logically equivalent to ϕ. For instance, if ϕ is

$$\mathscr{P}[T G \mathscr{Q}[G]],$$

where G is a 1-place predicate variable and $\mathscr{P}$, $\mathscr{Q}$ are predicate constants of type $\langle 1 \rangle$, then ϕ is logically equivalent to

$$\bigvee G(\mathcal{Q}[G] \wedge \wedge H(\mathcal{Q}[H] \to \square \wedge x(H[x] \leftrightarrow G[x]))$$
$$\wedge \mathscr{P}[G]) \vee (\neg \bigvee G(\mathcal{Q}[G] \wedge \wedge H(\mathcal{Q}[H] \to$$
$$\square \wedge x(H[x] \leftrightarrow G[x]))) \wedge \bigvee G(\square \wedge x \neg G[x] \wedge \mathscr{P}[G])).$$

The convenience of descriptive phrases is found in the construction of names of specific predicates. For instance, we can distinguish as follows expressions designating properties or 2-place predicates expressed by particular formulas (with respect to places marked by particular individual variables): if ϕ is a formula and u, v are distinct individual variables, understand by $\hat{u}\phi$ (which may be read 'the property of u such that ϕ') the term $\mathsf{T}G \wedge u \square (G[u] \leftrightarrow \phi)$, and by $\hat{u}\hat{v}\phi$ (read 'the predicate of u and v such that ϕ') the term $\mathsf{T}H \wedge u \wedge v \square (H[u, v] \leftrightarrow \phi)$, where G, H are respectively the first 1-place and the first 2-place predicate variables not occurring in ϕ. We can of course proceed upward to three variables or more; but – and this is more interesting – we can proceed downward to the empty sequence of variables. In particular, if ϕ is any formula, understand by $^\wedge\phi$ the term $\mathsf{T}G\square(G[\ ] \leftrightarrow \phi)$; this term designates the proposition expressed by the formula ϕ, may be read 'the proposition that ϕ' or simply 'that ϕ', and serves the purposes for which the term '$\bar{\phi}$' of Kaplan [1] was constructed.

It is clear from Definition IX that sentences of intensional languages, unlike those of pragmatic languages, may contain indirect components – that is, components of which the *intension* must be taken into account in determining the *extension* of the compound – of only one sort; and these are components standing within the scope of the particular operator $\square$. An equivalent construction would have taken the indirect context $^\wedge\phi$ rather than $\square\phi$ as basic, together with the notion of identity of propositions; we could then have defined $\square\phi$ as $^\wedge\phi = ^\wedge \wedge v_0 v_0 = v_0$.

Now let us see how to accommodate operators within intensional languages. (The observation that this can be done, as well as the present way of doing it, is due jointly to J. A. W. Kamp and me.) Suppose that L is any pragmatic language and $\langle A, F, R \rangle$ any possible interpretation for it. Let the operators N of L be mapped biuniquely onto predicate constants N' of type $\langle 0 \rangle$. Let L' be an intensional language of which the individual constants are those of L, and the predicate constants are those of L together with the symbols N', for N an operator of L. Let F' be such

that $\langle A, F' \rangle$ is a possible interpretation for the intensional language L',
$F \subseteq F'$, and for each operator N of L and each $i \in \mathbf{D}A$, F'_N, (i) is $\{\langle U \rangle : U$
is a $\langle \mathbf{D}A \rangle$-predicate and $\langle i, \{j : j \in \mathbf{D}A$ and $U(j) = \{\Lambda\}\}\rangle \in R_N\}$. Then we
can easily prove the following: if ϕ is a sentence of L, ϕ' is obtained from
ϕ by replacing each subformula of the form $N\psi$, where N is an operator
of L and ψ a formula of L, by

$$\vee G(\square (G[\,] \leftrightarrow \psi) \wedge N'[G]),$$

and $i \in \mathbf{D}A$, then ϕ is true with respect to i and the *pragmatic* interpretation $\langle A, F, R \rangle$ if and only if ϕ' is true with respect to i and the *intensional*
interpretation $\langle A, F' \rangle$.

We thus have a reduction of pragmatics to intensional logic which
amounts, roughly speaking, to treating 1-*place modalities* (that is,
relations between points of reference and sets of points of reference) as
properties of propositions. Conversely, every property of propositions
corresponds to a 1-place modality. Indeed, if $\langle A, F \rangle$ is an interpretation
for an intensional language and $\mathcal{X}$ is a property of propositions with
respect to $\langle A, F \rangle$ (that is, a $\langle \mathbf{D}A, U \rangle$-predicate, where U is the set of all
$\langle \mathbf{D}A \rangle$-predicates), then the corresponding 1-place modality will be the
set of pairs $\langle i, J \rangle$ such that $i \in \mathbf{D}A$ and there exists $Y \in \mathcal{X}(i)$ such that
$J = \{j : j \in \mathbf{D}A$ and $Y(j) = \{\Lambda\}\}$.

Let us be a little more precise about the sense in which intensional logic
can be *partially* reduced to pragmatics. Let L be an intensional language
of which the predicate constants are all of type $\langle 0 \rangle$ or $\langle s_0, \ldots, s_{n-1} \rangle$,
where $s_p = -1$ for all $p < n$, and let $\langle A, F \rangle$ be any interpretation
for L. Let the predicate constants $\mathcal{P}$ of L having type $\langle 0 \rangle$ be mapped
biuniquely onto operators $\mathcal{P}'$, and let N be an operator not among these.
Let L' be a pragmatic language of which the individual constants are those
of L, the predicate constants are those of L not having type $\langle 0 \rangle$, and the
operators consist of N together with the symbols $\mathcal{P}'$ for $\mathcal{P}$ a predicate
constant of L of type $\langle 0 \rangle$. Let F', R be such that $\langle A, F', R \rangle$ is a possible
interpretation for the pragmatic language L', $F' \subseteq F$, R_N is the set of pairs
$\langle i, J \rangle$ such that $i \in \mathbf{D}A$ and $J = \mathbf{D}A$, and for each predicate $\mathcal{P}$ of L of type
$\langle 0 \rangle$, $R_{\mathcal{P}'}$ is the set of pairs $\langle i, J \rangle$ such that $i \in \mathbf{D}A$ and there exists $Y \in F_{\mathcal{P}}(i)$
such that $J = \{j : j \in \mathbf{D}A$ and $Y(j) = \{\Lambda\}\}$. Then we can easily show that
if $i \in \mathbf{D}A$, ϕ is a sentence of L, ϕ' is obtained from ϕ by replacing each
subformula $\mathcal{P}[^\wedge\psi]$, where $\mathcal{P}$ is a predicate constant of type $\langle 0 \rangle$ and ψ

is a formula of L, by $\mathscr{P}'\psi$, and ϕ' is a sentence of the pragmatic language L' (this imposes certain limitations on the form of ϕ), then ϕ is true with respect to i and the *intensional* interpretation $\langle A, F \rangle$ if and only if ϕ' is true with respect to i and the *pragmatic* interpretation $\langle A, F', R \rangle$.

The fact that 1-place modalities coincide in a sense with properties of propositions is what lends interest to those modalities and provides intuitive sanction for using them to interpret operators. (A completely analogous remark would apply to many-place modalities and many-place operators if these had been included in our system of pragmatics.) The relations among various systems can be roughly expressed as follows. If we understand by *modal logic* that part of intensional logic which concerns formulas containing no predicate variables, then intensional logic can be regarded as *second-order modal logic*, and pragmatics is in a sense contained in it; indeed, pragmatics can be regarded as a first-order reduction of part of intensional logic.

Nothing of course compels us to stop at *second-order* modal logic. We could extend the present construction in a fairly obvious way to obtain various higher-order systems, even of transfinite levels. Only the second-order system, however, is required for the rather direct philosophical applications for which the present paper is intended to provide the groundwork.

For example, belief can be handled in a natural way within intensional logic. Let L be an intensional language containing a predicate constant $\mathscr{B}$ of type $\langle -1, 0 \rangle$. If $\langle A, F \rangle$ is a possible interpretation for L, we now regard the domain of A as the set of all possible worlds, A_i as the set of objects existing within the possible world i, and $F_c(i)$ as the extension of the nonlogical constant c within the world i. Then a $\langle DA \rangle$-predicate can reasonably be regarded as a proposition in the full philosophical sense, not merely the extended sense considered earlier, and the intension of a sentence with respect to $\langle A, F \rangle$ as the proposition expressed by that sentence (under the interpretation $\langle A, F \rangle$). We regard $\mathscr{B}$ as abbreviating 'believes', and accordingly regard $F_{\mathscr{B}}(i)$ as the set of pairs $\langle x, U \rangle$ such that x believes the proposition U in the possible world i. The proposal to regard belief as an empirical relation between individuals and propositions is not new. A number of difficulties connected with that proposal are, however, dispelled by considering it within the present framework; in particular, there remains no problem either of quantifying into belief contexts or of iteration of belief.[10] Consider the assertion 'there exists an object of which Jones believes that Robinson believes that it is perfectly spherical'. This involves both iteration and quantification into indirect contexts, but is represented in L (with respect to $\langle A, F \rangle$) by the simple sentence

$$\bigvee x(\mathsf{E}[x] \wedge \mathscr{B}[J, \, {}^{\wedge}\mathscr{B}[R, \, {}^{\wedge}S[x]]]),$$

where J and R are individual constants regarded as designating Jones and Robinson respectively and S is a predicate constant regarded as expressing the property of being perfectly spherical; or, if we prefer to avoid descriptive phrases, by the logically equivalent sentence

$$\bigvee x \bigvee G(\mathsf{E}[x] \wedge \mathscr{B}[J, G] \wedge \square(G[\,] \leftrightarrow \bigvee H(\mathscr{B}[R, H] \wedge$$
$$\square(H[\,] \leftrightarrow S[x])))).$$

Two objections might be raised. In the first place, what empirical sense can be assigned to belief as a relation between persons and propositions? As much, I feel, as is customary with empirical predicates. One can give confirmatory criteria for belief, though probably not a definition, id behavioristic terms. I present two unrefined and incompletely analyzen examples:

(1) If ϕ is any sentence expressing the proposition G, then the assertion that x assents to ϕ confirms (though certainly not conclusively) the assertion that x believes G.

(2) If ϕ is any formula with exactly one free variable that expresses the property H (in the sense that, for all $i \in \mathbf{D}A$, $H(i)$ is the set of possible individuals satisfying ϕ with respect to i and a given interpretation), then the assertion that x assents to ϕ when y is pointed out to x confirms (though again not conclusively) the assertion that x believes the proposition that $H[y]$.

A second objection might concern the fact that if ϕ and ψ are any logically equivalent sentences, then the sentence

$$\mathscr{B}[J, \, {}^{\wedge}\phi] \rightarrow \mathscr{B}[J, \, {}^{\wedge}\psi]$$

is logically true, though it might under certain circumstances appear unreasonable. One might reply that the consequence in question seems unavoidable if propositions are indeed to be taken as the objects of belief, that it sheds the appearance of unreasonableness if (1) above is seriously maintained, and that its counterintuitive character can perhaps be traced to the existence of another notion of belief, of which the objects are sentences or, in some cases, complexes consisting in part of open formulas.[11]

As another example, let us consider the verb 'seems', as in

u seems to be perfectly spherical to v.

We let L be as above, except that it is now to contain a predicate constant $\mathscr{S}$ of type $\langle -1, 1, -1 \rangle$; if $\langle A, F \rangle$ is a possible interpretation for L and $i \in \mathbf{D}A$, $F_{\mathscr{S}}(i)$ is to be regarded as the set of triples $\langle x, U, y \rangle$ such that, in the possible world i, x seems to y to have the property U. The formula displayed above would then be represented in L by the formula

$$\mathscr{S}[u, \hat{w}S[w], v].$$

We have made no attempt to *define* 'believes' or 'seems'. But that need not prevent us from clarifying the logical status of these verbs and the notions of logical truth and logical consequence for discourse involving them; and this would appear to be the main requirement for the evaluation of a number of philosophical arguments. The philosophical utility of intensional logic, however, is not in my opinion thereby exhausted; more important applications can be found in other areas, notably metaphysics and epistemology, and are to some extent discussed in Montague [3].

It is perhaps not inappropriate to sketch here an intermediate system, due to Dana Scott and me, which may be called *extended pragmatics*.[12] The symbols of an *extended pragmatic language* are drawn from the following categories:

(1) the logical constants of pragmatics,
(2) parentheses, brackets, commas,
(3) individual variables,
(4) individual constants,
(5) operators of degree $\langle m, n, p \rangle$, for all natural numbers m, n, p.

The set of *formulas* of such a language L is the smallest set Γ satisfying certain expected conditions, together with the condition that

$$Nu_0 \ldots u_{m-1}[\zeta_0, \ldots, \zeta_{n-1}, \phi_0, \ldots, \phi_{p-1}]$$

is in Γ whenever N is an operator of L having degree $\langle m, n, p \rangle$, $u_0, ..., u_{m-1}$ are distinct individual variables, each of $\zeta_0, ..., \zeta_{n-1}$ is either an individual constant of L or an individual variable, and $\phi_0, ..., \phi_{p-1}$ are in Γ. A *possible interpretation for an extended pragmatic language* L is a pair $\langle A, F \rangle$ satisfying conditions (1), (2), (4) of Definition I, and in addition such that (3') F is a function whose domain is the set of individual constants and operators of L, and (5') whenever N is an operator of L of degree $\langle m, n, p \rangle$, F_N is a $\langle \mathbf{D}A, U_0, ..., U_{n-1}, V_0, ..., V_{p-1} \rangle$-predicate, where each U_i (for $i < n$) is the union of the sets A_j for $j \in \mathbf{D}A$, and each V_i (for $i < p$) is the set of m-place $\mathbf{D}A$-predicates of members of the union of the sets A_j (for $j \in \mathbf{D}A$). The *extension* of an individual variable, an individual constant, or a formula with respect to a possible interpretation $\mathfrak{A}$ having the form $\langle A, F \rangle$ and at a point of reference $i \in \mathbf{D}A$ is characterized as in Definition II, together with a recursion consisting of clauses (1), (2), (4), (5) of Definition III, together with the following clause: if N is an operator of L of degree $\langle m, n, p \rangle$, $k_0, ..., k_{m-1}$ are distinct natural numbers, each of $\zeta_0, ..., \zeta_{n-1}$ is either an individual constant of L or an individual variable, and $\phi_0, ..., \phi_{p-1}$ are formulas of L, then $\mathrm{Ext}_{i,\mathfrak{A}}$ $(N v_{k_0} ... v_{k_{m-1}} [\zeta_0, ..., \zeta_{n-1}, \phi_0, ..., \phi_{p-1}])$ is $\{x : x \in U^\omega$ and $\langle \mathrm{Ext}_{i,\mathfrak{A}}(\zeta_0) (x), ..., \mathrm{Ext}_{i,\mathfrak{A}}(\zeta_{n-1}) (x), Y_{0,x}, ..., Y_{p-1,x} \rangle \in F_N(i)\}$, where, for each $q < p$ and $x \in U^\omega$, $Y_{q,x}$ is $\{\langle j, \{\langle y_0, ..., y_{m-1} \rangle : x_{y_0}^{k_0} ... {}_{y_{m-1}}^{k_{m-1}} \in \mathrm{Ext}_{j,\mathfrak{A}}(\phi_q)\} \rangle : j \in \mathbf{D}A\}$.

Thus, in particular, if N is an operator of degree $\langle 0, n, 0 \rangle$, then $\mathrm{Ext}_{i,\mathfrak{A}}(N[\zeta_0, ..., \zeta_{n-1}])$ is $\{x : x \in U^\omega$ and $\langle \mathrm{Ext}_{i,\mathfrak{A}}(\zeta_0) (x), ..., \mathrm{Ext}_{i,\mathfrak{A}} (\zeta_{n-1}) (x) \rangle \in F_N(i)\}$, and N will play the role of an n-place predicate constant; and if N has degree $\langle 0, 0, 1 \rangle$, then $\mathrm{Ext}_{i,\mathfrak{A}}(N[\phi])$ is $\{x : x \in U^\omega$ and $\langle \{\langle j, \{\Lambda\} \rangle : j \in \mathbf{D}A$ and $x \in \mathrm{Ext}_{j,\mathfrak{A}}(\phi)\} \cup \{\langle j, \Lambda \rangle : j \in \mathbf{D}A$ and $x \notin \mathrm{Ext}_{j,\mathfrak{A}}(\phi)\} \rangle \in F_N(i)\}$, and N will accordingly serve as a substitute for a (one-place) operator of pragmatics. Further, an operator of extended pragmatics of arbitrary degree $\langle m, n, p \rangle$ can be replaced within intensional logic by a predicate constant of type $\langle s_0, ..., s_{n-1}, t_0, ..., t_{p-1} \rangle$, where each s_i (for $i < n$) is -1 and each t_i (for $i < p$) is m.

Thus, in a sense, pragmatics is contained in extended pragmatics, which is in turn contained in intensional logic. We can regard extended pragmatics as providing another first-order reduction, more comprehensive than that supplied by ordinary pragmatics, of part of intensional logic. For instance, if $\mathscr{B}$ is, like 'believes', a predicate constant of type $\langle -1, 0 \rangle$

of intensional logic, we could replace $\mathscr{B}$ by an operator $\mathscr{B}'$ of degree $\langle 0, 1, 1 \rangle$ (of extended pragmatics) and express the assertion

$$\mathscr{B}[x, {}^{\wedge}\phi]$$

equivalently (under a suitable interpretation) by

$$\mathscr{B}'[x, \phi].$$

Similarly, if $\mathscr{S}$ is, like 'seems', a predicate constant of type $\langle 1, 1, -1 \rangle$, we could replace $\mathscr{S}$ by an operator $\mathscr{S}'$ of degree $\langle 1, 2, 1 \rangle$ and express the assertion

$$\mathscr{S}[u, \hat{w}\phi, v]$$

by

$$\mathscr{S}'w[u, v, \phi].$$

(It should be clear from this example, as well as from the general definition of extension, that the m variables immediately following an operator of degree $\langle m, n, p \rangle$ are to be regarded as *bound*.) There is of course no contention that all formulas of intensional logic involving $\mathscr{B}$ or $\mathscr{S}$ can be paraphrased within extended pragmatics; for instance, the assertion 'Jones believes something which Robinson does not believe' does not correspond to any formula of extended pragmatics.

We may now consider various technical properties of the three systems introduced in this paper. Notice first that the compactness theorem does not hold for intensional logic. In other words, let us call a set of sentences *satisfiable* if there is a nonempty interpretation $\mathfrak{A}$ and a point of reference i of $\mathfrak{A}$ such that all sentences in the set are true with respect to i and $\mathfrak{A}$; then it is not the case that for every set Γ of sentences of intensional logic,

(3)   if every finite subset of Γ is satisfiable, then Γ is satisfiable.

This is obvious in view of the reduction, at which we hinted earlier, of ordinary second-order logic to intensional logic, together with the well-known failure of the compactness theorem for second-order logic. On the other hand, let us call ϕ a *predicative* sentence if ϕ is a sentence of intensional logic not containing the descriptive symbol and such that (1) whenever G is a predicate variable, ψ is a formula, and $\wedge G\psi$ is a subformula of ϕ, there are $\mathcal{P}$, $\zeta_0, ..., \zeta_n$, χ such that $\mathcal{P}$ is a predicate constant, each ζ_i (for $i \leqslant n$) is either an individual constant, an individual variable, or a predicate variable, χ is a formula, ψ is the formula ($\mathcal{P}[\zeta_0, ..., \zeta_n] \to \chi$), and G is ζ_i for some $i \leqslant n$, and (2) whenever G is a predicate variable, ψ is a formula, and $\vee G\psi$ is a subformula of ϕ, there are $\mathcal{P}$, $\zeta_0, ..., \zeta_n$, χ satisfying the same conditions as in (1) except that ψ is now to be ($\mathcal{P}[\zeta_0, ..., \zeta_n] \wedge \chi$). For the *predicative* sentences of intensional logic we do have a compactness theorem; in other words, (3) holds for every set Γ of predicative sentences.[13] From this assertion we can infer full compactness theorems for pragmatics and extended pragmatics, in other words, the assertion that (3) holds for *every* set Γ of sentences of pragmatics and for *every* set Γ of sentences of extended pragmatics; we use reductions of the sort sketched above of those disciplines to intensional logic and notice that the reductions can be performed in such a way as to result exclusively in predicative sentences.

Similar remarks apply to the recursive enumerability of the logical truths of the three systems we have considered. We must, however, say a word about the meaning of recursive enumerability in this context. We have not required that the symbols from which our languages are constructed form a countable set; it would thus be inappropriate to speak of a Gödel numbering of all expressions. We may, however, suppose that a Gödel numbering satisfying the usual conditions has been given for a certain denumerable *subset S* of the set of all expressions; we may further suppose that all logical constants, the parentheses and brackets, the comma, all individual variables, all predicate variables, infinitely many n-place predicate constants (for each n), infinitely many predicate constants of each type, infinitely many 1-place operators, and infinitely many operators of each degree are in S, and that S is closed under the concatenation of two expressions. When we say that a set of expressions is recursive or recursively enumerable we shall understand that it is a subset of S which is recursive or recursively enumerable under our fixed Gödel numbering.

Let us identify a language with the set of symbols it contains; we may accordingly speak of recursive languages. It is then easily shown, by the same methods as those sketched in connection with compactness, that (1) there are recursive intensional languages of which the sets of logical truths are not recursively enumerable; (2) if L is any recursive intensional language, then the set of predicative sentences of L which are logically true is recursively enumerable; (3) if L is any recursive pragmatic language, then the set of all logical truths of L is recursively enumerable; (4) if L is any recursive extended pragmatic language, then the set of all logical truths of L is recursively enumerable.

On the basis of (2)–(4), together with a theorem of Craig [1], we can of course show for each of the three sets mentioned in (2)–(4) the existence of a recursive subset which axiomatizes the set in question under the rule of detachment. It would be desirable, however, to find natural and simple recursive axiomatizations of these sets. Of the three problems that thus arise one has been definitely solved: David Kaplan has recently axiomatized the set of logical truths of (ordinary) pragmatics. He has also axiomatized the set of logical truths of a system closely resembling extended pragmatics; and it is likely that when his axiomatization becomes available, it will be capable of adaptation to extended pragmatics. The problem, however, of axiomatizing predicative intensional logic remains open.

In connection with problems of axiomatizability it is perhaps not inappropriate to mention that all three of our systems are purely referential in one sense, specifically, in the sense that

$$(4) \qquad \bigwedge u \bigwedge v (u = v \rightarrow (\phi \leftrightarrow \phi'))$$

is logically true whenever u, v are individual variables, ϕ is a formula of the language in question, and ϕ' is obtained from ϕ by replacing a free occurrence of u by a free occurrence of v, but *not* purely referential in another sense: it is not generally true that whenever c, d are individual constants, ϕ is a formula of one of the languages under consideration, and ϕ' is obtained from ϕ by replacing an occurrence of c by d, the formula

$$(5) \qquad c = d \rightarrow (\phi \leftrightarrow \phi')$$

is logically true. It follows, of course, that the principle of universal instantiation does not always hold; it holds when one instantiates to variables but not in general when one instantiates to individual constants.

There is rather general (though not universal) agreement that (5) ought not to be regarded as logically true when modal and belief contexts are present; for consider the following familiar example of (5):

> If the Morning Star = the Evening Star, then Jones believes that the Morning Star appears in the morning if and only if Jones believes that the Evening Star appears in the morning.

This viewpoint has led some philosophers, however, to reject also the logical truth of (4). The desirability of maintaining (4) as a logical truth but not (5) was, to my knowledge, first explicitly argued in the 1955 talk reported in Montague [2], but has more recently been advanced in Føllesdal [1] and Cocchiarella [2], and in addresses of Professors Richmond Thomason and Dagfinn Føllesdal.

Let me conclude with a few historical remarks concerning intensional logic. The first serious and detailed attempt to construct such a logic appears to be that of Church [1]. Carnap had independently proposed in conversation that intensional objects be identified with functions from possible worlds to extensions of appropriate sorts, but that, in distinction from the later proposal of Kripke adopted in the present paper, possible worlds be identified with models. David Kaplan, in his dissertation Kaplan [1], pointed out certain deficiencies of Church's system, presented a modified version designed to correct these, and supplied a model theory for the revised system based on Carnap's proposal. Kaplan's system, however, suffered from the drawback indicated above involving the iteration of empirical properties of propositions; the difficulty stemmed largely from Carnap's suggestion that possible worlds be identified with models. More recent attempts by Charles Howard, David Kaplan, and Dana Scott (some preceding and some following the talk reported by the main body of the present paper) have avoided this difficulty but have shared with Kaplan [1] the drawback of not allowing unrestricted quantification over ordinary individuals. Without such quantification, however, I do not believe that one can treat ordinary language in a natural way or meet adequately Quine's objections to quantification into indirect contexts.

University of California, Los Angeles

BIBLIOGRAPHY

Elizabeth Anscombe, 'The Intentionality of Sensation: A Grammatical Feature' in *Analytical Philosophy*, Second Series (ed. by R. J. Butler), Oxford 1965. [1]

Yehoshua Bar-Hillel, 'Indexical Expressions', *Mind* 63 (1954) 359–379. [1]

Alonzo Church, 'A Formulation of the Logic of Sense and Denotation' in *Structure, Method, and Meaning* (ed. by Paul Henle, Horace M. Kallen, and Susanne K. Langer), New York 1951. [1]

Nino Cocchiarella, 'A Completeness Theorem for Tense Logic', *Journal of Symbolic Logic* 31 (1966) 689–690. [1]

Nino Cocchiarella, *Tense Logic: A Study of Temporal Reference* (doctoral dissertation, University of California at Los Angeles, 1966). [2]

William Craig, 'On Axiomatizability within a System', *Journal of Symbolic Logic* 18 (1953) 30–32. [1]

Herbert Feigl and Wilfrid Sellars (eds.), *Readings in Philosophical Analysis*, New York 1949. [1]

Dagfinn Føllesdal, *Referential Opacity and Modal Logic* (doctoral dissertation, Harvard University, 1961). [1]

Gottlob Frege, 'Über Sinn und Bedeutung', *Zeitschrift fur Philosophie und philosophische Kritik* 100 (1892) 25–50. English translation in Feigl and Sellars [1].

Leon Henkin, 'Completeness in the Theory of Types', *Journal of Symbolic Logic* 15 (1950) 81–91. [1]

David Kaplan, *Foundations of Intensional Logic* (doctoral dissertation, University of California at Los Angeles, 1964). [1]

Saul A. Kripke, 'Semantical Considerations on Modal Logic', *Acta Philosophica Fennica* 16 (1963) 83–94. [1]

Richard Montague, 'Well-Founded Relations; Generalizations of Principles of Induction and Recursion', *Bulletin of the American Mathematical Society* 61 (1955) 442. [1]

Richard Montague, 'Logical Necessity, Physical Necessity, Ethics, and Quantifiers', *Inquiry* 4 (1960) 259–269. [2]

Richard Montague, 'On the Nature of Certain Philosophical Entities', *The Monist* 53 (1969) 159–194. [3]

Richard Montague, 'Pragmatics' in *Contemporary Philosophy – La philosophie contemporaine* (ed. by R. Klibansky), La Nuova Italia Editrice, Florence 1968. [4]

Richard Montague and Donald Kalish, 'Remarks on Descriptions and Natural Deduction, Part I', *Archiv für mathematische Logik und Grundlagenforschung* 3 (1957) 50–64. [1]

Richard Montague and Donald Kalish, 'That', *Philosophical Studies* 10 (1959) 54–61. [2]

Richard Montague, Dana Scott, and Alfred Tarski, *An Axiomatic Approach to Set Theory*, Amsterdam (forthcoming). [1]

C. W. Morris, 'Foundations of the Theory of Signs' in the *International Encyclopedia of Unified Science*, vol. 1, no. 2, 1938. [1]

W. V. Quine, *Word and Object*, M.I.T. Press, Cambridge, Mass., 1960. [1]

Alfred Tarski, 'Projecie prawdy w językach nauk dedukcyjnych' (The concept of truth in the languages of the deductive sciences) in *Travaux de la Société des Sciences et des Lettres de Varsovie, Classe III*, no. 34 (1933); English translation in Tarski [3]. [1]

Alfred Tarski, 'Contributions to the Theory of Models, Part I', *Indagationes Mathematicae* 16 (1954) 572–581. [2]

Alfred Tarski, *Logic, Semantics, Metamathematics* (transl. by J. H. Woodger), Oxford 1956. [3]

REFERENCES

* This paper was delivered before the Southern California Logic Colloquium on January 6, 1967, and reports research partly supported by U.S. National Science Foundation Grant GP-4594. I should like to express gratitude to my student Dr. J. A. W. Kamp for a number of valuable suggestions beyond those explicitly acknowledged below, and to Mr. Tobin Barrozo for correcting an error. It should perhaps be mentioned that this paper was submitted to another journal on November 7, 1967, but was withdrawn after two and one-half years because of the great delay in its publication; it was thus intended to appear before either Montague [3] or Montague [4], for both of which it supplies a certain amount of background.

1 Other terms for these expressions include 'egocentric particulars' (Russell), 'token-reflexive expressions' (Reichenbach), 'indicator words' (Goodman), and 'noneternal sentences' (Quine, for sentences that are indexical).

2 For an account of the fundamental concepts of model theory see Tarski [2].

3 This work was reported in a talk I delivered before the U.C.L.A. Philosophy Colloquium on December 18, 1964. The treatment of special cases within the general framework of the present paper will be discussed in another publication.

4 Cocchiarella considered quantification only in connection with tense logic; his treatment may be found in the abstract Cocchiarella [1] and the unpublished doctoral dissertation Cocchiarella [2].

5 The idea of construing propositions, properties, and relations-in-intension as functions of the sorts above occurs first, I believe, in Kripke [1].

6 This simple and obvious approach is not the only possible treatment of 'thinks of', a phrase that has been discussed in the philosophical literature, for instance, in Anscombe [1], with incomplete success; but it is, I think, *one* possible treatment of *one* sense – the referential – of that phrase. For a treatment of the nonreferential sense see Montague [3].

7 Let us call an interpretation $\langle A, F, R \rangle$ *empty* if the union of the sets A_i for $i \in DA$ is the empty set. We have not excluded empty interpretations from consideration, and it might be feared that minor difficulties might consequently arise in connection with the notions introduced in Definition VII. Such fears would be unjustified; it can easily be shown that the definition given above of logical consequence is equivalent to the result of adding to it the restriction that $\mathfrak{A}$ be a nonempty interpretation. On the other hand, some of the criteria given above of truth and satisfaction would fail for empty interpretations; but the case of empty interpretations is excluded by the assumption 'x is a member of the union of the sets A_j'.

8 Recursion on well-founded relations was first explicitly introduced in Montague [1]; for a discussion of it see Montague, Scott, Tarski [1].

9 The present system could, however, be extended so as to contain a full theory of definite descriptions in any of the well-known ways, for instance, that of Montague and Kalish [1]. It is partly in order to avoid irrelevant controversy over the best treatment of descriptions that I introduce them so sparingly here.

10 Problems of the first sort have been pointed out many times by Quine, for instance, in Quine [1]; and problems of the second sort arose in connection with Kaplan [1], the system of which appeared incapable of being extended in such a way as adequately to accommodate iteration of belief.

[11] A partial treatment of such a notion may be found in Montague and Kalish [2]. The discussion there is, however, incomplete in that it fails to provide for such cases as those for which the confirmatory criterion (2) was designed – cases in which beliefs may concern objects for which the believer has no name.

[12] The outline of extended pragmatics did not occur in the original version of this paper, but was added after I had seen a treatment of modal logic developed by Scott in June, 1967, and had discussed it with him and David Kaplan. The principal difference between Scott's system and extended pragmatics is that in the former no allowance is made for quantification over individuals, but only over individual concepts.

[13] This assertion, the formulation of which is partly due to J. A. W. Kamp, can be shown rather easily on the basis of the completeness theorem for ω-order logic of Henkin [1], and is not peculiar to *second*-order modal logic: indeed, the compactness theorem would hold for the predicative sentences of a higher-order modal logic containing variables of all finite levels.

DAVID LEWIS

GENERAL SEMANTICS*

I. INTRODUCTION

On the hypothesis that all natural or artificial languages of interest to us can be given transformational grammars of a certain not-very-special sort, it becomes possible to give very simple general answers to the questions:

(1)   What sort of thing is a meaning?
(2)   What is the form of the semantic rules whereby meanings of compounds are built up from the meanings of their constituent parts?

It is not my plan to make any strong empirical claim about language. To the contrary: I want to propose a convenient format for semantics general enough to work for a great variety of logically possible languages. This paper therefore belongs not to empirical linguistic theory but to the philosophy thereof.

My proposals regarding the nature of meanings will not conform to the expectations of those linguists who conceive of semantic interpretation as the assignment to sentences and their constituents of compounds of 'semantic markers' or the like. (Katz and Postal, 1964, for instance.) Semantic markers are *symbols*: items in the vocabulary of an artificial language we may call *Semantic Markerese*. Semantic interpretation by means of them amounts merely to a translation algorithm from the object language to the auxiliary language Markerese. But we can know the Markerese translation of an English sentence without knowing the first thing about the meaning of the English sentence: namely, the conditions under which it would be true. Semantics with no treatment of truth conditions is not semantics. Translation into Markerese is at best a substitute for real semantics, relying either on our tacit competence (at some future date) as speakers of Markerese or on our ability to do real semantics at least for the one language Markerese. Translation into Latin might

Davidson and Harman (eds.), Semantics of Natural Language, 169–218. *All rights reserved*
Copyright © 1972 *by D. Reidel Publishing Company, Dordrecht - Holland*

serve as well, except insofar as the designers of Markerese may choose
to build into it useful features – freedom from ambiguity, grammar based
on symbolic logic – that might make it easier to do real semantics for
Markerese than for Latin. (See Vermazen, 1967, for similar criticisms).

The Markerese method is attractive in part just because it deals with
nothing but symbols: finite combinations of entities of a familiar sort out
of a finite set of elements by finitely many applications of finitely many
rules. There is no risk of alarming the ontologically parsimonious. But
it is just this pleasing finitude that prevents Markerese semantics from
dealing with the relations between symbols and the world of non-symbols
– that is, with genuinely semantic relations. Accordingly, we should be
prepared to find that in a more adequate method, meanings may turn out
to be complicated, infinite entities built up out of elements belonging to
various ontological categories.

My proposals will also not conform to the expectations of those who,
in analyzing meaning, turn immediately to the psychology and sociology
of language users: to intentions, sense-experience, and mental ideas, or
to social rules, conventions, and regularities. I distinguish two topics:
first, the description of possible languages or grammars as abstract
semantic systems whereby symbols are associated with aspects of the
world; and second, the description of the psychological and sociological
facts whereby a particular one of these abstract semantic systems is the
one used by a person or population. Only confusion comes of mixing
these two topics. This paper deals almost entirely with the first. (I discuss
the second elsewhere: Lewis, 1968b and 1969, Chapter V.)

My proposals are in the tradition of *referential*, or *model-theoretic*,
semantics descended from Frege, Tarski, Carnap (in his later works), and
recent work of Kripke and others on semantic foundations of intensional
logic. (See Frege, 1892; Tarski, 1936; Carnap, 1947 and 1963, § 9;
Kripke, 1963; Kaplan, 1964; Montague, 1960, 1968, and 1970c; Scott, 1970.)
The project of transplanting referential semantics from artificial to natural
languages has recently been undertaken, in various ways, by several philosophers and linguists (Davidson, 1967; Parsons, 1968; Montague,
1969, 1970a, and 1970b; Keenan, 1969.) I have no quarrel with these
efforts; indeed, I have here adapted features from several of them. I hope,
however, that the system set forth in this paper offers a simpler way to
do essentially the same thing. But simplicity is a matter of taste, and

simplicity at one place trades off against simplicity elsewhere. It is in these trade-offs that my approach differs most from the others.

II. CATEGORIALLY BASED GRAMMARS

A *categorial grammar* in the sense of Ajdukiewicz (Ajdukiewicz, 1935; Bar-Hillel, 1964, Part II) is a context-free phrase structure grammar of the following sort.

First, we have a small number of *basic categories*. One of these is the category *sentence* (S). Others might be, for instance, the categories *name* (N) and *common noun* (C). Perhaps we can get by with these three and no more; indeed, Ajdukiewicz went so far as to do without the category *common noun*. Or perhaps we might do better to use different basic categories; we will consider dispensing with the category *name* in favor of an alternative basic category *verb phrase* (VP), or perhaps *noun phrase* (NP).

Second, we have infinitely many *derived categories*. Whenever $c, c_1, ..., c_n$ ($n \geqslant 1$) are any categories, either basic or derived, we have a derived category which we will write $(c/c_1 ... c_n)$. (However, we will usually omit the outermost parentheses.)

Third, we have context-free phrase-structure rules of the form

$$c \rightarrow (c/c_1...c_n) + c_1 + \cdots + c_n$$

corresponding to each derived category. That is to say: for any categories $c, c_1, ..., c_n$, the result of concatenating any expression of category $(c/c_1...c_n)$, then any expression of category c_1, then..., and finally any expression of category c_n is an expression of category c. Accordingly, we will say that a $(c/c_1...c_n)$ *takes* a c_1 and ... and a c_n and *makes* a c. The phrase-structure rules are implicit in the system of derived categories.

Finally, we have a lexicon wherein finitely many expressions – words or word-like morphemes – are assigned to categories. The categories of these lexical expressions may be either basic or derived; unless some lexical expressions belong to derived categories, no non-lexical compound expressions can be generated. Notice that although there are infinitely many derived categories and infinitely many phrase-structure rules, nevertheless with any given lexicon all but finitely many categories and rules will be unemployed. This is true even though many lexica will generate infinitely many compound expressions.

To specify a categorial grammar, we need only specify its lexicon. The rest is common to all categorial grammars. Consider this lexicon:

$$
\left\{
\begin{array}{llll}
\langle a & (S/(S/N))/C\rangle & \langle pig & C\rangle \\
\langle believes & (S/N)/S\rangle & \langle piggishly & (S/N)/(S/N)\rangle \\
\langle every & (S/(S/N))/C\rangle & \langle Porky & N\rangle \\
\langle grunts & S/N\rangle & \langle something & S/(S/N)\rangle \\
\langle is & (S/N)/N\rangle & \langle the & (S/(S/N))/C\rangle \\
\langle loves & (S/N)/N\rangle & \langle which & (C/C)/(S/N)\rangle \\
\langle Petunia & N\rangle & \langle yellow & C/C\rangle
\end{array}
\right\}
$$

It gives us a categorial grammar which is simply a notational variant of this rather commonplace context-free grammar:

$$
\begin{array}{ll}
S \rightarrow \begin{cases} NP+VP \\ VP+Npr \end{cases} & Npr \rightarrow \begin{cases} Porky \\ Petunia \end{cases} \\[2ex]
 & NP \rightarrow something \\
VP \rightarrow \begin{cases} Adv+VP \\ Vt+Npr \\ Vs+S \end{cases} & Nco \rightarrow pig \\
 & VP \rightarrow grunts \\
NP \rightarrow Art+Nco & \\
Nco \rightarrow Adj+Nco & Vt \rightarrow \begin{cases} loves \\ is \end{cases} \\
Adj \rightarrow Rel+VP & \\
 & Vs \rightarrow believes \\
 & Art \rightarrow \begin{cases} a \\ every \\ the \end{cases} \\
 & Adj \rightarrow yellow \\
 & Adv \rightarrow piggishly \\
 & Rel \rightarrow which
\end{array}
$$

There are three peculiarities about the grammar. First, proper nouns are distinguished from noun phrases. Proper nouns or noun phrases may be subjects (though with different word order) but only proper nouns may be objects. Second, there is nothing to prevent inappropriate iteration of modifiers. Third, the word order is sometimes odd. We will see later how these peculiarities may be overcome.

The employed rules in this example are the eight phrase-structure rules corresponding to the eight employed derived categories.

In this example, I have used only derived categories of the form (c/c_1) that take a single argument. I shall adopt this restriction for the most part in practice, but not in principle.

It is apparent that categorial grammars of this sort are not reasonable grammars for natural language. For that matter, they are not reasonable grammars for most artificial languages either – the exception being symbolic logic in Polish notation. Hence, despite their elegance, categorial grammars have largely been ignored since the early 1950's. Since then, however, we have become interested in the plan of using a simple phrase-structure grammar as a base for a transformational grammar. The time therefore seems ripe to explore *categorially based transformational grammars*, obtained by taking an Ajdukiewicz categorial grammar as base and adding a transformational component. So far as I know, this proposal has been made only once before (Lyons, 1966), but it seems an obvious one.

It is obvious that by adding a transformational component to the categorial grammar of our example, we could rectify the word order and filter out inappropriate iterations of modifiers. Less obviously, we could provide for noun phrase objects by means of a transformational component together with a few additional lexical items – items that need never appear in the final generated sentences.

If reasonable categorially based transformational grammars can be given for all languages of interest to us, and if this can be done under the constraint that meanings are to be determined entirely by base structure, so that the transformational component is irrelevant to semantics, then it becomes extremely easy to give general answer to the questions: What is a meaning? What is the form of a semantic projection rule? Let us see how this can be done.

III. INTENSIONS FOR BASIC CATEGORIES

In order to say what a meaning *is*, we may first ask what a meaning *does*, and then find something that does that.

A meaning for a sentence is something that determines the conditions under which the sentence is true or false. It determines the truth-value of the sentence in various possible states of affairs, at various times, at various places, for various speakers, and so on. (I mean this to apply even

to non-declarative sentences, but postpone consideration of them.)
Similarly, a meaning for a name is something that determines what thing,
if any, the name names in various possible states of affairs, at various
times, and so on. Among 'things' we include things that do not actually
exist, but *might* exist in states of affairs different from the actual state of
affairs. Similarly, a meaning for a common noun is something that
determines which (possible or actual) things, if any, that common
noun applies to in various possible states of affairs, at various times,
and so on.

We call the truth-value of a sentence the *extension* of that sentence;
we call the thing named by a name the *extension* of that name; we call
the set of things to which a common noun applies the *extension* of that
common noun. The extension of something in one of these three categories depends on its meaning and, in general, on other things as well:
on facts about the world, on the time of utterance, on the place of utterance, on the speaker, on the surrounding discourse, etc. It is the meaning
which determines how the extension depends upon the combination of
other relevant factors. What sort of things determine how something
depends on something else? *Functions*, of course; functions in the most
general set-theoretic sense, in which the domain of arguments and the
range of values may consist of entities of any sort whatever, and in which
it is not required that the function be specifiable by any simple rule. We
have now found something to do at least part of what a meaning for a
sentence, name, or common noun does: a function which yields as output
an appropriate extension when given as input a package of the various
factors on which the extension may depend. We will call such an input
package of relevant factors an *index*; and we will call any function from
indices to appropriate extensions for a sentence, name, or common noun
an *intension*.

Thus an *appropriate intension for* a sentence is any function from indices
to truth-values; an *appropriate intension for* a name is any function from
indices to things; an *appropriate intension for* a common noun is any
function from indices to sets. The plan to construe intensions as extension-
determining functions originated with Carnap. (Carnap, 1947, § 40, and
1963.) Accordingly, let us call such functions *Carnapian intensions*. But
whereas Carnap's extension-determining functions take as their arguments
models or state-descriptions representing possible worlds, I will adopt the

suggestion (Montague, 1968; Scott, 1970) of letting the arguments be packages of miscellaneous factors relevant to determining extensions.

We may take indices as n-tuples (finite sequences) of the various items other than meaning that may enter into determining extensions. We call these various items *coordinates* of the index, and we shall assume that the coordinates are given some arbitrary fixed order.

First, we must have a *possible-world coordinate*. Contingent sentences depend for their truth value on facts about the world, and so are true at some possible worlds and false at others. A possible world corresponds to a possible totality of facts, determinate in all respects. Common nouns also have different extensions at different possible worlds; and so do some names, at least if we adopt the position (defended in Lewis, 1968a) that things are related to their counterparts in other worlds by ties of strong similarity rather than identity.

Second, we must have several *contextual coordinates* corresponding to familiar sorts of dependence on features of context. (The world coordinate itself might be regarded as a feature of context, since different possible utterances of a sentence are located in different possible worlds.) We must have a *time coordinate*, in view of tensed sentences and such sentences as 'Today is Tuesday'; a *place coordinate*, in view of such sentences as 'Here there are tigers'; a *speaker coordinate* in view of such sentences as 'I am Porky'; an *audience coordinate* in view of such sentences as 'You are Porky'; an *indicated-objects coordinate* in view of such sentences as 'That pig is Porky' or 'Those men are Communists'; and a *previous discourse coordinate* in view of such sentences as 'The aforementioned pig is Porky'.

Third, it is convenient to have an *assignment coordinate*: an infinite sequence of things, regarded as giving the values of any variables that may occur free in such expressions as 'x is tall' or 'son of y'. Each variable employed in the language will accordingly be a name having as its intension, for some number n, the *nth variable intension*: that function whose value, at any index i, is that thing which is the nth term of the assignment coordinate of i. That thing is the extension, or value, of the variable at i. (Note that because there is more than one possible thing, the variable intensions are distinct: nothing is both the n_1th and the n_2th variable intension for two different numbers n_1 and n_2.) The extensions of 'x is tall' of 'son of y' depend on the assignment and world coordinates of indices just as the extensions of 'I am tall' and 'son of mine' depend on the speaker and world coordinates. Yet the assignment coordinate cannot naturally be included among features of context. One might claim that variables do not appear in sentences of natural languages; but even if this is so, it may be useful to employ variables in a categorial base. In any case, I seek sufficient generality to accommodate languages that do employ variables.

Perhaps other coordinates would be useful. (See the Appendix.) But let us stop here, even though the penalty for introducing a superfluous coordinate is mere clutter, while the penalty for omitting a needed one is inadequacy. Thus an *index* is tentatively any octuple of which the first coordinate is a possible world, the second coordinate is a moment of time, the third coordinate is a place, the fourth coordinate is a person (or other creature capable of being a speaker), the fifth coordinate is a set of persons (or other creatures capable of being an audience), the sixth coordinate is a set (possibly empty) of concrete things capable of being pointed at, the seventh coordinate is a segment of discourse, and the eighth coordinate is an infinite sequence of things.

Intensions, our functions from indices to extensions, are designed to do part of what meanings do. Yet they are not meanings; for there are differences in meaning unaccompanied by differences in intension. It would be absurd to say that all tautologies have the same meaning, but they have the same intension: the constant function having at every index the value *truth*. Intensions are part of the way to meanings, however, and they are of interest in their own right. We shall consider later what must be added to an intension to obtain something that can do *all* of what a meaning does.

We may permit Carnapian intensions to be partial functions from indices, undefined at some indices. A name may not denote anything at a given possible world. 'Pegasus', for instance, denotes nothing at our world, so its intension may be taken as undefined at any index having our world as its world coordinate. A sentence that suffers from failure of presupposition is often thought to lack a truth-value (for instance in Strawson, 1950; Keenan, 1969; McCawley, 1969). If we adopt this treatment of presupposition, sentences susceptible to lack of truth-value should have intensions that are undefined at some indices. They might even have intensions that are undefined at *all* indices; a sentence with inconsistent presuppositions should have as its intension the empty function, defined at no index.

Hitherto I have spoken uncritically of 'things'. Things are name extensions and values of name intensions; sets of things are common-noun extensions and values of common-noun intensions; sequences of things are assignment coordinates of indices. Change the underlying set of things and we change the sets of extensions, indices, and Carnapian intensions. What, then, are things? Of course I want to say, once and for all: *everything* is a thing. But I must not say that. Not all sets of things can be things; else the set of things would be larger than itself. No Carnapian intension can be a thing (unless it is undefined at certain indices); else it would be a member of ... a member of itself. We must understand the above definitions of extensions, indices, and Carnapian intensions (and the coming definitions of compositional intensions, meanings, and lexica) as tacitly relativized to a chosen set of things. Can we choose the set of things once and for all? Not quite; no matter what set we choose as the set of things, the system of intensions defined over that set will not provide intensions for certain terms – 'intension', for instance – of the semantic metalanguage corresponding to that choice. Consider the language of this paper (minus this paragraph) with the extension of 'thing' somehow fixed; it is an adequate semantic metalanguage for some languages but not for itself. To do semantics for it, we must move to a second language in which 'thing' is taken more inclusively; to do semantics for that language we must move to a third language in which 'thing' is taken more inclusively still; and so on. Any language can be treated in a metalanguage in which 'thing' is taken inclusively enough; but the generality of semantics is fundamentally limited by the fact that no language can be its own semantic metalanguage (Cf. Tarski, 1936) and hence there can be no universal semantic metalanguage. But we can approach generality as closely as we like by taking 'thing' inclusively enough. For the remainder of this paper, let us proceed on the assumption that the set of things has been chosen, almost once and for all, as some very inclusive set: at least as the universe of some intended model of standard set theory with all the non-sets we want, actual or possible, included as individuals. Let us ignore the sequence of semantic metalanguages that still escape treatment.

In that case there is overlap between things, sets of things, and truth-values. (Not all sets of things can be things, but some should be.) More-over, there is overlap between sets and truth-values if we adopt the common conventions of identifying the truth-values *truth* and *falsity* with the numbers 1 and 0 respectively, and of identifying each natural number with the set of its predecessors. Thus the appropriate extensions and in-tensions for sentences, names, and common nouns overlap. The same function that is the intension of all contradictions is also the intension of the name 'zero' and of the common noun 'round square'. Such overlap, however, is harmless. Whenever we want to get rid of it, we can replace intensions by ordered pairs of a category and an intension appropriate for that category.

IV. INTENSIONS FOR DERIVED CATEGORIES

Turning to derived categories, it is best to foresake extensions and Carna-pian intensions in the interest of generality. Sometimes, for instance, a C/C – that is, an *adjective* – has an extension like that of a common noun: a set of things to which (at a given index) it applies. Probably 'married' is such an *extensional adjective*. But most adjectives do not have exten-sions. What is the set of things to which 'alleged' applies? An alleged Communist is not something which is, on the one hand, an alleged thing and, on the other hand, a Communist.

In general, an adjective takes a common noun to make a new, com-pound common noun; and the intension of the new common noun depends on the intension of the original common noun in a manner deter-mined by the meaning of the adjective. A meaning for an adjective, therefore, is something that determines how one common-noun intension depends on another. Looking for an entity that does what a meaning does, we are led to say that an appropriate intension for an adjective is any function from common-noun intensions to common-noun intensions. In more detail: it is a function whose domain and range consist of functions from indices to sets. Thus the intension of 'alleged' is a function that, when given as argument the intension of 'Communist', 'windshield', or 'chipmunk' yields as value the intension of the compound common noun 'alleged Communist', 'alleged windshield', or 'alleged chipmunk' respec-tively. Note that it would not work to use instead a function from common-noun extensions (sets) to common-noun extensions; for at certain indices 'Communist' and 'Maoist' have the same extension but 'alleged Communist' and 'alleged Maoist' do not – or, at other indices, vice versa.

More generally, let us say that an *appropriate intension for* a $(c/c_1...c_n)$, where c, c_1, ..., and c_n are any categories, basic or derived, is any n-place function from c_1-intensions, ..., and c_n-intensions to c-intensions. That is, it is any function (again in the most general set-theoretic sense) having as its range of values a set of c-intensions, having as its domain of first arguments the set of c_1-intensions, ..., and having as its domain of nth arguments the set of c_n-intensions. A $(c/c_1...c_n)$ takes a c_1 and ... and a c_n and makes a c by concatenation; correspondingly, a $(c/c_1...c_n)$-intension takes a c_1-intension and ... and a c_n-intension as arguments and makes a c-intension as function value. We will call these intensions for derived categories *compositional intensions*. (Intensions resembling some of my compositional intensions are discussed in Kaplan, 1964; in Scott, 1970; and – as appropriate intensions for adjectives and other modifiers – in Parsons, 1968 and Montague, 1970a. The latter discussion is due in part to J. A. W. Kamp.) The general form of the semantic projection rules for an interpreted categorial grammar is implicit in the nature of compositional intensions, just as the general form of the phrase-structure rules is implicit in the nomenclature for derived categories. The result of concatenating a $(c/c_1...c_n)$ with intension ϕ_0, a c_1 with intension ϕ_1, ..., and a c_n with intension ϕ_n is a c with intension $\phi_0(\phi_1...\phi_n)$.

We have considered already the derived category *adjective* C/C. For another example, take the derived category *verb phrase*, S/N.

A verb phrase takes a name to make a sentence. (We rely on the transformational component to change the word order if necessary.) An appropriate intension for a verb phrase – an S/N-intension – is therefore a function from name intensions to sentence intensions. That is, it is a function from functions from indices to things to functions from indices to truth values. The intension of 'grunts', for instance, is that function ϕ whose value, given as argument any function ϕ_1 from indices to things, is that function ϕ_2 from indices to truth values such that, for any index i,

$$\phi_2(i) = \begin{cases} \textit{truth} \text{ if } \phi_1(i) \text{ is something which grunts at the} \\ \quad \text{world and time given by the appropriate coor-} \\ \quad \text{dinates of } i \\ \textit{falsity} \text{ otherwise.} \end{cases}$$

Applying the projection rule, we find that the sentence 'Porky grunts' is true at just those indices i such that the thing named by 'Porky' at i grunts at the possible world that is the world coordinate of i at the time which is the time coordinate of i. (The appearance of circularity in this account is spurious; it comes of the fact that I am using English to specify the intension of a word of English.)

For another example, take the derived category *adverb* (of one sort), (S/N)/(S/N). An adverb of this sort takes a verb phrase to make a verb phrase; so an appropriate intension for such an adverb – an (S/N)/(S/N)-intension – is a function from verb-phrase intensions to verb-phrase intensions; or, in more detail, a function from functions from functions from indices to things to functions from indices to truth-values to functions from functions from indices to things to functions from indices to truth-values.

I promised simplicity; I deliver functions from functions from functions to functions to functions from functions to functions. And worse is in store if we consider the sort of adverb that modifies ordinary adverbs: the category ((S/N)/(S/N))/((S/N)/(S/N)). Yet I think no apology is called for. Intensions are complicated constructs, but the principles of their construction are extremely simple. The situation is common: look at any account of the set-theoretic construction of real numbers, yet recall that children often understand the real numbers rather well.

In some cases, it would be possible to find simpler intensions, but at an exorbitant cost: we would have to give up the uniform function-and-arguments form for semantic projection rules. We have noted already that some adjectives are extensional, though most are not. The extensional adjectives could be given sets as extensions and functions from indices to sets as Carnapian intensions. Similarly for verb phrases: we may call a verb phrase *extensional* iff there is a function ϕ from indices to sets such that if ϕ_1 is the (compositional) intension of the verb phrase, ϕ_2 is any name intension, ϕ_3 is $\phi_1(\phi_2)$, and i is any index, then

$$\phi_3(i) = \begin{cases} truth \text{ if } \phi_2(i) \text{ is a member of } \phi(i) \\ falsity \text{ otherwise.} \end{cases}$$

If there is any such function ϕ, there is exactly one; we can call it the Carnapian intension of the verb phrase and we can call its value at any index i the extension of the verb phrase at i. 'Grunts', for instance, is an extensional verb phrase; its extension at an index i is the set of things that grunt at the world and the time given by the world coordinate and the time coordinate of the index i. Verb phrases, unlike adjectives, are ordinarily extensional; but Barbara Partee has pointed out that the verb phrase in 'The price of milk is rising' seems to be non-extensional.

There is no harm in noting that extensional adjectives and verb phrases have Carnapian intensions as well as compositional intensions. However, it is the compositional intension that should be used to determine the intension of an extensional-adjective-plus-common-noun or extensional-verb-phrase-plus-name combination. If we used the Carnapian intensions, we would have a miscellany of semantic projection rules rather than the uniform function-and-arguments rule. (Indeed, the best way to formulate projection rules using Carnapian intensions might be to combine a rule for reconstructing compositional intensions from Carnapian intensions with the function-and-arguments rule for compositional intensions.) Moreover, we would sacrifice generality: non-extensional adjectives and verb phrases would have to be treated separately from the extensional ones, or not at all. This loss of generality would be serious in the case of adjectives; but not in the case of verb phrases since there are few, if any, non-extensional verb phrases.

For the sake of generality, we might wish to take account of selection restrictions by allowing a compositional intension to be undefined for some arguments of appropriate type. If we thought that 'green idea' should lack an intension, for instance, we might conclude that the intension of 'green' ought to be a partial function from common-noun intensions to common-noun intensions, undefined for such arguments as the intension of 'idea'. It proves more convenient, however, never to let the intension be undefined but rather to let it take on a value called the *null intension* (for the appropriate category). The null intension for the basic categories will be the empty function; the null intension for any derived category $(c/c_1...c_n)$ will be that $(c/c_1...c_n)$-intension whose value for any combination of appropriate arguments is the null intension for c. Thus the intension of 'green', given as argument the intension of 'idea', yields as value the null intension for the category C. The intension of the adverb 'furiously', given as argument the intension of 'sleeps', yields as value the null intension for the category S/N, and that in turn, given as value any name intension, yields as value the null intension for the category S. (I dislike this treatment of selection restrictions, but provide the option for those who want it.)

It is worth mentioning that my account of intensions for derived categories, and of the corresponding form for projection rules, is independent of my account of intensions for basic categories. Whatever S-intensions and N-intensions may be – even expressions of Markerese or ideas in someone's mind – it still is possible to take S/N-intensions as functions from N-intensions to S-intensions and to obtain the intension of 'Porky grunts' by applying the intension of 'grunts' as function to the intension of 'Porky' as argument.

V. MEANINGS

We have already observed that intensions for sentences cannot be identified with meanings since differences in meaning – for instance, between tautologies – may not carry with them any difference in intension. The same goes for other categories, basic or derived. Differences in intension, we may say, give us *coarse* differences in meaning. For *fine* differences in meaning we must look to the analysis of a compound into constituents and to the intensions of the several constituents. For instance 'Snow is white or it isn't' differs finely in meaning from 'Grass is green or it isn't' because of the difference in intension between the embedded sentences 'Snow is white' and 'Grass is green'. For still finer differences in meaning we must look in turn to the intensions of constituents of constituents, and so on. Only when we come to non-compound, lexical constituents can we take sameness of intension as a sufficient condition of synonymy. (See Carnap, 1947, § 14, on 'intensional isomorphism'; C. I. Lewis, 1944, on 'analytic meaning'.)

It is natural, therefore, to identify meanings with semantically interpreted phrase markers minus their terminal nodes: finite ordered trees having at each node a category and an appropriate intension. If we associate a meaning of this sort with an expression, we are given the category and intension of the expression; and if the expression is compound, we are given also the categories and intensions of its constituent parts, their constituent parts, and so on down.

Perhaps we would thereby cut meanings too finely. For instance, we will be unable to agree with someone who says that a double negation has the same meaning as the corresponding affirmative. But this difficulty does not worry me: we will have both intensions and what I call meanings, and sometimes one and sometimes the other will be preferable as an explication of our ordinary discourse about meanings. Perhaps some entities of intermediate fineness can also be found, but I doubt that there is any uniquely natural way to do so.

It may be disturbing that in our explication of meanings we have made arbitrary choices – for instance, of the order of coordinates in an index. Meanings are meanings – how can we *choose* to construct them in one way rather than another? The objection is a general objection to set-theoretic constructions (see Benacerraf, 1965), so I will not reply to it here. But if it troubles you, you may prefer to say that *real* meanings are *sui generis* entities and that the constructs I call 'meanings' do duty for real meanings because there is a natural one-to-one correspondence between them and the real meanings.

It might also be disturbing that I have spoken of categories without hitherto saying what they are. This again is a matter of arbitrary choice; we might, for instance, take them as sets of expressions in some language, or as sets of intensions, or even as arbitrarily chosen code-numbers. It turns out to be most convenient, if slightly unnatural, to identify categories with their own names: expressions composed in the proper way out of the letters 'S', 'N', 'C' (and whatever others we may introduce later in considering revisions of the system) together with parentheses and diagonal slashes. This does not prevent our category-names from being names of categories: they name themselves. All definitions involving categories are to be understood in accordance with the identification of categories and category-names.

Some might even wish to know what a *tree* is. Very well: it is a function that assigns to each member of the set of nodes of the tree an object said to *occupy* or be *at* that node. The nodes themselves are finite sequences of positive numbers. A set of such sequences is the set of *nodes of* some tree iff, first, it is a finite set, and second, whenever it contains a sequence $\langle b_1...b_k \rangle$ then it also contains every sequence that is an initial segment of $\langle b_1...b_k \rangle$ and every sequence $\langle b_1...b_{k-1}b_k' \rangle$ with $b_k' < b_k$. We regard $\langle \ \rangle$, the sequence of zero length, as the topmost node; $\langle b_1 \rangle$ as the b_1th node from the left immediately beneath $\langle \ \rangle$; $\langle b_1 b_2 \rangle$ as the b_2th node from the left immediately beneath $\langle b_1 \rangle$; and so on. We can easily define all the requisite notions of tree theory in terms of this construction.

Once we have identified meanings with semantically interpreted phrase markers, it becomes natural to reconstrue the phrase-structure rules of categorial grammar, together with the corresponding projection rules, as conditions of well-formedness for meanings. (Cf. McCawley, 1968.) Accordingly, we now define a *meaning* as a tree such that, first, each node is occupied by an ordered pair $\langle c\ \phi \rangle$ of a category and an appropriate intension for that category; and second, immediately beneath any non-terminal node occupied by such a pair $\langle c\ \phi \rangle$ are two or more nodes, and these are occupied by pairs $\langle c_0\ \phi_0 \rangle$, $\langle c_1\ \phi_1 \rangle$, ..., $\langle c_n\ \phi_n \rangle$ (in that order) such that c_0 is $(c/c_1...c_n)$ and ϕ is $\phi_0(\phi_1...\phi_n)$.

A meaning may be a tree with a single node; call such meanings *simple* and other meanings *compound*. Compound meanings are, as it were, built up from simple meanings by steps in which several meanings (simple or compound) are combined as sub-trees under a new node, analogously to the way in which expressions are built up by concatenating shorter expressions. We may call a meaning m' a *constituent of* a meaning m iff m' is a subtree of m. We may say that a meaning m is *generated by* a set of simple meanings iff every simple constituent of m belongs to that set. More generally, m is *generated by* a set of meanings (simple or compound) iff every simple constituent of m is a constituent of some constituent of m, possibly itself, which belongs to that set.

We shall in many ways speak of meanings as though they were symbolic expressions generated by an interpreted categorial grammar, even though they are nothing of the sort. The *category of* a meaning is the category found as the first component of its topmost node. The *intension of* a meaning is the intension found as the second component of its topmost node. The *extension at* an index i *of* a sentence meaning, name meaning, or common-noun meaning is the value of the intension of the meaning for the argument i. A sentence meaning is *true* or *false at i* according as its extension at i is *truth* or *falsity*; a name meaning *names at i* that thing, if any, which is its extension at i; and a common-noun meaning *applies at i* to whatever things belong to its extension at i. As we have seen, extensions might also be provided for certain meanings in derived categories such as C/C or S/N, but this cannot be done in a non-artificial, general way.

Given as fundamental the definition of truth of a sentence meaning at an index, we can define many derivative truth relations. Coordinates of the index may be made explicit, or may be determined by a context of utterance, or may be generalized over. Generalizing over all coordinates, we can say that a sentence meaning is *analytic* (in one sense) iff it is true at every index. Generalizing over the world and assignment coordinates and letting the remaining coordinates be determined by context, we can say that a sentence meaning is *analytic* (in another sense) *on* a given occasion iff it is true at every index i having as its time, place, speaker, audience, indicated-objects and previous-discourse coordinates respectively the time, the place, the speaker, the audience, the set of objects pointed to, and the previous discourse on that occasion. Generalizing over the time and assignment coordinates and letting the others (including world) be determined by context, we define *eternal truth* of a sentence meaning *on* an occasion; generalizing over the assignment coordinate and letting all the rest be determined by context, we define simply *truth on* an occasion; and so on.

We also can define truth relations even stronger than truth at every index. Let us call a meaning m' a *semantic variant* of a meaning m iff m and m' have exactly the same nodes, with the same category but not necessarily the same intension at each node, and, whenever a common intension appears at two terminal nodes in m, a common intension also appears at those two nodes in m'. Let us call m' an *s-fixed semantic variant of* m, where s is a set of simple meanings, iff m and m' are semantic variants and every member of s which is a constituent of m is also a constituent, at the same place, of m'. Then we can call a sentence meaning *s-true* iff every *s*-fixed semantic variant of it (including itself) is true at every index. If s is the set of simple meanings whose bearers we would classify as logical vocabulary, then we may call *s*-true sentence meanings *logically true*; if s is the set of simple meanings whose bearers we would classify as mathematical (including logical) vocabulary, we may call *s*-true sentence meanings *mathematically true*. Analogously, we can define a relation of *s*-fixed semantic variance between sequences of meanings; and we can say that a sentence meaning m_0 is an *s-consequence* (for instance, a *logical consequence* or *mathematical consequence*) of sentence meanings $m_1, \ldots$ iff, for every *s*-fixed semantic variant $\langle m_0' \, m_1' \ldots \rangle$ of the sequence $\langle m_0 \, m_1 \ldots \rangle$ and every index i such that all of $m_1', \ldots$ are true at i, m_0' is true at i. (The premises $m_1, \ldots$ may be infinite in number. Their order is insignificant.) These definitions are adapted from definitions in terms of truth in all logically or mathematically standard interpretations of a given language. However, we have been able to avoid introducing the notion of alternative interpretations of a language, since so far we are dealing entirely with meanings.

VI. GRAMMARS RECONSTRUCTED

Our system of meanings may serve, in effect, as a universal base for categorially based transformational grammars. There is no need to repeat the phrase-structure rules of categorial well-formedness as a base component in each such grammar. Instead, we take the meanings as given, and regard a grammar as specifying a way to encode meanings: a relation between certain meanings and certain expressions (sequences of sound-types or of mark-types) which we will call the *representing relation* determined by the grammar. We might just identify grammars with representing relations; but I prefer to take grammars as systems which determine representing relations in a certain way.

If we were concerned with nothing but transformation-free categorial grammars, we could take a grammar to consist of nothing but a *lexicon*: a finite set of triples of the form $\langle e \ c \ \phi \rangle$ where e is an expression, c is a category, and ϕ is an intension appropriate for that category. We may say that an expression e *represents* or *has* a meaning m *relative to* a lexicon **L** iff **L** contains items $\langle e_1 \ c_1 \ \phi_1 \rangle$, ..., $\langle e_n \ c_n \ \phi_n \rangle$ such that, first, e is the result of concatenating e_1, ..., e_n (in that order), and second, the terminal nodes of m are occupied by $\langle c_1 \ \phi_1 \rangle$, ..., $\langle c_n \ \phi_n \rangle$ (in that order).

We could instead have proceeded in two steps. Let us define a *(categorial) phrase marker* as a tree having categories at its non-terminal nodes and expressions at its terminal nodes. Then a phrase marker p represents or *has* a meaning m *relative to* a lexicon **L** iff p is obtained from m as follows: given any terminal node of the meaning m occupied by a pair $\langle c \ \phi \rangle$, place below it another node occupied by an expression e such that the item $\langle e \ c \ \phi \rangle$ is contained in the lexicon; then remove the intensions, replacing the $\langle c \ \phi \rangle$ pair at each non-terminal node by its unaccompanied category c. Note that the set of meanings thus representable relative to a lexicon **L** comprises all and only those meanings that are generated by

the set of simple meanings of the lexical items themselves; let us call it
the set of meanings *generated by* the lexicon **L**.

Next, we define the *terminal string* of a phrase marker p as the expression obtained by concatenating, in order, the expressions at the terminal
nodes of p. Thus we see that an expression e represents a meaning m
relative to a lexicon **L**, according to the definition above, iff e is the
terminal string of some phrase marker that represents m relative to **L**.

In the case of a categorially based transformational grammar, we have
not two steps but three. Such a grammar consists of a lexicon **L** together
with a *transformational component* **T**. The latter imposes finitely many
constraints on finite sequences of phrase markers. A sequence $\langle p_1...p_n \rangle$
of phrase markers that satisfies the constraints imposed by **T** will be
called a *(transformational) derivation of p_n from p_1 in* **T**. An expression e
represents or *has* a meaning m in a grammar $\langle$ **L T** $\rangle$ iff there exists a derivation $\langle p_1...p_n \rangle$ in **T** such that e is the terminal string of p_n and p_1
represents m relative to the lexicon **L**. If so, we will also call e a *meaningful expression*, p_n a *surface structure of e, p_{n-1}* and ... and p_2 *intermediate
structures of e, p_1* a *base structure of e*, and m a *meaning of e* (all *relative to*
the grammar $\langle$ **L T** $\rangle$). However, we will call any phrase marker p a *base
structure* in $\langle$ **L T** $\rangle$ iff it represents a meaning relative to **L**, whether or not it
is the base structure *of* any expression; thus we allow for base structures
which are filtered out by not being the first term of any derivation in **T**.

The representing relation given by a grammar $\langle$ **L T** $\rangle$ is by no means
a one-to-one correspondence between meanings and expressions. A given
expression might be *ambiguous*, representing several different meanings.
(If it represents several different but cointensive meanings, however, it
might be inappropriate to call it ambiguous; for the common notion of
meaning seems to hover between our technical notions of meaning and
of intension.) On the other hand, several expressions might be *synonymous*,
representing a single meaning. We might also call several expressions
completely synonymous iff they share all their meanings; synonymy and
complete synonymy coincide when we are dealing only with unambiguous
expressions. If several expressions represent different but cointensive
meanings, we may call them equivalent but not synonymous. If several
expressions not only represent the same meaning but also have a single
base structure, we may call them not only equivalent and synonymous
but also *paraphrases* of one another.

Given a representing relation, all the semantic relations defined hitherto for meanings carry over to expressions having those meanings. (If we like, they may carry over also to the base, surface, and intermediate structures between the meanings and the expressions.) Thus we know what it means to speak, relative to a given grammar and qualified in cases of ambiguity by 'on a meaning' or 'on all meanings', of the category and intension of any meaningful expression; of the extension at a given index of any expression of appropriate category; of the thing named by a name; of the things to which a common noun applies; of the truth at an index, truth on an occasion, analyticity, logical truth, etc. of a sentence; and so on.

We should note an oddity in our treatment of logical truth. A synonym of a logically true sentence is itself a logical truth, since it represents the same logically true meaning as the original. Hence a descendant by synonym-substitution of a logical truth is itself·a logical truth if the synonym-substitution is confined to single lexical items in the base structure; but not otherwise. 'All woodchucks are groundhogs' comes out logically true, whereas 'All squares are equilateral rectangles' comes out merely analytic (in the strongest sense).

A transformational component may constrain sequences of phrase markers in two ways. There is the local constraint that any two adjacent phrase markers in a derivation must stand in one of finitely many relations; these permitted relations between adjacent phrase markers are the *transformations*. There may also be global derivational constraints specifying relations between non-adjacent phrase markers or properties of the derivation as a whole. An example is the constraint requiring transformations to apply in some specified cyclic (or partly cyclic) order.

A transformation-free categorial grammar is a special case of a categorially based transformational grammar. It has a transformational component with no transformations or global constraints, so that the derivations therein are all and only those sequences $\langle p_1 \rangle$ consisting of a single phrase marker.

I will not attempt to say more exactly what a transformation or a transformational component is. Mathematically precise definitions have been given (for instance in Peters and Ritchie, 1969), but to choose among these would involve taking sides on disputed questions in syntactic theory. I prefer to maintain my neutrality, and I have no present need for a precise delineation of the class of transformational grammars. I have foremost in mind a sort of simplified *Aspects*-model grammar (Chomsky, 1965), but I have said nothing to eliminate various alternatives.

I have said nothing to eliminate generative semantics. What I have chosen to call the 'lexicon' is the *initial* lexicon. Words not in that lexicon might be introduced transformationally on the way from base to surface, if that seems desirable. It might even be that none of the initial lexical items ever reach the surface, and that all surface lexical items (expressions found at terminal nodes of surface structures) are introduced transformationally within derivations. In that case it would be appropriate to use a standardized initial lexicon in all grammars, and to rechristen my base structures 'semantic representations'. In that case also there might or might not be a level between base and surface at which word-introducing transformations are done and other transformations have not yet begun.

I have also said nothing to eliminate surface semantics. This may seem strange, since I have indeed said that meanings are to be determined by base structures alone. However, I rely here on the observation (Lakoff, 1970, § 3) that surface-structure interpretation rules are indistinguishable from global derivational constraints relating three levels: base structures (regarded as semantic representations), deep structures (an *intermediate* level), and surface structures. Deep structures might be ambiguous; a transformational grammar with base-deep-surface constraints might permit two derivations

$$\langle p_B^1 \cdots p_D \cdots p_S^1 \rangle$$
$$\langle p_B^2 \cdots p_D \cdots p_S^2 \rangle$$

differing at the base and surface but not at the deep level, but it might rule out other derivations of the forms

$$\langle p_B^2 \cdots p_D \cdots p_S^1 \rangle$$
$$\langle p_B^1 \cdots p_D \cdots p_S^2 \rangle.$$

In such a case base structure (and hence meaning) would be determined by deep and surface structure together, but not by deep structure alone. Similarly, we might have constraints relating base structure not only to deep and surface structure but also to structure at various other intermediate levels.

I have said nothing to eliminate a non-trivial phonological component;

but I would relocate it as part of the transformational component. The last few steps of a transformational derivation might go from the usual pre-phonological surface structure to a post-phonological surface structure whence the output expression can be obtained simply by concatenation of terminal nodes.

I have said nothing to eliminate an elaborate system of selection restrictions; but these will appear not as restrictions on the lexical insertions between meanings and base structures but as transformational filtering later on. There will be base structures representing the meanings of such questionable sentences as 'Seventeen eats beans' and 'He sang a pregnant toothbrush'. But these base structures need not be the first terms of any derivations, so these meanings may be unrepresented by sentences. If we like selection restrictions, we might match the lexicon to the transformational component in such a way as to filter out just those meanings that have the null intension.

I have not stipulated that only sentential meanings may be represented; that stipulation could be added if there is reason for it.

In fact, the *only* restriction I place on syntax is that transformational grammars should be categorially based. In other words: a transformational component should operate on a set of categorial phrase markers representing a set of meanings generated by some lexicon. But categorial bases are varied enough that this restriction is not at all severe. I claim that whatever familiar sort of base component you may favor on syntactic grounds, you can find a categorial base (i.e. a suitable part of the system of meanings, generated by a suitable chosen lexicon) that resembles the base you favor closely enough to share its attractive properties. Indeed, with a few preliminary rearranging transformations you can go from my categorial base structures to (notational variants of) more familiar base structures; then you can proceed exactly as before. I shall not marshall evidence for this claim; but I think that the following exploration of alternative categorial treatments of quantification will exhibit the close similarities between these categorial treatments and several alternative familiar base components. If it were necessary to choose between a categorial base that was convenient for semantics and a noncategorial base that was convenient for transformational syntax, I might still choose the former. But I deny the need to choose.

This completes the exposition of my proposed system of categories, intensions, and meanings. Now I shall consider how this system – either as is or slightly revised – might be applied to two difficult areas: the semantics of quantification and the semantics of non-declaratives. The treatments following are intended only as illustrations, however; many further alternatives are possible, and might be more convenient for syntax.

VII. TREATMENT OF QUANTIFICATION AND NOUN PHRASES

Let us consider such expressions as 'a pig', 'most pigs', 'seventeen pigs', 'roughly seventeen pigs', 'some yellow pig', 'everything', 'nobody', and the like. We call these *quantifier phrases* (presupposing that they should belong to a common category). What category in our system is this? What sort of intensions do quantifier phrases have?

Quantifier phrases combine with verb phrases to make sentences: 'Some pig grunts', 'Nobody grunts', 'Roughly seventeen pigs grunt', and the like. Names do this, since the category *verb phrase* is the derived category S/N. But quantifier phrases cannot be names, under our semantic treatment of names, because they do not in general name anything. ('The pig' could be an exception at indices such that exactly one pig existed at the world and time given by the index.) The absurd consequences of treating 'nobody', as a name, for instance, are well known (Dodgson, 1871). If a quantifier phrase combines with an S/N to make an S, and yet is not an N, it must therefore be an S/(S/N).

Except perhaps for one-word quantifier phrases – 'nobody', 'everything', and such – quantifier phrases contain constituent common nouns. These may be either simple, as in 'some pig' or compound, as in 'every pink pig that wins a blue ribbon'. Indeed, we may regard common nouns simply as predicates used to restrict quantifiers. (This suggestion derives from Montague, 1970a.) The expressions 'a', 'the', 'some', 'every', 'no', 'most', 'seventeen', 'roughly seventeen', and so on which combine with common nouns (simple or compound) to make quantifier phrases and which are variously called *quantifiers*, *determiners*, or *articles* must therefore belong to the category (S/(S/N))/C. And modifiers of quantifiers like 'roughly' which combine with certain quantifiers to make quantifiers, must belong to the category ((S/(S/N))/C)/((S/(S/N))/C). Selection restrictions by means of transformational filtering could be used to dispose of quantifiers like 'roughly the'.

The intension of 'some pig' may be taken as that function ϕ from S/N-intensions to S-intensions such that if ϕ_1 is any S/N-intension, ϕ_2 is the S-intension $\phi(\phi_1)$, and i is any index, then

$$\phi_2(i) = \begin{cases} \textit{truth} \text{ if, for some N-intension } \phi_3, \phi_3(i) \text{ is a pig and} \\ \qquad \text{if } \phi_4 \text{ is } \phi_1(\phi_3) \text{ then } \phi_4(i) \text{ is } \textit{truth} \\ \textit{falsity} \text{ otherwise.} \end{cases}$$

The intension of 'some' may be taken as that function ϕ from C-intensions to S/(S/N)-intensions such that if ϕ_1 is any C-intension, ϕ_2 is the S/(S/N)-intension $\phi(\phi_1)$, ϕ_3 is any S/N-intension, ϕ_4 is the S-intension $\phi_2(\phi_3)$, and i is any index, then

$$\phi_4(i) = \begin{cases} \textit{truth} \text{ if, for some N-intension } \phi_5, \phi_5(i) \text{ is a member} \\ \qquad \text{of } \phi_1(i) \text{ and if } \phi_6 \text{ is } \phi_3(\phi_5) \text{ then } \phi_6(i) \text{ is } \textit{truth} \\ \textit{falsity} \text{ otherwise.} \end{cases}$$

I spare you the intension of 'roughly'.

Other intensions might be specified for 'some pig' and 'some' that would differ from these only when a quantifier phrase was applied to a non-extensional verb phrase. If there are no non-extensional verb phrases in English, then the choice among these alternatives is arbitrary.

This treatment of quantifier phrases is motivated by a desire to handle simple sentences involving quantifier phrases as straightforwardly as possible, minimizing the use of transformations. But it raises problems. Quantifier phrases seemingly occur not only as subjects of sentences but also as objects of verbs or prepositions. And in all their roles – as subjects or as objects – they are interchangeable with names. That is why it is usual to have a category *noun phrase* comprising both quantifier phrases and names.

We might try the heroic course of doubling all our object-takers. We could have one word 'loves' which is an (S/N)/N and takes the object 'Petunia' to make the verb phrase 'loves Petunia'; and alongside it another 'loves' which is an (S/N)/(S/(S/N)) and takes the object 'some pig' to make the verb phrase 'loves some pig'. But we need not decide how much we mind such extravagant doubling, since it does not work anyway. It would give us one meaning for 'Every boy loves some girl': the weaker meaning, on which the sentence can be true even if each boy loves a different girl. But the sentence is ambiguous; where shall we get

a stronger meaning, on which the sentence is true only if a certain girl –
Zuleika, perhaps – is loved by all boys? (There are those who do not
perceive this ambiguity; but we seek a treatment general enough to
handle the idiolects of those who do.) The method of doubling object-
takers is a blind alley; rather we must look to the method of variable
binding, routinely used in the semantic analysis of standardly formulated
symbolic logic.

The quantifiers of symbolic logic belong to the category S/NS, taking
a name and a sentence to make a sentence. The name must be a variable;
other combinations could be disposed of by transformational filtering.
For instance, the logician's quantifier 'some' takes the variable 'x' and
the sentence 'grunts x' to make a sentence translatable into English as
'something grunts'. The logician's 'some' has as its intension that function
ϕ from N-intensions and S-intensions to S-intensions such that if ϕ_1 is
the nth variable intension for any number n, ϕ_2 is any S-intension, ϕ_3
is $\phi(\phi_1\phi_2)$, and i is any index, then

$$\phi_3(i) = \begin{cases} \textit{truth} \text{ if, for some index } i' \text{ that is like } i \text{ except perhaps} \\ \quad \text{at the } n\text{th term of the assignment coordinate,} \\ \quad \phi_2(i') \text{ is } \textit{truth} \\ \textit{falsity} \text{ otherwise;} \end{cases}$$

and such that if ϕ_1 is any N-intension that is not a variable intension and
ϕ_2 is any S-intension, then $\phi(\phi_1\phi_2)$ is the null intension. The intension
of the logician's quantifier 'every' is specified similarly, with 'for every
index i'...' replacing 'for some index i'...'.

It would be troublesome to employ logician's quantifiers in a grammar
for English. In the first place, these quantifiers are unrestricted, ranging
over everything. The base structure of 'Some pig grunts', for instance,
would come out as

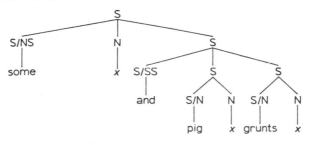

in which there is no constituent corresponding to 'some pig' and in which
'pig' and 'grunts' alike are put into the category S/N. (It was with
structures like this in mind that Ajdukiewicz saw fit to omit the category
C.) This attempt to dispense with quantifier phrases in favor of unrestricted quantifiers taking compound sentences is clumsy at best, and
fails entirely for quantifiers such as 'most' (see Wallace, 1965). In the
second place, by having the quantifier itself do the binding of variables,
we require there to be bound variables wherever there are quantifiers.
We get the unnecessarily complicated base structure

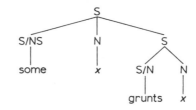

for 'Something grunts', whereas if we had employed quantifier phrases
which take verb phrases and do not bind variables, we could have had

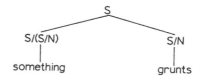

with three constituents instead of six and no work for the transformations
to do.

   It is not necessary, however, that the quantifier itself should bind
variables. We can stick with verb-phrase-taking quantifier phrases of the
category S/(S/N), restricted by constituent common nouns in most cases,
and bind variables when necessary – but *only* when necessary – by means
of a separate constituent called a *binder*: a certain sort of (S/N)/S that
takes a sentence and makes an extensional verb phrase by binding a
variable at all its free occurrences (if any) in the sentence. To every
variable there corresponds a binder. Suppose 'x' is a variable; we may
write its corresponding binder as '$\hat{x}$' and read it as 'is something x such
that'. (But presumably binders may best be treated as base constituents
that never reach the surface; so if the words 'is something x such that'

ever appear in a meaningful expression, they will be derived not from an '$\hat{x}$' in base structure but in some other way.) For instance, the following base structure using a binder is equivalent to 'grunts' and might be read loosely as 'is something x such that x grunts'.

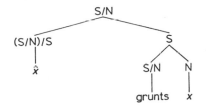

The following is a possible base structure for 'is loved by y'.

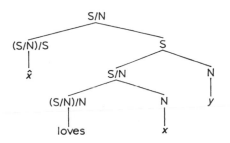

The following might be a base structure for 'Porky loves himself'. (Cf. McCawley, 1969.)

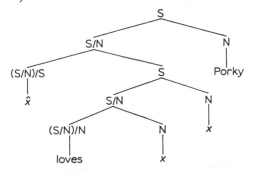

(Provided there is no ambiguity among our variables, we can use them in this way to keep track of coreferentiality, rather than subscripting the

names in

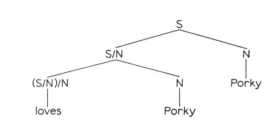

to indicate whether we are dealing with one Porky or two.)

If 'x' has the nth variable intension, then the corresponding binder '$\hat{x}$' has the nth *binder intension*: that function ϕ from S-intensions to S/N-intensions such that if ϕ_1 is any S-intension, ϕ_2 is the S/N-intension $\phi(\phi_1)$, ϕ_3 is any N-intension, ϕ_4 is the S-intension $\phi_2(\phi_3)$, i is any index, and i' is that index which has $\phi_3(i)$ as the nth term of its assignment coordinate and otherwise is like i, then $\phi_4(i) = \phi_1(i')$. It can be verified that this intension justifies the reading of '$\hat{x}$' as 'is something x such that'.

A finite supply of variables and binders, however large, would lead to the mistaken omission of some sentences. To provide an infinite supply by means of a finite lexicon, we must allow our variables and binders to be generated as compounds. We need only three lexical items: one simple variable having the first variable intension; an N/N having as intension a function whose value, given as argument the nth variable intension for any $n \geqslant 1$, is the $(n+1)$th variable intension; and an ((S/N)/S)/N having as intension a function whose value, given as argument the nth variable intension for any $n \geqslant 1$, is the nth binder intension. The first item gives us a starting variable; the second, iterated, manufactures the other variables; the third manufactures binders out of variables. However, we will continue to abbreviate base structures by writing variables and binders as if they were simple.

Variable-binding introduces a sort of spurious ambiguity called *alphabetic variance*. 'Porky loves himself' could have not only the structure shown but also others in which 'x' and '$\hat{x}$' are replaced by 'y' and '$\hat{y}$', or 'z' and '$\hat{z}$', etc. Since different variables may have different intensions, these structures correspond to infinitely many different but cointensive meanings for 'Porky loves himself'. The simplest way to deal with this nuisance is to define an ordering of any such set of meanings and employ transformational filtering to dispose of all but the first meaning in the set (according to the ordering).

Binders have occasionally been discussed by logicians, under the name 'abstraction operators' or 'lambda operators'. (Church, 1941; Carnap, 1958, § 33; Thomason and Stalnaker, 1968.)

Now we are in a position to complete our account of the category S/(S/N) of verb-phrase-taking quantifier phrases, using binders as needed. The base structure for 'Every boy loves Zuleika' may be simply

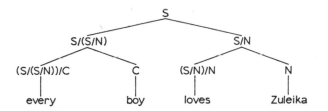

with no unnecessary variable-binding to make work for the transformational component. There is another base structure with variable-binding which we may read roughly as 'Every boy is something x such that x loves Zuleika'; it represents a different but equivalent meaning. We can either let these be another base structure and another (but equivalent) meaning for 'Every boy loves Zuleika' or get rid of them by transformational filtering. The base structure for 'Lothario loves some girl' is

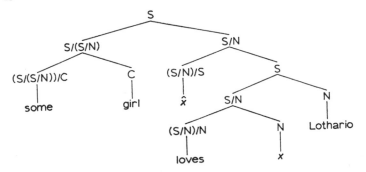

in which the quantifier phrase which is the surface object of 'loves' is treated as subject of a verb phrase obtained by binding the variable which is the base object of 'loves'. To reach an intermediate structure in which the quantifier phrase is relocated as the object of 'loves', we must have recourse to a transformation that moves the subject of a verb phrase made by variable binding into the place of one (the first?) occurrence of the bound variable and destroys the variable-binding apparatus. Note that, if desired, this transformation might apply *beneath* an intermediate level corresponding most closely to the ordinary level of deep structure. The two base structures for 'Every boy loves some girl' are

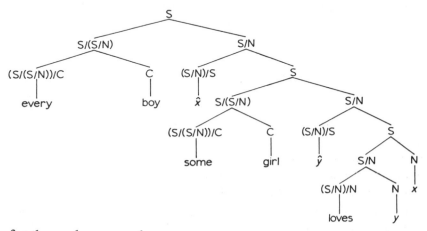

for the weak sense, and

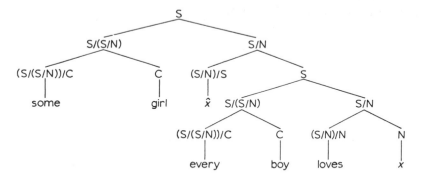

for the strong – Zuleika – sense.

It may be that quantifier-phrase objects should not be abandoned altogether. 'Lothario seeks a girl', in the sense in which it can be paraphrased as 'Lothario seeks a certain particular girl', can have the base structure

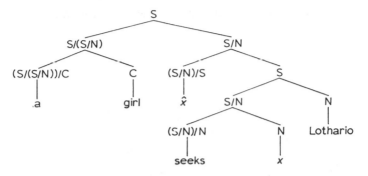

but what about the sense in which any old girl would do? We might give it the base structure

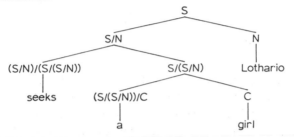

using a second 'seeks' that takes quantifier-phrase objects. The alternative is to let the word 'seeks' be introduced transformationally rather than lexically, as a transformational descendant of 'strives-to-find', so that the base structures would be

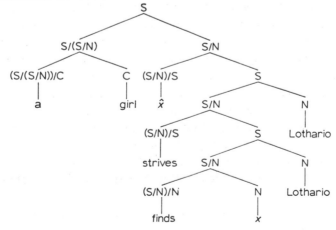

for the sense in which a certain particular girl is sought and

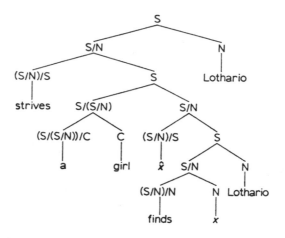

for the sense in which any old girl would do. But it is controversial whether we ought to let words be introduced transformationally in this way; and (as remarked in Montague, 1969) it is not clear how to apply this treatment to 'conceives of a tree'. Perhaps conceiving-of is imagining-to-exist, but perhaps not.

This completes one treatment of quantifier phrases, carried out with no modification of the system I originally presented. It is straightforward from the semantic point of view; however, it might result in excessive complications to transformational syntax. Ordinary bases have a category *noun phrase* which combines quantifier phrases and names; and transformations seem to work well on bases of that sort. By dividing the category of noun phrases, I may require some transformations to be doubled (or quadrupled, etc.). Moreover, my structures involving variable-binding are complicated and remote from the surface, so by doing away with quantifier-phrase objects I make lots of work for the transformational component. It might be, therefore, that this treatment is too costly to syntax. Therefore let us see how we might reinstate the combined category *noun phrase*. There are two methods: we might try to assimilate names to quantifier phrases, or we might try to assimilate quantifier phrases to names.

The method of assimilating names to quantifier phrases proceeds as follows. For every name in our lexicon, for instance 'Porky', we add to our lexicon a corresponding *pseudo-name* in the category S/(S/N). If the intension of the original name 'Porky' is the N-intension ϕ_1, then the intension of the corresponding pseudo-name 'Porky*' should be that function ϕ from S/N-intensions to S-intensions such that for any S/N-intension ϕ_2, $\phi(\phi_2) = \phi_2(\phi_1)$. As a result, a sentence such as 'Porky grunts' can be given either of the base structures

and will have the same intension either way. The category S/(S/N) may now be renamed *noun phrase*. It contains our former quantifier phrases together with our new pseudo-names. It does not contain names themselves. Names are now unnecessary as subjects, but still needed as objects; so the next step is to replace all name-takers except verb phrases by noun-phrase-takers. For instance, the category (S/N)/N of transitive verbs is to be replaced by the category (S/N)/(S/(S/N)) of pseudo-transitive verbs. The intensions of the replacements are related to the intensions of the originals in a systematic way which I shall not bother to specify. Names now serve no further purpose, having been supplanted both as subjects and as objects by pseudo-names; so the next step is to remove names from the lexicon. The category N is left vacant.

Since we have provided for noun-phrase objects for the sake of the pseudo-names, we can also have quantifier-phrase objects and so cut down on variable-binding. For instance, we have

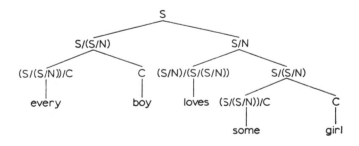

as the base structure for 'Every boy loves some girl' in the weak sense, leaving no work for the transformations. We cannot do away with variable-binding altogether, however. The base structure for 'Every boy loves some girl' in the strong – Zuleika – sense is now

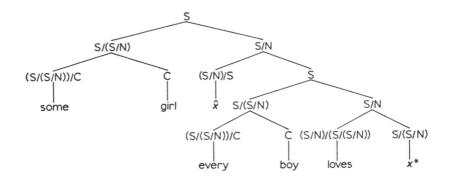

in which the seeming noun-phrase object 'some girl' is treated as subject of a verb phrase obtained by binding the pseudo-variable noun phrase 'x^*' which is the real object of 'loves'. Variables are names, of course, and therefore are replaced by pseudo-names just as any other names are; no change is made, however, in the corresponding binders.

So far we have not departed from the system I presented originally, and we *could* stop here. It is now advantageous, however, to take the step of eliminating the category N altogether and promoting the category *verb phrase* from a derived category S/N to a new basic category VP. Accordingly, the category of noun phrases becomes S/VP; the category of quantifiers becomes (S/VP)/C; the category of transitive verbs becomes VP/(S/VP); and the category which includes binders becomes VP/S.

We can also reopen the question of letting verb-phrase intensions be Carnapian rather than compositional. We rejected this simplification before, principally because it would require a projection rule which was not of our general function-and-arguments form; but that consideration no longer holds after names and verb-phrase-plus-name combinations are done away with. A lesser objection still applies: the simplification only works for extensional verb phrases. If any non-extensional verb phrases exist, they cannot go into our new basic category VP with Carnapian intensions. They will have to go into the category S/(S/VP) instead. The switch to Carnapian intensions for the now-basic verb phrases changes most other intensions in a systematic way which I need not stop to specify.

We turn last to the opposite method, in which quantifier phrases are assimilated to names to give an undivided category of noun phrases. This will require revising the extensions and intensions of names in a manner discussed by Mates (Mates, 1968) and Montague (Montague, 1969 and 1970b).

In the dark ages of logic, a story something like this was told. The phrase 'some pig' names a strange thing we may call the *existentially generic pig* which has just those properties that some pig has. Since some pig is male, some pig (a different one) is female, some pig is pink (all over), and some pig is grey (all over), the existentially generic pig is simultaneously male, female, pink, and grey. Accordingly, he (she?) is in the extensions both of 'is male' and of 'is female', both of 'is pink all over' and of 'is grey all over'. The phrase 'every pig' names a different strange thing called the *universally generic pig* which has just those properties that every pig has. Since not every pig is pink, grey, or any other color, the universally generic pig is not of any color. (Yet neither is he colorless, since not every – indeed not any – pig is colorless). Nor is he(?) male or female (or neuter), since not every pig is any one of these. He is, however, a pig and an animal, and he grunts; for every pig is a pig and an animal, and grunts. There are also the *negative universally generic pig* which has just those properties that no pig has (he is not a pig, but he is both a stone and a number), the *majority generic pig* which has just those properties that more than half of all pigs have, and many more. A sentence formed from a name and an extensional verb phrase is true (we may add: at an index i) if and only if the thing named by the name (at i) belongs to the extension of the verb phrase (at i); and this is so regardless of whether the name happens to be a name like 'Porky' of an ordinary thing or a name like 'some pig' of a generic thing.

This story is preposterous since nothing, however recondite, can possibly have more or less than one of a set of incompatible and jointly exhaustive properties. At least, nothing can have more or less than one of them *as its properties*. But something, a set, can have *any* combination of them *as its members*; there is no contradiction in that.

Let us define the *character* of a thing as the set of its properties. Porkys' character is that set which has as members just those properties that Porky has as properties. The various generic pigs do not, and could not possibly, exist; but their characters do. The character of the universally generic pig, for instance, is the set having as members just those properties that every pig has as properties.

A *character* is any set of properties. A character is *individual* iff it is a maximal compatible set of properties, so that something could possess all and only the properties contained in it; otherwise the character is *generic*.

Since no two things share all their properties (on a sufficiently inclusive conception of properties) things correspond one-to-one to their individual characters. We can exploit this correspondence to replace things by their characters whenever convenient. Some philosophers have even tried to eliminate things altogether in favor of their characters, saying that things are 'bundles of properties'. (Such a system is proposed as a formal reconstruction of Leibniz's doctrine of possible individuals in Mates, 1968.) We need not go so far. We will replace things by individual characters as extensions of names, and as members of extensions of common nouns. However, we may keep the things themselves as well, taking them to be related to their names via their characters. Having made this substitution, we are ready to assimilate quantifier phrases to names by letting them also take characters – in most cases, generic characters – as extensions. 'Porky' has as extension Porky's individual character; 'every pig' has as extension the generic character of the universally generic pig. Even 'nobody' has an extension: the set of just those properties that nobody has.

We revise the system of meanings as follows. Our basic categories are *sentence* (S), *noun phrase* (NP), and *common noun* (C). Appropriate extensions for sentences are truth values; appropriate extensions for noun phrases are characters, either individual or generic; appropriate extensions for common nouns are sets of individual characters. Intensions are as before: for basic categories, functions from some or all indices to appropriate extensions; for a derived category $(c/c_1...c_n)$, functions from c_1-intensions, ..., and c_n-intensions to c-intensions. A *name* is an NP that never has a generic character as its extension at any index. The category of quantifiers becomes NP/C; the category of verb phrases becomes S/NP. Object-takers take NP objects which may or may not be names. Some variable-binding still is required; the two base structures for 'Every boy

loves some girl' are

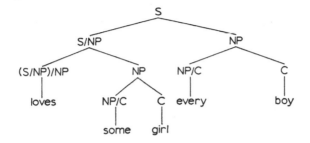

for the weak sense and

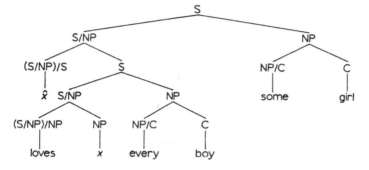

for the strong sense. Variables are names: the *n*th variable intension now becomes that NP-intension that assigns to every index *i* the character at the world coordinate of *i* of the thing that is the *n*th term of the assignment coordinate of *i*. The intensions of binders are revised to fit.

VIII. TREATMENT OF NON-DECLARATIVES

A meaning for a sentence, we said initially, was at least that which determines the conditions under which the sentence is true or false. But it is only declarative sentences that can be called true or false in any straightforward way. What of non-declarative sentences: commands, questions, and so on? If these do not have truth-values, as they are commonly supposed not to, we cannot very well say that their meanings determine their truth conditions.

One method of treating non-declaratives is to analyze all sentences, declarative or non-declarative, into two components: a *sentence radical* that specifies a state of affairs and a *mood* that determines whether the speaker is declaring that the state of affairs holds, commanding that it hold, asking whether it holds, or what. (I adopt the terminology of Stenius, 1967, one recent exposition of such a view.) We are to regard the sentences

> It is the case that you are late.
> Make it the case that you are late!
> Is it the case that you are late?

or more idiomatically

> You are late.
> Be late!
> Are you late?

as having a common sentence-radical specifying the state of affairs consisting of your being late, but differing in their moods: declarative, imperative, and interrogative. They might be given the base structures

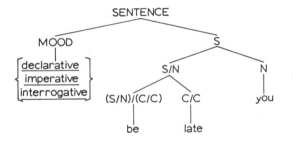

with S now understood as the category *sentence radical*. Different moods will induce different transformations of the sentence radical, leading to the different sentences above. The sentence radical is *not* a declarative sentence. If it is represented on the surface at all, it should be represented as the clause 'that you are late'. All that we have said about sentences should be taken as applying rather to sentence radicals. It is sentence radicals that have truth-values as extensions, functions from indices to truth-values as intensions, and meanings with the category S and an S-intension at the topmost node. We may grant that a declarative sentence is called true iff its sentence radical has the value *truth*; if we liked, we could also call an imperative or interrogative or other non-declarative sentence true iff its sentence radical has the value *truth*, but we customarily do not. Fundamentally, however, the entire apparatus of referential semantics (whether done on a categorial base as I propose, or otherwise) pertains to sentence radicals and constituents thereof. The semantics of mood is something entirely different. It consists of rules of language use such as these (adapted from Stenius, 1967):

Utter a sentence representing the combination of the mood *declarative* with an S-meaning *m* only if *m* is true on the occasion in question.

React to a sentence representing the combination of the mood *imperative* with an S-meaning *m* (if adressed to you by a person in a suitable relation of authority over you) by acting in such a way as to make *m* true on the occasion in question.

In abstract semantics, as distinct from the theory of language use, a meaning for a sentence should simply be a *pair* of a mood and an S-meaning (moods being identified with some arbitrarily chosen entities).

The method of sentence radicals requires a substantial revision of my system. It works well for declaratives, imperatives, and yes-no questions. It is hard to see how it could be applied to other sorts of questions, or to sentences like 'Hurrah for Porky!'

I prefer an alternative method of treating non-declaratives that requires no revision whatever in my system of categories, intensions, and meanings. Let us once again regard S as the category *sentence*, without discrimination of mood. But let us pay special attention to those sentential meanings that are represented by base structures of roughly the following form.

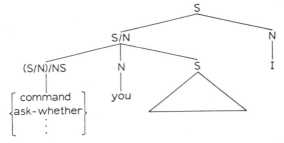

Such meanings can be represented by *performative sentences* such as these.

> I command you to be late.
> I ask you whether you are late.

(See Austin, 1962, for the standard account of performatives; but, as will be seen, I reject part of this account.) Such meanings might also be represented, after a more elaborate transformational derivation, by non-declaratives.

> Be late!
> Are you late?

I propose that these non-declaratives ought to be treated as paraphrases of the corresponding performatives, having the same base structure, meaning, intension, and truth-value at an index or on an occasion. And I propose that there is no difference in kind between the meanings of these performatives and non-declaratives and the meanings of the ordinary declarative sentences considered previously.

It is not clear whether we would classify the performative sentences as declarative. If not, then we can divide sentential meanings into declarative sentential meanings and non-declarative sentential meanings, the latter being represented both by performatives and by imperatives, questions, etc. But if, as I would prefer, we classify performatives as declarative, then the distinction between declarative and non-declarative sentences becomes a purely syntactic, surface distinction. The only distinction among meanings is the distinction between those sentential meanings that can only be represented by declarative sentences and those that can be represented either by suitable declarative sentences (performatives) or by non-declarative paraphrases thereof. Let us call the latter *performative sentential meanings*. I need not delineate the class of performative sentential meanings precisely, since I am claiming that they do *not* need to be singled out for special semantic treatment.

The method of paraphrased performatives can easily be extended to those non-declaratives that resisted treatment by the method of sentence radicals. Not only yes-no questions but other questions as well correspond to performative sentences. The sentences below

> I ask who Sylvia is.
> Who is Sylvia?

for instance, might have a common meaning represented by a base structure something like this.

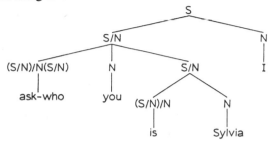

And the sentences

> I cheer Porky.
> Hurrah for Porky!

might have this base structure. (Thus the word 'Hurrah' would be introduced transformationally.)

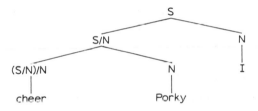

We may classify the sentential meanings represented by these base structures also as performative.

We noted at the outset that non-declaratives are commonly supposed to lack truth-values. The method of sentence radicals respects this common opinion by assigning truth-values fundamentally to sentence radicals rather than to whole sentences. We are under no compulsion to regard a non-declarative sentence as sharing the truth-value of its sentence radical, and we have chosen not to. The method of paraphrased performatives, on the other hand, does call for the assignment of truth-values to non-declarative sentences. The truth-value assigned is not that of the embedded sentence (corresponding to the sentence radical), however, but rather that of the paraphrased performative. If I say to you 'Be late!' and you are not late, the embedded sentence is false, but the paraphrased performative is true because I *do* command that you be late. I see no problem in letting non-declaratives have the truth-values of the performatives they paraphrase; after all, we need not ever mention their truth-values if we would rather not.

So far, I have assumed that performatives themselves do have truth-values, but that also has been denied. (Austin, 1962, Lecture I.) I would wish to say that 'I bet you sixpence it will rain tomorrow' is true on an occasion of utterance iff the utterer *does* then bet his audience sixpence that it will rain on the following day; and, if the occasion is normal in certain respects, the utterer does so bet; therefore his utterance is true. Austin says it is obviously neither true nor false, apparently because to utter the sentence (in normal circumstances) is to bet. Granted; but why is that a reason to deny that the utterance is true? To utter 'I am speaking' is to speak, but it is also to speak the truth. This much can be said in Austin's defense: the truth-values (and truth conditions, that is intensions) of performatives and their paraphrases are easily ignored just because it is hard for a performative to be anything but true on an occasion of its utterance. Hard but possible: you can be play-acting, practicing elocution, or impersonating an officer and say 'I command that you be late' falsely, that is, say it without thereby commanding your audience to be late. I claim that those are the very circumstances in which you could falsely say 'Be late!'; otherwise it, like the performative, is truly uttered when and because it is uttered. It is no wonder if the truth-conditions of the sentences embedded in performatives and their non-declarative paraphrases tend to eclipse the truth conditions of the performatives and non-declaratives themselves.

This eclipsing is most visible in the case of performative sentences of the form 'I state that ___' or 'I declare that ___'. If someone says 'I declare that the Earth is flat' (sincerely, not play-acting, etc.) I claim that he has spoken truly: he does indeed so declare. I claim this not only for the sake of my theory but as a point of common sense. Yet one might be tempted to say that he has spoken falsely, because the sentence embedded in his performative – the content of his declaration, the belief he avows – is false. Hence I do not propose to take ordinary declaratives as paraphrased performatives (as proposed in Ross, 1970) because that would get their truth conditions wrong. If there are strong syntactic reasons for adopting Ross's proposal, I would regard it as semantically a version of the method of sentence radicals, even if it employs base structures that look exactly like the base structures employed in the method of paraphrased performatives.

I provide only one meaning for the sentence 'I command you to be late'. Someone might well object that this sentence ought to come out ambiguous, because it can be used in two ways. It can be used to command; thus used, it can be paraphrased as 'Be late!', and it is true when uttered in normal circumstances just because it is uttered. It can be used instead to describe what I am doing; thus used, it cannot be paraphrased as an imperative, and it is likely to be false when uttered because it is difficult to issue a command and simultaneously say that I am doing so. (Difficult but possible: I might be doing the commanding by signing my name on a letter while describing what I am doing by talking.)

I agree that there are two alternative uses of this and other performative sentences: the genuinely performative use and the non-performative self-descriptive use. I agree also that the non-declarative paraphrase can occur only in the performative use. It still does not follow that there are two meanings. Compare the case of these two sentences.

> I am talking in trochaic hexameter.
> In hexameter trochaic am I talking.

The latter can be used to talk in trochaic hexameter and is true on any occasion of its correctly accented utterance. The former cannot be so used and is false on any occasion of its correctly accented utterance. Yet the two sentences are obviously paraphrases. Whether a sentence can be used to talk in trochaic hexameter is not a matter of its meaning. The distinction between using a sentence to talk in trochaic hexameter or not so using it is one sort of distinction; the distinction between using a performative sentence performatively and using it self-descriptively is quite another sort. Still I think the parallel is instructive. A distinction in uses need not involve a distinction in meanings of the sentences used. It can involve distinction in surface form; or distinction in conversational setting, intentions, and expectations; or distinction of some other sort. I see no decisive reason to insist that there is any distinction in meanings associated with the difference between performative and self-descriptive uses of performative sentences, if the contrary assumption is theoretically convenient.

We may ask to what extent the method of sentence radicals and the method of paraphrased performatives are compatible. In particular: given any sentence that can be analyzed into mood and sentence-radical, can we recover the mood and the sentence-radical intension from the meaning of the sentence according to the method of paraphrased performatives?

We almost can do this, but not quite. On the method of sentence radicals, the difference between the performative and self-descriptive uses of performative sentences *must* be treated as a difference of meanings. So given a performative sentence meaning, we will get two pairs of a mood and a sentence-radical intension corresponding to the two uses. Suppose we are given a performative sentential meaning represented by a base structure like this, for instance.

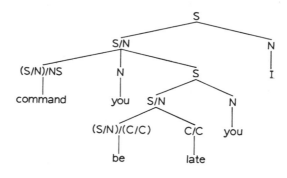

For the self-descriptive use, we do just what we would do for a non-performative sentence meaning: take the mood to be *declarative* and the sentence-radical intension to be the intension of the entire meaning. In this case, it would be the intension corresponding to the sentence radical 'that I command you to be late'. For the performative use, we take the mood to be determined by the (S/N)/NS-intension at node ⟨1 1⟩, and the sentence-radical intension to be the S-intension at node ⟨1 3⟩. In this case, these are respectively the intension of 'command', which determines that the mood is *imperative*, and the S-intension of the embedded sentence meaning, corresponding to the sentence radical 'that you are late'. Note here a second advantage, apart from fineness of individuation, of taking meanings as semantically interpreted phrase markers rather than as single intensions: we can recover the meanings of constituents from the meanings of their compounds.

APPENDIX: INDICES EXPANDED

Indices are supposed to be packages of everything but meaning that goes into determining extensions. Do we have everything? Let me speculate on several expansions of the indices that might prove useful.

First, consider the sentence 'This is older than *this*'. I might say it pointing at a 1962 Volkswagen when I say the first 'this' and at a 1963 Volkswagen when I say the second 'this'. The sentence should be true on such an occasion; but how can it be? Using the intension of 'this', with its sensitivity to the indicated-objects coordinate, we obtain the intension of the whole sentence; then we take the value of that intension at an index with world and contextual coordinates determined by features of the occasion of utterance. (We generalize over indices alike except at the assignment coordinate; but we can consider any one of these, since the assignment coordinate is irrelevant to the sentence in question.) This procedure ignores the fact that the indicated object changes part-way through the occasion of utterance. So the sentence comes out false, as it should on any occasion when the indicated object stays the same.

On a more extensional approach to semantics, a solution would be easy. We could take the two extensions of 'this' on the two occasions of its utterance and use these, rather than the fixed intension of 'this', to determine the truth-value of the sentence. The intension and the occasion of utterance of the sentence as a whole would drop out. But since the extensions of compounds are not in general determined by the extensions of their constituents, this extensional solution would preclude a uniform treatment of semantic projection rules.

An acceptable solution has been suggested to me by David Kaplan, as follows. Let the indicated-objects coordinate be not just one set of objects capable of being pointed at but an infinite sequence of such sets. Let the indicated-objects coordinate determined by a given occasion of utterance of a sentence have as its nth term the set of things pointed to at the nth utterance of 'this' during the utterance of the sentence so long as n does not exceed the number of such utterances, and let it be the empty set when n does exceed that number. Let there be an infinite sequence of constituents 'this$_1$', 'this$_2$',... with intensions such that 'this$_n$' depends for its extension at an index on the nth term of the assignment coordinate. So that the lexicon will remain finite, let all but 'this$_1$' be compounds generated by iterated application of a suitable N/N to 'this$_1$'. Let all members of the sequence appear as 'this' in surface structure. Use transformational filtering to dispose of all base structures except those employing an initial segment of the 'this'-sequence so arranged that if the subscripts were carried to the surface, they would appear in numerical order without repetition. Thus the only base structure for 'This is older than this' will be

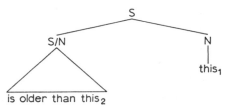

which will be true on occasions of the sort in question.

The solution must be modified to allow for the fact that 'this' is not the only demonstrative; I omit details. Similar difficulties arise, and similar solutions are possible, for other contextual coordinates: time, place, audience, and perhaps speaker.

Second, consider the sentence 'The door is open'. This does not mean that the one and only door that now exists is open; nor does it mean that the one and only door near the place of utterance, or pointed at, or mentioned in previous discourse, is open. Rather it means that the one and only door among the objects that are somehow prominent on the occasion is open. An object may be prominent because it is nearby, or pointed at, or mentioned; but none of these is a necessary condition of contextual prominence. So perhaps we need a *prominent-objects coordinate*, a new contextual coordinate independent of the others. It will be determined, on a given occasion of utterance of a sentence, by mental factors such as the speaker's expectations regarding the things he is likely to bring to the attention of his audience.

Third, consider the suggestion (Kaplan, 1968; Donnellan, 1970) that the extension of a personal name on a given occasion depends partly on the causal chain leading from the bestowal of that name on some person to the later use of that name by a speaker on the occasion in question. We might wish to accept this theory, and yet wish to deny that the intension or meaning of the name depends, on the occasion in question, upon the causal history of the speaker's use of it; for we might not wish to give up the common presumption that the meaning of an expression for a speaker depends only on mental factors within him. We might solve this dilemma (as proposed in Lewis, 1968b) by including a *causal-history-of-acquisition-of-names coordinate* in our indices and letting the intensions of names for a speaker determine their extensions only relative to that coordinate.

Fourth, we have so far been ignoring the vagueness of natural language. Perhaps we are right to ignore it, or rather to deport it from semantics to the theory of language-use. We could say (as I did in Lewis, 1969, Chapter V) that languages themselves are free of vagueness but that the linguistic conventions of a population, or the linguistic habits of a person, select not a point but a fuzzy region in the space of precise languages. However, it might prove better to treat vagueness within semantics, and we could do so as follows. (A related treatment, developed independently, is to be found in Goguen, 1969.)

Pretend first that the only vagueness is the vagueness of 'cool' and 'warm'; and suppose for simplicity that these are extensional adjectives. Let the indices contain a *delineation coordinate*: a positive real number, regarded as the boundary temperature between cool and warm things. Thus at an index i the extension of 'cool' is the set of things at the world and time coordinates of i having temperatures (in degrees Kelvin) less than or equal to the delineation coordinate of i; the extension of 'warm' is the set of such things having temperatures greater than the delineation coordinate. A vague sentence such as 'This is cool' is true, on a given occasion, at some but not all delineations; that is, at some but not all indices that are alike except in delineation and have the world and contextual coordinates determined by the occasion of utterance. But sentences with vague constituents are not necessarily vague: 'This is cool or warm, but not both' is true at all delineations, on an occasion on which there is a unique indicated object, even if the indicated object is lukewarm.

The delineation coordinate is non-contextual. It resembles the assignment coordinate, in that we will ordinarily generalize over it rather than hold it fixed. We may say that a sentence is *true over* a set s of delineations at an index i, iff, for any index i' that is like i except perhaps at the delineation coordinate, the sentence is true at i' if and only if the delineation coordinate of i' belongs to s. Given a normalized measure function over delineations, we can say that a sentence is *true to degree d* at *i* iff it is true at *i* over a set of delineations of measure *d*. Note that the degree of truth of a truth-functional compound of sentences is not a function of the degrees of truth of its constituent sentences: '*x* is cool' and '*x* is warm' may both be true to degree .5 at an index *i*, but '*x* is cool or *x* is cool' is true at *i* to degree .5 whereas '*x* is cool or *x* is warm' is true at *i* to degree 1.

Treating vagueness within semantics makes for simple specifications of the intensions of such expressions as 'in some sense', 'paradigmatic', '____ish', and '____er than'. The contemporary idiom 'in some sense', for instance, is an S/S related to the delineation coordinate just as the modal operator 'possibly' is related to the world coordinate. The intension of 'in some sense' is that function ϕ such that if ϕ_1 is any S-intension, ϕ_2 is $\phi(\phi_1)$, and *i* is any index, then

$$\phi_2(i) = \begin{cases} truth \text{ if, for some index } i' \text{ that is like } i \text{ except perhaps} \\ \quad \text{at the delineation coordinate, } \phi_1(i') \text{ is } truth \\ falsity \text{ otherwise.} \end{cases}$$

The comparative '____er than' is a $((C/C)/N)/(C/C)$ having an intension such that, for instance, '*x* is cooler than *y*' is true at an index *i* iff the set of delineations over which '*y* is cool' is true at *i* is a proper subset of the set of delineations over which '*x* is cool' is true at *i*. It follows that the sun is not cooler than Sirius unless in some sense the sun is cool; but that conclusion seems correct, although I do not know whether to deny that the sun is cooler than Sirius or to agree that in some sense the sun is cool. (This analysis of comparatives was suggested to me by David Kaplan.)

More generally, the delineation coordinate must be a sequence of boundary-specifying numbers. Different vague expressions will depend for their extensions (or, if they are not extensional, for the extensions of their extensional compounds) on different terms of the delineation. More than one term of the delineation coordinate might be involved for a single expression. For instance, the intension of 'green' might involve one term regarded as delineating the blue-green boundary and another regarded as delineating the green-yellow boundary. The former but not the latter would be one of the two terms involved in the intension of 'blue'; and so on around the circle of hues.

BIBLIOGRAPHY

Kazimierz Ajdukiewicz, 'Die syntaktische Konnexität', *Studia Philosophica* **1** (1935) 1–27; translated as 'Syntactic Connexion' in S. McCall, *Polish Logic*, Oxford 1967, pp. 207–231. Part I translated as 'On Syntactical Coherence', *Review of Metaphysics* **20** (1967) 635–647.

J. L. Austin, *How to Do Things with Words*, Harvard University Press, Cambridge, Mass., 1962.

Yehoshua Bar-Hillel, *Language and Information*, Addison-Wesley, Reading, Mass., 1964.

Paul Benacerraf, 'What Numbers Could Not Be', *Philosophical Review* **74** (1965) 47–73.

Rudolf Carnap, *Meaning and Necessity*, University of Chicago Press, Chicago, Illinois, 1947.

Rudolf Carnap, *Introduction to Symbolic Logic*, Dover, New York, 1958.

Rudolf·Carnap, 'Replies and Systematic Expositions', in P. Schilpp, *The Philosophy of Rudolf Carnap*, Open Court, La Salle, Illinois, 1963.

Noam Chomsky, *Aspects of the Theory of Syntax*, M.I.T. Press, Cambridge, Mass., 1965.

Alonzo Church, *The Calculi of Lambda Conversion*, Princeton University Press, Princeton, N.J., 1941.

Donald Davidson, 'Truth and Meaning', *Synthese* **17** (1967) 304–323.

Charles L. Dodgson, *Through the Looking-Glass*, London, 1871.

Keith Donnellan, 'Proper Names and Identifying Descriptions', *Synthese* **21** (1970) 335–358.

Gottlob Frege, 'Über Sinn und Bedeutung', *Zeitschrift für Philosophie und philosophische Kritik* **100** (1892) 25–50; translated as 'On Sense and Reference' in P. T. Geach and M. Black, *Translations from the Philosophical Writings of Gottlob Frege*, Blackwell, Oxford, 1960.

J. A. Goguen, 'The Logic of Inexact Concepts', *Synthese* **19** (1969) 325–373.

David Kaplan, *Foundations of Intensional Logic* (doctoral dissertation), University Microfilms, Ann Arbor, Michigan, 1964.

David Kaplan, 'Quantifying In', *Synthese* **19** (1968) 178–214.

Jerrold Katz and Paul Postal, *An Integrated Theory of Linguistic Descriptions*, M.I.T. Press, Cambridge, Mass., 1964.

Edward Keenan, *A Logical Base for English* (doctoral dissertation, duplicated), 1969.

Saul Kripke, 'Semantical Considerations on Modal Logic', *Acta Philosophica Fennica* **16** (1963) 83–94.

George Lakoff, 'On Generative Semantics' in *Semantics: An Interdisciplinary Reader in Philosophy, Linquistics, Anthropology and Psychology* (ed. by Danny Steinberg and Leon Jakobovits), Cambridge University Press, Cambridge, 1970.

Clarence I. Lewis, 'The Modes of Meaning', *Philosophy and Phenomenological Research* **4** (1944) 236–249.

David Lewis, 'Counterpart Theory and Quantified Modal Logic', *Journal of Philosophy* **65** (1968) 113–126. (1968a).

David Lewis, 'Languages and Language', to appear in the *Minnesota Studies in the Philosophy of Science*. (1968b).

David Lewis, *Convention: A Philosophical Study*, Harvard University Press, Cambridge, Mass., 1969.

John Lyons, 'Towards a "Notional" Theory of the "Parts of Speech"', *Journal of Linguistics* **2** (1966) 209–236.

Benson Mates, 'Leibniz on Possible Worlds' in *Logic, Methodology, and Philosophy of Science III* (ed. by B. van Rootselaar and J. F. Staal), North-Holland Publ. Co., Amsterdam, 1968.

James McCawley, 'Concerning the Base Component of a Transformational Grammar', *Foundations of Language* 4 (1968) 243–269.

James McCawley, 'Semantic Representation', paper presented to a symposium on Cognitive Studies and Artificial Intelligence Research, University of Chicago Center for Continuing Education, March 1969.

Richard Montague, 'Logical Necessity, Physical Necessity, Ethics, and Quantifiers', *Inquiry* 3 (1960) 259–269.

Richard Montague, 'Pragmatics' in *Contemporary Philosophy – La philosophie contemporaine* (ed. by R. Klibansky), La Nuova Italia Editrice, Florence 1968.

Richard Montague, 'Intensional Logic and Some of Its Connections with Ordinary Language', talk delivered to the Southern California Logic Colloquium, April 1969, and to the Association of Symbolic Logic meeting at Cleveland, Ohio, May 1969.

Richard Montague, 'English as a Formal Language I' in *Linguaggi nella società e nella tecnica,* Edizioni di Communità, Milan, 1970. (1970a).

Richard Montague, 'Universal Grammar', *Theoria* 36 (1970). (1970b).

Richard Montague, 'Pragmatics and Intensional Logic', *Synthese* 22 (1970) 68–94 (1970c).

Terence Parsons, *A Semantics for English* (duplicated), 1968.

P. Stanley Peters and R. W. Ritchie, *On the Generative Power of Transformational Grammars,* Technical Report in Computer Science, University of Washington, Seattle, Wash., 1969.

John R. Ross, 'On Declarative Sentences', *Readings in Transformational Grammar* (ed. by R. Jacobs and P. Rosenbaum), Blaisdell, Boston, Mass. (1970).

Dana Scott, 'Advice on Modal Logic' in *Philosophical Problems in Logic: Recent Developments* (ed. by Karel Lambert), D. Reidel Publishing Company, Dordrecht, 1970, pp. 143–173.

Erik Stenius, 'Mood and Language-Game', *Synthese* 17 (1967) 254–274.

P. F. Strawson, 'On Referring', *Mind* 59 (1950) 320–344.

Alfred Tarski, 'Der Wahrheitsbegriff in den formalisierten Sprachen', *Studia Philosophica* 1 (1936) 261–405; translated as 'The Concept of Truth in Formalized Languages' in Tarski, *Logic, Semantics, Metamathematics,* Oxford, 1956.

Richmond Thomason and Robert Stalnaker, 'Modality and Reference', *Noûs* 2 (1968) 359–372.

Bruce Vermazen, review of Jerrold Katz and Paul Postal, *An Integrated Theory of Linguistic Descriptions,* and Katz, *Philosophy of Language, Synthese* 17 (1967) 350–365.

John Wallace, 'Sortal Predicates and Quantification', *Journal of Philosophy* 62 (1965) 8–13.

REFERENCE

*This paper is derived from a talk given at the Third La Jolla Conference on Linguistic Theory, March 1969. I am much indebted to Charles Chastain, Frank Heny, David Kaplan, George Lakoff, Richard Montague, and Barbara Partee for many valuable criticisms and suggestions.

JOHN WALLACE

ON THE FRAME OF REFERENCE[1]

> Never ask for the meaning of a word in isolation, but
> only in the context of a sentence.
>
> G. FREGE

In philosophy we are sometimes interested in the invariants of intelligi-
bility. What do all good (adequate, successful, fair) interpretations of a
language, or of a person, have in common? What common reality is
projected by our understanding of each other?[2] What do persons share
that makes communication possible? Some voices in the tradition coach
us to look for answers in subject matter, or ontology (physical objects,
numbers, universals, propositions), in law governed relational systems
such as causality, in deep logical structures such as predication and
quantification, in universally applied concepts such as identity, truth,
order, and in language-wide principles of interchange, such as the
principle of extensionality. One may think here also of attitudes, such as
belief, that every person takes toward "propositions", of laws of deductive logic and, after Ramsey and de Finetti, of the calculus of probability.

From a semantical point of view, quantification, ontology, predication,
and extensionality form a single structure.[3] The semantical interpretation
of predication is that predicates are satisfied by objects, independently of
how objects are described; satisfiers of quantified sentences are determined by satisfiers of their predicate parts, relative to a universe of discourse. This semantical point of view is Tarski's; the referential structure
it brings to light is exactly represented in Tarski's theory of truth for
quantificational languages.

C. I. Lewis emphasized that the categories philosophy seeks to represent will likely be relative to socially shared functions or goals. We see
a partial reflection of this point in Tarski's theory: there the goal was a
theory of truth that explained a language-wide range of biconditionals of
the form of

'snow is white' is true ↔ snow is white.

A recursive theory of satisfaction, with its relativity to a universe of
discourse, emerged as a means to that end.

Davidson and Harman (eds.), Semantics of Natural Language, 219–252. *All rights reserved*
Copyright © 1972 by D. Reidel Publishing Company, Dordrecht-Holland

The question naturally arises: is the referential structure Tarski's theory represents categorial in character? Is it contained in every reasonable theory of truth? Or is it an artifact of Tarski's approach? Tarski alludes to the question in the following passage:

It may seem strange that we have chosen a roundabout way of defining the truth of a sentence, instead of trying to apply, for instance, a direct recursive procedure. The reason is that compound sentences are constructed from simpler sentential functions, but not always from sentences; hence no general recursive method is known which applies specifically to sentences.[4]

The purpose of this paper is to formulate and give evidence for a claim that under natural conditions a theory of truth is a recursive theory of satisfaction. The claim implies a strong form of the thesis of extensionality. If the claim is true, it provides a sense in which semantics for sentences is inseparable from extensional semantics for predicates and quantifiers.

The key idea is to play off against one another the familiar paradigms for the concepts of truth, satisfaction, and identity. In a form transparent to intuition, these are[5]:

(1)   '____' is true if and only if ____
(2)   '____' is satisfied by every____thing and nothing else
(3)   if x and y are in the universe of discourse and satisfy Eq, then x satisfies '____' if and only if y satisfies '____'.

The gaps in (1) are for sentences, in (2) and (3) for predicates. 'Eq' represents a canonical name of an open sentence (of the object language) containing two free variables. Notice that (3) is a metalinguistic form of the replacement schema for identity:

$$(x)\,(y)\,(x = y \rightarrow (Fx \leftrightarrow Fy)).$$

In essence, my claim will be this: if a finite theory puts enough conditions on 'true' to entail all instances of (1) (i.e., if it meets Tarski's Convention T) then it puts enough conditions on some relation 'satisfies' and on some name 'Eq' to entail (3) and all instances of (2). Tarski showed that satisfaction is a way to truth; I hope to persuade you that it is the way.

It should be emphasized that the relation 'satisfies' will not in general be a primitive of the metalanguage; it may be a complex open sentence that the theory's inventor never thought of and that appears in no theorems he called axioms. It is constructed from the theory's primitives and appears in its theorems. Similarly, 'Eq' will in general stand for a complex open sentence of the object language.

In the cases of languages that contain functional expressions (e.g., 'the father of') which (a) apply to quantifiable variables and (b) recursively to results of their own application, part (3) of the claim must be significantly weakened. In this case, identity still emerges in what is intuitively a "compact" bundle, but not always as a single sentence; the bundle will in general be an infinite class of sentences. This matter is intimately connected with Russell's theory of definite descriptions; it is discussed in Section VIII below.

Evidence for the claim is empirical. I discuss several non-Tarskian settings and strategies for truth theory to bring out why they should not be expected to generate counterexamples. Among the alternatives considered are: (1) the substitution interpretation of quantifiers ("a universal quantification is true if and only if all its substitution instances are true"); (2) straight semantics and possible world semantics for modal logic; (3) semantics for quotation marks (due to Raymond Smullyan); (4) variable free formulations of quantification theory (Schoenfinkel, Bernays, Quine); (5) Wang's strategy for systems with an infinite number of primitives; (6) semantics for languages that contain functional expression into which quantifications are made. Such empirical evidence is of course not conclusive. The additional analysis that would be needed to cast the claim in a form subject to mathematical proof (or refutation) seems quite difficult; I have not been able to carry it out.

The paper divides into nine sections. The first treats of adequacy conditions for truth theory. The second sets out the theory of satisfaction. Sections III–VIII take up the alternative approaches to truth theory mentioned in the preceding paragraph. Section IX explores philosophical implications of the formal-semantical structure isolated in what has come before it.

I. CONVENTION T AND PREDICATE CALCULUS

What is an adequate theory of truth? Tarski has made four points about the answer to this question.[6]

(1) The intuitive concept of truth is language-relative. This is obvious

if the concept of truth applies to sentences, and sentences are inscriptions or approximate geometric patterns; a pattern may be true in one language, false in another.

(2) A language cannot contain its own truth predicate; that is, "true-in-myself" is not a concept of any language. This point is an effect of the semantic paradoxed. It deepens point (1), by making it apparent that relativity of truth to language cannot be eliminated *simply* by positing intensional entities such as propositions; unless elaborate precautions are taken, these merely pave the road to paradox.

(3) Only complete, closed sentences of a language are true in that language. Sentence-like expressions that involve "unbound" pronouns e.g., 'I love you', indicator words, tense are not absolutely true or false; they are true or false relative to a way of fixing the references of these variable-like devices.

(4) Tarski's next point concerns the role of *partial definitions* of truth, i.e., sentences of the form of

'Lizzy is playful' is true if and only if Lizzy is playful,

in setting adequacy conditions for a theory of truth. Roughly, an adequate theory of truth for a given object language must explain each partial definition of truth. Suppose the metalanguage – the language *in* which truth theory is being given – is English; then a more exact statement of the adequacy condition is that the theory should explain each sentence obtained from the expression 'x is true if and only if *p*' by putting for '*x*' a structural-descriptive name of a sentence of the object language and for '*p*' a translation of that sentence into English. Here several notions have to be made definite before the adequacy of a proposed theory can be tested. Conspicuously, explanation, structural-descriptive name, and translation. But also the sense of 'if and only if' in the partial definitions, or more generally, the logical form of the partial definitions.

At this point it seems essential to bring in the idea of a logical calculus. Such a calculus carries with it accounts of sentence, logical consequence, theory, consistency and of the form of conditionals. It enables us to equate explanation with deducibility from a finite and consistent theory. Also, as part of its account of *sentence*, it may be expected to give a sense to the idea of *all* the sentences built on the vocabulary of a given sentence. It is not clear that a logical calculus is anything but an account of these notions and perhaps a few others of the same kind. The number of logical calculi that might be invented is very great; one can see this by reflecting on those that have actually been proposed and on the fact that logical calculi have "natural" fragments which are again logical calculi. This multiplicity is compounded by the difficulty in fixing the sense of 'logical constant' and thus of 'logical consequence'. Some limits can nevertheless be set.

Sentences must be of finite length. Because we are thinking of theories about natural language expressible in natural language.

Not too strong a sense of conditionality can be used in the partial definitions. For example, Lewis' strict implication would not be appropriate: it simply is not logically true that 'Lizzy is playful' is true-in-English if and only if (materially) Lizzy is playful, unless 'true-in-English', 'Lizzy', 'playful', ' 'Lizzy is playful' ', etc. are all logical constants. And taking all partial definitions into account, the implication in them is not strict unless *all* constant are logical constants. The material conditional itself seems strong enough; it is used in this connection by Tarski.

Logical consequence, on the other hand, must be stronger (i.e., connect more sentences) than truth-functional consequence, or no finite uniform explanation of all partial definitions will be possible. Each subset of the set of partial definitions is truth-functionally independent of its complement. And any consistent finite set of finite sentences has as its truth-functional consequences at most a finite set of partial definitions. Thus the logical calculus that underlies a truth theory must contain a finer analysis of consequence than mere truth-functional consequence. Very likely, it will be a predicate calculus.

It is worth noticing that one important decision about the logical form of the partial definitions has already been made (in points (1) and (2)): 'true' has the logical role of a predicate and not that of a sentential operator. In model logic where e.g., 'necessarily-true' is treated as a sentential operator it has ordinarily been thought plausible to take e.g., all instances of

$$\Box p \rightarrow p$$

as logical axioms. If true' were treated similarly,

$$\text{it is true that } p \leftrightarrow p$$

might also be taken as an axiom schema. The opportunity of asking for an explanation of the partial definitions would be lost. But we have taken the other approach; 'true' is a predicate; and the demand for a finite theory of truth is significant.

Why should an adequate theory of truth be finite? We want a theory of truth to be analytic or recursive, picking out a finite number of compoundable features of sentences whose effects on truth conditions are uniform. On the other hand, we want not to say in advance what the compoundable features and their effects are. A recursion we want; the shape or strategy of the recursion we want to leave open. The demand for a finite theory seems a – perhaps crude – way of satisfying both desires. To demand only that the theory be recursively axiomatizable is too weak: the set of partial definitions is itself recursive. But obviously no analysis is achieved by a theory that simply takes all "target" biconditionals as axioms.

The demands Tarski's Convention T places on a theory of truth are in some respects stronger than the ones discussed above.[7] It fixes the predicate calculi to be theories of types. And it demands that a *definition* of truth-in-L, having all partial definitions as consequences, be given in the language of type one higher than L. More generally, one may say that Tarski fixes the avenue along which strength is added to the object language, in forming the metalanguage, to be set theory; then he asks for an *explicit definition* of truth. For the purposes of this paper it seems desirable not to impose demands of this kind, but rather to leave as open as possible the means by which recursive or analytic theories are achieved.

We have yet to discuss the notions of translation and canonical description used in the characterization of *adequate theory of truth*. What is a good or correct translation between two languages is of course a difficult question on which there is little substantive agreement and less hard theory. In the case of truth theories taken up in this paper the general problem of translation is bypassed in two ways: (1) we shall usually be interested in cases where the object language is included in the metalanguage, e.g., ML = OL + a bit of recursive apparatus; in these cases we study the identity translation, which seems clearly to be a good one; (2) the main results of the paper extend to large classes of translations, but these classes can be characterized in terms of abstract structural features of translations, e.g., translations such that every sentence in a certain class of metalanguage sentences is a translation of something.

If we are thinking of translating natural languages, and of applying truth theory to natural languages, it seems reasonable to require that every sentence built from vocabulary that occurs in translations be a translation. Formally, if $S_1, ..., S_n$ are sentences of L_2 that translate some sentences of L_1 and if S_{n+1} is a sentence of L_2 built from vocabulary that occurs in $S_1, ..., S_n$ then S_{n+1} translates some sentence of L_1. The motivation for this requirement is that it is hard to see how one can have good reason to attribute to someone the ability to express, e.g., 'someone loves someone' and 'someone is taller than someone' without having good reason to attribute to him the ability to express e.g. 'someone loves someone taller than himself'. This requirement will be invoked from time to time in what follows.

In the *Wahrheitsbegriff* structural-descriptive names are obtained by spelling or, technically, the theory of concatenation, e.g. 'ay$^\wedge$bee$^\wedge$see' might naturally name the expression 'abc'. Alternatively, one might obtain structural-descriptive names by a system of Gödel numbering. Or thinking of sentences as shapes, one might describe them by equations à la Descartes. It will not be necessary for us to fix the details of structural-descriptive naming. I will represent the structural descriptive name of an expression by drawing a line over it. Thus $\overline{\text{Lizzy is playful}}$ represents the structural-descriptive name of 'Lizzy is playful'.

This section has had a generality that will completely drop out in what follows; we will be looking at particular truth theories formulated in familiar predicate calculi. It seemed worth emphasizing in a general setting the ideas that truth theory ties together: sentence, truth, consequence, conditionality, translation. In framing a theory we must jump to a simultaneous view of all these matters. As a side effect, this general view enables me to distinguish the theory of truth from another subject with which it can be confused, namely, the theory of models. We are interested in 'true-in-L' for various particular L; we are not interested in 'true in M' for variable M. Also, it is sufficient for our purposes that the notion of logical consequence be characterized proof theoretically; if it has in addition a model theoretic characterization, knowing that may deepen or speed our enquiries. But the basic condition of adequacy for truth theory could have been applied to modal languages in C. I. Lewis' day, before the invention of a model theory for them.

II. THE SATISFACTION INTERPRETATION

In setting out Tarski's theory of satisfaction I will assume that both object
language and metalanguage are built on the pattern of classical single
sorted quantification theory (formulated in the usual way with variables).[8]
The notion of logical consequence used will be ordinary first order consequence. I will pitch the discussion to the homophonic truth theory: the
metalanguage includes the object language and the theory implies

$$\text{True } (F) \leftrightarrow F$$

for each closed sentence $\ulcorner F \urcorner$ of the object language.

The intuitive recursion in the satisfaction interpretation of quantificational languages may be set out as follows ('sequence' is short for 'sequence of individuals from the universe of discourse of the object
language'):

Part I: Connectives
- (1) A negation is satisfied by a sequence if and only if what is
  negated is not satisfied by the sequence.
- (2) A conjunction is satisfied by a sequence if and only if both
  of the conjuncts are satisfied by the sequence.

Part II: Quantification
- (3) An existential quantification $\overline{(Ex_n)F}$ (of the open sentence
  F with respect to the nth variable) is satisfied by a sequence
  if and only if F is satisfied by at least one sequence that
  differs from the given one at most at the nth place.

Part III: Atomic predicates: suppose one atomic predicate 'before'; by
the convention introduced in the last section, the structural-
descriptive name of this predicate is represented by $\overline{\text{'before'}}$.
- (4) A predication of $\overline{\text{before}}$ with the variables x_m and x_n (in
  that order) is satisfied by a sequence if and only if the mth
  member of the sequence is before the nth member of the
  sequence.

In (4) we used on the right side of the biconditional the predicate named
on the left side. In general, the recursion contains a clause of this kind for
each atomic predicate of the object language. In recursions aimed at other

than the homophonic truth theory, we use on the right a translation of the predicate named on the left. Clauses for atomic predicates are sometimes called the *basis* clauses of the recursion.

This recursion can be precisely expressed in a metalanguage that contains in addition to predicates and logical apparatus of the object language (1) arithmetic, (2) syntactical apparatus for structural-descriptive names, (3) a two-place predicate 'Sat', (4) a one-place predicate 'Seq', (5) a two-place function sign 'Val'. Intuitively, Val (s, n) is the nth member of s. I assume also that the metalanguage contains a standard theory of identity. For convenience I will use 's', 's'', 's''' as variables ranging over sequences, 'f', 'g', as variables ranging over well-formed formulas (i.e., open or closed sentences), 'n', 'm' as variables ranging over natural numbers. This is not primitive notation and does not destroy the single-sorted character of the metalanguage, because the metalanguage contains predicates that express sequence, sentence, number. The expression

'$s \overset{n}{\approx} s'$' will abbreviate '$(m)$ $(m \neq n \rightarrow$ Val $(s, m) =$ Val $(s', m))$'; intuitively it means that the sequence s differs from the sequence s' at most at the nth place. Other notations used in the following first order representation of the recursion should be self-explanatory.

(1') s Sat neg $(f) \leftrightarrow \sim (s \text{ Sat } f)$

(2') s Sat conj $(f, g) \leftrightarrow (s \text{ Sat } f \ \& \ s \text{ Sat } g)$

(3') s Sat exquant $(f, \bar{x}_n) \leftrightarrow (Es') (s \overset{n}{\approx} s' \ \& \ s' \text{ Sat } f)$

(4') s Sat pred (before, $\bar{x}_m$, $\bar{x}_n) \leftrightarrow$ Val (s, m) is before Val (s, n).

In addition to these recursion clauses we must have in a theory of this kind assertions that are explicitly ontological in character. First, the assertion that there are sequences:

(5') $(Ex) (\text{Seq } x)$.

Second, an assertion that sequences vary freely over a certain range; this assertion has the form

$$Rx \rightarrow (Es') (s \overset{n}{\approx} s' \ \& \ \text{Val } (s', n) = x).$$

What it is appropriate to fill in for 'Rx' will vary from theory to theory, depending on the translation from object language to metalanguage. If we are aiming at the homophonic truth theory, 'Rx' must be replaced by a provably universal predicate, e.g., '$x=x$' or, better, omitted. Thus our last axiom is

(6') $(Es') (s \overset{n}{\approx} s' \ \& \ \text{Val} \ (s', n) = x)$.

(The free variables in (1')–(6') are of course supposed to receive the universality interpretation.)

Let us establish the convention that $\overline{Fx_{k_1}...x_{k_n}}$ has exactly the variables $\bar{x}_{k_1}, ..., \bar{x}_{k_n}$ free in it and that $\ulcorner F \text{Val} \ (s, k_1)...\text{Val} \ (s, k_n) \urcorner$ is the result of replacing those variables, in order, by the indicated terms. We can prove in the theory every sentence of the following form:

(A) $s \ \text{Sat} \ \overline{Fx_{k_1}...x_{k_n}} \leftrightarrow F \text{Val} \ (s, k_1)...\text{Val} \ (s, k_n)$.

Sentences of this form may be thought of as *partial definitions of satisfaction*. Notice that they make essential use of 'Val'.

The present theory gives '$s \ \text{Sat} \ f$' the intuitive sense: f comes out true when the reference of each of its free variables is fixed to be the value of that variable under s. Evidently, whether a sequence satisfies a sentence depends only on what the sequence assigns to numbers corresponding to variables free in the sentence. If the sentence is closed, whether it is satisfied by a sequence does not depend at all on what the members of the sequence are. A closed sentence is true if it is satisfied by every sequence, and false otherwise. Thus we can define:

(B) $\text{True} \ x =_{\text{df.}} (s) (\text{Seq} \ s \rightarrow s \ \text{Sat} \ x) \ \& \ x$ is a closed sentence .

Hilbert and Bernays observed that every first-order language with a finite primitive vocabulary of predicates (singular terms are excluded) contains an open sentence $\ulcorner Rxy \urcorner$ with two free variables such that

$(x) \ Rxx$

and all sentences of the form

$(x) (y) (Rxy \rightarrow (Fx \leftrightarrow Fy))$

are logically provable.[9] Intuitively, $\ulcorner Rxy \urcorner$ says that x and y are indistinguishable by atomic predicates of the language, relative to the ontology of the language. For example, if the only atomic predicate is 'before', the

Hilbert-Bernays method gives the open sentence

(z) ((x is before $z \leftrightarrow y$ is before z) & (z is before $x \leftrightarrow z$ is before y)) .

This method works also for the case in which the language contains constant singular terms – even if these are infinite in number. It does not work when there are functional expressions that take variables and into which one can quantify. This case is taken up in Section VIII below. Fom the point of view of truth theory, the object language predicate constructed by this method has the following properties, where for convenience 'Eq' will be treated as the structural-descriptive name of the predicate; it is assumed that the variables free in Eq are the first two variables of the language; Eq′ results from identifying the variables in Eq.

(C) s Sat Eq′

(D)   Val $(s, 1) = x$ & Val $(s, 2) = y$ & s Sat Eq $\rightarrow (s')\,(s'')\,(n)\,(f)$

$(s' \overset{n}{\approx} s''$ & Val $(s', n) = x$ & Val $(s'', n) = y \rightarrow (s'$ Sat $f \leftrightarrow s''$ Sat $f)$.

The latter statement is proved by induction on (the complexity of) f; the cases in the proof mirror in the straightforward way the basis and recursion clauses in the theory.

Five formulas now sum up the effects of a satisfactional truth theory that produces the homophonic partial definitions of truth.

(I)   True $(\overline{F}) \leftrightarrow F$

(II) (x) (True $(x) \leftrightarrow x$ is a closed sentence & (s) (Seq $s \rightarrow s$ Sat x))

(III) s Sat $\overline{Fx_{k_1} \dots x_{k_n}} \leftrightarrow F$ Val $(s, k_1) \dots$ Val (s, k_n)

(IV) s Sat Eq′

(V) $\langle x, y \rangle$ Sat Eq $\rightarrow (\langle \dots x \dots \rangle$ Sat $f \leftrightarrow \langle \dots y \dots \rangle$ Sat $f)$.

(V) is a perspicuous condensation of (D) obtained by exploiting the natural pointed bracket notation for sequences. Formulas (II), (IV), and (V) represent sentences provable from the theory of truth; (I) and (III) are schemata all of the instances of which are provable from the theory. These five formulas define the structure we now set out to discern in non-standard, non-satisfactional truth theories.

III. THE SUBSTITUTION INTERPRETATION

In exploring the substitution interpretation of quantifiers I will use the same background logic and the same aim for truth theory as in the preceding section: first-order languages, ordinary first order consequence, aimed at homophonic truth theory. Three substitutional strategies will be taken up; (1) the Naive, (2) the Hilbert-Bernays, and (3) the McKinsey.[10]

The intuitive recursion in the Naive substitution interpretation of quantificational languages may be set out as follows:

Part I: Connectives
            (1) A negation is true if and only if what is negated is not true.
            (2) A conjunction is true if and only if both of the conjuncts are true.

Part II: Quantification
            (3) An existential quantification $\overline{Ex_nFx_n}$ is true if and only if some substitution instance of $F\bar{x}_n$ is true.

The term 'substitution instance' is explained in terms of a substitution class (class of substitutes) and a syntactical operation ("substitution") that compounds members of the class with one-place open sentences. Typically the substitution class will consist of names or numerals and the syntactical operation will replace variables in open sentences by names (or numerals). But the substitution class *could* consist of e.g., parentheses[11]; substitution could be any constructive operation that takes triples consisting of a member of the substitution class, a variable, and an open sentence into closed sentences. In a self-explanatory notation, (1)–(3) might be expressed as follows:

(1′)   True (neg (f)) $\leftrightarrow \sim$ True (f)
(2′)   True (conj (f, g)) $\leftrightarrow$ (True (f) & True (g))
(3′)   True (exquant (f, v_n)) $\leftrightarrow (Ea)$ (s-class (a) & True (sub (a, v_n, f))).

the sense of 'sub (a, v_n, f)' is that a is substituted for all *free* occurrences of v_n in f, and only for these.

Basis clauses are so far lacking in the Naive theory: no use is made in (1′)–(3′) of atomic predicates. It is evident therefore that (1′)–(3′) do not entail the wanted partial definitions of truth, for these contain essential occurrences of atomic predicates. What must be added?

It is worth observing that it is not sufficient to add as axioms the partial definitions of truth for atomic sentences. For example, suppose we add as axioms:

True $\overline{\text{(Able is a man)}}$ ↔ Able is a man.

True $\overline{\text{(Baker is a man)}}$ ↔ Baker is a man.

True $\overline{\text{(Cain is a man)}}$ ↔ Cain is a man.

And so on. Now try to derive

True $\overline{((Ex)\,(x \text{ is a man}))}$ ↔ $(Ex)\,(x \text{ is a man})$.

I proceed by an informal method of natural deduction. First consider the conditional from left to right; assume

True $\overline{((Ex)\,(x \text{ is a man}))}$.

Then by (3′)

$(Ea)\,(S\text{-class}\,(a)\,\&\,\text{True}\,(a,\,\overline{x},\,\overline{x \text{ is a man}}))$.

But no path leads from here to the wanted partial definition. Next consider the conditional from right to left; assume

$(Ex)\,(x \text{ is a man})$.

If we try to work from here by applying the standard rule for existence quantifier elimination we get

m is a man

for some singular term 'm' *new to the theory*; in particular, 'm' ≠ 'Able', 'm' ≠ 'Baker', 'm' ≠ 'Cain', etc. Thus again the derivation fails to reach its goal.

What is sufficient is to add a notion of denotation and the following axioms:

(4)   A predication of $\overline{\text{man}}$ with a member of the substitution class, say a, is true if and only if the denotation of a is a man.

(5)   the denotation of $\overline{\text{Able}}$ = Able

            the denotation of $\overline{\text{Baker}}$ = Baker

            the denotation of $\overline{\text{Cain}}$ = Cain

            and so on for each member of the substitution class.

(6)   Everything is denoted by some member of the substitution class.

In a self-explanatory notation these appear as

(4′)   True (pred $(\overline{\text{man}}, a)$) $\leftrightarrow$ den (a) is a man.

(5′)   den $(\overline{\text{Able}})$ = Able

            den $(\overline{\text{Baker}})$ = Baker

            den $(\overline{\text{Cain}})$ = Cain

(6′) (Ea) (den $(a) = x$).

Notice that (6′) is the analogue of (6′) in the satisfactional truth theory. The converse of (6′)

$$(Ex)\,(\text{den}\,(a) = x)$$

is ensured by the functional notation for denotation. If the substitution class contains an infinite number of expressions, (5′) will contain an infinite number of sentences and so violate our requirement that a theory of truth be finite. In that case, all but a finite number of members of the substitution class must be viewed as complex and, typically, we will perform a subordinate recursion on denotation, e.g., the denotation of the result of applying 'the father' to a is the father of the denotation of a:

$$\text{den}\,(ap\,(\overline{\text{father of}}, a)) = \text{the father of (den}(a)).$$

Put another way, it would be natural in this situation to suppose an object language in which functional expressions are applied to constants, including results of their own application, but not to quantifiable variables. This is the situation to which the above recursion applies. (What happens when functional expressions are applied also to variables is discussed in Section VIII below; but see also the discussion of the Hilbert-Bernays theory later on in this section.)

With these additions and refinements the Naive theory is an adequate theory of truth. It proves each instance of

(I)   True $(\overline{F}) \leftrightarrow F$

and trivially it proves

(II) (x) (True $(x) \rightarrow x$ is a closed sentence).

And it is easy to find 'Seq', 'Sat', and 'Val' in it. A sequence is a sequence of members of the substitution class. 's Sat $(\overline{Fx_{k_1}...x_{k_n}})$' means that the result of substituting the k_1th, ..., k_nth member of s for the corresponding variables in $\overline{Fx_{k_1}...x_{k_n}}$ is True. Val (s, n) is the denotation of the nth member of s. Eq is obtained by the same method as the satisfaction theory. With these definitions, it is straightforward to verify that (III), (IV), and (V) are provable.

I think that some philosophers will resist the idea that (1)–(3) are not already an adequate account of truth conditions. Let me therefore underline what we have discovered about the Naive substitutional theory by connecting it with the philosophical problem of interpreting quantifications into opaque contexts. P. T. Geach has put forward the view that to give the truth conditions of (here I use Geach's numbering)

(10)   For some x, x is a man, and Johnson disbelieves that Ralph de Vere is a shopkeeper and does not disbelieve that x is a shopkeeper, and x is the same man as Ralph de Vere.

it is sufficient to say that it is true if and only if "we can find an interpretation in the category of proper names such that the formula

(9) x is a man, and Johnson disbelieves that Ralph de Vere is a shopkeeper and does not disbelieve that x is a shopkeeper, and x is the same man as Ralph de Vere

becomes a true proposition". Geach agrees of course that opaque contexts present serious logical difficulties. But he holds of (10) with regard to his interpretation of it: "We have specified its truth-conditions, and therefore its sense; its sense, as Frege would say, is the sense of: Such-and-such conditions are fulfilled."[12] The difference between what Geach requires of truth-conditions and what is required by Tarski's Convention (or by our slightly different conditions of adequacy) is easy to state: by Geach's lights, an ordinary sentence involving no semantical terms may have its truth-conditions given by a sentence that contains semantical terms, indeed, the concept of truth itself; by Tarski's lights, not. The Tarski demand is that a theory of truth explain partial definitions on the right sides of which no semantical terms occur. The effect of this demand is that we cannot be sure that we have specified the contribution to truth-conditions of one construction, e.g., quantification until we have specified the contribution of all constructions. Following Frege and Wittgenstein we might say: only in the context of a language does a construction really contribute to truth-conditions.

It should be noted that if the inadequacy of (1)–(3) as a theory of truth be taken as an objection to substitutional quantification, it is not the standard objection. The standard objection is that (3) is false for some languages with nameless objects in their ontology. The inadequacy we have found in (1)–(3) is not falsity but deductive weakness.

In volume two of their *Grundlagen der Mathematik* Hilbert and Bernays give a truth definition for (what has become) the standard first-order language of arithmetic: the system (Z) in which the primitive relation is '=', the primitive function signs are "''", ' + ', '.', and the primitive constant is '0'.[13] These function signs apply recursively to quantifiable variables as well as to the constant '0', so that strictly speaking discussion of the Hilbert-Bernays theory belongs in Section VIII; for reasons that will become apparent, it is useful to set out the theory and begin discussing it here. Their recursion follows a substitutional plan and has the important feature that for each degree n of quantificational complexity, the recursion applied to sentences of degree n or less can be carried out explicitly in the system (Z) itself. This shows that, though (Z) does not contain its own truth predicate, it does contain each finite approximation to its own truth predicate; i.e., not 'True-in-myself' but 'True-in-myself and of complexity n or less' for each n.

The Hilbert-Bernays recursion is in many points the same as that in the Naive substitutional theory. Theirs is more finely structured, to give the approximation results just cited. Their structural descriptive names are Gödel numbers; in particular, 2, 2.3, 2.3^2, etc., are the Gödel numbers of the numerals '0, '0'', '0''', etc. Their definition of denotation is such that it is easy to show

$$\text{den } (2. \, 3^n) = n;$$

thus immediately

$$(x) \, (Ey) \, (\text{den } (y) = x)$$

corresponding to (6′) in the Naive theory. The recursion on sentence structure is expressed in terms of a two-place predicate 'True*' which is added to (Z) as a primitive. The clause for existential quantification is

$$\text{True}^* \left(\text{exquant } (f, v_n), k + 1\right) \leftrightarrow (Ex) \left(\text{True}^* (\text{sub}(2.3^x, v_n, f), k)\right).$$

The k here indexes the complexity of f; it marks the finer analysis in the Hilbert-Bernays recursion. It is noteworthy that in this theory, as in the Naive theory, the clause for the quantifier, which is the keynote of a substitutional interpretation, uses only variables for expressions and numbers in making pronomial reference across the biconditional.

The basis clause for '=' is:

$$\text{True}^* \left(\text{pred } (\overline{=}, a, b), 0\right) \leftrightarrow \text{den } (a) = \text{den } (b).$$

The clauses for connectives are the natural ones.

Truth is defined essentially as follows

$$\text{True } (x) \leftrightarrow x \text{ is a closed sentence and True}^* (x, \text{compl. } (x))$$

(I) and (II) are now satisfied; (III) is recovered in the same way as in the Naive theory. (IV) and (V) are also obtainable: because the metalanguage, an extension of (Z), contains a standard theory of identity. Here it is important that the translation of '=', in the basis clause, is '=' itself. Actually, (V) would not be forthcoming in the system Hilbert and Bernays use; (V) requires an inductive proof in which 'True*' occurs essentially. Their axioms sanction inductive proofs only on the vocabulary of (Z), i.e., purely arithmetic vocabulary. This seems an artificial weakness.

McKinsey explicitly designed his theory to avoid use of the notion of satisfaction.[14] Comparing his theory with Tarski's he writes:

My own [theory] has the advantage that it defines truth without making use of the notion of the satisfaction of a sentential function by a set of entities; this feature is useful if one wants to give a semantic definition of the notions of logical necessity and logical possibility.

Tarski has commented that McKinsey's method "is not based on a preliminary definition of satisfaction."[15] This is certainly correct. What we have to check is whether satisfaction is implicit in the theory to which the method gives rise.

McKinsey's idea is (1) to mirror sentential structure in a set theoretic universe, (2) to define truth directly for the set-theoretic analogues of sentences, then (3) to define truth of a sentence as truth of its translation in the world of sets. Thus the sentence

>   Able is a man

is matched with the set-theoretic object

(7) $\langle$ Able, $\{x \mid x$ is a man$\}\rangle$

(i.e., the ordered pair whose first member is Able (the man!) and whose second member is the set of all men). The sentence

> (x) $(x$ is a man$)$

is matched with the *set* of pairs

> $\langle y, \{x \mid x$ is a man$\}\rangle$

for y in an explicitly specified, and perhaps infinite, range of variables; i.e., with

(8) $\{\langle y, \{x \mid x$ is a man$\}\rangle \mid y \in R\}$.

The set-theoretic analogues of closed sentences McKinsey calls *propositions*. The neat trick is that, e.g., an atomic proposition (like (7)) is true if and only if its first member belongs to its second member and e.g., a universal proposition like (8) is true if and only if all its members are true.

Open sentences as well as closed ones have translations in the world sets; translations of open sentences McKinsey calls *propositional functions*. This should suggest to us that we might be able to map *pairs* consisting of sequences of objects from the universe of discourse and sentences (open or closed) into propositions in such a way as to enable us to define

> s Sat $f =_{df}$ trans (s, f) is a true proposition.

The suspicion is correct; roughly, if f is an open sentence trans (s, f) is obtained from the propositional function that translates f by replacing its free variables with appropriate members of s. The requisite notion of replacement is in fact defined by McKinsey. 'Val' can be the same as in satisfactional truth theory. With these definitions, (I)–(V) are all forthcoming in McKinsey's theory.

The limits of substitutional quantification brought out in this section, if they are limits, are subtle. They do not bar someone from saying 'there are men' and meaning that some substitution instance of 'x is a man' is true-in-English. Of course not: *someone* might say 'bububu' and mean that. But if someone's sentence does mean that, then it has the structure, ontology and truth conditions that the sentence

> some substitution instance of 'x is a man' is true-in-English

has in my language, and not the structure and truth conditions the sentence

> there are men

has there.

IV. QUOTATION MARKS

Suppose we supplement pure quantification theory by adding quotation marks, with the understanding that the result of enclosing *any* expression (not necessarily well-formed) in quotation marks is a constant singular term. In the theory of deduction, quotation mark names are to be treated as atomic. Can we give an adequate theory of truth for a language built on this plan? I believe we can, by using the simple semantical rule

> the denotation of the result of enclosing any thing in quotes is the thing itself.[16]

In a self-explanatory notation:

(Q) $den \, (quot \, (x)) = x$

Then we easily prove

(1) $den \, (quot \, (\overline{before})) = \overline{before};$

if our metalanguage also contains quotation marks we can prove

(2) $den \, (quot \, ('before')) = \text{'before'}.$

We cannot prove sentences of the form of

(3) $den \, (quot \, (\overline{before})) = \text{'before'},$

for these would depend on some general connection between structural-descriptive names and quotation mark names. Since the present theory makes no provision for quantification into quotation marks – indeed, (Q) explicitly precludes such quantification – it could not possibly express such a connection.

Now to make an adequate theory of truth we must connect denotation with predication. From the satisfactional standpoint, it is best to expand the notion of value of a sequence to include the notion of denotation. Thus we could replace (A) by

(Q') $\text{Val}\,(s, \text{quot}(x)) = x$.

Then the connection with predication is effected by clause (4) of the satisfactional theory. From the substitutional standpoint, (Q) can stand as it is; the connection with predication is effected by clause (4) of the naive substitutional theory.

Quotation marks have been hailed as a paradigm of opacity, and rightly. But in the present theory, just because no sense is attached to quantification into quotation marks, (I)–(V) are all forthcoming, in the direct ways we have seen in the preceding sections.

V. VARIABLES EXPLAINED AWAY

Some devices that in English indicate cross reference – 'he', 'she', 'it', 'the former', 'the latter', 'the first', 'the second' – seem quite close to the variables of quantification theory. Other devices, such as relative clauses, reflexive pronouns, passive voice, and 'vice versa', serve the same purpose but do not seem at all variable-like. One naturally wonders whether some fresh device of cross reference, pushed to the limit as quantification theory pushes variables, might yield a new approach to the logic of generality. Presumably the new theory would be equivalent on some level with old-fashioned quantification theory; at the same time, it might open up new approaches to logical consequence and semantics.

It is not quite easy to see what such a reorientation of quantification theory would be like. A change to a canonical notation in which no signs look like variables would be, of course, irrelevant; Gödel numbering makes vivid the triviality of such changes. From the point of view of truth theory, the most striking reorientation would be a new recursion that produced the truth paradigms. Such a reorientation is implicit in Schoenfinkel's theory of combinators.[17]

Quine's working out of the combinator approach to quantification uses six constructions in addition to atomic predication.[18] These are conjunction, negation, derelativization (analogous to existential quantification), major inversion, minor inversion, and reflection. Intuitively, the last three of these constructions analyze the role of variables. The intuitive recursion runs as follows:

a sequence $\langle x_1, \ldots, x_n, y_1, \ldots, y_m, \ldots \rangle$ satisfies the conjunction of an n-place predicate, f, and an m-place predicate, g, if and only if $\langle x_1, \ldots, x_n, y_1 \ldots, y_m, \ldots \rangle$ satisfies f and $\langle y_1, \ldots, y_m, \ldots \rangle$ satisfies g

a sequence satisfies the negation of a predicate if and only if it does not satisfy the predicate

a sequence satisfies the derelativization of an $n + 1$-place predicate f if and only if some sequence that differs from the given one at most in the $n + 1$th place satisfies f

a sequence $\langle x_1, \ldots, x_n, \ldots \rangle$ satisfies the major inversion of an n-place predicate f if and only if $\langle x_n, x_1, \ldots, x_{n-1}, \ldots \rangle$ satisfies f

a sequence $\langle x_1, \ldots, x_n, \ldots \rangle$ satisfies the minor inversion of an n-place predicate f if and only if $\langle x_1, \ldots, x_{n-2}, x_n, x_{n-1}, \ldots \rangle$ satisfies f

a sequence $\langle x_1, \ldots, x_n, \ldots \rangle$ satisfies the reflection of an n-place predicate f if and only if $\langle x_1, \ldots, x_{n-1}, x_{n-1}, x_n, \ldots \rangle$ satisfies f

a sequence $\langle x_1, x_2, \ldots \rangle$ satisfies $\overline{\text{before}}$ if and only if x_1 is before x_2.

Notice that derelativization is a one-argument construction; unlike existential quantification, which is *of* an open sentence *with respect to* a variable.

Exact representation of this recursion would use a notion of *degree* with rules for computing degrees of complexes from degrees of their immediate parts, with degrees of atomic predicates being given outright.

For example,

$$\text{deg (conj } (f, g)) = \text{deg } (f) + \text{deg } (g)$$
$$\text{deg } \overline{(\text{before})} = 2.$$

Also, the representation would use simple functions for permuting and reflecting positions in sequences; e.g.,

$$\rho\,(\langle x_1, \dots, x_n, \dots \rangle, n) = \langle x_1, \dots, x_n, x_n, \dots \rangle.$$

It is worth noting that the functions involved here would be a complete set of permutations and reflections: if s and s' are sequences of the same elements, then for some composition φ of the simple functions, $\varphi(s) = s'$.

We have in mind using the Schoenfinkel-inspired recursion just summarized in giving a theory of truth for a quantificational language built with the usual variable notation. There are then many orthographically distinct formulas that are from the present point of view semantically identical, e.g., '$(Ex)\,(y)\,(x$ is before $y)$' and '$(Ey)(x)\,(y$ is before $x)$' and in general formulas obtainable from each other by alphabetic change of variables. Some syntactical recursive procedure will connect the structural description of a formula with the description – in terms of conjunction, derelativization, etc., – to which the semantical recursion directly applies. We will have something of the following form, where ϕ represents the syntactical recursive procedure:

$$s \text{ sat } \overline{Fx_{k_1} \dots x_{k_n}} \leftrightarrow s \text{ sat } \phi\,(\overline{Fx_{k_1} \dots x_{k_n}}).$$

Truth would be defined in the usual way:

$$\text{True }(x) =_{\text{df}} x \text{ is a closed sentence \& } (s)\,(\text{Seq}(s) \rightarrow s \text{ sat } x).$$

Now we cannot expect (III) to emerge automatically from this, especially since $\phi(f)$ may equal $\phi(g)$, even though $f \neq g$. It is obvious, however, that we can find a constructive operation ψ such that if we define

$$s \text{ Sat } Fx_{k_1} \dots x_{k_n} \leftrightarrow \psi\,(s, \overline{Fx_{k_1} \dots x_{k_n}}) \text{ sat } \overline{Fx_{k_1} \dots x_{k_n}}$$

all of (I)–(V) will be forthcoming.

VI. MODAL LOGIC

Modal logics supplement the classical stock of forms with at least one non-truth-functional sentential operator. I will consider the case in which one one-place operator, '□', is added; to fix ideas, the reader may give this operator the intuitive interpretation 'it is logically necessary that'. Two strategies are known for giving truth definitions for languages built on this pattern. One strategy uses a modal metalanguage and aims at the homophonic truth theory. The other uses classical quantification theory as form of metalanguage, and aims at the (heterophonic) truth theory which translates modal sentences into sentences about possible worlds. I will take up these strategies in turn.

When we are using modal sentences to give truth conditions of modal sentences, the natural recursion clause for necessitation is this:

> the necessitation of an open sentence f is satisfied by a sequence if and only if it is logically necessary that f is satisfied by the sequence.

Formally:

$$s \text{ Sat néc } (f) \leftrightarrow \square \, (s \text{ Sat} f).$$

This clause introduces a square on the right. In using it in tandem with other clauses to derive the truth paradigms, we must make replacements within the scope of the square; these replacements must be justified by the clauses and by the relation of logical consequence in the metalanguage. By the lights of consequence relations used in standard modal systems, the material biconditional does not support replacement within modal contexts. What *does* support replacement varies from system to system; in Lewis' S5 it is necessary material equivalence, or strict equivalence; there can be modal systems in which no sentential connective supports replacement in all contexts. Let us pursue the matter in S5. There we must strengthen *all* recursive clauses in the truth definition by prefixing a necessity sign to the biconditional; e.g., the clause for conjunction becomes

$$\square \, (s \text{ Sat conj } (f, g) \leftrightarrow (s \text{ Sat} f \, \& \, s \text{ Sat } g)).$$

(To see that the initial '□' is needed here the reader might try to prove without it 's Sat nec (conj $(f, g)) \leftrightarrow \square \, (s \text{ Sat } f \, \& \, s \text{ Sat } g)$'.)

Depending on the replacement properties of equality in the modal metalanguage, the recursive clause for existential quantification and the

clause laying down the universe of discourse may also have to be
strengthened. Thus the definition of 's differs from s' at most at n'
($s \approx^n s'$) might become '$m \neq n \rightarrow \Box$ (Val $(s, m) =$ Val (s', m))'.

Now if truth is defined in the usual way

$$\text{True } (x) \leftrightarrow x \text{ is a closed sentence } \& (s) (\text{Seq } s \rightarrow s \text{ Sat } x)$$

we find we are able to prove not only the truth paradigms

$$\text{True } (\bar{F}) \leftrightarrow F$$

but also their necessitations

$$\Box \, (\text{True } (\bar{F}) \leftrightarrow F).$$

As noted in Section I above, these are false if '$\Box$' means logical necessity.
They are false as well if '$\Box$' represents practically any other non-truth-
functional sentential operator, e.g., "Nikita believes that".

This shows, I think, that the homophonic strategy does not lead to
reasonable theories of truth for modal languages.

Let us turn then to possible world semantics.[19]

Possible world semantics for modal logic can be tailored to truth
theory in various ways. One can relativize the notion of satisfaction to
worlds. In recursive clauses for truth-functional connectives, worlds go
along as an idle parameter in the straightforward way. In recursive
clauses for quantifiers, worlds may do work or not, depending on what
view one takes of individuals existing in one world but not in some other.
Worlds come into their own in the clause for necessitation and in clauses
for atomic predicates. Thus we have

a sequence s satisfies $\ulcorner \Box f \urcorner$ in world w if and only if s satisfies
f in every world (or sometimes: in every world accessible from
w); a sequence s satisfies $\overline{x_{k_1} \text{ before } x_{k_2}}$ in w if and only if
Val (s, k_1) is before Val (s, k_2) in w.

The predicate 'before' that appears on the right in this clause is a *three-*
place predicate, the extra place being needed to absorb satisfaction's
relativity to worlds. In general, on this strategy the translation of an
n-place atomic predicate will have $n+1$ places. Alternatively, one can

introduce a counterpart relation between individuals and worlds[20]; e.g.,

> a sequence s satisfies $\overline{x_{k_1} \text{ before } x_{k_2}}$ in w if and only if the counterpart in w of what s assigns to k is before the counterpart in w of what s assigns to k_2.

There are many variations on these two main strategies.

It is noteworthy that either way the metalanguage is built on the pattern of classical single-sorted extensional quantification theory.

And either way the strategy we adopted from Hilbert and Bernays to establish (IV) and (V) breaks down: the sentence saying that x and y are indistinguishable by object language atomic predicates relative to object language ontology does not have the reflexivity and replacement properties of identity. But I think this is because of an expressive incompleteness of the object language: some of its sentences translate as sentences involving 'w is a world', 'x is before y in w', and perhaps 'w_1 is accessible from w_2'; or alternatively, 'x is before y' and 'x is a counterpart of y in w'. Yet some metalanguage sentences involving these predicates do not translate any object language sentences.[21] In particular, the Hilbert-Bernays definition of identity, formed now from metalanguage predicates that occur in translations of object language; if it did, (IV) and (V) would hold. Thus it seems to me that the failure of (IV) and (V) in the present context is an artifact of an artificial restriction on expressive power.

Dana Scott has counselled us as follows:

One often hears that modal (or some other) logic is pointless because it can be translated into some simpler language in a first-order way. Take no notice of such arguments. There is no weight to the claim that the original system must therefore be replaced by a new one. What is essential is to single out important concepts and to investigate their properties.[22]

If we are to do possible world theory at all, then it may very well be true that the original modal operator notation is an indispensable heuristic. In the same way the quotient, "dx/dt", notation in the differential calculus is indispensable for some people in working certain kinds of problems. But there is no pretense here that the operator notation, or the quotient notation, reflect logical form. Surely, fundamental questions of semantics and of the definability of identity, must be settled in full fundamental notation, not in the notation of a heuristically suggestive but derivative and incomplete fragment.

VII. DENUMERABLY MANY PRIMITIVES

We have a strong intuition that a language with more than finitely many primitives could not be learned, and thus that an adequate semantics must represent a natural language as having a finite number of atomic meaningful parts and also a finite number meaning-compounding constructions. We can describe formal languages, built on the pattern of ordinary quantification theory, that have as many atomic predicates as there are natural numbers. It is instructive to notice what happens to truth theory in such a case.

Suppose then a language with distinct one-place atomic predicates 'P_1', 'P_2', ... in a denumerable list. The direct strategy for giving a theory of truth for the language yields clauses for atomic predicates

$$s \operatorname{Sat} \overline{P_1 \ x_k} \leftrightarrow P_1 \operatorname{Val}(s, k)$$
$$s \operatorname{Sat} \overline{P_2 \ x_k} \leftrightarrow P_2 \operatorname{Val}(s, k)$$
$$\vdots$$

in an infinite list. But by our lights an adequate theory of truth must be finite. Or by Tarski's lights, it must be possible to gather the recursion into a definition of truth, which is of course impossible if an infinite primitive vocabulary is used in giving truth conditions.

Wang points out that for each natural number n we can define: is a true sentence built from predicates among the first n of the P's.[23] We simply confine attention to the clauses for connectives and quantifiers plus the first n basis clauses. But we cannot define by Wang's method

$$\text{True } (x, n)$$

for variable n. Thus we cannot define truth or give a finite theory of truth for the whole language.

We could introduce a two-place relation 'R' into the metalanguage and use it, together with a system of indices, to translate all the P's. Thus we might have the clause

$$s \operatorname{Sat} \text{ the result of putting } \bar{x}_k \text{ with the } n\text{th } \bar{P} \leftrightarrow R(\operatorname{Val}(s, k), n).$$

This single clause would deal with all the object languages atomic predicates. (IV) and (V) may fail in this situation, but for much the same reason as in possible world semantics for modal logic: there are meta-language sentences involving 'R' that translate no sentences of the object language; if this were not the case, the Hilbert-Bernays method for defining identity could be carried out.

VIII. QUANTIFYING INTO FUNCTION SIGNS

When a language contains function signs that apply to quantifiable variables and to results of their own application, the Hilbert-Bernays method of defining identity fails. It is clear why. Suppose the language contains a two-place predicate 'H' meaning 'heavier than' and a one-place function sign 'f' meaning 'the father of' (and no other primitive vocabulary). Then the Hilbert-Bernays method gives us

$$(z) ((Hxz \leftrightarrow Hyz) \,\&\, (Hzx \leftrightarrow Hzy))$$

i.e., 'x and y have the same weight'. But if x and y have the same weight, we still may be able to distinguish them by means of concepts of the language: x's father may weigh more than y, or than y's father, or than his grandfather, etc. In order to recover the replacement property for identity we should have to apply the Hilbert-Bernays method to all of the following forms:

$$H \,①\, ②$$
$$Hf(①)\, ②$$
$$H \,①\, f(②)$$
$$Hf(①)\, f(②)$$
$$Hf(f(①))\, ②$$
$$\vdots$$

and so on, an infinite list. Thus no definition can be given. The situation is even more complicated if the language contains a two-place function sign, say 'g'.

For then we have to consider

$$Hg\,(①\, ②)\, g(③\, ④)$$

and the like; that is, the number of argument places in the relevant forms increases (and without bound).

The set of basic forms to which the Hilbert-Bernays method must be applied is determined in a perfectly constructive way given the primitive vocabulary of the language in question. Let 'Eq' be a metalanguage predicate that represents this class of open sentences that results from applying the Hilbert-Bernays method to the stock of forms. This is a class of open sentences with the first two object language variables free. Let 'Eq''' represent the class of sentences obtained from Eq by identifying these variables. Then we have analogously to (IV) and (V):

(IV') $(x)\,(\text{Eq}'\ x \to s\ \text{Sat}\ x)$
(V') $(z)\,(\text{Eq}\ z \to \langle x, y \rangle\ \text{Sat}\ z) \to (f)\,(\langle \ldots, x, \ldots \rangle\ \text{Sat}\,f \leftrightarrow \langle \ldots y \ldots \rangle\ \text{Sat}\,f)$.

The natural satisfactional truth theory when functional expressions are present adds to the standard recursion on satisfaction a coordinate recursion on valuation. For example, one would add

$$\text{Val}\,(s, \text{ap}\,(\vec{f},\, x)) = \text{the father of}\,(\text{Val}\,(s, x))$$

where 'ap' represents the syntactical operation of applying a function-sign to its argument sign. When the truth theory is filled out in this way, we find we can prove (I), (II), (III), (IV'), (V').

And exactly the same thing holds true in the case of substitutional truth theory and possible world truth theory for modality (modulo the expressive incompleteness associated with modal languages). So the fundamental likeness of all known truth theories to satisfactional truth theory is undisturbed.

Associated with every function is a relation; e.g., with 'the father of', 'is a father of'. Putting this fact together with Russell's theory of definite descriptions [24] *and* the Hilbert-Bernays theory of identity, we get a translation of a language that contains function signs into one that does not; i.e., into a language built on the pattern of pure quantification theory: predicates, truth-functions, quantifiers. The scheme of translation is just Russell's, except that where he puts '$=$' we put the Hilbert-Bernays definition, using metalanguage predicates (a) that translate atomic object language predicates plus (b) metalanguage predicates associated with object language function signs. If Russell's theory of definite descriptions is true, this translation is good. Moreover, it is a translation we can reflect in a theory of truth. But with respect to this translation, the language that contains function signs is expressively incomplete in essentially the same way that modal languages were incomplete with respect to "possible world" translations, and languages with infinities of predicates were incomplete with respect to certain translations described in the preceding section. That is, there are metalanguage sentences built from vocabulary that occurs in translations but which are not themselves translations of any object language sentence. Since I think Russell's theory is true, I think this shows that functional expressions are not a fundamental form in language and that (I)–(V), not (I), (II), (III), (IV'), (V') is the likely frame of reference.

IX. CONSEQUENCES: TRUTH AND MEANING

The main outcome of the preceding sections may be summarized by reference to three schemata:

(1)   '____' is true if and only if ____
(2)   '____' is satisfied by all and only____things
(3)   if x and y satisfy Eq, then x satisfies '____' if and only if y satisfies '____'.

In (1) blanks are to be filled by closed sentences, in (2) and (3) by open ones. What we have found is that under natural conditions explanation of all relevant instances of (1) uses resources that define satisfaction and equality and explain all relevant instances of (2) and of (3).[25] It remains to connect this fact with philosophy.

Anyone who theorizes about meaning must come to terms with two ideas: (1) the compositional idea, that sentences and texts are complexes whose meanings are composed in regular ways from the meanings of their parts; (2) the holistic idea, that interpretation of language is constrained only in the large, that meaning attaches primarily to infinite systems of signs. The first idea is already flowering in Plato and Aristotle; it must be closely associated with the Greek's mastery of writing. The second was planted by Frege, and has been cultivated by Wittgenstein and by Quine. Quine writes, for example:

The statement, rather than the term, came with Frege to be recognized as the unit accountable to an empiricist critique. But what I am now urging is that even in taking the statement as unit we have drawn our grid too finely. The unit of empirical significance is the whole of science.[26]

The standard argument for the compositional character of meaning is that speakers sometimes understand sentences on first use. This argument can show, I think, that each speaker controls a recursive theory; but it lends no weight to the idea that all recursive theories open to all speakers share philosophically interesting structure. The traditional connection between compositional theories of meaning and metaphysics breaks down. There is a gap between the holistic and compositional approaches to meaning. Perhaps the point can be made vivid by returning to Frege. Two of the methodological principles that underlie his philosophy of arithmetic are, he says [27]:

Never to ask for the meaning of a word in isolation, but only in the context of a sentence;
Never to lose sight of the distinction between concept and object.

The first principle is the holistic one about meaning. What we are now being led to wonder is whether strict adherence to the first principle might not lead one to devalue the second, as depending on a structural distinction not determined by evidence that controls interpretation of a language.

Davidson has put forward the thesis that to interpret the language of an Other is to construct a theory of truth for it.[28] Davidson's thesis and the thesis of this paper together join the compositional and holistic approaches to theory of meaning. Davidson justifies Convention T – the demand for explanation of all biconditionals of 'X is true if and only if p' form – partly on holistic grounds, partly on grounds that mastery of a language should in principle flow from a finite theory. Any theory that meets this demand reads concepts, objects, and identity into the language interpreted: such is the thesis of this paper.

It should be noted that the emergence of concepts is not one thing, the emergence of objects another, the emergence of identity a third. Rather, (2) and (3) emerge, and strictly speaking there is no separating predication, ontology, and identity in them. To expect too sharp a separation of these aspects of meaning is to take up an extreme compositional theory of meaning – perhaps a museum theory in which words on the cases label the exhibits inside – that is not justified, at least not by the findings of this paper.

In the context of his theory of radical translation Quine has put forward indeterminacy theses concerning predication and reference.[29] These theses, as stated by Quine, are sharply local in character: e.g., there is no telling whether *this* native sentence segment is to be translated as 'rabbit' or as 'rabbit-stage'. The sort of determinacy of predication and reference implicit in (2)–(3) is global in character and in no way goes against Quine's local indeterminacy claims. It is worth emphasizing in this connection that though we have focused on homophonic truth theories in order to simplify exposition and fix ideas, this is in no way essential to the global determinacy results. All that is essential to those results is that all sentences on a certain vocabulary appear as right sides of partial definitions of truth. Similar determinacy attaches to even broader classes of truth theories; e.g., if quantifiers are relativized in passing from object language to metalanguage and, modulo this relativization, all sentences on a certain vocabulary appear as right sides of partial definitions.

Misgivings about the argument of this paper come, for me at least, from the role played in it by an antecedently chosen predicate calculus. This calculus fixes notions of sentence and consequence in the metalanguage. Wittgenstein put his finger on the worry:

114. (*Tractatus Logico-Philosophicus*, 4.5): "The general form of propositions is: This is how things are." – That is the kind of proposition that one repeats to oneself countless times. One thinks that one is tracing the outline of the thing's nature over and over again, and one is merely tracing round the frame through which we look at it.
115. A *picture* held us captive. And we could not get outside it, for it lay in our language and language seemed to repeat it to us inexorably.

Is what we have noticed any more than that quantification theory reads itself into any language it interprets? Somewhat, because we saw that modal predicate calculus does not provide a reasonable standpoint from which to interpret a language. And certainly quantification theory has considerable weight of intuition, well-established theory, and successful application behind it – which makes its selection as form of metalanguage less than arbitrary. Still, one would want a clearer view of the possible predicate calculi, and especially of the connection between truth and logical consequence, before concluding that (1)–(3) determine the frame of reference on which our world is spread out.[31]

Princeton University

REFERENCES

[1] Most of the material in this paper has been presented in classes and seminars or roughed out in short workpapers over the past four years. I am deeply indebted to students and friends who have suggested novel strategies, spotted errors and, more important, helped clarify the point of this work on truth theory. I cannot mention everyone who has helped in these ways but I must mention Nuel Belnap, Richard Grandy, Gilbert Harman, Richard Jeffrey, Sue Larson, David Lewis, Thomas Scanlon, Marc Temin, and Samuel Wheeler. To Donald Davidson I have a deeper debt: when I was a graduate student, his vision of the place of theory of meaning in philosophy and of the relation between a theory of truth and a theory of meaning set me to work on truth, meaning, and philosophy. I have had the benefit of countless discussions with him while the work reported in this paper was in process.

[2] This phrasing comes from C. I. Lewis, *Mind and the World Order*, New York 1965, p. 111.

[3] The singleness of the structure and its philosophical importance have been elucidated by W. V. Quine; see especially the middle chapters of *Word and Object*, Cambridge, Mass. 1960.

[4] A. Tarski, 'The Semantic Conception of Truth and the Foundations of Semantics' in *Readings in Philosophical Analysis* (ed. by H. Feigl and W. Sellars), New York 1949, p. 63. (This paper originally appeared in *Philosophy and Phenomenological Research* **4** (1944) 341–375.)

[5] This way of presenting the paradigms is borrowed from W. V. Quine, 'Notes on the Theory of Reference' in W. V. Quine, *From a Logical Point of View*, Cambridge, Mass. 1953, p. 134.

[6] A. Tarski, 'Der Wahrheitsbegriff in den formalisierten Sprachen', *Studia Philosophica* **1** (1936). This paper is translated under the title 'The Concept of Truth in Formalized Languages' in A. Tarski, *Logic, Semantics, Metamathematics*, Oxford 1956, pp. 152–278.

[7] I refer here to the precise condition of adequacy laid down by Tarski in the Wahrheitsbegriff; see especially Sections III and VI.

[8] The theory to be set out here is very close to one used by W. Craig and R. L. Vaught, 'Finite Axiomatizability Using Additional Predicates', *Journal of Symbolic Logic* **23** (1958) 289–308.

[9] D. Hilbert and P. Bernays, *Grundlagen der Mathematik* I, Berlin 1934, pp. 381ff. The Hilbert-Bernays elimination theory is very clearly explained by W. V. Quine, *Set Theory and Its Logic*, Cambridge, Mass. 1963, pp. 9–15.

[10] The substitution interpretation is discussed also in the following papers. B. Mates, 'Synonymity', *University of California Publications in Philosophy* **25** (1950) 201–226, esp. p. 223. This paper is reprinted, with original pagination, in *Semantics and the Philosophy of Language* (ed. by L. Linsky). P. T. Geach, *Reference and Generality*, Ithaca 1962, pp. 144–167. R. B. Marcus, 'Interpreting quantification', *Inquiry* **5** (1962) 252–259; and 'Modalities and Iktensional Languages' in *Boston Studies in the Philosophy of Science* (ed. by M. W. Wartofsky), Dordrecht 1963, pp. 77–96. D. Føllesdal, 'Interpretation of Quantifiers' in *Logic, Methodology, and Philosophy of Science III* (ed. by B. van Rootselaar and J. F. Staal), Amsterdam 1968, pp. 271–281. W. V. Quine, 'Reply to Professor Marcus' in W. V. Quine, *The Ways of Paradox*, New York 1966, pp. 175–182, and 'Ontological Relativity', *Journal of Philosophy* **65** (1968) 85–212, and 'Existence and Quantification' in *Fact and Existence* (ed. by J. Margolis), Oxford 1969,

pp. 1–17. W. Sellars, 'Grammar and Existence: A Preface to Ontology', *Mind* n.s. **69** (1960), reprinted in W. Sellars, *Science, Perception, Reality*, New York and London 1963, pp. 247–281. Some of these writers see in the substitution interpretation an ontological neutrality (Mates, Marcus, Quine, Sellars), some a congenialness to intensionality and modality (Marcus, Geach, Sellars) that distinguish it from the satisfaction interpretation. If my claim is correct, these supposed differences are illusory. But the reader must decide these matters for himself.

[11] The point about parentheses is Lesniewski's; see Quine, 'Existence and Quantification', p. 12.

[12] Geach, *Reference and Generality*; the first quotation is from p. 156, the second from p. 158.

[13] D. Hilbert and P. Bernays, *Grundlagen der Mathematik II*, Berlin 1939, pp. 329ff.

[14] J. C. C. McKinsey, 'A New Definition of Truth', *Synthese* **7** (1948–1949) 428–433. The quotation is from p. 428.

[15] Tarski, *Logic, Semantics, Metamathematics*, p. 246 (footnote).

[16] This rule is stated explicitly by R. M. Smullyan, 'Languages in which Self Reference is Possible', *Journal of Symbolic Logic* **22** (1957) 55–67.

[17] M. Schoenfinkel, 'Über die Bausteine der mathematischen Logik', *Mathematische Annalen* **92** (1942) 305–316. This paper is reprinted (with introductory comments by W. V. Quine) in *From Frege to Gödel: A Source Book in Mathematical Logic, 1879–1931* (ed. by J. van Heijenoort), Cambridge, Mass. 1967.

[18] W. V. Quine, 'Variables Explained Away', *Proceedings of the American Philosophical Society* **104** (1960) 343–347. This paper is reprinted in W. V. Quine, *Selected Logic Papers*, New York 1966, pp. 227–235. Similar work has been done by P. Bernays, 'Über eine natürliche Erweiterung des Relationenkalküls', in *Constructivity in Mathematics* (ed. by A. Heyting), Amsterdam 1959, pp. 1–14.

[19] The standard reference for possible world model theory is S. A. Kripke, 'A Completeness Theorem in Modal Logic', *Journal of Symbolic Logic* **24** (1959) 1–15. I do not know a paper in which possible world truth theory has been explicitly discussed.

[20] The counterpart idea comes from David K. Lewis, 'Counterpart Theory and Quantified Modal Logic', *Journal of Philosophy* **65** (1968) 113–126.

[21] David Lewis mentions this incompleteness, *ibid.*, p. 117. I do not know whether he would agree with the present point made on the basis of it.

[22] Dana Scott, 'Advice on Modal Logic' in *Philosophical Problems in Logic: Recent Developments* (ed. by Karel Lambert), Reidel, Dordrecht 1970, pp. 143–173.

[23] H. Wang, 'Truth Definitions and Consistency Proofs', *Transactions of the American Mathematical Society* **73** (1952) 243–275, esp. pp. 254–255. In fact, Wang appears to make the mistaken claim that a truth definition exists for the whole language. See Richard Montague's review, in *Journal of Symbolic Logic* **22** (1957) 365–367.

[24] B. Russell, 'On Denoting', *Mind* n.s. **14** (1905), 479–493. Reprinted in Russell, *Logic and Knowledge*, London 1958, and in Feigl and Sellars, *Readings in Philosophical Analysis*, and in Linsky, *Semantics and the Philosophy of Language*. For a recent treatment see Quine, *Word and Object*, sections 37 and 38.

[25] It will be well to note circumstances under which (1) does separate from (2) and (3). It separates when the object language has only a finite number of sentences: one can simply list their truth conditions. It separates when the object language has no quantifiers. It separates when the object language has quantifiers but only one-place predicates: its sentences fall into a finite number of truth-functional equivalence classes. It separates when each sentence is equivalent to a quantifier free sentence; i.e., when it

submits to elimination of quantifiers (see G. Kreisel and J. Krivine, *Elements of Mathematical Logic*, Amsterdam 1967, Ch. 4). It separates when truth in the object language is decidable. It seems likely that the language of a creature that knows and acts intentionally must include quantifications and relations essentially; Gödel showed that truth in a language that contains arithmetic is undecidable. Thus it seems likely that cases in which (1) separates from (2) and (3) are of limited philosophical interest.

[26] W. V. Quine, 'Two Dogmas of Empiricism' in Quine, *From a Logical Point of View*, pp. 20–46; the quotation is from p. 42.

[27] G. Frege, *The Foundations of Arithmetic*, Oxford 1959, p. x. This is a translation of *Die Grundlagen der Arithmetik* made by John L. Austin.

[28] D. Davidson, 'Truth and Meaning', *Synthese* **17** (1967) 304–323.

[29] See Quine, *Word and Object*, Ch. 2; and Quine, 'Ontological Relativity'.

[30] L. Wittgenstein, *Philosophical Investigations*, New York 1953, p. 48. This is a translation of *Philosophische Untersuchungen* made by G. E. M. Anscombe.

[31] My research was supported by Princeton University and the National Science Foundation.

SAUL A. KRIPKE

NAMING AND NECESSITY[1]

Lectures Given to the Princeton University Philosophy Colloquium

LECTURE I: JANUARY 20, 1970

I hope that some people see some connection between the two topics in
the title. If not, anyway, such connections will be developed in the course
of these talks. Furthermore, because of the use of tools involving reference
and necessity in analytic philosophy today, our views on these topics
really have wide-ranging implications for other problems in philosophy
that traditionally might be thought far-removed, like arguments over the
mind-body problem or the so-called 'identity thesis'. Materialism, in
this form, often now gets involved in very intricate ways in questions
about what is necessary or contingent in identity of properties – questions
like that. So, it is really very important to philosophers who may want
to work in many domains to get clear about these concepts. Maybe I will
say something about the mind-body problem in the course of these talks.
I want to talk also at some point (I don't know if I can get it in) about
substances and natural kinds.

The way I approach these matters will be, in some ways, quite different
from what people are thinking today (though it also has some points of
contact with what some people have been thinking and writing today,
and if I leave people out in informal talks like this, I hope that I will
be forgiven).[2] Some of the views that I have are views which may at first
glance strike some as obviously wrong. My favorite example is this
(which I probably won't defend in the lectures: for one thing it doesn't
ever convince anyone). It is a common claim in contemporary philosophy
that there are certain predicates which, though they are in fact empty –
have null extension – have it as a matter of contingent fact and not as a
matter of any sort of necessity. Well, *that* I don't dispute; but an example
which is usually given is the example of *unicorn*. So it is said that though
we have all found out that there are no unicorns, of course there *might*
have been unicorns. Under certain circumstances there *would* have been

Note: For addenda to this paper see pp. 763-769 in this volume.

Davidson and Harman (eds.), Semantics of Natural Language, 253–355. *All rights reserved*
Copyright © 1972 *by Saul A. Kripke*

unicorns. And this is an example of something I think is not the case. Perhaps according to me the truth should not be put in terms of saying that it is necessary that there be no unicorns, but just that we can't say under what circumstances there would have been unicorns. Further, I think that even if archeologists or geologists were to discover tomorrow some fossils conclusively showing the existence of animals in the past satisfying everything we know about the unicorns from the myth of the unicorn, that would not show that there were unicorns. Now I don't know if I'm going to have a chance to defend this particular view, but it's an example of a surprising one. (I actually gave a seminar in this institution where I talked about this view for a couple of sessions.) So, some of my opinions are somewhat surprising; but let us start out with some area that is perhaps not as surprising and introduce the methodology and problems of these talks.

The first topic in the pair of topics is naming. By a name here I will mean a proper name, i.e. the name of a person, a city, a country, etc. It is well known that modern logicians also are very interested in definite descriptions: phrases of the form 'the x such that ϕx', such as 'the man who corrupted Hadleyburg'. Now, if one and only one man ever corrupted Hadleyburg, then that man is the referent, in the logician's sense, of that description. We will use the term 'name' so that it does *not* include definite descriptions of that sort, but only those things which in ordinary language would be called proper names. If we want a common term to cover names and descriptions we may use the term 'designator'.

It is a point, made by Donnellan,[3] that under certain circumstances a particular speaker may use a definite description to refer, not to the proper referent, in the sense that I've just defined it, of that description, but to something else which he wants to single out and which he thinks is the proper referent of the description, but which in fact isn't. So, you may say "The man over there with the champagne in his glass is happy", though he actually only has water in his glass. Now, even though there is no champagne in his glass, and there may be another man in the room who does have champagne in his glass, the speaker *intended* to refer, or maybe, in some sense of 'refer', *did* refer, to the man he thought had the champagne in his glass. Nevertheless I'm just going to use the term 'referent of the description' to mean the object uniquely satisfying the conditions in the definite description. This is the sense in which it's been used in the logical tradition. So, if you have a description of the form 'the x such that ϕx', and there is exactly one x such that ϕx, that is the referent of the description.

Now, what is the relation between names and descriptions? There is a well known doctrine of John Stuart Mill, in his book *A System of Logic*, that names have denotation but not connotation. To use one of his examples, when we use the name 'Dartmouth' to describe a certain locality in England, it may be so called because it lies at the mouth of the Dart. But even, he says, had the Dart (that's a river) changed its course so that Dartmouth no longer lay at the mouth of the Dart, we could still with propriety call this place 'Dartmouth', even though the name may suggest that it lies at the mouth of the Dart. Changing Mill's terminology, perhaps we should say that a name such as 'Dartmouth' *does* have a 'connotation' to some people, namely, it *does* connote (not to me – I never thought of this) that any place called 'Dartmouth' lies at the mouth of the Dart. But then in some way it doesn't have a 'sense'. At least, it is not part of the *meaning* of the name 'Dartmouth' that the town so named lies at the mouth of the Dart. Someone who said that Dartmouth did not lie at the Dart's mouth would not contradict himself.

It should not be thought that every phrase of the form 'the x such that F-x' is always used in English as a description rather than a name. I guess everyone has heard about the Holy Roman Empire, which was neither holy, Roman nor an empire. Today we have the United Nations. Here it would seem that since these things can be so-called even though they are not Holy Roman United Nations, these phrases should be regarded not as definite descriptions, but as names. In the case of some terms, people might have doubts as to whether they're names or descriptions; like 'God' – does it describe God as the unique divine being or is it a name of God? But such cases needn't necessarily bother us.

Now here I am making a distinction which is certainly made in language. But the classical tradition of modern logic has gone very strongly against Mill's view. Frege and Russell both thought, and seemed to arrive at these conclusions independently of each other, that Mill was wrong in a very strong sense: really a proper name, properly used, simply was a definite description abbreviated or disguised. Frege specifically said that such a description gave the sense of the name.[4]

Now the reasons against Mill's view and in favor of the alternative view adopted by Frege and Russell are really very powerful; and it is hard to see – though one may be suspicious of this view because names don't seem to be disguised descriptions – how the Frege-Russell view, or some suitable variant, can fail to be the case.

Let me give an example of some of the arguments which seem conclusive in favor of the view of Frege and Russell. The basic problem for any view such as Mill's is how we can determine what the referent of a name, as used by a given speaker, is. According to the description view, the answer is clear. If 'Joe Doakes' is just short for 'the man who corrupted Hadleyburg', then whoever corrupted Hadleyburg uniquely is the referent of the name 'Joe Doakes'. However, if there is *not* such a descriptive content to the name, then how do people ever use names to refer to things at all? Well, they may be in a position to point to some things and thus determine the references of certain names ostensively. This was Russell's doctrine of acquaintance, which he thought the so-called genuine or proper names satisfied. But of course ordinary names refer to all sorts of people, like Walter Scott, to whom we can't possibly point. And our reference here seems to be determined by our knowledge of them. Whatever we know about them determines the referent of the name as the unique thing satisfying those properties. For example, if I use the name 'Napoleon', and someone asks, "To whom are you referring?", I will answer something like, "Napoleon was emperor of the French in the early part of the nineteenth century; he was eventually defeated at Waterloo", thus giving a uniquely identifying description to determine the referent of the name. Frege and Russell, then, appear to give the natural account of how reference is determined here; Mill appears to give none.

There are subsidiary arguments which, though they are based on more specialized problems, are also motivations for accepting the view. One is that sometimes we may discover that two names have the same referent, and express this by an identity statement. So, for example (I guess this is a hackneyed example), you see a star in the evening and it's called 'Hesperus'. (That's what we call it in the evening, is that right? – I hope it's not the other way around.) We see a star in the morning and call it 'Phosphorus'. Well, then, in fact we find that it's not a star, but is the planet Venus and that Hesperus and Phosphorus are in fact the same.

So we express this by 'Hesperus is Phosphorus'. Here we're certainly not just saying of an object that it's identical with itself. This is something that we discovered. A very natural thing is to say that the real content [is that] the star which we saw in the evening is the star which we saw in the morning (or, more accurately, that the thing which we saw in the evening is the thing which we saw in the morning). This, then, gives the real meaning of the identity statement in question; and the analysis in terms of descriptions does this.

Also we may raise the question whether a name has any reference at all when we ask, e.g., whether Aristotle ever existed. It seems natural here to think that what is questioned is not whether this *thing* (man) existed. Once we've got the thing we know that it existed. What really is queried is whether anything answers to the properties we associate with the name – in the case of Aristotle, whether any one Greek philosopher produced certain works, or at least a suitable number of them.

It would be nice to answer all of these arguments. I am not entirely able to see my way clear through every problem of this sort that can be raised. Furthermore, I'm pretty sure that I won't have time to discuss all these questions in these lectures. Nevertheless, I think it's pretty certain that the view of Frege and Russell is false.[5]

Many people have said that the theory of Frege and Russell is false, but, in my opinion, they have abandoned its letter while retaining its spirit, namely, they have used the notion of a cluster concept. Well, what is this? The biggest problem for Frege and Russell, the one which comes immediately to mind, is already mentioned by Frege himself. He said,

In the case of genuinely proper names like 'Aristotle' opinions as regards their sense may diverge. As such may, e.g., be suggested: Plato's disciple and the teacher of Alexander the Great. Whoever accepts this sense will interpret the meaning of the statement 'Aristotle was born in Stagira', differently from one who interpreted the sense of 'Aristotle' as the Stagirite teacher of Alexander the Great. As long as the nominatum remains the same, these fluctuations in sense are tolerable. But they should be avoided in the system of a demonstrative science and should not appear in a perfect language.[6]

So, according to Frege, there is some sort of looseness or weakness in our language. Some people may give one sense to the name 'Aristotle', others may give another. But of course it is not only that; even a single speaker when asked "What description are you willing to substitute for the name?" may be quite at a loss. In fact, he may know many things about him; but any particular thing that he knows he may feel clearly expresses a contingent property of the object. If 'Aristotle' meant *the man who taught Alexander the Great*, then saying 'Aristotle was a teacher of Alexander the Great' would be a mere tautology. But surely it isn't; it expresses the fact that Aristotle taught Alexander the Great, something we could discover to be false. So, *being the teacher of Alexander the Great* cannot be part of [the sense of] the name.

The most common way out of this difficulty is to say "really it is not a weakness in ordinary language that we can't substitute a *particular* description for the name; that's all right. What we really associate with the name is a *family* of descriptions." A good example of this is (if I can find it) in *Philosophical Investigations*, where the idea of family resemblances is introduced and with great power.

Consider this example. If one says 'Moses did not exist', this may mean various things. It may mean: the Israelites did not have a *single* leader when they withdiew from Egypt – or: their leader was not called Moses – or: there cannot have been anyone who accomplished all that the Bible relates of Moses – ... But when I make a statement about Moses, – am I always ready to substitute some *one* of those descriptions for 'Moses'? I shall perhaps say: by 'Moses' I understand the man who did what the Bible relates of Moses, or at any rate, a good deal of it. But how much? Have I decided how much must be proved false for me to give up my proposition as false? Has the name 'Moses' got a fixed and unequivocal use for me in all possible cases?[7]

According to this view, and a *locus classicus* of it is Searle's article on proper names,[8] the referent of a name is determined not by a single description but by some cluster or family. Whatever in some sense satisfies enough or most of the family is the referent of the name. I shall return to this view later. It may seem as an analysis of ordinary language quite a bit more plausible than that of Frege and Russell. It may seem to keep all the virtues and remove the defects of this theory.

Let me say (and this will introduce me to another new topic before I really consider this theory of naming) that there are two ways in which the cluster concept theory, or even the theory which requires a single description, can be viewed. One way of regarding it says that the cluster or the single description actually gives the meaning of the name; and when someone says 'Walter Scott', he means *the man such that such and such and such and such*.

Now another view might be that even though the description in some sense doesn't give the *meaning* of the name, it is what *determines its reference* and although the phrase 'Walter Scott' isn't *synonymous* with 'the man such that such and such and such and such', or even maybe with the family (if something can be synonymous with a family), the family or the single description is what is used to determine to whom some-one is referring when he says 'Walter Scott'. Of course, if when we hear his beliefs about Walter Scott we find that they are actually much more nearly true of Salvador Dali, then according to this theory the reference of this name is going to be Mr. Dali, not Scott. There are writers, I think, who explicitly deny that names have meaning at all even more strongly than I would but still use this picture of how the referent of the name gets determined. A good case in point is Paul Ziff in his *Semantic Analysis*, who says, very emphatically, that names don't have meaning at all, [that] they are not a part of language in some sense. But still, when he talks about how we determine what the reference of the name was, then he gives this picture. Unfortunately I don't have the passage in question with me, but this is what he says.[9]

The difference between using this theory as a theory of meaning and using it as a theory of reference will come out a little more clearly later on. But some of the attractiveness of the theory is lost if it isn't supposed to give the meaning of the name; for some of the solutions of problems that I've just mentioned will not be right, or at least won't clearly be right, if the description doesn't give the meaning of the name. For example, if someone said 'Aristotle does not exist' *means* 'there is no man doing such and such', or in the example from Wittgenstein, 'Moses does not exist', *means* 'no man did such and such', that might depend (and in fact, I think, does depend) on taking the theory in question as a theory of the meaning of the name 'Moses', not just as a theory of its reference. Well, I don't know. Perhaps all that is immediate now is the other way around: if 'Moses' means the same as 'the man who did such and such' then to say that Moses did not exist is to say that the man who did such and such did not exist, that is, that no one person did such and such. If, on the other hand, 'Moses' is not synonymous with any description, then even if its reference is in some sense determined by a description, statements containing the name cannot in general be *analyzed* by replacing the name by a description, though they may be materially equivalent to statements containing a description. So the analysis of singular existence statements mentioned above will have to be given up, unless it is established by some special argument, independent of a general theory of the meaning of names; and the same applies to identity state-ments. In any case, I think it's false that 'Moses exists' means that at all. So we won't have to see if such a special argument can be drawn up.[10]

Before I go any further into this problem, I want to talk about another distinction which will be important in the methodology of these talks. Philosophers have talked (and, of course, there has been considerable controversy in recent years over the meaningfulness of these notions) [about] various categories of truth, which are called 'a priori', 'analytic', 'necessary', – and sometimes even 'certain' is thrown into this batch. The terms are often used as if *whether* there are things answering to these concepts is an interesting question, but we might as well regard them all as meaning the same thing. Now, everyone remembers Kant (a bit) as making a distinction between 'a priori' and 'analytic'. So maybe this distinction is still made. In contemporary discussion very few people, if any, distinguish between the concepts of statements being a priori and their being necessary. At any rate I shall *not* use the terms 'a priori' and 'necessary' interchangeably here.

Consider what the traditional characterizations of such terms as 'a priori' and 'necessary' are. First the notion of a prioricity is a concept of epistemology. I guess the traditional characterization from Kant goes something like: *a priori* truths are those which can be known independently of any experience. This introduces another problem before we get off the ground, because there's another modality in the characterization of 'a priori', namely, it is supposed to be something which *can* be known independently of any experience. That means that in some sense it's *possible* (whether we do or do not in fact know it independently of any experience) to know this independently of any experience. And possible for whom? For God? For the Martians? Or just for people with minds like ours? To make this all clear might [involve] a host of problems all of its own about what sort of possibility is in question here. It might be best therefore, instead of using the phrase 'a priori truth', to the extent that one uses it at all, to stick to the question of whether a particular person or knower knows something a priori or believes it true on the basis of *a priori* evidence.

I won't go further too much into the problems that might arise with the notion of a prioricity here. I will say that some philosophers some-how change the modality in this characterization from *can* to *must*.

They think that if something belongs to the realm of *a priori* knowledge, it couldn't possibly be known empirically. This is just a mistake. Something may belong in the realm of such statements that can be known *a priori* but still may be known by particular people on the basis of experience. To give a really common sense example: anyone who has worked with a computing machine knows that the computing machine may give an answer to whether such and such a number is prime. No one has calculated or proved that the number is prime; but the machine has given the answer: this number is prime. We, then, if we believe that the number is prime, believe it on the basis of our knowledge of the laws of physics, the construction of the machine, and so on. We therefore do not believe this on the basis of purely *a priori* evidence. We believe it (if anything is *a posteriori* at all) on the basis of *a posteriori* evidence. Nevertheless, maybe this could be known *a priori* by someone who made the requisite calculations. So '*can* be known *a priori*' doesn't mean '*must* be known *a priori*'.

The second concept which is in question is that of necessity. Sometimes this is used in an epistemological way and might then just mean *a priori*. And of course, sometimes it is used in a physical way when people distinguish between physical and logical necessity. But what I am concerned with here is a notion which is not a notion of epistemology but of metaphysics, in some (I hope) nonpejorative sense. We ask whether something might have been true, or might have been false. Well, if something is false, it's obviously not necessarily true. If it is true, might it have been otherwise? Is it possible that, in this respect, the world should have been different from the way it is? If the answer is 'no', then this fact about the world is a necessary one. If the answer is 'yes', then this fact about the world is a contingent one. This in and of itself has nothing to do with anyone's knowledge of anything. It's certainly a philosophical thesis, and not a matter of obvious definitional equivalence, either that everything *a priori* is necessary or that everything necessary is *a priori*. Both concepts may be vague. That may be another problem. But at any rate they are dealing with two different domains, two different areas, the epistemological and the metaphysical. Consider, say, Fermat's last theorem – or the Goldbach conjecture. The Goldbach conjecture says that an even number greater than 2 must be the sum of two prime numbers. If this is true, it is presumably necessary, and, if it is false, presumably necessarily false. We are taking the classical view of mathematics here and assume that in mathematical reality it is either true or false.

If the Goldbach conjecture is false, then there is an even number, n, greater than 2, and for no primes p_1 and p_2, both $<n$, does $n = p_1 + p_2$. This fact about n, if true, is verifiable by direct computation, and thus is necessary if the results of arithmetical computations are necessary. On the other hand, if the conjecture is true, then every even number exceeding 2 is the sum of two primes. Could it then be the case that, although in fact every even number is the sum of two primes, there might have been an even number which was not the sum of two primes? What would that mean? Such a number would have to be one of 4, 6, 8, 10, ...; and, by hypothesis, since we are assuming Goldbach's conjecture to be true, each of these can be shown, by direct computation, to be the sum of two primes. Goldbach's conjecture, then, cannot be contingently true or false; whatever truth-value it has belongs to it by necessity.

But what we can say of course is that right now as far as we know, the question can come out either way. So, in the absence of a mathematical proof deciding this question, none of us has any *a priori* knowledge about this question in either direction. We don't know whether Goldbach's conjecture is true or false. So right now we certainly don't know anything *a priori* about it.

Perhaps it will be alleged that we *can* in principle know *a priori* whether it is true. Well, maybe we can. Of course an infinite mind which can search through all the numbers can or could. But I don't know whether a finite mind can or could. Maybe there just is no mathematical proof whatsoever which decides the conjecture. At any rate this might or might not be the case. Maybe there is a mathematical proof deciding this question; maybe every mathematical question is decidable by an intuitive proof or disproof. Hilbert thought so; others have thought not; still others have thought the question unintelligible unless the notion of intuitive proof is replaced by that of formal proof in a single system. Certainly no one formal system decides all mathematical questions, as we know from Gödel. At any rate, and this is the important thing, the question is not trivial; even though someone said that it's necessary, if true at all, that every even number is the sum of two primes, it doesn't follow that anyone knows anything *a priori* about it. It doesn't even seem to me to follow without some further philosophical argument (it is an interesting philosophical question) that anyone *could* know anything *a priori* about it. The 'could', as I said, involves some other modality. We mean that even if no one, perhaps even in the future, knows or will know *a priori* whether Goldbach's conjecture is right, in principle there is a way, which *could* have been used, of answering the question *a priori*. This assertion is not trivial.

The terms 'necessary' and '*a priori*', then, as applied to statements are *not* obvious synonyms. There may be a philosophical argument connecting them, perhaps even identifying them; but an argument is required, not simply the observation that the two terms are clearly interchangeable. (I will argue below that in fact they are not even co-extensive – that necessary *a posteriori* truths, and probably contingent *a priori* truths, both exist.)

I think people have thought that these two things must mean the same for these reasons. First, if something not only happens to be true in the actual world but is also true in all possible worlds, then, or course, just by running through all the possible worlds in our heads, we ought to be able with enough effort to see, if a statement is necessary, that it is necessary, and thus know it *a priori*. But really this is not so obviously feasible at all.

Secondly, I guess it's thought that, conversely, if something is known *a priori* it must be necessary, because it was known without looking at the world. If it depended on some contingent feature of the actual world, how could you know it without looking? Maybe the actual world is one of the possible worlds in which it would have been false. This depends on the thesis that there can't be a way of knowing about the actual world without looking which wouldn't be a way of knowing the same thing about every possible world. This involves problems of epistemology and the nature of knowledge; and of course it is very vague as stated. But it is not really *trivial* either. More important than any particular example of something which is alleged to be necessary and not *a priori* or *a priori* and not necessary, is to see that the notions are different, that it's not trivial to argue on the basis of something's being something which maybe we can only know *a posteriori*, that it's not a necessary truth. It's not trivial just because something is known in some sense *a priori*, that what is known is a necessary truth.

Another term used in philosophy is 'analytic'. Here it won't be too important to get any clearer about this in this talk. The common examples of analytic statements, nowadays, are like 'bachelors are unmarried'. Kant, (someone just pointed out to me) gives as an example 'gold is a yellow metal', which seems to me an extraordinary one, because it's something I think that can turn out to be false. At any rate, let's just make it a matter of stipulation that an analytic statement is in some sense true by virtue of its meaning and true in all possible worlds by virtue of its meaning. Then something which is analytically true will be both necessary and *a priori*. (That's sort of stipulative.)

Another category I mentioned was that of certainty. Whatever certainty is, it's clearly not obviously the case that everything which is necessary is certain. Certainty is another epistemological notion. Something can be known, or at least rationally believed, *a priori*, without being quite certain. You've read a proof in the math book; and, though you think it's correct, maybe you've made a mistake. You often do make mistakes of this kind. You've made a computation, perhaps with an error.

There is one more question I want to go into in a preliminary way. Some philosophers have distinguished between essentialism, the belief in modality *de re*, and a mere advocacy of necessity, the belief in modality *de dicto*. Now, some people say: Let's give you the concept of necessity.[11] A much worse thing, something creating great additional problems, is whether we can say of any particular that it has necessary or contingent properties, even make the distinction between necessary and contingent properties. Look, it's only a *statement* or a *state of affairs* which can be either necessary or contingent. Whether a *particular* necessarily or contingently has a certain property depends on the way it's described. This is perhaps closely related to the view that the way we refer to particular things is by a description. What is Quine's famous example? If we consider the number 9, does it have the property of necessary oddness? Has that number got to be odd in all possible worlds? Certainly it's true in all possible worlds, let's say, it couldn't have been otherwise, that *nine* is odd. Of course, 9 could also be equally well picked out as *the number of planets*. It is not necessary, not true in all possible worlds, that the number of planets is odd. For example if there had been eight planets, the number of planets would not have been odd. And so it's thought: Was it necessary or contingent that Nixon won the election? (It might seem contingent, unless one has some view of some inexorable processes....) But this is a contingent property of Nixon only relative to our referring to him as 'Nixon' (assuming 'Nixon' doesn't mean 'the man who won the election at such and such a time'). But if we designate Nixon as 'the man who won the election in 1968', then it will be a necessary truth, of course, that the man who won the election in 1968, won the election in 1968. Similarly whether an object has the same property in all possible worlds depends not just on the object itself but on how it is described. So it's argued.

It is even suggested in the literature, that though a notion of necessity may have some sort of intuition behind it (we do think some things could have been otherwise; other things we don't think could have been otherwise), this notion [of a distinction between necessary and contingent properties] is just a doctrine made up by some bad philosopher, who (I guess) didn't realize that there are several ways of referring to the same thing. I don't know if some philosophers have not realized this; but at any rate it is very far from being true that this idea [that a property can be held to be essential or accidental to an object independently of its description] is a notion which has no intuitive content, which means nothing to the ordinary man. Suppose that someone said, pointing to Nixon, 'That's the guy who might have lost'. Someone else says 'Oh no, if you describe him as 'Nixon', then he might have lost; but, of course, describing him as the winner, then it is not true that he might have lost'. Now which one is being the philosopher, here, the unintuitive man? It seems to me obviously to be the second. The second man has a philosophical theory. The first man would say, and with great conviction, "Well, of course, the winner of the election *might have been someone else*. The actual winner, had the course of the campaign been different, might have been the loser, and someone else the winner; or there might have been no election at all. So, such terms as 'the winner' and 'the loser' don't designate the same objects in all possible worlds. On the other hand, the term 'Nixon' is just a *name* of *this man*". When you ask whether it is necessary or contingent that *Nixon* won the election, you are asking the intuitive question whether in some counterfactual situation, *this man* would in fact have lost the election. If someone thinks that the notion of a necessary property (forget whether there *are* any necessary properties [and consider] just the *meaningfulness* of the notion[12]) is a philosopher's notion with no intuitive content, he is wrong. Of course, some philosophers think that something's having intuitive content is very inconclusive evidence in favor of it. I think it is very heavy evidence in favor of anything, myself. I really don't know in a way what more conclusive evidence one can have about anything, ultimately speaking. But, in any event, people who think the notion of accidental property unintuitive have intuition reversed, I think.

Why have they thought this? While there are many motivations for people thinking this, one is this: The question of essential properties so-called is supposed to be equivalent (and it is equivalent) to the question of identity across possible worlds. Suppose we have someone, Nixon, and there's another possible world where there is no one with all the properties Nixon has in the actual world. Which one of these other people, if any, is Nixon? Surely you must give some criterion of identity here. If you have a criterion of identity, then you just look in the other possible worlds at the man who is Nixon and the question whether in that other possible world Nixon has certain properties is well defined. It is also supposed to be well defined, in terms of such notions, whether it's true in all possible worlds, or there are some possible worlds in which Nixon didn't win the election. But, it's said, the problems of giving such criteria of identity are very difficult. Sometimes in the case of numbers it might seem easier (but even here it's argued that it's quite arbitrary). For example, one might say, and this is surely the truth, that if position in the series of numbers is what makes the number 9 what it is, then if (in another world) the number of planets had been 8, the number of planets would be a different number from the one it·actually is. You wouldn't say that that number then is to be identified with our number 9 in this world. In the case of other types of objects, say people, material objects, things like that, has anyone given a set of necessary and sufficient conditions for identity across possible worlds?

Really, adequate necessary and sufficient conditions for identity which do not beg the question are very rare in any case. Mathematics is the only case I really know of where they are given even *within* a possible world, to tell the truth. I don't know of such conditions for identity of material objects over time, or for people. Everyone knows what a problem this is. But, let's forget about that. What seems to be more objectionable is that this depends on the wrong way of looking at what a possible world is. One thinks, in this picture, a possible world as if it were like a foreign country. One looks upon it as an observer. Maybe Nixon has moved to the other country and maybe he hasn't, but one is given only qualities. One can observe all his qualities, but of course, one doesn't observe that someone is Nixon. One observes that something has red hair (or green or yellow) but not whether something is Nixon. So we had better have a way of telling in terms of properties when we run into the same thing again as we saw before; we had better have a way of telling, when we come across one of these other possible worlds, who was Nixon.

Some logicians in their formal treatment of modal logic may encourage this picture. A prominent example, perhaps, is myself. Nevertheless, intuitively speaking, it seems to me not to be the right way of thinking about the possible worlds. A possible world isn't a distant country that we are coming across, or viewing through a telescope, Generally speaking, another possible world is too far away. Even if we travel faster than light, we won't get to it. A possible world is *given by the descriptive conditions we associate with it*. What do we mean when we say 'In some other possible worlds I might not have given this lecture today'? We just imagine the situation where I didn't decide to give this lecture or decided to give it on some other day. Of course, we don't imagine everything that is true or false, but only those things relevant to my giving the lecture; but, in theory, everything needs to be decided to make a total description of the world. We can't really imagine that except in part; that, then, is a 'possible world'. Why can't it be part of the *description* of a possible world that it contains *Nixon* and that in that world *Nixon* didn't win the election? It might be a question, of course, whether such a world *is* possible. (Here it would seem, *prima facie*, to be clearly possible.) But, once we see that such a situation is possible, then we are given that the man who might have lost the election or did lose the election in this possible world is Nixon, because that's part of the description of the world. 'Possible worlds' are *stipulated*, not *discovered* by powerful telescopes. There is no reason why we cannot *stipulate* that, in talking about what would have happened to Nixon in a certain counterfactual situation, we are talking about what would have happened to *him*.

Of course, if someone makes the demand that every possible world has to be described in a purely qualitative way, we can't say, 'Suppose Nixon had lost the election', we could say instead 'suppose a man with a dog named Checkers, who looks like a certain David Fry impersonation, is in a certain possible world and loses the election', Well, does he re-semble Nixon enough to be identified with Nixon? A very explicit and blatant example of this way of looking at things is David Lewis' counter-part theory,[13] but the literature on quantified modality is replete with it.[14] Why need we make this demand? That is not the way we ordinarily think of counterfactual situations. We just say 'suppose this man had lost'. It is *given* that the possible world contains *this man*, and that in that world, he had lost. There may be a problem about what intuitions about possibility come to. But, if we have such an intuition about the possibility of *that* (*this man's* electoral loss), then it is about the possi-bility of *that*. It need not be identified with the possibility of a man looking like such and such, or holding such and such political views, or otherwise qualitatively described, having lost. We can point to the *man*, and ask what might have happened to *him*, had events been different.

It might be said 'Let's suppose that this is true. It comes down to the same thing, because whether Nixon could have had certain properties, different from the ones he actually has, is equivalent to the question of whether the criteria of identity across possible worlds include that Nixon does not have these properties'. But it doesn't really come to the same thing, because the usual notion of a criterion of transworld identity demands that we give purely qualitative necessary and sufficient con-ditions for someone being Nixon. If we can't imagine a possible world in which Nixon doesn't have a certain property, then it's a necessary condition of someone being Nixon. Or a necessary property of Nixon that he [has] that property. For example, supposing Nixon is in fact a human being, we might not imagine that there could have been a possible world in which he was, say, an inanimate object; perhaps it is not even possible for him not to have been a human being. Then it will be a necessary fact about Nixon that in all possible worlds where he exists at all, he is human or anyway he is not an inanimate object. This has nothing to do with any requirement that there be purely qualitative *sufficient* conditions for Nixonhood which we can spell out. And should there be? Maybe there is some argument that there should be, but we can consider these questions about *necessary* conditions without going into any question about *sufficient* conditions. Further, even if there were a purely qualitative set of necessary and sufficient conditions for being Nixon, the view I advocate would not demand that we find these conditions before we can ask whether Nixon might have won the election, nor does it demand that we restate the question in terms of such conditions. We can simply consider Nixon and ask what might have happened to him had various circumstances been different. So the two views, the two ways of looking at things, do seem to me to make a difference.

Notice this question, whether Nixon could not have been a human being, is a clear case where the question asked is not epistemological. Suppose Nixon actually turned out to be an automaton. That might happen. We might need evidence for whether Nixon is a human being or an automaton. But that is a question about our knowledge. The question of whether Nixon might have not been a human being, given that he is one, is not a question about knowledge, *a posteriori* or *a priori*. It's a question about, even though such and such things are the case, what might have been the case otherwise.

This table is composed of molecules. Might it not have been composed of molecules? Certainly it was a scientific discovery of great moment that it was composed of molecules (or atoms). But could anything be this very object and not be composed of molecules? Certainly there is some feeling that the answer to that must be 'no'. At any rate it's hard to imagine under what circumstances you would have this very object and find that it is not composed of molecules. A quite different question is whether it is in fact composed of molecules in the actual world and how we know this. (I will go into more detail about these questions about essence later on.)

I wish at this point to introduce something which I need in the methodology of discussing the theory of names that I'm talking about. We need the notion of 'identity across possible worlds' as it's usually and, as I think, somewhat misleadingly called,[15] to explicate one distinction that I want to make now. What's the difference between asking whether it's necessary that 9 is greater than 7 or whether it's necessary that the number of planets be greater than 7? Why does one show anything more about essence than the other? The answer to this might be intuitively 'Well, look, the number of planets might have been different from what it in fact is. It doesn't make any sense, though, to say that nine might have been different from what it in fact is'. Let's use some terms quasitechnically. Let's call something a *rigid designator* if in any possible world it designates the same object, a *non rigid* or *accidental designator* if that is not the case. Of course we don't require that the objects exist in all possible worlds. Certainly Nixon might not have existed if his parents had not gotten married, in the normal course of things. When we think of a property as essential to an object we usually mean that it is true of that object in any case where it would have existed. A rigid designator of a necessary existent can be called *strongly rigid*.

One of the intuitive theses I will maintain in these talks is that *names* are rigid designators. Certainly they seem to satisfy the intuitive test mentioned above: although someone other than the U.S. President in 1970 might have been the U.S. President in 1970 (e.g., Humphrey might have), no one other than Nixon might have been Nixon. In the same way, a designator rigidly designates a certain object if it designates that object wherever the object exists; if, in addition, the object is a necessary existent, the designator can be called *strongly rigid*. For example, 'the President of the U.S. in 1970' designates a certain man, Nixon; but someone else (e.g., Humphrey) might have been the President in 1970, and Nixon might not have; so this designator is not rigid.

In these lectures, I will argue, intuitively, that proper names are rigid designators, for although the man (Nixon) might not have been the President, it is not the case that he might not have been Nixon (though he might not have been *called* 'Nixon'). Those who have argued that to make sense of the notion of rigid designator, we must antecendently make sense of 'criteria of transworld identity' have precisely reversed the cart and the horse; it is *because* we can refer (rigidly) to Nixon, and stipulate that we are speaking of what might have happened to *him* (under certain circumstances), that 'transworld identifications' are unproblematic in such cases.[16]

The tendency to demand purely qualitative descriptions of counterfactual situations has many sources. One, perhaps, is the confusion of the epistemological and the metaphysical, between a prioricity and necessity. If someone identifies necessity with a prioricity, and thinks that objects are named by means of uniquely identifying properties, he may think that it is the properties used to identify the object which, being known about it *a priori*, must be used to identify it in all possible worlds, to find out which object is Nixon. As against this, I repeat: (1) Generally, things aren't 'found out' about a counterfactual situation, they are stipulated; (2) possible worlds need not be given purely qualitatively, as if we were looking at them through a telescope. And we will see shortly that the properties an object has in a counterfactual world have nothing to do with the properties used to identify it in the actual world.[17]

Does the 'problem'. of 'transworld identification' make any sense? Is it *simply* a pseudo-problem? The following, it seems to me, can be said for it. Although the statement that England fought Germany in 1943 perhaps cannot be *reduced* to any statement about individuals, nevertheless in some sense it is not a fact 'over and above' the collection of all facts about persons, and their behavior over history. The sense in which facts about nations are not facts 'over and above' those about persons can be expressed in the observation that a description of the world mentioning all facts about persons but omitting those about nations can be a *complete* description of the world, from which the facts about nations follow. Similarly, perhaps, facts about material objects are not facts 'over and above' facts about their constituent molecules. We may then ask, given a description of a non-actualized possible situation in terms of people, whether England still exists in that situation, or whether a certain nation (described, say, as the one where Jones lives) which would exist in that situation, is England. Similarly, given certain counterfactual vicissitudes in the history of the molecules of a table, T, one may ask whether T would exist, in that situation, or whether a certain bunch of molecules, which in that situation would constitute a table, constitute the very same table T. In each case, we ask criteria of identity across possible worlds for certain particulars in terms of those for other, more 'basic', particulars. If statements about nations (or tribes) are not *reducible* to those about other more 'basic' constituents, if there is some 'open texture' in the relationship between them, we can hardly expect to give hard and fast identity criteria; nevertheless, in concrete cases we may be able to answer whether a certain bunch of molecules would still constitute T, though in some cases the answer may be indeterminate. I think similar remarks apply to the problem of identity over time; here too we are usually concerned with determinacy, the identity of a 'complex' particular in terms of more 'basic' ones. (For example, if various parts of a table are replaced, is it the same object?[18])

Such conception of 'transworld identification', however, differs considerably from the usual one. First, although we can try to describe the world in terms of molecules, there is no impropriety in describing it in terms of grosser entities: the statement that *this table* might have been placed in another room is perfectly proper, in and of itself. We *need* not use the description in terms of molecules, or even grosser parts of the table, though we *may*. Unless we assume that some particulars are 'ultimate', 'basic' particulars, no type of description need be regarded as privileged. We can ask whether *Nixon* might have lost the election without further subtlety, and usually no further subtlety is required. Second, it is not assumed that necessary and sufficient conditions for what kinds of collections of molecules make up this table are possible; this fact I just mentioned. Third, the attempted notion deals with criteria of identity of particulars in terms of other *particulars*, not qualities. I can refer to the table before me, and ask what might have happened to it under certain circumstances; I can also refer to its molecules. If, on the other hand, it is demanded that I describe each counterfactual situation purely qualitatively, then I can only ask whether *a table*, of such and such color, and so on, would have certain properties; whether the table in question would be *this table*, table *T*, is indeed moot, since all reference to objects, as opposed to qualities, has disappeared. It is often said that, if a counterfactual situation is described as one which would have happened to *Nixon*, and if it is not assumed that such a description is reducible to a purely qualitative one, then mysterious 'bare particulars' are assumed, propertyless substrata underlying the qualities. This is not so: I think that Nixon is a Republican, not merely that he lies in back of Republicanism, whatever that means; I also think he might have been a Democrat. The same holds for any other properties Nixon may possess, except that some of these properties may be essential. What I do deny is that a particular is nothing but a 'bundle of qualities', whatever that may mean. If a quality is an abstract object, a bundle of qualities is an object of an even higher degree of abstraction, not a particular. Philosophers have come to the opposite view through a false dilemma: they have asked, are these objects *behind* the bundle of qualities, or is the object *nothing but* the bundle? Neither is the case; this table is wooden, brown, in the room, etc. It has all these properties and is not a thing without properties, behind them; but it should not therefore be identified with the set, or 'bundle', of its properties, nor with the subset of its essential properties. Don't ask: how can I identify this table in another possible world, except by its properties? I have the table in my hands,

I can point to it, and when I ask whether *it* might have been in another room, I am talking, by definition, about *it*. I don't have to identify it after seeing it through a telescope. If I am talking about it, I am talking about *it*, in the same way as when I say that our hands might have been painted green, I have stipulated that I am talking about greenness. Some properties of an object may be essential to it, in that it could not have failed to have them; but these properties are not used to identify the object in another possible world, for such an identification is not needed; nor need the essential properties of an object be the properties used to identify it in the actual world, if indeed it is identified in the actual world by means of properties (I have up to now left the question open).

So: the question of transworld identification makes *some* sense, in terms of asking about the identity of an object *via* questions about its component parts. But these parts are not qualities, and it is not an object resembling the given one which is in question. Theorists have often said that we identify objects across possible worlds as objects resembling the given one in the most important respects. On the contrary, Nixon, had he decided to act otherwise, might have avoided politics like the plague, through privately harboring radical opinions. Most important, even when we can replace questions about an object by questions about its parts, we need not do so. We can refer to the object and ask what might have happened to *it*. So, we do not begin with worlds (which are supposed somehow to be real, and whose qualities, but not whose objects, are perceptible to us), and then ask about criteria of transworld identification; on the contrary, we begin with the objects, which we *have*, and can identify, in the actual world. We can then ask whether certain things might have been true of the objects.

I mentioned the distinction between this question about the theory of naming as the theory of meaning or as a theory of reference. Let me give an example of this. Suppose someone stipulates that 100 degrees centigrade is to be the temperature at which water boils at sea level. This isn't completely precise because the pressure may vary at sea level. Of course, historically, a more precise definition was given later. But let's suppose that this were the definition. Another sort of example in the literature is that one meter is to be the length of S where S is a certain stick or bar in Paris. (Usually people who like to talk about these definitions then try to make 'the length of' into an 'operational' concept. But it's not important.)

Wittgenstein says something very puzzling about this. He says: "There is one thing of which one can say neither that it is one meter long nor that it is not one meter long, and that is the standard meter in Paris. But this is, of course, not to ascribe any extraordinary property to it, but only to mark its peculiar role in the language game of measuring with a meter rule."[19] This seems to be a very 'extraordinary property', actually, for any stick to have. I think he must be wrong. If the stick is a stick, for example, 39.37 inches long (I assume we have some different standard for inches), why isn't it one meter long? Anyway, let's suppose that he is wrong and that the stick is one meter long. Part of the problem which is bothering Wittgenstein is, of course, that this stick serves as a standard of length and so we can't attribute length to it. Be this as it may (well, it may not be), is the statement 'stick S is one meter long', a necessary truth? Of course its length might vary in time. We could make the definition more precise by stipulating that one meter is to be the length of S at a fixed time t_0. Is it then a necessary truth that stick S is one meter long at time t_0? Someone who thinks that everything one knows *a priori* is necessary might think: "This is the *definition* of a meter. By definition, stick S is one meter long at t_0. That's a necessary truth." But there seems to me to be no reason so to conclude, even for a man who uses the stated definition of 'one meter'. For he's using this definition not to *give the meaning* of what he called the 'meter', but to *fix the reference*. (For such an abstract thing as a unit of length, the notion of reference may be unclear. But let's suppose it's clear enough for the present purposes.) He uses it to fix a reference. There is a certain length which he wants to mark out. He marks it out by an accidental property, namely that there is a stick of that length. Someone else might mark out the same reference by another accidental property. But in any case, even though he uses this to fix the reference of his standard of length, a meter, he can still say, "if heat had been applied to this stick S at t_0, then at t_0 stick S would not have been one meter long."

Well, why can he do this? Part of the reason may lie in some people's minds in the philosophy of science, which I don't want to go into here. But a simple answer to the question is this: Even if this is the *only* standard of length that he uses,[20] there is an intuitive difference between the phrase 'one meter' and the phrase 'the length of S at t_0'. The first phrase is meant to designate rigidly a certain length in all possible worlds, which in the actual world happens to be the length of the stick S at t_0. On the other hand 'the length of S at t_0' does not designate anything rigidly. In some counterfactual situations the stick might have been longer and in some shorter if various stresses and strains had been applied to it. So we can say of this stick the same way as we would of any other of the same substance and length, that if heat of a given quantity had been applied to it, it would have expanded to such and such a length. Such a counterfactual statement, being true of other sticks with identical physical properties, will also be true of this stick. There is no conflict between that counterfactual statement and the definition of 'one meter' as 'the length of S at t_0', because the 'definition', properly interpreted, does *not* say that the phrase 'one meter' is to be *synonymous* (even when talking about counterfactual situations) with the phrase 'the length of S at t_0', but rather that we have *determined the reference* of the phrase 'one meter' by stipulating that 'one meter' is to be a *rigid* designator of the length which is in fact the length of S at t_0. So this does *not* make it a necessary truth that S is one meter long at t_0. In fact, under certain circumstances, S would not have been one meter long. The reason is that one designator ('one meter') is rigid and the other designator ('the length of S at t_0') is not.

What then, is the *epistemological* status of the statement 'Stick S is one meter long at t_0', for someone who has fixed the metric system by reference to stick S? It would seem that he knows it *a priori*. For if he used stick S to fix the reference of the term 'one meter', then as a result of this kind of 'definition' (which is not an abbreviative or synonymous definition), he knows automatically, without further investigation, that S is one meter long.[21] On the other hand, even if S is used as the standard of a meter, the *metaphysical* status of 'S is one meter long' will be that of a contingent statement, provided that 'one meter' is regarded as a rigid designator: under appropriate stresses and strains, heatings or coolings, S would have had a length other than one meter even at t_0. (Such statements as, 'Water boils at 100°C at sea level', can have a similar status.) So in this sense, there are contingent *a priori* truths. More important for present purposes, though, than accepting this example as an instance of the contingent *a priori*, is its illustration of the distinction between 'definitions' which fix a reference and those which give a synonym.

In the case of names one might make this distinction too. Suppose the reference of a name is given by a description or a cluster of descriptions. If the name *means the same* as that description or cluster of descriptions, it will not be a rigid designator. It will not necessarily designate the same object in all possible worlds, since other objects might have had the given properties in other possible worlds; unless (of course) we happened to use essential properties in our description. So suppose we say, 'Aristotle is the greatest man who studied under Plato'. If we used that as a *definition*, the name 'Aristotle' is to mean 'the greatest man who studied under Plato'. Then of course in some other possible world that man might not have studied under Plato and some other man would have been Aristotle. If, on the other hand, we merely use the description to *fix the referent* then that man will be the referent of 'Aristotle' in all possible worlds. The only use of the description will have been to pick out to which man we mean to refer. But then, when we say counterfactually 'suppose Aristotle had never gone into philosophy at all', we need not mean 'suppose a man who studied with Plato, and taught Alexander the Great, and wrote this and that, and so on, had never gone into philosophy at all', which might seem like a contradiction. We need only mean, 'suppose that *that man* had never gone into philosophy at all'.

It seems plausible to suppose that, in some cases, the reference of a name is indeed fixed *via* a description in the same way that the metric system was fixed.

When the mythical agent first saw Hesperus, he may well have fixed his reference by saying, "I shall use 'Hesperus' as a name of the heavenly body appearing in yonder position in the sky." He then has fixed the reference of 'Hesperus' by its apparent celestial position. Does it follow that it is part of the *meaning* of the name that Hesperus has such and such position at the time in question? Surely not: if Hesperus had been hit earlier by a comet, it might have been visible at a different position at that time. In such a counterfactual situation we would say that Hesperus would not have occupied that position, but not that Hesperus would not have been Hesperus. The reason is that 'Hesperus' rigidly designates a certain heavenly body and 'the body in yonder position' does not – a different body, or no body might have been in that position, but no other body might have been Hesperus (though another body, not Hesperus, might have been *called* 'Hesperus'). Indeed, as I have said, I will hold that names are always rigid designators.

Frege and Russell certainly seem to have the full blown theory according to which a proper name is not a rigid designator and is synonymous with the description which replaced it. But another theory might be that this description is used to determine a rigid reference. These two alternatives will have different consequences for the questions I was asking before. If 'Moses' *means* 'the man who did such and such', then, if no one did such and such, Moses didn't exist; and maybe 'no one did such and such' is even an *analysis* of 'Moses didn't exist'. But if the description is used to fix a reference rigidly, then it's clear that that is *not* what is meant by 'Moses didn't exist', because we can ask, if we speak of a counter-factual case where no one did indeed do such and such, say, lead the Israelites out of Egypt, does it follow that, in such a situation, Moses wouldn't have existed? It would seem not. For surely Moses might have just decided to spend his days more pleasantly in the Egyptian courts. He might never have gone into either politics or religion at all; and in that case maybe no one would have done any of the things that the Bible relates of Moses. That doesn't in itself mean that in such a possible world Moses wouldn't have existed. If so, then 'Moses exists' means something different from 'the existence and uniqueness conditions for a certain description are fulfilled'; and therefore this does not give an analysis of the singular existential statements after all. If you give up the idea that this is a theory of meaning and make it into a theory of reference in the way that I have described it, you give up some of the advantages of the theory. Singular existential statements and identity statements between names need some other analysis.

Frege should be criticized for using the term 'sense' in two senses. For he takes the sense of a designator to be its meaning; and he also takes it the way its reference is determined. Identifying the two, he supposes that both are given by definite descriptions. Ultimately, I will reject this second supposition too; but even were it right, I reject the first. A description may be used as synonymous with a designator, or it may be used to fix its reference. The two Fregean senses of 'sense' correspond to two senses of 'definition' in ordinary parlance. They should carefully be distinguished.[22]

I hope the idea of fixing the reference as opposed to actually defining one term as meaning the other is somewhat clear. There is really not enough time to go into every thing in great detail. I think, even in cases where the notion of rigidity versus accidentality of designation cannot be used to make out the difference in question, some things called definitions really intend to fix a reference rather than to give the meaning of a phrase, to give a synonym. Let me give an example. π is supposed to be the ratio of the circumference of a circle to its diameter. Now, it's something that I have nothing but a vague intuitive feeling to argue for: It seems to me that here this Greek letter is not being used as short for the phrase 'the ratio of the circumference of a circle to its diameter' nor is it even used as short for a cluster of alternative definitions of π, whatever that might mean. It is used as a name for a real number, which in this case is necessarily the ratio of the circumference of a circle to its diameter. Note that here both 'π' and the 'ratio of the circumference of a circle to its diameter' are rigid designators, so the arguments given in the metric case are inapplicable. (Well, if someone doesn't see this, or thinks it's wrong, it doesn't matter.)

Let me return to the question about names which I raised. As I said, there is a popular modern substitute for the theory of Frege and Russell; it is adopted even by such a strong critic of many views of Frege and Russell, especially the latter, as Strawson.[23] The substitute is that, although a name is not a disguised description it either abbreviates, or anyway its reference is determined by, some cluster of descriptions. The question is whether this is true. And as I say, there are stronger and weaker versions of this. The stronger version would say that the name is simply *defined*, synonymously, as the cluster of descriptions. It will then be necessary, not that Moses had any particular property in this cluster, but that he had the disjunction of them. There couldn't be any counterfactual situation in which he didn't do any of those things. I think it's clear that I think this is very implausible. People *have* said it – or maybe they haven't been intending to say that, but were using 'necessary' in some other sense. At any rate, for example, in Searle's article on proper names:

To put the same point differently, suppose we ask, 'why do we have proper names at all?' Obviously to refer to individuals. 'Yes but descriptions could do that for us'. But only at the cost of specifying identity conditions every time reference is made: Suppose we agree to drop 'Aristotle' and use, say, 'the teacher of Alexander', then it is a necessary truth that the man referred to is Alexander's teacher – but it is a contingent fact that Aristotle ever went into pedagogy (though I am suggesting that it is a necessary fact that Aristotle has the logical sum, inclusive disjunction, of properties commonly attributed to him).[24]

Such a suggestion, if 'necessary' is used in the way I have been using it in this lecture, must clearly be false. (Unless he's got some very interesting essential property commonly attributed to Aristotle.) Most of the things commonly attributed to Aristotle are things that Aristotle might not have done at all. In a situation in which he didn't do them, we would describe that as a situation in which *Aristotle* didn't do them. This is not a distinction of scope, as happens sometimes in the case of descriptions, where someone might say that the man who taught Alexander might not have taught Alexander; though it could not have been true that: the man who taught Alexander didn't teach Alexander. This is Russell's distinction of scope. (I won't go into it.) It seems to me clear that this is not the case here. Not only is it true *of* the man Aristotle that he might not have gone into pedagogy; it is also true that we use the term 'Aristotle' in such a way that, in thinking of a counterfactual situation in which Aristotle didn't go into any of the fields and do any of the achievements we commonly attribute to him, still we would say that was a situation in which *Aristotle* did not do these things.[25] Well there are some things like the date, the period he lived, that might be more imagined as necessary. Maybe those are things we commonly attribute to him. There are exceptions. Maybe it's hard to imagine how he could have lived 500 years later than he in fact did. That certainly raises at least a problem. But take a man who doesn't have any idea of the date. Many people just have some vague cluster of his most famous achievements. Not only each of these singly, but the possession of the entire disjunction of these properties, is just a contingent fact about Aristotle; and the statement that Aristotle had this disjunction of properties is a contingent truth.

A man might know it *a priori* in some sense, if he in fact fixes the reference of 'Aristotle' as the man who did one of these things. Still it won't be a necessary truth for him. So this sort of example would be an example where *a priority* would not necessarily imply necessity, if the cluster theory of names were right. The case of fixing the reference of 'one meter' is a very clear example in which someone, just because he fixed the reference in this way, can in some sense know *a priori* that the length of this stick is a meter without regarding it as a necessary truth. Maybe the thesis about *a priority* implying necessity can be modified.

It does appear to state some insight which might be important, and true, about epistemology. In a way an example like this may seem like a trivial counterexample which is not really the point of what some people think when they think that only necessary truths can be known *a priori*. Well, if the thesis that all *a priori* truth is necessary is to be immune from this sort of counterexample, it needs to be modified in some way. Unmodified it leads to confusion about the nature of reference. And I myself have no idea how it should be modified or restated, or if such a modification or restatement is possible.[26]

Let me state then what the cluster concept theory of names is. (It really is a nice theory. The only defect I think it has is probably common to all philosophical theories. It's wrong. You may suspect me of proposing another theory in its place; but I hope not, because I'm sure it's wrong too if it is a theory.) The theory in question can be broken down into a large number of theses, especially if you want to see how it handles the problem of identity statements, existence statements, and so on. There are more statements if you take it in the stronger version as a theory of meaning. The speaker is A.

(1)   To every name or designating expression 'X', there corresponds a cluster of properties, namely the family of properties ϕ such that A believes 'ϕX'.

This thesis is true, because it can just be a definition. Now, of course, some people might think that not everything the speaker believes about X has anything to do with determining the reference of 'X'. They might only be interested in a subset. But we can handle this later on by modifying some of the other features. So this thesis is correct, by definition. The theses that follow, however, are all, I think, false.

(2)   One of the properties, or some conjointly, are believed by A to pick out some individual uniquely.

This doesn't say that they do pick out something uniquely, just that A believes that they do. Another thesis is that he is correct.

(3)   If most, or a weighted most, of the ϕ's are satisfied by one unique object y, then y is the referent of 'X'.

Well, the theory says that the referent of 'X' is supposed to be the thing satisfying, if not all the properties, 'enough' of them. Obviously A could be wrong about some things about X. You take some sort of a vote. Now the question is whether this vote should be democratic or have some inequalities among the properties. It seems more plausible that there should be some weighting, that some properties are more important than others. A theory really has to specify how this weighting goes. I believe that Strawson, to my surprise, explicitly states that democracy should rule here, so the most trivial properties are of equal weight with the most crucial.[27] Surely it is more plausible to suppose that there is some weighting. Let's say democracy doesn't necessarily rule. If there is any property that's completely irrelevant to the reference we can disenfranchise it altogether, by giving it weight 0. The properties can be regarded as members of a corporation. Some have more stock than others; some may even have only non-voting stock.

(4)   If the vote yields no unique object, 'X' does not refer.

(5)   The statement, 'If X exists, then X has most of the ϕ's' is known *a priori* by the speaker.

(6)   The statement, 'If X exists, then X has most of the ϕ's' expresses a necessary truth (in the idiolect of the speaker).

(6) need not be a thesis of the theory if someone doesn't think that the cluster is part of the meaning of the name. He could think that though he determines the reference of Aristotle as the man who had most of the ϕ's, still there are certainly possible situations in which Aristotle wouldn't have had most of the ϕ's.

There are some subsidiary theses I was mentioning. These would give the analyses of singular existential statements, like 'Moses exists', means 'enough of the properties ϕ are satisfied'. Even the man who doesn't use the theory as a theory of meaning has some of these theses. For example, subsidiary to thesis 4, we should say that it is *a priori* true for the speaker that, if not enough of the ϕ's are satisfied, then 'X' does not exist. Only if he holds the view as a theory of meaning, rather than of reference, would it also be *necessarily* true that, if not enough of the ϕ's are satisfied, 'X' does not exist. In any case it will be something he knows *a priori*. (At least he will know it *a priori* provided he knows the proper theory of names.) Then there is also an analysis of identity statements along the same lines.

The question is, are any of these true? If true, they give a nice picture of what's going on. Preliminary to discussing these theses, let me mention that, often, when people specify which properties ϕ are relevant, they seem to specify them wrongly. That's just an incidental defect, though it is closely related to the arguments against the theory that I will give presently. Consider the example from Wittgenstein. What does he say the relevant properties are? "When one says 'Moses does not exist', this may mean various things. It may mean: the Israelites did not have a *single* leader when they withdrew from Egypt – or: their leader was not called Moses – or: there cannot have been anyone who accomplished all that the Bible relates of Moses ...." The gist of all this is that we know *a priori* that, if the Biblical story is substantially false, Moses did not exist. I have already argued that the Biblical story does not give *necessary* properties of Moses, that he might have lived without doing any of these things. Here I ask whether we know *a priori* that if Moses existed, he in fact did some or most of them. Is this really the cluster of properties that we should use here? Surely there is a distinction which is neglected in these kinds of remarks. The Biblical story might have been a complete legend, or it might have been a substantially false account of a real person. In the latter case, it seems to me that a scholar could say that he supposes that, though Moses did exist, the things said of him in the Bible are substantially false. Such things occur in this very field of scholarship. Suppose that someone says that no prophet ever was swallowed by a big fish or a whale. Does it follow, on that basis, that Jonah did not exist? There still seems to be the question whether the Biblical account is a legendary account of no person or a legendary account built on a real person. In the latter case, it's only natural to say that, though Jonah did exist, no one did the things commonly related to him. I choose this case because while Biblical scholars generally hold that Jonah did exist, the account not only of his being swallowed by a big fish but even going to Nineveh to preach or anything else that is said in the Biblical story is assumed to be substantially false. But nevertheless there are reasons for thinking this was about a real prophet. If I had a suitable book along with me I could start quoting out of it: 'Jonah, the Son of Amittai, was a real prophet, however such and such and such'. There are independent reasons for thinking this was not a pure legend about an imaginary character but one about a real character.[28]

These examples could be modified. Maybe all we believe is that *the Bible relates of him* that such and such. This gives us another problem, because how do we know whom the Bible is referring to? The question of our reference is thrown back to the question of reference in the Bible. This leads to a condition which we ought to put in explicitly.

(C) For any successful theory, the account must not be circular. The properties which are used in the vote must not themselves involve the notion of reference in a way that it is ultimately impossible to eliminate.

Let me give an example where the noncircularity condition is clearly violated. The following theory of proper names is due to William Kneale in an article called 'Modality, De Dicto and De Re'.[29] It contains, I think, a clear violation of noncircularity conditions.

Ordinary proper names of people are not, as John Stuart Mill supposed, – signs without sense. While it may be informative to tell a man that the most famous Greek philosopher was called Socrates, it is obviously trifling to tell him that Socrates was called Socrates; and the reason is simply that he cannot understand your use of the word 'Socrates' at the beginning of your statement unless he already knows that 'Socrates' means 'The individual called 'Socrates' '.[30]

Here we have a theory of the reference of proper names. 'Socrates' just means 'the man called 'Socrates'.' Actually, of course, maybe not just one man can be called 'Socrates', and some may call him 'Socrates' while others may not. Certainly that is a condition which under some circumstances is uniquely satisfied. Maybe only one man was called 'Socrates' by me on a certain occasion.

Kneale says it's trifling to tell someone that Socrates *was* called 'Socrates'. That isn't trifling on any view. Maybe the Greeks didn't call him 'Socrates'. Let's say that Socrates is called 'Socrates' by us – by *me* anyway. Suppose that's trifling. (I find it surprising that Kneale uses the past tense here; it is dubious that the Greeks *did* call him 'Socrates' – at least, the Greek name is pronounced differently. I will check the accuracy of the quotation for the next lecture.)

Kneale gives an argument for this theory. 'Socrates' must be analyzed as 'the individual called 'Socrates'', because how else can we explain the fact that it is trifling to be told that Socrates is called 'Socrates'? In some cases that's rather trifling. In the same sense, I suppose, you could get a good theory of the meaning of any expression in English and construct a dictionary. For example, though it may be informative to tell someone that horses are used in races, it is trifling to tell him that horses are called 'horses'. Therefore this could only be the case because the term 'horse', means in English 'the things called 'horses' '. Similarly with any other expression which might be used in English. Since it's trifling to be told that sages are called 'sages', 'sages' just means 'the people called 'sages''. Now plainly this isn't really a very good argument, nor can it therefore be the only explanation of why it's trifling to be told that Socrates is called 'Socrates'. Let's not go into exactly why it's trifling. Of course, anyone who knows the use of 'is called' in English, even without knowing what the statement means, knows that if 'quarks' means something then 'quarks are called 'quarks'' will express a truth. He may not know what it expresses, because he doesn't know what a quark is. But that does not have much to do with the meaning of the term 'quarks'.

We could go into this actually at great length. There are interesting problems coming out of this sort of passage. But the main reason I wanted to introduce it here is that as a theory of reference it would give a clear violation of the noncircularity condition. Someone uses the name 'Socrates'. How are we supposed to know to whom he refers? By using the description which gives the sense of it. According to Kneale, the description is 'the man called 'Socrates''. And here, (presumably, since this is supposed to be so trifling!) it tells us nothing at all. Taking it in this way it seems to be no theory of reference at all. We ask to whom does he refer by 'Socrates' and then the answer is given as, well he refers to the man to whom he refers. If this were all there was to the meaning of a proper name, then no reference would get off the ground at all.

So there's a condition to be satisfied; in the case of this particular theory it's obviously unsatisfied. The paradigm amazingly enough, is even sometimes used by Russell as the descriptive sense, namely: 'the man called 'Walter Scott''. Obviously if the only descriptive senses of names we can think of are of the form 'the man called such and such', 'the man called 'Walter Scott'', 'the man called 'Socrates' ', then whatever this relation of *calling* is is really what determines the reference and not any description like 'the man called 'Socrates''.

LECTURE II: JANUARY 22, 1970

Last time we ended up talking about a theory of naming which is given by a number of theses here on the board.

(1)   To every name or designating expression 'X', there corresponds a cluster of properties, namely the family of those properties ϕ such that A believes 'ϕX'.

(2)   One of the properties, or some conjointly, are believed by A to pick out some individual uniquely.

(3)   If most, or a weighted most, of the ϕ's are satisfied by one unique object y, then y is the referent of 'X'.

(4)   If the vote yields no unique object, 'X' does not refer.

(5)   The statement, 'If X exists, then X has most of the ϕ's' is known *a priori* by the speaker.

(6)   The statement, 'If X exists, then X has most of the ϕ's' expresses a necessary truth (in the idiolect of the speaker).

(C)   For any successful theory, the account must not be circular. The properties which are used in the vote must not themselves involve the notion of reference in such a way that it is ultimately impossible to eliminate.

(C) is not a thesis but a condition on the satisfaction of the other theses. In other words Theses (1)–(6) cannot be satisfied in a way which leads to a circle, in a way which does not lead to any independent determination of reference. The example I gave last time of a blatantly circular attempt to satisfy these conditions, was a theory of names mentioned by William Kneale. I was a little surprised at the statement of the theory when I was reading what I had copied down, so I looked it up again. I looked it up in the book to see if I'd copied it down accurately. Kneale *did* use the past tense. He said that though it is not trifling to be told that Socrates was the greatest philosopher of ancient Greece, it is trifling to be told that Socrates was called 'Socrates'. Therefore, he concludes, the name 'Socrates' must simply mean 'the individual called 'Socrates''. Russell, as I've said, in some places gives a similar analysis. Anyway as stated using the past tense, the condition wouldn't be circular, because one certainly could decide to use the term 'Socrates' to refer to whoever was called 'Socrates' by the Greeks. But, of course, in that sense it's not at all trifling to be told that Socrates was called 'Socrates'. If this is any kind of fact, it might be false. Perhaps we know that *we* call him 'Socrates'; that hardly shows that the Greeks did so. In fact, of course, they may have pronounced the name differently. It may be, in the case of this particular name, that transliteration from the Greek is so good that the English version is not pronounced very differently from the Greek. But that won't be so in the general case. Certainly it is not trifling to be told that Isaiah was called 'Isaiah'. In fact, it is false to be told that Isaiah was called 'Isaiah'; the prophet wouldn't have recognized this name at all. And perhaps the Greeks didn't call their country anything like 'Greece'. Suppose we amend the thesis so that it reads: it's trifling to be told that Socrates is called 'Socrates' by us, or at least, by me, the speaker. Then in some sense this is fairly trifling. I don't think it is necessary or analytic. In the same way, it is trifling to be told that horses are called 'horses' without this leading to the conclusion that the word 'horse' simply *means* 'the animal called a 'horse''. As a theory of the referent of the name 'Socrates' it will lead immediately to a vicious circle. If one was determining the referent of a name like 'Glunk' to himself and made the following decision, 'I shall use the term 'Glunk' to refer to the man that I call 'Glunk'', this would get one nowhere. One had better have some independent determination of the referent of 'Glunk'. This is a good example of a blatantly circular determination. Actually sentences like 'Socrates is called 'Socrates'' are very interesting and one can spend, strange as it may seem, hours talking about their analysis. I actually did, once, do that. I won't do that, however, on this occasion. (See how high the seas of language can rise. And at the lowest points too.) Anyway this is a useful example of a violation of the noncircularity condition. The theory will satisfy all of these statements, perhaps, but it satisfies them only because there is some independent way of determining the reference independently of the particular condition: being the man called 'Socrates'.

I have already talked about, in the last lecture, Thesis (6). Theses (5) and (6), by the way, have converses. What I said for Thesis (5) is that the statement that if X exists, X has most of the ϕ's is *a priori* true for the speaker. It will also be true under the given theory that certain converses of this statement hold true also *a priori* for the speaker, namely; if any unique thing has most of the properties ϕ in the properly weighted sense, it is X. Similarly a certain converse to this will be *necessarily* true, namely: if anything has most of the properties ϕ in the properly weighted sense, it is X. So really one can say that it is both *a priori* and necessary that something is X if and only if it uniquely has most of the properties ϕ. This really comes from the previous Theses (1)–(4), I suppose. And (5) and (6) really just say that a sufficiently reflective speaker grasps this theory of proper names. Knowing this, he therefore sees that (5) and (6) are true. The objections to Theses (5) and (6) will not be that some speakers are unaware of this theory and therefore don't know these things.

What I talked about in the last lecture is Thesis (6). It's been observed by many philosophers that, if the cluster of properties associated with a description is taken in a very narrow sense, so that only one property is given any weight at all, let's say one definite description to pick out the referent – for example, Aristotle was the philosopher who taught Alexander the Great – then certain things will seem to turn out to be necessary truths which are not necessary truths – in this case, for example, that Aristotle taught Alexander the Great. But as Searle said, it is not a necessary truth but a contingent one that Aristotle ever went into pedagogy. Therefore, he concludes that one must drop the original paradigm of a single description and turn to that of a cluster of descriptions.

To summarize some things that I argued last time, this is not the correct answer (whatever it may be) to this problem about necessity. For Searle goes on to say,

Suppose we agree to drop 'Aristotle' and use, say, 'the teacher of Alexander', then it is a necessary truth that the man referred to is Alexander's teacher – but it is a contingent fact that Aristotle ever went into pedagogy, though I am suggesting that it is a necessary fact that Aristotle has the logical sum, inclusive disjunction, of properties commonly attributed to him... .[31]

This is what is not so. It just is not, in any intuitive sense of necessity, a necessary truth that Aristotle had the properties commonly attributed to him. There is a certain theory, perhaps popular in some views of the philosophy of history, which might both be deterministic and yet at the same time assign a great role to the individual in history. Perhaps Carlyle would associate with the meaning of the name of a great man his achievements According to such a view it will be necessary, once a certain individual is born, that he is destined to perform various great tasks and so it will be part of the very nature of Aristotle that he should have produced ideas which had a great influence on the western world. Whatever the merits of such a view may be as a view of history or the nature of great men, it does not seem that it should be trivially true on the basis of a theory of proper names. It would seem that it's a contingent fact that

Aristotle ever did *any* of the things commonly attributed to him today, *any* of these great achievements that we so much admire. I must say that there is *something* to this feeling of Searle's. When I hear the name 'Hitler', I do feel it's sort of analytic that that man was evil. But really, probably not. Hitler might have spent all his days in quiet in Linz. In that case we would not say that then this man would not have been Hitler, for we use the name 'Hitler' just as the name of that man, even describing possible worlds. (This is the notion which I called a *rigid designator* in the previous talk.) Suppose we do decide to pick out the reference of 'Hitler', as the man who succeeded in having more Jews killed than anyone else managed to do in history. That is the way we pick out the reference of the name; but in another counterfactual situation where some one else would have gained this discredit, we wouldn't say that in that case that other man would have been Hitler. If Hitler had never come to power, Hitler would not have had the property which I am supposing we use to fix the reference of his name. Similarly, even if we define what a meter is by reference to the standard meter stick, it will be a contingent truth and not a necessary one that that particular stick is one meter long. If it had been stretched, it would have been longer than one meter. And that is because we use the term 'one meter' rigidly to designate a certain length. Even though we fix what length we are designating by an acci- dental property of that length, just as in the case of the name of the man we may pick the man out by an accidental property of the man, still we use the name to designate that man or that length in all possible worlds. The property we use need not be one which is regarded in any way as necessary or essential. In the case of a yard, the original way this property was picked out was, I think, the distance when the arm of King Henry I of England was outstretched from the tip of his finger to his nose. If this was the length of a yard, it nevertheless will not be a necessary truth that the distance between the tip of his finger and his nose should be a yard. Maybe an accident might have happened to foreshorten his arm; that would be possible. And the reason that it's not a necessary truth is not that there might be other criteria in a 'cluster concept' of yardhood. Even a man who strictly uses King Henry's arm as his one standard of length can say, counterfactually, that if certain things had happened to the King, the exact distance between the end of one of his fingers and his nose would not have been exactly a yard. He need not be using a cluster as long as he uses the term 'yard' to pick out a certain fixed reference to be that length in all possible worlds.

These remarks show, I think, the intuitive bizarreness of a good deal of the literature on 'transworld identification' and 'counterpart theory'. For many theorists of these sorts, believing, as they do, that a 'possible world' is given to us only qualitatively, argue that Aristotle is to be 'identified in other possible worlds', or alternatively that his counterparts are to be identified, as those things in other possible worlds who most closely resemble Aristotle in his most important properties. (Lewis, for example, says: "Your counterparts ... resemble you ... in important respects ... more closely than do the other things in their worlds ... weighted by the importance of the various respects and by the degrees of the similarities."[32]) Some may equate the important properties with those properties used to identify the object in the actual world.

Surely these notions are incorrect. To me Aristotle's most important properties consist in his philosophical work, and Hitler's in his murderous political role; both, as I have said, might have lacked these properties altogether. Surely there was no logical fate hanging over either Aristotle or Hitler which made it in any sense inevitable that they should have possessed the properties we regard as important to them; they could have had careers completely different from their actual ones. *Important* properties of an object need not be essential, unless 'importance' is used as a synonym for essence; and an object could have had properties very different from its most striking actual properties, or from the properties we use to identify it.

To clear up one thing which some people have asked me: When I say that a designator is rigid, and designates the same thing in all possible worlds, I mean that, as used in *our* language, it stands for that thing, when *we* talk about counterfactual situations. I don't mean, of course, that there mightn't be counterfactual situations in which in the other possible worlds people actually spoke a different language. One doesn't say that 'two plus two equals four' is contingent because people might have spoken a language in which 'two plus two equals four' meant that seven is even. Similarly, when we speak of a counterfactual situation, we speak of it in English, even if it is part of the description of that counterfactual situation that we were all speaking German in that counterfactual situation. We say, 'suppose we had all been speaking German' or 'suppose we had been using English in a nonstandard way'. Then we are describing a possible world or counterfactual situation in which people, including ourselves, did speak in a certain way different from the way we speak. But still, in describing that world, we use *English* with *our* meanings and *our* references. It is in this sense that I speak of it as having the same reference in all possible worlds. I also don't mean to imply that the thing exists in all possible worlds, just that the name refers rigidly to that thing. If you say 'suppose Hitler had never been born' then 'Hitler' refers, here, still rigidly, to something that would not exist in the counterfactual situation described.

Given these remarks, this means we must cross off Thesis (6) as incorrect. The other theses have nothing to do with necessity and can survive. In particular Thesis (5) has nothing to do with necessity and it can survive. If I use the name 'Hesperus' to refer to a certain planetary body when seen in a certain celestial position in the evening, it will not therefore be a necessary truth that Hesperus is ever seen in the evening. That depends on various contingent facts about people being there to see and things like that. So even if I should say to myself that I will use 'Hesperus' to name the heavenly body I see in the evening in yonder position of the sky, it will not be necessary that Hesperus was ever seen in the evening. But it may be *a priori* in that this is how I have determined the referent. If I have determined that Hesperus is the thing that I saw in the evening over there, then I will know, just from making that determination of the referent, that if there is any Hesperus at all it's the thing I saw in the evening. This at least survives as far as the arguments we have given go so far.

How about a theory where Thesis (6) is eliminated? Theses (2), (3), and (4) turn out to have a large class of counterinstances. Even when Theses (2)–(4) are true, Thesis (5) is usually false; the truth of Theses (3) and (4) is an empirical 'accident', which the speaker hardly knows *a priori*. That is to say, other principles really determine the speaker's reference, and the fact that the referent coincides with that determined by (2)–(4) is an 'accident', which we were in no position to know *a priori*. Only in a rare class of cases, usually initial baptisms, are all of (2)–(5) true.

What picture of meaning do these Theses ((1)–(5)) give you? The picture is this. I want to name an object. I think of some way of describing it uniquely and then I go through, so to speak, a sort of mental ceremony: By 'Cicero' I shall mean the man who denounced Cataline; and that's what the reference of 'Cicero' will be. I will use 'Cicero' to designate rigidly the man who (in fact) denounced Cataline, so I can speak of possible worlds in which he did not. But still my intentions are given by first, giving some condition which uniquely determines an object, then using a certain word as a name for the object determined by these conditions. Now there may be some cases in which we actually do this. Maybe, if you want to stretch and call it description, when you say: I shall call that heavenly body over there 'Hesperus'.[33] That is really a case where the theses not only are true but really even give a correct picture of how the reference is determined. Another case, if you want to call this a name, might be when the police in London use the name 'Jack' or 'Jack the Ripper' to refer to the man, whoever he is, who committed all these murders, or most of them. Then they are giving the reference of the name by a description.[34] But in many or most cases, I think the theses are false.[35] So let's look at them.

Thesis (1), as I say, is a definition. Thesis (2) says that one of the properties believed by A of the object or some conjointly are believed to pick out some individual uniquely. A sort of example people have in mind is just what I said: I shall use the term 'Cicero' to denote the man who denounced Cataline (or first denounced him in public, to make it unique). This picks out an object uniquely in this particular reference. Even some writers such as Ziff in *Semantic Analysis*, who don't believe that names have meaning in our sense, think that this is a good picture of the way reference can be determined.

Let's see if Thesis (2) is true. It seems, in some *a priori* way, that it's got to be true, because if you don't think that the properties you have in mind pick out any one uniquely – let's say they're all satisfied by two people – then how can you say which one of them you're talking about? There seem to be no grounds for saying you're talking about the one rather than about the other. Usually the properties in question are supposed to be some famous deeds of the person in question. For example, Cicero was the man who denounced Cataline. The average person, according to this, when he refers to Cicero, is saying something like 'the man who denounced Cataline' and thus has picked out a certain man uniquely. It is a tribute to the education of philosophers that they have held this thesis for such a long time. In fact, most people, when they think of Cicero, just think of a famous Roman orator, without any pretension to think either that there was only one famous Roman orator or that one must know something else about Cicero to have a referent for the name. Consider Richard Feynman, to whom many of us are able to refer. He is a leading contemporary theoretical physicist. Everyone *here* (I'm sure!), can state the contents of one of Feynman's theories so as to differentiate him from Gell-Mann. However, the man in the street, not possessing these abilities, may still use the name 'Feynman'. When asked he will say: well he's a physicist or something. He may not think that this picks out anyone uniquely. I still think he uses the name 'Feynman' as a name for Feynman.

But let's look at some of the cases where we do have a description to pick out someone uniquely. Let's say, for example, that we know that Cicero was the man who first denounced Cataline. Well, that's good. That really picks someone out uniquely. However, there is a problem, because this description contains another name, namely 'Cataline'. We must be sure that we satisfy the conditions in such a way as to avoid the non-circularity condition here. In particular, we must not say that Cataline was the man denounced by Cicero. If that is so, we will really not be picking out anything uniquely, we will simply be picking out a pair of objects A and B, such that A denounced B or B denounced A. We do not think that this was the only pair where such denunciations ever occurred; so we had better add some other conditions in order to satisfy the uniqueness condition.

If we say Einstein was the man who discovered the theory of relativity, that certainly picks out someone uniquely. One can be sure, as I said, that everyone *here* can make a compact and independent statement of this theory and so pick out Einstein uniquely; but many people actually don't know enough about this stuff, so when asked what the theory of relativity is, they will say: 'Einstein's theory', and thus be led into the most straightforward sort of vicious circle.

So Thesis (2), in a straightforward way, fails to be satisfied when we say Feynman is a famous physicist without attributing anything else to Feynman. In another way it may not be satisfied in the proper way even when it is satisfied: If we say Einstein was 'the man who discovered relativity theory', that does pick someone out uniquely; but it may not pick him out in such a way as to satisfy the noncircularity condition, because the theory of relativity may in turn be picked out as 'Einstein's theory'. So Thesis (2) seems to be false.

By changing the conditions ϕ from those usually associated with names by philosophers, one could try to improve the theory. There have been various ways I've heard; maybe I'll discuss these later on. Usually they think of famous achievements of the man named. Certainly in the case of famous achievements, the theory doesn't work. Some student of mine once said, 'Well Einstein discovered the theory of relativity'; and he determined the reference of 'the theory of relativity' independently by referring to an encyclopedia which would give the details of the theory. (This is what is called a transcendental deduction of the existence of encyclopedias.) But it seems to me that, even if someone has heard of encyclopedias, it really is not essential for his reference that he should know whether this theory is given in detail in any encyclopedia. The reference might work even if there had been no encyclopedias at all.

Let's go on to Thesis (3): If most of the ϕ's, suitably weighted, are satisfied by a unique object y, then y is the referent of the name for the speaker. (Now, since we have already established that Thesis (2) is wrong, why should any of the rest work? The whole theory depended on always being able to specify unique conditions which are satisfied. But still we can look at the other theses. The picture associated with the theory is that only by giving some unique properties can you know who someone is and thus know what the reference of your name is. Well, I won't go into the question of knowing who someone is. It's really very puzzling. I think you *do* know who Cicero is if you just can answer that he's a famous Roman orator. Strangely enough, if you know that Einstein discovered the theory of relativity and nothing about that theory, you can both know who Einstein is, namely the discoverer of the theory of relativity, and who discovered the theory of relativity, namely Einstein, on the basis of this knowledge. This seems to be a blatant violation of some sort of noncircularity condition; but it is the way we talk. It therefore would seem that a picture which suggests this condition must be the wrong picture.)

Suppose most of the ϕ's are in fact satisfied by a unique object. Is that object necessarily the referent of 'X' for A? Let's suppose someone says that Gödel is the man who proved the incompleteness of arithmetic, and this man is suitably well educated and is even able to give an independent account of the incompleteness theorem. He doesn't just say, 'Well, that's Gödel's theorem', or whatever. He actually states a certain theorem which he attributes to Gödel as the discoverer. Is it the case, then, that if most of the ϕ's are satisfied by a unique object y then y is the referent of the name 'X' for A? Let's take a simple case. In the case of Gödel that's practically the only thing many people have heard about him – that he discovered the incompleteness of arithmetic. Does it follow that whoever discovered the incompleteness of arithmetic is the referent of 'Gödel'?

Imagine the following blatantly fictional situation. (I hope Professor Gödel is not present.) Suppose that Gödel was not in fact the author of this theorem. A man named 'Schmidt', whose body was found in Vienna under mysterious circumstances many years ago, actually did the work in question. His friend Gödel somehow got hold of the manuscript and it was thereafter attributed to Gödel. On the view in question, then, when our ordinary man uses the name 'Gödel', he really means to refer to Schmidt, because Schmidt is the unique person satisfying the description, 'the man who discovered the incompleteness of arithmetic'. Of course you might try changing it to 'the man who *published* the discovery of the incompleteness of arithmetic'. By changing the story a little further one can make even this formulation false. Anyway most people might not even know whether the thing was published or got around by word of mouth. Let's stick to 'the man who discovered the incompleteness of arithmetic'. So, since the man who discovered the incompleteness of arithmetic is in fact Schmidt, we, when we talk about 'Gödel', are in fact always referring to Schmidt. But it seems to me that we are not. We simply are not. One reply, which I will discuss later, might be: You should say instead, 'the man to whom the incompleteness of arithmetic is commonly attributed', or something like that. Let's see what we can do with that later.

But it may seem to many of you that this is a very odd example, or that such a situation occurs rarely. This also is a tribute to the education of philosophers. Very often we use a name on the basis of considerable misinformation. The case of mathematics used in the fictive example is a good case in point. What do we know about Peano? What many people in this room may 'know' about Peano is that he was the discoverer of certain axioms which characterize the sequence of natural numbers, the so-called 'Peano axioms'. Probably some people can even state them. I have been told that these axioms are not actually due to Peano but to Dedekind. Peano was of course not a dishonest man. He includes them in his book with an accompanying credit in his footnotes. Somehow the footnote has been ignored. So on the theory in question the term 'Peano', as we use it, really refers to – now that you've heard it you see that you were really all the time talking about – Dedekind. But you were not. Such illustrations could be multiplied indefinitely.

Even worse misconceptions, of course, occur to the layman. In a previous example I supposed people to identify Einstein by reference to his work on relativity. Actually, I often used to hear that Einstein's most famous achievement was the invention of the atomic bomb. So when we refer to Einstein we refer to the inventor of the atomic bomb. But this is not so. Columbus was the first man to realize that the earth was round. He was also the first European to land in the western hemisphere. Probably none of these things are true, and therefore, when people use the term 'Columbus' they really refer to some Greek if they use the roundness of the earth, or to some Norseman, perhaps, if they use the 'discovery of America'. But they don't. So it does not seem that if most of the ϕ's are satisfied by a unique object y, then y is the referent of the name. This seems simply to be false.[36]

Thesis (4): If the vote yields no unique object the name does not refer.

Really this case has been covered before – has been covered in my previous examples. First, the vote may not yield a *unique* object, as in the case of Cicero or Feynman. Secondly, suppose it yields *no* object, that nothing satisfies most, or even any, substantial number, of the ϕ's. Does that mean the name doesn't refer? No: in the same way that you may have false beliefs about a person which may actually be true of someone else, so you may have false beliefs which are true of absolutely no one. And these may constitute the totality of your beliefs. Suppose, to vary the example about Gödel, no one had discovered the incompleteness of arithmetic – perhaps the proof simply materialized by a random scattering of atoms on a piece of paper – the man Gödel being lucky enough to have been present when this improbable event occurred. Further, suppose arithmetic is in fact complete. One wouldn't really expect a random scattering of atoms to produce a correct proof. A subtle error, unknown through the decades, has still been unnoticed – or perhaps not actually unnoticed, but the friends of Gödel .... So even if the conditions are not satisfied by a unique object the name may still refer. I gave you the case of Jonah last week. Biblical scholars, as I said, think that Jonah really existed. It isn't because they think that someone ever was swallowed by a big fish or even went to Nineveh to preach. These conditions may be true of no one whatsoever and yet the name 'Jonah' really has a referent. In the case above of Einstein's invention of the bomb, possibly no one really deserves to be called the 'inventor' of the device.

Thesis 5 says that the statement 'If X exists, then X has most of the ϕ's', is *a priori* true for A. Notice that even in a case where (3) and (4) *happen* to be true, a typical speaker hardly knows *a priori* that they are, as required by the theory. I *think* that my belief about Gödel *is* in fact correct and that the 'Schmidt' story is just a fantasy. But the belief hardly constitutes *a priori* knowledge.

What's going on here? Can we rescue the theory?[37] First, one may try and vary these descriptions – not think of the famous achievements of a man but, let's say, of something else, and try and use that as our description. Maybe by enough futzing around someone might eventually get something out of this[38]; however, most of the attempts that one tries are open to counterexamples or other objections. Let me give an example of this. In the case of Gödel one may say, 'Well, 'Gödel' doesn't mean 'the man who proved the incompleteness of arithmetic''. Look, all we really know is that most people *think* that Gödel proved the incompleteness of arithmetic, that Gödel is the man to whom the incompleteness of arithmetic is commonly attributed. So when I determine the referent of the name 'Gödel', I don't say to myself, 'by 'Gödel' I shall mean 'the man who proved the incompleteness of arithmetic, whoever he is''. That might turn out to be Schmidt or Post. But instead I shall mean 'the man who most people *think* proved the incompleteness of arithmetic'.

Is this right? First, it seems to me that it's open to counterexamples of the same type as I gave before, though the counterexamples may be more récherché. Suppose, in the case of Peano mentioned previously, unbeknownst to the speaker most people (at least by now) thoroughly realize that the number-theoretic axioms should not be attributed to him. Most people don't credit them to Peano but now correctly ascribe them to Dedekind. So then even the man to whom this thing is commonly attributed will still be Dedekind and not Peano. Still, the speaker, having picked up the old outmoded belief, may still be referring to Peano, and hold a false belief about Peano, not a true belief about Dedekind.

But second, and perhaps more significantly, such a criterion violates the noncircularity condition. How is this? It is true that most of us think that Gödel proved the incompleteness of arithmetic. Why is this so? We certainly say, and sincerely, 'Gödel proved the incompleteness of arithmetic'. Does it follow from that that we believe that Gödel proved the incompleteness of arithmetic – that we attribute the incompleteness of arithmetic to this man? No. Not just from that. We have to be *referring* to Gödel when we say 'Gödel proved the incompleteness of arithmetic'. If, in fact, we were always referring to Schmidt, then we would be attributing the incompleteness of arithmetic to Schmidt and not to Gödel – if we used the sound 'Gödel' as the name of the man whom I am calling 'Schmidt'.

But we do in fact refer to Gödel. How do we do this? Well, not by saying to ourselves, 'By 'Gödel' I shall mean the man to whom the incompleteness of arithmetic is commonly attributed'. If we did that we would run into a circle. Here we are all in this room. Actually in this institution [39] some people have met the man, but in many institutions this is not so. All of us in the community are trying to determine the reference by saying 'Gödel is to be the man to whom the incompleteness of arithmetic is commonly attributed'. None of us will get started with any attribution unless there is some independent criterion for the reference of the name other than 'the man to whom the incompleteness of arithmetic is commonly attributed'. Otherwise all we will be saying is, 'We attribute this achievement to the man to whom we attribute it', without saying who that man is, without giving any independent criterion of the reference, and so the determination will be circular. This then is a violation of the condition I have marked '*C*', and cannot be used in any theory of reference.

Of course you might try to avoid circularity by passing the buck. This is mentioned by Strawson, who says in his footnote on these matters that one man's reference may derive from another's.

The identifying description, though it must not include a reference to the speaker's own reference to the particular in question, may include a reference to another's reference to that particular. If a putatively identifying description is of this latter kind, then, indeed, the question, whether it is a genuinely identifying description turns on the question, whether the reference it refers to is itself a genuinely identifying reference. So one reference may borrow its credentials, as a genuinely identifying reference, from another; and that from another. But this regress is not infinite.[40]

I may then say, 'Look, by 'Gödel' I shall mean the man Joe thinks proved the incompleteness of arithmetic'. Joe may then pass the thing over to Harry. One has to be very careful that this doesn't come round in a circle. Is one really sure that this won't happen? If you could be sure yourself of knowing such a chain, and that everyone else in the chain is using the proper conditions and so is not getting out of it, then maybe you could get back to the man by referring to such a chain in that way, borrowing the references one by one. However, although in general such chains do exist for a living man, you won't know what the chain is. You won't be sure what descriptions the other man is using, so the thing won't go into a circle, or whether by appealing to Joe you won't get back to the right man at all. So you cannot use this as your identifying description with any confidence. You may not even remember from whom you heard of Gödel.

What is the true picture of what's going on? Maybe reference doesn't really take place at all! After all, we don't really know that any of the properties we use to the man are right. We don't know that they pick out a unique object. So what *does* make my use of 'Cicero' into a name of *him*? The picture which leads to the cluster-of descriptions theory is something like this: One is isolated in a room; the entire community of other speakers, everything else, could disappear; and one determines the reference for himself by saying – 'By 'Gödel' I shall mean the man, whoever he is, who proved the incompleteness of arithmetic'. Now you can do this if you want to. There's nothing really preventing it. You can just stick to that determination. If that's what you do, then if Schmidt discovered the incompleteness of arithmetic you *do* refer to him when you say 'Gödel did such and such'.

But that's not what most of us do. Someone, let's say, a baby, is born; his parents call him by a certain name. They talk about him to their friends. Other people meet him. Through various sorts of talk the name is spread from link to link as if by a chain. A speaker who is on the far end of this chain, who has heard about, say Richard Feynman, in the market place or elsewhere, may be referring to Richard Feynman even though he can't remember from whom he first heard of Feynman or from whom he ever heard of Feynman. He knows that Feynman was a famous physicist. A certain passage of communication reaching ultimately to the man himself does reach the speaker. He then is referring to Feynman even though he can't identify him uniquely. He doesn't know what a Feynman diagram is, he doesn't know what the Feynman theory of pair production and annihilation is. Not only that: he'd have trouble distinguishing between Gell-Mann and Feynman. So he doesn't have to know these things, but, instead, a chain of communication going back to Feynman himself has been established, by virtue of his membership in a community which passed the name on from link to link, not by a ceremony that he makes in private in his study: 'By 'Feynman' I shall mean the man who did such and such and such and such'.

How does this view differ from Strawson's suggestion, mentioned before, that one identifying reference may borrow its credentials from another? Certainly Strawson had a good insight in the passage quoted; on the other hand, he certainly shows a difference at least in emphasis from the picture I advocate, since he confines the remark to a footnote. The main text advocates the cluster-of-descriptions theory. Just because Strawson makes his remark in the context of a description theory, his view therefore differs from mine in one important respect. Strawson apparently must require that the speaker must *know* from whom he got his reference, so that he can *say*: 'By 'Gödel' I mean the man *Jones* calls 'Gödel''. If he does not remember how he picked up the reference, he cannot give such a description. The present theory sets no such requirement. As I said, I may well not remember from whom I heard of Gödel, and I may think I remember from which people I heard the name, but wrongly.

These considerations show that the view advocated here can lead to consequences which actually *diverge* from those of Strawson's footnote. Suppose that the speaker has heard the name 'Cicero' from Smith and others, who use the name to refer to a famous Roman orator. He later thinks, however, that he picked up the name from Jones, who (unknown to the speaker) uses 'Cicero' as the name of a notorious German spy and has never heard of any orators of the ancient world. Then, according to Strawson's paradigm, the speaker must determine his reference by the resolution, 'I shall use 'Cicero' to refer to the man whom Jones calls by that name', while on the present view, the referent will be the orator in spite of the speaker's false impression about where he picked up the name. The point is that Strawson, trying to fit the chain of communication view into the description theory, is forced to rely on what the speaker *thinks* was the source of his reference. If the speaker has forgotten his source, the device is unavailable to Strawson; if he misremembers it, Strawson's paradigm in his footnote can give the wrong results. On our view, it is not how the speaker thinks he got the reference, but the actual chain of communication, which is relevant.

I think I said the other time that philosophical theories are in danger of being false, and so I wasn't going to present an alternative theory. Have I just done so? Well, in a way; but my characterization has been far less specific than a real set of necessary and sufficient conditions for reference would be. Obviously the name is passed on from link to link. But of course not every sort of causal chain reaching from me to a certain man will do for me to make a reference. There may be a causal chain from our use of the term 'Santa Claus' to a certain historical saint, but still the children, when they use this, by this time probably do not refer to that saint. So other conditions must be satisfied in order to make this into a really rigorous theory of reference. I don't know that I'm going to do this because, first, I'm sort of too lazy at the moment; secondly, rather than giving a set of necessary and sufficient conditions which will work for a term like reference, I want to present just a *better picture* than the picture presented by the received views.

Haven't I been very unfair to the description theory? Here I have stated it very precisely – more precisely, perhaps, than it has been stated by any of its advocates. So then it's easy to refute. Maybe if I tried to state mine with sufficient precision in the form of six or seven or eight theses, it would also turn out that when you examine the theses one by one, they will all be false. That might even be so, but the difference is this. What I think the examples I've given show is not simply that there's some technical error here or some mistake there, but that the whole picture given by this theory of how reference is determined seems to be wrong from the fundamentals. It seems to be wrong to think that we give ourselves some properties which somehow qualitatively uniquely pick out an object and determine our reference in that manner. What I am trying to present is a better picture – a picture which, if more details were to be filled in, might be refined so as to give more exact conditions for reference to take place.

One might never reach a set of necessary and sufficient conditions. I don't know, I'm always sympathetic to Bishop Butler's 'Everything is what it is and not another thing' – in the nontrivial sense that philosophical analyses of some concept like reference, in completely different terms which make no mention of reference, are very apt to fail. Of course in any particular case when one is given an analysis one has to look at it and see whether it is true or false. One can't just cite this maxim to oneself and then turn the page. But more cautiously, I want to present a better picture without giving a set of necessary and sufficient conditions for reference. Such conditions would be very complicated, but what is true is that it's in virtue of our connection with other speakers in the community, going back to the referent himself, that we refer to a certain man.

There may be some cases where the description picture is true, where some man really gives a name by going into the privacy of his room and saying that the referent is to be the unique thing with certain identifying properties. 'Jack the Ripper' was a possible example which I gave. Another was 'Hesperus'. Yet another case which can be forced into this description is that of meeting someone and being told his name. Except for a belief in the description theory, in its importance in other cases, one probably wouldn't think that that was a case of giving oneself a description, i.e., 'the guy I'm just meeting now'. But one can put it in these terms if one wishes, and if one has never heard the name in any other way. Of course, if you're introduced to a man and told, 'That's Einstein', you've heard of him before, it may be wrong, and so on. But maybe in some cases such a paradigm works – especially for the man who first gives someone or something a name. Or he points to a star and says, 'That is to be Alpha Centauri'. So he can really make himself this ceremony: 'By 'Alpha Centauri' I shall mean the star right over there with such and such coordinates'. But in general this picture fails. In general our reference depends not just on what we think ourselves, but on other people in the community, the history of how the name reached one, and things like that. It is by following such a history that one gets to the reference.

More exact conditions are very complicated to give. They seem in a

way somehow different in the case of a famous man and one who isn't
so famous.[41] For example, a teacher tells his class that Newton was
famous for being the first man to think there's a force pulling things to the
earth; and I think that's what little kids think Newton's greatest achievement was. I won't say what the merits of such an achievement would be,
but, anyway, we may suppose that just being told that this was the sole
content of Newton's discovery gives the students a false belief *about
Newton,* even though they have never heard of him before. If on the other
hand the teacher uses the name, George Smith, who is in fact his next door
neighbor, and says that George Smith first squared the circle, does it
follow from this that the students have a false belief about the teacher's
neighbor? The teacher doesn't tell them that Smith is his neighbor, nor
does he believe Smith first squared the circle. He isn't particularly trying to
get any belief *about the neighbor* into the students' heads. He tries to
inculcate the belief that there was a man who squared the circle, but not
a belief about any particular man – he just pulls out the first name that
occurs to him – as it happens, he uses his neighbor's name. It doesn't
seem clear in that case that the students have a false belief about the
neighbor, even though there is a causal chain going back to the neighbor.
I am not sure about this. At any rate more refinements need to be
added to make this even begin to be a set of necessary and sufficient
conditions. In that sense it's not a theory, but is supposed to give a
better picture of what is actually going on.

A rough statement of a theory might be the following: An initial
baptism takes place. Here the object may be named by ostension, or the
reference of the same may be fixed by a description.[42] When the name is
'passed from link to link', the receiver of the name must, I think, intend
when he learns it to use it with the same reference as the man from whom
he heard it. If I hear the name 'Napoleon' and decide it would be a nice
name for my pet aardvark, I do not satisfy this condition.[43] (Perhaps
it is some such failure to keep the reference fixed which accounts for the
divergence of present uses of 'Santa Claus' from the alleged original use.)

Notice that the preceding outline hardly *eliminates* the notion of
reference; on the contrary, it takes the notion of intending to use the
same reference as a given. This is also an appeal to an initial baptism
which is explained in terms either of fixing a reference by a description,
or ostension (if ostension is not to be subsumed under the other category).[44]

(Perhaps there are other possibilities for initial baptisms.) Further, the George Smith case casts some doubt as to the sufficiency of the conditions. Even if the teacher does refer to his neighbor, is it clear that he has passed on his reference to the pupils? Why shouldn't their belief be about any other man named 'George Smith'? If he says that Newton was hit by an apple, somehow his task of transmitting a reference is easier, since he has communicated a common misconception about Newton.

To repeat, I may not have presented a theory, but I do think that I have presented a better picture than that given by description theorists.

I think the next topic I shall want to talk about is that of statements of identity. Are these necessary or contingent? The matter has been in some dispute in recent philosophy. First, everyone agrees that descriptions can be used to make contingent identity statements. If it is true that the man who invented bifocals was the first postmaster general of the United States – that these were one and the same – it's contingently true. That is, it might have been the case that one man invented bifocals and another was the first postmaster general of the United States. So certainly when you make identity statements using descriptions – when you say 'the x such that ϕx and the x such that ψx are one and the same', that can be a contingent fact. But philosophers have been interested also in the question of identity statements between names. When we say 'Hesperus is Phosphorus' or 'Cicero is Tully', is what we are saying necessary or contingent? Further, they've been interested in another type of identity statement, which comes from scientific theory. We identify, for example, light with electromagnetic radiation between certain limits of wavelengths, or with a stream of photons. We identify heat with the motion of molecules; sound with a certain sort of wave disturbance in the air; and so on. Concerning such statements the following thesis is commonly held. First, that these are obviously contingent identities: we've found out that light is a stream of photons, but of course it might not have been a stream of photons. Heat is in fact the motion of molecules; we found that out, but heat might not have been the motion of molecules. Secondly, many philosophers feel damned lucky that these examples are around. Now, why? These philosophers, whose views are expounded in a vast literature, hold to a thesis called the identity thesis with respect to some psychological concepts. They think, say, that pain is just a certain material state of the brain or of the body, or what have you – say the stimulation of C-fibres. (It doesn't matter what.) Some people have then objected, "Well, look, there's perhaps a *correlation* between pain and these states of the body; but this must just be a contingent correlation between two different things, because it was an empirical discovery that this correlation ever held. Therefore, by 'pain' we must mean something different from this state of the body or brain; and, therefore, they must be two different things."

Then it's said, "Ah, but you see, this is wrong! Everyone knows that there can be contingent identities." First, as in the bifocals and post-master general case, which I have mentioned before. Second, in the case, believed closer to the present paradigm, of theoretical identifications, such as light and a stream of photons, or water and a certain compound of hydrogen and oxygen. These are all contingent identities. They might have been false. It's no surprise, therefore, that it can be true as a matter of contingent fact and not of any necessity that feeling pain, or seeing red, is just a certain state of the human body. Such psychophysical identifications can be contingent facts just as the other identities are contingent facts. And of course there are widespread motivations – ideological, or just not wanting to have the nomological dangler of these mysterious connections not accounted for by laws of physics, one to one correlation between two different things – a material state and something of an entirely different kind – which lead people to want to believe this thesis.

I guess the main thing I'll talk about first is identity statements between names. But I hold the following about the general case. First, that characteristic theoretical identifications like 'Heat is the motion of molecules', are not contingent truths but necessary truths, and here of course I don't mean just physically necessary, but necessary in the highest degree – whatever that means. (Physical necessity, *might* turn out to be necessity in the highest degree. But that's a question which I don't wish to prejudge. At least for this sort of example, it might be that when something's physically necessary, it always is necessary *tout court*.) Second, that the way in which these have turned out to be necessary truths does not seem to me to be a way in which the mind-brain identities could turn out to be either necessary or contingently true. So this analogy has to go.

It's hard to see what to put in its place. It's hard to see therefore how to avoid concluding that the two are actually different.

Let me go back to the more mundane case about proper names. This is already mysterious enough. There's a dispute about this between Quine and Ruth Barcan Marcus.[45] Ruth Barcan Marcus says that identities between names are necessary. If someone thinks that Cicero is Tully, and really uses 'Cicero' and 'Tully' as names, he is thereby committed to holding that his belief is a necessary truth. She uses the term 'mere tag'. Quine replies as follows, "We may tag the planet Venus, some fine evening, with the proper name 'Hesperus'. We may tag the same planet again, some day before sunrise, with the proper name 'Phosphorus'. When we discover that we have tagged the same planet twice our discovery is empirical. And not because the proper names were descriptions."[46] First, Quine is right when we discovered that we tagged the same planet twice, our discovery was empirical. Another example I think Quine gives in another book is that the same mountain seen from Nepal and from Tibet, or something like that, is from one angle called Mt. Everest (you've heard of that); from another it's supposed to be called Gaurisanker. It can actually be an empirical discovery that Gaurisanker is Everest. (Quine says that the example is actually false. He got the example from Erwin Schrodinger. You wouldn't think the inventor of wave mechanics got things that wrong. I don't know where the mistake is supposed to come from. One could certainly imagine this situation as having been the case; and it's another good illustration of the sort of thing that Quine has in mind.)

What about it? I wanted to find a good quote on the other side from Mrs. Marcus in this book but I am having trouble locating one. Being present at that discussion, I remember[47] she advocated the view that if you really have names, a good dictionary should be able to tell you whether they have the same reference. So someone should be able, by looking in the dictionary, to say that Hesperus and Phosphorus are the same. Now this does not seem to be true. It does seem, to many people, to be a consequence of the view that identities between names are necessary. Therefore the view that identity statements between names are necessary has usually been rejected. Russell's conclusion was somewhat different. He did think there should never be any empirical question whether two names have the same reference. This isn't satisfied for ordinary names, but it is satisfied when you're naming your own sense datum, or something like that. You say, "Here, this, and that (designating the same sense datum by both demonstratives)." So you can tell that you're naming the same thing twice; the conditions are satisfied. Since this won't apply to ordinary cases of naming, ordinary 'names' cannot be genuine names.

What should we think about this? First, it's true that someone can use the name 'Cicero' to refer to Cicero and the name 'Tully' to refer to Cicero also, and not know that Cicero is Tully. So it seems that we do not necessarily know *a priori* that an identity statement between names is true. It doesn't follow from this that the statement so expressed is a contingent one if true. This is what I've emphasized in my first lecture. There are very strong feeling which lead one to think that, if you can't know something by *a priori* ratiocination, then it's got to be contingent: it might have turned out otherwise; but nevertheless I think this feeling is wrong.

Let's suppose we refer to the same heavenly body twice, as Hesperus and Phosphorus. We say Hesperus is that star over there in the evening; Phosphorus is that star over there in the morning. Actually Hesperus is Phosphorus. Are there really circumstances under which Hesperus wouldn't have been Phosphorus? Supposing that Hesperus is Phosphorus, let's try to describe a possible situation in which it would not have been. Well it's easy. Someone goes by and he calls two *different* stars Hesperus and Phosphorus. It may be even under the same conditions as prevailed when we introduced the names 'Hesperus' and 'Phosphorus'. But are those circumstances in which Hesperus is not Phosphorus or would not have been Phosphorus? It seems to me that they are not.

Now, of course I'm committed to saying that they're not, by saying that such terms as 'Hesperus' and 'Phosphorus', when used as names, are rigid designators. They refer in every possible world to the planet Venus. Therefore, in that possible world too, the planet Venus is the planet Venus and it doesn't matter what any other person has said in this other possible world. How should *we* describe this situation? He can't have pointed to Venus twice, and in the one case called it Hesperus and in the other Phosphorus, as we did. If he did so, then 'Hesperus is Phosphorus' would have been true in that situation too. He pointed maybe neither time to the planet Venus – at least one time he didn't point to the planet Venus, let's say when he pointed to Phosphorus. Then in that case we can certainly say that the name 'Phosphorus' might not have referred to Phosphorus. We can even say that in the very position when viewed in the morning that we found Phosphorus, it might have been the case that Phosphorus was not there – that something else was there, and that even, under certain circumstances it would have been *called* 'Phosphorus'. But that still is not a case in which Phosphorus was not Hesperus. There might be a possible world in which, a possible counterfactual situation in which, 'Hesperus' and 'Phosphorus' weren't names of the things they in fact are names of. Someone, if he did determine their reference by identifying descriptions, might even have used the very identifying descriptions we used. But still that's not a case in which Hesperus wasn't Phosphorus. For there couldn't have been such a case, given that Hesperus is Phosphorus.

Now this seems very strange, because in advance, we are inclined to say, the answer to the question whether Hesperus is Phosphorus might have turned out either way. So aren't there really two possible worlds – one in which Hesperus was Phosphorus, the other in which Hesperus wasn't Phosphorus – in advance of our discovering that these were the same? First, there's one sense in which things might turn out either way, in which it's clear that that doesn't imply that the way it finally turns out isn't necessary. For example, the four color theorem might turn out to be true and might turn out to be false. It might turn out either way. It still doesn't mean that the way it turns out is not necessary. Obviously, the 'might' here is purely 'epistemic' – it merely expresses our present state of ignorance, or uncertainty.

But it seems that in the Hesperus-Phosphorus case, something even stronger is true. The evidence I have before I know that Hesperus is Phosphorus is that I see a certain star or a certain heavenly body in the evening and call it Hesperus, and in the morning and call it Phosphorus. I know these things. There certainly is a possible world in which a man should have seen a certain star at a certain position in the evening and called it 'Hesperus' and a certain star in the morning and called it 'Phosphorus'; and should have concluded – should have found out by empirical investigation – that he names two different stars, or two different heavenly bodies. At least one of these stars or heavenly bodies was not Phosphorus, otherwise it couldn't have come out that way. But that's true. And so it's true that given the evidence that someone has antecedent to his empirical investigation, he can be placed in a sense in exactly the same situation, that is a qualitatively identical epistemic situation, and call two heavenly bodies 'Hesperus' and 'Phosphorus', without their being identical. So in that sense we can say that it might have turned out either way. Not that it might have turned out either way as to Hesperus's being Phosphorus. Though for all we knew in advance, Hesperus wasn't Phosphorus, that couldn't have turned out any other way, in a sense. But being put in a situation where we have exactly the same evidence, qualitatively speaking, it could have turned out that Hesperus was not Phosphorus; that is, in a counterfactual world in which 'Hesperus' and 'Phosphorus' were not used in the way that we use them, as names of this planet, but as names of some other objects, one could have had qualitatively identical evidence and concluded that 'Hesperus' and 'Phosphorus' named two different objects.[48] But we, using the names as we do right now, can say in advance, that if Hesperus and Phosphorus are one and the same then in no other possible world can they be different. We use 'Hesperus' as the name of a certain body and 'Phosphorus' as the name of a certain body. We use it as the name of those bodies in all possible worlds. If, in fact, they are the *same* body, then in any other possible world we have to use it as a name of that object. And so in any other possible world it will be true that Hesperus is Phosphorus. So two things are true: first, that we do not know *a priori* that Hesperus is Phosphorus, and are in no position to find out the answer except empirically. Second, this is so because we would have evidence qualitatively undistinguishable from the evidence we have and determine the reference of two names by the positions of two planets in the sky, without the planets being the same.

Of course, it won't be true in every other possible world that the star seen over there in the evening is the star seen over there in the morning, because there might have been possible worlds in which Phosphorus was not visible in the morning. But that shouldn't be identified with the statement that Hesperus is Phosphorus. It could only be so identified if you thought that it was a necessary truth that Hesperus is visible over there in the evening or that Phosphorus is visible over there in the morning. But neither of those are necessary truths even if that's the way we pick out the planet. These are the contingent marks by which we identify a certain planet and give it a name.

LECTURE III: JANUARY 29, 1970

What's been accomplished, if anything, up to now? First, I've argued that a popular view about how names get their reference in general doesn't apply. It is in general not the case that the reference of a name is determined by some uniquely identifying marks, some unique properties satisfied by the referent and known or believed to be true of that referent by the speaker. First, the properties believed by the speaker need not be uniquely specifying. Second, even in the case where they are, they may not be uniquely true of the actual referent of the speaker's use but of something else or of nothing. This is the case where the speaker has erroneous beliefs about some person. He does not have correct beliefs about another person, but erroneous beliefs about a certain person. In these cases the reference actually seems to be determined by the fact that the speaker is a member of a community of speakers who use the name. The name has been passed to him by tradition from link to link.

Second, I've argued, even if in some special cases, notably some cases of initial baptism, a referent *is* determined by a description, by some uniquely identifying property, what that property is doing in many cases of designation is not giving a synonym, giving something for which the name is an abbreviation; it is rather fixing a reference. It fixes the reference by some contingent marks of the object. The name denoting that object is then used to refer to that object even in referring to counterfactual situations where the object doesn't have the properties in question. An example was the case of a meter.

Finally, at the end of the talk last time we were talking about statements of identity. Statements of identity should seem very simple but they are somehow very puzzling to philosophers. I cannot be sure in my own case whether I have all the possible confusions that can be generated by this relation straightened out. Some philosophers have found the relation so confusing that they change it. It is for example thought that if you have two names like 'Cicero' and 'Tully' and say that Cicero is Tully, you can't really be saying of the object which is both Cicero and Tully that it is identical with itself. On the contrary 'Cicero is Tully' can express an empirical discovery, as we mentioned before. And so some philosophers, even Frege at one early stage of his writing, have taken identity to be a relation between names. Identity, so they say, is not the relation between an object and itself, but is the relation which holds between two names when they designate the same object.

This occurs even in the more recent literature. I didn't bring the book along, but J. B. Rosser, the distinguished logician, writes in his book, *Logic for Mathematicians*,[49] that we say that $x=y$ if and only if 'x' and 'y' are names for the same object. He remarks that the corresponding statement about the object itself, that it in no way differs from itself, is of course trivial; and so, presumably, cannot be what we mean. This is an especially unusual paradigm of what the identity relationship should be because it would apply very rarely. As far as I know, outside the militant black nationalist movement no one has ever been named 'x'. Seriously speaking, of course, 'x' and 'y' in the open sentence '$x=y$' are not names at all, they are variables. And they can occur with identity as bound variables in a closed sentence. If you say for every x and y, if $x=y$ then $y=x$, or something like that – no names occur in that statement at all, nor is anything said about names. This statement would be true even though the human race had never existed or, though it did exist, never produced the phenomenon of names.

If anyone ever inclines to this particular account of identity, let's suppose we gave him his account. Suppose identity *were* a relation in English between the names. I shall introduce an artificial relation called schmidentity (not a word of English) which I now stipulate to hold only between an object and itself.[50] Now then the question whether Cicero is schmidentical with Tully can arise, and if it does arise the same problems will hold for this statement as were thought in the case of the original identity statement to give the belief that this was a relation between the names. If anyone thinks about this seriously, I think he will see that therefore probably his original account of identity was not necessary, and probably not possible, for the problems it was originally meant to solve, and that therefore it should be dropped, and identity should just be taken to be the relation between a thing and itself. This sort of device can be used for a number of philosophical problems.

We have concluded that an identity statement between names, when true at all, is necessarily true, even though one may not know it *a priori*. Suppose we identify Hesperus as a certain star seen in the evening and Phosphorus as a certain star, or a certain heavenly body, seen in the morning; then there may be possible worlds in which two different planets would have been seen in just those positions in the evening and morning. However, at least one of them, and maybe both, would not have been Hesperus, and then that would not have been a situation in which Hesperus was not Phosphorus. It might have been a situation in which the planet seen in this position in the evening was not the planet seen in this position in the morning; but that is not a situation in which Hesperus was not Phosphorus. It might also, if people gave the names 'Hesperus' and 'Phosphorus' to these planets, be a situation in which some planet other than Hesperus was called 'Hesperus'. But even so, it would not be a situation in which Hesperus itself was not Phosphorus.[51]

Some of the problems which bother people in these situations, as I have said, come from an identification, or as I would put it, a confusion, between what we can know *a priori* in advance and what is necessary. Certain statements – and the identity statement is a paradigm of such a statement on my view – if true at all must be necessarily true. One does know *a priori*, by philosophical analysis, that *if* such an identity statement is true it is necessarily true.

One qualification: when I say 'Hesperus is Phosphorus' is necessarily true, I of course do not deny that there may have been situations in which there was no such planet as Venus at all, and therefore no Hesperus and no Phosphorus. In that case, there is a question of whether the identity statement 'Hesperus is Phosphorus' would be true, false, or neither true nor false.[52] And if we take the last option, is 'Hesperus = Phosphorus' necessary because it is never false, or should we require that a necessary truth be *true* in all possible worlds? I am leaving such problems outside my considerations altogether. If we wish to be careful and precise, we should replace the statement 'Hesperus is Phosphorus' by the conditional, 'If Hesperus exists then Hesperus is Phosphorus', cautiously taking only the latter to be necessary. Unfortunately this conditional involves us in the problem of singular attributions of existence, one I cannot discuss here. In particular, philosophers sympathetic to the description theory of naming often argue that one cannot ever say of an object that it exists. A supposed statement about the existence of an object really is, so it's argued, a statement about whether a certain description or property is satisfied. As I have already said, I disagree. Anyway, I can't really go into the problems of existence here.

I want to mention at this point that other considerations about *de re* modality, about an object having essential properties, can only be regarded correctly, in my view, if we recognize the distinction between *a prioricity* and necessity. One might very well discover essence empirically.

There are some examples of alleged essential properties in an article by Timothy Sprigge.

The internalist [which means the believer that there are some essential properties] says that the Queen must have been born of royal blood. [He means that *this person* must have been of royal blood.] The anti-essentialist says there would be no contradiction in a news bulletin asserting that it had been established that the Queen was not in fact the child of her supposed parents, but had been secretly adopted by them, and therefore the proposition that she is of royal blood is synthetic ...

For a time [the anti-essentialist] is winning. Yet there comes a time when his claims appear a trifle too far fetched. The internalist suggests that we cannot imagine that particular we call the Queen having the property of at no stage in her existence being human. If the anti-internalist admits this, admits that it is logically inconceivable that the Queen should have had the property of, say, always being a swan, then he admits that she has at least one internal property. If on the other hand he says that it's only a contingent fact that the Queen has ever been human, he says what it is hard to accept. Can we really consider it as conceivable that she should never have been human?[53]

This 'never' is supposed to be a qualification to get rid of the possibility of her right now being changed into a swan – by a wicked witch, I guess. (Or a benign witch.)

One confusion I find in this discussion is that in the first case Sprigge talks about whether there would be any contradiction in supposing that we had an *announcement* that the Queen was born of parents different from the ones she actually had. And in that there is no contradiction. Similarly, though, there is no contradiction in an *announcement* that the Queen, this thing we thought to be a woman, was in fact an angel in human form, or an automaton cleverly constructed by the royal family, who did not want the succession to pass to that bastard so-and-so, or something. Neither of these announcements represent things that we couldn't possibly *discover*, either. What is the question we are asking when we ask whether it's necessary, concerning this woman, that she should either have been of royal blood or have been human? (Royal blood is a little complicated, because in order for it to be necessary for her to have been of royal blood it has to be necessary that this particular family line at some time attained to royal power; but the latter fact seems to be a contingent. Therefore I suppose it *is* contingent that her blood should ever have been royal.)

Let's try and refine the question a little bit. The question really should be, let's say, could the Queen – could this woman herself – have been born of different parents from the parents from whom she actually came? Could she, let's say, have been the daughter instead of Mr. and Mrs. Truman? There would be no contradiction, of course, in an announcement that (I hope the ages do not make this impossible), fantastic as it may sound, she was indeed the daughter of Mr. and Mrs. Truman. I suppose there might even be no contradiction in the discovery that – it seems very suspicious anyway that on either hypothesis she has a sister called Margaret – that these two Margarets were one and the same person flying back and forth in a clever way. At any rate we can imagine discovering all of these things.

But let us suppose that such a discovery is not in fact the case. Let's suppose that the Queen really did come from these parents. Not to go into too many complications here about what a parent is, let's suppose that the parents are the people whose body tissues are sources of the biological sperm and egg. So you get rid of such recherché possibilities as transplants of the sperm from the father, or the egg from the mother, into other bodies, so that in one sense other people might have been her parents. If that happened, in another sense her parents were still the original king and queen. But other than that, can we imagine a situation in which it would have happened that this very woman came out of Mr. and Mrs. Truman? They might have had a child resembling her in many properties. Perhaps in some possible world Mr. and Mrs. Truman even had a child who actually became the Queen of England and was even passed off as the child of other parents. This still would not be a situation in which *this very woman* whom we call Elizabeth the Second was the child of Mr. and Mrs. Truman, or so it seems to me. It would be a situation in which there was some other woman who had many of the properties that are in fact true of Elizabeth. Now, one question is, in this world, was Elizabeth herself ever born? Let's suppose she wasn't ever born. It would then be a situation in which, though Truman and his wife have a child with many of the properties of Elizabeth, Elizabeth herself didn't exist at all. One can only become convinced of this by reflection on how you would describe this situation. (That, I suppose, means in many cases that you won't become convinced of this, at least not at the moment. But it is something of which I personally have been convinced.)

What right would you have to call this baby from completely different parents – in what sense would she be – *this very woman*? One can imagine, *given* the woman, that various things in her life could have changed: that she should have become a pauper; that her royal blood should have been unknown, and so on. One is given, let's say, a previous history of the world up to a certain time, and from that time it diverges considerably from the actual course. This seems to be possible. And so it's possible that even though she were born of these parents she never became queen. Even though she were born of these parents, like Mark Twain's character[54] she was switched off with another girl. But what is harder to imagine is her being born of different parents. It seems to me that anything coming from a different origin would not be this object.

In the case of this table,[55] we may not know what block of wood the table came from. Now could *this table* have been made from a completely *different* block of wood, or even of water cleverly hardened into ice – water taken from the Thames River? We could conceivably discover that, contrary to what we now think, this table is indeed made of ice from the river. But let us suppose that it is not. Then, though we can imagine making a table out of another block of wood or even from ice, identical in appearance with this one, and though we could have put it in this very position in the room, it seems to me that this is *not* to imagine *this* table as made of wood or ice, but rather it is to imagine another table, *resembling* this one in all external details, made of another block of wood, or even of ice.[56, 57]

These are only examples of essential properties.[58] I won't dwell on them further because I want to go on to the more general case, which I mentioned in the last lecture, of some identities between terms for substances, and also the properties of substances and of natural kinds. Philosophers have, as I've said, been very interested in statements expressing theoretical identifications; among them, that light is a stream of photons, that water is H_2O, that lightning is an electrical discharge, that gold is the element with the atomic number 79.

To get clear about the status of these statements we must first maybe have some thoughts about the status of such substances as gold. What's gold? I don't know if this is an example which has particularly interested philosophers. Its interest in financial circles is diminishing because of increased stability of currencies.[59] Even so gold has interested many people. Here is what Immanuel Kant says about gold. (He was a wealthy speculator who kept his possessions under his bed.) Kant is introducing the distinction between analytic and synthetic judgments, and he says: "All analytic judgments depend wholly on the law of contradiction, and are in their nature *a priori* cognitions, whether the concepts that supply them with matter be empirical or not. For the predicate of an affirmative analytic judgment is already contained in the concept of the subject, of which it cannot be denied without contradiction.... For this very reason all analytic judgments are *a priori* even when the concepts are empirical, as, for example, 'Gold is a yellow metal'; for to know this I require no experience beyond my concept of gold as a yellow metal. It is, in fact, the very concept, and I need only analyze it without looking beyond it."[60] I should have looked at the German. 'It is in fact the very concept' sounds as if Kant is saying here that 'gold' just *means* 'yellow metal'. If he says that, then it's especially strange, so let's suppose that that is not what he's saying. At least Kant thinks it's a *part* of the concept that gold is to be a yellow metal. He thinks we know this *a priori*, and that we could not possibly discover this to be empirically false.

Is Kant right about this? First, what I would have wanted to do would have been to discuss the part about gold being a metal. This, however, is complicated because first, I don't know too much chemistry. Investigating this a few days ago in just a couple of references, I found in a more phenomenological account of metals the statement that it's very difficult to say what a metal is. (It talks about malleability, ductibility, and the like, but none of these exactly work.) On the other hand, something about the periodic table gave a description of elements as metals in terms of their valency properties. This may make some people think right away that there are really two concepts of metal operating here, a phenomenological one and a scientific one which then replaces it. This I reject, but since the move will tempt many, and can be refuted only after I develop my own views, it will not be suitable to use 'Gold is a metal' as an example to introduce these views.

But let's consider something easier – the question of the yellowness of gold. Could we discover that gold was not in fact yellow? Suppose an optical illusion were prevalent, due to peculiar properties of the atmosphere in South Africa and Russia and certain other areas where gold mines are common. Suppose there were an optical illusion which made the substance appear to be yellow; but, in fact, once the peculiar properties of the atmosphere were removed, we would see that it is actually blue. Maybe a demon even corrupted the vision of all those entering the gold mines, (obviously their *souls* were already corrupt), and thus made them believe that this substance was yellow, though it is not. Would there on this basis be an announcement in the newspapers: "It has turned out that there is no gold. Gold does not exist. What we took to be gold is not in fact gold."? Just imagine the world financial crisis under these conditions. Here we have an undreamt of source of shakiness in the monetary system.

It seems to me that there would be no such announcement. On the contrary, what would be announced would be that though it appeared that gold was yellow, in fact gold has turned out not to be yellow, but blue. The reason is, I think, that we use 'gold' as a term for a certain *kind* of thing. Others have discovered this kind of thing and we have heard of it. We thus as part of a community of speakers have a certain connection between ourselves and a certain kind of thing. The kind of thing is *thought* to have certain identifying marks. Some of these marks may not really be true of gold. We might discover that we are wrong about them. Further, there might be a substance which has all the identifying marks we commonly attributed to identify the substance of gold in the first place, but which is not the same kind of thing, which is not the same substance. We would say of such a thing that though it has all the appearances we initially used to identify gold, it is not gold. Such a thing is, for example, as we well know, iron pyrites or fool's gold. This is not another kind of gold. It's a completely different thing which to the uninitiated person looks just like the substance which we discovered and called gold. We can say this not because we have changed the *meaning* of the term gold, and thrown in some other criteria which distinguished gold from pyrites. It seems to me that that's not true. On the contrary, we *discovered* that certain properties were true of gold in addition to the initial identifying marks by which we identified it. These properties, then, being characteristic of gold and not true of iron pyrites, show that the fool's gold is not in fact gold.

We should look at this in another example. It says somewhere in here:[61] "I say 'The word 'tiger' has meaning in English'.... If I am then asked 'What is a tiger?' I might reply 'A tiger is a large carnivorous quadrupedal feline, tawny yellow in color with blackish transverse stripes and white belly', (derived from the entry under 'tiger' in the *Shorter Oxford English Dictionary*.)" And now suppose someone says "You have just said what the word 'tiger' means in English." And Ziff asks "is that so?" and he says correctly, 'I think not." His example is, "Suppose in a jungle clearing one says 'look, a three-legged tiger!': must one be confused? The phrase 'a three-legged tiger' is not a *contradictio in adjecto*. But if 'tiger' in English meant, among other things, either quadruped or quadrupedal, the phrase 'a three-legged tiger' could only be a *contradictio in adjecto*." So, his example shows that if it is part of the concept of tiger that a tiger has four legs, there couldn't be a three-legged tiger. This is the sort of case which many philosophers tend to explain as a 'cluster concept'. Is it even a contradiction to suppose that we should discover that tigers *never* have four legs? Suppose the explorers who attributed these properties to tigers were deceived by an optical illusion, and that the animals they saw were from a three-legged species, would we then say that there turned out to be no tigers after all? I think we would say that in spite of the optical illusion which had deceived the explorers, tigers in fact have three legs.

Further, is it true that anything satisfying this description in the dictionary is necessarily a tiger? It seems to me that it is not. Suppose we discover an animal which, though having all external appearances of a tiger as described here, has an internal structure completely different from that of the tiger. Actually the word 'feline' was put in here, so it is not entirely fair. Let's suppose it were left out, for this example. That a tiger belongs to any particular biological family, anyway, was something we discovered. If 'feline' means just having the appearance of a cat, let's suppose that it does have the appearance of a big cat. We might find animals in some part of the world which, though they look just like a tiger, on examination were discovered not even to be mammals. Let's say they were in fact very peculiar looking reptiles. Do we then conclude on the basis of this description that some tigers are reptiles? We don't. We would rather conclude that these animals, though they have the external marks by which we originally identified tigers, are not in fact tigers, because they are not of the same species as the species which we called 'the species of tigers'. Now this, I think, is not because, as some people would say, the old concept of tiger has been replaced by a new scientific definition. I think this is true of the concept of tiger *before* the internal structure of tigers had been investigated. Even though we don't *know* the internal structure of tigers, we suppose – and let us suppose that we are right – that tigers form a certain species or natural kind. We then can imagine that there should be a creature which, though having all the external appearance of tigers, differs from them internally enough that we should say that it is not the same kind of thing. We can imagine it without knowing anything about this internal structure – what this internal structure is. We can say in advance that we use the term 'tiger' to designate a species, and that anything not of this species, even though it looks like a tiger, is not in fact a tiger.

Just as something may have all the properties by which we originally identified types and yet not be a tiger, so we might also find out tigers had *none* of the properties by which we originally identified them. Perhaps *none* are quadrupedal, none tawny yellow, none carniverous, and so on; all these properties turn out to be based on optical illusions or other errors, as in the case of gold. So the term 'tiger', like the term 'gold', does *not* mark out a 'cluster concept' in which most, but perhaps not all, of the properties used to identify the kind must be satisfied. On the contrary, possession of most of these properties need not be a necessary condition for membership in the kind, nor need it be a sufficient condition.

Since we have found out that tigers do indeed, as we suspected, form a single kind, then something not of this kind is not a tiger. Of course, we may be mistaken, in supposing that there is such a kind. In advance, we suppose that they probably do form a kind. Past experience has shown that usually things like this, living together, looking alike, mating together, do form a kind. If there are two kinds of tigers that have something to do with each other but not as much as we thought, then maybe they form a larger biological family. If they have absolutely nothing to do with each other, sometimes then there are really two kinds of tigers. This all depends on the history and on what we actually find out.

The philosopher I find most to recognize this sort of consideration (our thoughts on these matters developed independently) is Putnam. In an article called, "It Ain't Necessarily So',[67] he says of statements about species, that they are 'less necessary' (as he cautiously says) than statements like 'bachelors aren't married'. The example he gives is 'cats are animals'. And cats might turn out to be automata, or strange demons (not his example) planted by a magician. Suppose they turned out to be a species of demons. Then on his view, and I think also my view, the inclination is to say, not that there turned out to be no cats, but that cats have turned out not to be animals as we originally supposed. The original concept of cat is: *that kind of thing*, where the kind can be identified by paradigmatic instances. It is not something picked out by any qualitative dictionary definition. However, Putnam's conclusion is that statements like 'cats are animals' are 'less necessary' than statements like 'bachelors are unmarried'. Certainly I agree that the argument indicates that such statements are not known *a priori*, and hence are not analytic;[63] whether a given kind is a species of animals is for empirical investigation. Perhaps this epistemological sense is what Putnam means by 'necessary'. The question remains whether such statements are necessary in the non-epistemological sense advocated in these lectures. So the next thing to investigate is, (using the concept of necessity that I talked about): are such statements as 'cats are animals', or such statements as 'gold is a yellow metal' necessary?

So far I've only been talking about what we could find out. I've been saying we could find out that gold was not in fact yellow, contrary to what we thought. If one went in more detail into the concept of metals, let's say in terms of valency properties, one could certainly find out that though one took gold to be a metal, gold is not in fact a metal. Is it necessary or contingent that gold be a metal? I don't want to go into detail on the concept of a metal – as I said, I don't know enough about it. Gold apparently has the atomic number 79. Is it a necessary or a contingent property of gold that it has the atomic number 79? Certainly we could find out that we were mistaken. The whole theory of protons, of atomic numbers, the whole theory of molecular structure and of atomic structure, on which such views are based, could *all* turn out to be false. Certainly we didn't know it from time immemorial. So in that sense, gold could turn out not to have atomic number 79.

Given that gold *does* have the atomic number 79, could something be gold without having the atomic number 79? Let us suppose the scientists have investigated the nature of gold and have found that it is part of the very nature of this substance, so to speak, that it have the atomic number 79. Suppose we now find some other yellow metal, or some other yellow thing, with all the properties by which we originally identified gold, and

many of the additional ones that we have discovered later. An example
of one with many of the initial properties is iron pyrites, 'fool's gold.'
As I have said, we wouldn't say that this substance is gold. Consider a
possible world. Consider a counterfactual situation in which, let us say,
fool's gold or iron pyrites was actually found in various mountains in
the United States, or in areas of South Africa and the Soviet Union.
Suppose that all the areas which actually contain gold now, contained
pyrites instead, or some other substance which counterfeited the superficial properties of gold but lacked its atomic structure.[64] Would we say,
in this counterfactual situation, that in that situation gold would not
even be an element (because pyrites is not an element)? It seems to me
that we would not. We would instead describe this as a situation in which
a substance, say iron pyrites, which is not gold, would have been found
in the very mountains which actually contain gold and would have had the
very properties by which we commonly identify gold. But it would not be
gold; it would be something else. One should *not* say that it would still be
gold in this possible world, though gold would then lack the atomic number 79. It would be some other element, some other substance. (Once
again, whether people counterfactually would have *called* it 'gold' is irrelevant. *We* do not describe it as gold.) And so, it seems to me, this would
not be a case in which possibly gold might not have been an element, nor
can there be such a case (except in the epistemic sense of 'possible'.) Given
that gold *is* this element, any other substance, even though it looks like
gold and is found in the very places where we not in fact find gold, would
not be gold. It would be some other substance which was a counterfeit
for gold. In any counterfactual situation where the same geographical
areas were filled with such a substance, they would not have been filled
with gold. They would have been filled with something else.

So if this consideration is right, it tends to show that such statements
representing scientific discoveries about what this stuff *is* are not contingent
truths but necessary truths in the strictest possible sense. It's not just
that it's a scientific law, but of course we can imagine a world in which it
would fail. Any world in which we imagine a substance which does not
have these properties is a world in which we imagine a substance which is
not gold, provided these properties form the basis of what substance is.
In particular, then, present scientific theory is such that it is part of the
nature of gold as we have it to be an element with atomic number 79.

It will therefore be necessary and not contingent that gold be an element with atomic number 79. (We may also in the same way, then, investigate further how color and metallic properties follow from what we have found the substance gold to be: to the extent that such properties follow from the atomic structure of gold, they are necessary properties of it, even though they unquestionably are not part of the *meaning* of 'gold' and were not known with *a priori* certainty.)

Putnam's example 'cats are animals' comes under the same sort of heading. We have in fact made a very surprising discovery in this case. We have in fact found nothing to go against our belief. Cats are in fact animals! Then is this truth a necessary truth or a contingent one? It seems to me that it is necessary. Consider the counterfactual situation in which in place of these creatures – these animals – we have in fact little demons which when they approached us brought bad luck indeed. Should we describe this as a situation in which cats were demons? It seems to me that these demons would not be cats. They would be demons in a cat-like form. We could have discovered that the actual cats that we *have* are demons. Once we have discovered, however, that they are *not*, it is part of their very nature that, when we describe a counterfactual world in which there were such demons around, we must say that the demons would not be cats. It would be a world containing demons masquerading as cats. Although we could say cats *might turn out* to be demons, of a certain species, given that cats are in fact animals, any cat-like being which is not an animal, in the actual world or in a counterfactual one, is not a cat. The same holds even for animals with the appearance of cats but reptilic internal structure. Were such to exist, they would not be cats, but 'fool's cats'.

This has some relation also to the essence of a particular object. The molecular theory has discovered, let's say, that this object here is composed of molecules. This was certainly an important empirical discovery. It was something we didn't know in advance; maybe this might have been composed, for all we knew, of some ethereal entelechy. Now imagine an object occupying this very position in the room which *was* an ethereal entelechy. Would it be this very object here? It might have all the appearance of this object, but it seems to me that it could not ever be *this thing*. The vicissitudes of *this thing* might have been very different from its actual history. It might have been transported to the Kremlin. It might have already been hewn into bits and no longer exist at the present time. Various things might have happened to it. But whatever we imagine counterfactually having happened to it other than what actually did, the one thing we cannot imagine happening to this thing is that *it*, given that it is composed of molecules, should still have existed and not have been composed of molecules. We can imagine having discovered that it wasn't composed of molecules. But once we know that this is a thing composed of molecules – that this is the very nature of the substance of which it is made – we can't then, at least if the way I see it is correct, imagine that this thing might have failed to have been composed of molecules.

According to the view I advocate, then, terms for natural kinds are much closer to proper names then is ordinarily supposed. The old term 'common name' is thus quite appropriate for predicates marking out species or natural kinds, such as 'cow' or 'tiger', My considerations apply also, however, to certain mass terms for natural kinds, such as 'gold', 'water', and the like. It is interesting to compare my views to those of Mill. Mill counts both predicates like 'cow', definite descriptions, and proper names as names. He says of 'singular' names that they are connotative if they are definite descriptions but non-connotative if they are proper names. On the other hand, Mill says that *all* 'general' names are conno- tative; such a predicate as 'human being' is defined as the conjunction of certain properties which give necessary and sufficient conditions for humanity – rationality, animality, and certain physical features.[65] The modern logical tradition, as represented by Frege and Russell, seems to hold that Mill was wrong about singular names, but right about general names. More recent philosophy has followed suit, except that, in the case of both proper names and natural kind terms, it often replaces the notion of defining properties by that of a cluster of properties, only some of which need to be satisfied in each particular case. My own view, on the other hand, regards Mill as more-or-less right about 'singular' names, but wrong about 'general' names. *Perhaps* some 'general' names ('foolish', 'fat', 'yellow') express properties.[66] In a significant sense, such general names as 'cow' and 'tiger' do not, unless *being a cow* counts trivially as a property. Certainly 'cow' and 'tiger' are *not* short for the conjunction of properties a dictionary would take to define them, as Mill thought. Whether science can discover empirically that certain properties are *necessary* of cows, or of tigers, is another question, which I answer affirmatively.

Let's consider how this applies to the types of identity statements expressing scientific discoveries that I talked about before – say, that water is H_2O. It certainly represents a discovery that water is H_2O. We identified water originally by its characteristic feel, appearance and perhaps taste, (though the taste may usually be due to the impurities). If there were a substance, even actually, which had a completely different atomic structure from that of water, but resembled water in these respects, would we say that some water wasn't H_2O? I think not. We would say instead that just as there is a fool's gold there could be a fool's water; a substance which, though having the properties by which we originally identified water, would not in fact be water. And this, I think, applies not only to the actual world but even when we talk about counterfactual situations. If there had been a substance, which was a fool's water, it would then be fool's water and not water. On the other hand if this substance can take another from – such as the polywater allegedly discovered in the Soviet Union, with very different identifying marks from that of what we now call water – it is a form of water because it is the same substance, even though it doesn't have the appearances by which we originally identified water.

Let's consider the statement 'Light is a stream of photons' or 'Heat is the motion of molecules'. By referring to light, of course, I mean something which we have some of in this room. When I refer to heat, I refer not to an internal sensation that someone may have, but to an external phenomenon which we perceive through the sense of feeling; it produces a characteristic sensation which we call the sensation of heat. Heat *is* the motion of molecules. We have also discovered that increasing heat corresponds to increasing motion or molecules, or strictly speaking, increasing average kinetic energy of molecules. So temperature is identified with mean molecular kinetic energy. However I won't talk about temperature because there is the question of how the actual scale is to be set. It might just be set in terms of the mean molecular kinetic energy.[67] But what represents an interesting phenomenological discovery is that when it's hotter the molecules are moving faster. We have also discovered about light that light is a stream of photons; alternatively it is a form of electromagnetic radiation. Now we have identified light by the characteristic, internal visual impressions it can produce in us, that make us able to see. Heat, on the other hand, we originally identified by the characteristic effect on one aspect of our nerve endings or our sense of touch.

Imagine a situation in which human beings were blind or their eyes didn't work. They were unaffected by light. Would that have been a situation in which light did not exist? It seems to me that it would not. It would have been a situation in which our eyes were not sensitive to light. Some creatures may have eyes not sensitive to light. Among such creatures are unfortunately some people, of course; they are called *'blind'*. Even if all people had awful vestigial growths and just couldn't see a thing, the light might be around; but it would not be able to affect people's eyes in the proper way. So it seems to me that such a situation would be a situation in which there was light, but people could not see it. So, though we may identify light by the characteristic visual impressions it produces in us, this seems to be a good example of fixing a reference. We fix what light is by the fact that it is whatever, out in the world, affects our eyes in a certain way. But now, talking about counterfactual situations in which let's say, people were blind, we would not then say that since in such situations, nothing could effect their eyes, light would not exist; rather we would say that that would be a situation in which light – the thing we have identified as that which in fact enables us to see – existed but did not manage to help us see due to some defect in us.

Perhaps we can imagine, that by some miracle sound waves somehow enabled some creature to see. I mean, they gave him visual impressions just as we have, maybe exactly the same color sense. We can also imagine the same creature to be completely *insensitive* to light (photons). Who knows what subtle undreamt of possibilities there may be? Would we say that in such a possible world, it was sound which was light, that these wave motions in the air were light? It seems to me that, given our concept of light, we should describe the situation differently. It would be a situation in which certain creatures, maybe even those which were called people and inhabited this planet, were sensitive not to light but to sound waves, sensitive to them in exactly the same way that we are sensitive to light. If this is so, once we have found out what light is, when we talk about other possible worlds we are talking about this phenomenon in the world, and not using 'light' as a phrase *synonymous* with 'whatever gives us the visual impression – whatever helps us to see'; for there might have been light and it not helped us to see; and even something else might have helped us to see. The way we identified light *fixed a reference*.

And similarly for other such phrases, such as 'heat'. Here heat is something which we have identified, and picked out the reference of, by its giving a certain sensation, which we call the sensation of heat. We don't have a special name for this sensation other than as a sensation of heat. It's interesting that the language is this way. Whereas you might suppose it, from what I am saying, to have been the other way. At any rate, we identify heat and are able to sense it by the fact that it produces in us a sensation of heat. It might here be so important to the concept that its reference is fixed in this way, that if someone else detects heat by some sort of instrument, but is unable to feel it, we might want to say, if we like, that the concept of heat is not the same even though the referent is the same.

Nevertheless, the term 'heat' doesn't *mean* 'whatever gives people these sensations'. For first, people might not have been sensitive to heat, and yet the heat still have existed in the external world. Secondly, let us suppose that somehow light rays, because of some difference in their nerve endings, *did* give them these sensations. It would not then be heat but light which gave people the sensation which we call the sensation of heat.

Can we then imagine a possible world in which heat was not molecular motion? We can imagine, of course, having discovered that it was not. It seems to me that any case which someone will think of, which he thinks at first is a case in which heat – contrary to what is actually the case – was something other than molecular motion, would actually be a case in which some creatures with different nerve endings from ours inhabit this planet (maybe even we, if it's a contingent fact about us that we have this particular neural structure); and these creatures were sensitive to that something else, say light, in such a way that they felt the same thing that we feel when we feel heat. But this is not a situation in which, say, light would have been heat, or even in which a stream of photons would have been heat, but a situation in which a stream of photons would have produced the characteristic sensations which we call sensations of heat.

Similarly for many other such identifications, say, that lightning is electricity. Flashes of lightning are flashes of electricity. Lightning is an electrical discharge. We can imagine, of course, I suppose, other ways in which the sky might be illuminated at night with the same sort of flash without any electrical discharge being present. Here too, I am inclined to say, when we imagine this, we can imagine something with all the visual appearances of lightning but which is not, in fact, lightning. One could be told: this appeared to be lightning but it was not. I suppose this might even happen now. Someone might by a clever sort of apparatus produce some phenomenon in the sky which would fool people into thinking that there was lightning; but nevertheless no lightning was present. And you wouldn't say that phenomenon, because it looks like lightning, was in fact lightning. It was a different phenomenon from the lightning, which is the phenomenon of an electrical discharge; and this is not lightning but just something that deceives us into thinking that there is lightning.

What characteristically goes on in these cases of, let's say, 'heat is molecular motion'? There is a certain referent which we have fixed, for the real world and for all possible worlds, by a contingent property of it, namely the property that it's able to produce such and such sensations in us. Let's say it's a contingent property of heat that it produces such and such sensations in people. It's perhaps contingent that there should even have been people in this planet at all. So one doesn't know *a priori* what physical phenomenon, described in other terms – in basic terms of physical theory – is the phenomenon which produces these sensations. We don't know this, and we've discovered eventually that this phenomenon is in fact molecular motion. When we have discovered this we've discovered an identification which gives us an essential property of this phenomenon. We have discovered a phenomenon which in all possible worlds will be molecular motion – which could not have failed to be molecular motion, because that's what the phenomenon *is*.[68] On the other hand, the property by which we identify it originally, that of producing such and such a sensation in us, is not a necessary property but a contingent one. This very phenomenon could have existed, but due to differences in our neural structures and so on, have failed to be felt as heat. Actually, when I say *our* neural structures, as those of human beings, I'm really hedging a point which I made earlier; because of course, it might be part of the very nature of human beings that they have the neural structure which is sensitive to heat. Therefore this too could turn out to be necessary if enough investigation showed it. This I'm just ignoring, for the purpose of simplifying the discussion. At any rate it's not necessary, I suppose, that this planet should have been inhabited by creatures sensitive to heat in this way.

I will conclude with some remarks about the application of the foregoing considerations to the debate over the mind-body identity thesis. Before I do so, however, I wish to recapitulate the views I have developed, and perhaps add a point or two.

First, my argument implicitly concludes that certain general terms, those for natural kinds, have a greater kinship with proper names than is generally realized. This conclusion holds for certain for various species names, whether they are count nouns, such as 'cat', 'tiger', 'chunk of gold', or mass terms such as 'gold', 'water', 'iron pyrites'. It also applies to certain terms for natural phenomena, such as 'heat', 'light', 'sound', 'lightning', and, presumably, suitably elaborated, to corresponding adjectives – 'hot', 'loud', 'red'.

Mill, as I have recalled, held that although some 'singular names', the definite descriptions, have both denotation and connotation, others, the genuine proper names, had denotation but not connotation. Mill further maintained that 'general names', or general terms, had connotation. Such terms as 'cow' or 'human' are defined by the conjunction of certain properties which pick out their extension – a human being, for example is a rational animal with certain physical characteristics. The hoary tradition of definition by *genus* and *differentia* is of a piece with such a conception. If Kant did, indeed, suppose that 'gold' could be *defined* as 'yellow metal', it may well be this tradition which led him to the definition. ('Metal' would be the genus, 'yellow' the differentia. The differentia could hardly include 'being gold' without circularity.)

The modern logical tradition, as represented by Frege and Russell, disputed Mill on the issue of singular names, but endorsed him on that of general names. Thus *all* terms, both singular and general, have a 'connotation' or Fregean sense. More recent theorists have followed Frege and Russell, modifying their views only by replacing the notion of a sense as given by a particular conjunction of properties with that of a sense as given by a 'cluster' of properties, only *enough* of which need apply. The present view, directly reversing Frege and Russell, *endorses* Mill's view of *singular* terms, but *disputes* his view of *general* terms.

Second, the present view asserts, in the case of species terms as in that

of proper names, one should bear in mind the contrast between the
a priori properties carried with a term, the way its reference was fixed,
and the meaning of a term, and the analytic or necessary properties it
carries. For species, as for proper names, the way the reference of a term
is fixed should not be regarded as a synonym for the term. In the case of
proper names, the reference can be fixed in various ways. In an initial
baptism it is typically fixed by an ostension or a description. Otherwise,
the reference is usually determined by a chain, passing the name from
link to link. The same observations hold for such a general term as 'gold'.
If we imagine a hypothetical (admittedly somewhat artificial) baptism
of the substance, we must imagine it picked out as by some such 'definition' as, 'Gold is the substance instantiated by the items over there, or
at any rate, by almost all of them'. Several features of this baptism are
worthy of note. First, the identity in the 'definition' does not express a
(completely) necessary truth: though each of these items is, indeed,
essentially (necessarily) gold,[69] gold might have existed even if the items
did not. The definition does, however, express an *a priori* truth, in the
same sense as (and with the same qualifications applied as) '1 in. =length
of S': it *fixes a reference*. I believe that in general, terms for natural kinds
(e.g., animal, vegetable, and chemical kinds) get their reference fixed
in this way; the substance is defined as the kind instantiated by (almost
all of) a given sample. The 'almost all' qualification allows that some fools'
gold may be present in the sample. If the original sample has a small
number of deviant items, they will be rejected as not really gold. If, on
the other hand, the supposition that there is one uniform substance or
kind in the initial sample proves more radically in error, reactions can
vary: sometimes we may declare that there are two kinds of gold, sometimes we may drop the term 'gold'. (These possibilities are not supposed
to be exhaustive.) And the alleged new kind may prove illusory for other
reasons. For example, suppose some items (let the set of them be *I*)
are discovered and are believe to belong to a new kind *K*. Suppose that
later it is discovered that the items in *I* are, in fact, of a single kind; however, they belong to a previously known kind, *L*. Observational error
led to the false initial belief that the items in *I* possessed some characteristic
C excluding them from *L*. In this case we would surely say that the kind
K does not exist, in spite of the fact that it was defined by reference to a
uniform initial sample. (Note that if *L* had not previously been identified,

we might well have said that the kind K did exist, but that we were in error in supposing it to be associated with the characteristic C!) To the extent that the notion 'same kind' is vague, so is the original notion of gold. Ordinarily, the vagueness doesn't matter in practice.

In the case of a natural phenomenon perceptible to the senses, the way the reference is picked out is simple: 'Heat = that which is sensed by sensation S'. Once again, the identity fixes a reference: it therefore is *a priori*, but not necessary, since heat might have existed, though we did not. 'Heat', like 'gold', is a rigid designator, whose reference is fixed by its 'definition'. Other natural phenomena, such as electricity, are originally identified as the causes of certain concrete experimental effects. I do not attempt to give exhaustive characterizations here, only examples.

Third, in the case of natural kinds, certain properties, believed to be at least roughly characteristic of the kind and believed to apply to the original sample, are used to place new items, outside the original sample. ('Properties' is used here in a broad sense, and may include larger kinds: for example animality and felinity, for tigers.) These properties need not hold *a priori* of the kind; later empirical investigation may establish that some of the properties did not belong to the original sample, or that they were peculiarities of the original sample, not to be generalized to the kind as a whole. (Thus the yellowness of gold may be an optical illusion; or, more plausibly, though the gold originally observed was indeed yellow, it could turn out that some gold is white.) On the other hand, an item may possess all the characteristics originally used and fail to belong to the kind. Thus an animal may look just like a tiger, and fail to be a tiger, as mentioned above; distinct elements in the same column of the periodic table may resemble each other rather closely. Such failures are the exception; but, as in the periodic table, they *do* arise. (Sometimes a failure of the initial sample to have the characteristics associated with it may lead us to repudiate the species, as in the *I-K-L* case above. But this phenomenon is not typical, let alone universal; see the remarks on the yellowness of gold, or whether cats are animals.) *A priori*, all we can say is that it is an empirical matter whether the characteristics originally associated with the kind apply to its members universally, or even ever, and whether they are in fact, jointly sufficient for membership in the kind. (The joint sufficiency is extremely unlikely to be *necessary*, but it may be *true*. In fact, any animal looking just like a tiger is a tiger – as far as I know – though it is (metaphysically) *possible* that there should have been animals that resembled tigers but were not tigers. The universal applicability, on the other hand, may well be necessary, if true. 'Cats are animals' *has* turned out to be a necessary truth. Indeed of many such statements, especially those subsuming one species under another we know *a priori* that, if they are true at all, they are necessarily true.)

Fourth, scientific investigation generally discovers characteristics of gold which are far better than the original set. For example, a material object turns out to be (pure) gold if and only if the only element contained therein is that with atomic number 79. Here, the 'if and only if' can be taken to be *strict* (necessary). In general, science attempts, by investigating basic structural traits, to find the nature, and thus the essence (in the philosophical sense) of the kind. The case of actual phenomena is similar; such theoretical identifications as 'heat is molecular motion' are *necessary*, though not *a priori*. The type of property identity used in science seems to be associated with *necessity*, not with a prioricity, or analyticity: For all bodies x and y, x is hotter than y if and only if x has higher mean molecular kinetic energy than y. Here the coextensiveness of the predicates is *necessary*, but not *a priori*. The philosophical notion of attribute, on the other hand, seems to demand *a priori* (and analytic) coextensiveness as well as necessary coextensiveness.

Note that on the present view, scientific discoveries of species essence do not constitute a 'change of meaning'; the possibility of such discoveries was part of the original enterprise. We need not ever assume that the biologist's denial that whales are fish shows his 'concept of fishhood' to be different from that of the layman; he simply corrects the layman, discovering that 'whales are mammals, not fish' is a necessary truth. Neither 'whales are mammals' *nor* 'whales are fish' was supposed to be *a priori* or analytic in any case.

Fifth, and independently of the scientific investigations just mentioned, the 'original sample' gets augmented by the discovery of new items.[70] (In the case of gold, men applied tremendous effort to the task. Those who doubt the natural scientific curiosity of Man should consider this case. Only such anti-scientific fundamentalists as Bryan cast aspersions on the effort.) More important, the species-name may be passed from link to link, exactly as in the case of proper names, so that many who have seen little or no gold can still use the term. Their reference is determined by a causal (historical) chain, not by use of any items. I will make even less effort here to spell out an exact theory than in the case of proper names.

Usually, when a proper name is passed from link to link, the way the reference of the name is fixed is of little importance to us. It matters not at all that different speakers may fix the reference of the name in different ways, provided that they give it the same referent. The situation is probably not very different for species names, though the temptation to think that the metallurgist has a different concept of gold from the man who has never seen any may be somewhat greater. The interesting fact is that the way the reference is fixed seems overwhelmingly important to us in the case of sensed phenomena: a blind man who uses the term 'light', even though he uses it as a rigid designator for the very same phenomenon as we, seems to us to have lost a great deal, perhaps enough for us to declare that he has a different concept. ('Concept' here is used non-technically!) The fact that we identify light in a certain way seems to us to be *crucial*, even though it is not necessary; the intimate connection may create an *illusion* of necessity. I think that this observation, together with the remarks on property-identity above, may well be essential to an understanding of the traditional disputes over primary and secondary qualities.[71]

Let us return to the question of theoretical identification. Theoretical identities, according to the conception I advocate, are generally identities involving two rigid designators and therefore are examples of the necessary *a posteriori*. Now in spite of the arguments I gave before for the distinction between necessary and *a priori* truth, the notion of *a posteriori* necessary truth may still be somewhat puzzling. Someone may well be inclined to argue as follows: 'You have admitted that heat might have turned out not to have been molecular motion, and that gold might have turned out not to have been the element with the element with atomic number 79. For that matter, you also have acknowledged that Elizabeth II might have turned out not to be the daughter of George VI, or even to originate in the particular sperm and egg we had thought, and this table might have turned out to be made from ice made from water from the Thames. I gather that Hesperus might have turned out not to be Phosphorus. What then can you mean when you say that such eventualities are impossible? If Hesperus might have *turned out* not to be Phosphorus, then Hesperus might not have *been* Phosphorus, which Hesperus was not Phosphorus. And similarly for the other cases: if the world could have *turned out* otherwise, it could have *been* otherwise. To deny this fact is to deny the self-evident modal principle that what is entailed by a possibility must itself be possible. Nor can you evade the difficulty by declaring the 'might have' of 'might have turned out otherwise' to be merely epistemic, in the way that 'Fermat's Last Theorem might turn out to be true and might turn out to be false' merely expresses our present ignorance, and 'Arithmetic might have turned out to be complete' signals our former ignorance. In these mathematical cases, we may have been ignorant, but it was in fact mathematically impossible for the answer to turn out other than it did. Not so in your favorite cases of essence and of identity between two rigid designators: it really is logically possible that gold should have turned out to be a compound, and this table might really have turned out not to be made of wood, let alone of a given particular block of wood. The contrast with the mathematical case could not be greater and would not be alleviated even if, as you suggest, there may be mathematical truths which it is impossible to know *a priori*."

Perhaps anyone who has caught the spirit of my previous remarks can give my answer himself, but there is a clarification of my previous discussion which is relevant here. The objector is correct when he argues if I hold that this table could not have been made of ice, then I must also hold that it could not have turned out to be made of ice; *it could have turned out that P* entails that *P* could have been the case. What, then, does the intuition that the table might have turned out to have been made of ice or of anything else, that it might even have turned out not to be made of molecules, amount to? I think that it means simply that there might have been *a table* looking and feeling just like this one and placed in this very position in the room, which was in fact made of ice. In other words, I (or some conscious being) could have been *qualitatively in the same epistemic situation* that in fact obtains, I could have the same sensory evidence that I in fact have, about *a table* which was made of ice. The situation is thus akin to the one which inspired the counterpart theorists; when I speak of the possibility of the table turning out to be made of various things, I am speaking loosely. *This* table itself could not have had an origin different from the one it in fact had, but in a situation qualitatively identical to this one with respect to all the evidence

I had in advance, the room could have contained *a table made of ice* in place of this one. Something like counterpart theory is thus applicable to the situation, but it applies only because we are *not* interested in what might have been true of *this particular* table, but what might or might not be true of *a table* given certain evidence. It is precisely because it is *not* true that this table might have been made of ice from the Thames that we must turn here to qualitative descriptions and counterparts. To apply these notions to genuine *de re* modalities is, from the present standpoint, perverse.

The general answer to the objector can be stated, then, as follows: Any necessary truth, whether *a priori* or *a posteriori*, could not have turned out otherwise. In the case of some necessary *a posteriori* truths, however, we can say that under appropriate qualitatively identical evidential situations, an appropriate corresponding qualitative statement might have been false. The loose and inaccurate statement that gold might have turned out to be a compound should be replaced (roughly) by the statement that it is logically possible that there should have been a compound with all the properties originally known to hold of gold. The inaccurate statement that Hesperus might have turned out not to be Phosphorus should be replaced by the true contingency mentioned earlier in these lectures: two distinct bodies might have occupied in the morning and the evening, respectively, the very positions actually occupied by Hesperus-Phosphorus-Venus.[72] The reason the example of Fermat's Last Theorem gives a different impression is that here no analogue suggests itself, except for the extremely general statement that, in the absence of proof or disproof, it is possible for *a mathematical conjecture* to be either true or false.

I have not given any general paradigm for the appropriate corresponding qualitative contingent statement. Since we are concerned with how things might have turned out otherwise, our general paradigm is to redescribe both the prior evidence and the statement qualitatively and claim that they are only contingently related. In the case of identities, using two rigid designators, such as the Hesperus-Phosphorus case above, there is a simpler paradigm which is often usable to at least approximately the same effect. Let 'R_1' and 'R_2' be the two rigid designators which flank the identity sign. The '$R_1 = R_2$' is necessary if true. The references of 'R_1' and 'R_2', respectively, may well be fixed by non-

rigid designators 'D_1' and 'D_2' in the Hesperus and Phosphorus cases
these have the form 'the heavenly body in such-and-such position in the
sky in the evening (morning)'. Then although '$R_1 = R_2$' is necessary,
'$D_1 = D_2$' may well be contingent, and this is often what leads to the
erroneous view that '$R_1 = R_2$' might have turned out otherwise.

I finally turn to an all too cursory discussion of the application of the
foregoing considerations to the identity thesis. Identity theorists have
been concerned with several distinct types of identifications: of a person
with his body, of a particular sensation (or event or state of having the
sensation) with a particular brain state (Jones's pain at 06 : 00 was his
C-fiber stimulation at that time), and of *types* of mental states with
the corresponding *types* of physical states (pain is the stimulation of
C-fibers). Each of these, and other types of identifications in the literature,
present analytical problems, rightly raised by Cartesian critics, which
cannot be avoided by a simple appeal to an alleged confusion of synonymy
with identity. I should mention that there is of course no obvious bar,
at least (I say cautiously) none which should occur to any intelligent
thinker on a first reflection just before bedtime, to advocacy of some
identity theses while doubting or denying others. For example, some
philosophers have accepted the identity of particular sensations with
particular brain states while denying the possibility of identities between
mental and physical *types*. I will concern myself primarily with the type-
type identities, and the philosophers in question will thus be immune to
most of the discussion; but I will mention the other kinds of identities
briefly.

Descartes, and others following him, argued that a person or mind is
distinct from his body, since the mind could exist without the body.
He might equally well have argued the same conclusion from the premise
that the body could have existed without the mind.[73] Now the one response
which I regard as plainly inadmissible is the response which cheerfully
accepts the Cartesian premise while denying the Cartesian conclusion.
Let 'Descartes' be a name, or rigid designator, of a certain person, and
let 'B' be a rigid designator of his body. Then if Descartes were indeed
identical to B, the supposed identity, being an identity between two rigid
designators, would be necessary, and Descartes could not exist without
B and B could not exist without Descartes. The case is not at all comparable
to the alleged analogue, the identity of the first Postmaster General with

the inventor of bifocals. True, this identity obtains despite the fact that there could have been a first Postmaster General even though bifocals had never been invented. The reason is that 'the inventor of bifocals' is not a rigid designator; a world in which no one invented bifocals is not *ipso facto* a world in which Franklin did not exist. The alleged analogy therefore collapses; a philosopher who wishes to refute the Cartesian conclusion must refute the Cartesian premise, and the latter task is not trivial.

Let '*A*' name a particular pain sensation, and let '*B*' name the corresponding brain state, or the brain state some identity theorist wishes to identify with *A*. *Prima facie*, it would seem that it is at least logically possible that *B* should have existed (Jones's brain could have been in exactly that state at the time in question) without Jones feeling any pain at all, and thus without the presence of *A*. Once again, the identity theorist cannot admit the possibility cheerfully and proceed from there; consistency, and the principle of the necessity of identites using rigid designators, disallows any such course. If *A* and *B* were identical, the identity would have to be necessary. The difficulty can hardly be evaded by arguing that although *B* could not exist without *A*, *being a pain* is merely a contingent property of *A*, and that therefore the presence of *B* without pain does not imply the presence of *B* without *A*. Can any case of essence be more obvious than the fact that *being a pain* is a necessary property of each pain? The identity theorist who wishes to adopt the strategy in question must even argue that *being a sensation* is a contingent property of *A*, for *prima facie* it would seem logically possible that *B* could exist without any sensation with which it might plausibly be identified. Consider a particular pain, or other sensation, that you once had. Do you find it at all plausible that *that very sensation* could have existed without being a sensation, the way a certain inventor (Franklin) could have existed without being an inventor?

I mention this strategy because it seems to me to be adopted by a large number of identity theorists. These theorists, believing as they do that the supposed identity of a brain state with the corresponding mental state is to be analyzed on the paradigm of the contingent identity of Benjamin Franklin with the inventor of bifocals, realize that just as his contingent activity made Benjamin Franklin into the inventor of bifocals, so some contingent property of the brain state must make it into a pain.

Generally they wish this property to be one statable in physical or at least 'topic-neutral' language, so that the materialist cannot be accused of positing irreducible non-physical properties. A typical view is that *being a pain*, as a property of a physical state, is to be analyzed in terms of the 'causal role' of the state,[74] in terms of the characteristic stimuli (e.g., pinpricks) which cause it and the characteristic behavior it causes. I will not go into the details of such analyses, even though I usually find them faulty on specific grounds in addition to the general modal considerations I argue here. All I need to observe here is that the 'causal role' of the physical state is regarded by the theorists in question as a contingent property of the state, and thus it is supposed to be contingent property of the state that is a mental state at all, let alone that it is something as specific as a pain. To repeat, this notion seems to me self-evidently absurd. It amounts to the view that the *very pain I now have* could have existed without being a mental state at all.

I have not discussed the converse problem, which is closer to the original Cartesian consideration – namely, that just as it seems that the brain state could have existed without any pain, so it seems that the pain could have existed without the corresponding brain state. Note that *being a brain state* is evidently an essential property of B (the brain state). Indeed, even more is true: not only being a brain state, but even being a brain state of a specific type is an essential property of B. The configuration of brain cells whose presence at a given time constitutes the presence of B at that time is essential to B, and in its absence B would not have existed. Thus someone who wishes to claim that the brain state and the pain are identical must argue that the pain A could not have existed without a quite specific type of configuration of molecules. If $A = B$, then the identity of A with B is necessary, and any essential property of one must be an essential property of the other. Someone who wishes to maintain an identity thesis cannot simply *accept* the Cartesian intuitions that A can exist without B, that B can exist without A, that the correlative presence of anything with mental properties is merely contingent to B, and that the correlative presence of any specific physical properties is merely contingent to A. He must explain these intuitions away, showing how they are illusory. This task may not be impossible; we have seen above how some things which appear to be contingent turn out, on closer examination, to be necessary. The task, however, is obviously not child's play, and we shall see below how difficult it is.

The final kind of identity, the one which I said would get the closest attention, is the type-type sort of identity exemplified by the identification of pain with the stimulation of C-fibers. These identifications are supposed to be analogous with such scientific type-type identifications as the identity of heat with molecular motion, of water with hydrogen hydroxide, and the like. Let us consider, as an example, the analogy supposed to hold between the materialist identification and that of heat with molecular motion; both identifications identify two types of phenomena. The usual view holds that the identification of heat with molecular motion and of pain with the stimulation of C-fibers are both contingent. We have seen above that since 'heat' and 'molecular motion' are both rigid designators, the identification of the phenomena they name is necessary. What about 'pain' and 'C-fiber stimulation'? It should be clear from the previous discussion that 'pain' is a rigid designator of the type, or phenomenon, it designates: if something is a pain it is essentially so, and it seems absurd to suppose that pain could have been some phenomenon other than the one it is. The same holds for the term 'C-fiber stimulation', provided that 'C-fibers' is a rigid designator, as I will suppose here. (The supposition is somewhat risky, since I know virtually nothing about C-fibers, except that the stimulation of them is said to be correlated with pain.[76] The point is unimportant; if 'C-fibers' is not a rigid designator, simply replace it by one which is, or suppose it used as a rigid designator in the present context.) Thus the identity of pain with the stimulation of C-fibers, if true, must be *necessary*.

So far the analogy between the identification of heat with molecular motion and pain with the stimulation of C-fibers has not failed; it merely turned out to be the opposite of what is usually thought – both, if true, must be necessary. This means that the identity theorist is committed to the view that there could not be a C-fiber stimulation which was not a pain nor a pain which was not a C-fiber stimulation. These consequences are certainly surprising and counterintuitive, but let us not dismiss the identity theorist too quickly. Can he perhaps show that the apparent possibility of pain not having turned out to be C-fiber stimulation, or there being an instance of one of the phenomena which is not an instance of the other is an illusion of the same sort as the illusion that water might not have been hydrogen hydroxide, or that heat might not have been molecular motion? If so, he will have rebutted the Cartesian not, as in the conventional analysis, by accepting his premise while exposing the fallacy of his argument, but rather by the reverse – while the Cartesian argument, given its premise of the contingency of the identification, is granted to yield its conclusion, the premise is to be exposed as superficially plausible but false.

Now I do not think it likely that the identity theorist will succeed in such an endeavor. I want to argue that, at least, the case cannot be interpreted as analogous to that of scientific identification of the usual sort, as examplified by the identity of heat and molecular motion. What was the strategy used above to handle the apparent contingency of certain cases of the necessary *a posteriori?* The strategy was to argue that although the statement itself is necessary, someone could be *qualitatively* speaking, in the same epistemic situation as the original, and in such a situation a *qualitatively* analogous statement could be false. In the case of identities between two rigid designators, the strategy can be approximated by a simpler one: Consider how the references of the designators are determined; if these coincide only contingently, it is this fact which gives the original statement its illusion of contingency. In the case of heat and molecular motion, the way these two paradigms work out is simple. When someone says, inaccurately, that heat might have turned out not to be molecular motion, what is true in what he says is that someone could have sensed a phenomenon in the same way we sense heat, that is, feels it by means of its production of the sensation we call 'the sensation of heat', (call it 'S') even though that phenomenon was not molecular motion. He means, additionally, that the planet might have been inhabited by creatures who did not get S when they were in the presence of molecular motion, though perhaps getting it in the presence of something else. Such creatures would be, in some qualitative sense, in the same epistemic situation as we are, they could use a rigid designator for the phenomenon that causes sensation S in them (the rigid designator could even be 'heat'), yet it would not be molecular motion (and therefore not heat!), which was causing the sensation.

Now can something be said analogously to explain away the feeling that the identity of pain and the stimulation of C-fibers, if it is a scientific discovery, could have turned out otherwise? I do not see that such an analogy is possible. In the case of the apparent possibility that molecular motion might have existed in the absence of heat, what seemed really possible is that molecular motion should have existed without being *felt as heat*, that is, it might have existed without producing the sensation *S*, the sensation of heat. In the appropriate sentient beings is it analogously possible that a stimulation of C-fibers should have existed without being felt as pain? If this is possible, then the stimulation of C-fibers can itself exist without pain, since for it to exist without being *felt as pain* is for it to exist without there *being any* pain. Such a situation would be in flat out contradiction with the supposed necessary identity of pain and the corresponding physical state, and the analogue holds for any physical state which might be identified with a corresponding mental state. The trouble is that the identity theorist does not hold that the physical state merely *produces* the mental state, rather he wishes the two to be identical and thus *a fortiori* necessarily co-occurrent. In the case of molecular motion and heat there is something, namely, the sensation of heat, which is an intermediary between the external phenomenon and the observer. In the mental-physical case no such intermediary is possible, since here the physical phenomenon is supposed to be identical with the internal phenomenon itself. Someone can be in the same epistemic situation as he would be if there were heat, even in the absence of heat, simply by feeling the sensation of heat; and even in the presence of heat, he can have the same evidence as he would have in the absence of heat simply by lacking the sensation *S*. No such possibility exists in the case of pain or in other mental phenomena. To be in the same epistemic situation that would obtain if one had a pain *is* to have a pain; to be in the same epistemic situation that would obtain in the absence of a pain *is* not to have a pain. The apparent contingency of the action between the physical state and the corresponding brain state thus can be explained by some sort of qualitative analogue as obtained in the case of heat.

We have just analyzed the situation in terms of the notion of a qualitatively identical epistemic situation. The trouble is that the notion of an epistemic situation qualitatively identical to one in which the observer had a sensation *S* simply *is* one in which the observer had that sensation. The same point can be made in terms of the notion of what picks out the reference of a rigid designator. In the case of identity of heat with molecular motion the important consideration was that although 'heat' is a rigid designator, the reference of that designator was determined by an accidental property of the referent, namely the property of producing in us the sensation S. It is thus possible that a phenomenon should have been rigidly designated in the same way as a phenomenon of heat, with its reference also picked out by means of the sensation S without that phenomenon being heat and therefore without its being molecular motion. Pain, on the other hand, is not picked out by one of its accidental properties; rather it is picked out by the property of being pain itself, by its immediate phenomenological quality. Thus pain, unlike heat, is not only rigidly designated by 'pain' but the reference of the designator is determined by an essential property of the referent. Thus it is not possible to say that although pain is necessarily identical with a certain physical state, a certain phenomenon can be picked out in the same way we pick out pain without being correlated with that physical state. If any phenomenon is picked out in exactly the same way that we pick out pain, then that phenomenon *is* pain.

Perhaps the same point can be made more vivid without such specific reference to the technical apparatus in these lectures. Suppose we imagine God creating the world; what does He need to do to make the identity of heat and molecular motion obtain? Here it would seem that all He needs to do is to create the heat, that is, the molecular motion itself. If the air molecules on this earth are sufficiently agitated, if there is a burning fire, then the earth will be hot even if there are no observers to see it. God created light (and thus created streams of photons, according to present scientific doctrine) before He created human and animal observers; and the same presumably holds for heat. How then does it appear to us that the identity of molecular motion with heat is a substantive scientific fact, that the mere creation of molecular motion still leaves God with the additional task of making molecular motion into heat? This feeling is indeed illusory, but what *is* a substantive task for the Deity is the task of making molecular motion felt as heat. To do this He must create some sentient beings to insure that the molecular motion produces the sensation S in them. Only after he has done this will there be beings who can learn that the sentence 'Heat is the motion of molecules' expresses an *a posteriori* truth in precisely the same way that we do.

What about the case of the stimulation of C-fibers? To create this phenomenon, it would seem that God need only to create beings with C-fibers capable of the appropriate type of physical stimulation; whether the beings are conscious or not is irrelevant here. It would seem though, that to make the C-fiber stimulation correspond to pain, or be felt as pain, God must do something in addition to the mere creation of the C-fiber stimulation; He must let the creatures feel the C-fiber stimulation as *pain*, and not as a tickle, or as warmth, or as nothing, as apparently would also have been within His powers. If these things in fact are within His powers, the relation between the pain God creates and the stimulation of C-fibers cannot be identity. For if so, the stimulation could exist without the pain; and since 'pain' and 'C-fiber stimulation' are rigid, this fact implies that the relation between the two phenomena is not that of identity. God had to do some work, in addition to making the man himself, to make a certain man be the inventor of bifocals; the man could well exist without inventing any such thing. The same cannot be said for pain; if the phenomenon exists at all, no further work should be required to make it into pain.

In sum, the correspondence between a brain state and a physical state seems to have a certain obvious element of contingency. We have seen that identity is not a relation which can hold contingently between objects. Therefore, if the identity thesis were correct, the element of contingency would not lie in the relation between the mental and physical states. It cannot lie, as in the case of heat and molecular motion, in the relation between the phenomena (=heat =molecular motion) and the way it is felt or appears (sensation S), since in the case of mental phenomena there is no 'appearance' beyond the mental phenomenon itself.

Here I have been emphasizing the possibility, or apparent possibility, of a physical state without the corresponding mental state. The reverse possibility, the mental state (pain) without the physical state (C-fiber stimulation) also presents problems for the identity theorists which cannot be resolved by appeal to the analogy of heat and molecular motion.

I have devised similar problems more briefly for the equations of the self and the body and of particular mental events and particular physical events, without discussing possible countermoves to the same extent as in the type-type case. Suffice it to say that I suspect that the theorist who wishes to identify various particular mental and physical events will have to face problems fairly similar to those of the type-type theorist; he too will be unable to appeal to the standard alleged analogues.

That the usual moves and analogies are not available to solve the problems of the identity theorist is, of course, no proof that no moves are available. I certainly cannot discuss all the possibilities here. I suspect, however, that the present conditions tell heavily against the usual forms of materialism. Materialism, I think, must hold that a physical description of the world is a *complete* description of it, that any mental facts are 'ontologically dependent' on physical facts in the straightforward sense of following from them by necessity. No identity theorist seems to me to have made a convincing argument against the intuitive view that this is not the case.[77]

Department of Philosophy, The Rockefeller University, New York

REFERENCES

[1] In January and February of 1970, I gave the three talks at Princeton University transcribed here. As the style of the transcript makes clear, I gave the talks without a written text, and, in fact, without notes. The present text is lightly edited from the *verbatim* transcript; an occasional passage has been added to expand the thought, an occasional sentence has been rewritten, but no attempt has been made to change the informal style of the original. Many of the footnotes have been added to the original, but a few were originally spoken asides in the talks themselves.

I hope the reader will bear these facts in mind as he reads the text. Imagining it spoken, with proper pauses and emphases, may occasionally facilitate comp.ehension. I have agreed to publish the talks in this form with some reservations. The time allotted, and the informal style, necessitated a certain amount of compression of the argument, inability to treat certain objections, and the like. Especially in the concluding sections on scientific identities and the mind-body problem thoroughly had to be sacrificed. Some topics essential to a full presentation of the viewpoint argued here, especially that of existence statements and empty names, had to be omitted altogether. Further, the informality of the presentation may well have engendered a sacrifice of clarity at certain points. All these defects were accepted in the interest of early publication. I hope that perhaps I will have the chance to do a more thorough job later. To repeat, I hope the reader will bear in mind that he is largely reading informal lectures, not only when he encounters repetitions or infelicities, but also when he encounters irreverence or corn.

[2] Given a chance to add a footnote, I shall mention that Rogers Albritton, Charles Chastain, Keith Donnellan, and Michael Slote (in addition to philosophers mentioned in the text, especially Hilary Putnam), have independently expressed views with points of contact with various aspects of what I say here. Albritton called the problems of necessity and *a prioricity* in natural kinds to my attention, by raising the question whether we could discover that lemons were not fruits. (I am not sure he would accept all my conclusions.) The apology in the text still stands; I am aware that the list in this footnote is far from comprehensive. I make no attempt to enumerate those friends and students whose stimulating conversations have helped me. Thomas Nagel and

Gilbert Harman deserve special thanks for their help in editing the transcript.
³ Keith Donnellan, 'Reference and Definite Descriptions', *Philosophical Review* **75** (1966), pp. 281–304. See also Leonard Linsky, 'Reference and Referents', *Philosophy and Ordinary Language* (ed. by Caton) Urbana, 1963. Donnellan's distinction seems applicable to names as well as to descriptions. Two men glimpse someone at a distance and think they recognize him as Jones. 'What is Jones doing?' 'Raking the leaves'. If the distant leaf-raker is actually Smith, then in some sense they are *referring* to Smith, even though they both use 'Jones' *as a name of* Jones. In the text, I speak of the 'referent' of a name to mean the thing named by the name – e.g., Jones, not Smith – even though a speaker may sometimes properly be said to use the name to refer to someone else. Perhaps it would have been less misleading to use a technical term, such as 'denote' rather than 'refer'. My use of 'refer' is such as to satisfy the schema, 'The referent of '*X*' is *X*', where '*X*' is replaceable by any name or description. I am tentatively inclined to believe, in opposition to Donnellan, that his remarks about reference have little to do with semantics or truth-conditions, though they may be relevant to a theory of speech-acts. Space limitations do not permit me to explain what I mean by this, much less defend the view, except for a brief remark: Call the referent of a name or description in my sense the 'semantic referent'; for a name, this is the thing named, for a description, the thing uniquely satisfying the description.

Then the speaker may *refer* to something other than the semantic referent if he has appropriate false beliefs. I think this is what happens in the naming (Smith-Jones) cases and also in the Donnellan 'champagne' case; the one requires no theory that names are ambiguous, and the other requires no modification of Russell's theory of descriptions.

⁴ Strictly speaking, of course, Russell says that the names don't abbreviate descriptions and don't have any sense; but then he also says that, just because the things that we call 'names' do abbreviate descriptions, they're not really names. So, since 'Walter Scott'; according to Russell, does abbreviate a description,' Walter Scott' is not a name, and the only names that really exist in ordinary language are, perhaps, demonstratives such as 'this' or 'that', used on a particular occasion to refer to an object with which the speaker is 'acquainted' in Russell's sense. Though we won't put things the way Russell does, we could describe Russell as saying that names, as they are ordinarily called, *do* have sense. They have sense in a strong way, namely, we should be able to give a definite description such that the referent of the name, by definition, is the object satisfying the description. Russell himself, since he eliminates descriptions from his primitive notation, seems to hold in 'On Denoting' that the notion of 'sense' is illusory. In reporting Russell's views, we thus deviate from him in two respects. First, we stipulate that 'names' shall be names as ordinarily conceived, not Russell's 'logically proper names'; second, we regard descriptions, and their abbreviations, as having sense.

⁵ When I speak of the Frege-Russell view and its variants, I include only those versions which give a substantive theory of the reference of names. In particular, Quine's proposal that in a 'canonical notation' a name such as 'Socrates' should be replaced by a description 'the Socratizer' (where 'Socratizes' is an invented predicate), and that the description should then be eliminated by Russell's method, was not intended as a theory of reference for names but as a proposed reform of language with certain advantages. The problems discussed here will all apply, *mutatis mutandis*, to the reformed language; in particular, the question, 'How is the reference of 'Socrates' determined?' yields to the question, 'How is the extension of 'Socratizes' determined?' Of course I do not suggest that Quine has ever claimed the contrary.

[6] Gottlob Frege, 'On Sense and Nominatum', translated by Herbert Feigl in *Readings in Philosophical Analysis* (ed. by Herbert Feigl and Wilfrid Sellars), Appleton Century Crofts, 1949, p. 86.

[7] Ludwig Wittgenstein, *Philosophical Investigations*, translated by G. E. M. Anscombe, MacMillan, 1953, p. 79.

[8] John R. Searle, 'Proper Names', *Mind* 67 (1958), 166-73.

[9] Paul Ziff, *Semantic Analysis*, Cornell U.P., 1960, esp. pp. 85-89, 93-94, 104-105, 173-176.

[10] Those determinists who deny the importance of the individual in history may well argue that had Moses never existed, someone else would have arisen to achieve all that he did. Their claim cannot be refuted by appealing to a correct philosophical theory of the meaning of 'Moses exists'.

[11] By the way, it's a common attitude in philosophy to think that one shouldn't introduce a notion until it's been rigorously defined (according to some popular notion of rigor). Here I am just dealing with an intuitive notion and will keep on the level of an intuitive notion. That is, we think that some things, though they are in fact the case, might have been otherwise. I might not have given these lectures today. If that's right, then it is *possible* that I wouldn't have given these lectures today. Quite a different question is the epistemological question, how any particular person knows that I gave these lectures today. I suppose in that case he does know this is *a posteriori*. But, if someone were born with an innate belief that I was going to give these lectures today, who knows? Right now, anyway, let's suppose that people know this *a posteriori*. At any rate, the two questions being asked are different.

[12] The example I gave asserts a certain property – electoral victory – to be *accidental* to Nixon, independently of how he is described. Of course, if the notion of accidental property is meaningful, the notion of essential property must be meaningful also. This is not to say that there *are* any essential properties – though, in fact, I think there are. The usual argument questions the *meaningfulness* of essentialism, and says that whether a property is accidental or essential to an object depends on how it is described. It is thus *not* the view that all properties are accidental. Of course, it is also not the view, held by some idealists, that all properties are essential, all relations internal.

[13] David K. Lewis, 'Counterpart Theory and Quantified Modal Logic', *Journal of Philosophy* 65 (1968), 113-126. Lewis's elegant paper also suffers from a purely formal difficulty: on his interpretation of quantified modality, the familiar law $(y) ((x)A(x) \supset A(y))$ fails, if $A(x)$ is allowed to contain modal operators. (For example, $(\exists y) ((x) \Diamond (x \neq y))$ is satisfiable but $(\exists y) \Diamond (y \neq y)$ is not.) Since Lewis's formal model follows rather naturally from his philosophical views on counterparts, and since the failure of universal instantiation for modal properties is intuitively bizarre, it seems to me that this failure constitutes an additional argument against the plausibility of his philosophical views. There are other, lesser, formal difficulties as well. I cannot elaborate here.

Strictly speaking, Lewis's view is not a view of 'transworld identification'. Rather, he thinks that similarities across possible worlds determine a counterpart relation which need be neither symmetric nor transitive. The counterpart of something in another possible world is *never* identical with the thing itself. Thus if we say "Humphrey might have won the election (if only he had done such-and-such), we are not talking about something that might have happened to *Humphrey* but to someone else, a 'counterpart'." Probably, however, Humphrey could not care less whether someone *else*, no matter how much resembling him, would have been victorious in another possible world. Thus, Lewis's view seems to me even more bizarre than the usual notions of transworld identification that it replaces. The important issues, however, are common to the two views: the supposition that other possible worlds are like other dimensions of a more inclusive universe, that they can be given only by purely qualitative descriptions, and that therefore either the identity relation or the counterpart relation must be established in terms of qualitative resemblance.

Many have pointed out to me that the father of counterpart theory is probably Leibniz. I will not go into such a historical question here. It would also be interesting to compare Lewis's views with the Wheeler-Everett interpretation of quantum mechanics. I suspect that this view of physics may suffer from philosophical problems analogous to Lewis's counterpart theory; it is certainly very similar in spirit.

[14] Another *locus classicus* of the views I am criticizing, with more philosophical exposition than Lewis's paper, is a paper by David Kaplan on transworld identification. This paper has unfortunately never been published and no longer represents Kaplan's position.

[15] Misleadingly, because the phrase suggests that there is a special problem of 'transworld identification', that we cannot trivially stipulate whom or what we are talking about when we imagine another possible world. The term 'possible world' may also mislead; perhaps it suggests the 'foreign country' picture. I have sometimes used 'counter-factual situation' in the text; Michael Slote has suggested that 'possible state of the world' might be less misleading than 'possible world'. It is better still, to avoid confusion, not to say, 'In some possible world, Humphrey would have won' but rather, simply, 'Humphrey might have won'. The apparatus of possible worlds has (I hope) been very useful as far as the set-theoretic model-theory of quantified modal logic is concerned, but has encouraged philosophical pseudo-problems and misleading pictures.

[16] Of course I don't imply that language contains a name for every object. Demonstratives can be used as rigid designators, and free variables can be used as rigid designators of unspecified objects. Of course when we specify a counterfactual situation, we do not describe the whole possible world, but only the portion which interests us.

[17] See Lecture I, p. 273 (on Nixon), and Lecture II, pp. 287–289.

[18] There is some vagueness here. If a chip, or molecule, of a given table had been replaced by another one, we would be content to say that we have the same table. But if too many chips were different, we would seem to have a different one. The same problem can, of course, arise for identity over time.

Where the identity relation is vague, it may seem intransitive; a claim of apparent identity may yield an apparent non-identity. Some sort of 'counterpart' notion (though not with Lewis's philosophical underpinnings of resemblance, foreign country worlds, etc.), may have more utility here. One could say that strict identity applies only to the particulars (the molecules), and the counterpart relation to the particulars 'composed' of them, the tables. The counterpart relation can then be declared to be vague and intransitive. It seems, however, utopian to suppose that we will ever reach a level of ultimate, basic particulars for which identity relations are never vague and the danger of intransitivity is eliminated. The danger usually does not arise in practice, so we ordinarily can speak simply of identity without worry. Logicians have not developed a logic of vagueness.

[19] *Philosophical Investigations*, § 50.

[20] Philosophers of science may see the key to the problem in a view that 'one meter' is a 'cluster concept'. I am asking the reader hypothetically to suppose that the 'definition' given is the *only* standard used to determine the metric system. I think the problem would still arise.

[21] Since the truth he knows is contingent, I choose *not* to call it 'analytic', stipulatively requiring analytic truths to be both necessary and *a priori*. See footnote 63.

[22] Usually the Fregean sense is now interpreted as the meaning, which must be carefully distinguished from a 'reference fixer'.

We shall see below that for most speakers, unless they are the ones who initially give an object its name, the referent of the name is determined by a 'causal' chain of the communication rather than a description. Hartry Field has proposed that, for some of the purposes of Frege's theory, his notion of sense should be replaced by the chain which determines the reference.

In the formal semantics of modal logic, the sense of a term t is usually taken to be the (possibly partial) function which assigns to each possible world H the referent of t in H. For a rigid designator, such a function is constant. This notion of sense relates to that of 'giving a meaning', not that of fixing a reference. In this use of sense, 'one meter' has a constant function as its sense, though its reference is fixed by 'the length of S', which does not have a constant function as its sense.

Some philosophers have thought that descriptions, in English, are ambiguous, that sometimes they non-rigidly designate, in each world, the object (if any) satisfying the description, while sometimes they *rigidly* designate the object actually satisfying the description. (Others, inspired by Donnellan, say the description sometimes rigidly designates the object thought or presupposed to satisfy the description.) I find any such alleged ambiguities dubious. I know of no clear evidence for it which cannot be handled either by Russell's notion of scope or by the considerations alluded to in footnote 3 above.

If the ambiguity does exist, then in the supposed *rigid* sense of 'the length of S', 'one meter' and 'the length of S' designate the same thing in all possible worlds and have the same (functional) sense.

In the formal semantics of intensional logic, suppose we take a definite description to designate, in each world, the object satisfying the description. It is indeed useful to have an operator which transforms each description into a term which rigidly designates the object *actually* satisfying the description. David Kaplan has proposed such an operator and calls it 'Dthat'.

[23] P. F. Strawson, *Individuals*, Methuen, London, 1959, Ch. 6.

[24] Searle, *op. cit.* in Caton, *Philosophy and Ordinary Language*, p. 160.

[25] The facts that 'the teacher of Alexander' is capable of scope distinctions in modal contexts and that it is not a rigid designator are both illustrated when one observes that the teacher of Alexander might not have taught Alexander (and, in such circumstances, would not have been the teacher of Alexander). On the other hand, it is not true that Aristotle might not have been Aristotle, although Aristotle might not have been *called* 'Aristotle', just as 2×2 might not have been *called* 'four'. (Sloppy, colloquial speech, which often confuses use and mention, may, of course, express the fact that someone might have been called, or not have been called, 'Aristotle' by saying that he might have been, or not have been, Aristotle. Occasionally, I have heard such loose usages adduced as counterexamples to the applicability of the present theory to ordinary language. Colloquialisms like these seem to me to create as little problem for my theses as the success of the 'Impossible Missions Force' creates for the modal law that the impossible does not happen.) Further, although under certain circumstances Aristotle would not have taught Alexander, these are not circumstances under which he would not have been Aristotle.

[26] If someone fixes a meter as 'the length of stick S at t_0, then in some sense he knows

a priori that the length of stick *S* at t_0 is one meter, even though he uses this statement to express a contingent truth. But, merely by fixing a system of measurement, has he thereby *learned* some (contingent) *information* about the world, some new *fact* that he did not know before? It seems plausible that in some sense he did not, even though it is undeniably a contingent fact that *S* is one meter long. So there may be a case for reformulating the thesis that everything *a priori* is necessary so as to save it from this type of counterexample. As I said, I don't know how such a reformulation would go; the reformulation should not be such as to make the thesis trivial (e.g., by defining *a priori* as known to be *necessary* (instead of true) independently of experience); and the converse thesis would still be false.

Since I will not attempt such a reformulation, I shall consistently use the term *a priori* in the text so as to make statements whose truth follows from a definition which fixes a reference *a priori*.

27 Strawson, *op. cit.*, pp. 191–192. Strawson actually considers the case of several speakers, pools their properties, and takes a democratic (equally weighted) vote. He requires only a sufficient plurality, not a majority.

28 See, for example, H. L. Ginsberg, *The Five Megilloth and Jonah*, The Jewish Publication Society of America, 1969, p. 114: "The 'hero' of this tale, the prophet Jonah the son of Amittai, is a historical personage ... (but) this book is not history but fiction." The scholarly consensus regards all details about Jonah in the book as legendary and not even based on a factual substratum, excepting the bare statement that he was a Hebrew prophet, which is hardly uniquely identifying. Nor need he have been *called* 'Jonah' by the Hebrews; the '*J*' sound does not exist in Hebrew, and Jonah's historical existence is independent of whether we know his original Hebrew name or not. The fact that *we* call him Jonah cannot be used to single him out without circularity. The evidence for Jonah's historicity comes from an independent reference to him in II Kings; but such evidence could have been available in the absence of any such other references – e.g., evidence that all Hebrew legends were about actual personages. Further, the statement that Jonah is a legend about a real person might have been *true*, even if there were no evidence for it. One may say, "The Jonah of the book never existed," as one may say, "The Hitler of Nazi propaganda never existed." As the quotation above shows, this usage need not coincide with the historians view of whether Jonah ever existed. Ginsberg is writing for the lay reader, who, he assumes, will find his statement intelligible.

29 In Ernest Nagel, Patrick Suppes, and Alfred Tarski, *Logic, Methodology and the philosophy of Science: Proceedings of the 1960 International Congress*, Stanford University Press, 1962, 622–633.

30 Pp. 629–630.

31 Searle, 'Proper Names', in Caton, p. 160.

32 D. Lewis, *op. cit.*, pp. 114–115.

33 An even better case of determining the reference of a name by description, as opposed to ostention, is the discovery of the planet Neptune. Neptune was hypothesized as the planet which caused such and such discrepancies in the orbits of certain other planets. If Leverrier indeed gave the name 'Neptune' to the planet before it was ever seen, then he fixed the reference of 'Neptune' by means of the description just mentioned. At that time he was unable to see the planet even through a telescope. At this stage, an *a priori* material equivalence held between the statements 'Neptune exists' and 'some one planet perturbing the orbit of such and such other planets exists in such and such a position', and also such statements as 'if such and such perturbations are caused

by a planet, they are caused by Neptune' had the status of *a priori* truths. Nevertheless, they were not *necessary* truths, since 'Neptune' was introduced as a name rigidly designating a certain planet. Leverrier could well have believed that if Neptune had been been knocked off its course one million years earlier, it would cause no such perturbations and even that some other object might have caused the perturbations in its place.

34 Following Donnellan's remarks on definite descriptions, we should add that in some cases, an object may be identified, and the reference of a name fixed, using a description which may turn out to be false of its object. The case where the reference of 'Phosphorus' is determined as the 'morning star', which later turns out not to be a star, is an obvious example. In such cases, the description which fixes the reference clearly is in no sense known *a priori* to hold of the object, though a more cautious substitute may be. If such a more cautious substitute is available, it is really the substitute which fixes the reference in the sense intended in the text.

35 Some of the theses are sloppily stated in respect of fussy matters like use of quotation marks and related details. (For example, Theses (5) and (6), as stated, presuppose that the speaker's language is English.) Since the purport of the theses is clear, and they are false anyway, I have not bothered to set these things straight.

36 The cluster-of-descriptions theory of naming would make 'Peano discovered the axioms for number theory' express a trivial truth, not a misconception, and similarly for other misconceptions about the history of science. Some who have conceded such cases to me have argued that there are *other* uses of the same proper names satisfying the cluster theory. For example, it is argued, if we say, "Gödel proved the incompleteness of arithmetic," we are, of course, referring to Gödel, not to Schmidt. But, if we say, "Gödel relied on a diagonal argument in this step of the proof," don't we here, perhaps, refer to *whoever proved the theorem*? Similarly, if someone asks, "What did Aristotle (or Shakespeare) have in mind here?", isn't he talking about the author of the passage in question, whoever he is? By analogy to Donnellan's usage for descriptions, this might be called an 'attributive' use of proper names. If this is so, then assuming the Gödel-Schmidt story, the sentence 'Gödel proved the incompleteness theorem' is false, but 'Gödel used a diagonal argument is the proof' is (at least in some contexts) true, and the reference of the name, 'Gödel' is ambiguous. Since some counterexamples remain, the cluster-of-descriptions theory would still, in general, be false, which was my main point in the text; but it would be applicable in a wider class of cases than I thought. I think, however, that no such ambiguity need be postulated. It is, perhaps, true that sometimes when someone uses the name 'Gödel', his main interest is in whoever proved the theorem, and perhaps he refers to him. I do not think that this case is different from the case of Smith and Jones in footnote 3. If I mistake Jones for Smith, I may *refer* (in an appropriate sense) to Jones when I say that Smith is raking the leaves; nevertheless I do not use 'Smith' ambiguously, as a name sometimes of Smith and sometimes of Jones, but univocally as a name of Smith. Similarly, if I erroneously think that Aristotle wrote such-and-such passage, I may perhaps use 'Aristotle' to *refer* to the actual author of the passage, without supposing any ambiguity in my use of the name. In both cases, I will withdraw my original statement, and my original use of the name, if apprised of the facts. Recall that, in these lectures, 'referent' is used in the technical sense of the thing named by a name (or uniquely satisfying a description), and there should be no confusion.

37 It has been suggested to me that someone might argue that a name is associated with a 'referential' use of a description in Donnellan's sense. For example, although we

identify Gödel as the author of the incompleteness theorem, we are talking about him even if he turns out not to have proved the theorem. Theses (2)–(6) could then fail; but nevertheless each name would abbreviate a description, though the role of descriptions in naming would differ radically from that imagined by Frege and Russell. As I have said above, I am inclined to reject Donnellan's formulation of the notion of referential definite description. Even if Donnellan's analysis is accepted, however, it is clear that the present proposal should not be. For a referential definite description, such as 'the man drinking champagne', is typically withdrawn when the speaker realizes that it does not apply to its object. If a Gödelian fraud were exposed, Gödel would no longer be called the 'author of the incompleteness theorem' but he would still be called 'Gödel'. The description, therefore, does not abbreviate the name.

38 As Robert Nozick pointed out to me, there is a sense in which a description theory must be trivially true if any theory of the reference of names, spelled out in terms independent of the notion of reference, is available. For if such a theory gives conditions under which an object is to be the referent of a name, then it of course uniquely satisfies these conditions. Since I am not pretending to give any theory which eliminates the notion of reference in this sense, I am not aware of any such trivial fulfillment of the description theory and doubt that one exists. (A description using the notion of the reference of a name is easily available but circular, as we saw in our discussion of Kneale.) If any such trivial fulfillment were available, however, the arguments I have given show that the description must be one of a completely different sort from that supposed by Frege, Russell, Searle, Strawson and other advocates of the description theory.

39 Princeton University.

40 Strawson, op. cit., p. 181n.

41 The essential points of this example were suggested by Richard Miller.

42 A good example of a baptism whose reference was fixed by means of a description was that of naming Neptune in footnote 3. The case of a baptism by ostension can perhaps be subsumed under the description concept also. Thus the primary applicability of the description theory is that of initial baptism. Descriptions are also used to fix a reference is cases of designation which are similar to naming except that the terms introduced are not usually called names. The terms 'one meter', '100 degrees Centigrade', have already been given as examples, and other examples will be given later in these lectures. Two things should be emphasized concerning the case of introducing a name via a description in an initial baptism. First, the description used is not synonymous with the name it introduces but rather fixes its reference. Here we differ from the usual description theorists. Second, most cases of initial baptism are far from those which originally inspired the description theory. Usually a baptizer is acquainted in some sense with the object he names and is able to name it ostensively. Now the inspiration of the description theory lay in the fact that we can often use names of famous figures of the past who are long dead and with whom no living person is acquainted; and it is precisely these cases which, on our view, cannot be correctly explained by a description theory.

43 I can transmit the name of the aardvark to other people. For each of these people, as for me, there will be a certain sort of causal or historical connection between my use of the name and the Emperor of the French, but not one of the required type.

44 Once we realize that the description used to fix the reference of a name is not synonymous with it, then the description theory can be regarded as presupposing the notion of naming or reference. The requirement I made that the description used not

itself involve the notion of reference in a circular way is something else and is crucial if the description theory is to have any value at all. The reason is that the description theorist supposes that each speaker essentially uses the description he gives in an initial act of naming to determine his reference. Clearly, if he introduces the name 'Cicero' by the determination 'by 'Cicero' I shall refer to the man I call 'Cicero',' he has by this ceremony determined no reference at all.

Not all description theorists thought that they were eliminating the notion of reference altogether. Perhaps most realized that some notion of ostension, or primitive reference, is required to back it up. Certainly Russell did.

[45] Ruth Barcan Marcus, 'Modalities and Intensional Languages' (comments by W. V. Quine, plus discussion) Boston Studies in the Philosophy of Science, volume I, Reidel, Dordrecht, Holland, 1963, pp. 77 116.

[46] p. 101.

[47] p. 115.

[48] There is a more elaborate discussion of this point in the third lecture, where its relation to a certain sort of counterpart theory is also mentioned.

[49] New York, McGraw-Hill (1953), see Chapter VII, 'Equality'.

[50] Of course, the device will fail to convince a philosopher who wants to argue that an artificial language or concept of the supposed type is logically impossible. In the present case, some philosophers have thought that a relation, being essentially two-termed, cannot hold between a thing and itself. This position is plainly absurd. Someone can be his own worst enemy, his own severest critic and the like. Some relations are reflexive such as the relation 'no richer than'. Identity or schmidentity is nothing but the smallest reflexive relation.

I hope to elaborate on the utility of this device of imagining a hypothetical language elsewhere.

[51] Recall that we describe the situation in our language, not the language that the people in that situation would have used. Hence we must use the terms Hesperus and Phosphorus with the same reference as in the actual world. The fact that people in that situation might or might not have used these names for different planets is irrelevant. So is the fact that they might have done so using the very same descriptions as we did to fix their references.

[52] The same three options exist for 'Hesperus is Hesperus', and the answer must be the same as in the case of 'Hesperus is Phosphorus'.

[53] 'Internal and External Properties', Mind 71 (April, 1962), pp. 202–203.

[54] The Prince and The Pauper.

[55] Of course I was pointing to a wooden table in the room.

[56] A principle suggested by these examples is: If a material object has its origin from a certain hunk of matter, it could not have had its origin in any other matter. Some qualifications might have to be stated (for example, the vagueness of the notion of hunk of matter leads to some problems), but in a large class of cases the principle is perhaps susceptible of something like proof, using the principle of the necessity of identity for particulars. Let 'A' be a name (rigid designator) of a table, let 'B' name the piece of wood from which it actually came. Let 'C' name another piece of wood. Then suppose A were made from B, as in the actual world, but also another table D were simultaneously made from C. (We assume that there is no relation between A and B which makes the possibility of making a table from one dependent on the possibility of making a table from the other.) Now in this situation $B \neq D$; hence, even if D were made by itself, and no table were made from A, D would not be B. Strictly speaking, the 'proof'

uses the necessity of distinctness, not of identity. The same types of considerations that can be used to establish the former can, however, be used to establish the latter. (Suppose $A \neq B$; if A and B were both identical to some object C in another possible world, then $A = C$, $B = C$, hence $A = B$.) Alternatively, the principle follows from the necessity of identity plus the 'Brouwersche' axiom, or equivalently symmetry of the accesibility relation between possible worlds. In any event, the argument applies only if the making of D from C does not affect the possibility of making B from A, and vice-versa.

57 In addition to the principle that the *origin* of an object is essential to it, another principle suggested is that the *substance* of which it is made is essential. Several complications exist here. First, one should not confuse the type of essence involved in the question "What properties must an object retain if it is not to cease to exist, and what properties of the object can change while the object endures?", which is a temporal question with the question "What (timeless) properties could the object not have failed to have and what properties could it have lacked while still (timelessly) existing?" which concerns necessity and not time and which is our topic here. Thus the question of whether the table could have changed into ice is irrelevant here. The question whether the table could *originally* have been made of anything other than wood is relevant. Obviously this question is related to the necessity of the origin of the table from a given block of wood and whether that block, too, is essentially wood (even wood of a particular kind). Thus it is ordinarily impossible to imagine the table made from any substance other than the one of which it is actually made without going back through the entire history of the universe, a mind-boggling feat. (Other possibilities of the table not having been wooden have been suggested to me, including an ingenious suggestion of Slote's, but I find none of them really convincing. I cannot discuss them here.) A full discussion of the problems of essential properties of particulars is impossible here, but I will mention a few other points: (1) Ordinarily when we ask intuitively whether something might have happened to a given object, we ask whether the universe could have gone on as it actually did up to a certain time, but diverge in its history from that point forward so that the vicissitudes of that object would have been different from that time forth. *Perhaps* this feature should be erected into a general principle about essence. Note that the time in which the divergence from actual history occurs may be sometime before the object itself is actually created. For example, I might have been deformed if the fertilized egg from which I originated had been damaged in certain ways even though I presumably did not yet exist at that time. (2) I am not suggesting that only origin and substantial makeup are essential. For example, if the very block of wood from which the table was made had instead been made into a vase, the table never would have existed. So (roughly) *being a table* seems to be an essential property of the table. (3) Just as the question whether an object *actually* has a certain property (e.g. baldness), can be vague, so the question whether the object essentially has a certain property can be vague, even when the question whether it actually has the property is decided. (4) Certain counterexamples of the origin principle appear to exist in ordinary parlance. I am convinced that they are not genuine counter examples, but very exact analysis is difficult. I cannot discuss this here.

58 Peter Geach has advocated (in *Mental Acts*, London, Routledge and Kegan Paul, 1957, Section 16, and elsewhere) a notion of 'nominal essence' different from the type of essential property considered here. According to Geach, since any act of pointing is ambiguous, someone who baptizes an object by pointing to it must apply a sortal property to disambiguate his reference and to ensure correct criteria of identity over

time – for example, someone who assigns a reference to 'Nixon' by pointing to him must say, 'I use 'Nixon' as a name of that *man*', thus removing his hearer's temptations to take him to be pointing to a nose or a time-slice. The sortal is then in some sense part of the meaning of the name; names do have a (partial) sense after all, though their senses may not be complete enough to determine their references, as they are in description and cluster-of-descriptions theories. If I understand Geach correctly, his nominal essence should be understood in terms of *a prioricity*, not necessity, and thus is quite different from the kind of essence advocated here (perhaps this is part of what he means when he says he is dealing with 'nominal', not 'real', essences). So 'Nixon is a man', 'Dobbin is a horse', and the like would be *a priori* truths.

I need not take a position on this view here. But I would briefly mention the following: (1) Even if a sortal is used to disambiguate an ostensive reference, surely it need not be held *a priori* to be true of that object. Couldn't Dobbin turn out to belong to a species other than horses (though superficially he looked like a horse), Hesperus to be a planet, rather than a star, or Lot's guests, even if he names them, to be angels rather than men? Perhaps Geach should stick to more cautious sortals. (2) Waiving the objection in (1), surely there is a substantial gap between premise and conclusion. Few speakers do in fact learn the reference of a given name by ostension; and, even if they picked up the name by a chain of communication leading back to an ostension, why should the sortal allegedly used in the ostension be, in any sense, part of the 'sense' of the name for them? No argument is offered here. (An extreme case: A mathematician's wife overhears her husband muttering the name 'Nancy'. She wonders whether Nancy, the thing to which her husband referred, is a woman or a Lie group. Why isn't her use of 'Nancy' a case of naming? If it isn't, the reason is *not* indefiniteness of her reference.)

[59] I may have spoken too soon. That is what the financial pages said when these lectures were delivered, January, 1970.

[60] *Prolegomena to Any Future Metaphysics*, Preamble Section 2.b. (Prussian Academy edition, p. 267). My impression of the passage was not changed by a subsequent cursory look at the German, though I can hardly lay claim to any real competence here.

[61] Paul Ziff, *Semantic Analysis*, Ithaca, Cornell University Press, 1960, pp. 184–185.

[62] *Journal of Philosophy* 59, No. 22 (October 25, 1962), pp. 658–671. In subsequent work on natural kinds and physical properties, which I have not had a chance to see at the time of this writing, Putnam has done further work, which (I gather) has many points of contact with the viewpoint expressed here. As I mentioned in the text, there are some divergencies between Putnam's approach and mine; Putnam does not base his considerations on the apparatus of necessary versus *a priori* truths which I invoke. In his entire paper, 'The Analytic and the Synthetic', *Minnesota Studies in the Philosophy of Science*, vol. III, pp. 358–397, he seems closer to the 'cluster concept' theory in some respects, suggesting, for example, that it applies to proper names.

I should emphasize again that it was an example of Rogers Albritton which called my attention to this complex of problems, though Albritton probably would not accept the theories I have developed on the basis of the example.

[63] I am presupposing that an analytic truth is one which depends on *meanings* in the strict sense and therefore is necessary as well as *a priori*. If statements whose *a priori* truth is known via the fixing of a reference are counted as analytic, then some analytic truths are contingent; this possibility is excluded in the notion of analyticity adopted here. The ambiguity in the notion of analyticity of course arises from the ambiguity in the usual uses of such terms as 'definition' and 'sense'. I have not attempted to deal

with the delicate problems regarding analyticity in these lectures, but I will say that some (though not all) of the cases often adduced to discredit the analytic-synthetic distinction, especially those involving natural phenomena and natural kinds, should be handled in terms of the apparatus fixing a reference invoked here. Note that Kant's example, 'gold is a yellow metal', is not even *a priori*, and whatever necessity it has is established by scientific investigation; it is thus far from analytic in any sense.

[64] Even better pairs of ringers exist; for example, some pairs of elements of a single column in the periodic table which resemble each other closely but nevertheless are different elements.

[65] Mill, *op. cit.*

[66] I am not going to give any criterion for what I mean by a 'pure property', or Fregean intension. It is hard to find unquestionable examples of what is meant. Yellowness certainly expresses a manifest physical property of an object and, relative to the discussion of gold above, can be regarded as a property in the required sense. Actually, however, it is not without a certain referential element of its own, for on the present view yellowness is picked out and rigidly designated as that external physical property of the object which we sense by means of the *visual impression of yellowness*. It does in this respect resemble the natural kind terms. The phenomenological quality of the sensation itself, on the other hand, can be regarded as a *quale* in some pure sense. Perhaps I am rather vague about these questions, but further precision seems unnecessary here.

[67] Of course, there is the question of the relation of the statistical mechanical notion of temperature to, for example, the thermodynamic notion. I wish to leave such questions aside in this discussion.

[68] Some people have been inclined to argue that although certainly we cannot say that sound waves 'would have been heat' if they had been felt by the sensation which we feel when we feel heat, the situation is different with respect to a possible phenomenon, not present in the actual world, and distinct from molecular motion. Perhaps, it is suggested, there might be another form of heat other than 'our heat', which was not molecular motion; though no actual phenomenon other than molecular motion, such as sound, would qualify. Similar claims have been made for gold and for light. Although I am disinclined to accept these views, they would make relatively little difference to the substance of the present lectures. Someone who is inclined to hold these views can simply replace the terms 'light', 'heat', 'pain', etc., in the examples by 'our light', 'our heat', 'our pain' and the like. I therefore will not take the space to discuss this issue here.

[69] Assuming, of course, that they are all gold, as I say below, some may be fool's gold. We know in advance, *a priori*, that it is not the case that the items are *typically* fool's gold; and all those items which are actually gold are, of course, essentially gold.

[70] Obviously, there are also artificialities in this whole account. For example, it may be hard to say which items constitute the original sample. Gold may have been discovered independently by various people at various times. I do not feel that any such complications will radically alter the picture.

[71] To understand this dispute, it is especially important to realize that yellowness is not a dispositional property, although it is related to a disposition. Philosophers have often, for want of any other theory of the meaning of the term 'yellow', been inclined to regard it as expressing a dispositional property. At the same time, they have been bothered by the 'gut feeling' that yellowness is a manifest property, just as much 'right out there' as hardness or spherical shape. The proper account, on the present

conception is, of course, that the reference of 'yellowness' is fixed by the description 'that (manifest) property of objects which causes them, under normal circumstances, to be seen as yellow (i.e., to be sensed by certain visual impressions)' 'yellow', of course, does not *mean* 'tends to produce such and such a sensation'; if we had had different neural structures, if atmospheric conditions had been different, if we had been blind, and so on, then yellow objects would have done no such thing. If one tries to revise the definition of 'yellow' to be, 'tends to produce such and such visual impressions under circumstances C', then one will find that the specification of the circumstances C either circularly involves yellowness or plainly makes the alleged definition into a scientific discovery rather than a synonymy. If we take the 'fixes a reference' view, then it is up to the physical scientist to identify the property so marked out in any more fundamental physical terms that he wishes.

Some philosophers have argued that such terms as 'sensation of yellow', 'sensation of heat', 'sensation of pain', and the like, could not be in the language unless they were identifiable in terms of external observable phenomena, such as heat, yellowness, and associated human behavior. I think that this question is independent of any view argued in the text.

[72] Some of the statements I myself make above may be loose and inaccurate in this sense. If I say, "Gold *might* turn out not to be an element," I speak correctly; 'might' here is *epistemic* and expresses the fact that the evidence does not justify *a priori* (Cartesian) certainty that gold is an element. I am also strictly correct when I say that the elementhood of gold was discovered *a posteriori*. If I say, "Gold *might have* turned out not to be an element," I seem to mean this metaphysically and my statement is subject to the correction noted in the text.

[73] Of course, the body *does* exist without the mind and presumably without the person, when the body is a corpse. This consideration, if accepted, would already show that a person and his body are distinct. (See David Wiggins, 'On Being at the Same Place at the Same Time', *Philosophical Review*, Vol. 77 (1968), pp. 90–95'. Similarly, it can be argued that a statue is not the hunk of matter of which it is composed. In the latter case, however, one might say instead that the former is 'nothing over and above' the latter; and the same device might be tried for the relation of the person and the body. The difficulties in the text would not then arise in the same form, but analogous difficulties would appear. A theory that a person is nothing over and above his body in the way that a statue is nothing over and above the matter of which it is composed, would have to hold that (necessarily) a person exists if and only if his body exists and has a certain additional physical organization. Such a thesis would be subject to modal difficulties similar to those besetting the ordinary identity thesis, and the same would apply to suggested analogues replacing the identification of mental states with physical states. A further discussion of this matter must be left for another place. Another view which I will not discuss, although I have little tendency to accept it and am not even certain that it has been set out with genuine clarity, is the so-called functional state view of psychological concepts.

[74] Thomas Nagel and Donald Davidson are notable examples. Their views are very interesting, and I wish I could discuss them in further detail. It is doubtful that such philosophers wish to call themselves 'materialists'. Davidson, in particular, bases his case for his version of the identity theory on the supposed *impossibility* of correlating psychological properties with physical ones.

[75] For example, David Armstrong, *A Materialist Theory of the Mind*, London and New York, 1968, see the discussion review by Thomas Nagel, *Philosophical Review*

79 (1970), pp. 394–403; and David Lewis, 'An Argument for the Identity Theory', *The Journal of Philosophy*, pp. 17–25.

76 I have been surprised to find that at least one able listener took my use of such terms as 'correlated with', 'corresponding to', and the like as already begging the question against the identity thesis. The identity thesis, so he said, is not the thesis that pains and pain states are correlated, but rather that they are identical. Thus my entire discussion presupposes the anti-materialist points which I set out to prove. Although I was surprised to hear an objection which concedes so little intelligence to the argument, I have tried especially to avoid the term 'correlated' which seems to give rise to the objection. Nevertheless, to obviate misunderstanding, I shall explain my usage. Assuming, at least *arguendo*, that scientific discoveries have turned out so as not to refute materialism from the beginning, both the dualist and the identity theorist agree that there is a correlation or correspondence between mental states and physical states. The dualist holds that the 'correlation' relation in question is irreflexive; the identity theorist holds that it is simply a special case of the identity relation. Such terms as 'correlation' and 'correspondence' can be used neutrally without prejudging which side is correct.

77 Having expressed these doubts about the identity theory in the text, I should emphasize two things: first, identity theorists have presented positive arguments for their view, which I certainly have not answered here. Some of these arguments seem to me to be weak or based on ideological prejudices, but others strike me as highly compelling, arguments which I am at present unable to answer convincingly. Second, rejection of the identity thesis does not imply acceptance of Cartesian dualism. In fact, my view above that a person could not have come from a different sperm and egg from the ones from which he actually originated implicitly suggests a rejection of the Cartesian picture. If we had a clear idea of the soul or the mind as an independent, subsistent, spiritual entity, why should it have to have any necessary connection with particular material objects such as a particular sperm or a particular egg? A convinced dualist may think that my views on sperms and eggs beg the question against Descartes. I would tend to argue the other way; the fact that it is hard to imagine me coming from a sperm and egg different from my actual origins seems to me to indicate that we have no such clear conception of a soul or self. In any event, Descartes' notion seems to have been rendered dubious ever since Hume's critique of the notion of a Cartesian self. I regard the mind-body problem as wide open and extremely confusing.

KEITH S. DONNELLAN

PROPER NAMES AND IDENTIFYING DESCRIPTIONS*

I

There is an extremely plausible principle about proper names that many
philosophers up to the present have either assumed or argued for. I will
call it the 'principle of identifying descriptions'. One illustration of it is
in this passage from Strawson's *Individuals*:

... it is no good using a name for a particular unless one knows who or what is referred
to by the use of the name. A name is worthless without a backing of descriptions
which can be produced on demand to explain the application.[1]

The "backing of descriptions" Strawson speaks of supposedly functions
as the criterion for identifying the referent of a name, if it has one, or,
alternatively, for deciding that there is no referent. If I say, for example,
'Homer is my favorite poet', then, roughly speaking, the descriptions I
could supply in answer to the question, 'Who is Homer?', provide the
'backing of descriptions'. And these in turn either pick out a single individual as the referent of the name (as it occurs in my utterance) in virtue of
his fitting these descriptions or make it true that there is no referent – that
Homer did not exist.

While this initial statement of the principle needs refinement and the
acknowledgement of varients, it seems at first sight almost indisputable
that some such principle governs the referential function of proper names.
Must not a user of a proper name know to whom or what he is referring?
And what can this knowledge consist in if not the ability to describe the
referent uniquely?

Nevertheless, I believe the principle to be false. In the first sections of
the paper I will state the principle more precisely and fill in some of the
details of how it would have to operate. The exercise of trying to make it
more precise and giving various needed qualifications is enough, I think,
to rob it of some of its initial attractiveness. I will then, however, meet it
head-on by means of counter-examples. I will argue that (a) a proper name
may have a referent even though the conditions laid down by the principle

Davidson and Harman (eds.), Semantics of Natural Language, 356–379. *All rights reserved*
Copyright © 1972 *by D. Reidel Publishing Company, Dordrecht - Holland*

are not satisfied and (b) where the conditions are satisfied, the object that ought to be the referent according to the principle need not be the true referent. In the course of this I will suggest certain positive things about how the referent of a name is determined, though these will not amount to an alternative principle.

II

What I call the 'principle of identifying descriptions' should not be thought of as expressing the thesis that proper names have a sense (or meaning or connotation). (That thesis, I think, suffers in any case from vagueness about what is to count as showing that an expression has a sense.) Anyone who holds that proper names have a sense almost certainly subscribes to the principle, but the converse is doubtful. In his influential paper, 'Proper Names'[2], John Searle begins with the question, 'Do proper names have senses?', and he ends by saying that in a sense they do and in a sense they do not. Searle, however, though he would not without heavy qualification ascribe senses to proper names, is one of the prime examples of a philosopher who defends the principle I have in mind. In this he is in company with Frege who would have no reluctance in talking about the sense of a proper name.

The simplest application of the principle, to be sure, can be found in the view of someone such as Russell who holds that proper names are concealed definite descriptions. Russell says, "... the name 'Romulus' is not really a name [that is, in the 'narrow logical sense'] but a sort of truncated description. It stands for a person who did such-and-such things, who killed Remus, and founded Rome, and so on."[3] And again, "When I say, e.g., 'Homer existed', I am meaning by 'Homer' some description, say 'the author of the Homeric Poems'..."[4] Russell associates with the use of a name some definite description for which the name is a simple substitute – the same proposition would be expressed by a sentence containing the name as by the sentence formed from it by substituting the associated description for the name.

This tight connection between proper names and definite descriptions was rightly challenged by Searle in 'Proper Names'. Yet Searle still retains the backing of descriptions and these serve, as they would also for Russell, as criteria for identifying the referent, albeit in a looser and more complicated manner:

Suppose we ask the users of the name "Aristotle" to state what they regard as certain essential and established facts about him. Their answers would be a set of uniquely referring descriptive statements. Now what I am arguing is that the descriptive force of "This is Aristotle" is to assert that a sufficient but so far unspecified number of these statements are true of this object.[5]

Without doubt this departs significantly from Russell's simplistic view. It allows for (what surely we should allow for) the possibility, for example, of discovering that Aristotle was not the teacher of Alexander the Great without having to deny Aristotle's existence, which would be impossible on Russell's view if that description was part of the associated description for our use of 'Aristotle'. Only a 'sufficient number' of the things we believe about Aristotle need be true of some individual for him to be Aristotle.

But the flexibility introduced is limited. Vague and indeterminate as we may leave the notion of 'sufficient number', behind our use of a name a set of descriptions still operates to determine the referent. The formulation of the principle of identifying descriptions I shall give will allow both for Searle's looser and Russell's tighter connection between names and descriptions.

I should like to make one more general comment about the issue I am concerned with. The importance of the principle in question is not confined to a narrow issue about how proper names refer. It also has a bearing on the general problem of reference. For proper names constitute something like a test case for theories of reference. A peculiar feature of the situation is that two classical but opposing paradigms for referring expressions can both lead one to adopt the same theory about proper names. The model referring expression has been for many philosophers of language, I believe, a definite description (used 'attributively' in the terminology I used elsewhere[6]). An object is referred to in virtue of possessing uniquely the properties mentioned in the definite description. It is not hard to see how this standard leads to adopting the principle of identifying descriptions for proper names. Proper names are referring expressions, yet on the surface fail to exhibit any descriptive content. Given definite descriptions as the paradigm, one is forced to look under the surface (which amounts to looking into the user(s) of the name) for the 'backing of descriptions' that must be there.

The major alternative to a definite description as the paradigm of a referring expression is represented by Russell's and Wittgenstein's (in the *Tractatus*) notion of a name in the 'narrow logical sense'. Ordinary names, of course, are not names at all in this sense; they cannot meet the austere requirements of referring in some mysterious, unanalysable and absolutely direct way to their referents. And given this notion of 'genuine' names, Russell adduces very good reasons why no such ordinary name as 'Homer' or 'Aristotle' can be a genuine name. But some account has to be given of how ordinary names function. Russell saw no alternative but to treat them as concealed definite descriptions, what they name, if any-thing, being whatever is denoted by the concealed description. (Had he thought of Searle's perhaps more sophisticated view, there seems no reason why he should not have adopted that for 'ordinary' proper names.)

Strangely enough, then, two antagonistic models of what a genuine referring expression is like lead their proponents to the principle of identifying descriptions. Demonstrating that that principle is mistaken would not irrevocably descredit either model, but it would, I think, take away much of the motivation for adopting either. Ordinary proper names may not have as much claim to being genuine referring expressions as Russell's names 'in the strict logical sense' (could we but understand what those are and discover some of them), but as against definite descriptions it is hard to see how they could come out second best. If their mode of functioning, however, is not captured by the principle of identifying de-scriptions, if, that is, they do not name in much the same way a definite description denotes[7], then can definite descriptions possibly be model referring expressions?

And on the other side, if ordinary proper names are neither names 'in the strict logical sense', as they surely are not, nor concealed descriptions, then some other relationship will have to be recognized as holding between some singular expressions and what they stand for. In that case, much of the reason for supposing that there are such things as names 'in the strict logical sense' will be gone. For it is clear from Russell's writings, at least, that these are introduced in part because he felt that definite descriptions not *really* being referring expressions (but only denoting expressions), some other sort expression must serve the purpose of allowing us to talk directly about things in the world. If (ordinary) proper names do not function via the relationship of denoting nor through whatever relationship Russell's names are supposed to enjoy, then perhaps the way they do function represents the alternative Russell was seeking.[8]

III

The principle of identifying descriptions is a two-stage thesis, the second stage depending upon the first. It states, in the first place, that (with some qualifications to be noted later) the user(s) of a proper name must be able to supply a set of, as I shall call them, 'non-question-begging' descriptions in answer to the question, 'To whom (or what) does the name refer?' The important qualifier, 'non-question-begging', I will explain later[9]. I will call these descriptions that speakers supposedly must be able to supply 'the set of identifying descriptions'.

Secondly, the principle states that the referent of a proper name (as used by a speaker in some particular utterance), if there is one, is that object that uniquely fits a 'sufficient' number of the descriptions in the set of identifying descriptions. As a corollary, when no entity (or more than one) satisfies this condition, the name has no referent and a negative existential statement expressible by a sentence of the form 'N does not exist' (where 'N' is the name in question) will be true.

I have tried to state the principle so as to make it possible for alternative positions still to embody it. I should like to show that we ought not to accept *any* of the versions of it to be found in the literature. Thus, for reasons that will emerge, I leave it open in the first part whether the set of identifying descriptions is to be formed from what *each* speaker can supply or from what speakers collectively supply. In the second part, the 'sufficient number' of descriptions that an object must satisfy to be the referent might be *all* of them, as in Russell's view, or some *indeterminate number* of them, as in Searle's.

The counter-examples I later give are directed against the second part of the principle; they are designed to show that *even if* the user(s) of a name must be able to supply a set of identifying descriptions, as laid down by the first part, these descriptions do not provide necessary and sufficient conditions for what shall count as the referent. But the first part of the principle is not without difficulties. To strengthen my case against the principle I want first to point out some of these while formulating some of the needed qualifications to the principle as I have just stated it.

IV

There are two views on the source of the set of identifying descriptions that supposedly must back up the use of a proper name.

We find in Russell and Frege[10] the idea that different speakers who use the same name in an otherwise identical propositional context will most likely not express the same proposition (or thought, in Frege's terminology). This happens because very probably they do not associate with the name the same set of descriptions. The propositions might have different truth-values, because the speakers, with different sets of identifying descriptions, may be referring to different things[11]. Russell and Frege, in other words, look to the individual speaker for the set of identifying descriptions.

In contrast, Searle tells us that the set of identifying descriptions is formed from the descriptions users of the name give of what they refer to. And Strawson, in discussing this question[12], imagines a situation in which a name is used by a group in which each member "knows some distinguishing fact or facts, not necessarily the same ones, about Socrates, facts which each is prepared to cite to indicate whom he now means or understands, by 'Socrates'". He then suggests that we form a "composite description incorporating the most frequently mentioned facts" and continues, "Now it would be too much to say that the success of term-introduction within the group by means of the name requires that there should exist just one person of whom all the propositions in the composite description are true. But it would not be too much to say that it requires that there should exist one and only one person of whom some reasonable proportion of these propositions is true."[13] Given this difference of opinion, I allowed for alternatives in the statement of the principle.

Both means of determining the set of identifying descriptions contain difficulties. To take the Russell-Frege view first, it seems to me, though evidently not to them, absurd to suppose that a beginning student of philosophy, who has learned a few things about Aristotle, and his teacher, who knows a great deal, express different propositions when each says 'Aristotle was the teacher of Alexander'. Even if this can be swallowed, there are very unpleasant consequences. Given the second part of the principle of identifying descriptions the student and teacher possess different criteria for identifying Aristotle and even for establishing his existence. For the student Aristotle would be a person satisfying (substantially) some fairly small number of descriptions; for the scholar of philosophy a much larger number would determine the existence and identity of Aristotle. This means that if each affirm Aristotle's existence there is the theoretical possibility, at least, that one is correct and the other wrong. Yet suppose that the smaller supply of descriptions available to the student turns out generally to be incorrect (we can imagine him to be unfortunate enough to have been told mostly things about Aristotle that historians of Greek philosophy are mistaken about). Would he really be in error in saying that Aristotle existed? Should we say to him, if we uncover the errors, 'Your Aristotle doesn't exist, though Professor Smith's does.'?

Worse still, suppose that the few things the student has 'learned' about Aristotle are not only not true of the individual his teacher refers to, but turn out substantially to be true of, say, Plato. He has been told, perhaps, that Aristotle wrote the *Metaphysics* when, in fact, Plato wrote it and Aristotle cribbed it, etc. Should we say that he has all along been referring to Plato, though his teacher, for whom these few descriptions are not the only source of criteria for what the referent is, continues to refer to Aristotle? The principle of identifying descriptions seems to lead to that result when interpreted in this way.

The more liberal view that utilizes descriptions suppliable by users of the name, in the plural, is not in much better shape. In the first place, what group of speakers is to form the reference set from which the 'composite description' is to be drawn? Searle speaks of properties 'commonly' attributed to Aristotle. Commonly attributed by whom? By contemporary speakers? One thing seems certain: the speakers in question cannot be *all* those who have ever used the name 'Aristotle' to refer to Aristotle. Aside from the appearance, at least, of circularity, none of us would likely ever be in a position to know what properties that group would attribute to Aristotle. Childhood friends of Aristotle, who did not follow his subsequent career, would have a quite different set of descriptions of him from ours. I doubt that we shall ever know what those were. Using this *total* class of those who have ever spoken of Aristotle is a practical impossibility and can hardly form the basis for our use. (It would also seem to do violence to the motivation behind the principle of identifying descriptions – that users of a name should be able to supply criteria for identifying the referent.)

On the other hand, to limit the group of speakers whose descriptions will generate the 'composite description' to, say, those at a particular time yields consequences similar to those of the Russell-Frege view. Different times and ages might have different beliefs about Aristotle. And in conjunction with the second part of the principle of identifying descriptions it would be possible that the affirmation that Aristotle existed should have different truth-values from one time to another. Or, because of the particular beliefs they held, we could imagine that the people of one age, unknown to any of us, referred to Plato when they used the name 'Aristotle'. On the Frege-Russell view any two people using the same sentence containing the name 'Aristotle' and believing that they are referring to the same person, etc., very likely do not express the same proposition. The more liberal view only expands this possibility to different groups of people.

V

The first part of the principle of identifying descriptions tells us that users of a name must be in a position to supply a set of identifying descriptions. (For the sake of argument I will at times allow that this is so, although what positive remarks I make will imply that there is no necessity involved.) How are we to understand this? Strawson says, "... When I speak of 'preparedness to substitute a description for a name', this requirement must not be taken too literally. It is not required that people be very ready articulators of what they know."[14] I think he is surely right to allow us this latitude. Small children and even adults often use names without literally being able to describe the referent in sufficient detail to guarantee unique identification.

I imagine the reason philosophers who have discussed proper names so often use historical figures such as Aristotle, Homer, etc. is just that these names are introduced into our vocabulary via descriptions of facts about their bearers and most of us are prepared to give something like uniquely denoting descriptions. But it is less clear that we are ready to describe our friends, people we have met here and there, or even public figures of our times whose images have not yet been crystalized into a few memorable attributes. At the very least it would be an effort to insure that a description of someone we know fairly well and whose name we use often is both accurate and unique. The first part of the principle, then, seems to require of us a high level of ability – unless what counts as having the ability is very broad indeed. (Even though it is hardly like being able to describe the referent, the ability to *point* to the referent is usually included as if it were simply a variant.)

Construe it as broadly as you will, is there really a requirement that the user of a name be able to identify by description (or even by pointing) what the name refers to? The following example, which anticipates a bit some later results, may cast doubt on this. Suppose a child is gotten up from sleep at a party and introduced to someone as 'Tom', who then says a few words to the child. Later the child says to his parents, "Tom is a nice man". The only thing he can say about 'Tom' is that Tom was at a party. Moreover, he is unable to recognize anyone as 'Tom' on subsequent occasions. His parents give lots of parties and they have numerous friends named 'Tom'. The case could be built up, I think, so that nothing the child possesses in the way of descriptions, dispositions to recognize, serves to pick out in the standard way anybody uniquely. That is, we cannot go by the denotation of his descriptions nor whom he points to, if anyone, etc. Does this mean that there is no person to whom he was referring? It seems to me that his parents might perfectly well conjecture about the matter and come up with a reasonable argument showing that the child was talking about this person rather than that. For example, they might reason as follows: "He's met several people named 'Tom' at recent parties, but only Tom Brown did something that might make him say, 'Tom is a nice man'. Of course, Tom Brown isn't nice and he was just indulging in his usual sarcasm when he told him, 'You have a nice pair of parents', but the sarcasm wouldn't have registered."[15]

If this is a reasonable example, it seems the question of what a speaker referred to by using a name is not foreclosed by his inability to describe or even to recognize or point to the referent. The reasoning of the parents in this example is not aimed at finding out what descriptions the child could give, if only he were able to articulate them. I used a child in the example to sharpen the picture of someone with no descriptions or other means of identifying the referent uniquely; but adults also sometimes conjecture about other adults concerning what person they were referring to in using a name. Is it beyond doubt that in such instances the inquiry must ultimately be concerned with what descriptions the user of the name could supply? The examples later on will challenge this, yet even now examples such as the one I have given seem to me to make the requirement that every use of a name have behind it a backing of descriptions highly suspicious (even without relying on what appears to me beyond question, that no one has yet given a clear account of what the ability to describe a referent amounts to).

VI

Before turning to counter-examples one more preliminary issue should be settled. In stating the principle of identifying descriptions, I inserted the condition that the descriptions that 'back up' the use of a name should not be 'question-begging'. The qualification has vital significance because there are certain descriptions that a user of a name (providing he can articulate them) could always provide and which would always denote the referent of the name uniquely (providing there is one). No argument could be devised to show that the referent of a name need not be denoted by these descriptions. At the same time anyone who subscribes to the principle of identifying descriptions would hardly have these descriptions in mind or want to rely on them in defence of the principle. Some examples of what I shall count as 'question-begging' are the following:

(a)   'the entity I had in mind'
(b)   'the entity I referred to'
(c)   'the entity I believe to be the author of the *Metaphysics*'.

I think it is clear about (a) and (b) and only a little less so about (c) that if descriptions such as these are included in the 'backing of descriptions' the principle would become uninteresting.

Strawson, in fact, explicitly excludes descriptions such as (a): "[the speaker] cannot, for himself, distinguish the particular which he has in mind by the fact that it is the one he has in mind. So, there must be some description he could give, which need not be the description he does give, which applies uniquely to the one he has in mind and does not include the phrase, 'the one he has in mind'".[16] Although Strawson mentions a particular description, it is certain that he would exclude from consideration similar ones. In particular, (b) above surely would not count for him. The point of the 'backing of descriptions' is to explain how an object gets referred to by a proper name. Descriptions that fit the referent simply in virtue of the fact that the speaker did, in fact, refer to it or had it in mind as the object he meant to refer to are question-begging in answer to the question, 'who (or what) did you refer to?' in the same way that 'What I have in my hand' would be question-begging in answer to the question, 'What are you holding in your hand?'

It is only a little bit less obvious that descriptions of the form, 'the object I believe to be ϕ', such as (c) above, must likewise be excluded from the set of identifying descriptions.

Call descriptions such as 'the author of the *Metaphysics*' *primary* descriptions; call those such as 'the man I believed to be the author of the *Metaphysics*' *secondary* descriptions. Suppose that all primary descriptions the user(s) of a name can supply are false of everything. The backing of secondary descriptions would be useless in the same way that 'the object I had in mind' would be. For if I cannot rely on my primary descriptions to pick out uniquely what I refer to, trying to identify the referent via a description of the form 'the one I believed to be (though it is not) ϕ' would amount to no more than trying to identify *the object I had in mind* when I held that belief.

In what follows, then, I will count what I have called 'secondary' descriptions as question-begging.

VII

In the next sections I construct counter-examples to the principle of identifying descriptions. To do this I must show that there are possible situations in which the referent of a name does not satisfy the conditions the principle lays down or situations in which an entity satisfying those conditions is not the referent. The principle tells us that the referent of a name, if there is one, is that entity that fits some sufficient number of a certain set of descriptions, namely the set suppliable by the user(s) of the name. It is important to note that in denying this, one need not deny that there are some constraints on what the referent of a name may be – *some* description which it must fit. But this is only to allow that there may be a 'backing of descriptions' that serve as *necessary* conditions, while the principle tells us that such a backing of descriptions also serves as sufficient conditions.

Thus, I should want to argue, for example, that *theoretically* Aristotle might turn out to be a person who did *not* write the *Metaphysics*, was *not* the teacher of Alexander, etc.; that is to say, a person who does not fit 'a sufficient number' of the descriptions we, as users of the name, would now supply. But I need not argue that even theoretically he could turn out to be, say, a fishmonger living in Hoboken or Plato's dog (although in incautious moments I am inclined to believe in even this outlandish theoretical possibility). If anyone wants to maintain that our use of the name is such that being a human being or not living in modern times, etc. are *necessary* for being the referent of the name, I have no objection here to offer against a 'backing of descriptions' in that weaker sense. Such an attenuated backing would not *uniquely* identify the referent.

A word about the nature of the counter-examples is required, because they will undoubtedly seem artificial and possibly taken on their own not wholly convincing. Their artificiality is in part forced on me by the fact that I want to question not only the simple view of, say, Russell that sees a name as a simple substitute for a description, but also the looser and vaguer view of Searle and Strawson. The latter, however, uses the notion of an ill-defined 'sufficient' number of descriptions. Since the notion of 'sufficient' is ill-defined, it is necessary to invent examples in which, for instance, the referent of a name fits *no* description which is both unique to it and available to the speaker (other than 'question-begging' descriptions). Otherwise, a defender of the view might take refuge in those descriptions. To make sure that there are no remaining contaminating descriptions, the examples have to be fairly extreme ones in which the user(s) of a name are radically deceived about the properties of what they are talking about.

But if these 'pure' examples are in order in everything except their artificiality, then the fact that I do not tell more true-to-life stories should not be an objection. For however vague 'sufficient number' is left, one thing is certain: the Searle-Strawson view cannot be that the referent of a name is any entity that fits uniquely any *one* of the descriptions suppliable by the user(s) of the name. The whole purpose of this variant (as opposed to the stronger Russell view) is to allow that we could discover, e.g., that Aristotle did not teach Alexander without having to deny Aristotle's existence or that *someone else* was the teacher of Alexander. But if any *one* of the descriptions in the set of identifying descriptions counts always as 'sufficient', there will be an overwhelming number of cases in which there cannot be a unique referent for a name we use – all those instances in which we ascribe to the referent two or more properties which in fact are unique properties of more than one person.

VIII

The first counter-example is the most artificial (but perhaps the most pure). It is a situation in which a speaker uses a name to refer to something though what is referred to is not picked out uniquely by the descriptions available to the speaker. As well, there is something the speaker's descriptions denote uniquely, but that is not the referent.

Imagine the following circumstances: Perhaps in an experiment by psychologists interested in perception a subject is seated before a screen of uniform color and large enough to entirely fill his visual field. On the screen are painted two squares of identical size and color, one directly above the other. The subject knows nothing of the history of the squares – whether one was painted before the other, etc. Nor does he know anything about their future. He is asked to give names to the squares[17] and to say on what basis he assigns the names. With one complication to be noted later, it seems that the only way in which he can distinguish the squares through description is by their relative positions. So he might respond that he will call the top square 'alpha' and the bottom square 'beta'.

The catch in the example is this: unknown to the subject, he has been fitted with spectacles that invert his visual field. Thus, the square he sees as apparently on top is really on the bottom and *vice versa*. Having now two names to work with we can imagine the subject using one of them to say something about one of the squares. Suppose he comes to believe (whether erroneously or not doesn't matter) that one of the squares has changed color. He might report, 'Alpha is now a different color'. But which square is he referring to? He would describe alpha as the square on top. And if this is the only uniquely identifying description at his command then according to the principle I am attacking, he would have referred to the square that is on top. But given our knowledge of the presence and effect of the inverting spectacles and the ignorance of the subject about that, it seems clear that we should take him as referring to, not the square on top, but the one that seems to him erroneously to be on top – the one on the bottom. We know why he describes 'alpha' the way he does; we expect changes in the square on the bottom to elicit from him reports of changes in alpha, etc. I think it would be altogether right to say that although *he* does not know it, he is talking about the square on the bottom even though he would *describe* it as 'the square on top'. If this is right, we seem to have a case in which the speaker's descriptions of what he is referring to when he uses a name do not yield the true referent so long as we stick to what is denoted by the descriptions he gives. The referent is something different and the thing actually denoted is not the referent.

This counter-example to the principle of identifying descriptions depends upon the supposition that the subject's only description that could serve to pick out the referent uniquely is the one in terms of relative position. But it must be admitted that I have so-far neglected a description of alpha that he could supply, that is not question-begging, and that would in fact uniquely identify alpha despite the operation of the glasses. The subject could describe alpha as, 'the square that *appears* to me to be on top'. We must take 'appears' here in its phenomenological sense. If 'that appears to me to be on top' means 'that I believe to be on top' we would have a question-begging description. But in its phenomenological sense, alpha is the one that *appears* to him to be on top and, indeed, it is just because the square on the bottom is the one that appears to him to be on top that it is the referent of 'alpha'.

There is more than one way to modify the example in order to take care of this objection to it, but an easy way is by having the subject use the name 'alpha' a bit later having forgotten how alpha appeared to him, but recalling the position he took it really to have. Of course in our example as presented the subject would have no reason to suppose that there might be a discrepancy between the actual position of alpha and what position it appeared to him to have and so long as he remembered it as being the one on top, he would presumably say that that was also the way it appeared to him. What is needed is something to make him doubt that his recollection of what position he took alpha to have is an accurate guide to how it appeared to him.

Suppose then that our subject is an old hand at experiments of this sort and knows that inverting lenses are sometimes put into the spectacles he wears. Erroneously he believes he has a method of detecting when this happens. He goes through the experiment as previously described but with the mistaken belief that his spectacles have not been tampered with and that the squares have the position they appear to him to have. Later on he makes some statement such as, 'Alpha changed color at one point'. But while he remembers his judgment that alpha was the top square (and has absolute confidence in it), he cannot remember how alpha appeared to him at the time nor whether he had based his judgment on the assumption that his visual field was inverted or not. The subject's set of identifying descriptions thus no longer contains the *appearance* description and only the erroneous description of alpha as being the square on top remains as a uniquely identifying description.

IX

If the preceding counter-example was persuasive, then it will also suggest something positive. Its moral might be put this way: When a person describes something, as when he describes what he is referring to, *we* are not limited to looking for something that fits his descriptions uniquely (or fits them better than anything else). We can also ask ourselves, 'What thing would he *judge* to fit those descriptions, even if it does not really do so?' That question will utilize his descriptions, but will not be decided on the rigid basis of what is denoted, if anything, uniquely by them. In this particular example the influence of inverting spectacles was a deciding factor. We had to know *both* how he described the referent and, what he did not know, that the spectacles would influence his descriptions in a certain way. The role of his set of 'identifying descriptions' in determining the referent of his use of a name is not that which the principle of identifying descriptions gives it. It had its part, but the question asked about it was different: 'What do these descriptions denote uniquely (or best)?' vs. 'Why should he describe the referent in that way?'

The next counter-example[18] provides a somewhat different insight into how proper names function.

A student meets a man he takes to be the famous philosopher, J. L. Aston-Martin. Previously, the student has read some of the philosopher's works and so has at his command descriptions such as, "the author of 'Other Bodies'" and "the leading expounder of the theory of egocentric pluralism." The meeting takes place at a party and the student engages the man in a somewhat lengthy conversation, much of it given over, it turns out, to trying to name cities over 100000 in population in descending order of altitude above sea-level. In fact, however, although the student never suspects it, the man at the party is not the famous philosopher, but someone who leads the student to have that impression. (We can even imagine that by coincidence he has the same name.)

Imagine, then, a subsequent conversation with his friends in which the student relates what happened at the party. He might begin by saying, "Last night I met J. L. Aston-Martin and talked to him for almost an hour". To whom does he refer at this point? I strongly believe the answer should be, 'to the famous philosopher', and not, 'to the man he met at the party'. What the student says is simply false; a friend 'in the know' would be justified in replying that he did not meet J. L. Aston-Martin, but someone who had the same name and was no more a philosopher than Milton Berle.

Suppose, however, that the audience contains no such doubting Thomases, and that the rest of party was of sufficient interest to generate several more stories about what went on. The student might use the name 'J. L. Aston-Martin', as it were, incidently. For example: "... and then Robinson tripped over Aston-Martin's feet and fell flat on his face" or "I was almost the last to leave – only Aston-Martin and Robinson, who was still out cold, were left."

In these subsequent utterances to whom was the speaker referring in using the name, 'Aston-Martin?' My inclination is to say that here it was to the man he met at the party and not to the famous philosopher. Perhaps the difference lies in the fact that in the initial utterance the speaker's remark would only have a point if he was referring to the famous philosopher, while in the later utterances it is more natural to take him to be referring to the man at the party, since what happened there is the whole point.[19]

If in such examples as this there are *two* references made (or even if there is a strong inclination to say that there are) this is something unaccounted for by the principle of identifying descriptions.

To see this we need only ask what the student's set of identifying descriptions consists in each time he uses the name, first when he claims to have met Aston-Martin and later when he recounts events at the party that incidently involve the man he met there. In both cases the set of identifying descriptions would be the same. It will include, first of all, those descriptions of Aston-Martin he would have given prior to the party – the author of certain works, propounder of certain doctrines, etc. In addition, it would now contain various descriptions derived from meeting the spurious famous man at the party – the man who played the game about cities, whose feet Robinson tripped over, etc.

The full set of descriptions, available to him when he later talks about the party, would be the same whether he was asked, 'Who is Aston-Martin?', at the outset when he claims to have met Aston-Martin at the party or later on when the name occurs in recounting other events involving the man met at the party. *We* may say that the referent changes during the course of his conversation, but the speaker would not. And his full account, i.e. all the descriptions at his command, of who it is he refers to would remain the same. It would contain, for example, both "the author of 'Other Bodies'" and "the man I talked to at the party about cities."

This result, however, is inconsistent with the principle of identifying descriptions. On that principle, the *same* set of identifying descriptions can determine at most *one* referent. But in this example we seem to have two referents and only one set of identifying descriptions.

We extracted from the first counter-example the idea that the question we should ask is, 'What would the user(s) of the name describe in this way?' rather than, 'What (substantially) fits the descriptions they give?' Though these questions may usually have the same answer, the counter-example showed that they need not.

The present example, however, shows that even this distinction is not enough. It would do no good to ask about his set of identifying descriptions, 'Who would the speaker describe that way?' In the example the same set of identifying descriptions is related to two different referents. It seems then that the ultimate question is rather, 'What would the speaker describe in this way on this occasion?', where 'describe in this way' does not refer to his set of identifying descriptions, but to the predicate he ascribes to the referent; e.g., in the example, we might ask on one occasion, 'Who would he claim to have met at the party?', on another, 'Who would he want us to believe Jones tripped over at the party?' And although *his* answer, gleaned from his set of identifying descriptions, would be the same in either case, *we* may have reason to answer differently to each question.

X

It is instructive to look at the use of proper names in historical contexts if only to see why so many philosophers who discuss proper names appeal to examples of it. In general, our use of proper names for persons in history (and also those we are not personally acquainted with) is parasitic on uses of the names by other people – in conversation, written records, etc. Insofar as we possess a set of identifying descriptions in these cases they come from things said about the presumed referent by other people. My answer to the question, 'Who was Thales?' would probably derive from what I learned from my teachers or from histories of philosophy. Frequently, as in this example, one's identifying descriptions trace back through many levels of parasitic derivation. Descriptions of Thales we might give go back to what was said, using that name, by Aristotle and Herodotus. And, if Thales existed, the trail would not end there.

The history behind the use of a name may not be known to the individual using it. I may have forgotten the sources from whence I got my descriptions of Thales. Even a whole culture could lose this history. A people with an oral tradition in which names of past heroes figure would probably not be able to trace the history back to original sources. Yet, for all that, they may be telling of the exploits of real men in the past and they may possess knowledge of them and their deeds.

Yet, in such cases the history is of central importance to the question of whether a name in a particular use has a referent and, if so, what it is. The words of others, in conversation, books and documents can, like the inverting spectacles in a previous example, distort our view of what we are naming. But at the same time it can, to one who knows the facts, provide the means of uncovering the referent, if there is one.

The role of this history leading up to a present use of a name has almost always been neglected by those who accept the principle of identifying descriptions. The sort of description generally mentioned as helping to pick out, say, Thales, is such as 'the Greek philosopher who held that all is water'. Nothing is made of the fact that such descriptions are given by us derivatively. We might be pardoned if we supposed that the referent of 'Thales' is whatever ancient Greek happens to fit such descriptions uniquely, even if he should turn out to have been a hermit living so remotely that he and his doctrines have no historical connection with us at all.

But this seems clearly wrong. Suppose that Aristotle and Herodotus were either making up the story or were referring to someone who neither did the things they said he did nor held the doctrines they attributed to him. Suppose further, however, that fortuitously their descriptions fitted uniquely someone they had never heard about and who was not referred to by any authors known to us. Such a person, even if he was the only ancient to hold that all is water, to fall in a well while contemplating the stars, etc., is not 'our' Thales.

Or, to take the other possible outcome according to the principle of identifying descriptions, suppose no one to have held the ridiculous doctrine that all is water, but that Aristotle and Herodotus were referring to a real person – a real person who was not a philosopher, but a well-digger with a reputation for saying wise things and who once exclaimed. "I wish everything were water so I wouldn't have to dig these damned wells." What is the situation then regarding our histories of philosophy? Have they mentioned a non-existent person or have they mentioned someone who existed but who did not have the properties they attribute to him? My inclination is to say the latter. Yet ignoring the history of these uses of the name 'Thales', the principle of identifying descriptions would tell us that Thales did not exist. But then to whom were Aristotle and Herodotus referring? Surely we cannot conclude, 'to no one'. It seems to me to make sense that we should discover that Thales was afterall a well-digger and that Aristotle and Herodotus were deceived about what he did. That would not make sense, however, if we are forced to conclude in such a case that he did not exist. That is, if we neglect the fact that there is a history behind our use of the name 'Thales' or 'Aristotle' and concentrate only upon the descriptions we would supply about their life, their works and deeds, it is possible that our descriptions are substantially wrong without the consequence being that we have not been referring to any existent person.

It is significant that descriptions of the form 'N was referred to by A' should assume central importance in the case of uses of names that are parasitic on their use by others. Not only does the principle of identifying descriptions, as it has usually been defended, fail to prepare us for the special role of one type of description, but we now see that there is a quite ordinary sense in which a person might be ignorant of the nature of the entity he has referred to in using a name. While I do not want to classify descriptions of this form as 'question-begging' in the way in which 'the entity *I* have in mind' is question-begging, it seems nevertheless natural to say that in knowing only that Thales was a man referred to by Aristotle and Herodotus, I'm not in a position to *describe* the man Thales; that is, there is, I think, an ordinary use of 'describe' in which to say only 'the man referred to by Aristotle and Herodotus' is not yet to *describe* Thales. So it seems that we could be in the position of having referred to someone in using the name 'Thales', the same person in fact referred to by Aristotle and Herodotus, although we are not in the position of being able to describe him correctly.

Nevertheless, so long as the user of a name can fall back on such a description as 'the person referred to by Aristotle', the principle of identifying descriptions may be salvaged even if at expense of having to elevate one type of description to special status. But it is not at all clear that such descriptions will in general be available to the user of a name or that without them the failure of his other descriptions to identify the referent uniquely must mean that the name has no referent. In the case of individual people there are surely many who would, for example, identify Thales as the pre-socratic philosopher who held that all is water, but who do not know that he was referred to by Aristotle and Herodotus. And in fact they may not know even the immediate sources of their use of the name; that, for example, Thales was referred to by Mr. Jones, their freshman philosophy instructor. In case Thales was in fact the pre-socratic philosopher with that doctrine, such people surely know something about Thales and, in using the name, they have referred to him. But if, in fact, the attribution of this view to Thales is wrong and they are left without any descriptions that uniquely fit Thales, I do not believe it follows that they have not referred to anyone or that (in their use of the name) Thales did not exist. To be sure, they may have available to them some such description of Thales as, 'The one who is commonly believed to have been a pre-socratic philosopher who held that all is water.' But even this may not be true. Everyone may have come to believe that Thales did not have that doctrine. One could continue along these lines, I think, to deny an individual any identifying descriptions, even of the form 'The one referred to by so-and-so' that will serve uniquely to pick out Thales, without the consequence that he has not referred to anyone.

XI

The previous examples have concentrated on individuals and the set of descriptions they could supply. But I think there is no reason to suppose that, with a bit more stretching of the imagination, the same results could not be gotten for the whole of some group in which a name is used. Thus, those who would form the 'set of identifying descriptions' from a collective effort at description seem no better off to me.

Thus, we could imagine a future time, for example, when the plays we attribute to Shakespeare are available and it is believed that Shakespeare was their author, but little else is known about him – perhaps only that he was an actor in Elizabethan times – and, in particular, nothing about the documentation we rely upon in attributing the plays to him has survived. As we now view it, the people of this future generation would be correct in saying that Shakespeare wrote *Hamlet*. But suppose in fact the Baconian hypothesis is correct – Francis Bacon wrote those plays. What should an omniscient being who sees the whole history of the affair conclude about one of these future beings saying that Shakespeare wrote *Hamlet*? (Surely not that as they use 'Shakespeare' it refers to Bacon – Bacon was not an actor and they may know a great deal about Bacon, enough to insure that he could not have been an actor). It seems to me that the correct conclusion should be that (perhaps because we did not pay enough attention to the cryptologists who claim to find this message in the plays) we and they have made a mistake – we both believe that Shakespeare wrote the plays, though it was rather Bacon and not Shakespeare who is the Bard.

XII

As I have admitted, my counter-examples are necessarily somewhat artificial because of the vagueness of the position I want to attack. Yet, it seems to me that even artificial examples are sufficient because I take the principle of identifying descriptions to be a doctrine about how reference via proper names *must* take place. If these examples show that there are other possibilities for identifying the referent, they do their job. It is the idea that *only* a backing of descriptions identifying the referent by its fitting them (or some sufficient number of them) could serve to connect an object with a name that I question.

On the positive side my view is that what we should substitute for the question, 'What is the referent?' is 'What would the speaker be attributing that predicate to on this occasion?' Thus, in an early example, the parents of a child ask, 'Who would he say was a nice man at a party of ours?' when the child has said, 'Tom was a nice man.' *How* we answer such questions I do not have a general theory about. It seems clear to me that in some way the referent must be historically, or, we might say, causally connected to the speech act. But I do not see my way clear to saying exactly how in general that connection goes. Perhaps there is no exact theory.

The shift of question, however, seems to be important. One can explain why the principle of identifying descriptions has seemed so plausible, for example, while denying its validity. If a speaker says 'a is ϕ', where 'a' is a name, and we ask, "To what would he on this occasion attribute the predicate 'ϕ'?", asking him for descriptions would *normally* be the best strategy for finding out. Generally we know numbers of correct and even uniquely identifying descriptions of the referent of names we use. So others would naturally first rely on these and look for what best fits them.

To illustrate this, we can imagine the following games: In the first a player gives a set of descriptions and the other players try to find the object in the room that best fits them. This is analogous to the role of the set of identifying descriptions in the principle I object to. In the other game the player picks out some object in the room, tries to give descriptions that characterize it uniquely and the other players attempt to discover what object he described. In the second game the problem set for the other players (the audience in the analogue) is to find out what is being described, not what best fits the descriptions. Insofar as descriptions enter into a determination of what the referent of a name is, I suggest that the second game is a better analogy. In that game, on the normal assumption that people are unlikely to be badly mistaken about the properties of an object they are describing, the other players would usually first look for an object best fitting the descriptions given. But that need not always be the best tactics. They may notice or conjecture that the circumstances are such that the describer has unintentionally *mis*-described the object, the circumstances being such as distortions in his perception, erroneous beliefs he is known to hold, etc.

One final point: I earlier questioned whether we can really expect that there must be a backing of descriptions behind the use of a proper name.

Insofar as I offer an alternative to the principle of identifying descriptions, it has the merit of not requiring such a backing. If a speaker says 'a is ϕ', where 'a' is a name, the question of what he referred to does not hinge on what he can supply in the way of descriptions – though what descriptions he does give, if any, can constitute an important datum. It may be possible to answer the question, "To what would he on this occasion attribute the predicate 'is ϕ' ?", without any backing of descriptions.

Cornell University

REFERENCES

* I am indebted to students and colleagues for comments and suggestions, in particular Professor John Perry and Mr. Theodore Budlong. I believe also that some departure from the traditional alternatives in theories about reference and proper names is 'in the air' and that views along some of the lines I take in this paper I may share with others, although the view I attack is still the dominant one. I believe that Saul Kripke has a very similar position, at least insofar as denial of the prevalent theories go. And, indeed, I think I may owe one of my counter-examples to him through a second-hand source (although I did not understand the relevance until much later). David Kaplan's paper, 'Quantifying In', *Synthese* **19** (1969) 178–214, also seems to me to be in the same vein, though I am not sure I agree with a variety of details and the main purpose of the paper is not to mount an assault on theories of proper names.

1 P. F. Strawson, *Individuals*, Methuen & Co. Ltd., London, 1959, p. 20.

2 *Mind* **67** (1958) 166–173.

3 'Lectures on Logical Atomism' in *Logic and Knowledge* (ed. by Robert C. Marsh), George Allen & Unwin Ltd., London, 1956, p. 243.

4 *Ibid.*, p. 252.

5 'Proper Names', *op. cit.*, p. 171.

6 In 'Reference and Definite Descriptions', *The Philosophical Review* **75** (1966) pp. 281–304, and 'Putting Humpty Dumpty Together Again', *The Philosophical Review* **77** (1968) 203–215.

7 I assume here Russell's definition of denoting, which I think makes it a well-defined relation and ought always to be kept in mind in discussions of reference so that other relations may be compared with it: An entity X is denoted by a definite description, 'the ϕ', just in case X uniquely possesses the property designated by 'ϕ'.

8 Although I do not have space to develop it, my account of proper names in this paper seems to me to make what I called 'referential' definite descriptions (as discussed in 'Reference and Definite Descriptions', *op. cit.*) a close relative of proper names.

9 Below, Section VI.

10 E.g., in 'The Thought: A Logical Inquiry' (translated by A. M. and Marcelle Quinton), *Mind* **65** (1956) 289–311. Also in P. F. Strawson (ed.), *Philosophical Logic*, Oxford Readings in Philosophy, Oxford University Press, Oxford, 1967, pp. 17–38.

11 That is to say, *if* what they refer to is a function of the set of identifying descriptions each possesses. In that case there would be the logical possibility of each speaker's set picking out different objects, each possessing the properties one speaker would attribute to the referent, but not those the other would.

[12] *Individuals, op. cit.*, pp. 191–192.

[13] *Loc. cit.*

[14] *Ibid.*, p. 182, footnote 1.

[15] The last part of the remark is there simply to indicate that the parents need not even consider what the child says to be *true*; not only does the child not have a 'backing of descriptions', but the predicate in the sentence he uses need not apply. This connects up with the position suggested later in the paper.

[16] *Individuals, op. cit.*, p. 182.

[17] In the example as presented I have the subject of the experiment introduce the names. Nothing hinges on this. The experimenters could just as well use the names and give the subjects 'identifying descriptions'. Nor is there any importance in the fact that the example contains people, the experimenters, 'in the know'. For all that, everyone concerned might have the inverting spectacles on that I introduce.

[18] The idea behind this example originated with me from a conversation with Rogers Albritton in 1966 and may derive from Saul Kripke, who has, I believe, a view about proper names not dissimilar to the one in this paper.

[19] For the purpose of keeping the example within limits, I compress the two uses of the name, that I claim refer, unknown to the speaker, to two different people, into one conversation. I have sometimes, however, found it useful to make the case stronger intuitively by supposing that the person met at the party, for example, who is *not* the famous philosopher, becomes a longer term acquaintance of the speaker (who continues under the illusion that he is the famous man). In subsequent conversation, perhaps months or years later and after his friends have met the bogus philosopher, his use of the name is even more clearly a reference to the man he met at the party and whom he continues to see. Yet if he claimed to know, as in my example, J. L. Aston-Martin, in circumstances where it is clear that the point of the remark has to do with claiming to know a famous man, I still think we would suppose him to have referred to Aston-Martin, the famous philosopher, and not to man he met at the party, who later is one of his close acquaintances.

ROBERT C. STALNAKER

PRAGMATICS*

Until recently, pragmatics – the study of language in relation to the users
of language – has been the neglected member of the traditional three-part
division of the study of signs: syntax, semantics, pragmatics. The problems of pragmatics have been treated informally by philosophers in the
ordinary language tradition, and by some linguists, but logicians and
philosophers of a formalistic frame of mind have generally ignored
pragmatic problems, or else pushed them into semantics and syntax. My
project in this paper is to carve out a subject matter that might plausibly
be called pragmatics and which is in the tradition of recent work in formal
semantics. The discussion will be programmatic. My aim is not to solve
the problems I shall touch on, but to persuade you that the theory I sketch
has promise. Although this paper gives an informal presentation, the
subject can be developed in a relatively straightforward way as a *formal
pragmatics* no less rigorous than present day logical syntax and semantics.
The subject is worth developing, I think, first to provide a framework for
treating some philosophical problems that cannot be adequately handled
within traditional formal semantics, and second to clarify the relation
between logic and formal semantics and the study of natural language.

I shall begin with the second member of the triad, semantics. The
boundaries of this subject are not so clear as is sometimes supposed, and
since pragmatics borders on semantics, these boundaries will determine
where our subject begins. After staking out a claim for pragmatics, I shall
describe some of the tasks that fall within its range and try to defend a
crucial distinction on which the division between semantics and pragmatics is based.

I. SEMANTICS

If we look at the general characterizations of semantics offered by
Morris and Carnap, it will seem an elusive subject. Semantics, according
to them, concerns the relationship between signs and their *designata*. The
designatum of a sign, Morris writes, is what is "taken account of in virtue

*Davidson and Harman (eds.), Semantics of Natural Language, 380–397. All rights reserved
Copyright © 1972 by D. Reidel Publishing Company, Dordrecht-Holland*

of the presence of the sign". He also says "a *designatum* is not a thing, but a kind of object, or a class of objects".[1] Carnap is equally vague in giving a general characterization. The designatum of an expression, he says, is what he who uses it intends to refer to by it, "e.g., to an object or a property or a state of affairs. ... (For the moment, no exact definition for 'designatum' is intended; this word is merely to serve as a convenient common term for different cases – object, properties, etc., whose fundamental differences in other respects are not hereby denied.)"[2]

Though a clear general definition is hard to come by, the historical development of formal semantics is well delineated. The central problems in semantics have concerned the definition of truth, or truth conditions, for the sentences of certain languages. Formal semantics abstracts the problem of giving truth conditions for sentences away from problems concerning the purposes for which those sentences are uttered. People do many things with language, one of which is to express *propositions* for one reason or another, propositions being abstract objects representing truth conditions. Semantics has studied that aspect of language use in isolation from others. Hence I shall consider semantics to be the study of propositions.

The explication of *proposition* given in formal semantics is based on a very homely intuition: when a statement is made, two things go into determining whether it is true or false. First, what did the statement say: what proposition was asserted? Second, what is the world like; does what was said correspond to it? What, we may ask, must a proposition be in order that this simple account be correct? It must be a rule, or a function, taking us from the way the world is into a truth value. But since our ideas about how the world is change, and since we may wish to consider the statement relative to hypothetical and imaginary situations, we want a function taking not just the actual state of the world, but various possible states of the world into truth values. Since there are two truth values, a proposition will be a way – any way – of dividing a set of possible states of the world into two parts: the ones that are ruled out by the truth of the proposition, and the ones that are not.[3]

Those who find the notion of a *possible world* obscure may feel that this explication of proposition is unhelpful, since formal semantics generally takes that notion, like the notion of an individual, as primitive.[4] Some explanation is perhaps needed, but I am not sure what kind. Even without explanation, the notion has, I think, enough intuitive content to make it fruitful in semantics. I shall say only that one requirement for identifying a possible world is to specify a domain of individuals said to exist in that world.[5]

If we explain propositions as functions from possible worlds into truth values, they will have the properties that have traditionally been ascribed to them. Propositions are things that may be considered in abstraction on the one hand from particular languages and linguistic formulations (the sentences that express them), and on the other hand from the kinds of linguistic acts in which they figure (for example the assertions and commands in which a proposition is asserted or commanded). Thus once the homely intuition mentioned above has done its work, we may forget about assertions and consider propositions themselves, along with similar things such as functions taking individuals into propositions, and functions taking propositions into propositions.

Generally, the study of formal semantics has proceeded by first setting up a language, and then laying down rules for matching up the sentences of that language with propositions or truth values. But the languages are set up usually for no other purpose than to represent the propositions, or at least this is how formalized languages have been used by philosophers. Regimentation or formalization is simply a way to make clearer what the truth conditions are – what proposition is expressed by what is regimented or formalized. But with an adequate theory of propositions themselves, such philosophical analyses can proceed without the mediation of a regimented or formalized object language. Rather than translate a problematic locution into an object language in which it is clear what propositions are expressed by the sentences, one can simply state what proposition is expressed by that locution. The effect is the same. Unless one is concerned with proof theory, he may drop the language out altogether with no loss.

According to this characterization of semantics, then, the subject has no essential connection with languages at all, either natural or artificial. (Of course semantical theories are expressed *in* language, but so are theories about rocks.) This is not to deny the possibility of a *causal* relation between language and our conception of a proposition. It may be, for example, that the fact that we think of a possible world as a domain of individuals together with the ascription of properties to them is a result of the fact that our language has a subject-predicate structure. It is also not to deny that the study of the grammar of natural language may be a rich source of insight into the nature of propositions and a source of evidence for distinctions among propositions. If we find in grammar a device for marking a distinction of content, we may presume that there is a distinction of content to be marked. But whatever the causal or evidential story, we may still abstract the study of propositions from the study of language. By doing so, I think we get a clearer conception of the relation between them.

Though one may study propositions apart from language, accounting for the relation between language and propositions still falls partly within the domain of semantics. One of the jobs of natural language is to express propositions, and it is a semantical problem to specify the rules for matching up sentences of a natural language with the propositions that they express. In most cases, however, the rules will not match sentences directly with propositions, but will match sentences with propositions relative to features of the context in which the sentence is used. These contextual features are a part of the subject matter of pragmatics, to which I shall now turn.

II. PRAGMATICS

Syntax studies sentences, semantics studies propositions. Pragmatics is the study of linguistic acts and the contexts in which they are performed. There are two major types of problems to be solved within pragmatics: first, to define interesting types of speech acts and speech products; second, to characterize the features of the speech context which help determine which proposition is expressed by a given sentence. The analysis of illocutionary acts is an example of a problem of the first kind; the study of indexical expressions is an example of the second. My primary concern will be with problems of the second kind, but I shall say a few general things about the first before I go on to that.

Assertions, commands, counterfactuals, claims, conjectures and refutations, requests, rebuttals, predictions, promises, pleas, speculations, explanations, insults, inferences, guesses, generalizations, answers and lies are all kinds of linguistic acts. The problem of analysis in each case is to find necessary and sufficient conditions for the successful (or perhaps in some cases normal) performance of the act. The problem is a pragmatic one since these necessary and sufficient conditions will ordinarily involve the presence or absence of various properties of the context in which the act is performed[6], for example, the intentions of the speaker, the knowledge, beliefs, expectations or interests of the speaker and his audience, other speech acts that have been performed in the same context, the time of utterance, the effects of the utterance, the truth value of the proposition expressed, the semantic relations between the proposition expressed and some others involved in some way.

Almost all of the speech act types mentioned above involve the expression of a proposition, and in the first type of pragmatic problem, the identity of that proposition is taken to be unproblematic. In most cases, however, the context of utterance affects not only the force with which the proposition is expressed, but also the proposition itself. It may be that the semantical rules determine the proposition expressed by a sentence or clause only relative to some feature of the situation in which the sentence is used.

Consider a statement 'everybody is having a good time'. I assume that you understand the *sentence* well enough. Now assume also that you are omniscient with respect to people having a good time: you know for each person that ever lived and for each time up to now whether or not that person was having a good time at that time. Under these conditions, you may still be in doubt about the truth of the statement for at least two reasons: first, you do not know when it was made; second, you do not know what class of people it was made about. It is unlikely that the speaker meant everybody in the universe. He may have meant everybody at some party, or everyone listening to some philosophical lecture, and if so, then we have to know what party, or what lecture before we know even what was said, much less whether what was said is true.

Statements involving personal pronouns and demonstratives furnish the most striking examples of this kind. When you say "We shall overcome", I need to know who you are, and for whom you are speaking. If you say "that is a great painting", I need to know what you are looking at, or pointing to, or perhaps what you referred to in your previous utterance. Modal terms also are notoriously dependent on context for their interpretation. For a sentence using *can, may, might, must* or *ought*, to determine a proposition unambiguously, a domain of 'all possible worlds' must be specified or intended. It need not be *all* conceivable worlds in any absolute sense, if there is such a sense. Sentences involving modals are usually to be construed relative to all possible worlds consistent with the speaker's knowledge, or with some set of presuppositions, or with what is morally right, or legally right, or normal, or what is within someone's power. Unless the relevant domain of possible worlds is clear in the context, the proposition expressed is undetermined.

The formal *semantic* analysis of such concepts as universality and necessity isolates the relevant contextual or pragmatic parameters of an interpretation (as, for example, a domain of discourse in classical first order logic, a set of possible worlds and a relation of relative possibility on them in Kripke's semantics for modal logic), and defines truth conditions relative to these parameters. The second kind of pragmatic problem is to explicate the relation of these parameters to each other, and to more readily identifiable features of linguistic contexts.

The scheme I am proposing looks roughly like this: The syntactical and semantical rules for a language determine an interpreted sentence or clause; this, together with some features of the context of use of the sentence or clause determines a proposition; this in turn, together with a possible world, determines a truth value. An interpreted sentence, then, corresponds to a function from contexts into propositions, and a proposition is a function from possible worlds into truth values.

According to this scheme, both contexts and possible worlds are partial determinants of the truth value of what is expressed by a given sentence. One might merge them together, considering a proposition to be a function from context-possible worlds (call them points of reference) into truth values. Pragmatics-semantics could then be treated as the study of the way in which, not propositions, but truth values are dependent on context, and part of the context would be the possible world in which the sentence is uttered. This is, I think, the kind of analysis of pragmatics proposed and developed by Richard Montague.[7] It is a simpler analysis than the one I am sketching; I need some argument for the necessity or desirability of the extra step on the road from sentences to truth values. The step is justified only if the middlemen – the propositions – are of some independent interest, and only if there is some functional difference between contexts and possible worlds.

The independent interest in propositions comes from the fact that they are the objects of illocutionary acts and propositional attitudes. A proposition is supposed to be the common content of statements, judgments, promises, wishes and wants, questions and answers, things that are possible or probable. The meanings of sentences, or rules determining truth values directly from contexts, cannot plausibly represent these objects.

If O'Leary says "Are you going to the party?" and you answer, "Yes, I'm going", your answer is appropriate because the proposition you affirm is the one expressed in his question. On the simpler analysis, there is nothing to be the common content of question and answer except a truth value. The propositions are expressed from different points of reference, and according to the simpler analysis, they are different propositions. A truth value, of course, is not enough to be the common content. If O'Leary asks "Are you going to the party?" it would be inappropriate for you to answer, "Yes, snow is white."

When O'Leary says at the party, "I didn't have to be here you know", he means something like this: it was not necessary that O'Leary be at that party. The words *I* and *here* contribute to the determination of a proposition, and this proposition is what O'Leary declares to be not necessary. Provided he was under no obligation or compulsion to be there, what he says is correct. But if the proposition declared to be not necessary were something like the meaning of the sentence, then O'Leary would be mistaken since the sentence 'I am here' is true from all points of reference, and hence necessarily true on the simpler analysis.

Suppose you say "He is a fool" looking in the direction of Daniels and O'Leary. Suppose it is clear to me that O'Leary is a fool and that Daniels is not, but I am not sure who you are talking about. Compare this with a situation in which you say "He is a fool" pointing unambiguously at O'Leary, but I am in doubt about whether he is one or not. In both cases, I am unsure about the truth of what you say, but the source of the uncertainty seems radically different. In the first example, the doubt is about what proposition was expressed, while in the second there is an uncertainty about the facts.

These examples do not provide any criteria for distinguishing the determinants of truth which are part of the context from those which are part of the possible world, but they do support the claims that there is a point to the distinction, and that we have intuitions about the matter.

I certainly do not want to suggest that the distinction is unproblematic, or that it is not sometimes difficult or arbitrary to characterize certain truth determinants as semantic or pragmatic.[8] I want to suggest only that there are clear cases on which to rest the distinction between context and possible world, and differences in language use which depend on how it is made. To lend more detailed support to the suggestion, I shall first discuss a concept of *pragmatic presupposition* which is central to the characterization of contexts, as opposed to possible worlds, and second describe a kind of *pragmatic ambiguity* which depends on the distinction.

III. PRESUPPOSITIONS

The notion of presupposition that I shall try to explicate is a pragmatic concept, and must be distinguished from the semantic notion of pre-supposition analyzed by van Fraassen.[9] According to the *semantic* concept, a proposition P presupposes a proposition Q if and only if Q is necessitated both by P and by *not-P*. That is, in every model in which P is either true or false, Q is true. According to the *pragmatic* conception, presupposition is a propositional attitude, not a semantic relation. People, rather than sentences or propositions are said to have, or make, presuppositions in this sense. More generally, any participant in a linguistic context (a person, a group, an institution, perhaps a machine) may be the subject of a presupposition. Any proposition may be the object, or content of one.

There is no conflict between the semantic and pragmatic concepts of presupposition: they are explications of related but different ideas. In general, any semantic presupposition of a proposition expressed in a given context will be a pragmatic presupposition of the people in that context, but the converse clearly does not hold.

To presuppose a proposition in the pragmatic sense is to take its truth for granted, and to assume that others involved in the context do the same. This does not imply that the person need have any particular mental attitude toward the proposition, or that he need assume anything about the mental attitudes of others in the context. Presuppositions are probably best viewed as complex dispositions which are manifested in linguistic behavior. One has presuppositions in virtue of the statements he makes, the questions he asks, the commands he issues. Presuppositions are propositions implicitly *supposed* before the relevant linguistic business is transacted.

The set of all the presuppositions made by a person in a given context determines a class of possible worlds, the ones consistent with all the presuppositions. This class sets the boundaries of the linguistic situation. Thus, for example, if the situation is an inquiry, the question will be, which of the possible worlds consistent with the presuppositions is the actual world? If it is a deliberation then the question is, which of *those* worlds shall we make actual? If it is a lecture, then the point is to inform the audience more specifically about the location of the actual world within that class of possible worlds. Commands and promises are expected to be obeyed and kept within the bounds of the presuppositions. Since the presuppositions play such a large part in determining what is going on in a linguistic situation, it is important that the participants in a single context have the same set of presuppositions if misunderstanding is to be avoided. This is why presupposition involves not only taking the truth of something for granted, but also assuming that others do the same.

The boundaries determined by presuppositions have two sides. One cannot normally assert, command, promise, or even conjecture what is inconsistent with what is presupposed. Neither can one assert, command, promise or conjecture what is itself presupposed. There is no point in expressing a proposition unless it distinguishes among the possible worlds which are considered live options in the context.

Presuppositions, of course, need not be true. Where they turn out false, sometimes the whole point of the inquiry, deliberation, lecture, debate, command or promise is destroyed, but at other times it does not matter much at all. Suppose, for example, we are discussing whether we ought to vote for Daniels or O'Leary for President, presupposing that they are the Democratic and Republican candidates, respectively. If our real interest is in coming to a decision about who to vote for in the Presidential election, then the debate will seem a waste of time when we discover that in reality, the candidates are Nixon and Muskie. However, if our real concern was with the relative merits of the character and executive ability of Daniels and O'Leary, then our false presupposition makes little difference. Minor revisions might bring our debate in line with new presuppositions. The same contrast applies to a scientific experiment performed against the background of a presupposed theoretical framework. It may lose its point when the old theory is rejected, or it may easily be accommodated to the new theory. Sometimes, in fact, puzzlement is resolved and anomalies are explained by the discovery that a presupposition is false, or that a falsehood was presupposed. An experimental result may be more easily accommodated to the new presuppositions than to the old ones.

Normally, presuppositions are at least *believed* to be true. That is one reason that we can often infer more about a person's beliefs from his assertions than he says in them. But in some cases, presuppositions may be things we are unsure about, or even propositions believed or known to be untrue. This may happen in cases of deception: the speaker presupposes things that his audience believes but that he knows to be false in order to get them to believe further false things. More innocently, a speaker may presuppose what is untrue to facilitate communication, as when an anthropologist adopts the presuppositions of his primitive informant in questioning him. Most innocent of all are cases of fiction and pretending: speaker and audience may conspire together in presupposing things untrue, as when the author of a novel presupposes some of what was narrated in earlier chapters. In some contexts, the truth is beside the point. The actual world is, after all, only one possible world among many.

The shared presuppositions of the participants in a linguistic situation are perhaps the most important constituent of a context. The concept of pragmatic presupposition should play a role, both in the definition of various speech acts such as assertion, prediction, or counterfactual statement, and also in specifying semantical rules relating sentences to propositions relative to contexts.

IV. PRAGMATIC AMBIGUITY

The best example of the kind of ambiguity that I shall describe is given in Keith Donnellan's distinction between referential and attributive uses of definite descriptions.[10] After sketching an account of his distinction within the theory of pragmatics, I shall give some examples of other pragmatic ambiguities which have similar explanations.

Consider the following three statements, together with parenthetical comments on the contexts in which they were made:

(1)   Charles Daniels is bald (said about a philosopher named Charles Daniels by one of his friends).

(2)   I am bald (said by Charles Daniels, the man mentioned above).

(3)   The man in the purple turtleneck shirt is bald (said by someone in a room containing one and only one man in a purple turtleneck shirt, that man being Charles Daniels).

The question is, what proposition was expressed in each of these three cases? In the first case, since 'Charles Daniels' is a proper name, and since the speaker knows the intended referent well, there is no problem: the proposition is the one that says that *that* man has the property of being bald. In possible worlds in which that same man, Charles Daniels, is bald, the statement is true; in possible worlds in which he is not bald, the statement is false. What is the truth value in possible worlds where he does not exist? Perhaps the function is undefined for those arguments. We need not worry about it though, since the existence of Charles Daniels will be presupposed in any context in which that proposition is expressed.

The second statement expresses exactly the same proposition as the first since it is true in possible worlds where the referent of the pronoun, *I*, Charles Daniels, is bald, and false when he is not. To believe what is expressed in the one statement is to believe what is expressed in the other; the second might be made as a report of what was said in the first. To interpret the second *sentence*, one needs to know different things about the context than one needs to know to interpret the first, but once both statements are understood, there is no important difference between them.

In both cases, there is a pragmatic problem of determining from the context which individual is denoted by the singular term. The answer to this question fixes the proposition – the content of what is said. In case (1), a relatively unsystematic convention, the convention matching proper names to individuals, is involved. In case (2), there is a systematic rule matching a feature of the context (the speaker) with the singular term *I*. Different rules applied to different sentences in different contexts determine the same proposition.

What about the third case? Here there are two ways to analyze the situation corresponding to the referential and attributive uses of definite descriptions distinguished by Donnellan. We might say that the relation between the singular term "the man in the purple turtleneck shirt" and the referent, Charles Daniels, is determined by the context, and so the proposition expressed is the same as that expressed by statements (1) and (2). As with the term *I*, there are relatively systematic rules for matching up definite descriptions with their denotations in a context: the referent is the one and only one member of the appropriate domain who is *presupposed* to have the property expressed in the description. The rule cannot always be applied, but in the case described, it can be.

Alternatively, we might understand the rule picking out the denotation of the singular term to be itself a part of the proposition. This means that the relation between the definite description and its denotation is a function, not of the context, but of the possible world. In different possible worlds the truth value of the proposition may depend on different individuals. It also means that we may understand the proposition – the content of the statement – without knowing who the man in the purple turtleneck shirt is, although we may have to know who he is in order to know that it is true.

The simpler account of pragmatics which merges possible worlds with contexts cannot account for Donnellan's distinction. If one goes directly from sentence (together with context) to truth value, one misses the ambiguity, since the truth conditions for the sentence in a fixed context (in normal cases at least) coincide for the two readings. If one goes from sentence together with context to proposition, and proposition together with possible world to truth value, however, the ambiguity comes out in the intermediate step. There are at least three important differences between the referential and attributive uses of descriptions. These differences provide further argument for a theory which allows the distinction to be made and which gives some account of it.

First, in modal contexts and contexts involving propositional attitudes, the distinction makes a difference even for the *truth value* of statements in which descriptions occur. Compare

(4)   The man in the purple turtleneck shirt might have been someone else.

(5)   The man in the purple turtleneck shirt might have worn white tie and tails.

Both statements say approximately that a certain proposition was possibly true. But in each case there are two propositions that can be intended, and which one is chosen may make a difference in the truth value of the ascription of possibility to the proposition. If the first means, roughly, that Daniels might have been someone else, it is false, perhaps contradictory. On the other hand, if it means that someone else might have been the one wearing the turtleneck shirt (perhaps he almost lent it to me), then it may be true. The second statement can mean either that Daniels might have worn white tie and tails, or that it might have been the case that whoever was the one wearing a purple turtleneck shirt was *also* wearing white tie and tails. Clearly, the truth conditions are different for these two readings.

In a formal language containing modal or epistemic operators and descriptions, the distinction can be interpreted as a *syntactical* distinction. That is, statements (4) and (5) could each be formalized in two syntactically different ways with the description falling inside of the scope of the modal operator in one and outside the scope in the other.[11] But this procedure has two limitations: (a) it would be highly implausible to suggest that the *English* sentences (4) and (5) are syntactically ambiguous. There are no natural syntactical transformations of (4) and (5) which remove the ambiguity. (b) modal and propositional attitude concepts may be involved, not only as parts of statements, but as comments on them and attitudes toward them. The content of statement (3) above, which cannot be treated as syntactically ambiguous even in a formalized language, may be doubted, affirmed, believed or lamented. What one is doing in taking these attitudes or actions depends on which of the two readings is given to the statement.

Second, as Donnellan noted, the distinction makes a difference for the presuppositions required by the context in which the statement is made. In general, we may say that when a simple subject predicate statement is made, the existence of the subject is normally presupposed. When you say "the man in the purple turtleneck shirt is bald", you presuppose that the man in the purple turtleneck shirt exists. But of course the same ambiguity infects that statement of presupposition; how it is to be taken depends on what reading is given to the original statement. If the statement is given the referential reading, then so must be the presupposition. What is presupposed is that Daniels exists. If the statement is given the attributive reading, then the presupposition is that there is one and only one man (in the appropriate domain) wearing a purple turtleneck shirt. This is exactly the presupposition difference pointed out by Donnellan. Within the framework I am using, the different presuppositions can be seen to be instances of a single principle.

Third, the distinction is important if one considers what happens when the description fails to apply uniquely in the context. In *both* referential and attributive uses of descriptions, it is a presupposition of the context that the description applies uniquely, but if this presupposition is false, the consequences are different. In the case of referential uses, Donnellan has noted, the fact that the presupposition fails may have little effect on the statement. The speaker may still have successfully referred to someone, and successfully said something about him. When the presupposition fails in the attributive sense, however, that normally means that nothing true or false has been said at all. This difference has a natural explanation within our framework.

Where the rules determining the denotation of the singular term are considered as part of the context, what is relevant is not what is true, but what is presupposed. The definite description in statement (3) above, on the referential reading, denotes the person who is *presupposed* to be the one and only one man in a purple turtleneck shirt (in the relevant domain). If there is no one person who is presupposed to fit the description, then reference fails (even if some person does *in fact* fit the description uniquely). But if there is one, then it makes no difference whether that presupposition is true or false. The presupposition helps to determine the proposition expressed, but once that proposition is determined, it can stand alone. The fact that Daniels is bald in no way depends on the color of his shirt.

On the attributive reading, however, the rule determining the denotation of the description is a part of the proposition, so it is what is true that counts, not what is presupposed. The proposition is about whoever uniquely fits the description, so if no one does, no truth value is determined.

The points made in distinguishing these two uses of definite descriptions can be generalized to apply to other singular terms. Proper names, for example, are normally used to refer, but can be used in a way resembling the attributive use of definite descriptions. When you ask, "Which one is Daniels?" you are not *referring* to Daniels, since you do not presuppose of any one person that he is Daniels. When I answer "Daniels is the bald one" I am using "the bald one" referentially, and the name Daniels attributively. I am telling you not that Daniels is bald, but that he is Daniels. Using this distinction, we can explain how identity statements can be informative, even when two proper names flank the identity sign.

It has been emphasized by many philosophers that referring is something done by people with terms, and not by terms themselves. That is why reference is a problem of pragmatics, and it is why the role of a singular term depends less on the syntactic or semantic category of the term itself (proper name, definite description, pronoun) than it does on the speaker, the context, and the presuppositions of the speaker in that context.

The notion of pragmatic ambiguity can be extended to apply to other kinds of cases. In general, a sentence has the potential for pragmatic ambiguity if some rule involved in the interpretation of that sentence may be applied either to the context or to the possible world. Applied to the context, the rule will either contribute to the determination of the proposition (as in the case of the referential use of definite descriptions) or it will contribute to the force with which the proposition is expressed. Applied to the possible world, the rule is incorporated into the proposition itself, contributing to the determination of a truth value. Conditional sentences, sentences containing certain modal terms, and sentences containing what have been called parenthetical verbs are other examples of sentences which have this potential.

If a person says something of the form 'If A then B' this may be interpreted either as the categorical assertion of a conditional proposition or as the assertion of the consequent made conditionally on the truth of the antecedent. In the former case, a proposition is determined on the level of semantics as a function of the propositions expressed by antecedent and consequent. In the latter case, the antecedent is an additional presupposition made temporarily, either because the speaker wishes to commit himself to the consequent only should the antecedent be true, or because the assertion of the consequent would not be relevant unless the antecedent is true (as in, for example, "there are cookies in the cupboard if you want some").[12]

A sentence of the form 'It may be that P' can be interpreted as expressing a modal proposition, that proposition being a function of P, or it may be interpreted as making explicit that the negation of P is not presupposed in the context. In the latter case, P is the only *proposition* involved. The modal word indicates the force with which it is expressed.

A sentence of the form 'I suppose that P' may be meant as a report about a supposition of the speaker, or as a rather tentative assertion of P. To read it the second way is to treat *I suppose* as a *parenthetical verb*, since on this reading, the sentence is synonomous with 'P, I suppose'. The differences between these two readings are explored in Urmson's famous article on parenthetical verbs.[13]

Each of these examples has its own special features and problems. I do not want to suggest that they are instances of a common form. But the ambiguity, in each case, rests on the distinction between context and possible world.

V. CONCLUSION

Let me summarize the main points that I have tried to make. In section one I claimed that semantics is best viewed as the study of propositions, and argued that propositions may be studied independently of language. In section two I defined pragmatics as the study of linguistic acts and the contexts in which they are performed. Two kinds of pragmatic problems were considered; first, the definition of speech acts – the problem of giving necessary and sufficient conditions, not for the truth of a proposition expressed in the act, but for the act being performed; second, the study of the ways in which the linguistic context determines the proposition expressed by a given sentence in that context. The formulation of problems of the second kind depends on a basic distinction between contextual determinants of propositions and propositional determinants of truth. I argued that the distinction has an intuitive basis, and is useful in analyzing linguistic situations. In the final two sections, I tried to support this distinction, first by characterizing a pragmatic notion of presupposition that is a central feature of contexts as opposed to possible worlds, and second by describing a kind of pragmatic ambiguity which rests on the distinction.

In this sketch of a theory of pragmatics, I have relied on some undefined and problematic concepts, for example, possible worlds, contexts, and presuppositions. I have given some heuristic account of these concepts, or relied on the heuristic accounts of others, but I have made no attempt to reduce them to each other, or to anything else. It may be charged that these concepts are too unclear to be the basic concepts of a theory, but I think that this objection mistakes the role of basic concepts. It is not assumed that these notions are clear. In fact, one of the points of the theory is to clarify them. So long as certain concepts all have *some* intuitive content, then we can help to explicate them all by relating them to each other. The success of the theory should depend not on whether the concepts can be defined, but on whether or not it provides the machinery to define linguistic acts that seem interesting and to make conceptual distinctions that seem important. With philosophical as well as scientific theories, one may explain one's theoretical concepts, not by defining them, but by using them to account for the phenomena.

University of Illinois at
Urbana-Champaign

REFERENCES

* The research for and preparation of this paper was supported by the National Science Foundation, grant number GS-2574. I would like to thank Professors David Shwayder and Richmond Thomason for their helpful comments on a draft of this paper.
1 Charles W. Morris, *Foundations of the Theory of Signs*, Chicago 1938, pp. 4–5.
2 Rudolf Carnap, *Foundations of Logic and Mathematics*, Chicago 1939, p. 4.
3 See Dana Scott, 'Advice on Modal Logic' in *Philosophical Problems in Logic. Recent Developments* (ed. by Karel Lambert), D. Reidel Publishing Company, Dordrecht 1970, pp. 143–173.
4 This is not an inevitable strategy. Instead of taking individuals and possible worlds as primitive, defining properties and relations as functions from one to the other, one might take individuals, properties and relations as primitive and define possible worlds in terms of these.
5 A theory of possible worlds and propositions defined in terms of them is not committed to any absolute notion of synonymy or analyticity. Since propositions are functions taking possible worlds as arguments, a domain of possible worlds must be specified as the domain of the function. But the domain need not be *all* possible worlds in any absolute or metaphysical sense. We may leave open the possibility that the domain may be extended as our imaginations develop, or as discoveries are made, or as our interests change. Propositional identity is, of course, relative to the specification of a domain of possible worlds.
6 This is not necessarily so, however. Since speech act types can be *any* way of picking out a class of particular speech acts, one might define one in such a way that the context was irrelevant, and the problem of analysis reduced to a problem of syntax or semantics, as for example the speech act of uttering a grammatical sentence of English, or the speech act of expressing the proposition X.

[7] R. Montague, 'Pragmatics' in *Contemporary Philosophy – La philosophie contemporaine* (ed. by R. Klibansky), La Nuova Italia Editrice, Florence 1968, Vol. I, pp. 102–122. Montague uses the phrase 'point of reference' as does Dana Scott in the paper mentioned in note 3.

[8] Tenses and times, for example, are an interesting case. Does a tensed sentence determine a proposition which is sometimes true, sometimes false, or does it express different timeless propositions at different times? I doubt that a single general answer can be given, but I suspect that one's philosophical views about time may be colored by his tendency to think in one of these ways or the other.

[9] Bas C. van Fraassen, 'Singular Terms, Truth Value Gaps, and Free Logic', *Journal of Philosophy* 63 (1966) 481–495; and van Fraassen, 'Presupposition, Implication, and Self Reference', *Journal of Philosophy* 65 (1968) 136–151.

[10] Keith Donnellan, 'Reference and Definite Descriptions', *Philosophical Review* 75 (1966) 281–304.

[11] See R. Thomason and R. Stalnaker, 'Modality and Reference', *Noûs* 2 (1968) 359–372; and R. Stalnaker and R. Thomason, 'Abstraction in First Order Modal Logic', *Theoria* 34 (1968) 203–207.

[12] See R. Stalnaker, 'A Theory of Conditionals' in *Studies in Logical Theory* (ed. by Nicholas Rescher), Oxford 1968, pp. 98–112 for a semantical theory of conditional propositions. Nuel Belnap has developed a theory of conditional assertion in 'Conditional Assertion and Restricted Quantification', *Noûs* 4 (1970).

[13] J. O. Urmson, 'Parenthetical Verbs', *Mind* 61 (1952) 192–212.

JAAKKO HINTIKKA

THE SEMANTICS OF MODAL NOTIONS
AND THE INDETERMINACY OF ONTOLOGY

I. QUINE AGAINST POSSIBLE INDIVIDUALS

Many philosophers dislike possible individuals. Professor W. V. Quine
is a well-known case in point. According to him, possible individuals
create an ontological slum, "a breeding ground for disorderly elements".
At one point, he elaborated his apprehensions as follows: "Take, for
instance, the possible fat man in that doorway; and, again, the possible
bald man in that doorway. Are they the same possible man, or two
possible men? How do we decide? How many possible men are there in
that doorway? Are there more possible thin ones than fat ones? How
many of them are alike? Or would their being alike make them one? ...
Or ... is the concept of identity simply inapplicable to unactualized
possibles? But what sense can be found in talking of entities which cannot
meaningfully be said to be identical with themselves and distinct from
another? These elements are well-nigh incorrigible."[1]

Another aspect of this incorrigibility has subsequently been expounded
and argued for by Quine in *Word and Object*.[2] It is what Quine calls the
indeterminacy of ontology. This means that all physically possible evidence would not enable us to decide how another man is splitting up his
world into individuals, universals, and whatever other categories of
entities he might countenance. By the same token, all I say and do is
inevitably compatible with more than one way of structuring the world
conceptually. The reason why this is but another aspect of the old problem of possible individuals is not hard to appreciate. If I could spell
out, in the kind of behavioristic terms which Quine could accept, the
principles on which his questions concerning thin and fat possible men
could be answered, then these principles would describe the kind of linguistic behavior which goes together with one ontology rather than
another.[3]

II. THE REVIVAL OF POSSIBLE INDIVIDUALS

Recently, something like a resuscitation of possible individuals has nevertheless been taking place. For instance, in his 'Advice on Modal Logic' Dana Scott recommends to modal logicians a sandwich universe consisting of actual, potential, and virtual individuals.[4] The important domain *D* is the one which contains actual and potential but no virtual individuals. Of this class Scott writes: "I feel it is important to be thinking of *D* as *fixed in advance*" (his italics). According to Scott, we can quantify over *D*.

What is there to be said of this revival of possible individuals? It seems to me that it is not immune to challenges of the same type as Quine's and that it contains dangerous oversimplifications. There may be a sense in which the idea of possible individual can, and should, be restored to honor. Be this as it may, I am not convinced that the domain of possible individuals is anything we can start from in the sense of take for granted, at least not in some of the most important philosophical applications of modal logic. I am not sure, either, that all the possible individuals we in some sense have to deal with can eventually be pooled into one big happy domain. These are among the issues I shall try to discuss in this paper.

III. THE SEMANTICS OF MODALITY

The background of the recent renaissance of possible individuals is the development of a viable semantics for modal logics.[5] Many of the main ideas of this semantics can be discussed in terms of the vivid and precise idea of a 'possible world' which unfortunately has been partly pre-empted by logically minded metaphysicians from Leibniz to Heinrich Scholz.[6]

According to this semantics, understanding the attribution of necessity or possibility or a propositional attitude (to a person) in a given world turns on understanding which possible worlds are 'alternatives' to it. In the case of necessity and possibility, these alternatives to a given world *W* are those possible worlds that could have been realized instead of *W*. Possibility in *W* therefore amounts to truth in at least one of these alternatives to *W* and necessity to truth in all of them. For a propositional attitude *A*, attributed to *b*, these *A*-alternatives (with respect to *b*) to a given world *W* are all the possible worlds compatible with the presence of this attitude *A* in *b* (as a member of *W*). For instance, these might be all the worlds (epistemic alternatives) compatible with b's knowing what he knows in W, or the worlds (doxastic alternatives) compatible with what he believes in W.[7] Hence it is true in W that b knows that p if p is the case in all the possible worlds compatible with what b knows (and with his knowing it). Thus all attributions of propositional attitudes in W can be paraphrased in terms of the corresponding alternatives to W. In general, with a mild oversimplification one can say that all we want to say in the semantics of modal logics can be said in terms of the alternativeness relation.

IV. THE PROBLEM OF CROSS-IDENTIFICATION

This suggests at once an important reason why it is illicit to speak of well-defined individuals, whether possible or actual, in modal contexts without some further explanations. For the relatively unproblematic reality we face in the pragmatics of most modal notions, including especially prominently propositional attitudes, is a collection of possible worlds. We cannot, it is true, make actual observations of more than one possible world, to wit, of possible worlds other than the actual one. However, the other possible worlds can be described by conditional or counterfactual statements. What cannot be expressed by, or decided by means of, such statements about the observable or otherwise unproblematic features of possible worlds, is suspect or at least problematic in a much more radical way than possible worlds and their overt features.

This difficulty attaches, I claim, to the identity of 'possible individuals'. Each possible world contains a number of individuals (or, if you prefer the locution, manifestations of individuals) with certain properties and with certain relations to each other. We have to use these properties and relations to decide which member (if any) of a given possible world is identical with a given member of another possible world. Individuals do not carry their names in their foreheads; they do not identify themselves. We cannot – even counterfactually – observe bare particulars, only particulars clothed in their respective properties and interrelations. Ontological nudism may seem an attractive idea in the warm sunshine of a purely abstract semantics, but it is impossible to practice in the cold climate of a realistic pragmatics of modal logic.

The same point can be put as follows. Suppose, on the contrary, that one begins by postulating a fixed supply of prefabricated individuals. Then one obtains a semantics which could function as an actual means of communication, it seems to us, only if one could assume that there are no problems in principle about re-identifying one's individuals as they occur in the several possible worlds we are considering. Once this presupposition is made explicit, however, it is also seen at once how gratuitous it is for most philosophically interesting purposes.[8]

V. METHODS OF CROSS-IDENTIFICATION

Here the use of tense-logic as a conceptual paradigm, so fruitful in other walks of logic, is seriously liable to lead us astray. For in tense-logic the different 'possible worlds' are different contemporary slices of one and the same history of the world, and the identity of the members of the different slices is simply their ordinary identity as the same persons, physical bodies, or other equally familiar entities.

However, even here matters are in reality much more problematic than one first realizes. It is not clear to what degree it makes sense to speak of the continuing identity of an electron which after all can occasionally be thought of as a mere congestion of waves. Borderline cases of personal identity may be puzzling indeed, and the possible dependency of the criteria of continued personal identity on the criteria of bodily identity have caused much comment. In any case, it is clear that the identification (re-identification) of physical objects is as unproblematic (relatively speaking) as it apparently is only because our laws of nature serve to guarantee those continuity properties which in principle enable us to trace the continuous world line of an individual in space-time. Yet the applicability of these natural laws, or indeed any laws which can be used in the same way, has no logically (conceptually) necessary guarantee.

Of course similar continuity properties play a role in many other cross-identifications (identifications of individuals across the boundaries of possible worlds). However, they are not any longer capable of doing the whole job. The other considerations which here come into the play are somewhat less clear-cut and unproblematic. Instead of thinking of the model as following an individual along a continuous world-line in space-time one might in many cases more profitably think of one's identificatory task as being comparable to identifying the originals of the characters of a *roman à clef.* Indeed, in many circumstances a course of events described by a sufficiently realistic *roman à clef* might in fact be one of the 'alternatives' relevant to the semantics of modal logic. It might be an account of what might actually have happened or what will happen, for all that I know. (Think, for instance, of the novel which Harold Nicolson wrote in the thirties and which obviously and intentionally sought to anticipate, however fancifully, the events of the next few years, with the well-known actors on the stage of history continuing the roles they had been playing so far.) Than it would be one of my epistemic alternatives to the actual world. It is clear that our actual criteria of identifying a character in a *roman à clef* are multiple and not without some vagueness. (Think of what arguments lawyers might present in a libel suit prompted by such a novel!) Here it is especially clear, it seems to me, that for any serious philosophical purpose our criteria of cross-identification have to be given a long hard look and cannot simply be taken for granted. It is nevertheless also clear what the main criteria of cross-identification are. They might be labelled 'continuity plus similarity', for the considerations that go beyond continuity seem to rely largely on the sharing of properties and relations – be it sharing some especially important properties and relations or a sufficiently large number of them – or both.[9]

VI. INDIVIDUALS AND INDIVIDUATING FUNCTIONS

Nothing in all this nevertheless contradicts yet the possibility of eventually forming a class of entities very much like Scott's domain of possible individuals. Elsewhere, I have tried to spell out a trifle more carefully what happens when a semantics is developed systematically.[10] What becomes of an individual is now an atemporal and non-spatial 'world line' through several possible worlds. In equivalent terms each individual in the full sense of the word is now essentially a function which picks out from several possible worlds a member of their domains as the 'embodiment' of that individual in this possible world or perhaps rather as the *role* which that individual plays under a given course of events. These functions I have called individuating functions. They may of course be only partial ones: a well-defined individual existing in one world may fail to exist in another.

This possible failure to exist – this gappiness of the world lines – is the only form of unorthodox behavior some modal logicians allow to their possible individuals. I find it arbitrary to impose so strict a regimentation on the behavior of world lines, and I seem to detect a trace of Quine's patrician distaste of ontological slums in this prohibition of disorderly world lines. Certain limitations seem in order, however, in particular a prohibition against a world line's splitting when one moves from a possible world to its alternatives.[11]

Be this as it may, we can say that in any context of discussion – say, in considering a given statement p – we can make sense of an individual if and only if we can trace it through those possible worlds we are considering (however implicitly) in p. We may almost say that in such a context a well-defined individual *is* just a piece of world line. In any case, it goes together with one. Whenever it so happens that one of the individuating functions fails to have a value in the actual world, then it goes together with a merely possible individual, we might say.

VII. WELL-DEFINEDNESS OF INDIVIDUALS AND ITS LINGUISTIC EXPRESSIONS. THE OBJECTIVITY OF INDIVIDUATING FUNCTIONS

Not every free singular term (say, a) picks out from these possible worlds manifestations of one and the same individual. In fact, usually its references in different worlds are manifestations of different (well-defined) individuals. Such a term does not specify a well-defined individual in the context in question. For this reason we cannot instantiate or generalize with respect to such a singular term. The failure of the usual logical laws governing instantiation and generalization in such cases thus ceases to be a source of bewilderment and puzzle and becomes a matter of course.[12]

If we are speaking only of the alternatives to the actual world (plus, possibly, of this actual world itself), i.e. if there are no iterations of modal operations and if only one modal operator is present, then simple statements can be found to express explicitly that a term specifies a well-defined individual. These are statements of the type

(1) (Ex) b knows that $(a=x)$
(Ex) b perceives that $(a=x)$
(Ex) b remembers that $(a=x)$
(Ex) b believes that $(a=x)$
(Ex) necessarily $(a=x)$

When a success condition is not presupposed and when we are also talking about the actual world and not just its alternatives, we must make sure that the uniqueness of reference which (1) postulate extends to the actual world.

(2) (Ex) [(it appears to b that $(a=x)$) & $(a=x)$]
          (Ex) [(b believes that $(a=x)$) & $(a=x)$]

          ...

Several of these statement-forms have vernacular counterparts. For instance, the first four statements (1) can also be expressed as follows:

(1)* b knows who a is
          b perceives who a is.
          b remembers who a is
          b has an opinion of who a is

That (1) serve the purpose I claimed for them follows from the interpretation of our variables of quantification. They are assumed to range over genuine well-defined individuals. Because of this, '(Ex) b knows that $(a=x)$' has the force of saying that 'a' always picks out, from the several epistemic alternatives to the actual world, manifestations of *one and the same* individual x.

Thus no unusual sense of quantification is being assumed here, certainly nothing remotely like that *bête noire* of Quine's, substitutional quantification.[13] Rather, what we face here are the consequences of an objectual interpretation of quantification in a situation where one is considering several possible worlds. In this situation, the objectual interpretation immediately leads one to ask how one and the same individual appears in the different possible worlds. If a substitutional interpretation of quantification is assumed, '(Ex) b knows that $(a=x)$' will only have the force of saying that for a suitable substitution-value inserted for 'x' in 'b knows that $(a=x)$' the result is true. Obviously, 'a' will serve this purpose, making all of (1) trivially true. Hence we have here a clear-cut formal difference between the substitutional and objectual quantification.

Moreover, the translations (1)* will obviously be spoiled if a substitutional interpretation is presupposed. Hence we are committed in more than one way to the normal objectual reading of quantifiers.

Another side of the same coin is that quantifiers are in modal contexts

dependent on methods of cross-identification (i.e. on a supply of individuating functions), and their meaning will be relative to a given
method of cross-identification. (To be precise, this refers to quantifying
into a modal construction.)

In order for the truth-criteria of such statements as (1)–(2) to be objectively given, the supply of individuating functions (world lines) must also
be objectively given, at least relative to a fixed class of possible worlds.
I have argued that in a correct semantics for propositional attitudes this
objectively given supply of world lines is the main range of entities over
which we have to quantify.[14] They must therefore exist or at least subsist
in some objective fashion. Among them, there are the individuating functions which give rise to (merely) possible individuals. They must thus
also enjoy some sort of objective existence (or subsistence). Indeed, this
seems to vindicate possible individuals completely. For surely they can
be pooled together into one happy domain if we can even quantify over
them. What more can we possibly ask of a vindication of possible
individuals? No wonder that a reasonable semantics of modal logic seems
to reinstate possible individuals if it leads to this result.

VIII. THE RELATIVITY OF INDIVIDUALS

This, in fact, is the sense in which – and the extent to which – possible
individuals can be countenanced. We cannot go further, however. For
instance, if we as much as say that individuals and individuating functions
are just one and the same old things, we are already oversimplifying.
There are facts about the world lines that simply cannot be spelled out
in terms of prefabricated individuals. It seems to me that the situation
can be described in functional terms. (Of course, these terms have to be
taken to express logical rather than causal or temporal relationships.)
The world lines cannot be drawn so as to connect blank worlds. They
depend on the properties and relations that obtain in the several possible
worlds we are considering. They come about, as it were, only through
comparisons between these possible worlds. For this reason, we cannot
start from individuals. We can only arrive at them as outcomes of transworld comparisons.

All this is of course partly metaphorical. Since there is admittedly a
one-to-one correlation of some rough sort between possible individuals

(in any reasonable sense) and my individuating functions, all discussion of their relative priority may seem to resemble a dispute of the relative priority of hens vs. eggs.

There is a real issue here, however, or rather several issues. I shall by-pass the predominantly pragmatic point that the cross-identifications we in fact seem to be able to perform turn in reality on rather complicated processes. Instead, I want to argue that the primacy of individuating functions over possible individuals appears already on the level of semantics, provided we develop it with a view on certain applications of the greatest philosophical interest.

There are two main facts here, it seems to me, that are crucial for the applications I have in mind. The first is that the set of individuating functions is not given once and for all but is relative to a class of possible worlds.[15] It is objectively given, but only relative to this class. (This observation, if it can be sustained, is a partial semantical counterpart to the thesis – already aired in this paper – that individuating functions, i.e. world lines, depend functionally on those possible worlds they serve to tie together.) In other words, some world lines that run smoothly between a certain class of possible worlds may be impossible to continue to a wider class of possible worlds.[16] This fact (putative fact) I shall call the *relativity* of individuating functions or the relativity of world lines.[17]

This relativity, of course, is to be expected if the world lines are in the first place drawn (as it were) on the basis of similarities between the worlds and regularities holding in each of them. The members of the wider class of possible worlds may be dissimilar when compared with each other and irregular when examined alone.

It seems to me that when it is realized what the relativity of world lines means, it is immediately realized that this relativity obtains in our own conceptual system. In other (maybe somewhat more guarded) words, it has to be accepted if my general semantical framework is accepted. Otherwise one cannot have an opinion as to who *a* is unless one knows who that individual is in some guise or another or knows who *a* is unless everyone else also knows who *a* is under some suitable description or designation or other, and so on. I cannot help feeling that the main reason why the relativity of world lines has not been registered in the literature is a misplaced quest of mathematical elegance in one's logic.

IX. TECHNICAL CONSEQUENCES OF THE RELATIVITY

This point is worth elaborating, for the relativity of world lines has clear-cut consequences for our semantics.[18] The approach I have very briefly sketched may also be partly characterized by saying that in it we try to capture by means of explicit premises the precise conditions on which a singular term a will in a given context behave like a *bona fide* singular term of ordinary non-modal logic, i.e. obey the usual laws of instantiation and generalization.[12] It does so if and only if it picks out (apart from gaps) one and the same individual from all the possible worlds we are to consider. These possible worlds are determined by the context, and are relative to it. If we are merely considering what b believes or does not believe, we find the requisite condition in (1). If we are also considering the actual world, the condition is found in (2). If we are in addition considering what b believes (or fails to believe) that d knows or does not know, we are *ipso facto* considering epistemic d-alternatives to these doxastic b-alternatives, and the requisite condition has the form

$$(Ex) \, [(a=x) \, \& \, (b \text{ believes that } (a=x))$$
$$\& \, (b \text{ believes that } d \text{ knows that } (a=x))]$$

In general, the condition needed is a similar existentially quantified conjunction of modalized identities $(a=x)$. The modal prefixes of these identities indicate the classes of possible worlds as members of which a is being considered. These, in turn, are indicated by the several sequences of modal operators within the scope of which 'a' occurs in the sentence which constitutes the relevant context. (The prefixes are precisely these sequences except that the weaker operator in a pair of dual operators is always replaced by the stronger.)

All this is quite straightforward. However, it flies to the face of some of the most commonly used principles of modal logic. For instance, we cannot any more move from

(3) $\vdash (p(a/x) \supset q(a/x))$

to

(4) $\vdash ((Ex) \, p \supset (Ex) \, q)$

or to

(5) $\vdash ((x) \, p \supset (x) \, q)$

Since these are frequently used principles, some logicians have been reluctant to give them up. However, the need of doing so is a direct consequence of the relativity of world lines. Even if (3) is the case, (4) and (5) may fail to hold, for the simple reason that the uniqueness conditions presupposed in the antecedent of (4) for instantiation may be weaker than those required in its consequent. Hence the implication need not hold, although the corresponding implication holds for singular constants instead of variables. (In the case of constants, we need not worry about instantiation any more.) Similar (dual) remarks pertain to (5). Thus our approach forces us to give up some familiar and admittedly quite convenient and 'elegant' deductive principles.

X. THE FAILURE OF WORLD LINES FOR LOGICAL MODALITIES

What is remarkable about the relativity of world lines is nevertheless not its reality nor any of its technical by-products in our semantics, but rather its philosophical implications – or, more accurately, the philosophical suggestions it yields.

One of them I have already explained briefly elsewhere.[19] If world lines tend to break when extended further, there may eventually be no trans world heir lines left when all sorts of weird worlds are admitted into our class of possible worlds. In less metaphorical terms, if the world lines are to be drawn on the basis of similarities between worlds and of their intrinsic regularities, then this whole enterprise will break down when very dissimilar and irregular worlds have to be considered. And this is the case with logical modalities. Everyone will admit, I think, that logically possible worlds can be very, very irregular and entirely unlike each other. It is logically possible, for instance, that all the nice continuity properties which characterize the behavior of physical bodies vis-à-vis space and time should not obtain. This need not deter a logician from envisaging in purely abstract terms some unspecified system of world lines between them. However, every attempt to specify with any infinitesimal degree of realism how such world lines could conceivably be drawn in accordance with the criteria of individuation we normally use is doomed to fail. In connection with logical (analytical) modalities, individuating functions thus do not exist, if we presuppose a modicum of conformity with our actual ways with our concepts in other respects.

This implies that quantification makes no sense in a context of logical modalities, for quantification was seen to depend on a system of world lines. (To be precise, this affects only quantification *into* a context governed by operators for logical necessity and possibility.) Quine is thus seen to be right in his suspicion of quantified modal logic of *logical* modalities.[20] Quantifiers and *logical* modalities simply do not mix. In a context of logical modalities we cannot answer the questions that have to be answered in order for quantification to make sense, presupposing that the rest of our discourse is moderately realistic.

XI. RATIONALITY ASSUMPTIONS UNDERLYING PROPOSITIONAL ATTITUDES

This does not directly affect such other modalities, for instance propositional attitudes, as do not necessarily lead us into a comparable jungle of possible worlds. There may nevertheless be only a (vast) difference in degree rather than a difference in kind between logical modalities and (say) propositional attitudes. For one thing, logical modalities can occasionally be used in contexts (for instance, in a context where all talk is about numbers or other similar abstract entities) where the vagaries of cross-identification do not matter. For another, in discussing a man whose beliefs are few and irregular, we might fail to establish world lines and hence fail to make sense of quantification into *his* belief-contexts. We might perhaps say that some rudimentary rationality (in some rather weak sense) must be presupposed of someone's propositional attitudes in order for us to be able to use quantifiers and identity in discussing his attitudes. However, the fact that there is no a priori guarantee of such rationality does not make the general task of trying to make sense of quantification into contexts governed by operators expressing such attitudes any less interesting or important. However, other curious things happen in the case of propositional attitudes.

XII. THE INDETERMINACY OF ONTOLOGY

Consider, for the purpose of seeing what the situation is, people's systems of settled beliefs – their rational *Weltanschauungen*, one might say. When is an entity a member of the ontology of one such system of beliefs – say, of the beliefs *a* holds? This question is perhaps the main question one can ask concerning the individuals, possible and actual, that *a* countenances. In fact, one can almost paraphrase it by asking simply whether that entity *is* a member of *a*'s ontology.

Because of the relativity of world lines, the answer to this question is relative to the class of possible worlds we are considering. These are all the possible worlds compatible with *a*'s beliefs. Their totality determines precisely these beliefs, contentwise. Thus a man's ontology is relative to his beliefs in a radical sense. Not only does the selection of possible individuals that he believes to exist depend on his beliefs. Even the class of his *possible* (potential) individuals depends on his beliefs as to what predicates apply to what individuals. To determine my ontology, you would have to find out what my substantial beliefs are. In so far as these beliefs are behavioristically underdetermined, ontology is likewise indeterminate. Thus we have vindicated a thesis reminiscent of Quine's famous 'indeterminacy of ontology'. Our result is in fact very much like Quine's thesis in that in both cases the indeterminacy of ontology is essentially connected with the indeterminacy (if any) of beliefs. Our result is more limited than Quine's thesis, however, in that the relativity of a man's ontology to his beliefs matters only in so far as we are quantifying into a belief-context, i.e. explicitly or implicitly considering his beliefs. Even with this qualification, our result seems to amount to an important partial vindication of what Quine has been aiming at in speaking of the indeterminacy of ontology, for surely Quine's apprehensions about the inaccessibility of a jungle tribe's ontology are largely occasioned by the influence of the natives' beliefs on their linguistic behavior.[21] (Notice nevertheless that I have not discussed the question whether beliefs are really behavioristically underdetermined in the way Quine seems to think they are.)

XIII. REVIEW OF THE SITUATION

This result is also an additional reason for viewing with suspicion any facile postulation of a single unified domain of possible individuals, independent of people's beliefs and other propositional attitudes. Such a domain seems to me a completely unrealistic abstraction.

However, truth seems to lie between two extremes here. Although I agree with a version of Quine's relativity-of-ontology thesis, it seems to me that Quine's tendency to cast doubts on the use of quantifiers in each and every context in which the unreconstructed quantificational laws of instantiation and generalization do not hold (i.e. do not hold without supplementary premises) is not only exaggerated but misplaced. These laws fail as such as we are considering several possible worlds in their relation to each other and thus considering individuals as they appear in these different possible worlds. I have shown how these quantificational laws can be vindicated (formally *and* interpretationally) by means of supplementary premises. There is nothing in the failure of these laws to demonstrate the impossibility of quantified modal logic.

The possibility or impossibility of such logic hinges instead on the possibility of cross-identification, i.e. on the possibility of recognizing our individuals in their different roles in the different possible worlds our modal notions invite us to consider. It is here that Quine's critical arguments have their bite. A mere postulation of possible individuals does not help. Merely to assume a fixed set of individuals which are without any further ado presumed to crop up in the several worlds is to pretend that no problem is present, not to solve one. As was indicated above, this problem of cross-identification is unsolvable in the case of logical modalities, and Quine is therefore right in this favorite case of his. In the case of propositional attitudes, however, no insurmountable problems arise, provided that we recognize the important relativity of our methods of cross-identification (individuation) explained earlier. If we do so, we can even answer the pointed questions of Quine's which served to open this paper. For the purpose, we nevertheless need one more large-scale theoretical insight. Its scale is unfortunately too large for us to discuss it here, and forces us to leave it to another paper.[22]

REFERENCES

[1] W. V. Quine, *From a Logical Point of View*, Harvard University Press, Cambridge, Mass., 1953 (2nd ed., revised, 1961), p. 4.
[2] W. V. Quine, *Word and Object*, M.I.T. Press, Cambridge, Mass., 1960. For further elucidation of the precise nature of the indeterminacy of ontology and of radical translation, see also Quine's reply to Chomsky in *Words and Objections: Essays on the Work of W. V. Quine* (ed. by Donald Davidson and Jaakko Hintikka), D. Reidel Publishing Company, Dordrecht, 1969.
[3] Notice, however, that there may in principle be non-behavioristic ways of answering Quine's questions which therefore leave the behavioristic indeterminacy intact.
[4] Dana Scott 'Advice on Modal Logic', in *Philosophical Problems in Logic: Some*

Recent Developments (ed. by Karel Lambert), D. Reidel Publishing Company, Dordrecht, 1970. Richard Montague's highly important work in this area also uses the idea of 'prefabricated' domain of individuals which just show up in the different possible worlds one is considering; see e.g. Richard Montague, 'Pragmatics' in *Contemporary Philosophy – La philosophie contemporaine* Vol. I (ed. by R. Klibansky), La Nuova Italia Editrice, Florence, 1968, pp. 102–122 and Richard Montague, 'On the Nature of Some Philosophical Entities', *The Monist* **53** (1969) 159–194.

⁵ The first big wave of work in this area was largely due to Stig Kanger and Saul Kripke; see Stig Kanger, *Provability in Logic* (Stockholm Studies in Philosophy, Vol. I), Stockholm, 1957; Stig Kanger, 'The Morning Star Paradox', *Theoria* **23** (1957) 1–11; Stig Kanger, 'A Note on Quantification and Modalities', *ibid.* 133–134; Stig Kanger, 'On the Characterization of Modalities', *ibid.* 152–155; Saul Kripke, 'A Completeness Theorem in Modal Logic', *The Journal of Symbolic Logic* **24** (1959) 1–14; Saul Kripke, 'Semantical Considerations on Modal Logic' (*Proceedings of a Colloquium on Modal and Many-Valued Logics, Helsinki, 23–26 August, 1962*), *Acta Philosophica Fennica* **16** (1963) 83–94; Saul Kripke, 'Semantical Analysis of Modal Logic: I. Normal Modal Propositional Calculi', *Zeitschrift für mathematische Logik und Grundlagen der Mathematik* **9** (1963) 67–96; Saul Kripke, 'Semantical Analysis of Modal Logic: II, Non-Normal Modal Propositional Calculi' in *The Theory of Models* (Proceedings of the 1963 International Symposium at Berkeley, ed. by J. W. Addison, L. Henkin, and A. Tarski), Amsterdam 1965, pp. 206–220; Saul Kripke, 'The Undecidability of Monadic Modal Quantification Theory', *Zeitschrift für mathematische Logik und Grundlagen der Mathematik* **8** (1962) 113–116. See also Montague's work, partly mentioned above and partly referred to in these writings of his, and the work of E. J. Lemmon and Dagfinn Føllesdal. Most of my own published work here is collected in *Models for Modalities: Selected Essays*, D. Reidel Publishing Company, Dordrecht, 1969.

⁶ One danger here is to think of 'possible worlds' as being something weird and consequently philosophically suspect. Yet nothing is more commonplace in human life and in the life of science than to find someone considering several possibilities as to how some sequence of events might turn out (e.g. considering several possible outcomes of an experiment). Whoever does so, is dealing with as many 'possible worlds' in the general sense presupposed here.

It is instructive to see how pervasive and how unavoidable precisely analogous considerations are in the foundations of statistics, and how commonplace and innocent some of the intended applications of these concepts are. (Cf. e.g. L. J. Savage *The Foundations of Statistics*, John Wiley, New York, 1954, especially Savage's discussion of 'states of the world' on pp. 8–10 and of 'small worlds' on pp. 82–86.) An ontological standard which (in the name of science?) tries to exorcise possible worlds from our conceptual system is likely to make shambles of statistics and applied probability theory.

⁷ There seems to be a bad ambiguity here between compatibility with *what* someone believes (knows, remembers, etc.) and compatibility (also) with his believing (knowing, remembering, etc.) it. For many purposes, including those of the present paper, we can simply leave the ambiguity there. It only matters when further questions (concerning the details of the behavior of the alternativeness relation, especially its possible transitivity) are asked. Contrary to what has been claimed, I have never traded on the ambiguity myself. Here we can simply leave it alone. (Cf. Jaakko Hintikka, '"Knowing that One Knows" Reviewed', *Synthese* **21** (1970) 141–162.)

⁸ There are nevertheless explicit doctrines to the contrary. Sometimes it is thought

that our primary vehicle in referring to individuals are names (individual constants), and that they are mere labels without descriptive content. Then clearly we can refer to individuals only in so far as we have succeeded in pasting these labels on them. As far as our ways with singular terms go, we then have to think ourselves as being rather in the position of an Adam who has associated names with the various beasts because they had come to him to be identified. I have called this view of the functioning of our language 'logical Adamism'. (Cf. *Genesis* 2:19.) It is clear that if it were acceptable, all those individuals we can meaningfully talk about can be recognized everywhere by means of their identificatory labels which we (so to speak) have to think of as already being strung to them. It is equally clear, it seems to me, that this is an unrealistic way of thinking about the use of our language. The values of quantifiers will on any reasonable interpretation leave behind all the individuals we have already witnessed and labelled.

⁹ Suppose that we are given two characters in two different *romans à clef*, both compatible with all my beliefs and asked whether they are the same person (individual) or not. One thing we can try to do is to follow each of them back and forward in his respective *roman*. The possibility of doing so of course depends heavily on spatial and temporal continuity of individuals within each possible world. If we are lucky, we can trace the two characters to the common part of the two novels, i.e. the part which represents my positive beliefs about the world. If they coincide there, they are identical; if they are separate there, they are different.

This strategy may of course fail. Then we fall back on some suitable requirements of similarity between the two individuals. Such criteria of cross-identification do not seem very sharp nor very conclusive. However, this probably is as it should be. We are in this case dealing with two 'possible individuals' about whom I have no beliefs. No wonder there is little one can say of the identification of such underdetermined individuals between my belief-worlds (worlds compatible with what I believe).

¹⁰ See the essays included in *Models for Modalities* (Reference 5 above), especially 'Semantics for Propositional Attitudes' and 'Existential Presuppositions and Uniqueness Presuppositions'.

¹¹ For the pros and cons here, see my 'Existential Presuppositions and Uniqueness Presuppositions' (Reference 10 above). There it is also shown how this particular mode of good behavior on the part of individuals is connected with the problem of the substitutivity of individuals.

Gail Stine has claimed in effect that we cannot rule out splitting in the case of belief. (See 'Hintikka on Quantification and Belief', *Nous* 3 (1969) 349–408.) I am prepared to reserve judgement here, pending further discussion. This problem, vital to the evaluation of the Quine-Føllesdal position (as I am interpreting it), does not affect my constructive suggestions in this paper or elsewhere.

¹² The precise conditions on which the usual quantificational laws apply in different circumstances are studied in 'Existential Presuppositions and Uniqueness Presuppositions' (Reference 10 above). The next few paragraphs present only an intuitive summary of an analysis that can be made much tighter.

¹³ For Quine's distinction between objectual and substitutional quantification, see his new book, *Ontological Relativity*, Columbia University Press, New York, 1969, especially pp. 63–67, 104–108. See also W. V. Quine, *The Ways of Paradox and Other Essays*, Random House, New York, 1966, Ch. 14, and Ruth Barcan Marcus, 'Interpreting Quantification', *Inquiry* 5 (1962) 252–259, 'Modalities and Intensional Languages', *Synthese* 13 (1961) 303–322. I want to be especially emphatic here because

a substitutional interpretation of quantifiers has mistakenly been attributed to me.
[14] In 'Semantics for Propositional Attitudes' (Reference 10 above).
[15] Of course, formally one might very well try to handle the situation in terms of one big unified class of individuating functions. Then each of them would have to be thought of as being defined only for some subclass of the class of all possible worlds we are considering.
[16] Technically, this means – in rough-and-ready terms – that the kinds of auxiliary premises contemplated in Section VII above do not coincide but have to be distinguished from each other in almost all interesting cases.
[17] We might perhaps express the relativity involved here by saying that what counts as an individual depends on the context of-discussion. (The Prime Minister of Norway is a well-defined individual as far as Prof. Føllesdal's knowledge is concerned, for he knows who that high official of his country is, whereas the same Prime Minister unfortunately is not a well-defined individual as far as my knowledge and ignorance are concerned.)

This relativity of individuals has a terminological consequence which tends to create unnecessary confusion and perhaps even disagreement in this area. The inhabitants of each possible world, *when this world is considered alone*, are as good individuals as one can possibly hope. However, when our attention switches and we consider the same world (say) just as one particular alternative to another given world, these inhabitants suddenly become only so many 'embodiments' or 'manifestations' of the 'real' individuals who can also make their entrances and exits in other worlds, or perhaps rather so many different roles these individuals play. Hence referring to the good old inhabitants of one particular possible world as individuals may be perfectly appropriate in one context and yet quite misleading in another.

The same goes for the intuitive meaning one associates with the truth of an identity $a = b$ in some particular possible world. In one context, what is involved is a perfectly good identity between genuine individuals, while in another context only an identity between the ephemeral 'stages' or 'manifestations' of genuine individuals is what we ought to be thinking in terms of.

The main moral of this terminological and interpretational relativity is, it seems to me, that we need not be confused or misled by it.
[18] With the following (and with the preceding section) compare the related discussion in 'Existential Presuppositions and Uniqueness Presuppositions', Sections XVI–XVII.
[19] In 'Existential Presuppositions and Uniqueness Presuppositions', Section XIX.
[20] See e.g. W. V. Quine, *From a Logical Point of View* (Reference 1 above), Ch. 8; *Word and Object* (Reference 2 above), Ch. 6; *The Ways of Paradox and Other Essays*, Random House, New York, 1966, Chapters 13–15. Cf. also Dagfinn Føllesdal, 'Quine on Modality' in *Words and Objections* (Reference 2 above), with further references.
[21] This is especially clearly in evidence in *Ontological Relativity* (Reference 12 above).
[22] See Jaakko Hintikka, 'The Objects of Knowledge and Belief: Acquaintances and Public Figures', *Journal of Philosophy* **67** (1970).

BARBARA HALL PARTEE

OPACITY, COREFERENCE, AND PRONOUNS*

ABSTRACT. The problem discussed here is to find a basis for a uniform treatment of the relation between pronouns and their antecedents, taking into account both linguists' and philosophers' approaches. The two main candidates would appear to be the linguists' notion of coreference and the philosophers' notion of pronouns as variables. The notion of coreference can be extended to many but not all cases where the antecedent is non-referential. The pronouns-as-variables approach appears to come closer to full generality, but there are some examples of 'pronouns of laziness' which appear to resist either of the two approaches.

0. INTRODUCTION

The main concern of this paper is the relation between pronouns and their antecedents. A view widespread among linguists, first stated by Postal (1968), is that the relation is one of (presupposed) *coreference*. Philosophers tend to regard pronouns in the vernacular as generally analogous to variables in a logical notation, and many linguists are coming to share this view for at least some instances of pronouns. In order to dispute the adequacy of coreference as a basis for all pronominalization[1] (Section 2), it is necessary first to discuss the distinction between referential and non-referential noun phrases (Section 1). The treatment of pronouns as variables is brought up in Section 2.2.3, and the possibility of treating all pronouns in that way is discussed in Section 3.

1. REFERENTIAL AND NON-REFERENTIAL NOUN PHRASES

In both the philosophical and the linguistic literature there has been general recognition of the ambiguity of sentences like the following:

(1)   John would like to marry *a girl his parents don't approve of.*

The description of the ambiguity can take a variety of forms. Informally, we can say that in one case John has a particular girl in mind to marry, and the fact that his parents don't approve of her is descriptive information about that girl; in the other case, no particular girl is meant and it might

Davidson and Harman (eds.), Semantics of Natural Language, 415–441. *All rights reserved*
Copyright © 1972 by D. Reidel Publishing Company Dordrecht-Holland

even be the case that no such girl exists – here having the disapproval of his parents is not a description of a particular girl whose hand John is seeking but an attribute John will consider in his wife-hunting. Some linguists (e.g. Fillmore (1967)) have suggested that the ambiguity be represented as a distinction between two indefinite articles, distinguished by a feature [+/− Specific]. Some linguists and many philosophers prefer to represent the ambiguity as one of scope of an existential quantifier (in some sense realized as the indefinite article), i.e. as (2) vs. (3) or something of the sort.

(2)   ($\exists x$) (x is a girl John's parents don't approve of $\wedge$ John would like to marry x)

(3)   John would like ($\exists x$) (x is a girl John's parents don't approve of $\wedge$ John marries x)

Another way of describing the ambiguity follows the distinction made for definite noun phrases by Donnellan (1966) between a *referential* and an *attributive* use of a noun phrase, about which more will be said below. Still others have characterized the difference as stemming from whether or not there is a presupposition on the part of the speaker and/or on the part of John[2] that an object fitting the description actually exists.

These characterizations of the ambiguity of (1) are not unrelated to each other, and without further evidence there is no particular reason to regard any one of them as more incisive than any other. It is therefore helpful to consider what sorts of sentences (1) may be taken as exemplifying. The sentence contains the verbal expression *would like*, an expression which is commonly said to designate a 'propositional attitude' (e.g. Quine (1960)), like *believes*, *hopes*, and perhaps *tries*. Such verbs can be followed by sentences (which may be transformed into infinitive phrases or gerunds, depending on the syntactic requirements of the governing verb), and the noun phrase positions in these embedded sentences are *opaque*, according to Quine's definition ((1960), pp. 142–146), since substitution of coreferential terms in these positions does not necessarily preserve truth-value: cf. examples (4) and (5).

(4)   John believes that *Cicero* denounced Catiline.

(5)   John believes that *Tully* denounced Catiline.

The type of ambiguity exemplified by sentence (1) has quite commonly,

I believe, been held to occur only in opaque contexts. Thus further examples would typically be:

(6)   Dick Tracy believes that *a man with the third finger of his right hand missing* killed the Painted Lady.

(7)   Bill is trying to catch *a snipe*.

And it is ordinarily assumed, I think, that the indefinite noun phrases in the following sentences are unambiguous, having only the sense of 'a particular individual'.

(8)   John married *a girl his parents didn't approve of*.

(9)   Bill caught *a snipe*.

This view stems, I imagine, from thinking of the ambiguity in (1), (6), and (7) as characterized primarily by the presence or absence of the presupposition that an object fitting the given description exists. Clearly in (8) and (9), unlike (1) and (7), there is such a presupposition of existence. Sentences (1) and (7), but not (8) and (9), could be followed without anomaly by the clause 'but no such creature exists'.

I think there may be a confusion here, however, and that by comparing an ambiguity in definite noun phrases discussed by Donnellan (1966), one may come around to the view that opaque contexts just make particularly significant an ambiguity which is actually present in a much broader range of cases. Consider example (10):

(10)   John wants to murder *the man who lives in Apt. 3*.

The object of the embedded sentence is a definite noun phrase, and any interpretation of the sentence includes a presupposition that such a man exists. But there are still two different interpretations of the sentence which are quite parallel to the two interpretations of sentence (1). Under one interpretation, the object of John's hatred is a particular individual, and the definite description is being used by the speaker to refer to that individual. Under the other interpretation, John may not know who lives in Apt. 3, but because he lives directly below Apt. 3 and is fed up with the noise above him he has decided that he wants to kill whatever man it is that lives up there. This second use of the definite noun phrase is what Donnellan calls 'attributive' as opposed to referential. Now if it is true that this ambiguity is parallel to the ambiguity in (1), then there is something more than a presupposition of existence at stake, since both senses of

(10) include such a presupposition. Furthermore, it is quite easy to see that opacity is not necessary to produce ambiguities like those in (10). Consider (11), which is a slight variant of an example of Donnellan's:

(11)   *The man who murdered Smith* is insane.

There is no evident opacity involved, but there are still two ways the definite noun phrase may be understood: either the speaker is asserting of a particular individual, referred to by the definite noun phrase, that that individual is insane; or the speaker is asserting that whoever it is that murdered Smith is insane – i.e. the definite noun phrase gives a characterization of an individual not necessarily otherwise known[3], and the sentence asserts that whatever individual is so characterized may be further characterized as insane. But the existence of such an individual is still presupposed in both interpretations, since the use of the definite article always carries such a presupposition. Thus the distinction between the referential and attributive uses of noun phrases must be independent of the distinction between noun phrases with existential presuppositions and those without, at least for definite noun phrases.

Now let us turn back to the indefinite noun phrases. Consider (12):

(12)   John succeeded in marrying *a girl his parents didn't approve of*.

It seems to me that there is now a clear presupposition that such a girl exists, but that there are still two interpretations matching those of (1): i.e. either he succeeded in marrying *that girl* or he succeeded in marrying *such a girl*. I am not clear as to whether philosophers would typically regard 'succeed in' as setting up an opaque context or not; but I am quite sure that (8) and (9) would not be regarded as opaque, and just a little exercise of the imagination can, I think, convince one that they can be used as reports of success with the same ambiguity[4] as (12).

What I am trying to suggest is that the ambiguity exemplified by sentence (1) is restricted neither to indefinite noun phrases nor to opaque contexts; it is present in most of the examples considered so far, although one interpretation may be much more natural than the other in some contexts. The prominence of one or the other reading appears to depend on the relation between the significance of the description used in the noun phrases and whatever else is asserted in the sentence. The italicized noun phrases in the following sentences are most likely to be interpreted referentially, since their descriptive content has no particularly strong semantic relation to the content of the rest of the sentence, and is much more easily interpretable as intended to identify or partially identify a particular individual.

(13)   John is dating *a girl from Alabama that he met several summers ago*.

(14)   We left the dog tied to *the back fence*.

Names are almost always used referentially, since they have virtually no descriptive content; the same is true of indefinite noun phrases of the form *a certain x*.

In the non-referential, or attributive, use of a noun phrase, the concern is not with naming a particular object but with giving descriptive characteristics which are semantically significant as part of the content of the sentence. There may often be an associated object, as in (8), (9), (12) and in (15) below, and presumably with all the definite noun phrases. But in such cases the rest of the sentence is not simply about the object *qua* object, however; the particular description used is essential to the meaning of the sentence. An example which seems unambiguously non-referential may help to illustrate this point:

(15)   Since I heard that from *a doctor*, I'm inclined to take it seriously.

In (15) we may suppose that whatever it was that the speaker heard was something to which the special competence of doctors is relevant. If we replace *a doctor* by some other phrase, we get rather different interpretations of what sort of thing was heard:

(16)   Since I heard that from *a fellow who lives upstairs*, I'm inclined to take it seriously.

Note that the most natural interpretation is still attributive rather than referential; but now to make any sense of it we must assume that what was heard was something to do with conditions on the upper floors or the like – i.e. something to which this fellow's living upstairs has relevance. Why, by the way, are we disinclined to read either (15) of (16) as referential? Such an interpretation would be something like 'Since I heard it from x, I'm inclined to take it seriously', where x is a particular individual whom we identify to our hearer by some description. Now either the hearer also knows x or he doesn't; if he does, then we will use a definite noun phrase rather than an indefinite one; and if he doesn't, then we will want to find a description which indicates to our hearer why x's word is to be taken seriously – but this *is* to use the description attributively.

There are some interesting ways in which such a noun phrase can be interpreted referentially[5]. Suppose, for sentence (16), speaker and hearer share the information that all the fellows who live upstairs are engineering students who know all about engines and motors and such, and thus count as reliable sources of information about car troubles, for instance. Then (16) *may* be (although it still need not be) taken as referential, in that the speaker might just as well have said 'John Jones', but has chosen not to pick out for his hearer *which* member of this set they are both familiar with he is talking about. Then living upstairs is not itself what makes the fellow's word reliable, but simply provides a description which is sufficient to narrow down the class of possible referents to some whose reliability is accounted for by other characteristics.

If sentence (17) below is to be regarded as contained in sentence (15), the fact that *a doctor* in (15) is interpreted non-referentially would seem to offer further support to the claim that even a non-opaque sentence like (17) should be represented as ambiguous.

(17)   I heard that from *a doctor*.

Otherwise, if (17) is regarded as necessarily referential, (17) cannot be contained in (15). Furthermore, the following two-sentence discourse, which certainly contains (17), would be quite bizarre if *a doctor* could not be understood attributively.

(18)   I heard that from *a doctor*. That's why I'm inclined to take it seriously.

Having argued that the ambiguity in sentence (1) is quite general in both definite and indefinite noun phrases, let us return to the question of how it is to be regarded. The ambiguity does not depend on a presupposition of existence, as witnessed by all the examples with definite descriptions and by sentences like (12). The ambiguity also does not seem to be uniformly regardable as a scope difference, since (a) examples like (8), (9), and (11) have no place to vary scope; and (b) cases with definite noun phrases like (10) remain ambiguous even if the scope of the definite description is varied (i.e. *The man in Apt. 3 is such that* ... is still ambiguous).

The two remaining possibilities for representing the ambiguity, namely Fillmore's [± Specific] indefinite article and Donnellan's referential/ attributive distinction suffer only from the fact that the former is restricted to indefinites[6] and the latter to definites. It seems reasonable, therefore, to suggest that one or the other term be generalized to cover both the indefinite and the definite cases. I will continue to use the terms referential/ attributive or referential/non-referential for both cases (even though there may be some discomfort felt in using the term 'referential' for indefinites) since they are easiest to relate directly to the notion of coreference. Whether the ambiguity should be considered syntactic, semantic, or pragmatic, I still leave open.

2. SEMANTIC RELATIONS BETWEEN PRONOUNS AND THEIR ANTECEDENTS

2.1. *Linguistic Treatments of Pronouns; Coreference*

The linguistic literature on pronouns is extensive and increasing rapidly; I will give here only a brief sketch of the aspects most relevant to the present discussion.[7]

In the earliest transformational grammars, it was suggested that a pronominalization transformation optionally replaces a repeated noun phrase by a personal pronoun. Thus (20) could be derived from (19), and (22) from (21).

(19)   John lost *a black pen* yesterday and Bill found *a black pen* today.

(20)   John lost *a black pen* yesterday and Bill found *it* today.

(21)   I pushed *the empty box* and *the empty box* fell over.

(22)   I pushed *the empty box* and *it* fell over.

On such a view, all anaphoric pronouns were regarded as what Geach (1964) calls 'pronouns of laziness'; reference was considered irrelevant to the syntax.

Later the pronoun *one* was brought into the picture as an alternative replacement for a repeated indefinite noun phrase:

(23)   John lost *a black pen* yesterday and Bill found *one* today.

The contrast between *one* and the personal pronouns has been variously regarded. Some linguists consider (23) and (20) both to be directly derivable from (19), the choice of pronouns resulting in different semantic interpretations as to coreferentiality. Others argue that only (23) is directly derivable from (19), with (20) passing through an intermediate stage, (24) below, so that the difference in coreferentiality is pinned on the 'definitization transformation'.

(24)   John lost *a black pen* yesterday and Bill found *the black pen* today.

Following this latter tack, it has been suggested that the pronoun *one* in fact never replaces noun phrases at all, but only nouns, and does so regardless of whether the containing noun phrase is definite or indefinite. Examples (25) and (26) below show this possibility clearly, and example (23) can be regarded in the same way, since it can be argued that rules are independently needed which would change *a black one* to *a one* and then to *one*[8] (see UESP (1968)).

(25)   John lost a black *pen* yesterday and Bill found a gray *one* today.
(26)   I pushed the empty *box* and the full *one* fell over.

Postal (1968) was one of the first to seriously argue that reference should be represented in the syntactic structure, and that the formation of personal pronouns should depend on coreferentiality, not simply on formal identity. According to his proposals, the italicized noun phrases in (19) would carry referential indices, and (20) would be derived (via (24)) only if those indices were identical.

Other recent suggestions include the possibilities that definitization and pronominalization may not be transformational rules at all, so that all of the definite articles and personal pronouns in sentences (19)–(26) might be generated directly in the base component, with semantic rules assigning the possible anaphoric relations. But even within such an 'interpretive' approach to pronominalization, coreference is accepted as the fundamental relation to be assigned to a personal pronoun and its antecedent by such interpretive rules.

A first look at some sentences whose noun phrases can be interpreted non-referentially will support the view that coreference is the basis of the pronoun-antecedent relation. Consider the following sentences:

(27)   John was looking for *a gold watch* and Bill was looking for *a gold watch* too.

(28)   John was looking for *a gold watch* and Bill was looking for *the gold watch* too.

(29)   John was looking for *a gold watch* and Bill was looking for *it* too.

(30)   John was looking for *a gold watch* and Bill was looking for *one* too.

If both noun phrases in (27) are interpreted as referential, and the referents are the same, then (27) must be converted into either (28) or (29), which are synonymous. If both are referential but the referents are not the same, then (27) may optionally be converted to (30), but not to (28) or (29). The same is true if neither noun phrase is referential. It is hard, perhaps because of the parallel structure of the two clauses, to imagine an interpretation with one of the noun phrases referential and the other not. Such an interpretation may be possible for a sentence such as the following[9]:

(31)   She's marrying *a doctor* next week – someday I would like to marry *one* too.

If this can be interpreted with the first *a doctor* referential and the second non-referential, then it appears that the same pronominalization facts hold for such a case as for the cases where both noun phrases are non-referential or both are referential but with different referents.

It would appear from sentences (27)–(31) then that a personal pronoun is substituted for one of two noun phrases only when both noun phrases are referential and furthermore coreferential[10]; all other combinations appear to allow only pronominalization to *one*. In the following section, we will show that the situation is not so clear-cut.

2.2. *Pronouns with Non-Referential Antecedents*

2.2.1. *Definite Noun Phrases.* The following sentences are similar to (27)–(29) except for containing definite noun phrases:

(32)   John was looking for *the man who murdered Smith* and Bill was looking for *the man who murdered Smith* too.

(33)   ... and Bill was looking for *him* too.

Here both sentences are ambiguous as between referential and non-referential use of the noun phrases. (Whether it is possible here to interpret one noun phrase as referential and the other not is a question beyond the subtlety of my intuitions.) The puzzling thing about (33) is that *him* can occur in the interpretation where neither noun phrase is referential, although it couldn't in the corresponding indefinite case, (30). It is possible to maintain that coreferentiality is involved even in this non-referential case, however, by looking at the presuppositions involved in the use of the definite article with a singular noun phrase.

Compare (27) and (32) in the senses where neither noun phrase is referential. In both cases John and Bill will each consider their searches successful when they find something that fits the given description. However, the use of the indefinite article in *a gold watch* signals the presupposition that there may be more than one gold watch (or possibly none), whereas the use of the definite article in *the man who murdered Smith* signals a presupposition that there is one and only one such man. Hence in the definite case only, the object of John's search, to be consistent with the presuppositions of the sentence, *must* be coreferential with the object of Bill's search even though neither of them may have any idea what particular object that object is. The coreferentiality is here determined by inference from the presuppositions underlying the use of definite article. In the case where the noun phrases are used referentially, the coreferentiality could be determined simply by comparing the referents to see if they are the same; but the non-referential case suggests that the notion of coreferentiality that is playing a role in pronominalization is not dependent in this way on a prior identification of referents for the noun phrases.

Although the foregoing argument may seem a plausible way to save the primacy of coreferentiality, examples like the following appear to refute it.

(34)   John claimed to have found *the solution to the problem*, but Bill was sure he had found *it*.

(35)   Senator Green believed that he had nominated *the winner of the election*, but Senator White believed that she had nominated *him*.

(36)   John thought *the author of that book* was probably a man, but Bill thought *it* was more likely a woman.

Each of these sentences is ambiguous as between referential and non-referential use of the noun phrases. In the referential sense, the three sentences describe disputes over which of two people found a certain solution, which senator nominated a certain person, and what the sex of a certain known individual is, respectively; in all of these cases, coreference is involved in the ordinary way. In the non-referential senses, however, the disputes seem actually to be over the referents of the descriptive phrases. In (34), for instance, John claims that the thing he has found is the solution to the problem, while Bill claims that the solution is the thing he has found. Thus in spite of a presupposition that there is one and only one solution to the problem, the two noun phrases apparently have different referents. In (35), similarly, the non-referential sense involves an argument over who the winner of the next election will be, the one nominated by Green or the one nominated by White. Thus the argument appears to be over the referent of the noun phrase, so that again the two occurrences are not coreferential. Sentence (36) is similar, with the added twist that *it* is used here for a human, in spite of the fact that *he* is the usual sex-neutral human pronoun; the use of *it* may perhaps be explainable on the grounds that the gender in this case is not simply unknown but actually in dispute, and either *he* or *she* would seem to beg the question.

Sentences (34)–(36) in their non-referential senses thus appear to violate the principle of coreference. The noun phrase pairs appear instead to be 'codesignative', or 'cosignificant', but so presumably are the non-referential interpretations of the noun phrases in an indefinite case such as (27), and these do not allow personal pronouns. Thus sentences like (34)–(36) appear to constitute a real problem for any attempt to find a uniform basis for the pronoun-antecedent relationship.

It may be possible to argue that coreference is still the basic relation even in these cases by appealing to the sort of examples given in footnote 10, one of which is repeated below as (37). That is, if I can talk as in (37) about *my home* having been in one place and now being in another even though two different 'physical referents' are involved, it seems a small step to imagine a dispute taking place as to where my home is, as in (38).

(37)   *My home* was once in Maryland, but now *it*'s in Los Angeles.

(38)   John thinks *my home* is in Maryland, but Bill thinks *it*'s in Los Angeles.

Now in (38) the speaker is clearly not involved in the dispute, and there is therefore no reason to say that he assigns two different referents to the two noun phrases. But from (38) it is not such a large step to sentences (34)–(36), so perhaps we should conclude that the mere fact that a sentence describes a dispute over the referent of a noun phrase does not by itself establish non-coreferentiality. (The speaker may take sides in the dispute, but he cannot, as it were, take both sides at once.)

2.2.2. *Indefinite Noun Phrases.* Let us now turn to some examples which violate the earlier generalization suggested for pronominalization with indefinite antecedent. What was suggested on the basis of sentences (27)–(31) was that with indefinites, both referentiality and coreferentiality were required for the use of the personal pronoun; but in the examples given, there was no way to imagine coreferentiality holding independently of referentiality. But there is a class of sentences which has been discussed recently in the linguistic literature (e.g. Baker (1966), Karttunen (1968a, b,), Dean (1968)) where personal pronouns can have non-referential indefinite antecedents.

(39)   John wants to catch *a fish* and eat *it* for supper.
(40)   If John marries *a girl his parents disapprove of*, they will make life quite unpleasant for *her*.
(41)   I expect that John will buy *a car* and that he will drive *it* to work every day.

Sentences (39)–(41) are all perfectly well-formed and interpretable as having non-referential noun phrases in the antecedent position. They are clearly different from (29) – note that we could insert parenthetically 'any old fish' after 'a fish' in (39), but we could not insert 'any old gold watch' after 'a gold watch' in (29). How can we account for this pronominalization then?

We clearly cannot infer coreferentiality from any presuppositions here as we could for the non-referential reading of (33). What's happening here seems to be more complex: let us look particularly at sentence (40) and consider what sorts of noun phrase could paraphrase the final pronoun. I claim that (42) provides a rough paraphrase but (43) does not:

(42)   ..., they will make life quite unpleasant for *the girl he marries*.

(43)   ..., they will make life quite unpleasant for *the girl they disapprove of.*

From this we can conclude that the second clause of (40) carries a presupposition that John marries one and only one girl, since such a presupposition is generally signalled by the definite article, but does not presuppose that only one girl fits the description provided by the indefinite noun phrase in the first clause. (That the presupposition is still in some sense a hypothetical one is signalled by the use of a simple present tense *marries* in the final relative clause of (42) rather than a plain future *will marry*. This kind of tense shift is characteristic of if-clauses and other 'hypothetical' subordinate clauses.) Janet Dean (1968) has pointed out that for sentences like (39) and (41), the noun phrase most nearly equivalent to the pronoun is as in (44) and (45), not (46) or (47):

(44)   John wants to catch *a fish* and eat *the fish he catches* for supper.
(45)   ... and that he will drive *the car he buys* to work every day.
(46)   John wants to catch *a fish* and eat *the fish he wants to catch* for supper.
(47)   ... and that he will drive *the car that I expect him to buy* to work every day.

Thus one way of looking at these sentences is to say that in the first part of the sentence, the context describes a possible state of affairs or possible world in which an object of a certain sort is involved. Fulfillment of this state of affairs is in all these cases such that there would then be a unique object responsible for making the hypothetical world actual. I.e. in (39), where John wants to catch a fish, we know what defines success, namely the first fish he catches (whether or not he then catches others); similarly, the satisfaction of the antecedent of (40) involves John's getting married, which then establishes a unique girl to whom he is married (note that John's marriage would *not* establish a unique girl his parents disapprove of); in (41), if the first part of my expectation is fulfilled, there will then be a unique car whose purchase fulfilled that expectation.

The second part of the sentence, the part containing the pronoun, makes sense in all of these cases only when interpreted as presupposing the actualization of this possible state of affairs. That is, John can't eat a fish until he actually catches one; John's parents are not going to harrass such a girl until John has gotten married to one; John isn't expected to drive a car until he has bought one. Consequently the second part of the sentence presupposes the existence of the unique object which was responsible for actualizing the state of affairs – the caught fish, the married girl, the bought car. Coreference then is *not* directly between the noun phrase in the first part of the sentence and that in the second; the antecedent for the coreference is in fact not expressed *as a noun phrase* anywhere in the sentence. Coreference rather seems to be with that unique though hypothetical entity which would be crucially involved in actualizing the possible world characterized in the first part of the sentence.

Notice how this kind of account properly excludes (29) from being interpreted with the first noun phrase non-referential. The first part of the sentence could indeed describe a hypothetical state of affairs which would become actual on John's finding a gold watch. But the second half of the sentence does *not* presuppose the actualization of that state of affairs and hence does *not* presuppose the existence of a unique gold watch found by John.

Also excluded are (48) and (49) below (in a non-referential sense), since the hypothetical state of affairs described in the first clause cannot be correlated with a unique entity which could then be presupposed in the second clause.

(48)   *John probably won't catch *a fish*, though he'd like to eat *it* for supper.

(49)   *I expect that John will not buy *a car* and that he will not drive *it* to work every day.

But note the following sentence, which does allow pronominalization in a context superficially similar to that of (48).

(50)   John won't buy *a car* because he wouldn't have room for *it* in his garage.

Here the explanation, syntactically suggested by the conditional *wouldn't* in the second clause[11], seems to be that (50) is actually a result of ellipsis from something like (51):

(51)   John won't buy *a car* because if he did buy *a car*, he wouldn't have room for *it* in his garage.

Then the second *a car* can be seen to be a proper antecedent for the *it* exactly in the manner of (40).

Note the difference incidentally, between a second occurrence which presupposes actualization and a second occurrence which asserts it: only the former allows pronominalization if the first occurrence is non-referential.

(52)   John was trying to catch *a fish*. He wanted to eat *it* for supper.

(53)   John was trying to catch *a fish*. He finally caught *it*.

The second sentence of (53) is not a possible continuation of the discourse if *a fish* in the first is non-referential because it asserts instead of presupposing the actualization of the fish-catching.

The pair of sentences of (52) also show that pronominalization with non-referential indefinite antecedent is not a matter of both noun phrases being within the same opaque context, since neither *want* nor *try* in (52) is under the scope of the other. In fact, the second of a pair of non-referential noun phrases within a single opaque context does *not* ordinarily pronominalize to *it*, but only to *one*, just as in the non-embedded examples (27)–(31).

(54)   John wants to catch *a fish* or buy *one*.

(55)   If Susan married *a rich man* and Sally married *one* too, Clara would be jealous.

For this reason, the following examples are somewhat puzzling, since they do seem to involve a pair of noun phrases being within the same opaque context, without the second occurrence presupposing any sort of fulfillment of hypothesis.

(56)   The agency is looking for *a model* to use in the toothpaste ad; *she* must have red hair and freckles.

(57)   We need *a secretary* and we need *her* soon.

Note that (57) is very closely paraphrasable by (58):

(58)   We need *a secretary* and we need *one* soon.

It seems that (57) comes closer than (58) to presupposing that one will in fact find a secretary, but the second clause of (57) cannot be said to presuppose the actual finding in the way that the second clause of (39) or (52) presupposes the catching of a fish.

There are no straightforward syntactic clues that serve to identify those non-referential cases where pronominalization is appropriate; the following sentence pairs certainly have very similar superficial syntactic structure, and I know of no arguments for giving them clearly contrasting deep structures. Yet the pronoun in (59) is quite normal and that in (60) bizarre; (60) would sound natural with *one* instead of *him*.

(59)   Susan would like to marry *a millionaire* and run off with all his money. If she doesn't divorce *him* within a couple of years, her plan will probably go awry.

(60)   Susan would like to marry *a millionaire* and run off with all his money. If she doesn't meet *him* within a couple of years, her plan will probably go awry.

The only difference between (59) and (60) is that between the verb *divorce*, which presupposes marriage, and *meet*, which (in our culture at least) excludes that presupposition[12].

2.2.3. *Quantified Noun Phrases and Related Cases.* In all of the examples treated so far, it has been possible to regard the personal pronoun as in some sense a replacement for a noun phrase identical to the antecedent noun phrase, i.e. as a 'pronoun of laziness'. But when the antecedent contains a quantifier or a word like *only*, it is no longer semantically plausible to so regard the pronoun.

(61)   *No one* would put the blame on *himself*.

(62)   If *anyone* had been there, I would have seen *him* (*them*).

(63)   *Nearly every doctor* gives special attention to patients whose cases interest *him*.

Logicians have typically been much more concerned with pronouns of this sort than with the sorts exemplified earlier, and therefore need no introduction to the idea, found for instance in Quine (1960, 1961), that pronouns might be represented as bound variables. I discuss it here in part because it is still a relatively new approach within the linguistic literature, but more importantly in order to raise some questions about the domain of its applicability. Geach (1967) for one has made it clear that he does not regard all pronouns as corresponding to bound variables, but neither he nor anyone else that I know of has tried to draw a sharp line between those pronouns that can (or should) be regarded as bound variables, and those that cannot (or should not). As a preliminary to opening up this problem (to which I do not have a solution), I will indicate in this section some of the uses of pronouns to which the bound variable treatment seems particularly appropriate.

In sentences (61)–(63), the pronouns are clearly not substitutions for *no one, anyone,* and *nearly every doctor.* Furthermore, the question of who the pronouns refer to does not even seem to make sense. In the examples of the preceding section, singular pronouns appeared to have some sort of reference, even when the individual referred to was in some sense hypothetical. But in (61)–(63) the singular pronoun certainly does not refer to any one individual, even hypothetically. Nor, as Quine and Geach have pointed out, do the antecedents refer to any individual or any set; sentences (61) and (62) say something about the set of all people and (63) about the set of all doctors, but not because the italicized noun phrases in any sense *refer* to those sets.

The notation of quantificational logic was designed in part to represent perspicuously just such pronoun usage. Sentences (61)–(63) can be represented in something quite close to that notation with relatively little violence to their overt syntactic structure [13], e.g. as in (64)–(66) below:

(64)   Not (there is some person x) (x would put the blame on x)
(65)   ([for] any person x) (if x had been there, I would have seen x)
(66)   ([for] nearly every doctor x) (x gives special attention to patients whose case interests x)

Note that this sort of representation requires an overt distinction between the two roles simultaneously played by a quantified noun phrase in the vernacular, namely the binding by the quantifier and the role of the noun phrase as one of the arguments of some predicate. In the formula (65) there has in addition been a change in the relative scopes of the quantifier and the *if*, since the surface form of (62) does not show how the pronoun can be within the scope of the quantifier [14]. Whether such differences should be regarded as due to some sloppiness in natural language or as unnatural artifacts of the formal language is an open question.

Another instance of the usefulness of variables and binding to elucidate the role of pronouns is a classical example which is discussed by Geach (1962) and more recently by a number of linguists. The formulas below the two sentences suggest very roughly how variables may be involved.

(67)   Only *Lucifer* pities *Lucifer*:
         only for $x =$ Lucifer (x pities Lucifer)
(68)   Only *Lucifer* pities *himself*:
         only for $x =$ Lucifer (x pities x)

The non-referentiality of *himself* in (68) matches that of the prefix *self-* in (69) below:

(69)   Only Lucifer is self-pitying.

The following pair of examples appear at first blush to resemble the plain non-referential indefinite cases of the preceding section[15], since the antecedent is clearly non-referential in each case; but the semantic connection between pronoun and antecedent is clearly not of the 'hypothesis – presupposition of fulfillment' type.

(70)   John couldn't catch *a fish* if *it* jumped into his lap.
(71)   Susan wouldn't marry *a man with less than a million dollars*.
         if *he* were the last man alive.

Note that *a* in these two examples could be replaced by *any* and that the *if*'s are implicitly *even if*'s. Thus the sentences might be represented roughly as follows:

(72)   (any fish x) (even if x jumped into John's lap, John couldn't
         catch x)
(73)   (any man with less than a million dollars x) (even if x were the
         last man alive, Susan wouldn't marry x)

(The sentences (70) and (71) seem to be unusual in that *one* or *such a one* could be used instead of the personal pronouns with virtually no change in the total meaning of the sentence. But actually the usual difference between *one* and a personal pronoun is present here as well: if *one* were used in (70) or (71) it would be only by our understanding of the situation described by the sentence that we would infer any sort of sameness between a fish to be caught and a fish in the lap, or a man to be married and the last man alive.)

Another interesting case where the use of variables does not at first seem called for is the following ambiguous sentence, to be read with primary stresses (´) on *John* and *Bill* and weak stresses (˘) on *his wife*.

(74)   Jóhn was´ kissing hĭs wĭfe and *Bill* was kissing hĭs wĭfe too.

One's first impression is that all the noun phrases are referential, the ambiguity resting simply on whether the second *his* is *Bill's* or *John's*. If the second *his* is interpreted as *John's*, a purely referential reading seems quite appropriate. The stress pattern is then like that of (75):

(75)   Jóhn was kissing Mări and Bíll was kissing Mări too.

But I want to suggest that the other reading is not simply a substitution of *his* for *Bill's*. Suppose Mary is John's wife and Susan is Bill's wife; one cannot with the stress pattern of (74) and (75) say:

(76)   *Jóhn was kissing Mări and Bíll was kissing Sŭsan too.

Nor is *too* permissible in (76), at least not in the sense of 'and so was Bill'. The well-formed way to say something like (76) is as represented in (77); the same stress pattern is found in (78) and (79).

(77)   Jóhn was kissing Mári and Bíll was kissing Súsan.
(78)   Jóhn was kissing Jóhn's wĭfe and Bíll was kissing Bíll's wĭfe.
(79)   Jóhn was kissing hís wĭfe and Bíll was kissing hís wĭfe.

But (79) is not what we started with, i.e. the reading of (74) in which the second *his* seemed to be *Bill's*. Sentence (79) is indeed a case of fully referential noun phrases, and the two pronouns can be taken as substitutions for the respective nouns. But sentence (74) has a reading not yet accounted for, and it is here that the notion of variables comes into play.

The stress pattern of (74) is typical of conjoined sentences with contrasting subjects and identical predicates; hence it would be optimal from the point of view of the phonology to be able to represent *kissing his wife* identically in both clauses. One might suggest that it is only the superficial form of the words that counts in determining such a stress pattern, but then the pattern of (79) is unaccounted for. (Note that (75) has no analog to (79).) The rather unnatural paraphrase (80) below clearly has identical predicates on the two subjects. The evidence thus suggests that the reading of (74) in question must involve the binding of variables as in (81) rather than directly referential pronouns.

(80)   Jóhn was ŏwn-wĭfe-kĭssing and Bíll was ŏwn-wĭfe-kĭssing too.

(81)   (for $x=$ John and for $x=$ Bill) (x was kissing x's wife)[16]

The examples of this section serve to suggest some of the situations in which the notion of bound variables or something like it seems necessary to explain the pronoun-antecedent connection. Further relevant examples can be found in Karttunen (1969b). Next we turn to the question of how far this view can be extended.

3. THE PROBLEM OF TREATING PRONOUNS UNIFORMLY

The notion of coreferentiality, taken as holding between two noun phrases each of which has a referent, has been seen to cover only a subset of the uses of personal pronouns. The notion could be extended to include a sort of 'hypothetical coreferentiality' for the cases with non-referential indefinite antecedents, such as (39), (40), (41). Possibly it could also be extended to include the non-referential definite cases, except that it does not seem to be a satisfactory notion for examples like (34)–(36). Something like 'codesignation' seems to be more appropriate for such cases, but that kind of notion would clearly not be generalizable, both because it would apply equally well to pronominalization with *one* and because proper names, which certainly can be pronominalized with personal pronouns, presumably have reference but not designation.

The most serious problems for the notion of coreferentiality as a fully general basis for pronominalization arise in the cases that must be treated as variables. Certainly there is some kind of sameness between two instances of a single variable, but equally certainly it is not a sameness of reference, and furthermore the variable treatment requires breaking up the noun phrase into structurally very separate parts.

A striking counterexample to the claim that coreference might underly all pronominalization is provided by Karttunen (1969b); the *his* is to be interpreted as *his own*.

(82)   The man who gave *his paycheck* to his wife was wiser than the man who gave *it* to his mistress.

We must conclude that the notion of coreferentiality cannot provide a uniform basis for the treatment of pronouns. Since it fails primarily because of the need to treat some pronouns as variables, the most promising hope for a uniform treatment would seem to lie in regarding all pronouns as variables. Quine appears to hold such a position,[17] and Geach seems at least to regard it as possible, although in practice he often discriminates between pronouns as bound variables and pronouns of laziness. But as Karttunen points out, examples like (82) above are incompatible with the treatment of pronouns as variables, just as they are with the primacy of coreference. The *it* in (82) must be treated as a pronoun of laziness.[18]

If some pronouns must be treated as pronouns of laziness and others must not be, the problem is then to find either a clear criterion for distinguishing the two types or else some justification for regarding many pronouns as ambiguous. I have no solution to this problem, but I want to bring up some matters that seem relevant.

Geach (1962) argues that some pronouns which *could* be regarded as pronouns of laziness *should* rather be regarded as bound variables. His argument runs as follows (p. 128):

"(83)   If *any man* owns a donkey, *he* beats it.
 (84)   If *Smith* owns a donkey, *he* beats it.

The pronoun 'he' is replaceable by 'Smith' in (84) without changing the import of the proposition; it is not thus replaceable by 'any man' in (83); so it looks as if it were a pronoun of laziness in (84), but not in (83). All the same, (84) predicates of Smith precisely what (83) predicates of any man; both contain the same unambiguous complex predicable 'If − owns a donkey, he beats it', which is incomplete in sense, ... as any one-place predicable is until it is attached to a subject or quasi subject. On the other hand, the proposition:

 (85)   If Smith owns a donkey, Smith beats it.

contains the completely different predicable 'If − owns a donkey, Smith beats it'; ... Thus the wholly different sense of the predicable ... shows that even in (84) 'he' has a definite logical role of its own, and is not a mere pronoun of laziness − not a mere device for avoiding the repetition of 'Smith'."

Note, by the way, the misleadingness of the word 'mere' in the light of (82), where the pronoun must be treated as one of laziness precisely to account for its logical role.

The kind of argument used by Geach above can be extended to many other cases. For instance, the sentence (74) above (in the sense of (80)) provides a similar kind of evidence for positing a variable in (86), even though (86) in isolation could be handled simply as a case of a pronoun of laziness.

(86)   *John* was kissing *his* wife.

But Geach's claim that 'he' in (84) is unambiguously not a replacement for 'Smith' seems to me somewhat problematical. Consider a simple reflexive sentence like (87):

(87)   *Timmy* dressed *himself*.

By Geach's type of argument, the pronoun would not be regardable as a replacement for 'Timmy' because of sentences like (88):

(88)   *Only one two-year-old* dressed *himself*.

And yet to say that the predicable '——dressed Timmy' does not occur in (87) should preclude the possibility of discourses like (89) or (90) which seem perfectly well-formed:

(89)   Has anyone dressed Timmy yet? Yes, Timmy dressed himself.
(90)   Whoever dressed Timmy must be color-blind. Timmy dressed himself, so Timmy must be color-blind.

Similarly, the pronoun in (91) below could not, by Geach's kind of argument, be one of laziness because of sentences like (92), and yet should be so regardable if (91) is to be related to (93).

(91)   *John* set off a burglar alarm when *he* walked in.
(92)   *Someone* set off a burglar alarm when *he* walked in.
(93)   Something happened when *John* walked in.

Thus it would seem that Geach's line of argument should lead to the conclusion that many pronouns are syntactically ambiguous as between bound variables and pronouns of laziness. (The fact that most of the sentences may be semantically unambiguous would not be a crucial counter argument; cf. Geach's "cancelling-out fallacy" (1962).) Perhaps at this point some further more narrowly syntactic investigation of the relevant phenomena may prove to be of value. Certainly much more needs to be done to explain systematically the kinds of relations that can hold between a pronoun and its antecedent and the contexts in which the various relations can hold. What I have tried to do here is primarily to indicate some of the facts that need explaining and some of the problems that are likely to confront any attempts at simple explanations.

University of California, Los Angeles

BIBLIOGRAPHY

Bach, Emmon, 'Nouns and Noun Phrases' in *Universals in Linguistic Theory* (ed. by Emmon Bach and Robert T. Harms), Holt, Rinehart and Winston, Inc., New York, 1968, pp. 90–122.

Bach, Emmon, 'Anti-Pronominalization' (unpublished, University of Texas, Austin) 1969.

Bach, Emmon, 'Problominalization', *Linguistic Inquiry* 1 (1970) 121–122.

Bach, Emmon and Harms, Robert T., (eds.), *Universals in Linguistic Theory*, Holt, Rinehart and Winston, Inc., New York, 1968.

Baker, C. L., *Definiteness and Indefiniteness in English* (unpublished M.A. thesis, University of Illinois), 1966.

Dean, Janet, 'Nonspecific Noun Phrases in English' in Harvard Computational Laboratory Report No. NSF-20, Cambridge, Mass., 1968.

Donnellan, Keith, 'Reference and Definite Descriptions', *The Philosophical Review* 75 (1966) 281–304.

Fillmore, C. J., 'On the Syntax of Preverbs', *Glossa* 1 (1967) 91–125.

Geach, P. T., *Reference and Generality*, Cornell University Press, Ithaca, N.Y., 1962.

Geach, P. T., 'Intentional Identity', *Journal of Philosophy* 64 (1967) 627–632.

Geach, P. T., 'Quine's Syntactical Insights', *Synthese* 19 (1968) 118–129.

Kaplan, David, 'Quantifying In', *Synthese* 19 (1968–69) 178–214.

Karttunen, Lauri, *The Identity of Noun Phrases*, Rand Corporation Publication P-3756, Santa Monica, Calif., 1967.

Karttunen, Lauri, *What Do Referential Indices Refer to?*, Rand Corporation Publication P-3854, Santa Monica, Calif., 1968a.

Karttunen, Lauri, 'Co-Reference and Discourse' (read at the winter meeting, Linguistic Society of America, New York) 1968b.

Karttunen, Lauri, 'Migs and Pilots' (unpublished, University of Texas, Austin) 1969a.

Karttunen, Lauri, 'Pronouns and Variables' in *Papers from the Fifth Regional Meeting of the Chicago Linguistic Society* (ed. by Robert I. Binnick *et al.*), Dept. of Linguistics, University of Chicago, Chicago, Ill., 1969b.

Klima, E. S., 'Negation in English' in *The Structure of Language* (ed. by Jerry A. Fodor and Jerrold J. Katz), Prentice-Hall, Englewood Cliffs, N.J., 1964, pp. 246–323.

Langacker, Ronald, 'On Pronominalization and the Chain of Command' in *Modern*

438   BARBARA HALL PARTEE

Studies in English (ed. by David Reibel and Sanford Schane), Prentice-Hall, Englewood Cliffs, N.J., 1969, pp. 160–186.

McCawley, James D., 'The Role of Semantics in a Grammar' in *Universals in Linguistic Theory* (ed. by Emmon Bach and Robert T. Harms), Holt, Rinehart and
Winston, Inc., New York, 1968, pp. 124–169.

McCawley, James D., 'Where Do Noun Phrases Come from?', to appear in *Readings
in Transformational Grammar* (ed. by Roderick Jacobs and Peter S. Rosenbaum),
Blaisdell, Boston, Mass., forthcoming.

Postal, Paul M., 'On So-Called "Pronouns" in English' in *Georgetown University
Monograph Series on Languages and Linguistics*, Vol. 19 (ed. by Francis P. Dinneen,
S.J.), Washington, D.C., 1966, pp. 177–206.

Postal, Paul M., 'Cross-Over Phenomena: A Study in the Grammar of Coreference'
in *Specification and Utilization of a Transformational Grammar* (Scientific Report
No. 3), IBM Research Center, Yorktown Heights, N.Y., 1968.

Quine, W. V., *Word and Object*, M.I.T. Press, Cambridge, Mass., 1960.

Quine, W. V., *From a Logical Point of View*, Harvard University Press, Cambridge,
Mass., 1953, (2nd ed. 1961).

Ross, John R., *Constraints on Variables in Syntax* (unpublished Ph.D. dissertation,
M.I.T., Cambridge, Mass.), 1967.

Ross, John R., 'On the Cyclic Nature of English Pronominalization' in *To Honour
Roman Jakobson*, Vol. III, Mouton, The Hague, 1968, pp. 1669–1682.

Stockwell, R. P., Schachter, P. S., and Partee, B. H., *Integration of Transformational
Theories on English Syntax*, Government Document ESD-TR-68-419, Los Angeles,
1968 (UESP 1968).

REFERENCES

* Earlier versions of this paper, under various titles, were presented orally to the
Claremont Philosophical Discussion Group, the UCLA Linguistics Colloquium, the
IBM Watson Research Center, the IBM Systems Development Division at Endicott,
and at Princeton University. Criticisms and suggestions received on these occasions
have helped lead to many revisions and additions. I am particularly grateful for the
sympathetic encouragement given me by philosophers such as David Kaplan, Jack
Vickers, and Gilbert Harman in this attempt to communicate simultaneously with
linguists and philosophers.

The most important sources for the present work are the following: among linguists,
Postal (1968), for bringing the notion of coreference to prominence; Bach (1969, 1970),
for first pointing out some fundamental problems with the treatment of pronominalization as a substitution process; McCawley [1970, 1968], for his attempts to show logical
notation, including the use of variables, to be of linguistic relevance; and Karttunen
(1968a, b, 1969a, b), who has been exploring many of the same problems as are discussed here, and from whom a number of the examples below are taken or adapted
(some of which are originally due to Baker (1966)). Among philosophers, the main
sources are Quine (1960), for the notion of opacity and its relation to reference;
Donnellan (1966), for claiming a referential/attributive distinction in definite noun
phrases even in transparent contexts; and Geach (1962) for distinguishing 'pronouns
of laziness' from pronouns used like variables.

1 The term *pronominalization* suggests that pronouns arise by a syntactic process (of
substitution), and such was quite generally assumed to be the case by virtually all

linguists until quite recently. I retain the terminology here for want of a substitute, but everything I say here is meant to be quite independent of any proposals as to the syntactic treatment of pronouns.

2 In sentences like (1) it is important, but not always easy, to try to clearly distinguish the presuppositions, descriptions, etc. which may be ascribed to the speaker of the sentence from those which may be ascribed to the subject of the sentence. For the most part such distinctions are not drawn here, however.

3 Donnellan's claim for a referential/attributive ambiguity in definite noun phrases and my extension of it to indefinites both suffer from an oversimplification pointed out to me by David Kaplan (cf. Kaplan (1968–69)), namely the following: having a particular individual in mind (the 'referential' case) and knowing nothing about an individual other than some single descriptive phrase (the 'attributive' case) may be just two extremes on a continuum of 'vividness'. One may consider, for instance, the case of a detective tracking down a criminal and obtaining more and more clues, including perhaps fingerprints, voice recordings, photographs of varying clarity, etc. It is not at all clear at what point the detective, who may be described as 'looking for the man who did so-and-so', stops looking for 'whoever it is that did so-and-so' and starts looking for a particular individual. The appropriateness of the term 'ambiguity' for the referential/attributive distinction may be questioned on other grounds as well (see Reference 4), and nothing in what follows appears to hinge on acceptance of that term.

4 I have not met with universal agreement on this point. Donnellan himself suggests that sentences like (11) should be regarded as 'pragmatically ambiguous' and not syntactically ambiguous. For sentences like (8) and (9) the question of whether the term *ambiguity* is appropriate is complicated by the question of whether indefinite noun phrases can ever be said to refer. If one considers a sentence in isolation, ignoring the speaker's and hearer's roles, an indefinite noun phrase certainly cannot be said to refer in the way that a definite noun phrase can. But from the speaker's point of view, which is how Donnellan is looking at definite noun phrases, I would claim that a distinction very similar to Donnellan's can be drawn in the indefinite cases. Perhaps the indefinite cases analogous to Donnellan's 'referential' should be called 'semi-referential', since the speaker does not specify uniquely for the hearer what individual he has in mind.

5 This possibility was pointed out to me by Frank Heny.

6 From the point of view of Fillmore's original proposal, the [± Specific] distinction has another problem. Fillmore intended the feature both to mark the ambiguity of sentences like (1) and to control the *some/any* suppletion rule in negative sentences. Thus the sentence represented abstractly as (6-1) below would have two surface forms, (6-2) if the *some* was [+ Specific] and (6-3) if the *some* was [− Specific].

(6-1)   NEG John answered *some of the questions*.
(6-2)   John didn't answer *some of the questions*.
(6-3)   John didn't answer *any of the questions*.

But a sentence like (6-4) below is ambiguous in the same way as sentence (1), even though the *some* must be marked [+ Specific] or it would have changed to *any* (and thence to *none*: cf. Klima (1964)).

(6-4)   The teacher thinks that *some of the girls* won't pass the test.

In comments received after this paper was submitted, Lauri Karttunen has pointed out to me some fundamental inadequacies in the notion of a dichotomous feature like [±Specific]. Crucial examples, which were overlooked in part as a result of the simplification mentioned in Reference 2, might include

(6-5)   Sally believes that John would like to marry *a girl his parents don't approve of.*

(6-6)   Every teacher in the school is convinced that *one student* is responsible for all the disruptions.

Although I agree that a dichotomous feature is indeed inadequate, I am not convinced by Karttunen's arguments (which utilize the notion of a deleted performative verb) that all of the ambiguities can be treated as scope differences. At this point I have no satisfactory alternative hypothesis.

[7] In particular, almost nothing will be said here about the syntax proper of pronouns, e.g. the claim that personal pronouns are suppletive forms of definite articles (Postal (1966)), and the considerable literature on possible syntactic positions of a pronoun relative to its antecedent (e.g. Langacker (1969), Ross (1967, 1968), Bach (1969, 1970)). Nor will anything be said about the different conditions governing the use of reflexive and non-reflexive pronouns. For a fuller synopsis of both the syntactic and semantic treatment of pronouns, see UESP (1968) (183–252).

[8] It is argued in UESP (1968) that the step from *a one* to *one* involves suppletion of *a* by *one*, not simply the deletion of *a*.

[9] This example is due to Frank Heny.

[10] As some examples of Postal's have made clear, the relevant sense of coreferentiality is not sameness of physical object, but rather some sort of identity relative to the speaker's mental picture of the world. Relevant examples include:

(10-1)   *The alligator's tail* fell off, but *it* grew back.

(10-2)   *My home* was once in Maryland, but now *it*'s in L.A.

(10-3)   *The unicorn* carried the damsel to safety because she had shown *it* great kindness.

(Note, incidentally, how (10-2) seems to justify the adage that 'a house is not a home', since if *house* were substituted for *home*, the sentence would be true only if the actual physical object had been moved cross-country.)

[11] In general, the auxiliary *would*, except when expressing volition or habit, requires the presence of a subordinate clause with *if* or *unless*.

[12] There is even a difference in the interpretation of the phrase *within a couple of years* which correlates with the presence or absence of the presupposition of marriage: in (59) the phrase can be understood either as 'from now' or 'from the time of marriage'; in (60) it can only be 'from now'.

[13] Restricted rather than unrestricted quantification is necessary if the natural language syntax is to be preserved as far as possible, since otherwise additional clauses would be required (and in a case like (66), the form such additional clauses should take is not at all clear). The suggestion that the first, or binding, occurrence of a given variable occur in apposition to a (singular or general) term I take from Quine (1960).

[14] The change is logically justifiable by the equivalence between $((\exists x)\, Px) \supset Q$ and $(x)\,(Px \supset Q)$. Such equivalences seem reasonable candidates for inclusion in natural language semantics; within a 'generative semantics' framework they would presumably also have to be included in the syntax. It would be linguistically more desirable to account uniformly for the fact that *any* corresponds sometimes to an existential

quantifier and sometimes to a universal one, and perhaps to correlate this fact with the fact that quantifier phrases in the vernacular do not readily occur outside the scope of *if-then* as in (65). The ordinary logical notation appears to obscure rather than clarify such questions.

Since this paper was submitted, Prof. Quine has kindly reminded me that Quine (1960) contains a discussion of sentences like (62) with the proposal that *any* can be treated uniformly as a universal quantifier which 'always calls for the longer of two possible scopes' (p. 139). However, that claim would appear to be too strong as it stands, because of the ambiguity of sentences like the following, first brought to my attention by Frank Heny:

(14-1)   If *any of those books* can be used to fulfill the requirement, standards have certainly dropped.

[15] If their two clauses were inverted, with a corresponding interchange of pronoun and noun phrase (so that the pronoun still followed its antecedent), the sentences would indeed be of the type discussed in Section 2.2.2.

[16] The question of the form the variable-binding operator should take here and for examples like (84) below is a difficult one. Quine (1960) has shown how names used as singular terms can be eliminated in favor of names used only as general terms in predicates of the form 'is ———', so that (81) might be better represented as:

(16-1)   (for each person x) (if x is John or x is Bill, then x was kissing x's wife).

But such a representation is unlikely to receive much linguistic justification, both because of the introduction of an *if*-clause and, more importantly, because names are certainly not restricted to predicate position in natural language. On the other hand, a name used as a singular term does not have the power to bind variables and therefore could not be used to represent the sense of (80) as (81) does.

[17] Prof. Quine has corrected me on this point; his 'oft reiterated identification is merely the converse: variables are pronouns.'

[18] The conditions on the occurrence of non-coreferential pronouns of laziness as in Karttunen's example are not clear; note for instance that even though *his wife* in sentence (74) above has a possible non-referential interpretation, it cannot on that reading be pronominalized to *her*:

(18-1)   John was kissing *his wife* and Bill was kissing *her* too.

There are some speakers who find (82) impossible on the intended reading. If for such speakers there are no instances of pronouns which must be treated as pronouns of laziness, while for the rest of us there is no other way of accounting for examples like (82), then we are faced with the frustrating but unfortunately not uncommon situation of finding idiolectal variation in what would appear to be theoretically crucial examples.

METHODOLOGICAL REFLECTIONS ON
CURRENT LINGUISTIC THEORY

I want to make some broadly methodological remarks on a variety of issues. To begin with I'll talk of *rules*, and dwell a while on the distinction between *fitting* and *guiding*.

Imagine two systems of English grammar: one an old-fashioned system that draws heavily on the Latin grammarians, and the other a streamlined formulation due to Jespersen. Imagine that the two systems are *extensionally equivalent*, in this sense: they determine, recursively, the same infinite set of well-formed English sentences. In Denmark the boys in one school learn English by the one system, and those in another school learn it by the other. In the end the boys all sound alike. Both systems of rules *fit* the behavior of all the boys, but each system *guides* the behavior of only half the boys. Both systems *fit* the behavior also of all us native speakers of English; this is what makes both systems correct. But neither system guides us native speakers of English; no rules do, except for some intrusions of inessential schoolwork.

My distinction between fitting and guiding is, you see, the obvious and flat-footed one. Fitting is a matter of true description; guiding is a matter of cause and effect. Behavior *fits* a rule whenever it conforms to it; whenever the rule truly describes the behavior. But the behavior is not *guided* by the rule unless the behaver knows the rule and can state it. This behaver *observes* the rule.

But now it seems that Chomsky and his followers recognize an intermediate condition, between mere fitting and full guidance in my flat-footed sense of the word. They regard English speech as in some sense rule-*guided* not only in the case of the Danish schoolboys, but also in our own case, however unprepared we be to state the rules. According to this doctrine, two extensionally equivalent systems of grammatical rules need not be equally correct. The right rules are the rules that the native speakers themselves have somehow implicitly in mind. It is the grammarian's task to find the right rules, in this sense. This added task is set by demanding not just any old recursive demarcation of the right totality of well-formed

Davidson and Harman (eds.), Semantics of Natural Language, 442–454. All rights reserved
Copyright © 1972 by D. Reidel Publishing Company, Dordrecht-Holland

sentences, but rather a recursive demarcation of the right totality of trees. The trees used to be mere *ad hoc* scaffolding by the aid of which the grammarians, each in his own way, contrived to specify the objective totality of well-formed sentences. According to the new doctrine, the trees are themselves part of the objective linguistic reality to be specified.

We have all known that the native speaker must have acquired some recursive habit of mind, however unconscious, for building sentences in an essentially treelike way; this is evident from the infinitude of his repertoire. We can all go this far with Postal when, in his review of Dixon, he writes:

The claim that there are linguistic rules is simply the claim that individuals know their language and have not learned each of its sentences separately.[1]

His word 'claim', even, seems ill suited to anything so uncontroversial. What is more than trivial, in the new doctrine that I speak of, is rather the following: it imputes to the natives an unconscious preference for one system of rules over another, equally unconscious, which is extensionally equivalent to it.

Are the unconscious rules the same, even, from one native speaker to the next? Let us grant that the generated infinitude of well-formed sentences is itself the same for two natives. There may then seem to be a presumption of sameness of generating rules – just because any appreciably different but extensionally equivalent system of rules is apt to be prohibitively complex and artificial. However, this suggestion gets us nowhere. Insofar as it is true, the grammarian can just follow his old plan, after all, of settling for *any* system of rules, naturally the simpler the better, that demarcates the right infinite set of well-formed sentences. If the new doctrine of the grammarian's added burden has any content, it owes it to there being appreciably unlike and still comparably manageable systems of rules for generating the same infinite totality of well-formed sentences. From experiences with axiom systems in mathematics, incidentally, we can easily believe in the existence of such alternatives. In my parable of the Danish schoolboys I have already assumed the existence of just such alternative systems for English; though it should of course be said, if we are to be fussy about the facts, that Jespersen's grammar and that of the old-fashioned textbooks really fall short of extensional equivalence at some points.

We see then that the new doctrine of the grammarian's added burden raises the problem of evidence whereby to decide, or conjecture, which of two extensionally equivalent systems of rules has been implicitly guiding the native's verbal behavior. Implicit guidance is a moot enough idea to demand some explicit methodology. If it is to make any sense to say that a native was implicitly guided by one system of rules and not by another extensionally equivalent system, this sense must link up somehow with the native's dispositions to behave in observable ways in observable circumstances. These dispositions must go beyond the mere attesting to the well-formedness of strings, since extensionally equivalent rules are indistinguishable on that score. It could be a question of dispositions to make or accept certain transformations and not others; or certain inferences and not others.

Certainly I have no quarrel with dispositions. Nor do I question the notion of implicit and unconscious conformity to a rule, when this is merely a question of fitting. Bodies obey, in this sense, the law of falling bodies, and English speakers obey, in this sense, any and all of the extensionally equivalent systems of grammar that demarcate the right totality of well-formed English sentences. These are acceptably clear dispositions on the part of bodies and English speakers. The sticking point is this Chomskian midpoint between rules as merely fitting, on the one hand, and rules as real and overt guides on the other; Chomsky's intermediate notion of rules as heeded inarticulately. It is a point deserving of close methodological attention.

Ironically these same linguists have expressed doubt about the relatively clear and humdrum notion of a disposition to verbal behavior. Chomsky writes:

Presumably, a complex of dispositions is a structure that can be represented as a set of probabilities for utterances in certain definable "circumstances" ... But it must be recognized that the notion "probability of a sentence" is an entirely useless one ... On empirical grounds, the probability of my producing some given sentence of English ... is indistinguishable from the probability of my producing a given sentence of Japanese.[2]

I am puzzled by how quickly he turns his back on the crucial phrase "in certain definable 'circumstances'." Solubility in water would be a pretty idle disposition if defined in terms of the absolute probability of dissolving, without reference to the circumstance of being in water. Weight would be a pretty idle disposition if defined in terms of the absolute probability of falling, without reference to the circumstance of removal of support. Verbal dispositions would be pretty idle if defined in terms of the absolute probability of utterance out of the blue. I, among others, have talked mainly of verbal dispositions in a very specific circumstance: a questionnaire circumstance, the circumstance of being offered a sentence for assent or dissent or indecision or bizarreness reaction.

Chomsky's nihilistic attitude toward dispositions is the more puzzling in that I find it again in the newspaper account of his recent lectures in England, despite an intervening answer of mine[3] to the earlier statement. I seem to detect an echo of it also in a footnote in Postal's review of Dixon.[4] This rejection of dispositions would be bewildering by itself. It is doubly so when contrasted with the rather uncritical doctrine just previously considered – the doctrine of unconscious preferences among extensionally equivalent grammars. I'd like to think that I am missing something.

Now some more remarks on the task of the grammarian. What I have said suggests, too simply, the following notion of the grammarians' classical task: that it is the task of demarcating, recursively and in formal terms, the infinite totality of the well-formed strings of phonemes of the chosen language. It would seem from my remarks up to now that this is the basic or classical task, which, then, is added to if one insists further on some distinction between right and wrong rules, right and wrong trees subtending this same superficial mass of foliage. The trouble with thus stating the basic or classical task is that it presupposes some prior behavioral standard of what, in general, to aspire to include under the head of well-formed strings for a given community. What are the behavioral data of well-formedness? Passive observation of chance utterances is a beginning. The grammarian can extrapolate this corpus by analogical construction, and he can test these conjectures on an informant to see if they elicit only a manifestation of bewilderment. But of course the grammarian settles for no such criterion. Traditionally, at any rate, the grammarian has accepted wide ranges of sentences as grammatical which an informant would reject as bizarre. I think of sentences such as Carnap's example, 'This stone is thinking about Vienna.'

A more realistic characterization of the grammarians' classical task is an open-ended one. He does not have a prior behavioral criterion of well-formedness; he just has some sufficient behavioral conditions. Strings heard from natives count as well-formed, at least provisionally. So do sentences which, when tried on an informant, elicit casual and unbewildered responses. What I then picture the grammarian as doing is to devise as simple a formal recursion as he can which takes in all these confirmably well-formed strings and excludes all strings that would bring really excessive bizarreness reactions. He rounds out and rounds off his data. Sometimes of course he will even reject a heard string as ill-formed, thus rejecting a datum, if he can appreciably simplify his system in so doing; but it would be regrettable to do much of this.

In this somewhat melancholy version of the grammarian's task, I have held Chomsky's doctrine in abeyance. Chomsky believes that the linguistic community itself has a sense of grammaticality which the grammarian can and should uncover; that grammaticality is not just the grammarian's rounding off of performance data. Up to a point I agree; the native's disposition to bizarreness reactions is an implicit sense of grammaticality of a sort. But Chomsky would of course credit the native with a full and precise sense of grammaticality, this being of a piece with the native's purported fund of tacit rules – the native's purported bias even among extensionally equivalent grammars. Now this doctrine is interesting, certainly, if true; let me only mention again the crying need, at this point, for explicitness of criteria and awareness of method.

An attitude that is closely linked to this doctrine is a readiness to recognize linguistic universals. The problem of evidence for a linguistic universal is insufficiently appreciated. Someone says, let us suppose, that the subject-predicate construction occurs in all the languages he has examined. Now of course all those languages have been translated, however forcibly, into English and *vice versa*. Point, then, in those languages to the translations of the English subject-predicate construction, and you establish the thesis; the subject-predicate construction occurs in all those languages. Or is it imposed by translation? What is the difference? Does the thesis say more than that basic English is translatable into all those languages? And what does even this latter claim amount to, pending some standard of faithfulness and objectivity of translation?

To make proper sense of the hypothesis that the subject-predicate construction is a linguistic universal, we need an unequivocal behavioral criterion of subject and predicate. It is not enough to say that if we take these and these as subjects and those and those as predicates then there are ways of so handling the rest of the language as to get general English translations. The trouble is that there are extensionally equivalent grammars. Timely reflection on method and evidence should tend to stifle much of the talk of linguistic universals.

Insofar, on the other hand, as one is prepared to impute to the native a specific and detailed though inarticulate grammatical system, one is apt to conceive of the notions of subject and predicate and similar notions as objective and as unequivocally apprehended by the native himself. To conceive of them thus is no more of a strain, surely, than to suppose that the native favors one of two extensionally equivalent grammars over another. In all this there is no folly, I feel sure, that conscientious reflection on method and evidence cannot cure; but the cure is apt to take time.

I think it is instructive, before leaving this topic, to fit an idea of Geach's into the picture. Besides singling out the well-formed strings, Geach argues, our grammar must distinguish between proper and spurious components of well-formed strings. One of his examples of a spurious component was 'Plato was bald' in the context 'The philosopher whose most eminent pupil was Plato was bald.'[5] This demand is reminiscent of Chomsky's demand that the grammarian show how to generate not only the well-formed strings but the right trees. Yet Geach is not committed to finding a bias in the native community between extensionally equivalent grammars. I expect Geach's demand is reconcilable even with the humdrum view of the grammarian's task as the task merely of generating the well-formed strings; for the thing that Geach demands, the marking of the proper components of each well-formed string, would doubtless be a valuable auxiliary to the rules for generating further well formed strings. The same case can be made, more generally, for Chomsky's insistence that the grammarian's proper product is the whole tree rather than just the well-formed strings that it issues in. The argument is simply that rules for generating further well-formed strings (and trees) can then be formulated in terms of past trees and not just past well-formed strings. This is a strong argument, and it does not depend on any obscure doctrine to the effect that the natives tacitly prefer one system of grammar to another that is extensionally equivalent to it. It would be well to sort out these motives and benefits and see whether the obscure points of doctrine might not be cheerfully dropped.

Such an inquiry could, I suppose, convince us that there is indeed an unarticulated system of grammatical rules which is somehow implicit in the native mind in a way that an extensionally equivalent system is not. For me such a conviction would depend in part upon clarification of criteria.

To get down more nearly to cases, suppose again a language for which we have two extensionally equivalent systems of grammar; two extensionally equivalent recursive definitions of well-formed string. According to one of these systems, the immediate constituents of a certain sentence are 'AB' and 'C'; according to the other system they are 'A' and 'BC'. The enigmatic doctrine under consideration says that one of these analyses is right, and the other wrong, by tacit consensus of native speakers. How do we find out which is right?

An unimaginative suggestion might be: ask the natives. Ask them, in their language, whether the real constituents of 'ABC' are 'AB' and 'C'. Does this pose an embarrassing question of translation? Well, then let the native language be English. The essential problem remains; we do not really understand our own English question. We are looking for a criterion of what to count as the real or proper grammar, as over against an extensionally equivalent counterfeit. We are looking, in the specific case, for a test of what to count as the real or proper constituents of 'ABC', as against counterfeit constituents. And now the test suggested is that we ask the native the very question which we do not understand ourselves: the very question for which we ourselves are seeking a test. We are moving in an oddly warped circle.

Better and more imaginative suggestions may be forthcoming for determining, less directly, what to regard as the real constituents of 'ABC' from the point of view of tacit native grammar. I suggested a while ago that it could be a question of dispositions to make or accept certain transformations or inferences. But I want now to make use of the unimaginative suggestion as a point at which to take off on a tangent, leaving at last this whole question of a native bias toward one of two extensionally equivalent grammars.

The unimaginative suggestion was: ask the natives. The same question, and the same warped circle or one very much like it, are encountered from time to time in semantics. People like me challenge the notion of synonymy and ask for a criterion. What is synonymy? How do you tell whether two expressions are synonymous? Ask the natives. This essentially was Arne Næss's answer some decades ago, as I analyze it.[6] Moreover he suited the action to the word, disseminating questionnaires and claiming significantly uniform results. This was also essentially the answer more recently of Fodor and Katz,[7] as I analyze it; and I have sensed suggestions of it in Chomsky. Now a reason for pausing over this oddly warped circle is that an empirical investigation, however odd, that yields uniformities has a claim to attention. Grant for the sake of argument that Næss's questionnaire on synonymy yielded statistically significant uniformities; what do they mean? Do they show that Næss's laymen are pretty much alike on the score of their synonymy pairs, obscure though it be to us wherein synonymy consists? Do they show something also, or instead, about how Næss's laymen use the obscure word 'synonymy' or its paraphrases? Separation of these components presents an odd problem.

Essentially the same question is raised outside linguistics by work of Smith Stevens on subjective magnitudes.[8] For years he gathered subjective testimony of the pitch and loudness of sounds: whether this was twice as high as that, or half again as loud as that. He plotted these findings against the physical frequencies and volumes, and came out with significant correlations – not linear, but logarithmic. Significant, but of what? Was it uniformity of error in his subjects' effort to estimate physical frequency and volume? Or was it uniformity of subjective experience, coupled with uniformity of meaning attached to enigmatically subjective expressions like 'twice as high' and 'half again as loud'? Or did the subjective experience vary from subject to subject, while the meaning attached to the subjective expressions varied in a compensatory way? The uniformities surprise me and I am prepared to find them instructive, but I am at a loss to sort them out. It is the same warped circle.

Turning back to synonymy, or to the semantical notion of analyticity which is interdefinable with synonymy, I might mention also a questionnaire experiment which avoided the warped circle. Apostel and others[9] in Geneva compiled various lists of sentences. One list contained only sentences that the experimenters regarded as analytic. Other lists had varied and irrelevant motifs. Subjects were given these lists, untitled, and were asked to sort various further sentences into the appropriate lists. The experiment, much the same as one proposed more recently by Katz,[10] sought evidence of a felt similarity among analytic sentences, without benefit of title. The outcome was reported as at best indecisive.

A controversy over semantical notions has simmered for twenty years. Some of us have criticized these notions as insufficiently empirical. Others have defended the notions without improving them. Their defense has been visibly motivated by a sense of the indispensability of these notions in various applications. We would have been spared much of this rearguard action if the defenders of semantical notions had taken the criticism of these notions to heart, and sought seriously to get along without them. In one, certainly, of its most conspicuous applications the notion of synonymy is not needed; namely, in the definition of the phoneme. According to the familiar definition, what shows that two sounds belong to distinct phonemes is that the substitution of one for the other changes the meaning of some expression. Surely, however, meaning enough for this purpose is afforded by the innocent and uncontroversial notion of stimulus meaning.

The behavioral definition of stimulus meaning is as follows, nearly enough: the stimulus meaning of a sentence, for a given speaker, is the class of all stimulatory situations in the presence of which he will assent to the sentence if queried. Stimulus meaning is at its best among observation sentences. The behavioral definition of an observation sentence is as follows: an observation sentence is a sentence whose stimulus meaning is the same for just about all speakers of the language. Examples: 'It is raining', 'This is red', 'This is a rabbit'.

Sameness of stimulus meaning is no appreciable approximation to the general notion of synonymy to which semantics has aspired. Within observation sentences, however, sameness of stimulus meaning is synonymy enough. For distinguishing phonemes, consequently, it is enough; for surely, if two sounds belong to distinct phonemes, the meaning of some observation sentences will be changed by the substitution.

For that matter, phonemes can also no doubt be distinguished by appealing merely to well-formedness of expressions; by appealing, that is, to the capacity of a string of sounds to occur in the native stream of speech. Presumably, if two sounds belong to distinct phonemes, the substitution will render some coherent string of sounds incoherent. This way of defining the phoneme was proposed by Anders Wedberg,[11] and was already implicit, I think, in Zellig Harris. I wanted to bring in the definition in terms of stimulus meaning, however, as an example of how stimulus meaning can sometimes do the work that is desired of meaning or synonymy.

I turn, for the remainder of my remarks, to the notion of deep structure and its relation to logical analysis. Take, first, logical analysis. What do we do when we paraphrase a sentence by introducing logical symbols for truth functions and quantifiers? In principle it is the same as when in highschool algebra we were given some data about rowing up and down a river; we paraphrased the data into algebraic equations, with a view to solving these for the speed of the river. In principle it is the same also as programming a computer.

I find the phrase 'logical analysis' misleading, in its suggestion that we are exposing a logical structure that lay hidden in the sentence all along. This conception I find both obscure and idle. When we move from verbal sentences to logical formulas we are merely retreating to a notation that has certain technical advantages, algorithmic and conceptual. I mentioned the analogy of the computer; but essentially the same thing is happening in a more moderate way when in natural history we switch to the Latin binominals for genera and species, or when in relativity physics we paraphrase our temporal references into a spatial idiom using four dimensions. No one wants to say that the binominals of Linnæus or the fourth dimension of Einstein or the binary code of the computer were somehow implicit in ordinary language; and I have seen no more reason to so regard the quantifiers and truth functions.

What now of deep structure? If we believe that native speakers have a detailed though inarticulate grammatical system, specific even as between extensionally equivalent systems, then certainly we believe that deep structure, whatever there may be of it, is there to be uncovered. How to tell whether we are getting it right, whether we are matching the inarticulate native analysis or just carving out an extensional equivalent, is a methodological question that I have mentioned already.

If on the contrary we hold every grammar to be as authentic as every extensionally equivalent grammar, and to be preferred only for its simplicity and convenience, then deep structure loses its objectivity but need not lose its place. Deep structure, and the transformations to and from it, might still qualify as auxiliaries to the simplest and most convenient system we know for demarcating the class of well-formed strings. They would stay on in this role just as the trees would stay on, and Geach's discrimination of proper and improper ingredients.

Thus conceived, the grammarian's deep structure is similar in a way to logical structure. Both are paraphrases of sentences of ordinary language;

both are paraphrases that we resort to for certain purposes of technical convenience. But the purposes are not the same. The grammarian's purpose is to put the sentence into a form that can be generated by a grammatical tree in the most efficient way. The logician's purpose is to put the sentence into a form that admits most efficiently of logical calculation, or shows its implications and conceptual affinities most perspicuously, obviating fallacy and paradox.

These different purposes, the grammarian's and the logician's, are not in general best served by the same paraphrases; and for this reason the grammarian's deep structure is not to be identified with logical structure, suggestive though the one may be for the other. I have two major examples in mind to bring out the divergence.

One example is the elimination of singular terms other than variables. Let 'a' represent such a singular term – perhaps a proper name, perhaps a complex singular term – and let 'Fa' represent a sentence containing it. We can paraphrase 'Fa', to begin with, as '$(\exists x)(Fx . a = x)$'. In this way all singular terms, other than simple variables such as the 'x' here, can be confined to one specific manner of occurrence: occurrence to the left of '$=$'. Then, as a next step, we can reckon this identity sign to the singular term as an invariable suffix, thus re-parsing the singular term as a general term or predicate.

The advantages of this transformation are specific and limited. Laws of logic become simplified, through not having to provide for the instantiation of quantifications by terms other than variables. The simplification is the greater for the fact that the instantiations thus avoided were ones that depended awkwardly on existence assumptions. Certain gains in philosophical clarity ensue also. Variables, rather than names, come to be seen as the primary avenue of reference. Little puzzles about names that fail to name anything are swept aside.

This elimination of singular terms is not all good, however, even for logic and mathematics. Inference moves faster when we can instantiate quantifications directly by names and complex singular terms, rather than working through the variables and paraphrases. And complex singular terms are in practice vital for algebraic technique. An algebraist who was not free to substitute complex expressions directly for variables, or to substitute one side of a complex equality directly for the other, would soon give up.

The important point thus emerges that logical analysis itself – better, logical paraphrase – may go one way or another depending on one's specific logical purpose. The image of exposing an already present logical structure by analysis is a poor one. And when our interest turns to English grammar, again we are bound to find that the elimination of singular terms is to no purpose. Surely it yields no deep structure that would help to simplify an account of English grammar. Thus take the distinction between the referential and the non-referential use of singular terms. Work of Geach and Strawson suggests that this distinction is vital to an appreciation of English; but the logical paraphrase obliterates it utterly.

In my view the logical structure and the deep structure, or let me say the logician's paraphrases and the grammarian's paraphrase, differ not in kind but in detail and purpose. They differ in the same sort of way that the logician's two paraphrases differ from each other: one the austere and pellucid paraphrase containing no singular terms but variables, and the other the algorithmically efficient paraphrase bristling with complex singular terms.

The elimination of singular terms was one example of the difference between paraphrasing for logic and paraphrasing for grammar. Now the other example I have in mind is the treatment of time as a fourth dimension. A while ago I referred this to physics, but it is vital equally for logic and philosophy. A logic of tense is a towering triviality which we have no excuse to put up with if our concern is merely with the scientific use of language rather than with the scientific study of it. We program language into the simple neo-classical logic of truth functions and quantifiers, by eliminating tense and treating times on a par with places. The resulting simplification of formal logic may be sensed from this example, which I have used before: George V married Queen Mary; Queen Mary is a widow; therefore George V married a widow. We cease to have to provide against this kind of thing, among others.

Philosophical clarification ensues as well. Thus consider the following puzzles. How can things be related that do not coexist at any one time? How can a variable range now over things that no longer exist? or range ever over things that never coexist? How can a class have members that never coexist? How can a class, which is an abstract object, be said to change, as it must when its members change or cease to exist? We make a clean sweep of all such puzzles by dropping tense and treating all past, present, and future bodies as four-dimensional substances tenselessly scattered about in spacetime.

This is a paraphrase which, we see, works wonders for logic, philosophy, and physics as well, but presumably is not wanted for English grammar. A deep structure without tense seems unpromising, at any rate, as a means of simplifying a grammatical account of an Indo-European language. Here again, evidently, is a wide divergence between the structure that the logician is after and what the grammarian wants under the head of deep structure. And yet, reading Postal's typescript 'Coreferentiality and physical objects,' I begin to wonder whether the four-dimensional view might be useful sometimes in grammar too.

My previous example, the elimination of singular terms, spoke for pluralism not just as between logical structure and grammatical deep structure, but within logical structure; one logical paraphrase served one logical purpose, another another. Perhaps now there is a case also for pluralism within grammatical deep structure: one paraphrase might serve one grammatical purpose, another another. A paraphrase into the tenseless idiom of four dimensions might play an auxiliary role in connection with some grammatical twists, while a different deep structure, retaining tense, might still be exploited for other grammatical ends. So let me conclude with a plea against absolutism.

REFERENCES

[1] Paul Postal, review of Dixon, *Language*, 84–93, specifically p. 88.

[2] Noam Chomsky, 'Quine's Empirical Assumptions', *Synthese* **19** (1968) 53–68, specifically p. 57.

[3] W. V. Quine, 'Replies', *Synthese* **19** (1968) 264–321, specifically p. 280.

[4] Paul Postal, *op. cit.*, note 12.

[5] Peter Geach, 'Logical Procedures and the Identity of Expressions', *Ratio* **7** (1965) 199–205, specifically p. 201.

[6] Arne Næss, *Interpretation and Preciseness*, Dybwad, Oslo, 1953.

[7] Jerry Fodor and Jerrold Katz, 'The Structure of a Semantic Theory', *Language* **39** (1963) 170–210.

[8] S. S. Stevens, 'On the Psychophysical Law', *Psychological Review* **64** (1957) 153-181.

[9] L. Apostel, W. Mays, A. Morf, and J. Piaget, *Les liaisons analytiques et synthétiques dans le comportement du sujet*, Presses Universitaires, Paris 1937.

[10] Jerrold Katz, 'Some Remarks on Quine on Analyticity', *Journal of Philosophy* **64** (1967) 36–52.

[11] Anders Wedberg, 'On the Principles of phonemic Analysis', *Ajatus* **26** (1964) 235–253.

[12] Peter Geach, *Reference and Generality*, Cornell University Press, Ithaca, N.Y., 1962.

[13] P. F. Strawson, 'Singular Terms and Predication', *Synthese* **19** (1968) 97–117.

P. F. STRAWSON

GRAMMAR AND PHILOSOPHY[1]

One who speaks his native language fluently and correctly has acquired over a period of time that mastery of the language which he now has. During this period he was exposed, no doubt, to many sentences produced by others and to some correction of sentences he produced himself. But his mastery of the language does not consist merely in his being able to reproduce the sentences produced by others and, in their corrected forms, the sentences earlier produced by himself. It consists in his being able also to produce indefinitely many new sentences, knowing what they mean, and in being able to understand indefinitely many new sentences which are produced to him. It consists also in his being able to distinguish between sentences of his language which are fully 'correct' and literally significant sentences – however elaborate or stylistically unusual they may be – and sentences which deviate, in various ways or degrees, from full 'correctness' or literal significance; and perhaps to remark, with more or less explicitness, on how the sentences which deviate from correctness do so deviate.

It seems entirely reasonable to say that the possession, on the part of the fluent and correct speaker of a language, of these abilities to construct, interpret and criticize sentences implies the existence of a set or system of rules which the speaker has, in some sense, mastered. This does not imply that he consciously constructs or interprets sentences by the light of any such rules, nor that he could even begin to formulate such rules with any approach to full explicitness or to the maximum of system. Such rules may 'govern' his exercise of his abilities of sentence-construction and interpretation, and even of sentence-criticism, without his approaching full consciousness of such rules as governing such exercise. We should not expect of the fluent and correct speaker of a language, just because he is one, that he can state the theory of his practice.

Nevertheless the practice is there. And so it should be possible, for those who are minded to do so, to extract the theory and to state it with full explicitness and the maximum of system. This is the aim which the

Davidson and Harman (eds.), Semantics of Natural Language, 455–472. All rights reserved
Copyright © 1972 by D. Reidel Publishing Company, Dordrecht-Holland

new grammarians set themselves, the exponents of transformational generative grammar. A fully explicit and maximally systematic statement of the rules which 'govern' the fluent speaker's exercise of his capacities will supply the *theory* of that speaker's language. Such a theory may be called, in an extended sense of the word, a *grammar* of the language. It will contain three parts or components: a syntactic part; a semantic part; and a phonological part. Very roughly, and rather misleadingly, these parts may be said to be concerned respectively with structure, with sense and with sound; rather misleadingly, in so far as structure is itself quite largely determinant of sense. It is, on the whole, the syntactic or structural part which has received the most emphasis and aroused the most interest in the work of the transformational grammarians.

We are familiar, from traditional grammar, with some of the terms which are used in the new grammar to express facts about the structure of sentences. We are familiar, that is to say, with such grammatical *class-* or *category*-names as those of noun and noun-phrase, verb, preposition, adverb and adjective; and with the names of such grammatical *relations* as those of subject of sentence, subject of verb, object of verb, modifier of subject, modifier of verb and so on. Quite obviously a grasp of facts about structure, about grammatical relations in a sentence, enters into our understanding of sentences. To appreciate the difference in sense between 'John loves Mary' and 'Mary loves John' or between 'The old man sings a song' and 'The man sings an old song' *is* to grasp those structural facts which are expressed in the terminology of grammar by saying that 'John' is the subject and 'Mary' the object of the verb in the first sentence and vice versa in the second or that the adjective 'old' stands in attributive combination with 'man' in the third sentence and with 'song' in the fourth. In the kind of grammatical analysis which we do (or did) at school, we set out, in a prescribed form, facts of this kind about the grammatical relations which hold within the sentences we analyse. To that extent we set out their structure. Of course we may be rather bad at this exercise while perfectly well appreciating the differences in sense between such sentences; which illustrates merely the point that grasp of structure is not the same thing as ability to state explicitly what is grasped.

Grammatical structure, then, as well as the senses of individual words, is determinant of the sense or semantic interpretation of sentences. The central thesis of the transformational grammarians, the step which conditions the whole character of their theories, is the insistence that any adequate grammatical theory must recognize a distinction between the superficial syntactic structure of a sentence and its basic structure, between its deep grammar and its surface grammar. The motivation of this distinction goes very deep indeed, as we shall see hereafter. But we can easily be induced to see reason for it by noting, for example, that two sentences may be very similar in their superficial syntactic structure while, so to speak, the structure of their sense is very different; that in our understanding of such sentences we allow for differences in the grammatical relations of their elements which are simply not marked in the sentences as they stand. Chomsky gives as an example of this the pair of sentences, 'They persuaded John to leave' and 'They expected John to leave'. In our understanding of these sentences 'John' has a subject-like relation to the verb 'leave' in both; but while it also has an object-like relation to the main verb ('persuaded') of the first sentence, it has no such relation to the main verb ('expected') of the second. Thus we understand the elements of the sentences as differently related in the two cases; but there is no *manifest* structural difference between the sentences as they stand, corresponding to this understood difference. Again, a perhaps more striking way of making the distinction between deep and surface structure acceptable is to point to certain syntactically or structurally ambiguous sentences such as – to adapt an older example – 'The principal thing in his life was the love of women'. Though the ambiguity might well be removed by the context, the sentence, as it stands, leaves us uncertain as to whether it is his loving women or women loving him that is in question. Now both the unmanifest structural differences exemplified in the first kind of case and the syntactic ambiguities exemplified in the second would, it is held, be clearly and systematically exhibited in the representation of the deep, as opposed to the surface, structure of sentences. For *every* syntactic or structural relation between sentence-elements would be represented with total explicitness. A grammar of the desired kind will therefore assign at least two different deep structures to a syntactically ambiguous sentence; and will assign patently different deep structures to sentences which have a merely superficial identity of structure.

Looking for a moment beyond the confines of a single language, we may glimpse another and older kind of motivation for such a distinction. Just as surface similarity may conceal deep difference, so surface difference may conceal deep identity. Given two sentences in different languages, the one an accurate and adequate translation of the other, we may easily find grammatical constructions in the one which are absent in the other. But may we not want to say that the *fundamental* structural relationships thus differently displayed on the surface are exactly the same in both? The question how far we are prepared to press this thought has a bearing on the question whether we are prepared to entertain, and, if so, how we are prepared to use, the notion of a universal grammar. Evidently such a thought cannot be without interest for philosophers.

But this is to anticipate. Let us turn now to the question how facts about structure are actually presented by the transformational grammarians. Any answer I can give to this question in the present context must necessarily be incomplete and grossly simplified; but not, I hope, misleadingly so in relation to the further questions I wish to raise.

The syntactic component, then, of a grammar or theory of a language consists of a system of rules, permissive or mandatory, which operate, finally, on certain elements. These terminal materials are to be thought of as the minimal meaning units of the language, the atoms to be structured, as it were, by the syntax of the language. Chomsky calls these items formatives. No easy identification of formatives with any familiar idea is possible; but we need not concern ourselves here with their exact nature. Formatives are of two kinds, lexical and non-lexical. The first we may think of as corresponding to those general terms or proper names of the language of which the meaning is not in any way syntactically derived – such as the verbs 'sing' or 'love', the adjective 'red', the name 'Mary'. The latter are a more heterogeneous bunch and will include, for example, a formative named *Past*, for Past Tense.

The rules which operate, finally, on these materials are such that, for any sentence of the language, there is a path through the application of these rules the following of which path will yield us a complete exhibition both of the deep structure and of the surface structure of that sentence. This must not be misunderstood. It means no more than it says. It does not mean, for example, that the grammar provides us with a mechanical procedure for *finding* the deep structure of an antecedently given sentence or for *producing* a given sentence.[2] It means only that, in a complete grammar of the kind in question, there *is* some path through the rules which will yield these results. From what has already been said it will be clear that the rules are themselves of two kinds: those which yield deep structures and those which transform these into surface structures. With rules of the latter kind I shall not be much concerned. But I must say a little more about deep structure rules or rules of the base.

The terms in which the fundamental type of base-rules are framed have reassuring familiarity. They are the names of grammatical *classes* or *categories*, such as Sentence, Noun-Phrase, Predicate-Phrase, Noun, Verb, Adjective, Verbal Auxiliary, Prepositional Phrase *etc.* The results of applying the rules can be most easily represented by a kind of inverted tree-structure, in producing which we start from the basic symbol *S* (for Sentence) and branch out into constituent grammatical categories, then into constituents of those constituents and so on until we reach a point at which all the terminal category names are such that we can enter formatives directly under them. The rules permit the production of very simple diagrams of this kind – such as the diagram, say, for 'John smiled' – and, again, of diagrams of any degree of complexity. For they permit the re-introduction of the symbol *S* under a suitable constituent structure heading, such as noun-phrase, where it acts, in turn, as the head of another, subordinate branching diagram. The deep or base structure diagram of some actual sentence of the language is completed when, under the terminal category headings are entered appropriate formatives, the resulting string or sequence of formatives constituting the terminal sequence of the structure. Thus the non-lexical formative *Past* can be entered under the category heading *Verbal Auxiliary.* Lexical formatives are listed in a lexicon which assigns them to lexical categories like Noun, Verb and Adjective.

From a completed diagram of this kind, setting out a terminal sequence together with the pattern of its derivation, we can read off, with total explicitness, all those facts of grammatical structure which bear on the interpretation of the sentence whose deep structure it represents. The reason why we can do so – and this is a point of absolutely central importance – is that all those syntactical *relations* which, as we already know, are so largely determinant of the sense (or semantic interpretation) of sentences are *defined* in terms of the grammatical *categories* or *classes* and their permitted concatenations in deep structure diagrams. Chomsky is quite explicit on this important point. If we set aside the lexicon, the primary function of the rules of the base so far described is, he says, "that of defining the grammatical relations that are expressed in the deep structure and that therefore determine the semantic interpretation of a sentence."[3] Here, I repeat, we have a point of central importance. Most of the detail of what I have been saying can be safely forgotten is this is remembered.

The syntactic component of the theory, then, yields us both deep and surface structures of sentences. Now a word – no more – about their relations to the remaining components, the semantic and the phonological. The rules of the phonological component of the theory are applied to surface structures to yield the actual sound-rendering of a sentence. The information contained in the semantic component about the meanings of individual lexical items is supposed to combine with the structural information contained in the deep structure diagram to determine the full semantic interpretation of the sentence.[4]

1. So much by way of a sketch of the type of theory of a language envisaged by some transformational grammarians. Now I began this paper by summarising the linguistic ability of an ideally fluent and correct speaker of a language as the ability to understand, produce and criticize indefinitely many new sentences of his language. The theorists of transformational grammar, at least in their more cautious moments, do not claim that the possession of these linguistic abilities by an idealised speaker-hearer can be completely and adequately explained simply by crediting him with a 'tacit mastery' – or even by crediting him with an 'internal representation – of such a system of rules as such a theory would provide. They concede, or, rather, insist, that more is required for an adequate explanation. Let us, for the moment, postpone consideration of the question how the grammarians themselves think the provision of such a theory needs supplementing if the demand for adequate explanation is to be met; and let us consider, instead, a condition in respect of which a non-specialist critic might find that such a theory fell short of *his* demand for understanding. I shall name this the condition of perspicuousness.

Here we must turn once more to the consideration of the deep structures of sentences, so decisive, as Chomsky says, for their semantic interpretation. Deep structures are generated by the base rules of the syntactic component. If we set aside that part of the base (including the lexicon) which allows the completion of deep structures with terminal sequences, we are left essentially with the branching rules which introduce grammatical categories (Noun-Phrase, Verb, Prepositional Phrase, *etc.*) in various permitted concatenations. As remarked, Chomsky says that the importance of these rules and of the grammatical categories which they introduce consists primarily in the fact that they supply the basis for the definition of those grammatical *relations* which, as far as structural considerations go, are of decisive, though not exclusive, importance for the semantic interpretation of sentences. This is why the grammatical categories and the rules framed in terms of them *matter*. They matter because together they provide the terms in which the grammatical relations (subject-of, predicate-of, object-of, modifier-of *etc.*) can be defined for the given language. And these relations matter because of their decisive bearing on the semantic interpretation of sentences. But so far, if we keep the lexicon on one side, the grammar gives us no information about the significance of these grammatical relations independent of their definition in terms of the grammatical categories. The symbols for the grammatical categories, and the rules for framing structure diagrams containing them, are said to point forward to the grammatical relations, so important for understanding sentences; but the names of the grammatical relations point back, by definition, to the symbols for the grammatical categories and their arrangement; and, since the grammar is a fully explicit statement of rules, we must not suppose ourselves equipped with *any* understanding of *either* of these kinds of term except such as is given by the explicit rules of the grammar itself.

Of course the grammar, or theory of the language, as a whole, provides a way out of this circle of technical terms. It provides a way out because it contains a lexicon which, in its syntactic part, assigns lexical formatives to grammatical categories; and because it contains a semantic component which we may think of as containing all the remaining information about elements of the language which anyone must possess who understands the language. Now it is true, as critics have urged and grammarians acknowledged, that no satisfactory theoretical account has yet been given of the semantic component. But this point, thus generally stated, is not one I wish to labour. Let us simply assume that grasp of the rules of the theory, including grasp of the semantic component, would carry with it a complete grasp of the sense of all formatives, lexical and non-lexical alike. Then, since the grammar assigns individual formatives to grammatical categories, we see that the grammar provides for the immediate linking of the senses of formatives with grammatical categories; and hence it provides, mediately, for the linking of the senses of formatives with possible grammatical relations in deep structure, the relations which help to determine the sense of sentences. But – and this is the point on which my criticisms bear – of this apparently crucial set of connexions there is, in the grammar, no general theory whatever. There is simply the list of items in the lexicon without any account of general principles determining the assignment of those items to grammatical categories. Yet it is above all of this set of connexions that we might expect a general theory if we hoped that the grammar might satisfy the condition of perspicuousness.

It is worth while dwelling once more on the reasons why we might expect this. We are to remember that the primary importance of the grammatical categories and their permitted orderings in the deep structures of a language lies in the fact that they provide the terms in which the underlying grammatical functions and relations of elements in sentences can be defined – for the given language. And these functions and relations are functions and relations which any ordinary speaker of the language grasps implicitly in understanding the sentences he hears and produces. He grasps them implicitly, having – we may suppose – no explicit training in the grammar. Now how is his implicit grasp of these functions and relations connected with his knowledge of the meaning of the elements of his language? It is not to be supposed that his knowledge of the meaning of these elements is something quite separate from his grasp of the power of these elements to figure in those grammatical functions and in those grammatical relations which he must have an implicit grasp of in order to understand the sense of the sentences he hears and produces. His grasp of the meanings of the elements of the language, it seems, must include at least some grasp of their potential rôles in the grammatical relations of base structures. Suppose, then, there are intrinsic and general connexions between types of element-meaning and potentialities of grammatical rôle in deep, or base, structure.

In stating the principles of such connexion, we should, obviously, be linking semantic and syntactic considerations. Might we not also be laying the foundations, or some part of the foundations, of a general theory of grammar? In any case, a grammar which rested on, or incorporated, such principles would have a better claim than one which did not, to satisfy the condition of perspicuousness.

2. Thus, at least, we might reason. A little later I shall have to refine on this notion of perspicuousness. First, let us return, briefly, to Chomsky. As I have already hinted, he himself is the first to acknowledge that what he calls a "*descriptively* adequate" generative grammar of a language – such a theory as I described, in barest outline, in section 1 of this paper – would not by itself satisfy the condition of *explanatory* adequacy. To satisfy this condition we should need, he says, a theory of linguistic universals characteristic of human language in general; and we should need to show that this theory was related in a certain way to our descriptively adequate grammar, picking it out, as it were, from other possible grammars consistent with the "primary linguistic data". Now regarding these requirements we may be disposed to ask two questions. First, would their fulfilment finally yield a *complete* explanation of the idealised hearer-speaker's possession of his linguistic abilities – including it must be remembered, his ability to *understand* the indefinitely many sentences of the language? And, second, would their fulfilment involve – besides, doubtless, much else – the linking of semantic and syntactic considerations in somewhat the way just alluded to?

To neither question is the official answer entirely clear. But, as regards the first question, we may suppose that the fulfilment of the stated requirements would take us at least nearer to a complete explanation of the speaker-hearer's abilities.[5] And, in view of this, we may be surprised by the character of Chomsky's answer to the second question. For though he admits that "there is no reason to rule out *a priori*" the possibility that "substantive characterizations" of "the universal vocabulary from which grammatical descriptions are constructed" might ultimately have to refer "to semantic concepts of one sort or another",[6] yet his references to any such possibility are markedly cool. Thus he speaks of "vague and unsupported assertions about the 'semantic basis for syntax'" which "make no contribution to the understanding of these question."[7] Vague and unsupported assertions, of course, do not make much of a contribution to the understanding of anything. But if a general direction of inquiry seems promising, if indeed one can see no alternative to it, one should surely seek in that direction for assertions which are not vague and which one can support.

Chomsky himself remarks that it would be natural to expect that the ultimate framework for the characterization of the universal categories of grammar should be found in some features of the base. He has in mind what he calls *formal* features of the base. But the base includes the lexicon. And the lexicon includes lists of items capable of being entered directly under lexical category-headings in base structures. These items will be far less numerous than the entries in an ordinary dictionary of the language. For example, they will not include, in the category of nouns, formatives corresponding to our ordinary abstract nouns, 'sincerity' and 'destruction'; 'sincerity' and 'destruction' appear in sentences only as a result of a nominalising transformation.[8] Would it not seem very natural, then, to survey the restricted list of items in the lexicon with a certain question in mind: *viz.*, what semantical types of items are to be found in the lexicon, such that they can combine into sentences of which the deep structure requires minimum transformation to yield surface structure? And what correlations can be found between the semantical types of those items and the grammatical or syntactic categories to which they are there assigned? Or consider a more specific question. The grammatical category, Sentence, is basically divided, in the models of transformational grammar put forward by Chomsky, into Noun-Phrase and Predicate-Phrase, and this division immediately yields us, by definition, for basic structures, the relations of subject and predicate of a sentence. This point seems to bring us to the very brink of the question: What general semantic types of expression qualify for the basic subject- and predicate-rôles in simplest sentences? and why? An answer to this question, it might seem, could very well be at least a beginning towards a perspicuous characterization of this apparently fundamental grammatical relation; helping us, *e.g.*, to understand its extension, via nominalisations, to other, less simple cases. Yet no move is made towards confronting these questions, either in the more general or a more specific form.

3. I have said that it would seem natural enough, given their ultimate

theoretical concerns, for transformational grammarians to move in the direction I have indicated. Yet, on the other hand, there are reasons why it is natural that they should not. More than this: there are reasons why the questions I have just indicated as natural, though they are in the right spirit, are not yet in the right form. It is probably true that if genuinely explanatory foundations are to be provided for grammar, an attempt must be made to close the explanation-gap between semantico-logical features on the one hand and syntactic classifications and relations on the other. It is probably false that this attempt is best undertaken by first framing questions directly in terms of traditional syntactic categories and relations, such as those of noun and verb, object of the verb, *etc.* Let me first try to explain the grammarians' reluctance to undertake the necessary enterprise before explaining why the form of the enterprise is not to be so simply understood. The two points are closely, and subtly, interconnected.

First, let us recall that just as, on the one hand, the transformational grammarians tend to be severe critics of the philosophers of ordinary language for being insufficiently systematic, so, on the other, they are no less severe critics of those philosophers of language who derive their inspiration from formal logic and practise, or advocate, the construction of ideal languages; and their criticism of these last is that, though they are indeed systematic, they are insufficiently empirical.[9] For though the approach of the transformational grammarians is in one way highly abstract and theoretical, it is in another way thoroughly empirical. They are empirical linguists, grammarians – though in aspiration generalising grammarians – of actually given languages, inclined to be suspicious of theoretical notions except in so far as they can be used in *the construction of systems, or mechanisms, of rules* which will yield what is actually found in accepted sentences and will regularly mark the deviations in deviant ones. Thus, though it is characteristic of the transformational grammarian that he is willing to view the thought of a universal grammar, a general theory of language, with favour, yet he would – the example of Chomsky suggests – prefer to view the concepts which enter into such a theory as capable of being elucidated entirely in terms of the contribution they make to such working rule-mechanisms. Any other view of them is likely to be, from the grammarian's point of view, too vague and intuitive to satisfy his ideal of empirical clarity.

Thus the grammarian is apt to be inhibited from adopting an approach which the philosopher may be more ready to adopt, and which perhaps must be adopted if truly explanatory foundations are to be provided for grammar. Certain of the fundamental ideas of the transformational grammarians – the distinction between deep and surface structures, the notion of systematic transformational relations between them, the hint of a suggestion that the basic forms of functional relation are to be found in the simplest forms of deep structures – these will strike a responsive chord in the breast of any philosopher who has tried to reach through surface similarities of grammatical form to the semantico-logical differences which lie below them; that is, of any philosopher whatever. But when the question of explanatory foundations for grammar is raised against this background of shared ideas, the philosopher's response, it seems to me, should, at least at first, be to make the maximum use of his disreputable liberty from empirical constraints. Thus he need not be at all concerned, at least to begin with, with the actual formal arrangements by means of which functional relations are actually represented, whether in the base or at any other level, in a particular language. He will have, as the grammarian has, a conception of meaning-elements (the atoms to be structured) on the one hand; and of semantically significant modes of combination of them (syntactical relations) on the other. But he will be prepared from the start to use a vocabulary which is overtly semantic or, in a broad sense, logical, for the classification of elements, abstractly conceived; and this vocabulary will from the start stand in perspicuous connexion with his vocabulary of modes of combination or grammatical relations. Given these perspicuous connexions, he may next consider possible formal arrangements by means of which the combining functions might be discharged; and may finally relate these theoretical models of language to what is actually found in empirically given languages.

Here, then, is a programme for research in non-empirical linguistics, which may perhaps in the end pay empirical dividends. The procedure to be followed in pursuing such a programme will in some ways be reminiscent of the setting up of ideal languages by the logicians; but the purpose will be less restricted than that of the logicians. Quine says somewhere: don't expose more structure than you need expose. But the non-empirical grammarian will be concerned with every point at which structure is needed to contribute to overall meaning. Structure must be exposed at every point and understood at every point.

To say now a little more about details of procedure. Practically speaking it is inevitable that one should start with relatively simple models of language-types and work up to more complex ones. The vital distinction to be observed throughout is that between the intrinsic or essential grammar of a language-type and the alternative or variable grammars of that language-type. A language-type is defined by specifying (1) the semantic or broadly logical type of meaning-elements it contains and (2) the types of significant combinations into which they can enter to form sentences. These specifications determine *a priori* the essential grammar of the language-type, on the assumption that each sentence, at least in the base, must permit of a syntactically unambiguous reading. The rules of essential grammar will require that all combinations must somehow or other be indicated and, when necessary, differentiated; that if, *e.g.*, a sentence contains a number of elements which could be significantly clustered into different attributive groupings, then it must somehow be indicated which elements are to be taken with which; or, again, that in the case of an element signifying a non-symmetrical relation in combination with elements or clusters signifying its terms, the ordering of the term-signifying elements or clusters must somehow be indicated. These are requirements of essential grammar. But the essential grammar of a language-type in no way stipulates *how* such requirements are to be fulfilled. There lies open a choice among different ways of using such various formal devices as those of, *e.g.*, element-positioning, inflection, affixing or the use of special syntactic markers. In choosing one among various possible sets of formal arrangements adequate to the requirements of essential grammar, we should be choosing one of the possible variable or alternative grammars for the language-type in questions. When such a choice is made and codified, we have a complete and completely perspicuous grammar (or form of grammar) for that language-type; at the cost, of course, of not having the grammar of an actual language at all, but only of an ideally simplified type of language.

If we press these researches even a little way, we find that we need quite an elaborate vocabulary, or set of interrelated vocabularies, of theoretical notions. Thus we need, first, what might be called an ontological vocabulary. We need, second, a semantic vocabulary, or vocabulary for naming semantic types of elements and even for describing individual elements (elements being thoughout, as already said, rather abstractly conceived). Third, we need a functional vocabulary for naming the kinds of combination or relation into which elements may enter in sentences and the kinds of rôle which elements or combinations of elements may play in sentences. Fourth, and finally, we need a vocabulary of formal devices. Between, and within, the first three vocabularies, or batteries of notions, there are close interrelations and dependences. The fourth vocabulary stands rather apart from the rest in that we need to invoke it only when we move from essential to variable grammar. Specimen items belonging to the fourth vocabulary I have already mentioned, in referring to element-positioning, inflection, *etc.* Specimen items belonging to the ontological vocabulary might include space, time, particular continuant, situation, general character or relation; and some sub-classifications of these last, as, perhaps, of general characters into sorts, states, actions, properties, and of relations into, at least, symmetrical and non-symmetrical. Readiness to employ some such notions as these is inseparable from the use of the functional and semantic vocabularies. The functional notions must include those of major linkage of major sentence-parts into sentences and, for any language-type which is not of an idiotic simplicity, the notion of minor linkages of elements into sentence-parts. Major and minor linkages alike will have to be further distinguished into kinds, as also will the rôles which elements or parts may play, and the different relations in which they may stand to each other, inside these different combinations. The internal relations, the interlockings and overlappings of the functional vocabulary are most complex, and I shall not attempt to illustrate them here. The semantic vocabulary for a fairly restricted language-type might include three main classes of elements: (1) proper names for continuant particulars; (2) elements signifying general characters and relations; and (3) deictic elements. At least the second and third classes would be subdivided for a language-type of any richness, the second on lines already indicated in the ontological vocabulary, the third perhaps into elements for temporal deixis, for spatial deixis, for interlocutory deixis and for what might be called merely contextual deixis.

Now it will be noted that in listing these specimen items from the interrelated vocabularies of essential grammar, I have made no mention of of any of the traditional syntactic categories of noun, verb, adjective, preposition, *etc.* And this is no accident of selection or omission. The more complex the language-type, the more complex, certainly, will be the interrelated vocabularies necessary to specify the type and to state, as consequences of the specification, the requirements of its essential grammar. But, however complex those vocabularies become, they will never, so long as we remain at the level of essential grammar, include the traditional syntactic classifications I have mentioned. For those classifications, as understood by conventional modern grammarians, involve an essential reference to the formal arrangements by means of which grammatical relations are represented in variable grammar. The more rigorous the grammarian, the more he strives to explain such categories as noun and verb in terms of formal criteria: in terms of the types of inflection which expressions may undergo and their distribution in sentences, the positions they may standardly occupy in sentences relative to expressions of other categories. The statement of such criteria can, perhaps never be entirely purged of semantic notions; and it must be framed with some looseness if the traditional categories are to be applied over a range of languages. But the point remains that the conventional categories reflect the interaction, in actual languages, of semantic and functional factors with actually found formal factors; and therefore have no place in the study of essential grammars. This will not prevent the student of perspicuous grammar from observing how natural it is that certain types of formal arrangement, and hence perhaps certain conventional syntactic categories, should enter at the level of variable grammar. But it will be at that level that they will enter, and not before. And what holds for the conventional syntactic *categories* will hold also for the conventional syntactic *relations* in so far as their characterisation is inseparable from that of the conventional syntactic categories.

It will now, I hope, be clear why I earlier remarked that the task of finding explanatory foundations for grammar is not best approached by trying to establish direct links between semantico-logical notions and such traditional, or at least traditionally named, syntactic categories as the transformational grammarians employ in imagining base structures. If the names have anything like their normal significance, we must go behind or below them, to essential functions and classifications; and if they do not, it would be better to drop them in favour of a more perspicuous nomenclature. Some incidental advantages of emancipating ourselves, as we must, from these traditional categories are indeed obvious. We shall be readier for the discovery that such categories cannot be readily forced on some (from our point of view) remoter languages; and correspondingly less prone to draw from such a discovery romantic conclusions about profound differences between the conceptual schemes of speakers of such languages and our own.

Many questions arise about such a programme as I have sketched. The notion of an essential grammar is, evidently, a relative notion: an essential grammar is the essential grammar *of a specified language-type*. We may set aside the obvious fact that the only practicable way of proceeding is to start from relatively simple specifications and build up to more complex ones, essential and alternative grammars themselves becoming more complex at every stage. There are more fundamental questions to be faced regarding the specifications of relatively basic types of element and combination, the selection of basic functional and logico-semantic vocabularies. It is admitted that these selections cannot be wholly independent of each other, that every semantico-logical type carries with it a certain potentiality of syntactic function. Is it not to be feared (supposed) that any such selection as the theorist of perspicuous grammars will make is likely to be restrictively conditioned by features of those languages with which he is most familiar? that, at worst, the ontology which was to enter into the explanatory foundations of grammar will be nothing but the abstract reflection of the base of the ontologist's native and local grammar? And, if so, how does it stand with the idea of a *general* theory of human language – nothing less than which will satisfy the full demand for explanation?

To these questions I can give only dogmatic answers. First, even if such fears are to some extent justified, it by no means follows that there is nothing to be gained by pursuing the suggested approach. To achieve any fairly rich models of perspicuous grammar would, I think, be to achieve a great deal. Even though it did not directly supply us with substantive linguistic universals of a general theory, it might help us to look for them. It is no new thing to work towards a comprehensive theory by way of theories which are less than comprehensive, to reach an adequate explanation by way of discarding inadequate explanations. But, second, it seems to me that such fears are likely to be exaggerated. We are all animals of the same species with fundamentally similar nervous and cerebral organisations and it is not to be supposed either that the most general categories for the organisation of human experience are widely different or, correspondingly, that the basic logico-semantic types of element to be detected in human languages are so very widely different either. (This is not to say that detection will be easy.) The linguistic evidence may indeed *seem* to point to some fairly basic variations[10]; and it simply cannot be said, in advance of a much greater development of theory and research, what the best way of handling such apparent problems of variation will be. But no language could even set us a definite problem unless it were *understood* by some theorist of grammar; so it is scarcely to be feared (or hoped) that any which does set a definite problem could for ever escape the embrace of a unified theory.

One of the transformational grammarians suggests that a general theory of language, conceived as a quite self-contained empirical-linguistic study, would contain the solutions to a great range of traditional philosophical problems.[11] I have been suggesting that a general theory of language should not be above receiving help from philosophy as well as offering help to it. One of the most striking things about the transformational approach to grammar is that it does point so markedly in the direction I have indicated. To follow this direction does not seem to be a departure from empiricism, generously conceived, even though the proper title for such an endeavour might well be held to be, as I suggested earlier, Research in Non-Empirical Linguistics. Of course the empirical value of the constructions of the philosophical student of perspicuous grammars is finally subject to the checks of psychologists and linguists, working separately and in combination. But where these two very different studies meet, the philosopher, at least for a time, may also find a role; and that not the least promising which is at present available to him. And, finally, whatever the ultimate empirical value of his constructions, and even if they have none, he may be sure of finding them a fruitful source of a kind of question and answer which he characteristically prizes.

REFERENCES

[1] It will be obvious to any auditor of Professor Chomsky's John Locke lectures, delivered in Oxford this summer after the present paper was written, that he has moved from, or modified, some of the positions here attributed to him on the basis of his publications. However, with occasional qualifications, I have allowed the attributions

P. F. STRAWSON

to stand; the written, checkable word provides a firmer basis for discussion than the spoken, uncheckable word.

[2] See Chomsky, *Aspects of the Theory of Syntax*, p. 141.

[3] *Op. cit.*, p. 99. See also pp. 69, 117, 120, 141.

[4] This is one important point on which Chomsky has modified his views. He now allows that surface structure also may bear on semantic interpretation; so that two sentences with exactly the same deep structure diagram may nevertheless differ in meaning, the difference appearing only at the level of the transformations which yield surface structure. However, he adheres to his original view as regards those aspects of semantic interpretation which depend on the *grammatical relations;* and it is with these that the present paper is concerned.

[5] Leaving, one must suppose, a certain amount of work for psychologists and physiologists still to do.

[6] *Op. cit.* pp. 116–7.

[7] *Op. cit.* p. 78.

[8] It appears from the John Locke lectures that Chomsky no longer holds (or holds for all cases) that such abstract nouns appear as the result of nominalising transformation. Rather, he holds that there are underlying semantic or lexical elements, in themselves neither nominal nor, *e.g.*, verbal or adjectival, but capable of appearing in deep structures in either rôle. Nevertheless, there would appear to be grounds for awarding *some kind* of syntactical primacy to the verbal, or adjectival, over the nominal, rôle in such cases; and such an award will serve my present purpose, in whatever theoretical terms it is ultimately to be understood. My own guess, for what it is worth, is in line with Chomsky's later position, in so far as I see no reason why we should not, and much reason why we should, have a use for a notion of *nominalisation* which does not depend on that of *transformation*.

[9] See, for example, on both points, Katz, *Philosophy of Language*, Ch. 3.

[10] It may *seem* to suggest, for example, that in certain areas in which *we* are inclined to number concepts of sorts of objects among our *primary* concepts, the most nearly corresponding *primary* concepts of other language-speakers *may* be of a different and possibly more primitive kind, not yet determined either as concepts of certain sorts of objects or as concepts of sorts of activities or situations in which such objects may be typically involved.

[11] See Katz, *loc. cit.*

LEONARD LINSKY

ANALYTIC/SYNTHETIC AND SEMANTIC THEORY

ABSTRACT. A somewhat simplified version of Jerrold J. Katz's theory of the analytic/
synthetic distinction for natural languages is presented. Katz's account is criticized on
the following grounds. (1) the 'antonymy operator' is not well defined; it leaves certain
sentences without readings. (2) The account of negation is defective; it has the consequence that certain nonsynonymous sentences are marked as synonymous. (3) The
account of entailment is defective; it has the consequence that analytic sentences entail
synthetic ones. (4) Katz's account of "indeterminable sentences" is criticized; it has the
consequence that certain logical truths are not marked as analytic. (5) Katz's semantics
provides no account of truth, so that he is unable to show that analytic sentences are
true and that 'indeterminable' sentences are not.

In his book, *The Philosophy of Language*,[1] Jerrold Katz attempts to provide an account of the analytic/synthetic distinction for natural languages.
He offers a solution to what, in his first paper on this topic, he calls
"Quine's Problem". I shall present enough of the Katz-Fodor semantic
theory to explain Katz's account of the analytic/synthetic distinction. I
shall then present a critical analysis and evaluation of this portion of
Katz's book. Full details of the Katz-Fodor semantic theory will not be
presented; instead a simplified version will be offered. But none of the
simplifications will be relevant to the points of criticism which will
subsequently be made.

The chief technical concept employed by Katz is that of the semantic
marker. It is the analogue in semantics of such syntactic categories as
'Adjective', 'Noun Phrase', 'Verb', and these latter are called syntactic
markers. The dictionary component of semantic theory will list not only
syntactic markers in its lexical entries for words (or morphemes) but also
semantic markers such as '(Male)', '(Human)', '(Animate)'. Some semantic markers are complex such as '((Male) ∪ (Female))'. These are all
expressed as "Boolean functions" of simple semantic markers. Some
words (or morphemes) have identical dictionary entries except for a difference in semantic markers. For example, the entry for 'woman' is identical
with the entry for 'man' except that one entry has the marker '(Female)'
where the other has '(Male)'. The second sub-component, beside the

Davidson and Harman (eds.), Semantics of Natural Language, 473–482. *All rights reserved*

lexicon, of the semantic component of the linguistic description of a language is the projection rule sub-component.

Katz says "A dictionary entry consists of a set of lexical readings associated with a phonological representation of a morpheme and a set of syntactic markers. These syntactic markers provide the information necessary to determine whether the lexical reading associated with a morpheme M is to be assigned to an occurrence of M in an underlying phrase marker. We proposed that the assignment take place just in case the syntactic categorization of M in the underlying phrase marker ascribes to M exactly those syntactic markers that appear in the set of syntactic markers in the entry for M. The determination of whether or not such a condition is satisfied in the case of any particular phrase marker is made on the basis of the purely formal operation of checking to determine if each symbol in the set of syntactic markers for the lexical item M has a formally identical counterpart among those symbols that label nodes dominating the occurrence of the item in the phrase marker." The operation described in the last sentence is the work of one of Katz's projection rules called "Rule (I)" (p. 163).

Once Rule I has assigned all of the admissible readings which the terminal elements in the underlying phrase marker of a sentence may take the other projection rules operate to assign 'derived readings' to each of the increasingly larger constituents of the sentence in question. Taking as input from the syntactic component abstract representations for each of the well formed sentences of the language (together with their underlying phrase markers), the semantic component of the linguistic description will, in the manner indicated, assign a semantic interpretation (set of readings) to every sentence in the language. Other semantic concepts and relations are defined in terms of the notion of a reading. A sentence is synonymous with another sentence if, and only if, they have the same readings. A sentence is ambiguous if, and only if, it has more than one reading etc.

The notion of analyticity which Katz attempts to reconstruct is the Kantian one. We will confine our account (again for simplicity) to syntactically noncompound copula sentences of the Subject + Predicate type. Katz is able to replace Kant's vague appeal to grammar by exact definitions of the relevant syntactic relations. The grammatical relation 'subject of the sentence S' is defined as follows: "The string of words σ is the subject of S just in case σ is the whole string of terminal elements in the underlying phrase marker for S that is dominated by a node labeled 'Noun Phrase' and this node is immediately dominated by a node labeled 'sentence' which is dominated by nothing." The definition of the relation 'predicate of the sentence S' is obtained by replacing the words 'subject' and 'Noun Phrase' in each of their occurrences by 'predicate' in the definition just given (p. 192).

The definitions of analyticity and contradictoriness depend upon the notion of an antonymous n-tuple of semantic markers. Under the general notion of antonymy are many specific types of antonymy relations. An example is the relation of sex antonymy that holds between a pair of expressions just in case they have identical readings except that where the reading of one has the semantic marker '(Male)' the other has the semantic marker '(Female)'. Examples are 'bride' and 'groom', 'aunt' and 'uncle', 'the cow in the barn', 'the bull in the barn'. But most specific antonymy relations hold for n-tuples of expressions, not for pairs. For example "species antonymous cases" like: 'child', 'cub', 'puppy', 'kitten', 'cygnet', etc., or an age-antonymous n-tuple: 'baby', 'toddler', 'child', 'adolescent', 'adult', etc.

The antonymy concepts required by us are developed in two stages. First, we must group semantic markers into antonymous n-tuples, i.e., n-tuples of incompatible semantic markers. "This is accomplished" says Katz "by the notation which semantic theory will prescribe for the formulation of semantic markers." Semantic markers will be required to be so represented that membership in any n-tuple of antonymous semantic markers can be uniquely determined on the basis of formal features of the symbols that comprise semantic markers. For example the antonymous pair '(Male)' and '(Female)' are represented as (say) '(S^m)' and '(S^f)'. Thus two semantic markers belong to the same antonymous n-tuple if, and only if, they have the same base symbol. The definitions which concern us are the following. Let 'R_1' stand for a reading for the subject of a syntactically noncompound sentence S, and 'R_2' stand for a reading of the predicate of S and '$R_{1,2}$' stand for the reading of the whole sentence S which results from the amalgamation of R_1 and R_2. Then:

(D7) S is analytic on the reading $R_{1,2}$ if, and only if, every non-complex semantic marker in R_2 also occurs in R_1; for any complex semantic marker $((M) \cup (M_2) \cup \ldots \cup (M_n))$ in R_2 there is an M_i, $1 \leqslant i \leqslant n$, in R_1; and the reading R_1 does not contain any antonymous semantic markers (p. 194).

(D9) S *is contradictory on a reading* $R_{1,2}$ if, and only if, the reading R_1 contains a semantic marker (M_i) and the reading R_2 contains a semantic marker (M_j) such that (M_i) and (M_j) are different semantic markers belonging to the same antonymous n-tuple of semantic markers, and the reading R_1 does not itself contain any antonymous semantic markers (p. 198).

(D11) S *is synthetic on a reading* $R_{1,2}$ if, and only if, there is a reading $R_{1,2}$ assigned to S's sentence-constituent such that S is neither analytic nor contradictory on $R_{1,2}$ and R_1 does not contain any antonymous semantic markers (p. 198).

These definitions rest crucially on the relation of antonymy between semantic markers. Is there any gain in explicating analyticity and contradictoriness in terms of the notion of meaning-incompatibility involved in the concept of antonymy? Is not antonymy as much in need of explication as analyticity itself? Katz's procedure leaves him unopen to the charge of explicating analyticity and contradictoriness in terms of a concept equally in need of explication, for semantic markers belong to the same n-tuple of antonymous semantic markers if, and only if, they have a specified shape. "Two semantic markers belong to the same antonymous n-tuple of semantic markers if, and only if, one has the form (M^{α_i}) and the other has the form (M^{α}_j), where $i \neq j$, $1 \leqslant i \leqslant n$ and $1 \leqslant j \leqslant n$." (p. 197). In other words the question as to whether a pair of semantic markers is antonymous, is to be answered by inspection of the list of the antonymous n-tuples of the language in question. The markers are antonymous if, and only if, they both appear in the same n-tuple in this list. Thus we escape what may be called 'Quine's circle' by appeal to a list. But how do we know which items to include on our list? This is not a question which is answered or needs to be answered within semantic theory. It is a question as to how one *discovers* a correct theory and the answer to that question is totally irrelevant to the question of the truth or adequacy of the theory discovered. It does not matter how Katz or anyone else discovers his list of antonymous semantic markers so long as the list is correct.

Consider the sentence, 'A spinster is a woman'. On Katz's account, it is correctly marked 'analytic' for the semantic markers in its predicate are (say) '(Human)', '(Animal)', '(Female)', '(Physical Object)', and each of these markers also appears in the reading for its subject. Again, 'A spinster is a man' is, for Katz, contradictory because it contains the marker '(Male)' in the reading for its predicate and this belongs to the same antonymous couple as '(Female)' which appears in the reading for its subject. Finally consider 'My father is a king'. Since it has the semantic marker '(Monarch)' in the reading for its predicate which does not appear in the reading for its subject, our sentence is not analytic. Since there are no markers in its predicate which are antonymous with any in its subject it is not contradictory, therefore it is synthetic. One final example. Consider the sentence 'That man is a person'. The predicate contains the complex semantic marker '((Male)∪(Female))' together with a number of other noncomplex semantic markers, each of which appears in the reading for the subject of our sentence. But since the semantic marker '(Male)' which is included in our complex marker also appears in the reading for 'that man' our sentence satisfies Katz's definition of analyticity and is so marked.

We have now defined 'analytic sentence', 'contradictory sentence' and 'synthetic sentence'. Our next task is to show that these sentences are so related that the negation of an analytic sentence is contradictory, the negation of a synthetic sentence is synthetic and the negation of a contradictory sentence is analytic. This is accomplished on the basis of a dictionary entry for 'not'. As a preliminary step an operator 'A/(−)' called the "antonymy operator" is defined. Let (M^{α_1}), (M^{α_2}), ..., (M^{α_n}) be an antonymous n-tuple of semantic markers, then

$$A/(M^{\alpha_i}), \text{ for } 1 \leqslant i \leqslant n = ((M^{\alpha_1}) \cup (M^{\alpha_2})$$
$$\cup ... \cup (M^{\alpha_i - 1}) \cup (M^{\alpha_i + 1}) \cup ... \cup (M^{\alpha_n})) \text{ (p. 199)}.$$

Notice that $A/A/(M^{\alpha_i}) = (M^{\alpha_i})$.

Katz's lexical entry for 'Neg' is very complicated. What is here offered is a simplification adequate for the discussion which follows. The entry is a rule for constructing from the reading for a sentence a reading for the negation of that sentence. 'S' stands, as before, for syntactically simple subject-predicate sentences. Semantic markers in the reading for the predicate of such a sentence which are neither identical with nor antonymous with any in the reading for its subject, I shall call "independent" markers.

(i)   If S is synthetic, there are semantic markers in its predicate which are independent. Let these be $(M_1), (M_2), ..., (M_n)$. To form the reading for the *negation* of S, replace these markers by $A/(M_1) \cup A/(M_2) \cup ... \cup A/(M_n)$.

(ii)   If S is contradictory, there are semantic markers in the reading for its predicate which belong to the same antonymous n-tuple of semantic markers as semantic markers in the reading for its subject. Let these be $(M_1), (M_2), ..., (M_n)$. Form the reading for the *negation* of S by replacing these markers by $A/(M_1) \cup A/(M_2) \cup ... \cup A/(M_n)$. Erase all independent semantic markers in the reading for the predicate of S.

(iii)   If S is analytic, all semantic markers in the reading of its predicate are in the reading for its subject. Let the markers in the reading for the predicate of S be $(M_1), (M_2), ..., (M_n)$. Form the reading for the *negation* of S by replacing these markers by $A/(M_1) \cup A/(M_2) \cup ... \cup A/(M_n)$ (p. 201).

These definitions are open to criticism. According to the definition, $A/(M^\alpha)$ for each semantic marker (M^α) is the remainder of the n-tuple of antonymous semantic markers of which (M^α) is a member. But (M^α) may itself be complex, in particular it may be a disjoint marker such as '((Male) $\cup$ (Female))' which includes all of the simple semantic markers in the sex antonymous couple. But what then is $A/((Male) \cup (Female))$? The definition leaves this question unanswered; thus there is no way to show that the negation of 'A man is a spouse' is synthetic and in fact 'A man is not a spouse' is simply not provided with any reading whatever.

Clause (ii) also suffers. It marks nonsynonymous sentences as synonymous. Consider the sentence (1) 'My father is a queen'. This is contradictory (on one reading) for the predicate contains the marker '(Female)' and the subject '(Male)'. The predicate also contains the marker '(Monarch)'. Under clause (ii) all independent markers (e.g., '(Monarch)') in the predicate are "nullified", and '(Female)' becomes '(Male)'. Thus we get the reading for (2) 'My father is not a queen' as analytic. The trouble is that now (2) has the same reading as (3) 'My father is a male', and thus is marked as synonymous with it, but (2) and (3) are not synonymous. There is no way to avoid this difficulty except by erasing the erasure clause in (ii). But the erasure clause cannot be removed without having the negations of contradictory sentences turn into synthetic sentences. Consider (1) with '(Monarch)' not erased by clause (ii). Then (2) would be synthetic for it would still have this marker in its predicate and not in its subject.[2]

We turn now to the problem of entailment. "The philosophical problem is to so construct the definition of this notion that the so-called paradoxes of material implication are not derivable and yet entailments that are acceptable can be predicted from the definition." (p. 205). The problem is solved by extending semantic theory to include the following definitions:

(D13) S_1 entails S_2 on a reading if, and only if, there is a conditional S_3 of which S_1 is the antecedent and S_2 is the consequent and S_3 is analytic on a reading or S_3 is metalinguistically true on a reading (p. 205).

The task now is to define "analyticity" for conditional sentences 'CS'. Let S_1 and S_2 stand respectively for the antecedent and the consequent sentences of CS. Let R_1 be a reading for S_1 and R_2 for S_2, and $R_{1,2}$ be the amalgamated reading for CS. Let R_1 and R_2 be formed from readings $R \operatorname{subj}_1$ and $R \operatorname{pred}_1$ and $R \operatorname{subj}_2$ and $R \operatorname{pred}_2$ respectively. Finally let $R \operatorname{const}_i \phi R \operatorname{const}_j$ hold just in case every noncomplex semantic marker in $R \operatorname{const}_j$ also occurs in $R \operatorname{const}_i$ and for any complex semantic marker $((M_1) \cup (M_2) \cup \ldots \cup (M_n))$ in $R \operatorname{const}_j$ there is an (M_k) in $R \operatorname{const}_i$ such that $1 \leqslant k \leqslant n$, and $R \operatorname{const}_i$ does not contain any antonymous semantic markers[3] (p. 206).

(D15)   *CS is analytic on the reading $R_{1,2}$ if, and only if, it is both the case that $R \operatorname{subj}_1 \phi R \operatorname{subj}_2$ and that $R \operatorname{pred}_1 \phi R \operatorname{pred}_2$* (p. 206).

An example of an analytic conditional is, 'If that person is a spinster then that person is female'. We omit Katz's account of analyticity for syntactically compound non-copula sentences since it involves nothing in principle new which is relevant to the subsequent discussion. An important category of sentences in Katz's account of analyticity contains those he calls 'indeterminable sentences'.

(D19)   *S is indeterminable on the reading $R_{1,2}$ if*, and only if, *S* has
         a reading $R_{1,2}$ and R_1 contains two different semantic markers
         from the same antonymous *n*-tuple (p. 211).

We thus obtain the following classification of sentences. On a given
reading a sentence may be either anomalous, indeterminable, or determinable. If it is determinable, it is either analytic, synthetic, or contradictory. What is the *rationale* for the inclusion of the category of indeterminable sentences? Consider the sentence 'A female king is male'.
If we ignore the clause in the definitions which excludes the case in which
the reading for the subject has semantic markers from the same antonymous *n*-tuple, this sentence is marked both 'analytic' and 'contradictory'.
This is not possible according to the presystematic notion of the analytic/
synthetic distinction which is being reconstructed, so Katz excludes it
from both categories and labels it 'indeterminable'.

Now Katz sees the following difficulty for himself. The sentence 'Any
person who is female and not female is generous' must, on his view, be
marked 'indeterminable'. But its translation into elementary logic
'$(x) ((Fx \ \& \sim Fx) \supset Gx)$' is a valid sentence. Other sentences marked 'indeterminable' will be correctly translated into sentences of elementary
logic which are logically false, e.g., 'Some female man is generous'. Katz
seeks to avoid these difficulties by denying that the relevant sentences
can be translated at all into the notation of elementary logic. This conclusion is, of course, absurd. On the other hand, there is no good reason
for Katz to adopt it, for what is wrong with translating a sentence marked
'indeterminable' into a logical truth or a logical falsehood? No reason is
given for Katz's assumption that it is wrong. Of course it would be wrong
to translate truths into falsehoods or falsehoods into truths but it has
not been shown that there is anything wrong with translating 'indeterminable' sentences into sentences with truth-values.

There is, however, a problem which Katz does not see in connection
with translation and indeterminable sentences. It is that some logical
truths are not marked 'analytic'. For example, 'All females who are not
females are generous' is not marked 'analytic' by Katz's theory. Certainly
such an account cannot claim to be a solution to "Quine's problem" about
the analytic/synthetic distinction, for Quine regards the logical truths and
their substitution instances as providing the only clear cases of analyticity.

Katz assumes throughout his discussion that sentences his theory marks as indeterminable do not have truth-values, but there is nothing in his theory to justify this assumption, for Katz's semantics gives no account whatever of the notion of truth. For the same reason, there is no way within his explication of analyticity to show that analytic sentences are true and contradictory ones false.

The most serious difficulty which arises for Katz's account of analyticity and entailment is that on this account analytic sentences entail synthetic ones. Consider the sentence (4) 'A spinster is a woman'. This sentence is analytic, but it entails (5) 'A person is a woman'. It can readily be seen that (5) is both synthetic and entailed by (4). All of the semantic markers in the predicate of (5) are included in the predicate of (4) for these predicates are identical. The subject of (5) contains the disjoint marker '((Male) $\cup$ (Female))' in its reading, and according to the definition of analyticity for conditional sentences it follows that the conditional with (4) as antecedent and (5) as consequent is analytic if any one of the simple markers in this complex marker is included in the reading for the subject of (4). But (4) has the marker '(Female)' in the reading for its subject. Therefore the analytic sentence (4) entails (5), which is synthetic, for the predicate of (5) contains the marker '(Adult)' in its reading and this marker does not occur in the reading for its subject.[4]

A somewhat different case is the following. The sentence (6) 'My father is a queen' is contradictory (on one reading). Its negation (7) 'My father is not a queen' is marked as analytic (on that reading). But (7) entails (8) 'Someone is not a queen' and (8) is synthetic, so once again we see that on Katz's account, analytic sentences entail synthetic ones.

Although Katz gives a detailed account of the analytic/synthetic distinction for some classes of sentences, he does not provide an account of this distinction for all sentences. He implies that, e.g., the sentence 'The table is not round and square' is analytic (p. 218), but none of the definitions supplied are even relevant to this case. (The dictionary entry for 'Neg' supplies readings only for the negations of syntactically noncompound subject-predicate sentences). Perhaps Katz would not wish to claim that the procedures he has employed or anything like them can be extended to other classes of sentences. But if that is the case we are left completely uninformed as to how Katz's program is to be carried out. On the other hand, I have shown above that the procedures he does use yield unacceptable results for the classes of cases for which they are designed.

University of Chicago

REFERENCES

[1] Jerrold J. Katz, *The Philosophy of Language*, Harper and Row, New York and London, 1966. All quotations in this paper are from this book.

[2] Similar results are obtainable without use of the erasure clause. Consider the sentence (1′) 'An uncle is an aunt'. The negation of (1′), by clause (ii) of the entry for 'Neg' is the analytic sentence (2′) 'An uncle is not an aunt'. Since '(Female)' in the reading of the predicate of (1′) has been replaced by A/(Female), i.e. '(Male)', in forming the reading for the predicate of (2′), there is nothing in the reading for (2′) to distinguish it from the reading for (3′) 'An uncle is an uncle'. Katz's definitions thus lead to the conclusion that (3′) and (2′) are synonymous.

[3] 'R subj$_1$' and 'R pred$_1$' stand respectively for readings for the subject and predicate of S_1. Similarly for 'R subj$_2$' and 'R pred$_2$'; and generally, 'R const$_i$' and 'R const$_j$' stand for readings for the same unspecified constituent (e.g., Subject) of S_i and S_j.

[4] Another route to the same conclusion is this: The sentence 'A spinster is a person' is analytic. Therefore, R subj$_4 \phi R$ subj$_5$. Since pred$_4$ = pred$_5$, R pred$_4 \phi R$ pred$_5$. Therefore (4), which is analytic, entails (5) which is synthetic.

P. T. GEACH

A PROGRAM FOR SYNTAX

The program for syntax which I describe here is not one I can claim as specially my own. The two basic ideas are due to Frege: analysis of an expression into a main functor and its argument(s), and distinction among categories of functors according to the categories of arguments and values. The development of a handy notation for categories, and of an algorithm to test whether a string of expressions will combine into a complex expression that belongs to a definite category, is due to the Polish logicians, particularly Ajdukiewicz. My own contribution has been confined to working out details. So my program is not original, but I think it is right in essentials; and I am making propaganda for it by working it out in some particular instructive examples. I think this is all the more called for because some recent work in syntax seems to have ignored the insights I am trying to convey.

I shall begin with some thoughts from Aristotle's pioneering treatise on syntax, the *De Interpretatione*. Aristotle holds that the very simplest sort of sentence is a two-word sentence consisting of two heterogeneous parts – a name, and a predicative element (rhēma). For example, 'petetai Sōkratēs', 'Socrates is flying'. This gives us an extremely simple example for application of our category theory:

$$
\begin{array}{cc}
\text{petetai} & \text{Sōkratēs} \\
s/n & n \\
\end{array}
$$
$$s$$

The two-word Greek expression as a whole belongs to the category s of sentences; 'petetai' is a functor that takes a single name (of category n) 'Sōkratēs' as argument and yields as a result an expression of category s. Ajdukiewicz represented functorial categories by a fractional notation: α/β would be the category of a function that operates upon a single argument of category β to yield an expression of category α, so that we have a "multiplying out" of category indices. This notation becomes awkward to print when indices become complex; so following a suggestion of my

Leeds colleague Dr. T. C. Potts I shall henceforth rather write ': $\alpha\beta$' for such a functorial category. (This device makes bracketing theoretically superfluous, but in practice I shall insert parentheses sometimes to facilitate reading.) Our first rule then is the multiplying-out rule:

$$:\alpha\beta\ \beta \rightarrow \alpha$$
For instance, $:$sn n $\rightarrow$ s.

Aristotle observed that one may get a sentence from a rhēma like 'petetai' not only by combining it with a name but also by combining it with a quantified phrase like 'pās anthrōpos', 'every man'. He further observed that these two types of sentence behave quite differently under negation; the negation of 'petetai Sōkratēs is 'ou petetai Sōkratēs', when the negation 'ou' attaches to the rhēma 'petetai'; the negation of 'pās anthrōpos petetai' is 'ou pās anthrōpos petetai', where the negative attaches to the quantified phrase 'pās anthrōpos'. This is a profound insight, ignored by those who would lump together proper names and phrases like 'every man' as Noun Phrases; we have two different syntactical categories. It is easy to find in the Ajdukiewicz scheme another category that will yield the category s when combined with the category $:$sn; for we shall have, by the general rule, $::$s$:$sn $:$sn $\rightarrow$ s. But this is not enough to exhaust the Aristotelian insight. We should wish to make 'ou petetai' 'does not fly' a syntactically coherent sub-string of 'ou petetai Sōkratēs', and on the other hand to make 'ou pās anthrōpos' 'not every man' a syntactically coherent sub-string of 'ou pās anthrōpos petetai'. But by the Ajdukiewicz criteria for a string's being syntactically coherent (SC), neither string will come out as SC. To negation 'ou', we must assign the category $:$ss of a sentence-forming operator upon sentences; and neither the category-indices '$:$ss $:$sn' of 'ou petetai' nor the indices '$:$ss $:$s$:$sn' of 'ou pās anthrōpos' multiply out by Ajdukiewicz' rule to a single index of the whole expression. These are two particular cases of a general fact, noticed by medieval logicians: that a sentence may contain a *formale*, formal element – Ajdukiewicz' main functor – negation of which *is* negation of the whole proposition.

Intuitions about the SC nature of sub-strings are fallible, but are *pro tanto* evidential; we need to check our general theories of syntax against such intuitions, and also to correct our intuitions against wider insights. By the two-way process we may hope to get steadily closer to truth. In this case, we can satisfy the demands of intuition if we supplement the Ajdukiewicz multiplying-out rule with a recursive rule:

$$\text{If} \quad \alpha\,\beta \rightarrow \gamma, \quad \alpha : \beta\delta \rightarrow :\gamma\delta.$$

This already covers the Aristotelian and medieval cases. For suppose the main functor of a sentence is of category $:s\beta$, so that we have a sentence by adding a β expression. We then have by our recursive rule:

$$\text{Since} \quad :ss \; s \rightarrow s, \quad :ss \; :s\beta \rightarrow :s\beta.$$

And this covers all cases in which negation, of category $:ss$, operates upon a sentence of structure $:s\beta\ \beta$. The string of expressions categorized as:

$$:ss \; :s\beta\ \beta,$$

may be split up in two ways into SC sub-strings; namely, we may regard negation $(:ss)$ as operating on the whole sentence categorized as $:s\beta\ \beta$; or, we may regard it as combining with the $:s\beta$ expression to form a complex $:s\beta$ expression, which then combines with the β expression to form a sentence. The two Aristotelian examples are covered by this account if we take $\beta = :sn$ and $\beta = :s:sn$.

Such possibilities of multiple analysis do not mean that we have a syntactically ambiguous string. We have a single "proper series of indices", as Ajdukiewicz calls it, for a given sentence; the different ways of multiplying out the indices reveal two different but equally legitimate ways of dissecting out an SC sub-string from a larger SC string.

The Ajdukiewicz scheme allows for functors that take more than one argument. In the present discussion it will be enough to consider functors that take two arguments of the same category: if this category is β and α is the category of the functor plus its two arguments, I give the functor the category $:\alpha(2\beta)$. We get in Ajdukiewicz the rule for multiplying out with such category indices:

$$:\alpha(2\beta)\ \beta\ \beta \rightarrow \alpha.$$

Once again I add a recursive rule:

$$\text{If} \quad \alpha\,\beta\,\beta \rightarrow \gamma, \quad \text{then} \quad \alpha : \beta\delta\, :\beta\delta \rightarrow :\gamma\delta.$$

A medieval example may serve to illustrate the newly introduced categories. 'John or James came' need not be transformed into 'John came or James came' before we investigate its SC character; we can show it to be SC as it stands. But we cannot treat it as having the same simple subject-predicate structure as 'John came', only having a complex subject 'John or James' instead of the single name 'John'. For whereas the negation of 'John came' attaches to the predicate 'came', 'John or James came' has to be negated by negating 'or' – '*neither* John *nor* James came'. So my medieval writer justly took 'or' to be here the *formale* or main functor. 'John or James' may be regarded as a restricted existential quantification – 'for some x in the universe {John, James}, x...'; so we assign to it, just as we do to 'pās anthrōpos' or 'every man', the category :s:sn. The functor 'or' will then be assigned the category :(:s:sn) (2n), which combines with two names of category n to yield an :s:sn expression; and this in turn combines with the predicate 'came' of category :sn to yield a sentence. Negation, of category :ss, will combine with a functor of category :(:s:sn) (2n) to yield a functor of the same category; we see this by twice applying our recursive rule:

:ss s → s
ergo, :ss :s:sn → :s:sn
ergo, :ss :(:s:sn) (2n) → :(:s:sn) (2n).

I shall now briefly sketch how the traditional apparatus of Parts of Speech get reshaped in an Ajdukiewicz grammar. I shall consider only some of the traditional list.

I. VERBS

Intransitive verbs like 'come' or 'petetai' may be categorized as :sn. A transitive verb along with its noun-object, a phrase like 'loves Socrates', will likewise be of category :sn; 'loves' itself is thus most conveniently categorized as ::snn. 'Every Greek loves Socrates' then admits of a double dissection into SC sub-strings; we need this, because we need to recognize both 'loves Socrates' and 'every Greek loves' as SC expressions that may recur in other contexts e.g. in the relative clauses 'who loves Socrates' and 'that every Greek loves'. (When symbolizing a piece of argument stated in the vernacular, we might find it convenient to represent either recurrent phrase by the same one-place predicate letter each time it occurred.) In fact, 'loves Socrates' gets categorized as ::snn n, which multiplies out to :sn by the Ajdukiewicz rule; and then 'Every Greek loves Socrates' will be categorized as :s:sn :sn, which multiplies out to s. On the other hand, 'every Greek loves' gets categorized as :s:sn ::snn; this multiplies out to :sn by our recursive rule:

Since :s:sn :sn → s, :s:sn ::snn → :sn.

So 'Every Greek loves Socrates' comes out as :sn n, and thus again as s. Once again, we have two equally legitimate analyses, not a syntactic ambiguity.

II. CONJUNCTIONS

The term 'connective' is preferable, since 'conjunction' is indispensable as a name for one of the truth-functions. Traditional grammar distinguishes subordinating and coordinating connectives; in one case, e.g. with 'if', the connective is felt to go with the clause that follows it; in the other case, e.g. 'and', 'or', the connective is felt to be joining two clauses, not going with one rather than the other. No such distinction is needed for the binary sentence-connectives in a formal system, which may very well be taken to be all of one category; but for analysis of the vernacular it seems better to recognize a syntactical distinction between the two sorts of connectives. A subordinating connective would be of category ::sss; so such a connective together with the clause following it would be of category ::sss s, i.e. :ss, which is the category of a sentence-forming operator upon a sentence. A coordinating connective, on the other hand, would be of category :s(2s). A string categorizable as :s(2s) s s has as a whole the category s; but just as the category indices ':s(2s) s' do not multiply out to a single index, so we need not take either 'John ran and' or 'and Jane rode' to be an SC substring of 'John ran and Jane rode'.

Grammarians have often taken sentences in which a coordinating connective joins expressions other than sentences to be derived from sentences in which the same connective joins sentences. I regard this view as wholly erroneous. Our theory of categories does not restrict the possible arguments of an :s(2s) connective to a pair of sentences; on the contrary, by our recursive rule we have that a pair of the category :sβ may also be so connected to form a third:

Since :s(2s) s s → s, :s(2s) :sβ :sβ → :sβ, whatever category β may be.

And so we obtain a correct analysis of a sentence like:

> All the girls admired, but most boys detested, one of the
> saxophonists.

This is not equivalent, as a moment's thought shows, to:

> All the girls admired one of the saxophonists, but most boys
> detested one of the saxophonists,

and cannot sensibly be regarded as a transformation of it. The expressions
'all the girls admired' and 'most boys detested' are in fact each assignable
to the category :sn, as we saw before regarding 'every Greek loved'; so
the coordinating connective 'but' can combine them to form a single
string of category :sn. Since 'one of the saxophonists' is plainly a quantifying expression like 'every man', it is of category :s:sn; this is the main
functor, operating upon 'All the girls admired, but most boys detested',
of category :sn, to yield a sentence. The change of intonation pattern
marked by the second comma, as contrasted with the smooth run in the
sentence:

> All the girls were thrilled, but most boys detested one of the
> saxophonists,

is easily explained: 'most boys detested one of the saxophonists' is an
SC substring (in fact a sentence) in the latter example but not in the for-
mer, and the change of intonation shows our feeling for this. (Just as
'Plato was bald' has a different intonation pattern when it stands by itself
and when it comes as part of 'The man whose most famous pupil was
Plato was bald'; in the latter context it is patently not an SC string.)

Similarly, a subordinating connective along with the clause following
it will come out, as I said, in the category :ss, that of a sentence-forming
operator upon sentences; but it does not follow that such a unit can be
read only as attached to an entire main clause; on the contrary, we must
sometimes so regard it as attached to an expression of another category.
A good medieval example of syntactical ambiguity brings out this point:

> Every man dies when just one man dies.

This could be true (and was once, in this sense, a presumption of English
law) as denying the possibility of quite simultaneous deaths; in the other

possible sense, it could be true only if there were just one man, so that his death was the death of every man. The first sense requires us to take the subordinating connective plus its clause, 'when just one man dies', as going not with 'Every man dies' but just with 'dies', as we may see from the paraphrase:

> It holds of every man that he dies when just one man dies (namely he himself and nobody else).

The second sense affirms that the universal death of mankind happens along with the death of one and only one man; here, the whole sentence 'Every man dies' is operated on by the sentence-forming operator 'when just one man dies'.

III. ADVERBS

Some adverbs, as the name suggests, are verb-forming operators upon verbs, and are thus of category :(:sn) (:sn). Thus 'passionately protested' comes out as of the same category with 'protested' (I am taking this as an intransitive verb of category :sn) but also 'passionately loved' comes out as of the same category with 'loved', namely ::snn, for we have:

$$\text{Since } :(:sn)(:sn) :sn \rightarrow :sn, \; :(:sn)(:sn) ::snn \rightarrow ::snn.$$

And as in the other example we have a double possibility of analysis that corresponds to no syntactical ambiguity: 'passionately/loved Mary' and 'passionately loved/Mary' alike work out as SC, and here once more we are just picking out subordinate SC strings in alternative ways from an SC string.

Two adverbs can be joined by a coordinating connective – 'passionately and sincerely', 'improbably but presumably'. On the other hand a combination like 'passionately and presumably' sounds like nonsense. It is nonsense; it involves a confusion of syntactical categories. For an adverb like 'improbably' or 'presumably' is to be taken, in at least some cases, not as modifying the verb, but as modifying the whole sentence – its category must thus be :ss. Two adverbs of category :ss can be joined with the connective 'but' of category :s(2s); for by our recursive rule:

$$\text{Since } :s(2s) \, s \, s \rightarrow s, \; :s(2s) :ss :ss \rightarrow :ss.$$

So 'improbably but presumably' comes out as a complex adverb of category :ss. Again, by our recursive rule:

$$\text{Since } :s(2s) \, s \, s \rightarrow s, \; :s(2s) :sn :sn \rightarrow :sn$$
$$\text{Since } :s(2s) :sn :sn \rightarrow :sn, \; :s(2s) :(:sn) (:sn) :(:sn) (:sn)$$
$$\rightarrow :(:sn) (:sn).$$

So 'passionately and sincerely' comes out as of category :(:sn) (:sn), like its component adverbs. But an operator of category :s(2s) can take only two arguments of like category; so if we attempt to join with 'and' the adverbs 'passionately', of category :(:sn) (:sn), and 'presumably', of category :ss, we get syntactical nonsense.

IV. PREPOSITIONS

A prepositional phrase may be an adverb of category :(:sn) (:sn), like 'in London' in 'Raleigh smoked in London'; if so the preposition in the phrase is of category ::(:sn) (:sn)n. On the other hand, in the sentence 'Nobody except Raleigh smoked', 'nobody except Raleigh', like plain 'nobody', is a quantifying expression, of category :s:sn. So 'except Raleigh' is a functor turning one quantifying expression into another – thus, of category :(:s:sn) (:s:sn); and 'except' itself is of category ::(:s:sn) (:s:sn) n. As before, expressions of the same category can be joined with coordinating connectives but not expressions unlike in category; for example, we may assume that 'before' and 'after' are both of category ::(:sn)(:sn)n, so 'before or after' is well-formed, as we may see:

$$\text{Since } :s(2s) \, s \, s \rightarrow s, \quad :s(2s) :sn :sn \rightarrow :sn$$
$$\textit{ergo,} \quad :s(2s) :(:sn) (:sn) :(:sn) (:sn)$$
$$\rightarrow :(:sn) (:sn)$$
$$\textit{ergo,} \quad :s(2s) ::(:sn) (:sn)n ::(:sn) (:sn)n$$
$$\rightarrow ::(:sn) (:sn)n.$$

But though 'Nobody smoked before or after Raleigh' is well-formed, 'Nobody smoked before or except Raleigh' is syntactical nonsense, because 'before' and 'except' differ in category.

The preposition 'by' is of different category, again, in the use it has with the passive construction; 'was hit by' must be regarded as formed by a logical operation upon 'hit', and the functor is of category :(::snn) (::snn), since ::snn is the category of 'hit'. The word "governed" by 'by' is thus not syntactically connected with it, since ':(::snn) (::snn)' and 'n' do not multiply out to give a single index. Why anyone should call a 'by'phrase an Adverbial of Manner I can only dimly imagine, calling to mind half-remembered school exercises in parsing. (How, in what manner, was Caesar killed? By Brutus. Very well then, 'by Brutus' is an Adverbial of Manner, just like 'brutally'!)

The categorizing of prepositions, however, raises very serious difficulties for our whole theory of categories – difficulties which I think can be overcome only by introducing a further powerful, recursive, procedure for establishing that an expression is SC. For example, 'some city' like 'every man' is of category :s:sn; but if we assign 'in' to category ::(:sn) (:sn)n, not only is the functor incapable of taking 'some city' as an argument as it can take 'London', but also the whole sentence 'Raleigh smoked in some city' cannot be made out to be SC by any way of multiplying out the category indices of 'Raleigh' (n), 'smoked' (:sn), 'in', and 'some city'. The only arrangement of the indices that multiplies out to 's' is this:

:s:sn	::(:sn) (:sn) n	n	:sn
(some city)	(in)	(Raleigh)	(smoked)

but this gives rather the syntactical analysis of 'Some city smoked in Raleigh'.

Our recursive procedure is supplied by the well-known logical device – well expounded e.g. in Quine's *Methods of Logic* – of introducing a predicate as an interpretation of a schematic letter in a schema. If 'F' is of category :sn, the schema 'F(London)' will be SC and of category s. Now if 'F(London)' is SC, so will '(Some city)F' be – since ':s:sn :sn' gives 's'. We now reason thus: We have seen how to assign categories to the expressions in 'Raleigh smoked in London' so as to show it is SC and of category s. We may accordingly assign 'Raleigh smoked in —[1]' as the interpretation of the one-place predicate letter 'F' in the SC schema 'F(London)'. But then also the corresponding interpretation of the SC schema '(Some city)F' will be SC; and this interpretation is the sentence 'Raleigh smoked in some city'; so this sentence is also SC.

Some quite short sentences require a number of steps like this to show they are SC. I shall give an example presently; but I must first explain how to categorize the reflexive pronouns in '-self'. Such a pronoun can be attached to a transitive verb of category ::snn to yield a one-place predicate of category :sn. We have already seen two ways of so attaching an expression to a transitive verb; both ':s:sn ::snn' and '::snn n' multiply out to ':sn'. But a reflexive pronoun plainly is not either a name, or a quantifying expression like 'every man'. Nor is it a mere proxy or substitute for an expression of one of these categories; we might take 'himself' in 'Judas hanged himself' to go proxy for 'Judas', but there is nothing 'himself' would be taken as proxy for in 'The Apostle who hanged himself went to Hell', and plainly 'hanged himself' is not syntactically different in the two sentences. The only category that gives the right result is ::sn::snn, since ::sn::snn ::snn → :sn. We may now consider our example, recalling ones of medieval vintage:

> Every number or its successor is even.

We begin with the clearly well-formed sentence: '8 or 3 is even'. If we give the numerals the category n of proper names (shades of Frege!) then 'is even' will be of category :sn and this sentence will be of the same syntax in essentials as our previous example 'John or James came'.

Since '8 or 3 is even' is SC, we may take '8 or $\underline{1}$ is even' as the interpretation of the one-place predicate letter 'F' (category :sn) in the SC schema 'F(3)'. Now if 'F(3)' is SC, then if we assign to '5's successor' the quantifier category :s:sn (there are arguments for doing this, but I omit them for simplicity of exposition), the schema '(5's successor) F' will be SC. But the corresponding interpretation of *this* schema will be the sentence:

> 8 or 5's successor is even.

So this sentence is SC.

We now treat '$\underline{1}$ or $\underline{2}$'s successor is even' as the interpretation of the two-place predicate letter 'R' in the schema 'R(8,5)'. If 'R' is of category ::snn, and each of '8', '5' is of category n, this schema is SC. But then also the result of operating on 'R' with a reflexive pronoun, 'R($\underline{1}$, itself)', will be an SC *one*-place schematic predicate; since we just saw that is how the reflexive pronoun works, to turn a two-place predicate into a one-place predicate. And the corresponding interpretation of 'R($\frac{1}{}$, itself)' will be:

$\frac{1}{}$ or itself's successor is even.

So this counts as an SC one-place predicate. English accidence of course demands that one rewrite 'itself's' as 'its'.

Finally, since we may treat '$\frac{1}{}$ or its successor is even' as an interpretation of the one-place predicate letter G, and since with the quantifying expression 'Every number' prefixed we get an SC schema '(Every number) G', we get as the relevant interpretation of this schema:

Every number or its successor is even.

So *this* is an SC sentence; which was to be proved.

Grammarians may find my interpretation of this sentence extremely farfetched. They should consider, however, that it does correspond to the obviously correct paraphrase:

It holds of every number that it or its (own) successor is even.

Moreover, other analysis, more comfortable to the ideas that come natural to grammarians, lead us into a bog of absurdity. We cannot construe our sentence on the model of:

Every man or every woman will be shot.

For this is equivalent to 'Every man will be shot or every woman will be shot'; but no such equivalence holds in our case – the irrelevant falsehood 'Every number is even' has nothing to do with the syntax of our example. (Nor need 'Every man or every woman will be shot' itself be construed as *short for* a disjunction of sentences, though it is *equivalent* to one; for it is easily shown by our rules that the two quantifying expressions 'every man' and 'every woman', of category :s:sn, can in their own right be joined by 'or', category :ss, to form an expression of that same category.) As for taking 'number or its successor' as a complex term, that lets us in at once, as my medieval predecessors noticed, for an absurd "syllogism":

Every number is a (number or its successor).
Every (number or its successor) is even.
ergo: Every number is even!

V. RELATIVE PRONOUNS

Quine and I have both repeatedly argued that the use of relative pronouns may fruitfully be compared to that of bound variables. The question is, though, which kind of expressions throws light on the syntax of the other kind; the syntax of bound variables is very complicated and un-perspicuous, as we may see e.g. from the need for rules in logic books to guard against unintended "captures" of variables in formulas introduced by substitution. Ajdukiewicz attempted to modify his scheme of cate-gories so as to assign categories to quantifiers that bind variables; but his theory is manifestly inadequate – it takes no account of the fact that a variable is bound to a quantifier containing an *equiform* variable: for Ajdukiewicz '(x) (Fxy)' would not differ syntactically from '(z) (Fxy)', so far as I can see.

It occurred to me that some light might be thrown on the matter by constructing a simple combinatory logic, on the lines of Quine's paper 'Variables explained away'. I cannot claim any algorithmic facility in working with combinators, but I have reached results encouraging enough to be worth reporting.

To translate into a combinatory notation the English sentence:

Anybody who hurts anybody who hurts him hurts himself.

I began with an obvious translation of this into quantifier notation (variables restricted to persons; '$H\underline{}^{1}\,\underline{}^{2}$' = '$\underline{}^{2}$ hurts $\underline{}^{1}$'):

$$(x)\,((y)\,(Hxy \rightarrow Hyx) \rightarrow Hxx)$$

and then devised the following set of combinators:

'Univ': when a predicate followed by a string of variables has prefixed to it a universal quantifier binding just the last variable of the string, we may instead delete the last variable and prefix 'Univ'; e.g. '(x) (Fx)' becomes 'Univ F' and '(x) (Ryx)' becomes 'Univ Ry'.

'Imp': if the antecedent of a conditional consists of a predicate followed by a string of variables, and the consequent consists of a predicate follow-ed by just the same string, then we may instead write 'Imp' followed by the two predicates followed by the string of variables. E.g. '$Rxy \rightarrow Sxy$' becomes 'Imp R S xy'; '$Fz \rightarrow Gz$' becomes 'Imp F G z'.

'Ref': if a predicate is followed by a string of variables ending with repetition of a variable, we may instead delete the repetition and prefix 'Ref' to the predicate. E.g. 'Rxx' becomes 'Ref Rx', and 'Syxx' becomes 'Ref Syx'.

'Cnv': the result of prefixing 'Cnv' to a predicate followed by a string of two or more variables is tantamount to the result of switching the last two variables of the string. E.g. 'Ryx' may be rewritten as 'Cnv R xy', and 'Rxyx' as 'Cnv R xxy'.

We now eliminate, step by step, the variables in the above formula. 'Hxy → Hyx' may be rewritten as 'Hxy → Cnv H xy', and then as 'Imp H Cnv H xy'.

So '(y) (Hxy → Hyx)' may be rewritten as '(y) (Imp H Cnv H xy)' and thus as 'Univ Imp H Cnv H x'.

'Hxx' may be rewritten as 'Ref H x'; so since '(y) (Hxy → Hyx)' may be rewritten as 'Univ Imp H Cnv Hx', '((y) (Hxy → Hyx) → Hxx)' may be rewritten as:

$$\text{Imp Univ Imp H Cnv H Ref H } x\,.$$

Finally, to get an equivalent of the whole formula, we get the effect of the prenex '(x)' by deleting the final 'x' and prefixing 'Univ':

$$\text{Univ Imp Univ Imp H Cnv H Ref H}\,.$$

It is fairly easy to see how the symbols of this string should be assigned to categories. 'Univ F', when 'F' is one-place, is a sentence of the same form as 'Everyone smokes'; 'Univ', like 'everyone', is of category :s:sn. 'H', like the transitive verb 'hurts' that it represents, is of category ::snn. 'Imp' is a connective that combines two predicates to form a predicate with the same number of places; it is thus of category ::sn(2:sn). 'Ref', like a reflexive pronoun, reduces a predicate of $n+1$ places to a predicate of n places; it is thus of category ::sn(::snn). And 'Cnv' turns a many-place predicate into one of the same number of places; it is thus of category :(::snn)(::snn). (It might seem as if these assignments of categories were too restrictive of the arguments these functors would be allowed to operate on. But in view of our recursive rules this is not so. For example, 'Imp' could combine two predicates of category ::snn to form a third:

$$::\text{sn}(2:\text{sn}) :\text{sn} :\text{sn} \rightarrow :\text{sn}$$
$$\textit{ergo, } ::\text{sn}(2:\text{sn}) ::\text{snn} ::\text{snn} \rightarrow ::\text{snn}.)$$

We may now check that the above string is, as Ajdukiewicz would say, well-formed throughout and of category s. 'Cnv H' is of category ::snn, since we have

$$: (::snn) (::snn) ::snn \rightarrow ::snn .$$

So 'Imp H Cnv H' is of category ::snn, since we have:

$$::sn(2:sn) :sn :sn \rightarrow :sn .$$

Hence, by the recursive rule:

$$::sn(2:sn) ::snn ::snn \rightarrow ::snn .$$

So 'Univ Imp H Cnv H' is of category :sn, since we have:

$$:s:sn :sn \rightarrow s$$
$$ergo, \ :s:sn ::snn \rightarrow :sn .$$

Now also 'Ref H' is of category :sn, since we have:

$$::sn(::snn) ::snn \rightarrow :sn .$$

Hence 'Imp Univ Imp H Cnv H Ref H' is of category sn

$$::sn(2:sn) :sn :sn \rightarrow :sn .$$

Finally, since 'Univ' is of category :s:sn, the category of the whole works out as s.

Now this string of predicates and combinators can at once be translated, word for word, into pidgin English:

Univ	Imp	Univ	Imp	H	Cnv H	Ref H
anybody	who	anybody	who	hurt	get hurt by	hurt self.

(Some small changes of word order were made to improve this mock-up of English: 'Cnv' was rendered by 'get' before the argument of the functor and 'by' after it, and 'Ref' by 'self' after rather than before the argument of this functor.) I suggest, therefore, on the strength of this example (and of others I have not space for here) that we may hope to get a good mock-up of the use of relative pronouns in the vernacular by exercises in combinatory logic.

An interesting confirmation of this conjecture comes to us when we observe that in the above sentence 'Univ Imp' is an SC sub-string:

Univ   Imp
:s:sn   :(:sn) (2:sn) → :s(2:sn),

by our recursive rule since :s:sn :sn → s.

Accordingly, we could definitionally introduce a new combinator of category :s(2:sn), say 'Unimp', and rewrite our string as 'Unimp Unimp H Cnv H Ref H'. The new string may also be translated straight into pidgin English:

Unimp	Unimp	H	Cnv H	Ref H
Whoever	whoever	hurt	get hurt by	hurt self.

And this seems to give a correct account of the logical syntax of the relative pronoun 'whoever'. Of course these results are most unnatural from the point of view of school grammar; in 'anybody who hurts...' the major division would be taken to come not after 'who' but after 'anybody', and 'who hurts...' would be taken as an SC sub-string somehow "modifying" 'anybody'. But if we are to get a scientific insight into syntax we mustn't be afraid to break Priscian's head. As Descartes said, *manum ferulae subduximus* – we no longer need hold out our hand to be caned by pedants.

Such are some specimens of the work I have done to carry out this Polish program. Much more remains to be done; it is like fitting together a huge jig-saw puzzle. But I hope I may have persuaded some readers that further following of this path is worth while.

University of Leeds,
University of Pennsylvania

JAMES D. McCAWLEY

A PROGRAM FOR LOGIC

1. CONSTITUENT STRUCTURE IN LINGUISTICS AND LOGIC

Chomsky's *Aspects* (1965) described and presented justification for a model of linguistic structure according to which the relation between sentences (or better, the surface structures of sentences) and their semantic structures was mediated by a level of DEEP STRUCTURE: a grammar consisted of a BASE COMPONENT, which was a set of rules that specified what deep structures were possible in the language in question, a TRANSFORMATIONAL COMPONENT, which was a system of rules that specified how deep structures corresponded to surface structures[1], and a SEMANTIC COMPONENT, which was a system of rules that associated a set of semantic representations to each deep structure. Since the appearance of *Aspects*, there have been two opposing lines of development in transformational grammar, the principal differences between which relate to the syntax/ semantics dichotomy which the theory of *Aspects* presupposes. In the remainder of this paper, I will ignore the line of development represented by the recent works of Chomsky and Jackendoff (see e.g. Chomsky, 1970), which upholds the dichotomy between syntax and semantics, and will concentrate on the other line of development, represented by the recent works of Ross, Lakoff, Postal, and myself, which rejects any dividing line between syntax and semantics (such as the level of 'deep structure' had constituted) or any distinction between 'transformations' and 'rules of semantic interpretation'.

My chief reason for pursuing a conception of grammar in which there is no dividing line between syntax and semantics is that in all significant respects in which putative deep structures proposed within the framework of *Aspects* have differed from semantic structure, they have been shown to be wrong. I will illustrate this sweeping conclusion with an example that I consider fairly typical. Katz and Postal (1964) proposed that negative clauses have a deep structure as in Figure 1, in which the negative clause is composed of three constituents: the negative element

Davidson and Harman (eds.), Semantics of Natural Language, 498–544. *All rights reserved*
Copyright © 1972 by D. Reidel Publishing Company, Dordrecht-Holland

and the two elements (a noun-phrase and a verb-phrase) of which the corresponding positive clause would be composed. I will argue below that negative clauses have a different constituent structure, namely that of the negative element plus a sentence (rather than plus the pieces of a sentence), as in Figure 2. The deep structure given in Figure 1 can be shown wrong and that in Figure 2 right (at least, right in the respect in

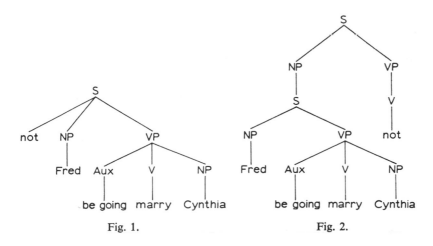

Fig. 1.   Fig. 2.

which it differs from Figure 1) by the following argument. It is possible for the pronoun *it* to have a clause for its antecedent, as in

(1)   Max told me that Eleanor had eloped with Schwartz, but I refused to believe it.

Lakoff in unpublished work has demonstrated that this type of *it* (though not all uses of personal pronouns) must be derived from a copy of its antecedent by a transformation which applies to a structure containing two identical embedded sentences and replaces one of them by *it*. Consider now the sentence

(2)   Fred isn't going to marry Susan, even though the fortune-teller predicted it.

The *it* would generally be taken as standing for *Fred is going to marry Susan*[2], which means that in the derivation of (2), the pronominalization transformation must apply to a structure containing two copies of whatever underlies *Fred is going to marry Susan*. Under the proposal of Figure 2, (2) would have a deep structure containing two copies of such an embedded sentence, but under the proposal of Figure 1 it would not. Thus, the proposal of Figure 2 allows the pronominalization transformation that figures in (1) to apply in the derivation of (2) in such a way as to correctly associate it with its semantic structure, whereas the proposal of Figure 1 does not allow any known formulation of pronominalization which would give a uniform treatment of the occurrence and interpretation of *it* in (1) and (2). This treatment of negation makes the further prediction that a negative clause makes its positive counterpart available to be the antecedent of *it* but a positive clause does not make its negative counterpart available to be the antecedent of *it*. This prediction seems to be borne out by the facts: the *it* of

(3)   Fred is going to marry Susan, even though the fortune teller predicted it.

cannot refer to the proposition that Fred isn't going to marry Susan (unless, of course, that proposition has been mentioned earlier in the discourse; in that case, it is the earlier mention and not the first clause of (3) that provides the antecedent of *it*).

The above argument that negative clauses arise from an underlying structure in which the negative element is outside of the corresponding positive clause[3] relies heavily on the notion of CONSTITUENT STRUCTURE, which is indicated in the various diagrams by lines[4]. The reasons for taking syntactic representations to be TREES rather than STRINGS are first, that the transformations that associate underlying and surface structures function in terms of units (which can in principle be of arbitrarily great internal structure) such as are represented by the non-terminal nodes in such structures; for example, the transformation of EXTRAPOSITION optionally moves an embedded sentence to the end of its clause, as illustrated by the following pairs of sentences (in the first sentence of each pair, extraposition has not applied; in the second, it has):

(4)(a)   That Harry was arrested shocks me.
   (b)   It shocks me that Harry was arrested.
(5)(a)   Why Max hit me is not known.
   (b)   It is not known why Max hit me.

Secondly, different groupings of the same elements are not equivalent (as they are in e.g. Ajdukiewicz's work); a transformation may have the effect of changing the grouping of elements, but once it has been changed, it stays changed in subsequent stages of the derivation of the sentence. For example, there is a transformation in English which combines an

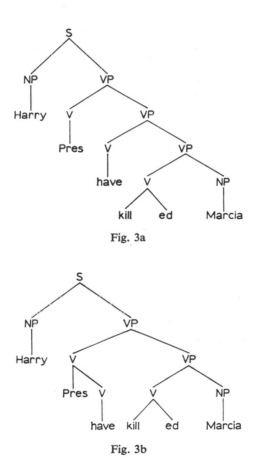

Fig. 3a

Fig. 3b

'auxiliary verb' with an adjacent tense element, thus converting the tree of Figure 3a into that of Figure 3b.[5] All subsequent transformations treat Pres +*have* as a unit but do not treat *have* (tenseless)+*kill*+*ed*+ *Marcia* as a unit: note the results of the transformations which position the negative element, give rise to question word order, and delete certain repeated items:

(6)(a)   John hasn't killed Marcia. (*John doesn't have killed Marcia)
  (b)   Has John killed Marcia? (*Does John have killed Marcia?)
  (c)   John has killed his wife, and so has Bill. (*... and so does Bill).

The asterisked examples are what would result if these transformations treated *have* as grouped together with *killed Marcia* rather than as grouped together with the present tense element.

I maintain that not only syntactic structure but also semantic structure involves the grouping of elements rather than just their linear sequence. In particular, to the extent that 'semantic structure' will coincide with what has been called 'logical form', it will have to specify the grouping of elements in order that it be possible to formulate rules of inference that work right. For example, take the following familiar rules of inference:

(7a) $p \vee q$ ('$\vee$' is 'inclusive' *or*)
        $\dfrac{-p}{q}$ ('$-$' is negation)

(7b) $\dfrac{p \cdot q}{p}$ ('$\cdot$' is *and*)

If one uses these rules of inference in connection with formulas written according to the usual conventions for 'leaving out parentheses', he cannot simply substitute any string of symbols for p or q and get a valid inference; for example,

(8)(a) $\dfrac{p \cdot q \vee r}{-p \cdot q}$ $\dfrac{p \cdot q \vee r}{p}$
          $\quad\quad r$

are not valid inferences. The purpose of this example is to show that the grouping of symbols which according to the 'conventions for leaving out parentheses' need not be indicated explicitly continues to function in any use that one makes of the formulas in question: the various rules of inference make reference not just to a string of symbols that has a − or a ∨ or a. in the middle but to the negation or the *or*-conjunction or the *and*-conjunction[6] of certain sentences, which is to say that they make reference to the constituent structure of the sentences that they are applied to. This, incidentally, demonstrates the point which I assumed above, that semantically a negative clause is composed of the negative element plus the sentence that it negates rather than of the negative element plus the pieces that make up that sentence. In addition, the so-called 'Polish parentheses-free notation', which is often said to eliminate even the restricted use of parentheses which the above-mentioned 'conventions for leaving out parentheses' cannot eliminate, is actually unable to do without some explicit indication of constituent structure if conjunctions of more than three items are allowed, e.g. the formula

(9)   And Or *p q r s*

would give no clue as to whether the *r* is bound by the *And* (i.e. And (Or *p q*)*r s*)) or by the *Or* (i.e. And(Or *p q r*)*s*)). I will argue later that the proposal that all multi-termed conjunctions be treated as iterated two-term conjunctions is misguided and that in order to allow one to state rules of inference in their fullest generality and to be able to provide the input necessary for the correct application of syntactic rules, a system of semantic representation must involve conjunctions of arbitrarily many terms. I accordingly conclude that no adequate system of semantic representation can be 'parentheses-free' and will henceforth assume that the syntactic and semantic structures that I will refer to are trees rather than strings; I will occasionally write proposals for semantic structure in linear form, but these strings of symbols are to be taken as merely informal abbreviations for trees.

2. SOME PROPERTIES OF SEMANTICALLY BASED TRANSFORMATIONAL GRAMMAR

In this section, I will assume that every sentence[7] has a semantic structure and a surface syntactic structure, both of which are LABELED TREES (i.e. they specify the grouping of units into larger units and the category membership of those units). I will examine reflexive pronouns in English and on the basis of their behavior draw some conclusions about how semantic structure must be related to surface structure.

Since there are cases in which a sentence with a reflexive pronoun can be paraphrased by a sentence containing something non-reflexive in place of it, e.g.

(10)(a)   Max$_i$ believes himself$_i$ to be a werewolf.
    (b)   Max$_i$ believes that he$_i$ is a werewolf.[8]

I will assume that the difference between reflexive pronouns and non-reflexive items is not present in semantic structure and thus that a grammar of a language must have rules that relate surface structures with reflexive pronouns to more abstract structures that do not contain reflexive pronouns. Under the assumption that (10a) and (10b) have the same semantic structure, it is clear that semantic structure is not sufficient to determine whether a given item is realized as a reflexive pronoun, since if one interchanges reflexive and ordinary pronouns in (10a–b), the results are ungrammatical:

(11)(a)   *Max$_i$ believes that himself$_i$ is a werewolf.
    (b)   *Max$_i$ believes him$_i$ to be a werewolf.

Evidently, the possibility of using a reflexive depends on whether one avails himself of the option provided by English grammar of moving

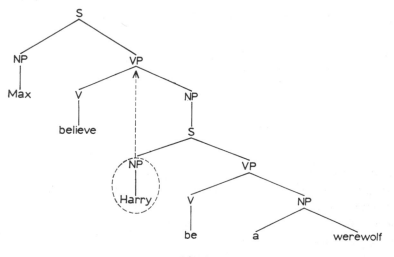

Fig. 4

the subject of certain subordinate clauses into the main clause (Figure 4), giving such variants as

(12)(a) Max believes that Harry is a werewolf.
 (b) Max believes Harry to be a werewolf.

These examples suggest that the rule for using reflexive pronouns is that (as proposed in Lees and Klima, 1963) a reflexive is used in place of one of two coreferential NP's if they are in the same clause. I have already shown that the condition 'in the same clause' does not refer to the clauses of semantic structure. It likewise does not refer to the clauses of surface structure. To see this, note first that infinitive expressions act like separate clauses in not generally allowing reflexives whose antecedent is outside the expression:

(13)(a) *Harry$_i$ forced Susan to kiss himself$_i$.
 (b) *Harry$_i$ wants Susan to kiss himself$_i$.
 (c) *John promised Margaret$_i$ to kiss herself$_i$.
 (d) *Cynthia seems to me$_i$ to like myself$_i$.
 (e) *Agnes$_i$ believes John to have insulted herself$_i$.

However, there are also sentences in which a reflexive in an infinitive expression does have its antecedent outside that expression:

(14)(a) Harry forced Susan$_i$ to denounce herself$_i$.
 (b) Harry$_i$ wants to kill himself$_i$.
 (c) Fred$_i$ promised Margaret to wash himself$_i$.
 (d) Cynthia$_i$ seems to me to admire herself$_i$.
 (e) Agnes believes Fred$_i$ to have shot himself$_i$.

The sentences which allow reflexives have either had a NP which is co-referential with the reflexive deleted (a, b, c) or been subjected to a transformation that moves either the reflexive or its antecedent into a higher clause (d, e), as illustrated in Figure 5a–b. While (13a–c) have likewise undergone the deletion of a NP and (13d–e) a movement of material into the main clause, the difference is that in (14a–e) the reflexive and its antecedent were in the same clause prior to the application of that transformation, but such is not the case with (13a–e). This indicates that the rule for using reflexives has to do with the structure of these sentences prior to the deletion or movement in question. The rule cannot simply

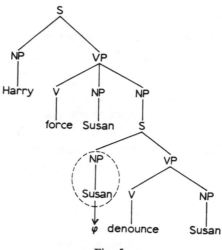

Fig. 5a

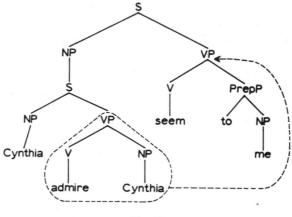

Fig. 5b

be based on the surface structure of the sentences, since the ungrammatical (13c) and the grammatical (14a) have exactly the same surface structure except for the choice of nouns and verbs. The fact that *force* and *promise* show different patterns in the use of reflexives is the result of their having different conditions for the deletion of the subject of the embedded sentence: the subject of the embedded sentence is deleted if it is coreferential with the indirect object of *force* or if it is coreferential with the subject of *promise*. Thus, the conditions for using reflexives have to do with something intermediate between semantic structure and surface structure. The conception of grammar which I will assume in what follows is one in which the rules relating semantic structure to surface structure (henceforth called *transformations*) virtually all have to do with intermediate stages between semantic structure and surface structure. Using the term DERIVATION to refer to a sequence of trees that lead from semantic structure to surface structure, each transformation may be thought of as a specification of how a certain stage of a derivation may ('optional transformation') or must ('obligatory transformation') differ from the next stage.[9]

The discussion of exx. 10–14 has touched on an important aspect of the way in which transformations interact with each other. I have shown that in the derivation of (10a), raising must apply before reflexivization, and that in the derivation of (14e), reflexivization must apply before raising. This, however, does not mean that there is no restriction on the order in which reflexivization and raising apply: when two transformations are such that one applies earlier in some derivations and the other applies earlier in other derivations (as is the case with reflexivization and raising), the two classes of derivations differ as to the relative 'heights' of the clauses which are affected, and an application of either transformation to a 'lower' clause takes precedence over an application of either of them to a 'higher' clause. For example, in the derivation of (14e), reflexivization affects the subordinate clause and applies before raising, which affects the main clause. In cases like (10a), where both transformations affect the same clause, they apply in a fixed order, in this case, raising first and then reflexivization. Such considerations lead to the proposal that at least some of the transformations of the language form what Chomsky (1965) called a CYCLE: a system of rules which have a fixed order governing their application to any one clause and such that the application of any

508 JAMES D. MCCAWLEY

of them to a 'lower' clause precedes the application of any of them to a 'higher' clause. A demonstration that not all transformations of English belong to a cycle is given in Ross (1967) and is reported in slightly revised form in McCawley (1970a). The conception of a grammar which Ross arrived at (and which he, Lakoff, and I currently subscribe to) is that the transformations form two systems: a cycle, whose rules interact in the manner just described, and a system of post-cyclic transformations, which interact in a somewhat simpler manner: they come in a linear order, and all applications of any one of them precede all applications of the next one. While little of the material to follow will be incomprehensible without an understanding of this conception of how transformations are ordered, there will be a couple of places where I have occasion to mention the notion of cycle.

3. ON THE NOTION 'GENERALIZATION'

My sweeping statement that in all respects where deep structures proposed within the framework of *Aspects* have differed from semantic structure they can be shown to be wrong crucially depends on a notion that is worth devoting some time to, namely that of '(linguistically) significant/ valid generalization'. Many of the arguments against putative deep structures are based on demonstrations that they make it impossible to give a single rule which covers all cases of a phenomenon and that they thus 'miss the generalization'. As an example[10], compare two analyses of imperative sentences such as

(15)   Shut the door.

In the one analysis, the sentence is treated as having an underlying subject *you*, which is deleted by a transformation[11]. Under such an analysis, the reflexive pronoun in

(16)   Wash yourself.

and the deletion of the subject in the embedded clause of

(17)   Promise Harry to wash yourself.

arise by the same rules that create reflexives and delete embedded subjects in declarative sentences. Under the second analysis, which no one to my knowledge has seriously proposed, imperatives have no underlying subject, a reflexive pronoun is introduced in place of a noun phrase which either is coreferential to an earlier NP in the same clause or is second person and in the main clause of an imperative sentence, and the subject of the sentential complement of *promise* is deleted when it is coreferential with the subject of *promise* or when it is second person and *promise* is the main verb of an imperative. The fault with the second proposal is that it treats the reflexivization and deletion in (16–17) as if they had nothing to do with coreferentiality, as if it were purely accidental that in imperatives reflexivization of NP's in the main clause and deletion of the subject of the complement of *promise* affect second person items rather than, say, first person plurals or expressions denoting baseball players or expressions denoting an even number of objects. According to the first proposal, (16–17) illustrate the interaction of several extremely general rules of grammar; according to proposal two, (16–17) illustrate rules specific to imperatives which only by coincidence have an effect similar to that of some much more general rules of English.

A more topical example of an argument that one analysis captures a generalization which another misses is the argument which rejects the deep structures proposed in *Aspects* for NP's (according to which a NP such as *every philosopher* or *many Armenians* is present as such in deep structure) in favour of an alternative in which, as in most modern proposals for 'logical structure', quantifiers are outside of the clauses that they appear in in surface structure, and, since *every philosopher* and *many Armenians* are constituents in surface structure and indeed can be shown to be NP's, there is a transformation of QUANTIFIER LOWERING, which attaches the quantifier to one of the NP's which is indexed by the variable that it binds.

The proposal of an external source for quantifiers makes it possible for exactly the same rule that introduces reflexives into quantifier-free sentences to account for where reflexives occur or do not occur in sentences with quantifiers, e.g. Geach's celebrated examples

(18)(a)   Every philosopher contradicts himself.

  (b)   Every philosopher contradicts every philosopher.

and likewise for exactly the same rule which deletes the subject of an embedded sentence in a quantifier-free structure to account for where deletion takes place or does not in sentences containing quantifiers, e.g.

(19)(a)   Every American wants to be rich.
　　(b)   Every American wants every American to be rich.

It makes no sense to treat (18b) as differing from (18a) in having a deep
structure with non-coreferential tokens of *every philosopher* where (18a)
has coreferential tokens of *every philosopher*, in the way that transformational grammarians have often treated

(20)(a)   Harry kicked himself.
　　(b)   Harry kicked Harry.

as differing through (20b) having a deep structure with two non-coreferential tokens of *Harry* where (20a) has coreferential tokens of *Harry*,
as in Figure 6. Since the two surface tokens of *every philosopher* in (18b)
refer to the same set of philosophers (to the extent that it makes sense to

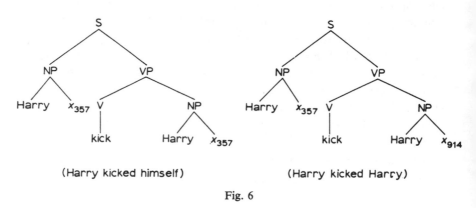

Fig. 6

speak of them referring at all), it is nonsense to speak of them as non-
coreferential. Thus, the types of deep structure proposed in *Aspects* give
no clue as to how one could assign different deep structures to (18a–b)
nor how one could formulate a rule of reflexivization that would apply
in the derivation of (18a) but not that of (18b). The proposal that quantifiers originate outside of the clauses that they are manifested in has no
such difficulties: taking Figures 7a–b as a first approximation to the deep
structures of (18a–b) (they will be modified considerably in Section 5),
the derivations yield exactly the correct outputs, without any revision of

the reflexivization rule being necessary, under the assumptions (which are well supported) that reflexivization and quantifier lowering are in the cycle. In McCawley (1970b), I show that the presence of reflexives in (21a, c) and their absence in (21b, d):

(21)(a)   Only Lyndon pities himself.
    (b)   Only Lyndon pities Lyndon.
    (c)   Only Lyndon pities only himself.
    (d)   Only Lyndon pities only Lyndon.

follows automatically if (21a–d) are derived respectively from structures along the lines of[13]

(22)(a) $Only_x(Lyndon, Pity(x, x))$
    (b) $Only_x(Lyndon, Pity(x, Lyndon))$
    (c) $Only_x(Lyndon, Only_y(x, Pity(x, y))$
    (d) $Only_x(Lyndon, Only_y(Lyndon, Pity(x, y))$

and reflexivization and the rule which combines 'Only' with the corresponding NP (I suspect that that rule can be taken in in a generalized formulation of quantifier lowering) are both in the cycle, with the 'Only'-rule ordered before reflexivization.

It should be emphasized here that the arguments under discussion are

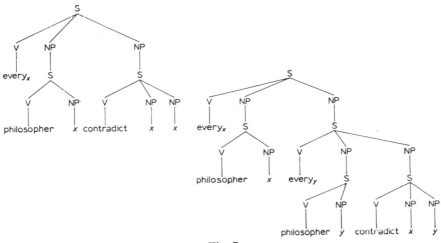

Fig. 7

concerned not merely with considerations of 'elegance' but have in principle empirical consequences: if some analogue to the rules of a grammar is learned by a person in his acquisition of his native language, the proposal of *Aspects* implies that one must know more about reflexives in order to have mastery over sentences like (18a) than in order to have mastery over sentences like (20a), i.e. that it is possible that one could know how to use reflexives with 'simple' antecedents and know what quantifiers meant without knowing how to use reflexives with quantified antecedents; the proposals made here imply that that is not possible.

Before going on, I should mention a peculiar way in which the term 'generalization' has been used by such linguists as Chomsky and Halle and point out that it has no relationship to what I am discussing here. Chomsky and Halle in many works (e.g. Chomsky and Halle, 1968) describe an 'abbreviatory convention' whereby consecutive rules of a grammar that have any elements in common are combined into a single expression in which the non-shared parts are written inside curly brackets, e.g. a sequence of rules of the form

$$A \rightarrow B \;/\; \underline{\quad} C \;(\text{'A becomes B when followed by C'})$$
$$A \rightarrow D \;/\; \underline{\quad} E$$

is abbreviated to

$$A \rightarrow \begin{Bmatrix} B \;/\; \underline{\quad} C \\ D \;/\; \underline{\quad} E \end{Bmatrix}$$

While they speak of this notation as 'expressing a generalization', I can see no justification for that locution. Indeed, curly brackets are applicable only in cases where I would normally speak of 'missing a generalization', e.g. the analysis of sentences like (16–17) which I ridiculed above, whose rules for introducing the reflexive element-*self* could be combined by curly brackets into the expression

$$\text{Attach } self \;/\; \begin{Bmatrix} NP_i \; X \; NP_i \\ \# \; V \; X \; NP_{2\,\text{pers}} \end{Bmatrix} \underline{\quad}$$

Curly brackets would be equally applicable in the absurd case suggested above, in which reflexivization affected not NP's which are second person but NP's which denote baseball players. Curly brackets have been described accurately by Lakoff as 'a formal device for expressing the claim that no generalization exists'. I will henceforth ignore curly brackets on the grounds that all rules in which they have been employed either are sequences of unrelated rules which purely by accident have parts in common or are simply wrong.

4. ON THE NON-EQUIVALENCE OF SOME 'NOTATIONAL VARIANTS'

I have already mentioned several cases in which linguistic facts argue for a 'deep structure' which in the respect at issue agrees with what can be demonstrated on the basis of logical considerations to be the 'logical structure' of the sentence. There are, however, many cases where there are alternative proposals for logical structure which no facts of logic allow one to choose between. For example, as far as logic is concerned, it is a matter of taste or of convenience with regard to ulterior (e.g. mathematical) motives whether one uses 'Polish' notation, in which predicates precede their arguments and 'operators' precede that which they combine, or 'Italian' notation (to coin a much needed term, whose choice is based on the proportion Łukasiewicz : predicates first :: Peano : predicates second) in which a predicate appears after its first argument[14] and 'connectives' such as *and, or*, and *if-then* (but generally not quantifiers) are written between the things that they connect.

While the choice between such alternatives may be purely arbitrary when viewed purely from a logician's point of view, it often ceases to be so if one takes 'logical structure' to be not merely a hypothesized input to logical rules of inference but also an input to a system of syntactic transformations which relate the content of a sentence to its surface syntactic structure in a given language. Different proposals for 'deep structure' have different implications as to what system of transformations is needed to relate them to the corresponding surface structures, and facts about surface structures in a language in combination with universal principles concerning what transformations are possible in a language and how they may be organized often allow one to reject a proposal for 'deep structure' on the grounds that it conflicts with otherwise valid universals about transformations. In particular, there is an argument of this type (McCawley, 1970a) that English requires deep structures with the verb at the beginning of the clause rather than the verb-second order that appears in all prior transformational literature on English except only for the work of Fillmore. If in fact 'deep structure' can be identified with semantic structure and if the argument just alluded to is valid, then an adequate semantic representation (at least for English) has the form of 'Polish' rather than 'Italian' notation. Before sketching an argument for underlying verb-first order in English, two points should be made. First, my reference to universal principles about transformations presupposes that one of the goals of linguistics is to provide as tight as possible a characterization of what a 'possible grammar' is. Rather than allowing a transformation to be any mapping at all of trees onto trees, one must exclude from the class of possible transformations all types of transformations which cannot be shown to be demanded by the facts (rather than just consistent with the facts) of some language: the fact that a system of transformations correctly associates semantic structures to surface structures in a given language does not justify calling the transformations it contains 'possible transformations'. One of the arguments for underlying verb-first order in English is based on the fact that while it is possible to formulate transformations that correctly associate semantic structures to surface structures regardless of whether semantic structures have verb-first or verb-second order (obviously, if there is a system of transformations that correctly associates semantic structures of the one kind to surface structures, there is also a system of transformations that would do the same for semantic structures of the other kind, namely a system of transformations consisting of the first system of transformations preceded by a transformation that moves the verb from first to second position or vice versa), the proposal of verb-first order allows much tighter constraints to be imposed on the class of 'possible transformations' than does the proposal of verb-second order. Secondly, it is an open question whether considerations of the syntax of other languages would lead one to make the same choice between 'equivalent' systems of semantic representation as do considerations of English syntax. For example, I know of nothing in Japanese syntax that would give any reason for setting up any order of constituents other than that with the verb at the end of the clause. Indeed, in McCawley (1970a), I stated that there appear to be two distinct underlying word-order types, namely verb-first and verb-last. In this case, there is the alternative of saying that there really is a common semantic structure for all languages, namely one in which the verb is unspecified as to its left-right orientation with respect to its arguments, and that languages differ as regards rules for imposing an order on partially unordered structures. However, to date no facts about English or Japanese have been adduced which provide any evidence for an underlying structure in which the verb is unspecified as to orientation with respect to its arguments, nor against such structures. The argument which is to follow is really an argument that if semantic structures are oriented trees, English must have underlying verb-first order.

If English has verb-first order in semantic structure, there will have to be a transformation which changes that order into the surface verb-second order, or at least, that does so in those clauses which have verb-second order: the proposal of underlying verb-first order allows one to say that the verb-first order of yes-no questions comes about through the non-application of the transformation just mentioned rather than through the application of a rule that changes $NP - V - X$ into $V - NP - X$. If there is a transformation which changes verb-first order into verb-second order, then the transformations which apply before it apply to structures having verb before subject and those which apply after it apply to structures having subject before verb (except in the questions, etc. to which the rule does not apply). The hypothesis of underlying verb-first order can thus be confirmed or disconfirmed by determining which transformations are significantly different if they apply to structures with verb-first rather than verb-second (there are, of course, many transformations for which either the position of the verb is totally irrelevant, e.g. extraposition and reflexivization, or involves only a trivial difference in the formulation of the transformation, e.g. quantifier lowering – if, as I argue below, quantifiers should be assigned to the category V (= 'predicate'), then quantifier lowering will move the quantifier to the right if its input has verb-first but to the left if it has verb-second) and determining whether the transformations which are significantly 'simpler' if they apply to verb-first structures must apply before all the transformations which are significantly 'simpler' if they apply to verb-second structures. This in fact turns out to be the case. The transformation which forms passive clauses moves only one NP if it applies to verb-first structures but moves two NP's if it applies to verb-second structures; the transformation which inserts the *there* of existential clauses need only insert the *there* if it applies to verb-first structures but must in addition move the subject from before the verb to after the verb if it applies to verb-second structures; three transformations which move material out of a subordinate clause (the 'raising' transformation illustrated by example (12b) and two others that have not been discussed here) move it to the left regardless of the role that the subordinate clause plays in the main clause if they apply to inputs with verb-first order but with verb-second order they must move material to the left when the subordinate clause is the object and to the right when it is the subject of the main clause. These transformations precede the few transformations which are at all 'simpler' if they apply to verb-second structures, e.g. PARTICLE SEPARATION, which (usually optionally) moves the 'particle' of composite verbs such as *look up* and *kick out* after their objects, as in

(23)   He looked the price up.
(24)   They kicked the beggar out.

The 'simplicity' to which I alluded above is of greater significance than just the formulation of the rules in question, since the versions of these rules which apply to verb-second structures happen to be the best examples of certain rule types (e.g. transformations which perform more than one 'elementary operation and transformations which have a non-uniform effect on the things that they apply to) which now can probably be done away with entirely. Thus, if English (and, presumably, all other languages with surface verb second order) is analyzed as having underlying verb-first order, the notion 'possible transformation' can be much more tightly constrained than would otherwise be the case.

5. CONJOINING AND QUANTIFICATION

It may seem strange to call the argument presented in the last section an argument that English requires 'Polish' and not 'Italian' semantic representations, since the argument said nothing about 'logical operators' such as negation, quantifiers, and 'connectives', which are what all of the fuss about Polish notation has been about. I in fact maintain that these are all V's (predicates) and that the above argument in fact covers their orientation as well as that of things that it is less unsettling to hear called predicates. I take the position that things must be assigned to the same category unless one is forced to do otherwise and that (as pointed out by Lakoff, 1965; see also Bach, 1968) most traditional category distinctions (e.g. the verb/adjective distinction) can be viewed as a difference in the applicability of some transformation or other to items which combine in the same way with other things and which are otherwise subject to the same transformations (e.g. the difference between verbs and adjectives is that adjectives but not verbs are subject to a transformation which inserts the copula *be*). Negation combines with other elements of semantic structure in the same way as do some things which are manifested as verbs in the ordinary sense, e.g. the *happen* of

(25)   Two plus two happens to be four.

In either case the item in question combines with a sentence to yield a sentence (i.e. is of Ajdukiewicz's type *s/s*); in either case the element

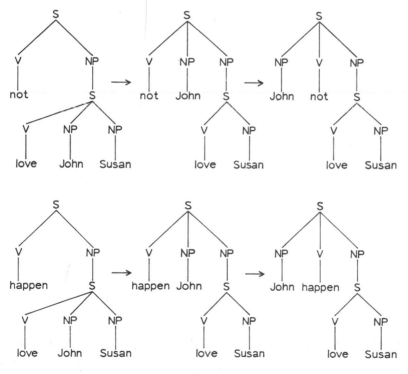

Fig. 8

triggers a transformation which moves the first NP of the embedded sentence into the main sentence (Figure 8). The difference between the syntax of *not* and *happen* appears simply to be that English has transformations which prevent *not* from getting the verbal inflections that English morphology does not allow it to have: if there is an 'auxiliary verb' present, it is put before *not*, as in *Harry can't swim*, and otherwise *do* is inserted as a semantically empty bearer of verbal inflections, as in *I don't like eggs*. There are languages in which the negative element is morphologically a verb (e.g. Finnish) or an adjective (e.g. Japanese). In both Finnish and Japanese, a sentence meaning *Harry wants to drink beer* and a sentence meaning *Harry doesn't drink beer* have the same surface structure except for the choice of 'want' or 'not': in Finnish, 'want' and 'not' are both inflected as verbs and are followed by an infinitive, and in Japanese, 'want' and 'not' are both inflected as adjectives and appear compounded with the main verb of their complement. The policy which I have adopted regarding the labelling of nodes localizes the difference between English, Finnish, and Japanese as one of morphology plus those syntactic rules which owe their existence to morphological details of the language. I will thus henceforth take the labeling of the negative element as V to be fairly adequately justified and hence take the arguments of the preceding section as applying also to the underlying orientation of negation relative to what is negated. The remainder of this section will be devoted to a somewhat tentative and incomplete analysis of quantifiers and coordinating conjunctions (I will have nothing to say about the one other item which generally figures in a discussion of 'Polish' notation, namely 'if ... then') in which I will show that at least two putative underlying structures for coordination are consistent with what is known about coordination and a large variety of putative underlying structures for quantifiers are consistent with what is known about quantification, but that there are also some facts which support the conclusion that coordination and quantification are the same thing, only one of the possibilities for the underlying structure of conjoined sentences and only one of the possibilities for the underlying structure of quantified sentences are consistent with that conclusion, and the elements which underlie both quantifiers and conjunctions under that analysis (e.g. the same element underlies both *one* and exclusive *or*) are in a configuration which makes it natural to label them 'V'.

The first step in this argument is a demonstration that an adequate system of semantic representation must allow coordination of arbitrarily many sentences at a time, rather than the coordination of two terms at a time, which logicians have generally confined themselves to. The use of the English word *or* that most closely matches the logician's 'exclusive *or*' yields a true sentence if and only if exactly one of the conjuncts is true; for example, the presupposition of a question such as

(26)   Did Andy study physics, chemistry, or geo\logy? (\ denotes fall in pitch)

is that Andy studied exactly one of the three subjects. While exclusive *or* satisfies the 'associative law'

(27) $(p \ v_e \ q) \ v_e \ r = p \ v_e (q \ v_e \ r)$,   ($v_e$ is 'exclusive *or*')

which is often given by logicians as justification for 'leaving out parentheses' in multi-termed conjunctions, the result of iterated binary conjoining with v_e is a sentence which is true not only if exactly one of the conjuncts is true but if any odd number of them are (to my knowledge, the only logician to mention this point in print is Reichenbach (1947)). Thus, if semantic representation is to contain a conjunction which matches the 'exclusive' use of English *or*, that conjunction will have to be allowed to combine with arbitrarily many conjuncts: iterated binary conjoining (indeed, iterated *n*-or-less-ary conjoining, for any specific *n*) of a set of conjuncts has different truth conditions from the result of conjoining them all at once with the English word *or* in its 'exclusive' sense. Moreover, I am reasonably sure that there is no language with a conjunction which fits the truth table of iterated binary exclusive *or*, i.e. is true when an odd number of its conjuncts are true but false when an even number of them are true. Since there is no known way in which the combinatory possibilities of exclusive *or* in semantic structure differ from those of *and* and inclusive *or*, presumably these too would then have to be allowed to combine with arbitrarily many conjuncts rather than with just two. This conclusion is confirmed by the fact that[15]

(28)(a)   And (p, q, r)
   (b)   And $(p, \text{And } (q, r))$
   (c)   And $((\text{And } (p, q), r)$

although they have the same truth conditions (namely, are true when all three of p, q, r are true and false otherwise), correspond to different conceptions of what the various conjuncts have in common, which have different surface realizations in English, e.g.

(29)(a) Tom voted for Cleaver, and he voted for O'Dwyer, and Bill voted for O'Dwyer.

(b) Tom voted for Cleaver, and he and Bill voted for O'Dwyer.

(c) Tom voted for Cleaver and O'Dwyer, and Bill voted for O'Dwyer.

Ross (1967) has proposed a treatment of conjoining in transformational grammar which fits quite closely the conclusions just drawn. He has deep structures of the form

(30)

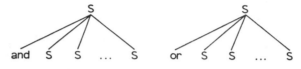

and derives the surface forms of sentences with underlying conjoined clauses through the following transformations:

> Conjunction reduction, which replaces a conjoined structure whose conjuncts are identical except for one term by a simple structure with a conjoined constituent in place of that term (Figures 9a, b). Conjunction distribution, which attaches a copy of a conjunction to each of its conjuncts, e.g. the tree of Figure 9b is converted into that of Figure 9c.
>
> Various rules of conjunction deletion. In English, the first conjunction in the output of conjunction distribution is deleted except when it is replaced by *both* or *either*, which Ross takes to be positional variants of *and* and *or* respectively, and there is the option of deleting all but the last copy of the conjunction (i.e. either *tennis, and golf, and football* or *tennis, golf, and football* is a possible output).

Conjunction reduction is necessary because of sentences such as

(31)   John has been named vice-president and seems pleased with himself.

in which the conjuncts do not correspond to coherent pieces of semantic

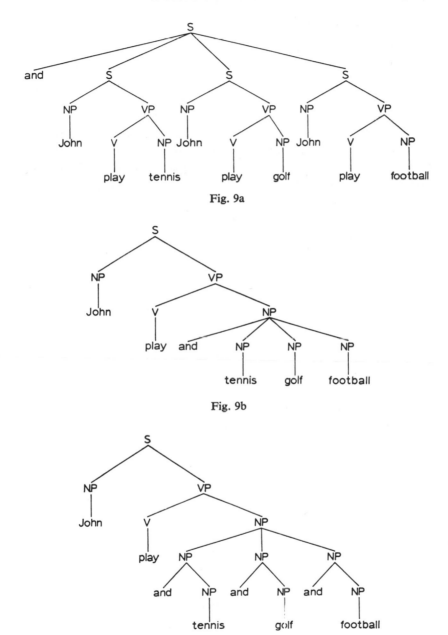

Fig. 9a

Fig. 9b

Fig. 9c

structure and arise only through the action of transformations. Conjunction distribution must have the effect indicated because English conjunctions are pronounced as part of the same phrase as the following conjunct (i.e. it is possible to make a pause before the conjunction but not after it) and because there is only one 'degree of freedom' in the choice of conjunctions in a single conjoined structure: if one of the conjuncts in a conjoined structure has *and* before it, all the other conjuncts must have either *and* or a positional variant of it (*both* or zero) before them[16]. Ross conjectures that all languages have conjunction reduction and conjunction distribution and that the differences between conjoined structures in different languages reside in what rules the language has that delete conjunctions or replace them by positional variants and in whether conjunctions precede or follow the conjuncts. He notes that in clear cases of languages with underlying verb first order, conjunctions precede conjuncts, and in clear cases of languages with underlying verb last order (e.g. Japanese, in which a pause can generally be made after but not before a conjunction), conjunctions follow conjuncts. This correlation between the order of verbs and the order of conjunctions is partially explained by the conclusion to be drawn below that conjunctions are predicates and is strengthened by the fact that in verb-second languages, which presumably can all be argued to have underlying verb-first order, as in English, conjunctions work the same way as in verb-first languages.

Conjunction reduction gives rise to surface structures in which things other than sentences are conjoined, e.g. the conjoined NP's of (29) and the other conjoined constituents of

(32)   John plays the guitar and sings folksongs.
(33)   The policeman kicked and clubbed Sam.

However, it is well-known that not all conjoined constituents can be derived from conjoined S's, as illustrated by the celebrated example

(34)   The king and the queen are an amiable couple.

One example whose analysis is somewhat controversial is

(35)   John and Harry are similar,

which cannot be derived merely through conjunction reduction, since

(36)   *John is similar and Harry is similar (too).

is ungrammatical, except where it makes an elliptical reference to something mentioned earlier, e.g.

(37)   Fred does nothing but smoke hashih and play the sarod;
         John is similar;

this kind of interpretation of (36) is irrelevant to the point under discussion.
It is occasionally proposed (Gleitman, 1964) that (35) is derived from a
conjoined structure which also underlies

(38)   John is similar to Harry and Harry is similar to John.

via a transformation which creates reciprocal pronouns

(39)   John and Harry are similar to each other.

and a transformation which deletes reciprocals (and any attached preposition) after certain verbs and adjectives. However, there is a major
difficulty in applying that analysis to an analogue of (35) whose subject
had more than two conjuncts: as Goodman (1951:125) has pointed out,
the proposition that any two members of a group are similar does not
imply that the members of the group are similar, since a member of a
group might be similar to each other member in a different respect and
there thus might be no similarity shared by all the members, e.g. Tom and
Dick might be similar by virtue of looking like Humphrey Bogart, Dick
and Harry might be similar by virtue of being confirmed wife-beaters,
and Harry and Tom might be similar by virtue of being connoisseurs
of pornography, but there might be nothing significant which all three
have in common. Another case where a conjoined noun phrase cannot
be derived by Gleitman's proposal without setting up a source which is
true under different conditions that it is pointed out in Quang (1970):

(40)   John and Louise kissed.

cannot be derived from the same source as

(41)   John and Louise kissed each other.,

since (40) may be a report of a single kiss in which both John and Louise
participate actively, whereas (41) must be a report of at least two events,
one or more in which John is the agent and one or more in which Louise
is the agent.

Consequently (as concluded in Lakoff and Peters, 1969), it is necessary that there be some source for conjoined constituents besides the conjoined sentences which provide the source for the conjoined constituents that are derived by conjunction reduction. However, the range of conjoined constituents that cannot be derived from conjoined sentences via conjunction reduction (and/or other transformations) is rather small: the conjoined constituent is always a conjoined NP, and the conjunction is always *and*.

An apparent counterexample to the first of these claims is the sentence

(42)   I have often eaten pizza and been sick an hour later.,

which has what eppears to be conjoined VP but is not paraphraseable by

(43)   ?I have often eaten pizza, and I have often been sick an hour later.

However, (42) is a problem only if one accepts the analysis (Chomsky, 1965) in which auxiliary verbs originate within the clause where they appear in surface structure; under the alternative analysis (Ross, 1969a; McCawley, in press) in which auxiliary verbs (including tenses) originate as the verbs of higher clauses, (42) is derived from an underlying structure containing the embedded conjoined clause 'I eat pizza at t and I be sick one hour later than t', which undergoes conjunction reduction before I is raised into the higher clause which provides the *have* (and the still higher clause which provides the present tense).

Some apparent counterexamples to the second claim are

(44)   I want a Cadillac or a Mercedes.
(45)   A camera or a pair of binoculars is permitted.
(46)   Nixon or Humphrey is a frightening choice.

(44–5)   are obviously different in meaning from

(47)   I want a Cadillac or I want a Mercedes.
(48)   A camera is permitted or a pair of binoculars is permitted.,

and the corresponding sentence in the case of (46) is incoherent:

(49)   *Nixon is a frightening choice or Humphrey is a frightening choice.

I maintain that in each of these cases there is an embedded sentence which has undergone conjunction reduction and whose verb (and perhaps more) has then been deleted. That sentences with *want* and a non-sentential object are derived by the deletion of either *have* or *get* from a sentential object is confirmed by the existence of sentences such as

(50)   I want a Cadillac by tomorrow.,

which contains an adverb which does not modify the verb *want* but rather the verb which I claim has been deleted. It is even possible to say [17]

(51)   He wanted a Cadillac by tomorrow.,

in which *by tomorrow* occurs with a past tense verb, a situation which does not occur unless the verb is one (such as *want*) which allows one to derive an apparently 'simple' clause from an underlying structure containing an embedded clause that has a time adverb. A similar piece of evidence supports the claim that (45) involves a deleted *have*: in

(52)   A camera or a pair of binoculars is permitted in one's cabin baggage.,

the locative adverb specifies not the place where the permission is given but part of what is permitted (namely, to have a camera or a pair of binoculars in one's cabin baggage). In (46), it is not clear what has been deleted (possibly (46) comes from something like [[[one choose Nixon]$_s$ or [one choose Humphrey]$_s$]$_s$ be a frightening choice]$_s$), but a fact can be adduced which confirms the claim that pieces of an underlying embedded sentence have been deleted, namely that in

(53)   Nixon and Agnew or Humphrey and Muskie is a frightening choice.,

the verb must be in the singular, although a subject in which plural items are conjoined with *or* normally takes plural number agreement:

(54)   Nixon and Agnew or Humphrey and Muskie have/*has been elected.

However, a sentential subject takes singular number agreement, even when deletion transformations reduce it to a plural noun phrase, as pointed out by Ross (1969b):

(55)   Susan is dating several boys, but which boys isn't/*aren't known.

These two restrictions on 'underivable' conjoined structures are connected with the following observations (McCawley, 1968b): (i) in all
environments where a conjoined NP is allowed, a simple plural NP is
also allowed, e.g.

(56)   Those men are similar.,

(ii) there are certain verbs and adjectives which do not admit a singular
subject (e.g. *similar*), and (iii) even a plural noun phrase will not do as
subject of such a verb or adjective unless it denotes a set of two or more
things: *scissors, trousers*, etc. are grammatically plural regardless of the
number of pairs of scissors, etc. being referred to, and the difference in
grammaticality between

(57)   Joe and Fred each bought a pair of trousers; the trousers are
         similar.
(58)   *Joe bought a pair of trousers; the trousers are similar.

has to do with whether *the trousers* refers to one pair or to more than one.
My conclusion was that the restriction on *similar*, etc. impose on their
subjects is that the subject purport to refer to a set of two or more individuals and that thus the NP's which meet such a condition are those
which can be used to refer to a set, either by describing its members
(plural NP) or by enumerating its members (conjoined NP with *and*).
I thus conclude that the conjoined constituents which cannot be derived
from conjoined sentences are precisely those which are used to enumerate
the elements of a set and that conjoined constituents in surface structure
have exactly two sources in semantic structure: sentential conjunction
and description of sets by enumeration. I will provisionally represent the
latter by a portion of semantic structure in which a NP-node dominates
a sequence of NP-nodes and will treat *and* (the only possible conjunction)
as to be inserted by a transformation, e.g.

(59)

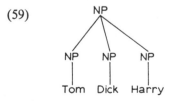

Having concluded that semantic representation should involve pieces like (59), a slight revision of Ross's underlying structure for conjoined sentences now presents itself: rather than a conjoined structure with n conjuncts being represented as an $(n+1)$-ary branching structure (the conjunction on the first branch and the n conjuncts on the second through $(n+1)$-th branches), it could be represented as a binary branching structure: on one branch the conjunction, and on the other branch a NP which enumerates a set of n sentences:

(60)

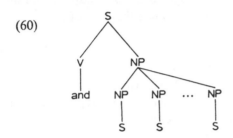

At this point it is hard to see any linguistic evidence which would choose between (60) and (30), since conjunction distribution (whose formulation would be only trivially different under the two proposals) would give the same output in either case and thus any such evidence would have to relate to a stage of a derivation prior to conjunction distribution. One small piece of evidence for (60) is provided by sentences such as

(61)   Either John is an idiot, or you are lying, or both.,

in which *both* refers to the set of sentences enumerated in the preceding part of the sentence; however, the facts relating to the possibility of pronouns, etc. referring to the sets of sentences involved in the proposal of (60) do not give the kind of evidence that would provide a clear case for (60), since ordinary pronouns generally are not possible:

(62)   ??Either John is an idiot, or you are lying, or both of them.
(63)   *John said that Amsterdam was in Liberia and Los Angeles was in Finland, and I disagreed with one of them.

One somewhat unusual piece of evidence that I can offer for (60) relates to the formulation of rules of inference in logic. Logicians are generally content to formulate rules of inference that are sufficient to cover the inferences that are desired, regardless of whether these rules of inference are formulated 'in fullest generality'. A number of commonly encountered rules of inference are in fact special cases of more general rules of inference that could be formulated. For example,

(64) $\dfrac{\text{And}(p, q)}{p}$

makes reference to a two-term conjunction and to its first term, whereas in fact from an *and*-conjunction of any length one can validly deduce any one of its conjuncts. One might try to formulate that rule of inference as

(65) $\dfrac{\text{And}(p_1, p_2, ..., p_n)}{p_i \,(1 \leqslant i \leqslant n)}$

but there the condition $1 \leqslant i \leqslant n$ is tacked on in such a way as to leave its status unclear. Since it really amounts to the premise that p_i is one of the conjuncts that appears in the overt premise, it can be reformulated as

(66)   And M
            $\dfrac{p \text{ belongs to } M}{p,}$

where M is used to denote a set of sentences. Similarly, the proposal of (60) allows the rule

(67) $\dfrac{p}{p \vee q}$

to be reformulated in the more general form

(68) p
            $\dfrac{p \text{ belongs to } M}{\text{Or } M.}$

Later, I will show that if sets of propositions are allowed to be defined by means other than enumeration, (66) and (68) remain valid and take in as special cases some familiar rules of inference relating to quantifiers.

In Section 2, I presented an argument that quantifiers must originate outside of the clauses which they appear in in surface structure. The tree which I drew there as a suggestion of the source of quantifiers is only one of a large number of possibilities which are consistent with that conclusion. An obvious possibility to consider is an underlying structure matching the analysis which Russell and numerous logicians have given to quantifiers, in which universal and existential quantifiers would originate in structures such as

(69)

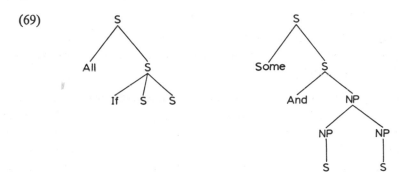

One difficulty with this proposal is that it does not provide for the existential presupposition that sentences with quantifiers other than *any* have in ordinary English: not only is

(70)   All unicorns have accounts at the Chase Manhattan Bank.

infelicitous because of violation of the presupposition (for which *all* is responsible) that there are unicorns, rather than being (as the more mathematically minded logicians often claim) 'vacuously' true, but the sentence

(71)   Some egg-laying mammals have webbed feet.

is odd if used in a discourse in which the existence of egg-laying mammals has not yet been established; (71) can be used to convey the information that there are mammals with webbed feet but (if one is playing fair) not to convey the information that there are egg-laying mammals, i.e. if one were to use (71) in order to convey that information, he would be engaging in an act comparable to surreptitiously handing a person a note that said 'You are supposed to already know that there are egg-laying mammals; don't give any indication that you didn't know'. In the case of the universal quantifier, it is possible to get the existential presupposition into a structure like (69) by taking the embedded 'connective' to be not the material implication which Russell used but rather something corresponding to the English *whenever*, which does have the existential presupposition needed[18]. However, I know of no such strategem for getting the existential presupposition into the underlying structure of existential clauses. A more serious difficulty with (69) is provided by sentences like

(72)   At least some Americans want Nixon to invade New Zealand.
(73)   Some, if not all, Americans want Nixon to invade New Zealand.

If *some* combines semantically with the conjoined sentence 'x is an American and x wants Nixon to invade New Zealand', *at least* in (72) should refer to a scale on which the different things that that sentence can be combined with appear, and (74) implies that *all* is on that scale; but *all* does not combine with 'x is an American and x wants Nixon to invade New Zealand' in the sentence

(74)   All Americans want Nixon to invade New Zealand.

Lakoff (1965) has proposed an alternative underlying structure for quantifiers which matches the surface structure of such slightly archaic sentences as

(75)   The students who want Nixon deposed are many.,

in which a quantifier is predicated of a NP whose relative clause provides the eventual main clause:

(76)   Many students want Nixon deposed.

While this analysis is plausible in the case of quantifiers which refer to the (absolute or relative) number of individuals with a certain property, it is much less so in the case of *all*, *every*, *each*, *any*, and *some*. The implausibility which I find here does not have to do with the ungrammaticality even in archaic-sounding English of

(77)   *The philosophers who contradict themselves are every.,

etc. (as will be clear from the analyses presented above, I have no objection to underlying structures in which an item appears in a position where the corresponding English word is not allowed in surface structure) but has rather to do with the idea that 'everyhood' is a property of a set of philosophers. That it is not is shown by the fact that if the set of philosophers who contradict themselves happens to be identical with the set of wife-beaters who smoke pipes, one cannot deduce from (18a) that

(78)   Every wife-beater smokes a pipe.

Thus, if 'the set of philosophers who contradict themselves' is involved in the semantic structure of (18a), more than just that set and the quantifier will have to appear, e.g. *every* might be a relationship between a set (e.g. the set of all philosophers) and a putative subset (the set of all philosophers who contradict themselves) which exhausts the whole set.

While I have no substantial objection to the analysis suggested in the last sentence, I see no obvious advantage which it has over another proposal that has been made, that a quantifier is a relation between two sentences (rather than between two sets defined by those sentences), as I proposed in McCawley (1970c):

(79)

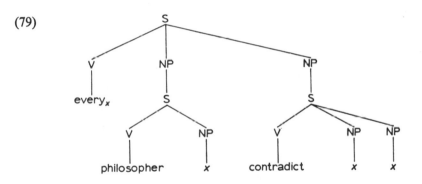

One thing that might be adduced as an advantage of the former proposal over the latter is that the former, by using set construction operations, provides a more natural account of the existential presupposition of quantified sentences: the presupposition is simply that the 'subject' of *every*, etc. denote a non-empty set. However, that is no argument, since under the former proposal, the 'object' of *every* is also given by a set description, and that set not only is not presupposed to be non-empty but can indeed be asserted to be empty:

(80)   No philosopher contradicts himself.

Thus, under either proposal, the existential presupposition does not follow from the structure proposed but must be imposed as a condition that one but not the other argument of the quantifier must meet.

There is another possible underlying structure for quantifiers, a somewhat wild one, which I will argue is correct and which in fact automatically provides for the existential presupposition. Under this analysis, a quantifier is predicated not of a set of individuals but of a set of propositions, e.g. in the case of (18a), *every* would be predicated of the set of all propositions '*x* contradicts *x*' for which *x* is a philosopher. Under the assumption that a NP which defines a set by definite description has as its immediate constituents a NP (which gives the 'general term' of the set) and a S (which gives the conditions which the variable(s) in that expression must meet for the corresponding 'value' of the general term to be in the set), the semantic structure of (18a) is [19]

(81)

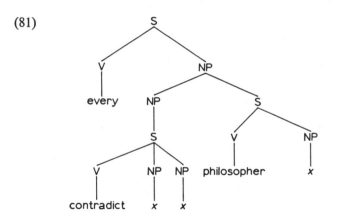

I emphasize that I am not talking about a set of English sentences of the form 'NP contradicts (him)self' but about a set of propositions, the membership of a proposition in the set having nothing to do with whether any expression exists for referring to the individual that figures in that proposition. Under this proposal, the existential presupposition is simply the presupposition that the set of propositions be non-empty (the only way that it could be empty is for there to be no *x* such that '*x* is a philosopher' is true, i.e. for there to be no philosophers), and the proposal allows that presupposition to be treated as a special case of a principle whereby all sets mentioned in semantic representations are presupposed non-empty [20]. That principle is illustrated by the oddity of the sentences

(82a)   Harry is an expert on the prime numbers between 32 and 36.
(82b)   Harry is an expert on the operas of Johannes Brahms.,

which are odd because they mention a set which is known to be empty.

The strongest case for this last proposal comes from the fact that it is essentially the only possible analysis which allows one to treat quantifiers and conjunctions as special cases of the same thing, differing only in whether the set of sentences that is involved in either case is defined by enumeration or by a definite description, and certain facts which argue that quantifiers and conjunctions in fact are the same thing. I first note that if universal quantifiers are identified with And and existential quantifiers with Or, then when applied to sets of sentences defined by definite descriptions, the generalized rules of inference proposed above yield familiar rules of inference having to do with quantifiers; for example, (66) includes the familiar

(83) $\dfrac{\text{All}_{x:f(x)}g(x)}{\dfrac{f(a)}{g(a)}}$

since the first premise of (83) consists of And applied to the set of all propositions $g(x)$ for which $f(x)$ and the second premise gives the condition under which $g(a)$ is in that set; thus (66) covers such classical cases as 'All men are mortal; Socrates is a man; therefore, Socrates is mortal'. Similarly, (68) includes the rule of existential generalization as a special case. That rule, when stated in terms of 'restricted' quantification [21] would take the form

(84) $\dfrac{\dfrac{g(a)}{f(a)}}{\text{Exists}_{x:f(x)}g(x)}$

whose second premise is the condition for $g(a)$ to be a member of the set of all $g(x)$ for which $f(x)$, and whose conclusion is Or applied to that set.

One syntactic reason for identifying *and* with universal quantifiers and *or* with existential quantifiers has been called to my attention by

Quang Phuc Dong, who notes that curses may be conjoined with *and*
but not with *or*, and allow *and* and universal quantifiers but not *or* or
existential quantifiers in their 'object':

(85)   Goddamn Nixon and/*or fuck Laird.
(86)   Goddamn Nixon and/*or Laird.
(87)   Fuck all/(every one)/*some/*one of those imperialist butchers.

Quang's observation appears to be a special case of a more general
restriction on performative verbs: sentences with a performative verb
can be conjoined with *and* but not with *or* and allow *and* and universal
quantifiers but not *or* or existential quantifiers in their subject and indirect object:

(88)   I promise you that I'll help you, and/*or I assure you that
        you won't have any trouble.
(89)   I promise you and/*or Harry that I'll empty the garbage.
(90)   I promise all/(every one)/*one/*some of you that I'll stop
        kicking my dog.
(91)   My partners and/*or I promise that we'll help you.
(92)   All/(every one)/*one/*some of us promise(s) that we'll/he'll
        help you.

Also, while

(93)   I promise that I'll help every one of you.

has a scope ambiguity (either it is a single promise which is fulfilled by
helping every one of the persons to whom it is adressed, or it is several
simultaneously made promises, one for each of those persons, to help
that person),

(94)   I promise that I'll help one of you.

only allows an interpretation as a promise which is fulfilled by helping
one of the persons to whom it is addressed. These facts would all follow
from a restriction that a performative verb is allowed to appear in the
complement of And but not in the complement of Or[22].
    There is at least one language, namely Japanese, in which some uni-
versal quantifiers involve the same morpheme that is used for *and* and

some existential quantifiers involve the same morpheme which is used for *or*. Universal quantifiers are formed from an indefinite pronoun plus *mo* (e.g. *itumo* 'always', *dokomo* 'everywhere') except that suppletive forms appear in place of some of the expected combinations (*minna* 'everyone', *zenbu* 'everything'), and existential quantifiers are formed from an indefinite pronoun plus *ka* (e.g. *ituka* 'sometime', *dokoka* 'somewhere'); *mo* is used for the *and* of sentence conjunction [23] and *ka* is used for *or*. *Mo* and *ka* appear as suffixes but with *mo* following case markers and *ka* preceding them, regardless of whether they are used as conjunctions or quantifiers: *Tookyoo ni mo Oosaka ni mo* 'both in Tōkyō and in Ōsaka', *doko ni mo* 'everywhere (locative)', *Tookyoo ka Oosaka ka ni* 'in either Tōkyō or Ōsaka', *doko ka ni* 'somewhere (locative)'.

In addition, the kinds of 'selectional restrictions' that predicates impose on their arguments are such that if there were no elements of the type that I claim *and/all* is, that fact would be a gap that would require explaining: there are predicates which require that their subject denote a set (e.g. *similar*) and predicates which require that their subject be sentential (e.g. *not* or *imply*), and there is nothing to exclude the possibility of a predicate which imposes these two restrictions simultaneously. Moreover, if conjunctions are analysed as in (60) but quantifiers are not treated as being the same as conjunctions, conjunctions would have a selectional restriction of a type otherwise unknown: a restriction that a set-denoting NP define that set by enumeration.

Facts about the use of *respective* and *respectively* also provide evidence for identifying *and* with a universal quantifier. Transformational grammarians have generally derived sentences like

(95)   John and Harry gave Susan and Alice respectively candy and flowers respectively.

from an underlying conjoined structure by means of a generalized version of conjunction reduction which allows the conjuncts to differ in more than one constituent and creates conjoined constituents at all the places where the original conjuncts differ, as in the derivation of (95) from a structure which also underlies

(96)   John gave Susan candy and Harry gave Alice flowers.

In place of each of the conjoined NP's in (95) it is possible to get a plural NP with *respective* instead of *respectively:*

(97)   John and Harry gave their respective girlfriends candy and flowers respectively.

(98)   John and Harry gave Susan and Alice respectively their respective lollipops.

(99)   Those boys gave Susan and Alice respectively candy and flowers respectively.

(100)   John and Harry gave their respective girlfriends their respective lollipops.

(101)   Those boys gave Susan and Alice respectively their respective lollipops.

(102)   Those boys gave their respective girlfriends candy and flowers ·respectively.

(103)   Those boys gave their respective girlfriends their respective lollipops.

Since *respective* and *respectively* may co-occur in the same sentence (exx. 97–102), one cannot say that *respectively* arises through a transformation unless he is also willing to let *respective* arise through the same transformation, since otherwise one would have to treat *respectively* as arising differently in (97–102) than it does in (95), which is absurd. But what about (103), which contains only plural NP's and *respective?* If *respectively* is created by a conjunction-reduction transformation, then the *respective*'s of (103) will also have to arise through that same transformation, since otherwise the *respective*'s of (103) would have to arise in a different way from those of (97–102), which is absurd. While one might want to propose that NP's like *those men* are derived from conjoined singular NP's that differed in reference (i.e. from *that man$_1$ and that man$_2$* or from *that man$_1$ and that man$_2$ and that man$_3$* or from any of the infinitely many other such expressions), there are sentences like (103) for which that strategem cannot be employed:

(104)   The approximately 50 boys that I talked to gave their respective girlfriends their respective lollipops.

(104) not only can not reasonably be derived from a conjoined source but

could hardly be given a semantic representation other than one in which a universal quantifier whose 'range' is denoted by *the approximately 50 boys that I talked to* is applied to the propositional function *x gave x's girlfriend x's lollipop*. Therefore, whatever mechanism is responsible for the introduction of *respective* and *respectively* must treat clauses conjoined with *and* the same way that it treats universally quantified clauses.

Having said that, however, I am not much closer to an explicit description of where *respective(ly)* comes from. An obvious proposal to make (and which I in fact made in McCawley, 1968b) is that sentences with *respectively* are really quantified rather than conjoined structures but involve functions defined by enumeration rather than functions given by general expressions such as '*x*'s girlfriend', e.g. to represent the semantic structure of (95) as

(105) $\text{All}_{x:x \text{ belongs to } \{\text{John, Harry}\}}$ x gave $f(x)\,g(x)$, where f is defined by '$f(\text{John}) = \text{Susan}$, $f(\textit{Harry}) = \text{Alice}$' and g by '$g(\text{John}) = \text{candy}$, $g(\text{Harry}) = \text{flowers}$'.

However, that proposal is open to a really overwhelming objection, namely that the 'values' of the functions that it requires can perfectly well be transformationally derived constituents, i.e. constituents which do not exist at the stage of the derivation (semantic structure) which (105) is supposed to correspond to, e.g.

(106)   John and Harry respectively have been arrested for smuggling pot and happen to be in jail for indecent exposure.

The facts that I have just presented create a major dilemma, and while I am not prepared to give a detailed resolution of that dilemma, I am prepared to offer a program that I think will eventually provide a resolution of the dilemma and in the process further confirmation of my claim that quantifiers and conjunctions are the same thing. One thing that has been missing from my observations so far about *respective(ly)* is a consideration of cases where the *respective(ly)* construction may not be used even though the conjoined structure from which (according to the 'classical' treatment of *respective(ly)*) it ought to correspond to is perfectly normal, e.g.

(107)(a)   The score is tied and Yastrzemski is at bat.
       (b)*The score and Yastrzemski are tied and at bat respectively.

(108)(a) The sun is shining and the birds are singing.
(b)*The sun and the birds are shining and singing respectively.
(109)(a) Truman was President and the war was almost over.
(b)*Truman and the war were President and almost over respectively.

The cases where *respective(ly)* is good are cases where the conjoined constituents not merely have the same 'grammatical function' in the input to the putative transformation but also have the same 'pragmatic function', in the sense that (96) can be used to report several instances of 'a boy giving a girl a present', where 'a boy' corresponds to a role in this general formula which is filled by *John* in one case and by *Harry* in the other case, but (107a) cannot be described as reporting several instances of anything like, say 'something doing something', which has a constituent matching *the sun* in the one case and *the birds* in the other. There is a type of sentence in which the relation between 'general formula' and 'specific cases' is made explicit, using such words as *for example*, *namely*, *specifically*, and *in particular*; the cases in which such a sentence is possible appear to be exactly the cases in which *respectively* may be used:

(110)   Several boys gave their girlfriends presents; for example, John gave Susan candy and Harry gave Alice flowers.
(111)   *Several things were doing things; for example, the sun was shining and the birds were singing.
(112)   Two of my friends are in trouble; specifically, John has been arrested for smuggling pot, and Harry happens to be in jail for indecent exposure.

The last point is closely connected with Wierzbicka's (1967) observation that (contrary to not only popular belief but the explicit statements of many linguists and logicians) not just any clauses of the same 'type' can be conjoined and that many of the standard examples which have been given of conjoined clauses are abnormal because of there not being any 'general' proposition of which the conjuncts can be taken as special cases, e.g.

(113)   *Plato currit et Sortes est albus.

(114)   *I wrote my grandmother a letter yesterday and six men can fit in the back seat of a Ford.

In the case of (107–9), there are 'general' propositions of which the conjuncts can be taken as special cases, say, 'two conditions relating to the progress of the game prevailed', 'two phenomena are making the atmosphere pleasant', 'two conditions relating to international politics prevailed', but in none of these cases can a plausible 'general' proposition be found which is exemplified by the conjuncts and which contains a constituent matching the inadmissible conjoined constituents of the (b) sentences. I thus propose that an adequate analysis of conjoining must make crucial use of the 'general' propositions which Wierzbicka proposed, that in fact the underlying structure of a conjoined sentence must specify what 'general' proposition the conjuncts exemplify, and that conjunction reduction in the generalized version discussed in connection with (95) is dependent on the conjuncts not merely having the same 'syntactic form' at the point where conjunction reduction applies (and (106) appears to leave no alternative to having some kind of conjunction reduction transformation apply in the derivation of sentences with *respectively*) but also on the conjoined constituents which the transformation creates corresponding to constituents in the 'general formula'. If this program for the investigation of conjoined structure leads where I conjecture it will, it will show conjoining and quantification to be identical in an even stronger sense than I had proposed above: not only will both be predicated of sets of propositions, but in both cases the semantic structure will have to contain an expression giving the 'general form' of the members of that set, the difference being whether all propositions of that form come into consideration or only specially designated ones.

6. CONCLUDING REMARKS

The main point of this paper has been that considerations of either logic alone or linguistics alone leave one having to make a large number of highly arbitrary choices in choosing among the various alternative proposals that could be made for the semantic structure of various sentences but that if considerations of both logic and linguistics are employed together, the range of possibilities for semantic structure is drastically narrowed, though not so drastically as to eliminate everything from consideration, i.e. the linguist's concerns and the logician's are consistent with each other. The resulting picture of semantic structure is different in many respects from what either linguists or logicians are used to operating with, and I have found the experience of starting with a linguist's conception of semantics and proceeding in the direction of these conclusions mind-expanding.

One thing which linguistics may contribute to logic is stimulation to study the logical properties of items that logicians generally ignore (e.g. is it valid to argue 'Goddamn all imperialist butchers; Nixon is an imperialist butcher; therefore goddamn Nixon'?) and to consider more mundane items such as conjunctions in connection with the full range of things which they combine with (e.g. the conjoined epithets which figured in one of the arguments above; if the *and* of that argument is the same *and* that figures in conjoined declarative sentences, as it surely is, one cannot get away with reducing *and* to truth tables, although one might, *pace* Prior, be able to get away with reducing it to rules of inference).

I should also emphasize that no account of quantifiers can be considered adequate unless it covers a much broader range of quantifiers than just the three (*all, some, one*) which I considered. One major defect in the above treatment is that I have treated all 'universal' quantifiers as if they were semantically the same; see Vendler's 'Each and every, any and all' (1968) for a highly insightful account of the ways in which those four words differ. In the case of *several, many, five*, etc., I conjecture that their use as 'existential quantifiers' is a combination of a 'pure' existential quantifier which asserts the existence of a set and a description of the size of that set; however, I have neither a proposal for the details of such an analysis nor any linguistic facts which provide any support for it. One matter that could conceivably be the undoing of my proposal that quantifiers and conjunctions are the same thing is the fact that there are no conjunctions corresponding to *several, many, five*, etc. nor to such things as *all but one, almost all, at least seven*, and *at most ten*. What I have said above should be taken with at least a dash of soy sauce until someone succeeds in explaining in a manner consistent with my proposals the lack of a conjunction **shmor* which yields a true sentence if and only if at least two of its conjuncts are true.

University of Chicago

BIBLIOGRAPHY

Emmon Bach, 'Nouns and Noun Phrases', in *Universals in Linguistic Theory* (ed. by E. Bach and R. T. Harms), Holt, Rinehart and Winston, New York, 1968, pp. 91–122.

Emmon Bach and Robert T. Harms (eds.), *Universals in Linguistic Theory*, Holt, Rinehart and Winston, New York, 1968.

Noam A. Chomsky, *Aspects of the Theory of Syntax*, MIT Press, Cambridge, Mass., 1965.

Noam A. Chomsky, 'Deep Structure, Surface Structure, and Semantic Interpretation', in *Studies in General and Oriental Linguistics* (ed. by R. Jakobson and S. Kawamoto), TEC, Tokyo, 1970.

Noam A. Chomsky and Morris Halle, *The Sound Pattern of English*, Harper and Row, New York, 1968.

Lila R. Gleitman, 'Coordinating Conjunctions in English', *Language* 41 (1965), 260–93.

Nelson Goodman, *The Structure of Appearance*, Harvard University Press, Cambridge, 1951.

Jerrold J. Katz and Paul M. Postal, *An Integrated Theory of Linguistic Descriptions*, MIT Press, Cambridge, Mass., 1964.

George Lakoff, *On the Nature of Syntactic Irregularity*. Indiana University dissertation, 1965. Published by Holt, Rinehart, and Winston, New York, as *Irregularity in Syntax*, 1970.

George Lakoff, in press, 'On Generative Semantics', to appear in *Semantics, An Interdisciplinary Reader*, (ed. by Danny Steinberg and Leon Jakobovits) Cambridge University Press, 1970a.

George Lakoff, in press, *Global Rules*, to appear in *Language*, 1970b.

George Lakoff and Stanley Peters, 'Phrasal Conjunction and Symmetric Predicates', in Reibel and Schane (1969), 113–42.

Robert B. Lees and Edward S. Klima, 'Rules for English Pronominalization', *Language* 39 (1963), 17–28. Reprinted in Reibel and Schane, 145–59.

James D. McCawley, 'Concerning the Base Component of a Transformational Grammar', *Foundations of Language* 4 (1968a), 243–69.

James D. McCawley, 'The Role of Semantics in a Grammar', in *Universals in Linguistic Theory* (ed. by Bach and Harms), (1968b), 125–69.

James D. McCawley, 'English as a VSO Language', *Language* 46 (1970a), 286–99.

James D. McCawley, 'Semantic Representation' in *Cognition: A Multiple View* (ed. by Paul Garvin), Spartan Books, New York, 1970b, 227–47.

James D. McCawley, 'A Note on English Reflexives', *Journal of Philosophical Linguistics*, vol. 1, No. 2, 1970c.

James D. McCawley, 'Tense and Time Reference in English', in *Studies in Linguistic Semantics* (ed. by Charles J. Fillmore and D. Terence Langendoen), Holt, Rinehart and Winston, New York, in press.

Quang Phuc Dong, 'Phrases anglaises sans sujet grammatical apparent', *Languages* 14 (1969), 44–51.

Quang Phuc Dong, 'A Note on Conjoined Noun Phrases', *Journal of Philosophical Linguistics* (1970), vol. 1, no. 2, 31–40.

David A. Reibel and Sanford A. Schane, *Modern Studies in English*, Prentice Hall, New York 1969.

Hans Reichenbach, *Elements of Symbolic Logic*, MacMillan, New York, 1967.

John Robert Ross, 'Constraints on Variables in Syntax', MIT dissertation, 1967.

John Robert Ross, 'Autiliaries as Main Verbs', *Journal of Philosophical Linguistics* **1** (1969a), 77–102.

John Robert Ross, 'Guess who', *Papers from the Fifth Meeting, Chicago Linguistic Society*, Univ. of Chicago, 1969b.

Zeno Vendler, 'Each and Any, Every and All' in *Linguistics in Philosophy*, Cornell Univ. Press, Ithaca, 1968, 70–96.

Anna Wierzbicka, *Against Conjunction Reduction*, Mimeographed, MIT., Mass., 1967.

REFERENCES

[1] Things are somewhat more complicated than this statement makes them sound, in that it is possible for a deep structure to be perfectly well-formed but for there to be no way for the transformations to associate a surface structure with it, as in the case of a deep structure for a question that would ask for the x such that 'You were talking to Susan and x'. The sentence that one might expect to correspond to that deep structure, namely **Who(m) did you talk to Susan and?*, is not grammatical, its ungrammaticality following from the general principle (Ross, 1967) that transformations may not move material out of a coordinate structure. In the example in question, the transformation which moves interrogative elements to the beginning 'of the clause would have to move the *who(m)* of the coordinate structure *Susan and who(m)* to the beginning of the clause (since it is an obligatory transformation) but is not allowed to do so (since otherwise Ross's constraint would be violated), and hence no surface structure at all results.

[2] It could be taken as standing for *Fred isn't going to marry Susan* under conditions which would make that interpretation consistent with the use of *even though* e.g. if one believed that Fred did everything in his power to falsify the fortune-teller's predictions.

[3] I have only provided an argument for that one detail of Figure 2. Later I will provide some reason for labeling *not* as V. Two details of Figure 2 which I would argue are wrong are the place of *be going to* (which I maintain is, like *not*, the 'main verb' of a higher clause; see Ross (1969a) and McCawley (in press)) and the order of the elements of the clauses (the facts of English, combined with some considerations of universal grammar, demand an underlying order in which every V comes first in its clause; see McCawley (1970a), part of the argument of which is summarized in Section 4 below).

[4] On the notion of tree and its relation to syntax, see McCawley (1968a).

[5] The tree of Figure 3a is a fairly late stage in the derivation of the sentence *Harry has killed Marcia;* for details of the derivation, see McCawley (in press).

[6] I will use 'conjunction' in accordance with the traditions of grammar rather than of logic and will thus use it to take in what logicians have called 'conjunction' and 'disjunction', which I will refer to as *and*-conjunction and *or*-conjunction respectively.

[7] It will develop that I should be talking about sentence tokens rather than sentence types. A 'semantic structure' will thus specify not the 'meaning' of a sentence but the 'content' of a token of a sentence, e.g. *It's raining* will have different 'content' depending on when and where it is said.

[8] I will use paired subscripts to indicate presupposed coreferentiality. The fact that (10b) and other examples also allow an interpretation in which the indicated coreferentiality relations do not hold is of no relevance to the arguments presented here.

[9] Lakoff (in press, b) has adduced several examples where, unlike the cases discussed here, two consecutive stages of a derivation are allowed to differ in the way a trans-

formation prescribes only if certain conditions are met at some third stage of a derivation.

[10] The treatment of 'generalization' which I present here is largely due to to David M. Perlmutter.

[11] Since the semantic structure of an imperative will presumably have to indicate that it is an order or request to the person it is addressed to to do the action in question, the approach taken here lets one avoid having a special rule to delete *you* and to subsume that deletion under the general principle of deletion which was alluded to in the discussion of (14a).

[12] While Chomsky proposed the use of referential indices in *Aspects*, neither there nor anywhere else has he ever drawn a tree that exhibited them explicitly. Thus, Figure 6 is drawn in accordance with what Chomsky said in *Aspects* about indices but is not modeled after any of the diagrams that appear there.

[13] I do not mean in (22a–d) to suggest that 'only' is semantically primitive. Whether it is derived from a combination of semantically more primitive elements or not has no effect on reflexivization.

[14] This statement suggests more uniformity than actually exists. Many logicians who write a 2-place predicate between its arguments write a 1-place predicate before its argument, and there is no consistent 'Italian' tradition for predicates of more than 2 places.

[15] I write And(p, q, r) rather than p And q And r, since I have in mind the combination of three terms with a single 'operator' and the latter formula misleadingly suggests that there are two 'operators'.

[16] This does not exclude the possibility of one of the conjuncts in a conjoined structure being itself a conjoined structure, as in *I talked to Tom, and either Bill or Dick, and Harry*.

[17] This example is based on a related example of Masaru Kajita's.

[18] I am grateful to Östen Dahl for this observation.

[19] Under this proposal, the variable is bound not by the quantifier (as in the earlier proposals) but by the set-construction operation. In the earlier proposals, I indicated which variable a quantifier bound by attaching that variable to it as a subscript. It thus appears as if (81) is deficient and should be supplemented by, say, an extra NP node under the higher NP node, the extra node dominating a copy of the variable in question and thus indicating what is being quantified over. However, if one knows beforehand which symbols are 'constants' and which are 'variables', it is not necessary to have such an extra NP (or for that matter, to have subscripts on quantifiers under a proposal of 'restricted quantification' such as that embodied in (79), though such subscripts can not be dispensed with in a proposal of 'unrestricted quantification' such as would be involved in (69)), since it is then possible to state a principle which will decide whether variables are being employed 'coherently' and, if so, decide which variable each set-construction operation binds. Specifically, the 'condition' of any set-construction operation must contain exactly one variable which is not contained in the 'condition' of any 'higher' set-description operation (that variable is then the variable which the set-description operation binds), and that variable must also occur in the 'general term' of that set-description operation. Regardless of whether semantic structures explicitly indicate which variable each set-description operation (or quantifier) binds, it will be necessary (at least from a linguist's point of view) to have something like that principle, since it is necessary to exclude as semantically ill-formed a putative semantic structure in which a variable is bound by more than one quantifier (all$_x$ some$_x$ (x lives in Tucson)) or in which the 'condition' does not involve the bound variable

('for all x such that Philadelphia is in North America, x is allergic to cucumbers') or in which the 'general term' does not involve the bound variable ('for all x such that x is a hydrogen molecule, Beethoven's fourth symphony is in Bb major'). The first clause of the principle excludes the first two kinds of anomaly, the second clause the third kind.

[20] I emphasize that I am speaking of the language of ordinary speakers of English, not the language of mathematicians.

[21] The more familiar version of existential generalization has to do with 'unrestricted quantification':

$$\frac{g(a)}{\text{Exists}_x g(x)}$$

[22] I wish to include words such as *Goddamn* (which Quang (1969) calls 'quasi-verbs') among performative verbs. While they fail some of the familiar tests for performative-hood, e.g. they do not admit *hereby*, they certainly seem to fit the defining characteristic of performative verbs, namely that of specifying the illocutionary force of the sentence in which they appear.

[23] Japanese has a variety of morphemes which can be translated as *and*. *Mo* appears as a suffix to a NP but represents sentence conjunction, e.g.

> Nedan mo yasukute, sina mo ii. 'The price is low and the quality is good'.
> Taroo mo Ziroo mo dekaketa. 'Both Taroo and Jiroo went out'.

In conjoined NP's which are not derived by conjunction reduction, a different conjunction is used:

> Taroo to Ziroo to ga dekaketa. 'Tarō and Jirō went out (together)'.

GEORGE LAKOFF

LINGUISTICS AND NATURAL LOGIC*

ABSTRACT. Evidence is presented to show that the role of a generative grammar of a natural language is not merely to generate the grammatical sentences of that language, but also to relate them to their logical forms. The notion of logical form is to be made sense of in terms a 'natural logic', a logical for natural language, whose goals are to express all concepts capable of being expressed in natural language, to characterize all the valid inferences that can be made in natural language, and to mesh with adequate linguistic descriptions of all natural languages. The latter requirement imposes empirical linguistic constraints on natural logic. A number of examples are discussed.

I. THE CORRESPONDENCE BETWEEN LOGICAL AND GRAMMATICAL STRUCTURE

For better or worse, most of the reasoning that is done in the world is done in natural language. And correspondingly, most uses of natural language involve reasoning of some sort. Thus it should not be too surprising to find that the logical structure that is necessary for natural language to be used as a tool for reasoning should correspond in some deep way to the grammatical structure of natural language. Take the following example.

(1)   The members of the royal family are visiting dignitaries.
(2)   Visiting dignitaries can be boring.
(3)   a. Therefore, the members of the royal family can be boring.
        b. Therefore, what the members of the royal family are doing can be boring.

Example (1) is a classical case of a structurally ambiguous sentence. The phrase 'visiting dignitaries' can either be a noun phrase consisting of a head noun 'dignitaries' preceded by a modifier 'visiting', or it can be a verb phrase with the verb 'visit' and the object noun 'dignitaries'. The same structural ambiguity occurs in sentence (2). Corresponding to each of these grammatical analyses, we find a pattern of deduction. Thus if 'visiting' is assumed to be a modifier of the head noun 'dignitaries', then (3a) follows as a logical consequence. On the other hand, if 'visiting' is

Davidson and Harman (eds.), Semantics of Natural Language, 545–665. *All rights reserved*

taken to be a verb followed by a direct object, then (3b) follows as a logical consequence.

Whenever sentences of a form superficially similar to (1) and (2) can have only one of these grammatical analyses, then only one of the patterns of deduction appears. For example, consider the following case.

(4)　　　The members of the royal family are sniveling cowards.
(5)　　　Sniveling cowards can be boring.
(6)　　　a.　Therefore, the members of the royal family can be boring.
　　　　　b. *Therefore, what the members of the royal family are doing can be boring.

In (4) and (5) 'sniveling' can only be considered a modifier of 'cowards'; it cannot be considered a transitive verb. Correspondingly, from (4) and (5) one can conclude (6a), but (4) and (5) do not lead to the conclusion (6b).

(7)　　　The members of the royal family are smuggling brickbats.
(8)　　　Smuggling brickbats can be boring.
(9)　　　a. *Therefore, the members of the royal family can be boring.
　　　　　b.　Therefore, what the members of the royal family are doing can be boring.

In (7) and (8) the reverse is true. 'Smuggling' is only a transitive verb in (7) and not a modifier of 'brickbats'. Consequently, from (7) and (8), (9a) does not follow as a logical consequence, but (9b) does.

This is a trivial example of a case where there is a correspondence between grammatical structure and logical structure. It does, however, raise an interesting question. Is this an accidental case? Or is there some necessary connection between the grammatical structures of these sentences and the corresponding logical structures? Intuitively, one would guess that the connection was not accidental. If this is true, one would like such a fact to be represented in a theory of linguistic structure. Not all theories of linguistic structure guarantee that such a correspondence is not accidental. For example, the theory given in Chomsky's *Syntactic Structures* leaves open the question as to whether such correspondences are accidental. The reason is that, in that theory, the sentences of English are to be generated by rules that do not take into account the meaning of the sentences. Any rules relating English sentences to their logical forms would be independent of the rules assigning those sentences grammatical structures, though the rules assigning logical form might or might not depend on the grammatical structures assigned by rules of grammar. To the extent to which a theory of grammar assigns grammatical form independently of meaning, to that extent that theory will be making the claim that any correspondence between grammatical form and logical form is accidental.

II. OVERLAPPING RULES

It is sometimes assumed, as it was in *Syntactic Structures*, that the rules that generate the grammatical sentences of English, separating them from the ungrammatical sentences and assigning them their grammatical structure, are distinct from the rules that relate English sentences to their corresponding logical forms. In the past several years, a considerable amount of evidence has been discovered which indicates that this is not true. In some cases, the rules which determine which sentences are grammatical or ungrammatical are identical to rules relating the surface form of an English sentence to its logical form. Consider the sentences of (1).

(1) a. Sam smoked pot last night.
     b. Last night, Sam smoked pot. (=a)

It is clear that (1a) is related to (1b) by a rule of grammar which moves an adverb to the front of the sentence. This much is uncontroversial. Let us call such a rule 'adverb-preposing'. In the simple case, adverb-preposing moves an adverb to the front of its own clause, as in (1b). However, there are cases where adverb-preposing moves the adverb to the front of a higher clause, as in (2) and (3).

(2) a. I think Sam smoked pot last night.
     b. Last night, I think Sam smoked pot. (=a)
(3) a. It is possible that Sam will leave town tomorrow.
     b. Tomorrow, it is possible that Sam will leave town.

However, there are cases where adverb-preposing may not move the adverb to the front of a higher clause, depending on what the verb or adjective in the higher clause is. When this restriction on adverb-preposing is violated, the result can be an ungrammatical sentence.[1]

(4)   a. I realize that Sam will leave town tomorrow.
       b. *Tomorrow, I realize that Sam will leave town. (≠a)
(5)   a. It is mistaken that Sam smoked pot last night.
       b. *Last night, it is mistaken that Sam smoked pot. (≠a)

'Realize' and 'mistaken' do not permit adverb-preposing from a lower clause in my speech. In (4b) and (5b), violation of this constraint on adverb-preposing leads to ungrammatical sentences. Thus, the rule of adverb-preposing, constrained as indicated, must be a rule of grammar, since it plays a role in distinguishing grammatical from ungrammatical sentences. Now consider examples (6) and (6').

(6)   a. I mentioned that Sam smoked pot last night.
       b. Last night, I mentioned that Sam smoked pot. (≠a)
(6')   a. I mentioned that Sam will smoke pot tomorrow.
       b. *Tomorrow, I mentioned that Sam will smoke pot. (≠a)

(6'b) shows that 'mention' is also a verb that does not permit adverb-preposing from a lower sentence. In (6b) on the other hand, we have a grammatical sentence which looks just like the sentence that would be formed by preposing the adverb 'last night' to the front of (6a). However, (6b) does not have the meaning of (6a). In (6b) 'last night' does not modify 'smoked', but rather 'mentioned'. The reason is obvious. 'Last night' in (6b) originates in the same clause as 'mentioned' and moves to the front of its own clause by adverb-preposing. On the other hand, 'tomorrow' in (6'b) cannot originate in the same clause as 'mentioned', since 'tomorrow' requires a future tense and 'mentioned' is in the past tense. Although 'tomorrow' can originate as a modifier of 'will smoke', it cannot move to the front of the higher clause, since adverb-preposing from a lower clause is blocked by 'mention'. The fact that 'mention' blocks adverb-preposing from a lower clause also accounts for the fact that (6b) cannot be understood as a paraphrase of (6a). Note however, that the same rule with the same constraint in the case of (6'b) yields an ungrammatical sentence, while in the case of (6b) it blocks a certain interpretation of a grammatical sentence. Here we have a case where the violation of a rule of grammar does not guarantee that the sentence generated will be un-grammatical. The violation only guarantees that the sentence will be ungrammatical relative to a given reading. A sentence will be fully un-grammatical only if it is ungrammatical relative to all readings. This suggests that the role of rules of grammar is not simply to separate out the grammatical from the ungrammatical sentences of English, but also to pair surface forms of sentences with their corresponding meanings, or logical forms. Thus, rules like adverb-preposing appear to have two functions: to generate the grammatical sentences, filtering out the un-grammatical sentences, while at the same time relating the surface forms of sentences to their corresponding logical forms, while blocking any incorrect assignments of logical form to surface form.

This can be seen somewhat more clearly in the case of *if*-clauses. It is often assumed that sentences of the form

$$\text{If } S_1, \quad \text{then} \quad S_2,$$

are to be translated into a logical form like

$$S_1 \supset S_2$$

or something of that sort, perhaps with a different connective. This view is mistaken. As Jerry Morgan has observed, *if*-clauses behave just like other adverbial clauses (e.g., *when*-clauses, *because*-clauses, etc.) with respect to low level syntax. In particular, *if*-clauses undergo the rule of adverb-preposing. Adverb-preposing derives (7b) from (7a).

(7)   a. Sam will smoke pot, if he can get it cheap.
        b. If he can get it cheap, *then* Sam will smoke pot.   (=a)

Morgan (1970) has proposed that the 'then' of 'if-then' is inserted by transformation after the *if*-clause has been preposed. This view is sub-stantiated by examples like (8) and (9).

(8)   a. I think Sam will smoke pot, if he can get it cheap.
        b. If he can get it cheap, *then* I think Sam will smoke pot.
           (=a)
(9)   a. It is possible that Sam will smoke pot, if he can get it cheap.
        b. If he can get it cheap, *then* it is possible that Sam will smoke
           pot.   (=a)

In (8) and (9) adverb-preposing has moved the *if*-clause to the front of a higher clause. The *if*-clause in (8b) originates inside the object complement of 'think', as in (8a). Thus (8b) can be synonymous to (8a). Similarly, the *if*-clause in (9b) originates inside the sentential complement of 'possible' and so (9b) can be synonymous to (9a). Note, however, where the 'then' appears. In (8b) and (9b) 'then' appears in front of the higher clause. This corroborates Morgan's claim that 'then' is inserted after adverb-preposing.[2]

As we saw above, certain verbs and adjectives block the application of adverb-preposing from below. The examples we gave were 'realize', 'mistaken', and 'mention'. Examples (10) and (11) show that adverb-preposing blocks in the same cases with *if*-clauses.

(10) a. I realize that Sam will smoke pot, if he can get it cheap.
    b. *If he can get it cheap, *then* I realize that Sam will smoke pot. ($\neq$a)

(11) a. It is mistaken that Max smokes pot if he can get it cheap.
    b. *If he can get it cheap, *then* it is mistaken that Max smokes pot. ($\neq$a)

In (12) we have a case parallel to (6) above.

(12) a. Max mentioned that Sam will resign if Sue is telling the truth.
    b. If Sue is telling the truth, *then* Max mentioned that Sam will resign.

The *if*-clause in (12b) is understood only as modifying 'mention' and not as modifying 'resign'.

It should be clear from these examples that sentences of the form

If S_1, then S_2.

are not necessarily to be translated as

$S_1 \supset S_2$.

If one permitted such a translation from surface form to logical form, then a sentence such as (9b), which has a logical form something like (13), would be given a logical form like (14).

(13) $\Diamond (p \supset q)$
(14) $p \supset (\Diamond q)$.

Classical logical fallacies are often results of such mistaken translations.

It should be clear from these remarks that the rule of adverb-preposing, which we have seen is a rule of grammar, plays a crucial role in relating surface forms to their logical forms. It follows that the rules determining which sentences are grammatical and which, ungrammatical are not distinct from the rules relating logical forms and surface forms. The rule of adverb-preposing is a rule which does both jobs.

Adverb-preposing is interesting in other respect as well. For example, it can be used to show that there are cases where material which is understood but does not appear overtly in the sentence, and which can only be determined from context, must appear in underlying grammatical structure and must be deleted by a rule of grammar. Consider the following case.

(15)   a. I'll slug him, if he makes one more crack like that.
        b. If he makes one more crack like that, I'll slug him.
        c. One more crack like that, and I'll slug him.

(15c) is understood in the same way as (15a) and (15b), that is, it is understood as an if-then construction. In (15c) 'he makes' is understood, though it does not appear overtly in the sentence. The question is whether 'he makes' in (15c) is to be deleted by a rule of grammar or to be supplied by a rule mapping surface form into logical form, which is not a rule of grammar. Further examples show that the missing material in such constructions is determinable only from context, that is, only from what is presupposed by the speaker. Consider, for example, (16).

(16)   a. One more beer, and I'll leave.
        b. If I drink one more beer then I'll leave.
        c. If you drink one more beer then I'll leave.
        d. If you pour one more beer down my back, then I'll leave.

and so on.

Sentence (16a) can be understood, depending upon the context, as any of (16b, c, d, etc.). Yet it can be shown that noun phrases such as 'one more beer' as in (16a) must be derived by deletion from full clauses. Consider examples (17), (18), (19) and (20).

(17)   a. It's possible that I'll slug him if he makes one more crack
            like that.

    b.   If he makes one more crack like that, then it's possible that I'll slug him.

    c.   One more crack like that, and it's possible that I'll slug him.

(18)   a.   I think that I'll slug him if he makes one more crack like that.

    b.   If he makes one more crack like that, then I think I'll slug him.

    c.   One more crack like that and I think I'll slug him.

(19)   a.   I realize that I'll slug him if he makes one more crack like that.

    b.   *If he makes one more crack like that, then I realize that I'll slug him.

    c.   *One more crack like that and I realize that I'll slug him.

(20)   a.   It's mistaken that I'll slug him if he makes one more crack like that.

    b.   *If he makes one more crack like that, then it's mistaken that I'll slug him.

    c.   *One more crack like that and it's mistaken that I'll slug him.

(21)   a.   I mentioned that I would slug him if he made one more crack like that.

    b.   *If he made one more crack like that, then I mentioned that I would slug him.

    c.   *One more crack like that and I mentioned that I would slug him.

It should be clear from such examples that constructions like (15c) are derived from preposed *if*-clauses, since they are paraphrases and obey the same grammatical constraints. It follows that noun phrases like 'one more crack' in (15c) are derived from full underlying clauses and that the 'and' in this construction is not an underlying 'and' but rather an underlying 'if-then'. (16a) is an instance of exactly the same construction. Moreover, it shows exactly the same constraints. Consider the examples of (22).

(22)   a.   One more beer and I'll leave.

    b.   One more beer and I think I'll leave.

    c.   One more beer and it's possible that I'll leave.
    d. *One more beer and I'll realize that I'll leave.
    e. *One more beer and it's mistaken that I'll leave.
    f. *One more beer and I mentioned that I would leave.

These cases provide strong evidence that constructions such as (16a) must be derived from if-then clauses and that noun phrases such as 'one more beer' be derived from the full underlying *if*-clause. If there were no *if*-clause present in the syntactic derivation of sentences like (16a), then the facts of (22) would be inexplicable. Consequently, it follows that the understood matter in such sentences is recoverable only from context; it must be present in order to form a full clause at the time of adverb-preposing, and hence must be deleted by a rule of grammar. Thus rules of deletion in grammar must be sensitive to context, that is, to what is presupposed by the speaker. Let us now return to the facts of (1)–(14).

From a consideration of these facts we have reached conclusion 1.

CONCLUSION 1: The rules of grammar, which generate the grammatical sentences of English, filtering out the ungrammatical sentences, are not distinct from the rules relating the surface forms of English sentences to their corresponding logical forms.

The reason for this is that adverb-preposing must do both jobs at once. The only way conclusion 1 could be avoided would be to assume that there were two rules which did the same job as adverb-preposing and had exactly the same constraints and that one was a rule of grammar and the other a rule relating surface forms to logical forms. This would necessarily involve stating the same rule twice, and thus missing a significant generalization.

CONCLUSION 2: Conclusion 1 provides support for the theory of generative semantics, which claims that the rules of grammar are identical to the rules relating surface forms to their corresponding logical forms.

At present, the theory of generative semantics is the only theory of grammar that has been proposed that is consistent with conclusion 1.

It should be noted that both of the above conclusions depend upon a form of argumentation upon which just about all of the linguistics of the past decade and a half depends, namely, that if a given theory necessarily requires that the same rule be stated twice, then that theory is wrong. Not just inelegant, but empirically incorrect. It was on the basis of just such an argument that the theory of classical phonemics was shown to be incorrect (see Halle, 1959 and Chomsky, 1964). If one agrees that classical phonemics has been shown to be wrong on the basis of such arguments, one must accept conclusions 1 and 2.

Of course, there may be some people who do not mind if a given theory necessarily forces one to state the same rule twice. Indeed, there may be individuals who actually prefer such theories. Such people will not accept arguments of the form given, and will thus not accept the usual counter-arguments to classical phonemics nor either of the conclusions reached above. Of course, in the absence of such arguments, it is not clear what sort of empirical evidence, if any, could possibly bear on the question of whether grammar is related to logic and if so, how. So far as I can see, there could be no such evidence. If so, then the question ceases to be an empirical one, and by refusing to accept such arguments, one is deciding a priori, by fiat, that there is no relation between grammar and logic. Anyone who wishes to claim that the question of whether grammar and logic are related is an empirical one has the burden of showing what sort of evidence and what sort of arguments could bear on the question. What is interesting about the form of argumentation which we have been using (and which is generally accepted in generative linguistics) is that it does permit empirical considerations to be brought to bear on the issue.

III. QUANTIFIERS

Consider sentences (1) through (4).

 (1) That archaeologist discovered nine tablets. (AMB)

 (2) All the boys carried the couch upstairs. (AMB)

 (3) Every boy carried the couch upstairs. (UNAMB)

 (4) That archaeologist discovered few tablets. (UNAMB)

(1) is ambiguous. It can mean either that the archaeologist discovered a group of nine tablets or that the number of tablets that he discovered altogether totalled nine, though they may not have been in a group. (2) has the same ambiguity. It can mean either that a group consisting of all the boys carried the couch upstairs or that each of the boys carried the couch upstairs. (3) and (4) do not have these ambiguities. (3) cannot

have the reading that a group consisting of every boy carried the couch upstairs. It can only mean that each boy carried the couch upstairs. Similarly, (4) cannot mean that the archaeologist found a group of tablets which didn't have many tablets in it. It can only mean that the total number of tablets that the archaeologist found was few. We will refer to these readings as the 'group-reading' and 'quantifier-reading' respectively.

Suppose now that we embed sentences like (1) and (2) inside the object of a verb like 'believe'. We would expect additional scope of quantification ambiguities. These show up in the quantifier-readings, but not in the group-readings. For example, consider (5) and (6).

(5)   Sam believed that that archaeologist discovered nine tablets.
(6)   a. Sam believed that the number of tablets that that archaeologist discovered was nine.
        b. Sam believed that that archaeologist discovered a group of nine tablets.
        c. The number of tablets that Sam believes that that archaeologist discovered is nine.
        d. Of a group of nine tablets, Sam believed that that archaeologist discovered them.

(5) is ambiguous in three ways. It can have the reading of (6a), where the scope of the quantifier is inside the scope of 'believe'. Or it can have the reading of (6c), where the scope of the quantifier is outside the scope of 'believe'. Or it can have the reading of (6b), the group-reading, where the group is understood as being inside the scope of 'believe'. However, it may not have the reading of (6d), where the group is understood as being outside the scope of 'believe'. The quantifier 'all' works the same way, as examples (7) and (8) show.

(7)   Sam believed that all the boys carried the table upstairs.
(8)   a. Sam believed that the boys who (individually) carried the table upstairs included all the boys.
        b. Sam believed that a group consisting of all the boys carried the table upstairs.
        c. The boys who Sam believes carried that table upstairs includes all the boys.
        d. Of a group consisting of all the boys, Sam believed that they (jointly) carried the table upstairs.

(7) may have the readings of (8a, b, and c), but not (d). I have no idea of how the group reading is to be represented formally. But whatever its formal representation is to be, the possibility of scope ambiguities, as is the norm with quantifiers, must be excluded.

Now let us consider some implications of the above facts. Let us begin with sentences like (9) and (10).

(9)   Everyone likes someone.
(10)   Someone is liked by everyone.

In my speech, though not in that of all speakers of English, (9) and (10) have different meanings.[1] (9) would have a logical form something like that of (11), while (10) would have to have a logical form something like that of (12).[2]

(11)

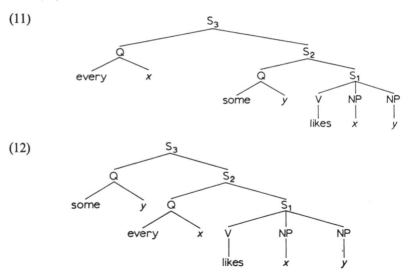

(12)

To relate the logical forms of the sentences and their corresponding surface forms, there would have to be a rule of quantifier-lowering, which in (11) would lower 'some' onto the NP with the index y and the 'every' onto the NP with the index x. The same rule would apply in (12). In my speech, though not in that of many other speakers, there is a constraint on possible pairs of logical forms and surface forms which says that when two quantifiers appear in the same surface clause, the leftmost quantifier must be the higher one in the logical form of the sentence. That constraint accounts for the difference in meaning between (9) and (10) in my speech.

Any account of the relationship between the logical form and the surface form of sentences like (9) and (10) must include a rule essentially like quantifier-lowering (or, if one prefers, its inverse, which I will call 'quantifier-raising'). Quantifier-lowering (or quantifier-raising, if one prefers) will be a movement rule. That is, it will move a quantifier over a stretch of tree. Movement rules have been studied in great detail by John R. Ross (Ross, 1967). Ross discovered that movement rules (in particular, chopping rules, of which quantifier-lowering would be one) obeyed certain very general constraints. One of these constraints, known as the coördinate structure constraint, states that no movement rule may move an element into or out of one conjunct of a coördinate structure. For example, consider examples (13) through (15).

(13)   a.   John and Bill are similar.
       b.   John is similar to Bill.

(14)   a.   *Who is John and similar?
       b.   Who is John similar to?

(15)   a.   *Bill, John and are similar.
       b.   Bill, John is similar to.

In (13a) the subject is the coördinate NP 'John and Bill'. In (13b) there is no coördinate NP. Consider the NP in the position of 'Bill' in these examples. Suppose we try to question that NP. This is possible in (14b), where 'Bill' would not be part of a coördinate structure, but it is impossible in (14a), where one would be questioning an element of a coördinate structure. Or consider topicalization, as in (15). In (15b) 'Bill' can be moved to the front of the sentence, since it is not part of a coördinate structure, but in (15a), where 'Bill' would be part of a coördinate structure, it cannot be moved to the front of the sentence. Now let us return to the rule of quantifier-lowering and to the distinction between the group-reading and the quantifier-reading of 'nine' and 'all'. In cases of true quantification, where scope of quantification is involved, the rule of quantifier-lowering would apply, moving the quantifier down to the NP containing the appropriate variable. Thus, 'some' in (11) would move down to the NP containing the variable y. One would predict that, in such cases, Ross's coördinate structure constraint would apply. That is, if the variable were contained in a coördinate NP, the rule of quantifier-lowering would be blocked. This, however, would only be the case for true quantifiers, and not for quantifiers with a group-reading, since the group-reading involves no scope of quantification, and hence no rule of quantifier-lowering. As one would guess, this is exactly what happens, as (16) and (17) show.

(16)   a.   John and nine boys are similar.   (UNAMB)
       b.   John and all the girls are similar.   (UNAMB)
       c.   *John and every linguist are similar.
       d.   *Few philosophers and John are similar.

(17)   a.   John is similar to nine boys.   (AMB)
       b.   John is similar to all the boys.   (AMB)
       c.   John is similar to every linguist.   (UNAMB)
       d.   Few philosophers are similar to John.   (UNAMB)

Compare (17a) with (16a). (17a) is ambiguous. It can mean either that nine boys share a single property with John or that there are nine boys who share some property or other with John. (16a) however only has the former reading. In (16a) the shared property must be the same, as in the group-reading of (17a). (16a) cannot have the reading that John shares different properties with each of the nine boys. The same is true of (16b) and (17b). This is predictable, since the true quantifier reading of (16a and b) is ruled out by the application of the coördinate structure constraint to the rule of quantifier-lowering, leaving only the group-reading for (16a and b). Since the quantifiers 'every' and 'few' do not have group-readings, but only quantifier readings, sentences (16c) and (16d) are ungrammatical, because in order to derive such sentences, the rule of quantifier-lowering would have to violate the coördinate structure constraint. Compare these with (17c and d) where there is no coördinate structure and where, correspondingly, the sentences are grammatical. The rule of quantifier-lowering not only obeys Ross's coördinate structure constraint, but also Ross's other constraints on movement transformations, as would be expected. For details, see G. Lakoff (1970).

Now let us consider what these facts show. First, they reveal the existence of a group-reading for quantifiers of certain sorts, the logical form of which is unknown. All we know about it is that it does not involve scope of quantification. Secondly, we have seen that the rules relating sentences with true quantifiers to their corresponding logical forms must obey Ross's constraints on movement transformations. These are constraints on grammatical rules, such as question-formation and topicalization (see (14) and (15)). Thus, the rules relating the surface forms of sentences containing true quantifiers to their logical forms obey the same constraints as ordinary grammatical rules. This should not be surprising, since violations of the rule of quantifier-lowering lead to ungrammatical sentences, as in (16c) and (16d). Thus, quantifier-lowering seems to do double duty. It not only accounts for the difference between grammatical and ungrammatical sentences (compare (16c and d) with (17c and d)), but it also serves to relate the logical form of sentences to the corresponding surface forms. Note also that the same rule constrained in the same way will block the generation of the sentences in (16c) and (16d), but only block the corresponding readings for the sentences of (16a and b), it will not yield an ungrammaticality in the case of (16a and b), but only restrict the possibilities for what those sentences can mean. Here we have another case that shows that the rules of grammar, which separate grammatical from ungrammatical sentences, are not distinct from the rules which relate logical forms and surface forms. Consequently, we reach the same conclusions from these facts as we did from the facts considered in the previous section.

IV. PERFORMATIVE VERBS

In Sections II and III we saw that the rules of adverb-preposing and quantifier-lowering do double duty in that they serve both to distinguish the grammatical from the ungrammatical sentences of English and to relate the surface forms of sentences to their corresponding logical forms. They thus serve to confirm what has come to be called the theory of generative semantics.[1] Generative semantics claims that the underlying grammatical structure of a sentence *is* the logical form of that sentence, and consequently that the rules relating logical form to surface form are exactly the rules of grammar. If the theory of generative semantics is correct, then it follows that the study of the logical form of English sentences is indistinguishable from the study of grammar. This would mean that empirical linguistic considerations could affect decisions concerning how

the logical form of a sentence is to be represented. It would also mean
that, on linguistic grounds, the logical forms of sentences are to be
represented in terms of phrase structure trees. In this section, we will
consider the question of how linguistic considerations can bear on the
question of how the illocutionary force of a sentence is to be represented
in logical form. In particular, we will consider some of the linguistic
evidence which indicates that the illocutionary force of a sentence is to
be represented in logical form by the presence of a performative verb,
which may or may not appear overtly in the surface form of the sentence.
This should not be too surprising in the case of imperatives or questions.
It is clear that sentences like 'I order you to go home', in which there is
an overt performative verb, namely 'order', enters into the same logical
relations as a sentence like 'Go home' in which there is no overt performative verb in the surface form. Linguistic arguments in favor of such
an analysis of imperatives can be found in R. Lakoff (1968). It should
also not be too surprising that the logical form of questions should be
represented in a similar way. On the other hand, it might be assumed that
statements should be distinguished in their logical form from imperatives,
questions, etc. by the absence of any such performative verb (or modal
operator). However, there is considerable evidence to show that even
statements should be represented in logical form by the presence of some
performative verb with a meaning like 'say' or 'state'. Thus, it is claimed
that the logical forms of imperatives, questions, and statements should
be represented as in (A).[2]

(A)

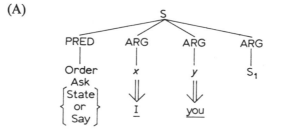

In (A), S_1 represents the propositional content of the command, question,
or statement. Note that in statements it is the propositional content,
not the entire sentence, that will be true or false. For example, if I say to
you 'I state that I am innocent', and you reply 'That's false', you are

denying that I am innocent, not that I made the statement. That is, in sentences where there is an overt performative verb of saying or stating or asserting, the propositional content, which is true or false, is not given by the sentence as a whole, but rather by the object of that performative verb. In 'I state that I am innocent', the direct object contains the embedded sentence 'I am innocent', which is the propositional content. Thus, even in statements, it should not be surprising that the illocutionary force of the statement is to be represented in logical form by the presence of a performative verb.

In the analysis sketched in (A), the subject and indirect object of the performative verbs are represented in logical form by the indexical expressions x and y. Rules of grammar will mark the subject of the performative verb as being first person and the indirect object as being second person. Thus, logical forms need not contain any indication of first person or second person, as distinct from third person. If there are other instances of the indexical expressions x and y in S_1, they will be marked as being first and second person respectively by the grammatical rule of person-agreement, which makes a NP agree in person with its antecedent. Thus all occurrences of first or second person pronouns will be either the subject or indirect object of a performative verb or will arise through the rule of person-agreement. The analysis given in (A) and the corresponding account of first and second person pronouns makes certain predictions. Since the structure given in (A) is exactly the same structure that one finds in the case of non-performative verbs of ordering, asking, and saying, it is predicted that rules of grammar involving ordinary verbs of these classes, which occur overtly in English sentences, may generalize to the cases of performative verbs, even when those verbs are not overtly present in the surface form of the sentence, as in simple orders, questions, and statements. Since the analysis of simple statements is likely to be the most controversial, let us begin by considering some of the grammatical evidence indicating that simple statements must contain a performative verb of saying in their logical forms. Consider sentences like (1)[3].

(1)   Egg creams, I like.

In (1), the object NP 'egg creams' has been moved to the front of the sentence by a rule of topicalization. Let us consider the general conditions under which this rule can apply. Consider (2) through (4).

(2)   John says that egg creams, he likes.

(3)   *The fact that egg creams, he likes bothers John.

(4)   *John dreamed that egg creams, he liked.

(2) shows that the rule must be able to occur inside the objects of verbs of saying. However, as (3) and (4) show, this rule does not generally apply inside complement constructions, either subject complements or object complements. It is limited to the objects of verbs of saying (actually, a somewhat larger class including verbs of saying). Without an analysis such as (A), one would have to state two environments in which the rule could apply, that is, one would have to say that the rule applies either in the objects of verbs of saying or in simple declarative sentences. Under the analysis given in (A), these two conditions for the application of the rule would be reduced to a single general condition, namely, that the rule applies in the objects of verbs of saying. This rule, as generalized, would then predict the ungrammaticality of (5a).

(5)   a. *Egg creams, I state that I like.
         b. Egg creams, I stated that I liked.

In (5a) the performative verb 'state' appears overtly. In the derivation of (5a), topicalization is not being applied inside the object of that verb of saying; instead the NP 'egg creams' is moved to the front of the sentence as a whole. In (5b), on the other hand, the performative verb of saying does not appear overtly. The verb 'stated', a non-performative, past-tense usage, appears instead. Since there is no overt performative verb of saying in (5b), the analysis of (A) requires that (5b), in logical form, be embedded inside the object of a performative verb of saying which is not overtly present in the sentence. That is, the logical form of (5b) would contain two occurrences of the verb 'state', as in 'I state to you that I stated that I liked egg creams'. Under this analysis, the NP 'egg creams' in (5b) would have been moved by topicalization to the front of the object of the understood performative verb. Without an analysis like that in (A), it would be impossible to state the general conditions under which topicalization applies or to explain the difference between (5a) and (5b).

Now consider sentence (6).[4]

(6)   Never have I seen such impudence.

(6) is derived from the structure underlying 'I have never seen such impudence', first by a rule moving 'never' to the front and then by the rule of auxiliary inversion, which moves 'have' to a position in front of 'I'. Since the inversion of the auxiliary is automatic when a negative adverb precedes, we will be concerned only with the conditions under which that adverb can be fronted, as it is in (6). Now consider (7) through (9).

(7)   John said that never had he seen such impudence.

(8)   *The fact that never had he seen such impudence bothered John.

(9)   *John dreamed that never had he seen such impudence.

As (7) shows, the rule may apply inside the objects of verbs of saying. As (8) and (9) show, the rule in general does not apply inside either subject or object complements. It applies in embedded sentences only in the objects of verbs of saying. Without an analysis of simple declaratives as given in (A), we would have to say that there was no single general condition under which the rule applied, but rather that it applied either in the objects of verbs of saying or in simple declarative sentences. Again, a generalization is being missed. With the analysis given in (A), we can state a single general condition, namely, that the rule applies only in the object of verbs of saying. This general principle now provides an explanation for the difference between (10a) and (10b).

(10)   a. *Never do I say to you that I have seen such impudence.
        b. Never did I say to you that I had seen such impudence.

Both sentences have first person subjects. The only difference between them is that in (a) the verb 'say' is in the present tense, which is marked by 'do', while in (b) the verb 'say' is in the past tense, which is marked by 'did'. In the present tense with a first person subject and a second person indirect object, the verb 'say' is used performatively. In the past tense, it is not being used performatively. Thus in (10a), a performative verb occurs overtly in the sentence, while in (10b) there is no overt performative verb. The analysis of (A) would claim that (10b) would be embedded in logical form inside the object of a performative verb of saying. Thus 'never' in (10b) is being moved to the front of an object of a verb of saying. Since a performative verb of saying appears overtly in (10a), the analysis of (A) would claim that (10a) is not embedded inside the object of some performative verb of saying which did not appear overtly. Thus 'never' in (10a) would be moved to the front of the sentence as a whole, not to the front of the object of a verb of saying. (10a) would therefore be a violation of the general principle governing the fronting of such adverbs. Again, without an analysis such as (A), it would be impossible to state the general condition under which the rule applies and to provide an explanation for the difference between (10a) and (10b).

Now consider (11).

(11)   He did *so* eat the hot dog.

The emphatic morpheme 'so', with extra heavy stress, can occur in simple sentences, as (11) shows. In complex sentences, it may not always occur.

(12)   John said that he did *so* eat the hot dog.
(13)   *The fact that he did *so* eat the hot dog bothered John.
(14)   *John dreamed that he did *so* eat the hot dog.
(15)   *John thought that he did *so* eat the hot dog.

As (12) shows, the emphatic *so* may also occur in the objects of verbs of saying. However, as (13) through (15) show, emphatic *so*, in general, cannot occur inside sentential complements, either in subject or object position. It is restricted to complements which are objects of verbs of saying. Once more, without an analysis such as (A), one could not state a general condition for the occurrence of this morpheme. One would have to say that it occurred in two distinct environments, namely, in the objects of verbs of saying and in simple declarative sentences. However, with the analysis of (A), it is possible to state the single general condition that the emphatic morpheme *so* occurs inside the objects of verbs of saying. Thus we have seen that there are two movement rules and one condition on the occurrence of a morpheme which require, for their general statement, an analysis such as (A). In addition to the arguments given above, another variety of grammatical arguments can be given in support of the analysis of (A).

There are certain expressions which, when they appear in simple sentences, require the presence of a second person pronoun.[5]

(16)   Shove it up your (*my, *her, *their) ass.

However, when this expression is embedded inside the direct object of a verb that takes indirect object, the second person restriction no longer holds. Instead, the pronoun must agree in number, person, and gender which the indirect object of the verb inside whose direct object the expression is embedded.[5a]

(17)   John told *Sue* to shove it up *her* (*your, *my, *his) ass.

In (17), the pronoun 'her' must have as its antecedent the indirect object of 'tell', namely, 'Sue'. Without an analysis such as (A), there would have to be two distinct constraints on the occurrence of the pronoun in 'shove it up ____'s ass', namely, that in a simple sentence it must be second person, but when embedded it must agree in person, number, and gender with the indirect object of the next highest verb. However, under the analysis given in (A), two distinct conditions would no longer be required. Instead, the statement governing what happens in embedded sentences would suffice for both cases. The pronoun would only be required to agree with the indirect object of the next highest verb. In the case of the simple sentence, as in (16), the indirect object would always be second person. Exactly the same argument can be made for the construction 'Watch ____'s step'.

(18)   Watch your (*my, *his, *her) step.
(19)   John told Sue to watch her (*your, *my, *his) step.

There are many other constructions of this sort which can either be embedded or occur in a simple surface sentence. Each one of them provides grammatical evidence in favor of the analysis given in (A), since they all work like the cases given above.

There are also constructions, which, in unembedded sentences, require first person pronouns.

(20)   I'll (*you'll, *she'll, *he'll) be damned if I'll eat batwings on
        toast.

The construction '____'ll be damned if ...' in its nonliteral sense, is one of these, in non-reported speech. When such constructions are embedded, the constraint requiring first person pronouns disappears. In its place there appears a constraint which requires that the pronoun agree with the subject of the next highest verb in gender, number, and person. Once more, without an analysis such as (A), two separate conditions would be required. With an analysis like (A), only one condition would be required, i.e., that the pronoun agree with the next subject of the next highest verb. In simple sentences, that will be the subject of the performative verb of saying, which will always be first person.

There are still other cases where a construction, when unembedded, requires either a first person or a second person pronoun.

(22)   It would be wise to wash yourself (myself, *himself, *themselves).

When constructions like 'It would be wise to wash ____self' are embedded, that constraint is lifted. Instead, the construction must have a pronoun which agrees in person, number, and gender with either the subject or the indirect object of the next highest verb.

(23)   John told Sue that it would be wise to wash herself (himself, *yourself, *myself).

Again, two separate principles would be required without (A), while with (A), a single general principle can be stated, namely that the pronoun must agree with either the subject or the indirect object of the next highest verb. Such cases provide extremely strong evidence in favor of an analysis like (A). Without (A), unnecessary duplication would be required in many rules. With (A), the general principles can be stated. Note, incidentally, that in each of the above cases the general principle did not involve a restriction on the occurrence of first or second person pronouns. Rather, the restriction on first and second person pronouns in unembedded sentences was *predicted* in each case from the behavior of the construction in embedded sentences.

Another class of arguments in favor of (A) involves adverbial expressions which modify the performative verbs which are understood, but which may not be present in the sentence as uttered.[6] Consider (24) through (26).

(24)   Why is John leaving, since you know so much?
(25)   Since I'm tired, go home.
(26)   John has left, in case you haven't heard.

The adverbial clause 'Since you know so much' in (24) does not modify the verb 'leave'. The adverbial clause 'since I'm tired' in (25) does not modify the verb 'go'. And in (26) 'In case you haven't heard' does not modify 'left'. Sentences (24) through (26) become much clearer when one considers their paraphrases, as in (27) through (29).

(27)   Since you know so much, I'm asking you why John is leaving.
(28)   Since I'm tired, I order you to go home.
(29)   In case you haven't heard, I'm telling you John has left.

In (27) through (29), the understood performative verbs of (24) through (26) have been supplied. In (27) 'since you know so much' obviously modifies 'ask'. It provides the reason why I am asking, which is exactly the same function that the phrase serves in (24). In (28) 'since I'm tired', obviously modifies 'order'. It provides the reason why I am giving the order, which is exactly what the corresponding expression does in (25). In (29), 'in case you haven't heard' modifies 'tell'. It gives the reason why I am telling you that information. This expression performs the same function in (26). Without an analysis like (A), there would be no way of specifying what the adverbial clauses in (24) through (26) modify. In fact, (24) would provide an extremely difficult problem. In (24) the adverbial clause is a reason adverbial, while the question being asked is a why-question. Simple sentences cannot contain both a why-question and a reason adverbial. Without an analysis like (A), one would be hard pressed even to explain why (24) should be grammatical at all.

Let us now turn to questions. (A) makes the claim that all direct questions are really indirect questions in logical form, that is, that sentences like 'Who left, have the same logical form as 'I ask you who left'. Certain facts about questions which were discovered by Leroy Baker tend to corroborate this view. Consider (30).

(30)   Who knows where John bought which books?

(30) is ambiguous. That is, it can be understood as asking for answers of two different sorts. In one sense, (30) can be asking for the addressee to supply a subject of 'know'. Under this reading, an appropriate answer would be 'Irving knows where John bought which books'. In the other reading (30) is asking for two pieces of information. That is, the speaker requires as an answer both a subject of 'know' and a specification of the books. Under such a reading, an appropriate answer to (30) would be 'Irving knows where John bought *Principia Mathematica* and Max knows

where John bought *Das Kapital*. Exactly the same ambiguity occurs in (31).

(31)   Bill asked me who knew where John bought which books.

(31) allows one to see somewhat more clearly what is going on here. It appears that verbs like 'ask' and 'know', which take indirect questions, act like operators binding the items which they question.[7] The reason for the ambiguity in (31) is that three items are being questioned, while there are only two verbs doing the binding. The third item may be bound by either of the verbs. Thus in (31), 'ask' binds 'who' and 'know' binds 'where'. 'Which books' may be bound either by 'ask' or by 'know'. Hence the ambiguity.[8]

(31) shows that verbs taking indirect questions bind the items that they question. But what of direct questions? (30) exhibits the same ambiguity as (31). Under analysis (A), this is not surprising, since under analysis (A), (30) would be embedded inside the object of a performative verb of asking. The performative verb would then act as a binder, binding 'who' on one reading and on the other reading binding both 'who' and 'which books'. Without an analysis like (A), there could be no non-ad hoc uniform analysis of binding in questions. In addition, both direct and indirect questions exhibit the movement of an interrogative pronoun to the front of some clause.

(32)   Who did Sam say that Bill ordered Max to hit?
(33)   Max asked Sue who Sam said Bill ordered Max to hit.

In (32), the pronoun is moved to the front of the sentence as a whole. In (33), the pronoun is moved only to the front of the clause which is the direct object of the verb of asking. Without an analysis like (A), one would have to state two distinct conditions for the application of that rule. With analysis (A), we can state only one condition, namely, that the interrogative pronoun is moved to the front of the clause which is the direct object of that verb of asking which binds that interrogative pronoun. Again, analysis (A) allows one to state a generalization that would otherwise be missed.

In this section we have provided a number of arguments, on linguistic grounds, that the underlying grammatical structure of imperatives, questions, and statements must be represented as in (A). All of these arguments involved linguistic generalizations which could be stated if (A) was accepted, but which could not be stated otherwise. Under the generative semantics hypothesis, for which we provided arguments in Sections II and III, the underlying grammatical structure of each sentence would be identical with its logical form. Therefore the logical forms of imperatives, questions, and statements would have to look like (A) if all of these grammatical arguments are accepted.

The analysis of (A) not only permits the statement of grammatical generalizations, but it also permits one to simplify formal semantics. Consider, for example, the notion of an 'index' as given by Scott (1969). Scott assumed that indices would include among their coordinates specifications of the speaker, addressee, place, and time of the utterance, so that truth conditions could be stated for sentences such as 'Bring what *you now* have to *me* over *here*'. Under an analysis such as (A), the speaker and addressee coordinates could be eliminated from Scott's indices. Moreover, if (A) were expanded, as it should be, to include indications of the place and time of the utterance, then the place and time coordinates could be eliminated from Scott's indices.[9] Truth conditions for such sentences could then be reduced to truth conditions for sentences with ordinary adverbs of place and time. Moreover, truth conditions for sentences such as 'I am innocent' and 'I state that I am innocent' could be generalized in terms of the notion 'propositional content', namely, S_1 in (A). Thus, (A) can be motivated from a logical as well as a grammatical point of view.

V. PRESUPPOSITIONS

Natural language is used for communication in a context, and every time a speaker uses a sentence of his language to perform a speech act – whether an assertion, question, promise, etc. – he is making certain assumptions about that context.[1] For example, suppose a speaker utters the sentence of (1a).

(1)   a. Sam realizes that Irv is a Martian.
          b. $+R^+(S) \rightarrow +S$.

(1a) presupposes that Irv is a Martian. In general, the verb 'realize' presupposes the truth of its object complement. We will represent this as in (1b). In (1b) we let S stand for the object complement of 'realize', namely

'Irv is a Martian' in (1a).[2] R^+ stands for 'realize' and the superscripted plus indicates that positive form of S is to be presupposed under normal conditions. The arrow '→' indicates the relation 'presupposes'.

When (1a) is negated, the complement of 'realize' is still presupposed, as (2a) shows.

(2)   a. Sam doesn't realize that Irv is a Martian.
       b. $-R^+(S) \rightarrow +S$.

The minus sign in (2b) indicates that the sentence containing 'realize' is negated.

Certain grammatical constructions also involve presuppositions. Compare (3a) and (4a).

(3)   a. If Irv is a Martian, I'm leaving.
       b. $+IF^{0,0}(S_1, S_2) \rightarrow 0S_1 \& 0S_2$.
(4)   a. Since Irv is a Martian, I'm leaving.
       b. $+SI^{+,0}(S_1, S_2) \rightarrow +S_1 \& 0S_2$.

The simple if-then construction, as in (3a), does not presuppose that either of the sentences it contains is true. This is indicated in (3b) by superscripting the two zeros to the right of IF. '$0S_1$' indicates that neither S_1 nor its negative is presupposed. (4a), unlike (3a) does involve a presupposition. In (4a) the since-clause is presupposed to be true, though the other clause is not presupposed to be true, but rather asserted. As (5a) shows, the same presupposition relations hold when (4a) is negated.

(5)   a. It is not the case that, since Irv is a Martian, I'm leaving.
       b. $-SI^{+,0}(S_1, S_2) \rightarrow +S_1 \& 0S_2$.

Let us now turn to cases where the negative of a given sentence is presupposed. As (6a) shows, the object complement of the verb 'pretend' is presupposed to be false.

(6)   a. Irv is pretending that he is sick.
       b. $+P^-(S) \rightarrow -S$.

Counterfactual presuppositions will be represented by a superscripted minus, as in (6b). For many speakers, verbs requiring negative presuppositions, such as 'pretend', act quite differently under negation than verbs like 'realize' which require positive presuppositions. Consider (7a).

(7) a. Irv is not pretending that he is sick.
  b. $-P^-(S) \to 0S$ Dialect A
  c. $-P^-(S) \to -S$ Dialect B.

For speakers of what I shall call Dialect A, (7a) makes no presupposition of either the truth or falsity of its complement. For speakers of Dialect B, (7a) presupposes the falsity of its complement. I happen to be a speaker of Dialect A. Incidentally, I am assuming that 'pretend' is unstressed in (7a). If it is stressed, the stress is understood contrastively and (7a) is normally taken in both dialects to either presuppose or assert the truth, not the falsity, of the complement of 'pretend'.

Counterfactual conditionals are not subject to such variation, so far as I have been able to determine.

(8) a. If Irv were a Martian, I'd be running away from here.
  b. $+IFC^{-,-}(S_1, S_2) \to -S_1 \& -S_2$.
(9) a. It is not the case that if Irv were a Martian, I'd be running away from here.
  b. $-IFC^{-,-}(S_1, S_2) \to -S_1 \& -S_2$.

In a simple counterfactual conditional, as in (8a), the negative of both clauses is presupposed. Thus (8a) presupposes both that Irv is not a Martian and that I am not running away from here. The same presuppositions are made in (9a), where the counterfactual conditional is negated.

Verbs like 'realize' and 'pretend' are to be contrasted with verbs like 'ask' as in (10a) and (11a).

(10) a. I asked whether Harry had left.
  b. $+A^0(S) \to 0S$.
(11) a. I asked Harry to leave.
  b. $+AT^0(S) \to 0S$.

In (10a) we have 'ask whether' and in (11a) we have 'ask to'. Both verbs act the same with respect to the presuppositions of their complements. Neither of them presupposes either the truth or the falsity of their complement. The same is true for their negations.

It is very often the case that a presupposed sentence presupposes still another sentence. Consider (12a).

(12)   a. Few men have stopped beating their wives.
          b. Some men have stopped beating their wives.
          c. Some men have beaten their wives.

(12a) presupposes (12b) and (12b), in turn, presupposes (12c). As it turns out, (12a) also presupposes (12c). Thus it would appear, at least in this case, that the presupposition relation is transitive. If S_1 presupposes S_2, and S_2 presupposes S_3, then S_1 presupposes S_3. We will refer to (12b) as a 'first order presupposition' of (12a), and to (12c) as a 'second order presupposition' of (12a). As it turns out, first order presuppositions must be distinguished from second and higher presuppositions. The evidence for this comes from a set of odd constructions in English which I will refer to as 'qualifications'. Consider (13).

(13)   Few men have stopped beating their wives, if any at all have.

(13) consists of (12a), with the qualifying phrase 'if any at all have' tacked on. Though (12a) presupposes (12b), (13) does not presuppose (12b). In fact, the job of the qualifying phrase is to cancel the presupposition of (12b). Similarly, the sentence, 'Sam has stopped beating his wife' presupposes 'Sam has beaten his wife'. Yet in (14), the qualifying phrase has cancelled out this presupposition.

(14)   Sam has stopped beating his wife, if he has ever beaten her at all.

What is particularly interesting about qualifying phrases is that they can cancel out only first-order presuppositions, not second-order or higher-order presuppositions. Thus, given the sentence of (12a) we cannot tack on a qualifying phrase cancelling out a second-order presupposition (12c).

(15)   *?Few men have stopped beating their wives, if any have ever beaten them at all.

(15) is decidedly strange, if intelligible at all, while (13) and (14) are perfectly normal. Compare (15) to (16), where a first order presupposition is cancelled by the same qualifying phrase as in (15).

(16)   Few men have beaten their wives, if any have ever beaten them at all.

Some further examples of qualifying phrases are given in (17).

(17)   a. Few girls are coming, or maybe none at all are.

        b. If the FBI were tapping my phone, I'd be paranoid, but

            then $\begin{cases} \text{I am anyway.} \\ \text{*they are anyway.} \end{cases}$

        c. If Irv weren't a Martian, I'd still be running away.

        d. If Irv still were a Martian, I'd be running away.

Note that in (17b) the negative presupposition associated with the second clause of a counterfactual condition can be cancelled by a qualifying phrase, but the presupposition corresponding to the first clause may not. In (17c) the word 'still' acts as a qualifying phrase for the second clause of the counterfactual conditional. Compare (17c) with (8a). In (8a), the simple counterfactual conditional, the negative of the second clause is presupposed. But in (17c) the positive of the second clause is presupposed, though the negative of the first clause is still presupposed. Note that 'still' used as a qualifying phrase cannot be inserted into the first clause of a counterfactual conditional, as (17d) shows. Though (17d) is grammatical, 'still' can be understood there only in its ordinary sense, and not as a qualifying phrase.[2a]

We can define first-order presuppositions in terms of the concept 'immediately presupposes'. Thus, we will say that 'S_1 immediately presupposes S_2, if and only if S_1 presupposes S_2 and there is no S_3 such that S_1 presupposes S_3 and S_3 presupposes S_2'. This of course does not solve the deeper problem of how qualifying phrases are to be represented in logical form without contradictions arising. It only provides a way of restricting what the content of a qualifying clause can be.

In addition to qualifications, there is another construction discovered by Paul Neubauer and myself which differentiates first-order from second- and higher-order presuppositions. Consider (18).

(18)   a. Sam stopped beating his wife, and it is odd that he stopped beating his wife.

        b. Sam stopped beating his wife, and it is odd that he ever beat her at all.

In the second clauses of (18a and b), the speaker is making a comment about the first clause. In (18a) it is a comment about the entire first clause, while in (18b) it is a comment about the presupposition of the first clause.

However, if such comments are made about second-order presuppositions, they come out sounding like non-sequiturs.

(19)   a. Few men have stopped beating their wives, and it is odd
            that any at all have.
        b. *?Few men have stopped beating their wives, and it is odd
            that any ever beat them at all.

In (19a), the comment is about a first-order presupposition, while in (19b) it is about a second-order presupposition. The comment in (19b) is a non-sequitur. Or take another case.

(20)   a. John won't stop beating his wife until tomorrow, and it
            is odd that he will even stop then.
        b. *John won't stop beating his wife until tomorrow, and it
            is odd that he ever beat her at all.

(20b) contains a clear non-sequitur, where a comment is being made about a second-order presupposition.[3]

So far, we have seen that first-order presuppositions must be distinguished from second- and higher-order presuppositions, and we have seen, in the case of (12), that in certain cases the presupposition relation is transitive. Let us consider further cases of presuppositions of presuppositions to see whether the presupposition relation is transitive in general. Consider (21a).

(21)   a. Max realized that he was pretending that he was sick.
        b. $+R^+(P^-(S)) \to +P^-(S)$ (first order)
        c. $+P\text{-}(S) \to A(-S)$ (second order)
        d. $+R^+(P^-(S)) \to A(-S)$ (by transitivity).

In (21a) we have 'pretend' inside the complement of 'realize'. Here the presupposition relation appears to be transitive. The first order presupposition of (21a) is that Max was pretending to be sick. That in turn presupposes that Max assumes he was not sick. And indeed (21a) presupposes that Max assumes he was not sick.

The situation is somewhat more complicated when 'realize' is embedded inside the object complement of 'pretend'. Consider (22a).

(22)   a. Sue pretended that her boss realized that she had an I.Q.
            of 180.

   b. $+P^-(R^+(S)) \to A(-R^+(S))$ (first order)
   c. $A^-(R^+(S)) \to A(+S)$ (second order)
   d. $+P^-(R^+(S)) \to A(+S)$ (by transitivity).

In my speech, (22a) presupposes that Sue had an I.Q. of 180, so the pre-supposition relation again appears to be transitive. However, there are some speakers who find it hard to make judgments about (22a) and some for whom transitivity seems to fail in such cases. Moreover, in my speech, transitivity fails when the subject of 'realize' is the same as the subject of 'pretend'.

   (23)   a. Max pretended that he realized that he was sick.
           b. $+P^-(R^+(S)) \to A(-R^+(S))$ (first order)
           c. $A(-R^+(S)) \to A(+S)$ (second order)
           d. $+P^-(R^+(S)) \to A(0S)$ (transitivity fails).

In my speech, (23a) does not presuppose that Max assumed he was sick. Consequently, the presupposition relation is not always transitive for all speakers.

   Let us now turn to counterfactual conditionals. In (24a) 'realize' is embedded in the if-clause of a counterfactual conditional.

   (24)   a. If I had realized that Harry had survived, I'd have gone
              home.
           b. $+IFC^{-,-}(R^+(S_1), S_2) \to -R^+(S_1) \& -S_2$
                                            (first order)
           c. $-R^+(S_1) \to +S_1$ (second order)
           d. $+IFC^{-,-}(R^+(S_1), S_2) \to +S_1$ (by transitivity).

(24a) presupposes the negative of both clauses, that is, that I didn't realize that Harry had survived and that I didn't go home. That I didn't realize that Harry survived presupposes, in turn, that Harry survived, as (24c) indicates. Since (24a) presupposes that Harry survived, it appears that transitivity holds when 'realize' is embedded in the if-clause of the counterfactual conditional.

   The situation is somewhat more complex when 'realize' is embedded in the then-clause of a counterfactual conditional. If the complement of 'realize' is not identical with the content of the if-clause, then transitivity holds, otherwise it fails.

(25)   a. If Harry had left, Sue would have realized that he was the
            thief.
         b. $+\text{IFC}^{-,-}(S_1, +R^+(S_2)) \rightarrow -S_1 \& -R^+(S_2)$
                                                        (first order)
         c. $-R^+(S_2) \rightarrow +S_2$ (second order)
         d. $+\text{IFC}^{-,-}(S_1, +R^+(S_2)) \rightarrow +S_2$ (by transitivity).

Since (25a) presupposes that Harry is the thief, the presupposition relation
is transitive in (25a). However, transitivity fails in case the complement
of 'realize' is identical to the content of the if-clause, as Morgan (1969)
has observed. Consider (26a).

(26)   a. If Harry had left, Bill would have realized it.
         b. $+\text{IFC}^{-,-}(S_1, +R^+(S_1)) \rightarrow -S_1 \& -R^+(S_1)$
                                                        (first order)
         c. $-R^+(S_1) \rightarrow +S_1$ (second order)
         d. $+\text{IFC}^{-,-}(S_1, +R^+(S_1)) \rightarrow -S_1$ (transitivity fails).

The first order presupposition of (26a) is the negative of both clauses,
namely that Harry didn't leave and that Bill didn't realize that Harry left.
But 'Bill didn't realize that Harry left' presupposes that Harry left, as
(26c) indicates. But this contradicts the first order presupposition. Thus,
if transitivity held in this case, we would have a contradiction. But (26a)
isn't contradictory. (26a) only presupposes that Harry didn't leave. That
is, the second-order presupposition of (26c) does not go through. Thus,
transitivity of the presupposition relation fails in such cases.[3a]
   Now consider what happens when 'pretend' is embedded inside one of
the clauses of a counterfactual conditional. Consider (27a).

(27)   a. If Irv had pretended that he was sick, he'd have been
            excused.
         b. $+\text{IFC}^{-,-}(P^-(S_1), S_2) \rightarrow -P^-(S_1) \& -S_2$
                                                        (first order)
         c. $-P^-(S_1) \rightarrow A(0S_1)$ (second order)
         d. $+\text{IFC}^{-,-}(P^-(S_1), S_2) \rightarrow A(0S_1)$ (transitivity holds).

In (27a) 'pretend' is embedded in the if-clause of the counterfactual conditional, and transitivity holds.[4] The first order presuppositions of (27a)
are the negations of the two clauses, namely, that Irv didn't pretend that

he was sick and that he wasn't excused. As in (27c) 'Irv didn't pretend that he was sick' presupposes he neither assumed that he was nor was not sick. (27a) also makes no presupposition as to whether Irv was or was not sick. Thus, transitivity holds. But in (28a) the situation is rather different, at least in Dialect A.[5]

(28) a. If Sue had been in trouble, Irv would have pretended that he was sick.

   b. $+IFC^{-,-}(S_1, P^-(S_2)) \rightarrow -S_1 \& -P^-(S_2)$

             (first order)

   c. $-P^-(S_2) \rightarrow A(0S_2)$ (expected second order)

   d. $+IFC^{-,-}(S_1, P^-(S_2)) \rightarrow A(-S_2)$ (transitivity fails).

The first order presuppositions of (28a) are given in (28b), namely that Sue was not in trouble and that Irv didn't pretend that he was sick. In Dialect A, 'Irv didn't pretend that he was sick' would presuppose he neither assumed that he was nor was not sick. However, (28a) presupposes that Irv assumed that he was not sick, as indicated in (28d). This transitivity fails in Dialect A when 'pretend' is embedded in the then-clause of a counterfactual conditional. However, this case is somewhat more complicated than (26a). In (26a), we can simply say that transitivity fails, and that the presupposition that one would have expected from (26c) does not arise. That accounts for all the facts of (26a). However, simply blocking the presupposition relation of (28c) will not account for the facts of (28a). In (28a), we must in addition account for the fact that it is presupposed that Irv assumed that he was not sick. There are no obvious non-ad hoc ways of accounting for this.

Let us now turn to predicates which make no particular presupposition about the truth or falsity of their complements. First consider 'ask whether'. In (29a) 'realize' is embedded inside the complement of 'ask whether'.

(29) a. I asked Sam whether he realized that he was sick.

   b. $A^0(R^+(S)) \rightarrow 0R^+(S)$ (first order)

   c. $0R^+(S) \rightarrow ?$ (undefined)

   d. $A^0(R^+(S)) \rightarrow +S$ (transitivity seems to fail).

So far we have indicated the lack of a presupposition by a zero, as in (29b) for cases where no presupposition is made, no second order presupposition is defined, at least as we have defined the presupposition relation. Thus (29c) is undefined. However, (29a) makes a positive presupposition, namely, that Sam was sick. Thus, given the way we have defined the lack of a presupposition, transitivity seems to fail for (29a). Suppose, however, that we redefine what is meant by the lack of a presupposition as meaning that either a positive or a negative presupposition is permitted, as in (30b).

(30) a. I asked Sam whether he realized that he was sick.
  b. $A^{+\vee-}(R^+(S)) \rightarrow R^+(S) \vee -R^+(S)$ (first order)
  c. $+R^+(S) \rightarrow +S$ (second order)
  d. $-R^+(S) \rightarrow +S$ (second order)
  e. $A^{+\vee-}(R^+(S)) \rightarrow +S \vee +S(\equiv +S)$ (by distribution and transitivity).

If, in addition, we add an axiom of distribution saying that the presupposition of a disjunction entails the disjunction of the presuppositions, then transitivity holds for (30a).

(31) Distribution
  $(S_1 \rightarrow (S_2 \vee S_3)) \supset ((S_1 \rightarrow S_2) \vee (S_1 \rightarrow S_3))$.

(30a) presupposes that either Sam realized that he was sick or that he didn't realize that he was sick. But both of those sentences presuppose that Sam was sick. Therefore, by distribution and transitivity, it follows that (30a) should presuppose that Sam was sick, which it does.

Distribution and transitivity also work in the case where 'pretend' is embedded inside 'ask whether'.[6]

(32) a. I asked Sam whether he was pretending that he was sick.
  b. $AW^{+\vee-}(P^-(S)) \rightarrow +P^-(S) \vee -P^-(S)$ (first order)
  c. $+P^-(S) \rightarrow A(-S)$ (second order)
  d. $-P^-(S) \rightarrow (A(+S) \vee A(-S))$ (second order)
  e. $AW^{+\vee-}(P^-(S)) \rightarrow (A(+S) \vee A(-S))$ (by distribution and transitivity).

(32a) presupposes that either Sam pretended that he was sick or Sam didn't pretend that he was sick, as shown in (32b). 'Sam pretended that he was sick' presupposes that Sam assumed he was not sick, as given in

(32c), but 'Sam didn't pretend that he was sick' presupposes that he either assumed he was sick or assumed he wasn't sick, as shown in (32d). Therefore by distribution and transitivity, no particular presupposition is made.

Just as we saw above that there are cases where transitivity fails, so there are cases involving distribution where transitivity fails. Consider (33a), in Dialect A, which is the interesting dialect.

(33)   I asked Sam to pretend that he was sick.

    b. $AT^{+\vee-}(P^-(S)) \rightarrow (+P^-(S) \vee -P^-(S))$

                                                       (first order)

    c. $+P^-(S) \rightarrow A(-S)$ (second order)

    d. $-P^-(S) \rightarrow (A(+S) \vee A(-S))$ (second order)

    e. $AT^{+\vee-}(P^-(S)) \rightarrow A(-S)$ (transitivity fails).

In (33a) we have 'pretend' embedded inside 'ask to'. In Dialect A, 'ask to' works rather differently with respect to this phenomenon than 'ask whether'. 'Ask to' has the same first order presupposition as 'ask whether', namely that either Sam will pretend that he is sick or that Sam will not pretend that he is sick. This is shown in (33b). Given the principles of distribution and transitivity, one would expect that (33a) would have the same second-order presuppositions as (32a). These are indicated in (33c and d). Thus we would expect that (33a) would make no presupposition as to whether Sam assumed he was or was not sick. However (33a) presupposes that Sam assumed he was not sick, at least in Dialect A. Thus the principles of distribution and transitivity would appear not to fit in this case. Again, the principle at work here is mysterious.

Although we do not know how (33a) works, we can use the fact that it does work as indicated to account for an otherwise mysterious fact in Dialect A. Consider (34a).

(34)   a. Nixon refused to try to shut Agnew up.

    b. REFUSE (S).

(34a) entails (though does not presuppose) (35a).

(35)   a. Nixon didn't try to shut Agnew up.

    b. $-S$.

Thus, if someone refuses to do something which involves an act of the will and which he has control over, then it is entailed that he didn't do it.

In such situations, sentences of the form (34b) entail sentences of the form (35b). Now consider (36a) and (37a).

(36)   a. Nixon refused to pretend that he tried to shut Agnew up.
         b. REFUSE $(P^-(S))$.
(37)   a. Nixon didn't pretend that he tried to shut Agnew up.
         b. $-P^-(S)$.

(36a) entails (37a). (37a) has the form of (37b). As we have seen above, sentences of that form in Dialect A make no presupposition about the truth or falsity of their complements, as indicated in (38a).

(38)   a. $-P^-(S) \rightarrow (A(+S) \vee A(-S))$
         b. Either Nixon assumed that he tried to shut Agnew up or that he didn't try to shut Agnew up.

Thus, we would expect sentences like (36a) not to presuppose or entail anything about the complement of 'pretend'. That is, we would expect (36a) to say nothing about whether Nixon assumed that he tried or did not try to shut Agnew up. However, (36a) does presuppose that Nixon assumed that he did not try to shut Agnew up, as indicated in (39)

(39)   REFUSE $(P^-(S)) \rightarrow A(-S)$.

This would appear to be a mystery. However, as Robin Lakoff has pointed out (personal communication), (36a) presupposes that someone asked Nixon to pretend that he tried to shut Agnew up. In general, sentences with 'refuse' presuppose corresponding sentences with 'ask to', as indicated in (40a).

(40)   a. REFUSE $(P^-(S)) \rightarrow$ AT$(P^-(S))$
         b. AT $(P^-(S)) \rightarrow A(-S)$.

As we saw above in (33a), when 'pretend' is embedded inside 'ask to', the negative of the complement of 'pretend' is presupposed, as indicated in (40b). Thus, if the principles of distribution and transitivity hold for 'refuse' and 'ask to', we can explain why (36a) presupposes that Nixon assumed that he did not try to shut Agnew up. Thus the problem of (36a) reduces to a previously unsolved problem. Note incidentally, that the question of whether distribution and transitivity hold for the pair of predicates 'refuse' and 'ask to' is separate from the question of whether those principles hold for the pair 'ask to' and 'pretend'. They seem to hold for the former pair, but they do not hold for the latter pair.

Most of the cases we've considered so far are examples where truth or falsity of some embedded sentence is presupposed. However, in (40a), this is not the case. What is presupposed is not the truth of the complement of 'refuse', but rather another sentence containing that complement. There are many such cases. For example, as Don Larkin (personal communication) observed, the verb 'agree' when it takes an infinitive complement, presupposes a request. Thus, 'Harry agreed to leave' presupposes that someone asked Harry to leave. Similarly, 'agree' with the complementizer 'that' presupposes a statement. 'Harry agreed that Marvin was a louse' presupposes that someone stated that Marvin was a louse. The difference between the verbs 'fear' and 'hope' lies in the fact that the former presupposes a sentence containing 'bad', while the latter presupposes a sentence containing 'good'. For example, 'Sam fears that Max will come' presupposes that Sam believes that it will be bad for someone for Max to come, while 'Sam hopes that Max will come' presupposes that Sam believes that it will be good for someone for Max to come.

A rather complicated but particularly interesting example of this sort involves the word 'even', which has been discussed in detail by Horn (1969).

(41)   a. Even John came.
        b. John came. (assertion)
        c. It was expected that John would not come. (presupposition)
        d. Other people than John came. (presupposition)

(41a) asserts (41b). It presupposes (41c and d). What is particularly interesting is that while (41c), as expected, acts like a first-order presupposition of (41a), (41d) acts like a higher-order presupposition, even though it is not presupposed by (41c). We can tell this by testing possible negative-attitude comments and qualifying phrases. The presupposition of (41c) may be cancelled by a qualifying phrase, while that of (41d) may not.

(42)   a. Even John came, but then maybe it was to be expected.
        b. *Even John came, $\begin{cases} \text{but then maybe no one else did} \\ \text{if anyone else came.} \end{cases}$

In (42a) the qualifying phrase 'but then...' cancels the presupposition of
(41c). But any attempt to cancel the presupposition of (41d) by a qualifying phrase yields an ungrammatical sentence, as in (42b). When 'even' is
mixed with a verb like 'stop', which presupposes the truth of its complement, it is still the case that the presupposition of negative expectation
associated with 'even' must be first-order, while the presupposition of
'stop' must be higher-order. Compare (43) and (44).

(43)   John has stopped beating his wife, if he ever beat her at all.
(44)   a. *Even John has stopped beating his wife, if he ever beat
            her at all.
         b. Even John has stopped beating his wife, but then maybe
            it was to be expected.

In (43), where there is no 'even', the qualifying phrase cancels the presupposition of the truth of the complement of 'stop'. However, if 'even'
is added, as in (44a), then the same qualifying phrase cannot cancel the
presupposition of the truth of the complement of 'stop'. Compare (44a)
with (44b), where it is possible to cancel the presupposition of negative
expectation associated with 'even'. Thus we have a case where a certain
construction requires two presuppositions, one of which must be first-
order, the other of which isn't second-order, but acts as if it were.

(41d) also acts like a second-order presupposition of (41a) with respect
to the phenomenon of negative-attitude comments. Consider (45).

(45)   a. Even John came, and it was odd that he did.
         b. Even John came, and it was odd that it wasn't expected.
         c. *Even John came, and it was odd that anyone else did.

In (45a and b) we have comments on the assertion and first-order presupposition, as expected. But the comment of (45c) is ruled out, just as
if it were a comment on a second-order presupposition.

It should be noted, incidentally, that not all first-order presuppositions
can be qualified.

(46)   a. *Sam realized that Sue had gonorrhea, if she ever did.
         b. *Irv regretted leaving home, if he ever left at all.

The general conditions under which first-order presuppositions can be
qualified are not known at present, however, Horn (1970, and personal

communication) has made an extremely insightful suggestion which works in a large number of cases. Compare (47) and (48).

(47) a. Sixty per cent of the students are striking, if not more.
      b. *Sixty per cent of the students are striking, if not less.
(48) a. *Only sixty percent of the students are striking, if not more.
      b. Only sixty percent of the students are striking, if not less.

Horn observes that in (47a) the qualifying phrase is making an assertion 'in the same direction' as the main assertion of the sentence. That is, the main assertion is a positive assertion giving a certain percentage. The qualifying phrase is in a sense 'still more positive', giving an even higher percentage. Thus, in some intuitive sense of the term, the qualifying phrase is making an assertion in the same direction as the main clause. Now consider (49), which accords with the analysis presented in Horn (1969).

(49) a. Only sixty percent of the students are striking.
      b. No more than sixty percent of the students are striking. (assertion)
      c. Sixty percent of the students are striking. (presupposition)

Horn notes that (49b), the asserted part of (49a), is a negative statement. Thus, the qualifying phrase in (48b) would be going 'in the direction of' the assertion of the main clause, while the qualifying phrase in (48a) would not. Thus, Horn suggests that qualifying phrases cancelling out the presupposition of the main clause are permitted only if the assertion they make is 'in the same direction' as the assertion of the main clause, that is, toward greater universality, either in the positive or negative direction. Obviously, the notion 'in the same direction as' has not yet been made into a formal notion. Still, it is clear that there is something to it. If formalized, it would appear to account for such facts as the following, as Horn has observed.

(50) a. Sam goes swimming sometimes, if not often.
      b. *Sam goes swimming often, if not sometimes.

In (50a), we have a positive statement, with a qualifying phrase going in the direction of greater universality. In (50b) we have a positive statement, with a qualifying phrase going in the direction of less universality, and so the sentence is impermissible.

(51) a. Sam seldom goes swimming, if he ever does.
      u. *Sam never goes swimming, if he seldom does.

In (51a) we have a negative statement in the main clause and a qualifying phrase in the direction of greater negative universality, namely, 'John seldom swims' versus 'John never swims'. In (51b), this is not the case, and the qualifying phrase is disallowed.

Horn's account of this phenomenon also provides an explanation for the difference between (52a) and (52b).

(52) a. John doesn't beat his wife anymore, if he ever did.
      b. *John still beats his wife, if he ever did.

Both 'John doesn't beat his wife anymore' and 'John still beats his wife' have the first-order presupposition that John beat his wife at some point in the past. Thus, without Horn's hypothesis, one would guess that the same qualifying phrase could be used to cancel out both. But this fails in (52b). Horn's hypothesis, however, accounts for this. In (52a), the main clause is making a negative statement, namely, that at present John doesn't beat his wife. The qualifying phrase suggests that 'John doesn't beat his wife' may not only be true at present, but may have been true at all times in the past. Thus it is in the direction of greater (negative) universality. In (52b), however, the assertion is made that at present John does beat his wife, and thus the qualifying phrase does not constitute an extension of that assertion into the past, but rather suggests the contrary. Incidentally, Horn's hypothesis also appears to account for the sentences of (46), since the qualifying phrases there also seem not to go 'in the same direction as' the assertion.

It should be noted in addition that negative-attitude comments work differently than qualifications in cases like (46).

(53) a. Sam realized that Sue had gonorrhea, and it is surprising that she did.
      b. Irv regretting leaving home, and it is strange that he ever left.

Thus, it would appear that negative-attitude comments allow all first-order presuppositions, while qualifications are limited by Horn's hypothesis.

A particularly interesting phenomenon, observed by Morgan (1969), is that of embedded presuppositions. We can approach the problem by considering (54) and (55).

(54)   a. Nixon is pretending that everyone realizes that he is a homosexual.

       b. $P^-(R^+(S)) \to A(+S)$.

(55)   a. Nixon is pretending that he is a homosexual.

       b. $P^-(S) \to A(-S)$.

In (54a) it is presupposed that Nixon is a homosexual, as indicated in (54b). This should be clear from the discussion above. In (55a) it is presupposed that Nixon is not a homosexual, as is indicated in (55b). Now consider (56a).

(56)   a. Nixon is pretending that he is a homosexual and that everyone realizes it.

       b. $P^-(S \ \& \ R^+(S))$ (first order)

       c. $P^-(S) \ \& \ P^-(R^+(S))$ (by distribution over conjunction)

       d. $A(-S) \ \& \ A(+S)$ (conjunction of the presuppositions of c).

(56a) contains a conjunction inside the complement of 'pretend'. The conjunction is 'Nixon is a homosexual and everyone realizes that Nixon is a homosexual'. Since the presupposition of 'Nixon is pretending that he is a homosexual' is that he is not a homosexual, and since the presupposition of 'Nixon is pretending that everyone realizes that he is a homosexual' is that he is a homosexual, one would expect that (56) would have contradictory assumptions, as indicated in (56d). However, (56a) is not contradictory at all. What went wrong? Lest anyone think that the step from (56b) to (56c) was unjustified, note that (56a) has the same meaning as (57), which has the overt structure of (56c).

(57)   Nixon is pretending that he is a homosexual and he is pretending that everyone realizes it.

Morgan has suggested that the difficulty with (56a) lies in our assumptions that only sentences as a whole may presuppose other sentences.

Morgan suggests that embedded sentences may have presuppositions that entire sentences may not have. He notes that a verb like 'pretend' in essence defines a possible world (actually a class of worlds) such that the sentential complement of 'pretend' is true in that world. Morgan claims, correctly I think, that the way we understand (56a) is that 'Nixon is a homosexual' is true in the world of Nixon's pretense, but is presupposed to be false with respect to the world of the speaker. If Morgan is right, then we must distinguish between presuppositions of the entire sentence and presuppositions of embedded sentences. Unfortunately, we have no idea of how to represent embedded presuppositions at present in such a way that the relationship between presuppositions of embedded sentences and presuppositions of entire sentences can be stated naturally. [7a]

The question now arises as to how presuppositions are to be represented in terms of logical form. There is a precedent for incorporating presuppositions into the logical form of the sentences that presuppose them. For example, Von Wright and others have employed what is called a 'dyadic modal logic', using formulas such as those in (58).

(58)   a. $L\,(p/q)$
          b. $O\,(p/q)$.

(58a) is to be read 'p is necessary, given that q', and (58b) is to be read 'p is obligatory, given that q'. So far as I can tell, the reading 'given that q' is equivalent to 'presupposing q'. The notation in (58) is equivalent to representing the propositional and presuppositional content of a sentence by an ordered pair. This happens to be the approach I took in (G. Lakoff, in press). However, having an ordered pair of sentences is equivalent to having a relation between two sentences.[8] In the above discussion, we have represented such relation by '→'. Let us consider how we can make sense of this in terms of a relationship between the surface form of a sentence and its logical form, assuming that that relationship is to be given by rules of grammar. Let S_1 and S_2 stand for the surface forms of two sentences, and let $\mathcal{L}_1$ and $\mathcal{L}_2$ stand for the underlying forms of the corresponding sentences. Suppose now that S_1 is a sentence whose main verb is 'realize'. For instance, suppose S_1 is 'Sam realizes that Harry is a fink' and S_2 is 'Harry is a fink'. Then we will say that the surface form S_1 can be related to the logical form $\mathcal{L}_1$ only if the relation '→' holds between $\mathcal{L}_1$ and $\mathcal{L}_2$, as indicated in (59) and (60).

(59) $\mathscr{L}_1 \rightarrow \mathscr{L}_2$
         $\vdots$ $\vdots$
         S_1 S_2

(60)

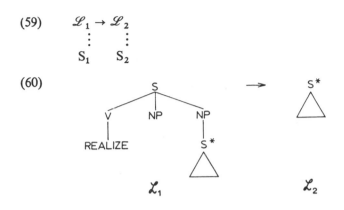

Thus the presupposition relation, as strictly defined, will hold only between logical forms of sentences and not between surface forms. We will, however, speak of the presupposition relation holding between two sentences, S_1 and S_2, if the relation '→' holds between their corresponding logical forms. In this formulation presuppositions need not be considered part of the logical forms of sentences. In the cases where rules of grammar interact with presuppositions, such rules will be stated as transderivational constraints.[9]

On the basis of the above discussion, we can draw the following conclusions.

CONCLUSION 1: An account of the logical form of a sentence must include an account of the presuppositions of that sentence. The question is left open as to whether presuppositions should best be represented as separate logical forms, related to the main assertion by '→' or whether they should be incorporated into logical forms, as I believe they are in dyadic modal logic.

CONCLUSION 2: The presupposition relation is usually transitive, though transitivity fails in a number of cases. Thus, one cannot assume that there will be a simple, unrestricted axiom of transitivity for the relation '→'. Moreover, the restrictions on transitivity will differ from dialect to dialect, just as rules of grammar do.[10]

CONCLUSION 3: First-order presuppositions will have to be distinguished from higher-order presuppositions.

CONCLUSION 4: If Horn's hypothesis is correct, logical forms must be given in such a way that the notion 'in the same direction as' or 'in the direction of greater (positive or negative) universality' can be stated formally for *all* relevant cases in natural language.

CONCLUSION 5: If Morgan's proposal is correct, logical forms must include some method of representing embedded presuppositions.

CONCLUSION 6: A method must be found for representing qualifications of first-order presuppositions without contradicting those presuppositions.[11]

VI. BAKER'S CONJECTURE AND NATURAL LOGIC

So far we have been speaking about 'logical forms' of English sentences as though the term meant something. However, it makes sense to speak of the logical forms of sentences only with respect to some system of logic. And systems of logic are constructed with specific aims in mind – there are certain concepts one wants to be able to express, inferences one wants to be able to account for, mysteries one wants to explain or explain away, fallacies one wants to avoid, philosophical problems one wants to elucidate. Most of the attempts made in recent years to provide logics for given fragments of English have been motivated by a desire to shed light on philosophical problems that require that certain concepts (e.g., logical necessity, change in time, obligation, etc.) be expressed and inferences (e.g., what is logically necessary is true) be accounted for.[1]

In this study we have set an additional goal. In Section I, we saw that there was some connection between grammar and reasoning, and we inquired as to whether it was accidental, and if not, just what the connection was. In Sections II and III, we saw that the connection was not accidental and we got an inkling as to what it was. We saw that the rules relating logical forms to the corresponding surface forms of English sentences must be identical to certain rules of English grammar, at least in the case of quantifiers and conditionals. These results were relative to another goal: that significant generalizations (especially linguistic ones) be expressed, that the same rule not be stated twice. From these results, and from a large number of other results not considered here,[2] we adopted the hypothesis known as 'generative semantics', which states that the rules of grammar are just the rules relating logical forms to surface forms of sentences. In Sections IV and V, we saw that such assumptions led to some rather interesting conclusions about logical form.

To recapitulate, we have made the following assumptions:

(i) We want to understand the relationship between grammar and reasoning.

(ii) We require that significant generalizations, especially linguistic ones, be stated.

(iii) On the basis of (i) and (ii), we have been led tentatively to the generative semantics hypothesis. We assume that hypothesis to see where it leads.

Given these aims, empirical linguistic considerations play a role in determining what the logical forms of sentences can be. Let us now consider certain other aims.

(iv) We want a logic in which all the concepts expressible in natural language can be expressed unambiguously, that is, in which all non-synonymous sentences (at least, all sentences with different truth conditions) have different logical forms.[3]

(v) We want a logic which is capable of accounting for all correct inferences made in natural language and which rules out incorrect ones. We will call any logic meeting the goals of (i)–(v) a 'natural logic'. As should be obvious, the construction of a full, nonfragmental natural logic is not an immediate practical goal. In fact, it may not even be a possible goal. Linguistic considerations alone, not to mention logical considerations, rule this out. For example, assumptions (ii) and (iii) require that a full, descriptively adequate grammar of English is required for there to be a natural logic. That is, all the relevant generalizations concerning the relation between logical forms and surface forms must be known. It would be ludicrous to think of this as a practical goal to be accomplished within the next several centuries, if it is possible at all. Serious grammatical studies are in their infancy. Moreover, the study of intensional logics has just gotten off the ground. So it should be clear that no one is about to successfully construct a full natural logic. The goals of (i)–(v) define a subject matter, and its viability depends not upon being able to construct full logics, but upon whether it leads to interesting results. The study of natural logic constitutes a program without an end in sight (like most programs) and the question to be asked is whether it is an interesting program.

If it makes sense to study a subject matter based on the assumptions of (i)-(v), one might expect that these assumptions might interact in some empirically observable way. For example, if the rules of grammar are just those rules that relate logical forms and surface forms, and if it makes sense to speak of logical forms of sentences only in terms of some system of logic – with axioms, rules of inference, etc. – then it might be the case there might be an interaction between grammatical phenomena and logical phenomena. Perhaps there are grammatical constraints that are, for example, dependent upon one's choice of axioms. In fact, an example of such a phenomenon has been proposed by Baker (1969).

Baker considered cases like:

(1)   I would rather go.

(2)   *I would*n't* rather go.

(3)   I did*n't* meet anyone who would*n't* rather go.

He noted that 'affirmative polarity' items like *would rather*, which cannot occur when one negative is present, can occur in some cases when two negatives are present.[3a] He first attempted to describe this phenomenon by saying that the item in question must be commanded by an even number of negatives. Faced with a number of counterexamples to this proposal, he observed that many of the double negation cases he had considered were logically equivalent to positive sentences, while none of the counterexamples were. He then conjectured that perhaps the distribution of affirmative polarity items like 'would rather' was determined by a principle involving logical equivalences. This conjecture, if true, would be a case of the above sort.

Let us begin by considering some apparent confirming instances of Baker's conjecture.

(4)   *I did*n't* meet the man who would*n't* rather go.

(5)   *I did*n't* meet anyone who claimed that he would*n't* rather go.

(6)   *I did*n't* claim that I met anyone who would*n't* rather go.

(7)   *I did*n't* claim that I would*n't* rather go.

Although (3) seems intuitively to be logically equivalent to a positive sentence, (4)–(7) seem not to be. Despite the occurrence of double negatives, *would rather* cannot occur in such cases. For example, in (6) the intervening complement construction with *claim* between the two negatives keeps the sentence from being logically equivalent to a positive sentence. Now compare (8a and b).

(8)   a. *I do*n't* claim that I met anyone who would*n't* rather go.
        b. I do*n't* think that I met anyone who would*n't* rather go.

The difference between (8a) and (8b) can be explained by the fact that *think* and not claim undergoes the rule of *not*-transportation, which moves a *not* from within the complement of *think* to the next highest clause. The existence of such a rule has been demonstrated beyond a reasonable doubt by R. Lakoff (1969).[4] Thus, the occurrence of (8b) follows from the occurrence of (9).

(9)   I thought that I had*n't* met anyone who would*n't* rather go.

If Baker's conjecture is correct, it provides still more confirming evidence for *not*-transportation. Note that it is exactly those verbs that take *not*-transportation that can occur in the position of *think* in (8b).

An especially interesting class of confirming instances arises in the case of modal equivalences. For example,

(10) $\sim$ NECESSARY (S) $\equiv$ POSSIBLE $\sim$ (S).

Baker's conjecture would predict that, just as one can get (11),

(11)   It is possible that I would rather go.

one should be able to get (12):

(12)   It is *not* necessarily true that I would*n't* rather go.

It is rather remarkable that this prediction is borne out. Compare (12) with (13), which is not logically equivalent to a positive sentence.[5]

(13)   *It is *not* probable that I wouldn't *rather* go.

This 'confirmation' of Baker's conjecture raises some questions in itself. If 'logical equivalences' are involved here, just what sort of logic are they associated with? Baker speaks only of the predicate calculus. The above examples seem to indicate that his conjecture would have to be extended to some system of modal logic, presumably quantified modal logic. Let us consider for a moment what this means. Suppose, like formalist logicians, we were to think of a logic as simply an arbitrary formal system, with operators chosen from an arbitrary vocabulary and logical equivalences defined in some arbitrary way. From this point of view, first-order predicate calculus and quantified modal logic are simply two out of an infinite variety of possible logics. Why should the distribution of 'affirmative polarity' items like *would rather* depend on the translation of English sentences into any of these particular logics? After all, one could always construct some logic or other where any sentence containing two negatives was logically equivalent to a positive. Suppose, for example, we constructed a logic which contained a predicate SNURG. Suppose, in addition, that we defined the following logical equivalence:

(14) $\sim$ PROBABLE $\sim$ (S) $\equiv$ SNURG (S).

With respect to this arbitrary logic, (13) would be logically equivalent to a positive sentence. Should the fact that one can always construct such a logic be taken as showing that Baker's conjecture makes no sense? If there is always a logic in which any sentence with two negatives is logically equivalent to a positive sentence, then doesn't Baker's conjecture cease to be an empirical hypothesis?

I think that one would have to agree that Baker's conjecture does not make any sense if one conceives of logics as simply arbitrary formal systems. It is only with respect to natural logic that Baker's conjecture makes sense. In natural logic, the operators and atomic predicates would not be chosen from an arbitrary vocabulary, but would be limited to those that could occur in the logical forms of sentences of natural languages. That is, they would be limited in part on empirical linguistic grounds. Moreover, logical equivalence could not just be arbitrarily set down; rather they would be just those necessary to characterize the notion 'valid inference' for natural language arguments. Presumably, the predicate SNURG would not be a possible atomic predicate and (14) would not be a possible equivalence. From this point of view, the fact that Baker's, conjecture holds, say, for the logical equivalence in (10), indicates that (10) is not an arbitrary logical equivalence like (14), but rather that it has an empirical basis in human reasoning.

Let us turn to some more complicated examples like those discussed in Baker's paper.[6]

(15)   It's *not* possible for Sam to convince Sheila that he would*n't* rather go.

(16)   It's *not* possible for Sam to make Sheila believe that he would*n't* rather go.

(17) ?*It's *not* possible for Sam to make Sheila claim that he would-
n't rather go.

(18) ?*It's *not* possible for Sam to make Sheila hope that he would-
n't rather go.

Clearly nothing from first-order predicate calculus tells us that (15) and
(16) are logically equivalent to positive sentences, while (17) and (18) are
not. Suppose we consider what might be required of natural logic for
Baker's conjecture to account for (15)–(18). Let us start with a very rough
approximation of what the relevant par. f the logical structure of (15)
might look like.

(I)

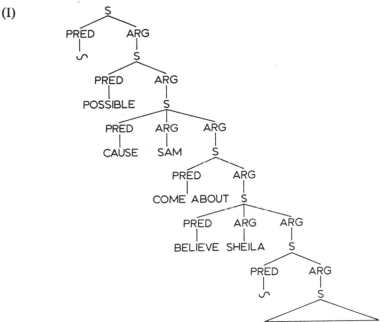

(I) makes use of the fact that *convince* in (15) means *cause to come to
believe*. The PREDs in (I) are meant to be first approximations to atomic
predicates that would occur in logical forms of natural language sentences; they are not meant to be words of English or predicates chosen
from an arbitrary vocabulary.

Note that the two occurrences of '∼' in (I) are separated by a consider-able distance. The question to be raised is this: Would natural logic contain appropriate logical equivalences which would enable the two negatives to be moved into adjacent positions so that an appropriately restricted version of the Law of Double Negation might cancel them out? Suppose natural logic contained the equivalence of (19), which is essen-tially the same as (10).

(19)   ∼ POSSIBLE (S) ≡ NECESSARY ∼ (S).

(19) states that (I) is equivalent to (II). The effect is to move the '∼' down a clause.

(II)

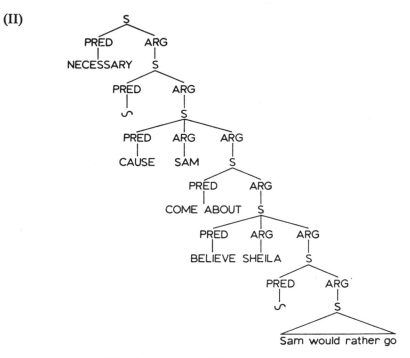

Now suppose natural logic contained (20).

(20)   ∼ CAUSE (S) ≡ ALLOW ∼ (S).

If one has it in one's power to bring about some situation *S*, then not to cause *S* is equivalent to allowing the situation *not S* to persist. (20)

(III)

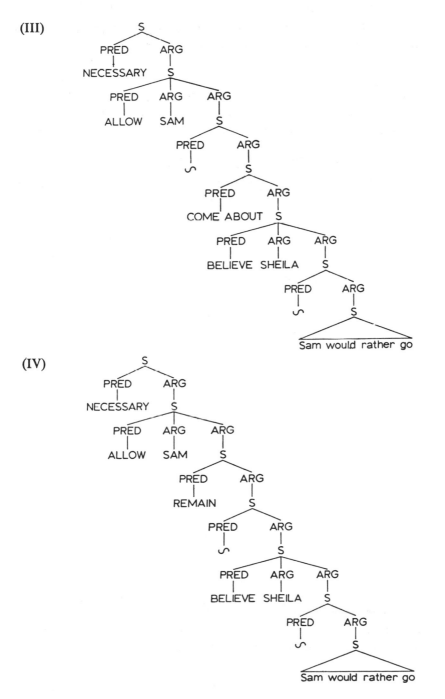

(IV)

states that (II) is equivalent to (III). Again, the '~' moves down a clause. Suppose now that (21) was an equivalence of natural logic.

(21)   ~ COME ABOUT (S) ≡ REMAIN ~ (S).

If appropriately formulated, (21) would state that (III) was equivalent to (IV), in which '~' is moved down still another notch.

Moreover, suppose that natural logic contained the equivalence of (22).

(22)   ~ BELIEVE (S) ≡ BE OPEN TO ~ (S).

This would state that (IV) was equivalent to (V), where the two occurrences of '~' are in adjacent sentences.

(V)

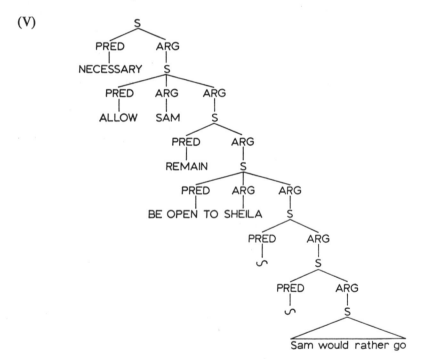

Though it is clear that the Law of Double Negation does not apply with full generality in natural language (*John is not unhappy* is not equivalent to *John is happy*), it is equally clear that in a restricted range of cases the Law of Double Negation does apply. Assuming that (V) is such a case, then (V) would be equivalent to (VI), which contains no negatives.

(VI) would be a partially specified semantic representation for something like (23).

(23)   It is necessary for Sam to allow Sheila to remain open to the idea that he would rather go.

So far as I can tell, (23) is logically equivalent to (15); that is, I do not see how one can be true and the other false (on the appropriate readings).

If (19)–(22) were equivalences of natural logic, then Baker's conjecture could account for the grammaticality of (15) and (16). But what about the ungrammaticality of (17) and (18), which differ from (16) only in that they contain *claim* and *hope* rather than *believe*? In order for these to be

(VI)

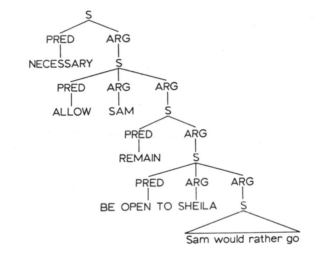

ruled out under Baker's conjecture, it would have to be the case that natural logic did *not* contain logical equivalences for *claim* and *hope* parallel to (22), which involves *believe*. That is there could *not* occur in the inventory of atomic predicates for the semantic representations of natural languages two predicates which we will call BLIK and BNIK, such that (24) and (25) were equivalences in natural logic.

(24) $* \sim$ CLAIM (S) $\equiv$ BLIK $\sim$ (S)
(25) $* \sim$ HOPE (S) $\equiv$ BNIK $\sim$ (S).

Baker's conjecture seems to require that there be no natural logic equivalences like (24) and (25). The absence of such equivalences would keep the '∼' from moving down into the clause below *claim* or *hope*, thus making it impossible for the two negatives to come to be in adjacent clauses and thereby ruling out the possibility that they could cancel out by the Law of Double Negation.[6a]

Whether Baker's conjecture is right or wrong remains to be seen. But I think that this discussion has at least shown that it makes sense, even for very complicated cases like (15)–(18). I'm not sure how seriously one should take the supposed equivalences of (19)–(22). If considered in detail, they would undoubtedly prove inadequate. Perhaps they could be fixed up, or perhaps an entirely different set of equivalences would do the job. However, (19)–(22) are at least plausible; they are not wild or far-fetched. Nor is it far-fetched to think that there are no natural logic equivalences like (24) and (25).

Baker's conjecture, given that it makes sense, raises questions of the utmost importance both for linguists and for logicians interested in human reasoning. For linguistics, its consequences are remarkable, since it claims that the *distribution of morphemes* (e.g., would rather) is determined not simply by which other elements and structures are present in the same sentence, or even in a transformational derivation of that sentence, but in addition by logical equivalences. As far as logic is concerned, Baker's conjecture would, if correct, show that natural logic is a field with real subject matter. At any rate, it would show that there was a relation between grammaticality and logical equivalence. Proposed equivalences for natural logic might be tested by constructing the appropriate sentences and seeing whether they were grammatical or not.

One apparent difficulty with the conjecture is that there are some cases where affirmative-polarity items are acceptable, but where there are no fairly obvious and reasonably plausible logical equivalences that can be invoked to yield a positive sentence. For example,

(26)   I wonder if there is anyone who would*n't* rather go home.
(27)   Is there anyone who would*n't* rather go home?
(28)   Anyone who would*n't* rather go home now is crazy.

(26) and (27) seem to be rhetorical questions and to presuppose a negative answer, which would contain two negatives of the appropriate sort. (28) seems to involve some sort of negative judgment, which again would

contain two negatives. Perhaps there is a constraint to the effect that the negative presupposition or judgment of such sentences must be logically equivalent to a positive. It is clear that the conjecture alone is insufficient and that there are other conditions involved.[7] This does not invalidate the conjecture; it merely limits its scope of applicability. But even in such a limited form, the conjecture would lose none of its theoretical significance. If the distribution of morphemes is determined *even in part* by logical equivalences, then all of the consequences stated above still follow. There would have to be a natural logic, including some equivalences and excluding others.

VII. LEXICAL DECOMPOSITION VERSUS MEANING-POSTULATES

Lexical items are not undecomposable wholes with respect to the logical forms of the sentences that they appear in. We can see this clearly in a sentence like (1).

(1)   Sam has always loved his wife.

(1) is ambiguous. It can have the meaning of either (2a) or (2b).

(2)   a. Sam has always loved the person he is now married to.
         b. Sam has always loved whoever he was married to at that time.

Suppose that Sam has had several wives, and that he may or may not have loved his previous wives, though he has always loved the woman he is presently married to. (1) has the reading of (2a). On the other hand, suppose that Sam did not love his present wife before he married her, but that whenever he was married to a woman, he loved her at that time. Then (1) has the reading of (2b). (2a) and (2b) can be represented as (3a) and (3b), respectively, where t_0 is the time of the utterance and 'LOVE' is assumed (for the sake of discussion) to be a 3-place predicate where 'x loves y at time t'.

(3)   a. SAY (I, you, t_0, ($\forall t$ (LOVE (Sam, Ix (WIFE $(x$, Sam, $t_0))$), t)))
            $t < t_0$
         b. SAY (I, you, t_0, ($\forall t$ (LOVE (Sam, Ix (WIFE $(x$, Sam, $t)$, t))).
            $t < t_0$

Note that 'wife' must also be a 3-place predicate including a time-index.

In fact the only difference between (3a) and (3b) lies in what that time-index is. In (3a) it is t_0, the time of the utterance, while in (3b) it is the variable t, which is bound by the universal quantifier of 'always'. Thus, the portion of the logical form corresponding to 'wife' in (1) must contain a time-index, though no reflex of this time-index appears overtly in (1). It follows that lexical items cannot be undecomposable with respect to the logical forms of the sentences that they appear in. The question therefore arises as to which lexical items are decomposable and what they are to be decomposed into.

In (Lakoff, 1965), it was proposed that certain verbs were decomposable not only with respect to the logical forms of the sentences they appeared in, but also with respect to the grammatical structures of those sentences. For example, it was proposed that sentences of the form (4a) were to be decomposed essentially into structures of the form (4b) and that the rules relating (4b) to (4a) were to be transformational rules of English grammar.

(4)   a. x persuaded y to hit z.

         b.

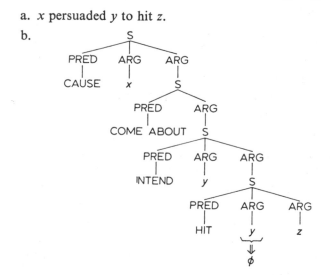

Including some refinements due to McCawley, the derivation of (4a) from (4b) would precede as follows. First, the rule of equi-NP-deletion would delete the second occurrence of y, as indicated in (4b). Then, the y which is the subject of 'INTEND' would undergo the rule of subject-raising, yielding (4c).

The rule of subject-raising is the rule that relates sentences like 'It is

(4)   c.   (by subject-raising of *y*)

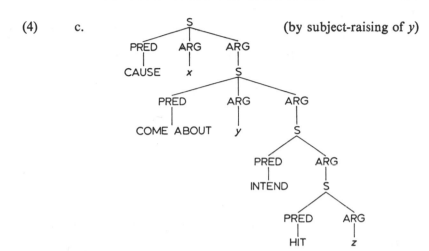

likely for John to go' and 'John is likely to go'. Then the rule of predicate-lifting would raise 'INTEND', yielding (4d).

(4)   d.   (by predicate-lifting of INTEND)

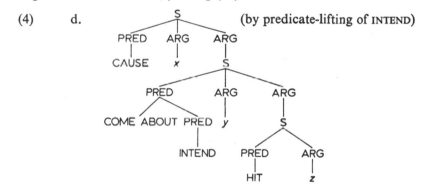

The rule of subject-raising again applied to *y* would yield (4e), and another application of predicate-lifting would yield (4f).

The lexical item *persuade* would substitute for the predicate CAUSE-COME ABOUT-INTEND. Aside from the rule of predicate-lifting, all of the rules used in this derivation and in similar derivations are needed anyway in English grammar. Moreover, structures like (4b) are also needed independently in English grammar. That is, there must be a verb 'cause' which is a two-place predicate, a verb 'come about' which is a one-place predicate, and a verb 'intend' which is a two-place predicate. Thus, we can reduce the structures of sentences containing 'persua de' toindepend-

(4)   e.   (by subject-raising of *y*)

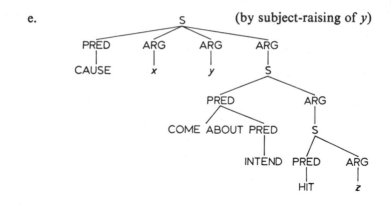

(by predicate-lifting of COME ABOUT-INTEND)

(4)   f.

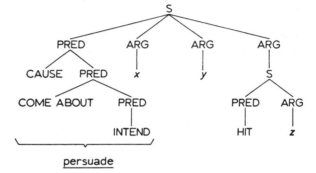

persuade

(5)   a. *x* persuaded *y* that *y* hit *z*.

          b.

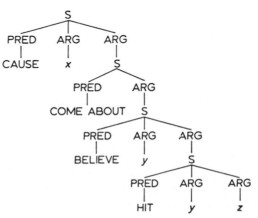

ently needed structures by, for the most part, independently needed rules.

So far, we have only considered 'persuade to', and not 'persuade that'. The former means 'cause to come to intend', while the latter means 'cause to come to believe'. Consequently, it was proposed that sentences like (5a) be derived by similar means from structures like (5b), where 'BELIEVE' appears instead of 'INTEND'.

Fillmore has added to analyses such as these considerations of presuppositions. For example, Fillmore observed that (6a),

(6)   a. x accused y of stealing z.

asserts that x said that y was responsible for stealing z and presupposes that it was bad for y to steal z. We might represent such an analysis as in (6b).

(6)   b.

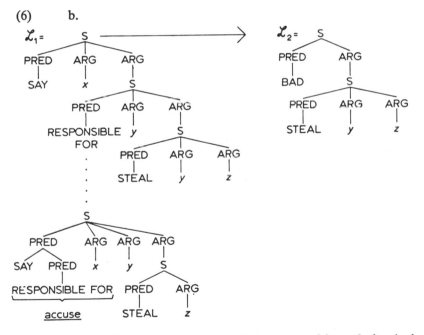

In (6b) the logical form $\mathscr{L}_1$ is related by the presupposition relation '→' to $\mathscr{L}_2$, and $\mathscr{L}_1$ is related by transformational rules of English grammar to the surface form of (6a). The lexical item 'accuse' is substituted in for the derived predicate 'SAY-RESPONSIBLE FOR' under the condition that the corresponding logical form $\mathscr{L}_1$ presupposes $\mathscr{L}_2$, where the encircled S's in $\mathscr{L}_2$ and $\mathscr{L}_1$ are identical.

Fillmore observed that the verbs 'accuse' and 'criticize' differ minimally in that what is part of the assertion of 'accuse' is the presupposition of 'criticize' and vice versa.

(7)   a. *x* criticized *y* for stealing *z*.

That is, (7a) asserts that *x* said that it was bad for *y* to steal *z* and presupposes that *y* was responsible for stealing *z*. (7a) might be given the corresponding analysis of (7b).

(7)   b.

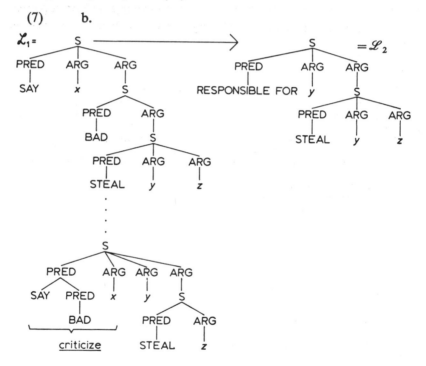

Similar analyses have been proposed by many others, including especially Binnick, Gruber, McCawley, and Postal.

Such proposals as the above make empirical claims as to the relationship between logical form and grammatical structure. These proposals seem especially appealing from the logical point of view, since they obviate the necessity for stating certain axioms (and/or rules of inference) in natural logic to account for certain inferences. For example, from (5a), 'x persuaded y that y hit z', it follows that y came to believe that he hit z. Under an analysis such as (5b), no special axiom for 'persuade' is necessary. The independently needed axioms for 'CAUSE' will do the job. However, there is at least one other proposal under which this will also be true, which does not involve grammatical analyses like those given above. Before we consider this proposal, let us take up some preliminary considerations. Consider the question of whether the logical form of a sentence, as we have been considering that term, is a representation of the meaning of that sentence. Consider, for example, sentences of the form 'x requires y to do S_1' and 'x permits y to do S_1'. Let us, for the sake of argument, consider these sentences as having the logical forms (8a) and (8b), respectively.

(8)   a.

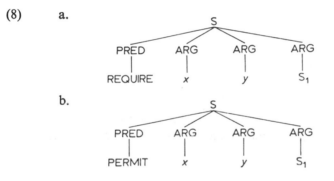

b.

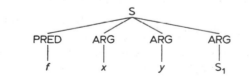

These logical forms differ only in the specification of the predicate. 'REQUIRE' and 'PERMIT' are to be understood not as words of English, but as symbols for certain atomic predicates. The symbols we have chosen happen to be English words in capital letters, but they could just as well have been a box and a diamond, or any other arbitrary symbols. Thus, in effect, both (8a) and (8b) have the same form, namely that of (8c),

(8)   c.

except that they contain different arbitrary symbols indicating atomic predicates.

Considering this, in what sense can we say that (8a) and (8b) reflect the different meanings of the sentences given above?

Note that (8a) and (8b) are not isolated cases. Any two sentences whose logical forms have the same geometry will raise the same questions. For example, consider sentences of the form 'It is certain that S_1' and 'It is possible that S_1'. Let us assume that these sentences have logical forms like those of (9a) and (9b) respectively.

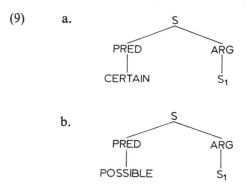

Both of these have basically the same form, namely that of (9c), except that they contain different arbitrary symbols indicating the atomic predicate of the sentence.

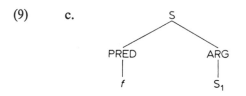

Again, how can we say that (9a) and (9b) represent different logical forms corresponding to different meanings?

It is clear that there is more to representing meanings than simply providing logical forms of sentences. In addition, we must provide certain axioms, or 'meaning-postulates', which indicate how certain atomic predicates are related to other atomic predicates. For example, we would want to include meaning-postulates like those in (10), but not like those in (11).

(10)   a. $\text{REQUIRE}(x, y, S_1) \supset \text{PERMIT}(x, y, S_1)$
       b. $\text{CERTAIN}(S_1) \supset \text{POSSIBLE}(S_1).$
(11)   a. $^*\text{PERMIT}(x, y, S_1) \supset \text{REQUIRE}(x, y, S_1)$
       b. $^*\text{POSSIBLE}(S_1) \supset \text{CERTAIN}(S_1).$

If something is required, then it is permitted, but not vice versa. And if something is certain, then it is possible, but not vice versa. Such axioms, or meaning postulates, together with the logical forms of the sentences and other appropriate logical apparatus will, hopefully, characterize a class of models in terms of which truth conditions for the sentences can be given. It is only in terms of such models that the logical forms of sentences can be said to represent meanings. Providing logical forms is only half of the job. At least as much work is involved in finding the right meaning-postulates, truth definitions, etc. Including analyses such as those in (4), (5), (6), and (7) as part of English grammar lessens the job of providing meaning-postulates. The question now arises as to whether there might not be a possible trade-off between the work done by rules of English grammar and the work done by meaning-postulates.

Suppose someone were to claim, for example, that the grammatical analyses of (4), (5), (6), and (7) were incorrect for English grammar, and that the paraphrase relations accounted for by such analyses could be done just as well by the use of meaning postulates. Instead of the grammatical analyses of (4) and (5), one might propose that 'persuade' in both cases be represented in logical form by atomic predicates (PERSUADE_1 and PERSUADE_2), and consequently that the verb 'persuade' was not decomposable in terms of English grammar. Instead, one might propose that the job done by the grammatical analyses of (4) and (5) could be done just as well or better by meaning-postulates like (12a) and (12b).

(12)   a. $\forall x, y, z(\text{PERSUADE}_1(x, y, z) \equiv \text{CAUSE}(x, (\text{COME ABOUT}$
            $(\text{BELIEVE}(y, z))))$
       b. $\forall x, y, z(\text{PERSUADE}_2(x, y, z) \equiv \text{CAUSE}(x, (\text{COME ABOUT}$
            $(\text{INTEND}(y, z)))).$

Similarly, one might say that the analyses given in (6) and (7) were not to be part of English grammar, but instead, that the work done by such analyses should be captured by meaning-postulates such as (13a) and (13b).

(13)   a. $\forall x, y, z(\text{ACCUSE}(x, y, z) \equiv \text{SAY}\,[x, (\text{RESPONSIBLE FOR}\,(y, z)/$
$$\text{BAD}(z)])$$
     b. $\forall x, y, z(\text{CRITICIZE}(x, y, z) \equiv \text{SAY}\,[x, (\text{BAD}(z)/$
$$\text{RESPONSIBLE FOR}\,(y, z)]).$$

In (13) the '/' represents the presupposition relation, as in dyadic modal logic.

The problem posed by such an alternative proposal is whether there is any empirical evidence favoring one proposal or the other. In other words, are there any empirical considerations which limit the role of meaning-postulates? It should be noted at the outset that there are certain immediate differences between these proposals. One of these is that rules of grammar may operate on structures containing either atomic predicates or lexical items with actual phonological shapes. Meaning-postulates on the other hand are defined only in terms of structures containing atomic predicates, variables, etc., but not lexical items with phonological shapes. (4f) thus differs in an important way from (12). In (4f), the complex predicate CAUSE – COME ABOUT – INTEND is represented by the phonological shape *persuade*. Similarly, the complex predicate CAUSE – COME ABOUT – BELIEVE is to be represented by the same phonological shape. In (12a) and (12b) however, we have atomic predicates PERSUADE$_1$ and PERSUADE$_2$. These are not to be confused with the single phonological form *persuade*. PERSUADE$_1$ and PERSUADE$_2$ are arbitrary symbols standing for atomic predicates; they are different symbols and have nothing whatever to do with each other. They are as different as '!' and '?'. Consequently, no regularities which can be stated only in terms of the phonological forms of lexical items can be stated by meaning-postulates, though it is possible that such regularities might be stated by rules of grammar. Another difference is that grammatical transformations are subject to certain constraints, such as Ross' constraints on movement transformations. There is no reason to believe that meaning-postulates should be subject to such constraints. Another difference is that under the meaning-postulate hypothesis there will be many more atomic predicates than under the lexical decomposition hypothesis. In fact, every lexical verb, will correspond to an atomic predicate. Since the stock of lexical verbs varies tremendously from language to language, the meaning-postulate hypothesis requires that the overwhelming proportion of meaning-postulates will vary from language to language. Thus, there will not be a single natural logic for natural language in general, but rather a vastly different one for each different natural language.

Given such differences between the proposals, we can begin to consider what sorts of empirical evidence could confirm or disconfirm either of these proposals. Let us start with the observation that rules of grammar may describe regularities involving both atomic predicates and phonological forms, while meaning-postulates may state regularities involving atomic predicates but not phonological forms. Robert Binninck and Charles Fillmore, working independently, have noted certain regularities having to do with the lexical items 'come' and 'bring'. Consider (14).

(14) come   bring = CAUSE to *come*
      come about   bring about = CAUSE to
                                        come about
      come up (for discussion)   bring up = CAUSE to *come*
                                        up
      come to (awaken)   bring to = CAUSE to *come* to
      come together   bring together = CAUSE to
                                        come together
      come in (land, of an airplane)   bring in = CAUSE to *come* in
      come out (of a newspaper)   bring out = CAUSE to *come*
      etc.   out

bring = CAUSE – to – *come*, where CAUSE is an atomic predicate
      and *come* is the phonological form corresponding to
      a lexical item.

The ordinary sense of 'come' is related to the ordinary sense of 'bring' by a predicate of direct causation, which, as in (14), we represent as CAUSE. In addition, there are many idiomatic expressions containing the phonological form *come*, whose corresponding causative has the phonological form *bring*. (14) contains an abbreviated list of such cases. Binnick (1969) lists many additional similar cases. There are also a number of cases in which the correspondence does not hold, for example, 'John came at me with an ax' does not have the corresponding '*Harry brought John at me with an ax'. There are several other cases where the correspondence fails. However, the overwhelming preponderance of such cases works as in (14). There are enough of such cases to require that a rule be stated relating the cases with 'come' and the cases with 'bring' (though there will, of course, be exceptions to any such rule). In the lexical decomposition framework, the rule of predicate-lifting will create complex predicates such as 'CAUSE – *come*'. The regularity is that 'bring' substitutes for such a complex predicate.[1] Such an analysis is possible only under the lexical decomposition hypothesis. In the meaning-postulate hypothesis, no such regularity can be stated. The reason is that logical forms do not contain phonological shapes.[2] Thus the predicates 'BRING ABOUT', 'BRING UP', and 'BRING TO', will all be separate and distinct symbols for atomic predicates, having nothing whatever in common. Similarly 'COME ABOUT', 'COME UP', and 'COME TO', will also be symbols for atomic predicates having nothing whatever in common. Consequently, the regularity concerning their phonological shapes cannot be stated in terms of the meaning-postulate hypothesis. Hence, we have at least one case where a lexical decomposition of the sort we have discussed above is required on

(15)   a. LIQUEFY (x, y).
            b.

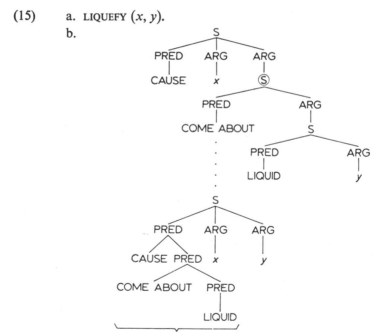

liquefy

linguistic grounds. Otherwise a linguistic regularity would have to go unstated.

Another case providing confirmation of the lexical decomposition hypothesis is given in Lakoff (1968). Under the lexical decomposition hypothesis, sentences of the form (15a) receive an analysis like that in (15b). (15a) means that x caused y to liquefy, and 'y liquefied' means that y came to be liquid. If the transitive verb 'liquefy' is taken to be an atomic predicate in a logical form like (15a) then the intransitive sentence 'y liquefied' would not be represented as a subpart of (15a). However it would be represented as a sentence in (15b), as the encircled S in (15b) indicates.

Now consider (16a).

(16)   a. The metal liquefied, but it took me an hour to bring *it* about.

        b. The chemist liquefied the metal in an hour, but it would have taken me a week to bring *it* about.

In (16a) the *it* takes as its antecedent the sentence 'the metal liquefied'. Now look at (16b). In (16b) the *it* is understood as taking as its antecedent not 'the chemist liquefied the metal', but, as before, 'the metal liquefied'. If the transitive verb 'liquefy' is represented in logical form as an atomic predicate, then there would be no antecedent for the 'it' in (16b). If, however, sentences with the transitive verb 'liquefy' are represented as in (15b), then the encircled S could serve as an antecedent for 'it' in (15b). For further arguments in favor of the lexical decomposition hypothesis on the basis of syntactic facts, see (Postal, 1970) and (Lakoff, in press).[3]

The fact that the meaning-postulate hypothesis provides for a great many more atomic predicates than the lexical decomposition hypothesis suggests another argument in favor of lexical decomposition. Consider sentences like (17a).

(17)   a. Sam kicked the door open.
        b. Sam caused the door to come to be open, by kicking it.

(17a) essentially has the meaning of (17b). In (17b) 'kick' is used in its basic sense, that of striking with the foot. If (17a) is derived from a grammatical structure like that suggested by (17b), then the same sense of 'kick' will appear in both sentences, and only one atomic predicate (or perhaps a complex one) will be required for 'kick'. However, if 'kick' in (17a) is taken to be undecomposable, as the meaning-postulate hypothesis would require, then one would need more than one atomic predicate corresponding to the verb 'kick'. The one needed for (17a) would be quite peculiar in that it would have to act as a sentential operator, that is, it would have to take a sentential complement as its object, as indicated in (18).

(18)

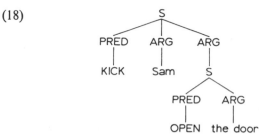

The same would be true of not only of 'kick', but also of verbs like 'scrub', 'beat', and many others.

(19)   a. Sam scrubbed the floor clean.
        b. Sam caused the floor to become clean, by scrubbing it.
(20)   a. Sam beat Harry into submission.
        b. Sam caused Harry to submit, by beating him.

(17a), (19a) and (20a) all show a regularity in their paraphrases. Sentences of the form (21a) have paraphrases of the form (21b).

(21)   a. Sam VERBed x ADJ.
        b. Sam caused x to come to be ADJ, by VERB-ing x.

If sentences like (21a) are derived by grammatical transformation from structures underlying sentences of the form (21b), then verbs like 'kick', 'scrub', and 'beat', will not have to be represented as sentential operators in the *a* sentences, but can be given their simple senses, as in the *b* sentences. Only with the lexical decomposition hypothesis can we avoid the oddness of calling 'kick' in (17a) a sentential operator.

Moreover, since the relationship between sentences of the forms (21a and b) is not regular, there is a further argument in favor of the lexical decomposition hypothesis. Under that hypothesis, the relationship between (21b) and (21a) will be given by transformational rules. Since grammatical rules can have lexical exceptions, such semi-productive relationships can be described by rules of grammar. However, the notion of a lexical exception makes no sense for meaning-postulates. There can be no semi-productive meaning-postulates.

Let us now consider the arguments from the point of view of constraints on transformational rules. According to the meaning-postulate hypothesis, the notion 'possible lexical item' is to be characterized in terms of possible meaning-postulates. Under the lexical decomposition hypothesis however, the notion 'possible lexical item' is to be characterized partially in terms of constraints on transformational rules. There is no reason to believe that constraints on transformational rules should be the same as constraints on meaning postulates. We know a good deal about constraints on transformational rules, and, so far as we can tell, they do in part determine the concept of a possible lexical item. Consider, for example, Ross's coordinate structure constraint. Ross's coordinate structure constraint, under the lexical decomposition hypothesis, makes certain predictions about possible lexical items. For example, it predicts that there cannot be a lexical item 'accusate' such that 'x accusated y that S_1' means that 'x said that S_1 and that y was guilty'.

(22)

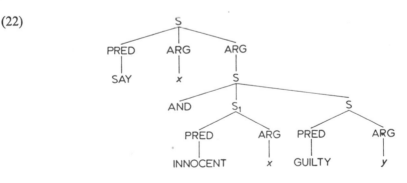

(23)   a. x accused y that S_1.
        b. x said that S_1 and that y was guilty.
(24)   a. x accused y that x was innocent.
        b. x said that x was innocent and that y was guilty.

Under the lexical decomposition hypothesis, this claim follows since the coordinate structure constraint will prevent 'GUILTY' in (22) from undergoing predicate-lifting up to 'SAY'. To my knowledge, there are no lexical items like 'accusate' in any language, and I think it is a fair guess to say that no natural language will ever turn up with one. This is a natural consequence of the lexical decomposition hypothesis. However, under the meaning-postulate hypothesis, it would be possible to have a meaning postulate like (25), which assigned such a meaning to 'accusate'.

$$(25) \qquad \text{ACCUSATE}(x, y, S_1) \equiv \text{SAY}(x, \text{AND}(\text{INNOCENT}(x)), \text{GUILTY}(y)).$$

The only way to keep the meaning-postulate hypothesis from permitting such possible lexical items would be to impose something corresponding to Ross's coordinate structure constraint on meaning-postulates. Considerations of this sort also seem to lead to the correctness of the lexical decomposition hypothesis.

Referential opacity phenomena may also ultimately provide arguments in favor of the lexical decomposition hypothesis. For example, as Quine has pointed out, the verb 'look for' has an opaque object.

(26)   a. Oedipus is looking for his mother.
        b. Oedipus is looking for Jocasta.
(27)   a. Oedipus is trying to find his mother.
        b. Oedipus is trying to find Jocasta.

That is, sentences like (26a) are ambiguous, and may or may not mean the same thing as (26b), even granted that Jocasta is Oedipus's mother. Quine has attempted to explain this on the basis that (26a) is synonymous with (27a), where there is an embedded sentence, and which therefore, allows for an ambiguity in the scope of quantification. Any such explanation of opacity phenomena assumes the lexical decomposition hypothesis, that is, it assumes that 'look for' is not an atomic predicate in logical form. Though I currently believe that such an account is in the right direction, there are certain apparent difficulties. Consider (28) and (29).

(28)   a. Oedipus admires his mother.
        b. Oedipus admires Jocasta.

(29)   a. Oedipus hates his mother.
          b. Oedipus hates Jocasta.

(28a) can be true and (28b) false, even though I know that Jocasta is
Oedipus's mother. The same is true of (29a) and (29b). Thus, both (28)
and (29) display opacity phenomena, though it is not obvious that verbs
like 'admire' and 'hate' can be paraphrased in terms of two independently
needed atomic predicates. In other words, it is not clear that there are in
natural language atomic predicates 'WURF' and 'GLIP' such that 'admire'
means 'WURF-to-GLIP', and such that there are sentences like (30a and b)
displaying the same difference in meaning as (28a and b).

(30)   a. Oedipus WURFs to GLIP his mother.
          b. Oedipus WURFs to GLIP Jocasta.

In an arbitrary system, one could always make up such predicates, but
that is beside the point. The question here is an empirical one. Is there
any evidence that such atomic predicates actually exist in the logical forms
of sentences of a natural language? This does not necessarily mean that
there must actually be in some language single lexical items directly
corresponding to these predicates. However, it is required, at the very
least, that such predicates appear elsewhere. For example, there might
be a number of other verbs which can be decomposed in terms of one or
the other of these predicates. And, presumably, there would be meaning-
postulates relating these atomic predicates and others that we know to
exist. However, at present, there is no reason to believe that atomic
predicates 'WURF' and 'GLIP' exist in natural language. If they do not,
then it might be difficult ultimately to use opacity evidence such as that
given above to argue for the correctness of the lexical decomposition
hypothesis. But more on this below.

   I think it is clear that there are a range of cases where lexical decomposition is necessary. In addition, it is also clear that certain meaning-
postulates are necessary, for example those in (10). The question is where
to draw the line. The examples given above suggest certain guidelines.
In the analyses offered above, certain atomic predicates kept recurring:
CAUSE, COME ABOUT, SAY, GOOD, BAD, BELIEVE, INTEND, RESPONSIBLE FOR,
etc. These are all sentential operators, that is, predicates that take sentential complements. It seems clear that we would want these, or predi-

cates like these, to function as atomic predicates in natural logic. Since these keep recurring in our analyses, it is quite possible that under the lexical decomposition hypothesis the list would end somewhere. That is, there would be only a finite number of atomic predicates in natural logic taking sentential complements. These would be universal, and so meaning-postulates would not vary from language to language. Moreover, verbs like 'kick' or 'scrub' in (17a) and (19a) would be ruled out as sentential operators, since they could be analyzed in terms of already existing sentential operators, as in (17b) and (19b). This seems to me to be an important claim. Kicking and scrubbing are two out of a potentially infinite number of human activities. Since the number of potential human activities and states is unlimited, natural logic will have to provide an open-ended number of atomic predicates corresponding to these states and activities. Hopefully, this can be limited to atomic predicates that do not take sentential complements. It is hard for me to visualize how one could construct a model for a logic with an unlimited number of sentential operators, and correspondingly an axiom system for such a logic. It seems to me that under the lexical decomposition hypothesis we have a fighting chance of limiting sentential operators to a finite number, fixed for all natural languages.

Moreover, it is possible that there may be empirical support for such a position coming from linguistics. Consider, for example, the possible derivational endings in natural languages. Certain languages have causative endings, others inchoative endings, others have endings meaning 'try', or 'want', etc. That is, to a certain extent, there is a correspondence between possible derivational endings and the finite number of sentential operators proposed under the version of the lexical decomposition hypothesis presented above. For example, there are languages with a causative derivational ending (let us use -ga for the sake of discussion) such that there would be a sentence of the form 'John open-ga the door', meaning 'John caused the door to open'; but to my knowledge there is no language containing a derivational ending -ga such that 'John open-ga the door' means 'John kicked the door open'. Under our hypothesis, this would follow from the fact that CAUSE is one of the finite number of sentential operators in natural logic, while KICK is not. Such a possible empirical confirmation of the above version of the lexical decomposition hypothesis certainly deserves further study.

One more thing: In Section VI we gave some examples of potential meaning postulates which, under Baker's conjecture, would not exist in natural logic. These were all cases where there was no dual for certain predicates, e.g., PROBABLE, CLAIM, and HOPE. At the same time, it was observed that three were lexical items corresponding to duals of other predicates, e.g., NECESSARY-POSSIBLE, etc. In order to make the claims of Chapter VI into an empirical hypothesis, we need to add at least one more constraint to the theory of lexical insertion. That is, we need to say that there are no lexical items of the structure of (31).

(31)

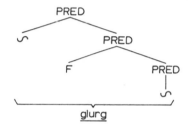

That is, there are no lexical items 'glurg' which mean 'not F not', for some atomic predicate F.[4] That is, if there is a word for the dual of an atomic predicate, then that dual exists as an atomic predicate. Note that the converse is not required to be true. That is, natural logic may contain the dual of an atomic predicate, even though no existing natural language actually contains a word corresponding to that dual. However, the claim would be made that such a dual would be a possible lexical item in a possible natural language, if not an actual one. Facts like those given in Section VI might be used to determine whether or not such a dual existed, even though there were no actual word for it.

CONCLUSION I: There is more to meaning than logical form. Meaning-postulates, as well as other logical apparatus, are needed.

CONCLUSION II: There are empirical limits on the use of meaning-postulates. There are some cases where lexical decomposition is required on linguistic grounds.

HYPOTHESIS: Natural language employs a relatively small finite number of atomic predicates that take sentential complements (sentential operators). These do not vary from language to language. They are related to each other by meaning-postulates that do not vary from language to language.

VIII. MEANING-POSTULATES, POSSIBLE WORLDS, AND PRONOMINAL REFERENCE

As we saw above, natural logic will require certain meaning-postulates and theorems and will rule out certain others, as indicated in (1) and (2).[1]

(1)　　a.　CERTAIN(S) ⊃ POSSIBLE(S)
　　　　b.　*POSSIBLE(S) ⊃ CERTAIN(S).
(2)　　a.　REQUIRE(x, y, S) ⊃ PERMIT(x, y, S)
　　　　b.　*PERMIT(x, y, S) ⊃ REQUIRE(x, y, S).

If something is certain, then it's possible, but not vice versa.[1a] And if x requires y to do something, then x permits y to do it, but not vice versa. And as (3) shows, POSSIBLE and CERTAIN are duals, as are PERMIT and REQUIRE.

(3)　　a.　POSSIBLE(S) ≡ ∼ CERTAIN(∼ S)
　　　　b.　PERMIT(x, y, S) ≡ ∼ REQUIRE(x, y, ∼ S).

For any natural logic containing these concepts, truth conditions will be required. One way of providing truth conditions for such cases is to employ a model containing possible worlds and alternativeness relations holding between worlds. For each dual pair there will be one alternativeness relation. Let R_1 be the alternativeness relation corresponding to CERTAIN and POSSIBLE. Then we can define truth conditions for CERTAIN(S) and POSSIBLE(S) as in (4).

(4)　　a.　CERTAIN(S) is true in w_0 ↔ ($\forall w$) ($w_0 R_1 w$ ⊃ S is true in w)
　　　　b.　POSSIBLE(S) is true in w_0 ↔ ($\exists w$) ($w_0 R_1 w$ ⊃ S is true in w).

For cases like REQUIRE and PERMIT we will need an alternativeness relation for each different pair of subject and indirect object. For the sake of discussion, let us fix the subject and indirect object for REQUIRE and PERMIT and call the corresponding alternativeness relation R_2.[2] Then we can state truth conditions as in (5).

(5)　　a.　REQUIRE(a, b, S) is true ↔ ($\forall w$) ($w_0 R_2 w$ ⊃ S is true in w)
　　　　b.　PERMIT(a, b, S) is true ↔ ($\exists w$) ($w_0 R_2 w$ ⊃ S is true in w).

Thus, a sentence of the form 'a requires b to do S' is true just in case S is true in all worlds related to the actual world by R_2. In this way, we can assign truth conditions for the entire sentence based on the truth conditions for its parts. Moreover, the nature of the alternativeness relation (that is, whether it is transitive, reflexive, symmetric, or whatever) will depend upon what meaning-postulates there are for the corresponding operators. In other words, the meaning-postulates will determine which worlds are related to which other worlds.

A priori, one might think that such considerations would have nothing whatever to do with linguistics. But as it turns out, such matters are crucially important for the solution of certain very deep and difficult linguistic problems. Baker (1966) raised the problem of when a pronoun can refer back to an unspecified noun phrase. For example, he noted that while 'John wants to catch *a fish* and he wants to eat *it*' is grammatical, '*John wants to catch *a fish* and he will eat *it*' is not.[2a] Karttunen (1968) suggested that some notion of 'discourse referent' would be necessary for such problems. Although he did not come close to solving the problem, he did point out a great number of interesting examples, upon which a good deal of the following is based. Consider (6).

(6)   a. It's certain that Sam will find *a girl* and possible that he will kiss *her*.
       b. *It's possible that Sam will find *a girl* and certain that he will kiss *her*.[3]

In (6a), 'a girl' can be the antecedent of 'her', but not in (6b). If one compares (6) with (1), one finds a correspondence. Somehow, the grammaticality of (6a) corresponds to the valid meaning-postulate of (1a), while the ungrammaticality of (6b) corresponds to the invalid meaning-postulate of (1b). Looking at the possible world model, it becomes clear why. The truth conditions for 'It's certain that Sam will find a girl' say that that sentence is true just in case Sam finds a girl in every possible world related to by R_1 to w_0, which we might take to be the actual world. If 'Sam finds a girl' is true in a world, then there must exist in that world a girl that Sam found. And because of the truth conditions for CERTAIN, that girl will exist in *every* world w related by R_1 to w_0, the actual world. Now consider the truth conditions for 'It is possible that he will kiss her'. That will be true just in case 'he kisses her' is true in *some* possible world w related to w_0 by R_1. Since we already know that there will be an appropriate girl in every world, w, we are guaranteed that a referent for 'her' exists in each world w, and that in each world the pronoun will have an antecedent.

In (6b), however, this is not the case. The truth conditions for 'It's possible that Sam will find a girl' say that there will exist *some* world w related by R_1 to w_0 in which 'Sam finds a girl' is true. Thus, there will be some world in which such a girl exists, though it is not guaranteed that such a girl will exist in all worlds w related by R_1 to w_0. Now if one considers the truth conditions for 'It is certain that he will kiss her' we see that in order for that to be true 'He kisses her' will have to be true in *all* worlds w related to w_0 by R_1, and so a referent for 'her' will have to exist in all worlds w. Since the pronoun must have an antecedent, the referent of the antecedent must also exist in all w.

However, we have just seen that that is not the case. We cannot guarantee that the referent of the antecedent will be in all the worlds containing the referent for the pronoun. In just this case, the pronoun-antecedent relation is blocked, and ungrammaticality results. (7) is a similar case.

(7)   a. It is possible that Sam will kiss the girl that it is certain that he will find.
        b. *It is certain that Sam will kiss the girl that it is possible that he will find.

The general principle, I think, is clear.

(8)   The antecedent must have a referent in all the worlds in which the anaphoric noun phrase (or pronoun) has a referent.

(8) will work for cases like (6). (7) appears to be slightly different. However, if one recalls that restrictive relative clauses are always presupposed, then it becomes clear that the head noun phrase of the relative clause, 'the girl' in (7a) is acting as an anaphoric noun phrase. This can be seen clearly in (7'), where the phenomena of (6) and (7) are combined.[4]

(7')   a. It is certain that Sam will find a girl and it is possible that he will kiss the girl that it is certain that he will find.
        b. *It is possible that Sam will find a girl and it is certain Sam will kiss the girl that it is possible that he will find.

Given an appropriate analysis of relative clauses, principle (8) should do the job.

So far we have seen cases where possible pronoun-antecedent relations are determined by the meaning-postulates of (1). Let us now turn to the meaning-postulates of (2).

(9) a. You are permitted to kiss the girl you are required to find.
  b. *You are required to kiss the girl you are permitted to find.
(9') a. You are required to find a girl and permitted to kiss the girl you are required to find.
  b. *You are permitted to find a girl and you are required to kiss the girl you are permitted to find.
(10) a. You are required to find *a girl* and permitted to kiss *her*.
  b. *You are permitted to find *a girl* and required to kiss *her*.[5]

These cases are parallel to the sentences cited above. Consider (10a). The truth definition for REQUIRE and PERMIT and the postulate of (2a) guarantee that the worlds in which the things you are required to do are true will be a subset of the set of worlds in which the set of things you are permitted to do are true, but not vice versa. Thus, in (10a) every world in which 'her' has a referent will also be a world in which 'a girl' has a referent, and therefore 'a girl' may be an antecedent for 'her' in (10a) by principle (8). This is not the case in (10b) however, because, given the truth definitions in (2), 'her' in (10b) may have reference in worlds related by R_2 to w_0 in which 'a girl' has no referent. Thus (10b) will violate condition (8). (9) and (9') work the same way.

Now consider (11).

(11) a. CERTAIN(S) $\supset$ S
  b. *POSSIBLE(S) $\supset$ S
  c. (*)REQUIRE$(a, b, S) \supset$ S.

It is not unreasonable to assume that (11a) will be a postulate of natural logic, while (11b) will not. (11c) will not be a postulate of natural logic, although for a fixed a and b, an assumption of this form may be made in certain instances by certain speakers. For example, a speaker may assume that b will do everything that a requires him to do. Now consider (12).

(12) a. It is certain that Sam will find *a girl*, and he will kiss *her*.
  b. *It is possible that Sam will find *a girl* and he will kiss *her*.
  c. (*)Sam is required to find *a girl* and he'll kiss *her*.

Given out truth definitions and principle (8), the grammaticality of (12a) will follow from the postulate of (11a). Correspondingly, the lack of grammaticality of (12b) will follow from the lack of validity of (11b). Whether or not (12c) will be considered grammatical, will depend on whether or not it is assumed that in this instance, Sam will do what he is required to do.

(13)   a.   Sam will kiss the girl who it is certain that he'll find.
         b.   *Sam will kiss the girl who it is possible that he'll find.
         c.   (*)Sam will kiss the girl who he is required to find.

The facts of (13) follow accordingly.

So far, we have considered only postulates and theorems in which modal operators are not mixed. Now let us turn to cases in which they are mixed.

(14)   INTEND$(x, S) \supset$ BELIEVE$(x, ($POSSIBLE$(S))$.

(14) appears to be a good candidate for a theorem, if not a postulate of natural logic. Let us assume that truth definitions for INTEND and BELIEVE are given as in (14′), using alternativeness relations R_i and R_b respectively.[6]

(14′)   a. INTEND(a, S) is true $\leftrightarrow (\forall w) (w_0\ R_i\ w \supset S$ is true in $w)$
         b. BELIEVE(a, S) is true $\leftrightarrow (\forall w) (w_0\ R_b\ w \supset S$ is true in $w)$.

Given (14), (14′) and other obvious postulates involving INTEND and BELIEVE, principle (8) will then account for the grammaticality of the sentences in (15).

(15)   a.   Sam intends to find *a girl* and he believes that it's possible that he'll kiss *her*.
         b.   Sam believes that it's possible that he'll kiss the girl he intends to find.

Given the fact that (16) will be neither a postulate nor a theorem of natural logic,

(16)   *BELIEVE$(x, $POSSIBLE$(S)) \supset$ INTEND(x, S)

it follows from principle (8) that sentences of (17) will be ungrammatical.

(17)   a.   *Sam believes that it's possible that he'll find *a girl* and he intends to kiss *her*.

b. *Sam intends to kiss the girl he believes it's possible that he'll find.

Incidentically, the effect of (14) can be captured by placing the following restriction on the alternativeness relations of R_1, R_b, and R_i:

(18) $(\forall w) [w_0 \, R_i \, w_2 \supset (\exists w_1) (w_0 \, R_b \, w_1 \, \& \, w_1 \, R_1 \, w_2)]$.

Postulates like (14) give the meanings of certain concepts such as INTEND in terms of the meaning of other concepts such as BELIEVE and POSSIBLE. This raises certain interesting questions. For example, are there any modal concepts whose meaning is not defined in terms of other modal concepts. Let us call such concepts if they exist 'primitive concepts'.

(19)   F is a *primitive concept* if and only if natural logic contains no meaning-postulates of the form 'F(S) $\supset \phi$', where ϕ contains modal operators which are not identical to the dual of F.

In natural logic, it is an empirical question as to whether primitive concepts exist. Moreover, it is conceivable that there is a hierarchy of concepts, defined by (20).

(20)   F is *more primitive than* G if and only if there are meaning-postulates (or theorems) of the form 'G(S) $\supset \phi$', where ϕ contains F, but there are no meaning-postulates (nor theorems) of the form 'F(S) $\supset \phi$', where ϕ contains G.

A priori, we cannot tell whether natural logic will contain a hierarchy such as that defined by (20). Again, it is an empirical question. If natural logic contains primitive concepts and a concept hierarchy, what does this say about the nature of the human mind? Would such primitive concepts also be psychologically primitive in some significant sense? Would there be a corresponding psychological hierarchy in some significant sense of the term? One could also imagine that there might be linguistic correlates of such notions. For instance, would every natural language contain words or morphemes corresponding directly to the primitive concepts? Would it be the case in every natural language that if it contained a word for a concept at some point on the hierarchy it would contain words for all concepts higher on the hierarchy? It seems to me that these are questions worth investigating.

Another question raised by natural logic concerns the notion of a 'natural semantic class'. The truth conditions for modal operators taken together with the postulates and theorems which mention those operators may be considered as defining natural semantic classes containing those operators. Postulates or theorems of a certain form may impose certain linguistically significant semantic classifications. Correspondingly, truth conditions of a certain form may also impose linguistically significant semantic classifications.

(21)   a. $\Box(S_1 \supset S_2) \supset (\Box S_1 \supset \Box S_2)$
         b. $\Box S \supset S$
         c. $\Box S \supset \Diamond S$
         d. $\Box S \supset \Box\Box S$
         e. $\Box\Box S \supset \Box S$
         f. $S \supset \Box \Diamond S$
         g. $\Diamond S \supset \Box \Diamond S.$

(22)   a. $\Box S$ is true in $w_0 \leftrightarrow (\forall w)\, (w_0\, Rw \supset S$ is true in $w)$
         b. $\Diamond S$ is true in $w_0 \leftrightarrow (\exists w)\, (w_0\, Rw \supset S$ is true in $w)$.

(21) shows a number of the possible shapes of postulates and theorems. The box, $\Box$, represents an arbitrary modal operator and the diamond, $\Diamond$, represents its dual. Postulates or theorems of these forms will be true of various different modal operators. Moreover, various modal operators will have truth conditions of the form shown in (22), for different alternativeness relations R. Thus, as a first approximation, we can consider the definition of 'linguistically significant semantic class' as given in (23).

(23)   Two modal operators, $\Box_1$, and $\Box_2$, will be said to be in the same 'linguistically significant semantic class' if some postulate or theorem listed in (21) is true of both $\Box_1$ and $\Box_2$, or if they have truth conditions of the same form.

(23) is just an approximation to this notion. For example, I have taken statements of the forms given in (21) as the only significant ones for defining linguistically significant semantic classes, though there is no question in my mind that the list given in (21) is incomplete or incorrect in certain respects. Moreover, I have only considered truth conditions of the form given in (22), though again I do not doubt that truth condi-

tions of other forms will be significant. Furthermore, (23) is an if-statement, not an if-and-only-if-statement. However, it may be the case that with the right list of postulates and theorems and with the right list of truth definition forms, (23) can be strengthened to be an if-and-only-if condition.

Let us take an example of how the truth conditions of (22) and the postulates and theorems of (21) can be said to impose a linguistically significant semantic classification. Consider (24) and (25).

(24)   a. Sam may leave.
       b. It is possible that Sam will leave.
       c. It is permitted for Sam to leave.
(25)   a. Sam may leave.
       b. It is possible for Sam to leave.
       c. It is required that Sam leave.

First consider (24). (24a) may have the meaning either of (24b) or (24c). That is, the lexical item 'may' can have the meaning of either 'possible' or 'permitted'. As (4b) and (5b) above show, POSSIBLE and PERMIT have truth conditions of the same form, namely, that of (22b). In addition, they share certain postulates and theorems of the same form. Consider (26).

(26)   a'. $(\Diamond S_1 \supset \Diamond S_2) \supset \Diamond (S_1 \supset S_2)$
      c. $\Box S \supset \Diamond S$
      e'. $\Diamond S \supset \Diamond \Diamond S.$

(26a') is deducible from the dual of (21a) above given (21c), (26c) is identical to (26c) above, and (26e') is the dual of (26e) above. Now consider (27) and (28), which seem to be valid.

(27)   a'. $(\text{POSSIBLE}(S_1) \supset \text{POSSIBLE}(S_2)) \supset \text{POSSIBLE}(S_1 \supset S_2)$
      c. $\text{CERTAIN}(S) \supset \text{POSSIBLE}(S)$
      e'. $\text{POSSIBLE}(S) \supset \text{POSSIBLE}(\text{POSSIBLE}(S))$
(28)   a'. $(\text{PERMIT}(a, b, S_1) \supset \text{PERMIT}(a, b, S_2) \supset$
                                $\supset \text{PERMIT}(a, b, (S_1 \supset S_2))$
      :. $\text{REQUIRE}(a, b, S_1) \supset \text{PERMIT}(a, \iota, S_1)$
      e'. $\text{PERMIT}(a, b, S) \supset \text{PERMIT}(a, b, (\text{PERMIT}(a, b, S))).$

(27) and (28) show that POSSIBLE and PERMIT share at least three postulates and theorems of the same form, namely, those of the forms given in (26). Robin Lakoff, observing these facts, raised the question of whether it was an accident that the two concepts of possibility and permission could be expressed by the same word 'may'. She suggested that it was no accident. One would like to be able to say that such cases are possible only if the concepts involved, in this case possibility and permission, are in the same linguistically significant semantic class. According to the definition of semantic classes given in (23), the concepts of permission and possibility would be in the intersection of at least four linguistically significant semantic classes. That is to say, their meanings have great deal in common. Thus, as R. Lakoff has suggested, a single lexical item may be used to represent two concepts only if those concepts are in the same semantic class. Moreover, one might add, the more of such classes two concepts are in, the more natural it is for the same lexical item to represent those concepts. Note that this makes a rather interesting claim. Namely, that there will be no natural language in which the same lexical item will represent the two concepts of permission and certainty, or the two concepts of requirement and possibility. That is, it is no accident that while (24b and c) above may be represented as the same sentences, (24a), (25b and c) above may not be represented as the same sentence, (25a).[7]

To consider another example, somewhat less formally, the logic of time and the logic of place will have a great deal in common. The logic of time will involve a linear dimension, while the logic of place will involve three linear dimensions. Notions such as 'later than' and 'farther from' will both be irreflexive, asymmetric and transitive. In both cases, there will be an axiom of density. Just as there will be a postulate saying that if S is always true, then S is sometimes true, there will be a postulate saying that if S is true everywhere, then S is true somewhere. And so on. The logic of time and the logic of place will have many postulates in common. Correspondingly, it is not surprising that the same grammatical constructions are very often used for both. Consider the prepositions 'at', 'within', 'up to', 'around', etc. These prepositions can be used to represent corresponding spacial and temporal concepts. By principle (23), this is to be expected, since such concepts will fall into natural classes due to the similarity of spacial and temporal postulates.

IX. MISCELLANEOUS TOPICS

A. *Manner Adverbs*

It has been proposed by Reichenbach and, more recently by Parsons, that adverbs of manner such as 'carefully' are operators that map a predicate into another predicate.

(1)   Sam sliced the salami carefully.

(2)

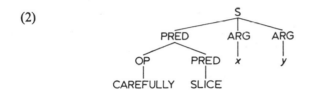

Thus (1) would, under such a scheme, be represented as (2). In Lakoff (1965) it was suggested that sentences like (1) are to be derived transformationally from structures like that underlying (3).

(3)   Sam was careful in slicing the salami.

That is, it was claimed that 'carefully' was not an underlying adverb, but rather a transitive adjective, as in (3), or in other words, a two-place predicate relating an agent and an action. This might be represented roughly as in (4).

(4)

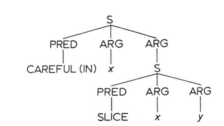

Thus we might ask whether the logical form of sentences like (1) should be more like (2) or like (4). What sort of empirical evidence bears upon an issue of this kind?

As we noted in Section IV, there is a difference in meaning between (5a) and (5b).

(5)   a. Every boy likes some girl.
        b. Some girl is liked by every boy.
(6)   a. $\forall x(\exists y(\text{LIKE}(x, y)))$
        b. $\exists y(\forall x(\text{LIKE}(x, y)))$.

(5a) has a logical form like (6a), while (5b) has a logical form like (6b). As we noted above, there is a regularity in these cases, at least in my speech. When two quantifiers are in the same surface structure clause, the leftmost one is understood as having wider scope. As it turns out, this principle is not simply limited to quantifiers, but also works with adverbs, and with adverbs mixed with quantifiers.[1] Consider, for example, the difference between (7a) and (7b).

(7)   a. Sam sliced all the bagels carefully.
        b. Sam carefully sliced all the bagels.

Here 'all' and 'carefully' appear in the same surface structure clause. As in (5), the leftmost of these elements as understood as having wider scope.[2] Thus, if we assume that sentences with 'carefully' such as (1) have a logical

(8)   a.

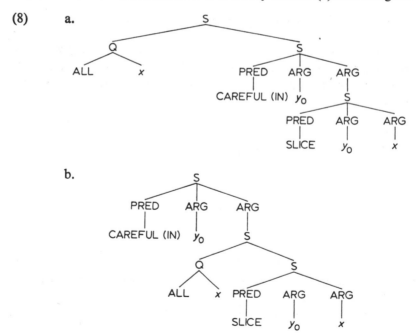

        b.

form such as (4) above, then we can state the difference between the logical forms of (7a) and (7b) as (8a) and (8b).

If, on the other hand, we assume that (1) has a logical form like (2), then there is no apparent way to provide a logical form which shows the distinction between (7a) and (7b). We conclude from this that manner adverbs such as 'carefully' are not to be represented in logical form as operators mapping predicates into predicates, but rather as sentential operators, that is, predicates taking sentential complements.

B. *Absolutely*

Consider the two occurrences of 'anyone' in (1a) and (1b).

> (1) a. Anyone can cook Peking duck.
>   b. Sam didn't see anyone.

It is generally acknowledged that the "anyone" in (1a) is an instance of a universal quantifier, as in (2).

> (2) $\forall x(x$ can cook Peking duck).

Many linguists have assumed, on the other hand, that the 'anyone' in (1b) is a variant of 'someone', which occurs in certain contexts, for example, in the presence of the negative, as in (1b). However, Quine has suggested that both occurrences of 'anyone' are instances of universal quantifiers and that there is a constraint on 'anyone' to the effect that it always takes the widest scope it can. According to Quine's proposal, (1b) should be represented as (3a), whereas according to other proposals (1b) should be represented as (3b).

> (3) a. $\forall x(\sim (\text{Sam saw } x))$
>   b. $\sim (\exists x(\text{Sam saw } x))$.

Since (3a) and (3b) are logically equivalent, it doesn't make much difference from the viewpoint of logic alone, and one could decide the matter arbitrarily. But if one were considering how such sentences were to be represented, not in terms of first-order predicate calculus, but in terms of a natural logic, which involves empirical linguistic considerations, the question would become an empirical one. Is there a right way and a wrong way to represent (1b)? In fact, would one want both universal and existential quantifiers as primitives in natural logic, or could one get away with one of these, and if so, which one? Let us consider one sort of argument that might bear on such questions.

Quine has argued that treating (1b) as having the form of (3a) rather than (3b) would make for a uniform treatment of 'any'. However, there is some syntactic evidence which goes counter to Quine's proposal. This depends on certain properties of the word 'absolutely', which were first uncovered by Östen Dahl (1970) and investigated more thoroughly by Robin Lakoff. Consider (4). As (4a) shows, 'absolutely' can modify a universal quantifier. But 'absolutely' cannot modify an existential quantifier, as (4b) shows, though it can modify a negative existential, as (4c) shows.

(4)   a. Sam hates absolutely everyone.
        b. *Sam hates absolutely someone.
        c. Sam hates absolutely no one.

As Robin Lakoff has observed, application of this test to the sentences of (1) shows that 'absolutely' can modify 'anyone' in (1a), but not in (1b).

(5)   a. Absolutely anyone can cook Peking duck.
        b. *Sam didn't see absolutely anyone.

If it correct that 'absolutely' goes with universal but not existential quantifiers, that would indicate that (1b) should be given a logical form like (3b) with an existential quantifier, rather than one like (3a) with a universal quantifier. This conclusion is further substantiated by the fact that other occurrences of 'anyone', as in (6a and b), may not take 'absolutely'.

(6)   a. *Did absolutely anyone leave?
        b. *If absolutely anyone leaves, Sam will commit suicide.

The constraints on 'absolutely' have even more interesting consequences. Dahl noticed that they were not restricted to constraints on quantifiers, and pointed out cases like (7), (8), and (9).

(7)   a. That is absolutely necessary.
        b. *That is absolutely possible.
(8)   a. That is absolutely required.
        b. *That is absolutely permitted.
(9)   a. You absolutely must go.
        b. *You absolutely may go.

Dahl made the extremely interesting proposal that the facts of (7) through (9) followed from the constraints involving quantifiers, since in a possible world semantics, the *a* sentences would be statements about *all* alternative worlds, while the *b* sentences would be statements about *some* possible alternative worlds. 'Absolutely' would go with universal quantification over possible alternative worlds, but not with existential quantification. Under this fascinating proposal, facts about grammaticality of English sentences would follow from facts about the truth conditions for such sentences in a possible world semantics.

Unfortunately a damper, at least a tentative one, has been thrown on this alluring proposal by some further facts uncovered by Robin Lakoff. As (10) shows, the negatives of the above *b* sentences may also take 'absolutely'.

(10)   a. That is absolutely impossible.
        b. That is absolutely not permitted.
        c. You absolutely may not go.

This is entirely in line with what happens in quantification, as (4c) shows. However, there are a number of cases where 'absolutely' can occur and which seem essentially to be of the same sort as the above cases, but which involve neither universal quantifiers nor negative existentials, nor predicates that can be understood (at least not in any obvious way) in terms of a possible world semantics. Consider (11) through (13).

(11)   a. That is absolutely fascinating.
        b. *That is absolutely interesting.
        c. That is absolutely uninteresting.
(12)   a. I absolutely love snails.
        b. *I absolutely like snails.
        c. I absolutely loathe snails.
(13)   a. That's absolutely wonderful.
        b. *That's absolutely good.
        c. That's absolutely terrible.

Each of these cases seems to involve some sort of scale. In (11) it is a scale of interest running from the uninteresting through the relatively and very interesting up to the fascinating. 'Uninteresting' and 'fascinating' seem to represent end-points (or at least distant parts) of the scale. It is these that can be modified by 'absolutely'. Similarly (12) and (13) seem to involve scales of fondness and goodness respectively. However, there seems to be no obvious way in which one can associate the *a* sentences with universal quantifiers, the *b* sentences with existentials, and the *c* sentences with negative existentials, though that is what would be required in order to reduce these cases to the quantifier cases. In the absence of such an analysis, R. Lakoff has suggested that the restrictions on 'absolutely' are to be understood in terms of such scales, and restricted so that they go with the extremes on such scales. She suggests moreover that quantifiers are really special cases of such scalar predicates, and that 'all' and 'none' can also be understood as end-points on a scale. What follows from this is that quantifiers must be cross-classified with predicates (that is, adjectives and verbs). This suggests that they are in the same category as adjectives and verbs, in other words, that quantifiers are predicates. This might be taken as more support for the claim to that effect, as made in Lakoff (1965), Carden (1968) and (1970), and McCawley (1970). On the other hand, it may be the case that predicates on these scales are not to be represented in logical form as atomic predicates, but are rather to be decomposed into quantifier expressions which range over a scale and an atomic predicate which defines the scale. If the latter analysis is correct, we would expect to find scope differences involving the understood quantifiers that range over such scales. However, there is no known evidence for such an analysis.[1]

Incidentally, there are cases where a word may be understood either literally or figuratively, and the possibilities for the occurrence of 'absolutely' or 'absolute' will depend not on the occurrence of the word itself but on whether either of its meanings is understood as the end point on some scale. Consider for example (14) through (17).

(14)   a. Sam is an absolute elephant.
        b. *Sam is an absolute wombat.
(15)   a. Sadie is running an absolute whorehouse.
        b. *Sadie is running an absolute apartment house.
(16)   a. Moe is an absolute bastard.
        b. *Moe is an absolute illegitimate child.

'Elephant' can be taken in its literal sense, in which case (14a) is meaningless. It would be absurd to assert (14a) of an elephant named Sam. (14a) said of a person named Sam, means that he is enormous. That is because we have come to associate elephants with what is, from the point of view of our culture, their most outstanding property, their size. (14b) is strange, because it cannot be taken literally and because, in our culture (or at least in my subculture), wombats are not viewed as having any special defining property. In a culture where, say, wombats represented the quintessence of smelliness, (14b) would be perfectly fine. Thus our ability to understand sentences like those in (14) depend in part on our cultural assumptions. (15) and (16) are similar cases. (15a) is not understood literally. It is not the sort of thing you would say of a madame. It might be the sort of thing you would say figuratively if Sadie had a number of promiscuous daughters. (15b) is strange because in our culture there is no way of understanding it figuratively, though perhaps those with different cultural assumptions or wilder imaginations may find (15b) perfectly fine. (16) works in the same way.

C. *Presuppositions and Propositional Functions*

An *n*-place propositional function is a function mapping a sequence of *n* individuals into a proposition. In some instances two or more of the individuals may be coreferential. (1) and (2) below are two common ways of representing propositional functions.

(1) $f(x, y, x)$.
(2) $f(\_\_, \_\_, \_\_)$.

Propositions may be formed from (1) and (2)[1] either by substituting individual constants for the variables in (1) or the slots in (2), or by binding the variables or the slots by quantifiers. In (1), coreference is indicated by the use of the same variable letter, x. This indicates that the first and third places refer to the same individual. In the notation used in (2), this is indicated by drawing a line between the first and third places. It should be noted that, although the 'f' in (1) and (2) may be an atomic predicate, it need not be. For example, (1) or (2) may be a representation of an extremely complex sentence, as in (3).

(3) x's sister thought that the man who kicked y was disturbed by the fact that x was rich.

In terms of tree structures, we will consider (1) to be an abbreviation for any complex sentence containing three arguments, the first and third of which are coreferential, as indicated in (4).

(4)

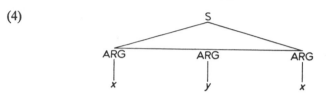

It should be noted that the indication of coreference, whether a specification of identical variable letters or a line between the slots, is considered an integral part of a propositional function. Thus, (5) through (9) below all represent different propositional functions.

(5) $f(x, y, z)$ $f(\underline{\quad}, \underline{\quad}, \underline{\quad})$

(6) $f(x, x, z)$ $f(\underline{\quad}, \underline{\quad}, \underline{\quad})$

(7) $f(x, y, y)$ $f(\underline{\quad}, \underline{\quad}, \underline{\quad})$

(8) $f(x, y, x)$ $f(\underline{\quad}, \underline{\quad}, \underline{\quad})$

(9) $f(x, x, x)$ $f(\underline{\quad}, \underline{\quad}, \underline{\quad})$.

Let us now consider some facts concerning the word 'before'. Consider (10).

(10)   a. Before Sue punched anyone, she was miserable.
         b. Before Sue punches anyone, she'll get drunk.

(10a) presupposes that Sue punched someone, and (10b) presupposes that Sue will punch someone. In sentences of this sort, the content of the before-clause is presupposed, as in (11a).

(11)   a. BEFORE $(S_1, S_2) \rightarrow S_1$
         b. $S_1 = (\exists x) (\text{PUNCH (Sue, } x))$.

Note that in (10a and b), S_1 is understood as being a sentence containing an existential quantifier binding a propositional function.

Under somewhat different conditions, which aren't completely understood, before-constructions presuppose the negative of the content of the before-clause. Consider (12).

(12)   a. Before Sue punched anyone, she left the party.
         b. Before Sue punches anyone, she'll fall asleep.

(12a) presupposes that Sue didn't punch anyone and (12b) presupposes
that she won't punch anyone. We can represent this as in (13a).

(13)   a. BEFORE (S_1, S_2) → ~ S_1 (under certain conditions)
         b. $S_1 = (\exists x)$ (PUNCH (Sue, x)).

Again, S_1 is understood as containing an existential quantifier binding a
propositional function. Note that (11a) and (13a) both involve identity
conditions. The S_1 which is the first argument of BEFORE must be identical
to the S_1 which is presupposed in (11) and whose negation is presupposed
in (13a).

Now let us turn to (14) and (15).

(14)   a. *Before Sue punched *anyone, he* got her to leave the party.
         b. *Before Sue punches *anyone, he*'ll make sure she falls asleep.
(15)   a. *Before Sue punched *anyone,* Max tried to convince *him*
            to leave.
         b. *Before Sue punches *anyone,* I'll try to convince *him* to
            leave.

In each of these sentences there is an occurrence of 'anyone' in the before-
clause and a pronoun 'he' in the other clause. In each case, 'he' cannot
have 'anyone' as its antecedent. There are various possible explanations
of this. In (14a) it is assumed that Sue didn't punch anyone and therefore
there would be no individual for 'he' to refer to. However, such an
explanation will not account for the facts of (15), since in (15) it is presupposed that Sue did (or will) punch someone. This leaves us two
possible explanations for the ill-formedness of (15). These depend on
what logical forms one attempts to provide for the sentences of (15). We
can, for example, assume that there is some sort of quantifier outside of
BEFORE binding two occurrences of a variable, one in each clause, as in
(16a).

(16)   a. (Qx) (BEFORE $(f(x), g(x))$)
         b. *BEFORE $((\exists x) f(x), g(x))$.

On the other hand, we can assume, as in (15b), that there is an existential
quantifier inside the first clause binding a variable inside that clause, and
that there is another occurrence of that variable inside the second clause.
Unfortunately, in such constructions as (16b), the quantifier in the first

clause cannot bind the variable in the second clause. Thus, if such an analysis is necessary, we have an explanation for why the sentences of (15) are ungrammatical. However, one can always retreat to an analysis like (16a). As it turns out, (16a) also offers us an explanation for the ungrammaticality of (15). Recall that both sentences of (15) must presuppose the content of the before-clause, as in (11a) above. This would give us a presupposition-relation as given in (17a).

(17)   a. $[(Qx) (\text{BEFORE } (f(x), g(x))] \rightarrow (\exists x) f(x)$
          b. $[(Q\underbrace{\quad}) (\text{BEFORE } (f(\underbrace{\quad}), g(\underbrace{\quad}))] \rightarrow (\exists\underbrace{\quad}) f(\underbrace{\quad})$
          c. $\text{BEFORE } (f(\underbrace{\quad}), g(\underbrace{\quad}))$
          d. $f(\underbrace{\quad})$.

(17a) is equivalent to (17b), using the slot-and-line notation for propositional functions instead of the identical-variable-letter notation. However, (17b) cannot be a schema of the form (11a). Note that the expression in the square brackets of (17b) contains the propositional function of (17c), in which two slots are joined by a line. If that line, the indication of coreference, is an integral part of the propositional function, then the expression of (17d) is not a proper subpart of (17c). That is, if we call (17d) S_1, then S_1 does not occur as a proper subpart of (17c). Consequently (17b) cannot be an instance of (11a), or any similar statement. The reason is that there can be no identity statement between anything on the right side of the arrow in (17b) and anything on the left side of the arrow. One propositional function, say that of (17d), cannot be identical to part of another propositional function, say that of (17c). Thus, assuming that the line connecting the slots, the indication of coreference, is an integral part of a propositional function, we have an explanation for the ungrammaticality of the sentences of (15). Under no possible analysis can 'him' in (15) be bound by the quantifier corresponding to 'any' in (15). Thus analyses like (16a) are ruled out, as well as analyses like (16b).

So far, everything works pretty much as it should. The assumption that the indication of coreference is an integral part of a propositional function and that (17d) is not a proper subpart of (17c) has paid dividends.

Unfortunately, the market is about to collapse. Consider (18).

(18)   Before Sue punches *anyone*, she tries to get *him* to leave.

'Any' in (18) might well be said to be understood as a universal quantifier. Thus (18) might be given the form of (19).

(19) $(\forall x)$ BEFORE $(f(x), g(x))$.

Now, (18) presupposes that Sue punches people. Thus we should have an instance of (11a). The presupposition relation of (18) is given in (20).

(20)   a. $[(\forall x)$ BEFORE $(f(x), g(x))] \rightarrow (\exists x)(fx)$
            b. $[(\forall\underline{})$ BEFORE $(f(\underline{}), g(\underline{}))] \rightarrow (\exists\underline{})f(\underline{})$.

Unfortunately, neither (20a) nor (20b) can be an instance of (11a). (20e) and (20b) are of the same form as (17a and b) above. As we saw, under the assumption that the indication of coreference, the line between the slots, is an integral part of a propositional function, there cannot be any identity condition between the expression on the right of the arrow in (20b) or any of the propositional function it contains and any part of the expression on the left. Thus it is impossible for (20a) to be an instance of (11a), or any similar statement. In fact, it would be impossible to account for the presupposition relation in (18) generally, since any general account must contain an identity condition between a proposition or a propositional function in the expression on the left side of the arrow and a proposition or propositional function in the expression on the right side of the arrow – if it is true that (17d) cannot be a proper subpart of (17c). Thus, given our assumptions, we can neither account for the grammaticality of (18), nor can we state a general rule accounting for the presuppositions of before-constructions. Something is wrong. And what appears to be wrong is the assumption that the indication of coreference is an integral part of the structure of the propositional function. That is, we need to be able to say that (17d) is a proper subpart of (17c). This leaves us with two problems. Why is (15) ungrammatical but (18) grammatical? And how can we represent coreference in a propositional function in such a way that the indication of coreference is not a proper part of the structure of the propositional function?

Before concluding let us consider some further examples.

(21)   a. Whenever *someone* comes to the door, I let *him* in.
            b. $(\exists x)(x$ comes to the door).

(21a) presupposes (21b). How can 'him' in (21a) be found by the quanti-

fier corresponding to 'some', at the same time as there is an identity-condition between (21b) and the content of the whenever-clause of (21a) '
Now let us turn to an even more complex case.

(22)   a. Before Mary realizes that *someone* has broken into her
            room, *he*'ll have stolen her jewels.
         b. Mary will realize that someone has broken into her room.
         c. Someone has broken into her room.

(22a) presupposes (22b) which in turn presupposes (22c). In (22a) 'some-one' is inside the complement of the factive verb 'realize' which is in turn inside a before-clause. However, the quantifier corresponding to 'some' seems to be binding a variable corresponding to 'he' in the second clause of (21a). How is this possible? Note, incidentally, that the quantifier corresponding to 'some' in (22a) cannot be outside of the before-clause, as in (19). Thus it would appear that we have a situation in (22a) like that of (16b), which is impossible, given our current notions about how the binding of variables works. (23) presents even more difficulties.

(23)   a. *Before Mary claims that *someone* has broken into her
            room, *he*'ll have stolen her jewels.
         b. *Before Mary claims that *someone* has broken into her
            room, she'll claim that *he* stole her jewels.
         c. After Mary claims that *someone* has broken into her
            room, she'll claim that *he* stole her jewels.

Note that with 'claim' instead of 'realize', (23a) is ungrammatical. One might guess that this would follow from the facts of Section VIII, since it is not guaranteed that 'he' will have an antecedent in the appropriate worlds. However, it is not that simple, as (23b and c) indicate. These sentences indicate that time relations are somehow involved. A further complication arises in (24).

(24)   Before Mary realizes that *someone* has broken into her room,
         he will have stolen her jewels and her mother will have re-
         ported *it* to the police.

(24) is a continuation of (22). Note the occurrence of 'it' in (24). 'It' is understood as 'someone has stolen her jewels' not as 'he has stolen her jewels' nor as 'the man who broke into the room has stolen her jewels'.

This would provide problems for the view that 'he' in (22a) is not the reflex of a variable bound by the quantifier corresponding to 'some' but rather the reduction of a definite description such as 'the man who broke into her room'. Here too, there would be difficulties in stating the identity-condition between the sentence that 'it' is understood as representing and the sentence which is the antecedent of 'it'. Under any analysis of the logical forms of sentences like (24), there will be difficulties.

D. *Counterparts and Propositional Functions*[1]

The problem of identifying individuals across possible worlds is a particularly vexing one. I would like to add some further vexations. Consider sentence (1).

(1)   I dreamt that I was Brigitte Bardot and that I kissed me.

(1) is interesting in a number of ways. First, the sentence '*I kissed me' is ungrammatical in isolation, though it occurs embedded in (1). Secondly, it is usually the case that all first-person singular pronouns refer to the same individual, the speaker. However, the 'I' which is the subject of 'kiss' and the 'me' which is the object of 'kiss' refer to different individuals. Moreover, there is a difficulty in making an identification between the speaker in the world of the utterance and the referent of 'I' in the world of the dream. In the dream, Brigitte Bardot is a counterpart of the speaker. However, in some sense, the speaker is also his own counterpart. It appears that what one needs is not simply a single counterpart relation for identifying individuals across possible worlds, but two counterpart relations. That is, the individual must be distinguished from his body. In (1), the 'I' which is the subject of 'kiss' has the body-counterpart of Brigitte Bardot, but is the individual-counterpart of the speaker. 'Me', in (1), has the body-counterpart of the speaker. Thus it would appear as though we must distinguish individual-counterparts from body-counterparts.

(1) is also interesting from a purely grammatical point of view. Why should the subject of 'kiss' be 'I' rather than 'she'? Or why should the object of 'kiss' be 'me' rather than 'him'? In order to account for these facts, it would appear that the rule of person-agreement in English must state that any counterpart of the first-person is marked with the first-person morpheme, whether it is an individual-counterpart or a body-

counterpart. Thus it would appear that the rule of person-agreement in English must involve the notion of counterparts. Secondly, why do we get 'I kissed me' rather than 'I kissed myself'? Note that in the world of the dream, the referent of 'I' and the referent of 'me' are different individuals; they are not coreferential. Thus it would appear that the rule of reflexivization in English requires a coreferentiality relationship rather than a counterpart relationship. It is rather interesting that the notion 'counterpart', which was introduced to handle problems of trans-world identity in possible world models, should play a role in English grammar.

There are still further counterpart relations that must be distinguished. Consider (2).

(2)   I dreamt that I was playing the piano.

(2) can be understood in one of two ways. In one reading, my dream consists of feeling myself seated at the piano, seeing the keyboard in front of me, feeling my fingers hitting the keys, etc. I am a participant in the dream. On the other reading, I see, as in a movie, someone who looks like me seated at a piano, playing. In this reading, I am an observer. These two readings have correlates in English grammar. Consider (3).

(3)   a. I enjoyed playing the piano.   (participant)
           b. I enjoyed my playing the piano.   (observer)

In (3a), the subject of 'play' has been deleted by the rule of equi-NP-deletion. In (3b) the subject of 'play' has not been deleted by the rule of equi-NP-deletion. (3a) and (3b) mean different things. They have readings corresponding to the two readings of (2) given above. In (3a), I enjoyed my participation in playing the piano, while in (3b) I enjoyed the fact that I did it. In (3a), the relationship between the subject of 'enjoy' and the subject of 'play' might be called a participant-counterpart relation, while in (3b) one has an observer-counterpart relation. In English, the rule of equi-NP-deletion only operates in a case of participant-counterpart relation. Thus we have another rule of English in which the notion 'counterpart' plays a crucial role. (4) is another example of this sort.

(4)   a. I wanted to be president.   (participant)
           b. I wanted myself to be president.   (observer)

In (4a), equi-NP-deletion has taken place and we get a participant-reading, while in (4b) equi-NP-deletion has not taken place and we get an observer-reading. Note that (4a) can be true and (4b) false.

(5)   I wanted to be president, but I didn't want myself to be president.

(5) is not contradictory. I may want to be president because I am power-hungry, while not wanting myself to be president because I am lazy and corrupt, and it would be bad for the country. Thus it seems clear that one must distinguish a participant-counterpart relation from an observer-counterpart relation.

The above considerations have important consequences for the concept of a propositional function. Consider (6).

(6)   a. Everyone wants to be president.
        b. Everyone wants himself to be president.

Without a distinction between participant-counterparts and observer-counterparts, one would normally expect to represent (6a) something like (7a) or (7b).

(7)   a. $(\forall x)\ (x\ \text{wants}\ (x\ \text{be president}))$
        b. $(\forall \underline{\ \ })\ (\underline{\ \ }\ \text{wants}\ \underline{\ \ }\ \text{be president}).$

However, that is also how one would have to represent (6b). But they mean different things, and one can be true while the other is false. Hence, they must have different logical forms. However, given the notion of a propositional function as indicating identity only through using either the same variable letter, or lines connecting slots, there is no way of differentiating (6a) from (6b) in logical form. Consequently, our present notion of what a propositional function is will be inadequate for natural logic, since in natural logic (6a) and (6b) must both be given logical forms and the difference between them represented systematically.

One more thing: Lewis' notion that the counterpart of an individual in another world is that individual who shares the most properties with, or is most like, the first individual. Thus the counterpart of me in another world would be the person in that world who is most like me, according to Lewis' suggestion, while your counterpart in another world would be the person who is most like you. However, it is clear from (8) below that this notion of 'counterpart' is inadequate.

(8)   If I were you and you were me, I'd hate you.

E. *Individual and Class Coreference*[1]

Plural NPs in English may indicate either aggregates of individuals or classes. Consider (1).

(1)   a. Former servicemen are neurotic.
          b. Former servicemen are numerous.

In (1a) we have a plural NP indicating an aggregate of individuals. (1a) predicates 'is neurotic' of each individual former serviceman. In (1b), on the other hand, we have the same plural NP representing a class. 'Numerous' is predicated not of the individual former serviceman, but of the class of former servicemen. That is, (1b) says that the class of former servicemen is large.

Corresponding to each of the two ways in which we can understand plural NPs there are two ways in which we can understand plural pronouns referring back to those NPs. Consider (2).

(2)   a. I like *former servicemen*, but the fact that *they* are neurotic disturbs me.
          b. I like *former servicemen*, but the fact that *they* are numerous disturbs me.

In (2a), 'they' is understood as representing an aggregate of individuals and, as in (1a) above, 'neurotic' is predicated of each of those individuals. In (2b), 'they' is understood as representing a class and 'numerous', as in (1b) above, is understood as predicating something of that class. Since there is presumably some sort of identity relation between a pronoun and its antecedent, one would suspect that, since the pronouns in (2a) and (2b) are understood in different ways, their antecedents would also be understood in different ways. But this does not seem to be true. In both (2a) and (2b), I am saying that I like individual servicemen, not the class of servicemen. The problem becomes clearer in (3).

(3)   Whenever you put *former servicemen* in a room, *they* start discussing the fact that *they* are numerous.

In (3) there are two occurrences of 'they'. The first occurrence of 'they' refers to the individual servicemen, while the second occurrence of 'they' refers to the class of former servicemen. If pronouns bear some sort of identity relation to their antecedents, how can these two pronouns have the same antecedent? Perhaps one might guess that the pronouns were somehow or other grammatically identical, though they referred to different things. (4), however, shows that this is not the case.

(4)   a.   Whenever you put *former servicemen* in a room, *they* start discussing *their* numerousness.
        b.   Whenever you put *former servicemen* in a room, *they* start discussing *their* own problems.
        c.   *Whenever you put *former servicemen* in a room, *they* start discussing *their* own numerousness.

(4a) is just like (3) except that 'numerous' has been nominalized. In (4b) we find that 'their' refers to the individuals, not to the class, and it may be followed by 'own', the possessive marker in English. However, in (4c) 'their' may not be followed by 'own'. The reason is that reflexive markers like 'own' can only occur where there are propositional functions with the same variable, as in (5a). The fact that 'own' cannot occur in (4c) shows that (4c) does not contain a propositional function like (5a), but rather one like (5b).

(5)   a. x starts discussing x's numerousness.
        b. x starts discussing y's numerousness.

There must be different variables for the individuals and for the class. It should be noted that both sorts of pronouns may not only have as an antecedent a plural NP which is interpreted as an aggregate of individuals, but may also have as an antecedent a plural NP interpreted as a class.

(6)   a. Because *former servicemen* are numerous, *they* are neurotic.
        b. *Former servicemen* used to be numerous, but now *their* size is diminishing.

The problem is, how can one represent plural NPs and plural pronouns in such a way as to distinguish reference to individuals from reference to classes as (4) above requires, while also indicating the appropriate way in which a plural pronoun is related to its antecedent. Clearly, identity of reference will not do the job.

F. *Definite Descriptions*

In recent years there has been an adverse reaction of a non-Strawsonian sort to Russell's theory of descriptions. Logicians such as Lambert, and more recently Van Fraassen, Kaplan, Montague, and Scott have claimed that the problem of nonreferring definite descriptions such as 'the present king of France' can be avoided without claiming that definite descriptions are not really terms, that is, without a Russellian analysis. Taking the description operator '*Ixfx*' as a primitive, they provide a truth definition for it such that '*Ixfx*' is undefined if there is no individual a in the domain of x such that '*fa*' is true. In short, they use truth definitions to circumvent Russell's problem.[1]

There is no question that the cases of nonreferring definite descriptions brought up by Russell can be handled in this way. However, there are cases in English of definite descriptions that do refer which cannot be handled by considering the description operator as a primitive. Thus, it would appear that the technique described above cannot be extended to natural logic, since natural logic would have to deal with the following sentences.

(1)   *The man who doesn't expect it* will be elected.
(2)   The usual men were meeting in *the usual place*.

The problem in (1) is the pronoun *it* inside the definite description, which refers to something outside the definite description. If the description operator is not taken as a primitive, (1) might be described as in (3).

(3) $(\exists!x)[(\sim [x \text{ expects } (x \text{ will be elected})] \& (x \text{ will be elected}))]$.

Under such an analysis, the *it* would arise though the deletion of '*x* will be elected' under a condition of identity with the other occurrence of that phrase, by normal rules of grammar. If, however, (1) is represented as in (4),

(4) $[Ix(\sim [x \text{ expects } (x \text{ will be elected})])]$ will be elected,

the normal rule of pronominalization cannot operate, since there is no sentence-identity.

(2) presents a much worse problem, since it contains two occurrences

of the word 'usual', while the logical form of the sentence would contain only one.[2] Thus (2) might be represented as in (5).

(5) $\exists x_1 \cdots x_n \, \exists ! y \, [(\text{Usual} \, (x_1 \cdots x_n \text{ meet at } y)) \, \& \, (x_1 \cdots x_n \text{ were meeting at } y)]$.

The difficulty here is that 'usual' is predicated of an expression containing both y and $x_1 \cdots x_n$, and in addition there must be another expression containing both. So far as I can tell, there is no way to represent the logical form of (2) if one takes the definite description operator as primitive. And things get even worse if one considers sentences like (6).

(6) The usual men want to meet at *the usual place*.

(6) shows a scope ambiguity. It can have the reading of either (7) or (8).

(7) $\exists x_1 \cdots x_n \, \exists ! y \, ([\text{Usual} \, (x_1 \cdots x_n \text{ meet at } y)] \, \& \, [x_1 \cdots x_n \text{ want} \, (x_1 \cdots x_n \text{ meet at } y)])$

(8) $\exists x_1 \cdots x_n \, \exists ! y \, ([\text{Usual} \, (x_1 \cdots x_n \text{ want} \, (x_1 \cdots x_n \text{ meet at } y))] \, \& \, [x_1 \cdots x_n \text{ want} \, (x_1 \cdots x_n \text{ meet at } y)])$.

In (7), the men usually do meet at the given place, while in (8) they usually want to meet at the given place. So far as I can see, it is absolutely impossible to represent the ambiguity of (6) using a primitive definite description operator.

The following sentences should also give pause to anyone wishing to maintain that description operators are primitives.

(9) John and Bill live in *the same house*.
(10) John and Bill want to live in *the same house*. (ambiguous)
(11) The usual boys made love to *the same girl* in *the usual place*. (ambiguous)
(12) The usual boys believed that they made love to *the same girl* in *the usual place*. (multiply ambiguous).

Similar difficulties will, of course, arise with Bach-Peters sentences like (13).

(13) *The boy who deserves it* will get *the prize he wants*.

Anyone who wishes to propose a theory of definite descriptions for natural logic will have to take sentences like these into account.

X. CONCLUDING REMARKS

Natural logic is by no means new. The study of logic began and developed as an attempt to understand the rules of human reasoning (which is characteristically done in natural language). The discovery and development of symbolic logic can be viewed in part as the discovery that the regularities involved in human reasoning cannot be stated in terms of the surface forms of sentences of natural languages. One needs instead special logical forms containing quantifiers, variables, etc. To check on the correctness of an argument each surface form of each natural language sentence must be associated with a corresponding logical form, and rules of logic apply to the logical forms, not the surface forms.

The development of logic has followed a pattern common to many fields. As formal techniques are developed for dealing with certain aspects of the field's subject matter, that subject matter tends to shrink until it encompasses only those aspects of the original subject matter that the techniques developed can cope with. The development of the predicate calculus had this effect. For many logicians, logic, the study of human reasoning, became the study of those aspects of human reasoning capable of being dealt with by the techniques of predicate calculus. This was both good and bad. It was good, very good, in that it led to remarkable developments in the foundations of mathematics and a very deep understanding of how logical systems work. Unfortunately, the concentration on the development of known techniques had the consequence that most of the original subject matter of logic was ignored, if not forgotten. The recent development of modal logic, I think, has taken a large step toward remedying this situation. Although most modal logicians have, quite rightly, concentrated their effort on refining and developing the techniques made available by Kripke and others, this has been accompanied by a good deal of effort toward applying those techniques to deal with a wider and wider range of natural language constructions: imperatives, questions, tenses, and so on. It seems to me that recent developments in modal logic, together with recent developments in linguistics, make the serious study of natural logic possible. Just as modal logic will enable us to study seriously the logic of a very large number of natural language concepts, so the techniques of generative grammar and, more recently, generative semantics, will enable us to study to a great extent the rules relating logical forms to surface forms for sentences of natural languages. It seems clear that neither the techniques that have been developed in modal logic up to now, nor those of generative semantics, will be capable of doing their respective jobs in the long run. Just as there are natural language phenomena which are beyond the scope of intensional logic, so there are natural language phenomena which are beyond the scope of global grammatical rules. This, of course, does not mean that either modal logic or generative semantics should be abandoned. Rather they should be vigorously developed to find out how far they can be extended and precisely what their limitations are. However, I think it is most important, both for linguists and for logicians who are interested in the subject matter of natural logic, not to lose sight of the ultimate goal. This is especially important, since the short-term goals of linguists and modal logicians are bound to be in conflict. Take, for example, the goals discussed by Dana Scott in his 'Advice on Modal Logic'. Scott is interested in setting up foundations for a general quantified intensional logic. His goals are therefore different in many respects from the goals of natural logic. He has limited his aims to something he thinks can be done in the foreseeable future, and that excludes a wide range of phenomena that actually occur in natural language. He is not attempting to deal with presuppositional phenomena nor with non-intensional concepts. Nor does he seem interested in having his results mesh with the results of linguistics, as any natural logic must. For instance, one of Scott's principle aims is the elegance and the simplicity of the system of intensional logic he is developing. Since he feels that there are no known three-valued logics that are sufficiently elegant for his tastes, he advises modal logicians to ignore three-valued logics for the present. But natural logic involves presuppositions, and so will require a three-valued logic. Here is a short-term conflict. Moreover, if it were to turn out that Scott's concept of elegance were to lead to some result incompatible with stating some linguistic generalization, there is no doubt in my mind that he, as well as other logicians, would consider logical elegance as more important than linguistic generalizations.[1] I, of course, would disagree, but then I am a linguist.

I do not intend these remarks as being a criticism of Scott or of anyone else. I have chosen to discuss Scott's remarks partly because they are typical of the attitude of many good practicing logicians, and partly because he happened to put them down on paper. So far as short-term goals are concerned, Scott's seem to me to be not unreasonable for someone in his position. Good logic will undoubtedly be served through the refinement and vigorous development of the present techniques of modal logic. However, if one is interested in natural logic and in its long-term goals, then there are courses other than Scott's that one can follow. One can attempt to extend logic to deal with presuppositions, and there are a number of able logicians involved in this enterprise. One can study the group-reading of quantifiers mentioned in Section II above. One can study the logic of scalar predicates such as *like-love, interesting-fascinating*, etc., and how they are related to the quantifiers *some-all*. (One measure of success for such an endeavor would be the ability to state a general rule governing the occurrence of the word 'absolutely'.) In addition to studies in the logic of time, one might attempt parallel studies in the logic of location and linear dimensions in general, e.g., weight, cost, etc. One might study the various counterpart relations: individual-counterparts, body-counterparts, participant-counterparts, and observer-counterparts. Are all of these different types really necessary? Do they overlap in any way? What properties do they have? Can one use the notion of counterpart to revise our current notion of propositional function so as to make it adequate for doing natural logic? In short, there are many new things that logicians might be doing if they are interested in the goals of natural logic.

   Natural logic, taken together with linguistics, is the empirical study of the nature of human language and human reasoning. It can have right and wrong answers. For example, as we saw in Section IXA above, any treatment of manner adverbs as operators mapping predicates into predicates is simply wrong. It is wrong because in principle it cannot provide different logical forms for sentences that require them – on logical grounds (see Example (7) in IXA and Footnote 2 in that section). An analysis of logical form can be wrong because it does not account for the logical facts. But under the assumptions of natural logic, analyses of logical form can be inadequate for other reasons. If, for example, an analysis of the logical form of some sentence or class of sentences does not permit the statement of some significant linguistic generalization, then that analysis is inadequate on linguistic grounds. Take, for instance, the case of scalar predicates. As we saw above, the word 'absolutely' can occur with words indicating extreme points of a scale (*fascinating, uninteresting*), but not some intermediate point on the scale (*interesting*). We saw that the same was true of quantifiers (*all* and *none* versus *some*), and that, in this sense, quantifiers seemed to act like scalar predicates. Although quantifiers have been very well studied, scalar predicates have not. There is at present no known analysis of the logical forms of both quantifiers and scalar predicates such that the similarities between them are brought out. Consequently, we cannot say for sure that we have an adequate analysis of the logical forms of quantifiers such as *all, some*, and *none*, in the absence of a corresponding analysis of the logical forms of scalar predicates. Further study may show either that the traditional analysis of quantifiers is essentially correct, or that it is partly correct, or that it is entirely wrong, depending on how the study of scalar predicates turns out. One of the criteria for the correctness of such analyses of logical form will be the extent to which the similarities between quantifiers and scalar predicates are brought out. Unless these similarities are made sufficiently explicit so that a general rule governing the occurrence of 'absolutely' can be stated, our analyses of these concepts must be considered inadequate on linguistic grounds. Under the assumptions of natural logic, logical analyses must be linguistically adequate and vice versa. Thus the criteria for adequacy in natural logic are rather stringent. Since the criteria for adequacy of both linguistics and logic must be met at once, the inherent interest of natural logic is so much the greater.

In recent years, much attention has been paid to the ontological claims made by logical systems. Since a natural logic will undoubtedly contain just about all of the things most commonly questioned in such discussions – quantifications over propositions, classes, non-existent individuals, etc. – we ought to consider what it would mean to adopt some particular natural logic as being 'correct'. Are we saying that the universe contains non-existent or hypothetical individuals? If natural logic requires, in part, a possible world semantics, would we be claiming that the universe contains possible worlds? Certainly not. Recall that natural logic is a theory, a theory about the logical structure of natural language sentences and the regularities governing the notion of a valid argument for reasoning in natural language. That is, it is a theory about the human mind, not a theory about the universe. If natural logic requires a possible world semantics, then that might mean that people conceive of things in terms of possible worlds, not that the physical universe contains possible worlds. If natural logic requires quantification over propositions, then that means that people can conceive of propositions as entities, not that there are propositional entities floating around in the universe. If natural logic requires that space and time be independent dimensions, then it is claimed that people conceive of space and time as independent dimensions, not that space and time are independent dimensions (which we know they are not). If one wants a logic capable of dealing with the physical facts of a Einsteinian universe, then it seems pretty sure that one doesn't want a natural logic. This is not to say that the ontological commitments of a natural logic are irrelevant or uninteresting. Quite the contrary. Though a natural logic, if one could be constructed, would not make claims about the universe, it would make claims about the way human beings conceive of the universe. And in the gap between the way the universe is and the way people conceive of the universe, there is much philosophy.

University of Michigan

BIBLIOGRAPHY

Lennart Åqvist, *A New Approach to the Logical Theory of Interrogatives, Part I: Analysis*, Uppsala 1965.
Emmon Bach and Robert T. Harms (eds.), *Universals in Linguistic Theory*, Holt, Rinehart and Winston, New York 1968.
C. Leroy Baker, 'Definiteness and Indefiniteness in English', University of Illinois master's thesis, 1966.
C. Leroy Baker, *Indirect Questions in English*, University of Illinois doctoral dissertation, 1968.
C. Leroy Baker, 'Double Negatives', *Linguistic Inquiry* (1970).
C. Leroy Baker, 'Notes on the Description of English Questions: The Role of an Abstract Question Morpheme', 1970b, in *Foundations of Language*.
Nuel Belnap, 'An Analysis of Questions', TM-1287/000/000, Systems Development Corporation, 1957.
Robert Binnick, *Studies in the Derivation of Predicative Structures*, University of Chicago Dissertation, 1969.
Guy Carden, 'English Quantifiers', Harvard master's thesis, 1968.
Guy Carden, *Idiolect Variation and Logical Predicates in English*, Harvard doctoral dissertation, 1970a.
Guy Carden, 'A Note on Conflicting Idiolects', *Linguistic Inquiry* (1970b).
Brian Chellas, *The Logical Form of Imperatives*, Stanford doctoral dissertation, Perry Lane Press, 1969.
Noam Chomsky, *Syntactic Structures*, Mouton, The Hague, 1957.
Noam Chomsky, 'Current Issues in Linguistic Theory', in *The Structure of Language*

(ed. by Jerry A. Fodor and Jerrold J. Katz), Prentice-Hall, Englewood Cliffs, N.J., 1964.

Östen Dahl, 'Some Notes on Indefinites', *Language*, 1970.

Donald Davidson, 'The Logical Form of Action Sentences' in *The Logic of Decision and Action* (ed. by Nicholas Rescher), University of Pittsburgh Press, Pittsburgh, Pennsylvania, 1966.

Charles Fillmore, 'Verbs of Judging: An Exercise in Semantic Description', *Papers in Linguistics* (1969).

Charles Fillmore, 'Types of Lexical Information' to appear in *Semantics: An Inter-disciplinary Reader in Philosophy, Linguistics, Anthropology and Psychology* (ed. by Leon Jakobovits and Danny Steinberg), Cambridge University Press, Cambridge.

Jerry A. Fodor and Jerrold J. Katz (eds.), *The Structure of Language*, Prentice-Hall, Englewood Cliffs, N.J., 1964.

H. P. Grice, *The Logic of Conversation*, Berkeley mimeo, 1968.

Morris Halle, *The Sound Pattern of Russian*, Mouton, The Hague 1959.

Jaakko Hintikka, *Knowledge and Belief*, Cornell University Press, Ithaca, N.Y., 1962.

Laurence Horn, 'A Presuppositional Analysis of "Only" and "Even"' in *Papers from the Fifth Regional Meeting of the Chicago Linguistic Society*, University of Chicago Press, Chicago, Ill., 1969.

Laurence Horn, 'Ain't It Hard Anymore?' in *Papers from the Sixth Regional Meeting of the Chicago Linguistic Society*, University of Chicago Press, Chicago, Ill., 1970.

Laurence Horn, *Studies in the Semantics of Negation*, U.C.L.A. doctoral dissertation, in preparation.

G. E. Hughes and M. J. Cresswell, *An Introduction to Modal Logic*, Methuen, 1968.

Richard Jeffrey, *Formal Logic*, McGraw-Hill, New York 1967.

David Kaplan, 'Quantifying In', *Synthese* **19** (1968–69).

Lauri Karttunen, 'Problems of Reference in Syntax', University of Texas mimeograph, 1969.

Edward Keenan, *A Logical Base for English*, University of Pennsylvania doctoral dissertation, 1969.

Edward L. Keenan, 'Names, Quantifiers, and a Solution to the Sloppy Identity Problem', University of Pennsylvania, Unpublished, 1970.

Edward L. Keenan, 'Quantifier Structures in English', to appear in *Foundations of Language*.

Saul Kripke, 'Semantical Considerations on Modal Logic', *Acta Philosophica Fennica* **16** (1963).

George Lakoff, *On the Nature of Syntactic Irregularity*, Report NSF-16, Harvard University Computation Laboratory, 1965; reprinted as *Irregularity in Syntax*, Holt, Rinehart and Winston, New York 1970.

George Lakoff, 'Some Verbs of Causation and Change' in Report NSF-20, 1968.

George Lakoff, 'Presuppositions and Relative Grammatically' in *Philosophical Linguistics, Series I* (ed. by William Todd), Great Expectations, Evanston, Ill., 1969.

George Lakoff, 'Repartee', *Foundations of Language* (1970).

George Lakoff, 'On Generative Semantics' in *Semantics: An Interdisciplinary Reader in Philosophy, Linguistics, Anthropology and Psychology* (ed. by Leon Jakobovits and Danny Steinberg), Cambridge University Press, Cambridge, in press.

George Lakoff, *Generative Semantics*, Holt, Rinehart and Winston, New York, in preparation.

George Lakoff, 'Some Thoughts on Transderivational Constraints', to appear.

George Lakoff and Peter Railton, 'Some Types of Presupposition and Entailment in Natural Language', University of Michigan mimeo, 1970.

Robin Lakoff, *Abstract Syntax and Latin Complementation*, M.I.T. Press, Cambridge, Mass., 1968.

Robin Lakoff, 'A Syntactic Argument for *Not*-Transportation' in *Papers from the Fifth Regional Meeting of the Chicago Linguistic Society*, University of Chicago Press, Chicago, Ill., 1969.

Karel Lambert, 'Notes on E!III: A Theory of Descriptions', *Philosophical Studies* (1962).

Karel Lambert, *The Logical Way of Doing Things*, Yale University Press, New Haven, Conn., 1969.

Ronald Langacker, 'An Analysis of Questions', U.C.S.D. mimeograph, 1969.

E. J. Lemmon, 'Deontic Logic and the Logic of Imperatives', *Logique et analyse* **29** (1965).

E. J. Lemmon and Dana Scott, *Intensional Logic* (preliminary draft of initial chapters by E. J. Lemmon), Stanford mimeograph, 1966.

David Lewis, 'General Semantics', this volume, p. 169.

David Lewis, 'Counterpart Theory and Quantified Modal Logic', *Journal of Philosophy* (1968).

Gerald J. Massey, *Understanding Symbolic Logic*, Harper and Row, 1969.

James D. McCawley, 'The Role of Semantics in a Grammar' in *Universals in Linguistic Theory* (ed. by Emmon Bach and Robert T. Harms), Holt, Rinehart and Winston, New York 1968.

James D. McCawley, 'Lexical Insertion in a Transformational Grammar without Deep Structure' in *Papers from the Fourth Regional Meeting of the Chicago Linguistic Society*, University of Chicago Press, Chicago, Ill., 1968a.

James D. McCawley, 'Meaning and the Description of Languages', *Kotoba no Uchii* 1968b.

James D. McCawley, 'Semantic Representations', to appear in *Cognition: A Multiple View* (ed. by Paul Garvin), Spartan Books, New York.

James D. McCawley, 1972 'A Program for Logic', this volume, p. 498.

Richard Montague, 'Pragmatics and Intensional Logic', U.C.L.A. mimeograph, 1967.

Richard Montague, 'English as a Formal Language I', U.C.L.A. mimeograph, 1968.

Jerry Morgan, 'On the Treatment of Presupposition in Transformational Grammar' in *Papers from the Fifth Regional Meeting of the Chicago Linguistic Society*, University of Chicago Press, Chicago, Ill., 1969.

Jerry Morgan, 'On the Derivation of If-Clauses', University of Michigan mimeograph, 1970.

Jerry Morgan, *Presuppositional Structure*, University of Chicago doctoral dissertation, in preparation.

Terence D. Parsons, *A Semantics for English*, University of Illinois at Chicago Circle mimeograph, 1968.

Paul Postal, 'The Surface Verb "Remind"', *Linguistic Inquiry* (1970).

A. N. Prior, *Time and Modality*, Oxford University Press, Oxford 1957.

A. N. Prior, *Past, Present, and Future*, Oxford 1967.

A. N. Prior, *Time and Tense*, Oxford 1968.

W. V. Quine, *Word and Object*, M.I.T. Press, Cambridge, Mass., 1960.

W. V. Quine, *Ontological Relativity*, Columbia University Press, New York 1969.

Hans Reichenbach, *Elements of Symbolic Logic*, Macmillan, New York 1947.

Nicholas Rescher, *The Logic of Commands*, Dover, 1966.

John R. Ross, *Constraints on Variables in Syntax*, M.I.T. doctoral dissertation, 1967.

John R. Ross, 'On Declarative Sentences' in *Readings in English Transformational Grammar* (ed. by Roderick Jacobs and Peter S. Rosenbaum), Blaisdell, Boston, 1970.

Dana Scott, 'The Logic of Tenses', Stanford mimeograph, December 1965.

Dana Scott, 'An Outline for Quantified Intensional Logic', Stanford mimeograph, June 1967.

Dana Scott, 'Advice on Modal Logic', Stanford dittograph, in *Philosophical Problems in Logic: Some Recent Developments* (ed. by Karel Lambert), Reidel, Dordrecht, 1970.

Dana Scott, 'Formalizing Intensional Notions', Stanford mimeograph, 1968.

Robert Stalnaker, 'Pragmatics', this volume, p. 380.

P. F. Strawson, *Introduction to Logical Theory*, Methuen, 1952.

John Tinnon, 'A Minimal System of Modal Logic', in preparation.

William Todd (ed.), *Philosophical Linguistics, Series I*, Great Expectations, Evanston, Ill., 1969.

G. H. von Wright, *Logical Studies*, Routledge and Ketan Paul, London 1957.

G. H. von Wright, *Norm and Action*, Routledge and Kegan Paul, London 1963.

REFERENCES

* This work was partially supported by grant GS-2939 from the National Science Foundation to The University of Michigan. This work is the result of lengthy and informative conversations with the following persons: Lee Bowie, Wallace Chafe, Charles Fillmore, Georgia Green, Gilbert Harman, Lawrence Horn, Robin Lakoff, James D. McCawley, Jerry Morgan, Paul Neubauer, Paul Postal, Peter Railton, John R. Ross, John Tinnon and Bas Van Fraassen. In addition, I have relied heavily on observations of C. Leroy Baker and Lauri Karttunen. They are in no way responsible for any mistakes I may have made.

Section II

1 The conditions under which adverb-preposing is blocked vary somewhat from person to person. The assignment of asterisks in the following examples corresponds to the author's speech. Readers whose idiolects disagree with these examples can easily construct similar examples in their own speech. The argument in this section does not depend on the particular examples given being correct for all dialects, but only on the *existence* of examples of this sort for *some* dialects.

2 It should be noted that adverb-preposing can optionally move the adverb to the front of its own clause as well as to the front of the higher clause.

> a. I think that, if he can get it cheap, *then* Sam will smoke pot.
> b. It is possible that, if he can get it cheap, *then* Sam will smoke pot.

The point here is that *then* is introduced following preposing, and that the placement of *then* depends on how far the *if*-clause has been preposed. It should be noted, incidentally that the *if*-clause may also be preposed to the front of a clause more than one sentence up the tree.

> c. If he can get it cheap, *then* I think it's possible that Sam will smoke pot.

These are just the cases where other adverbs can prepose:

    d. Tomorrow, I think it's possible that Sam will smoke pot.

Section III

[1] For a fuller account of dialect differences see (G. Lakoff, in press) and (Carden, 1970a, 1970b).

[2] In (G. Lakoff, 1965), (G. Lakoff, 1970), (G. Lakoff, in press), and (McCawley, to appear) it was argued that quantifiers are predicates, not simply operators of the usual sort. Though I still maintain such a position, I am leaving the issue aside here for the sake of avoiding controversy.

    In (11) and (12), V is meant to indicate atomic predicates and NP, arguments. The tree structure reflects the bracketings of most normal logical notation.

Section IV

[1] For discussions of generative semantics, see (Lakoff, in press), (Lakoff, in preparation), (McCawley, 1968), and (Postal, 1970).

[2] I will consider hierarchical structures like (A) to be equivalent to expressions like: ORDER (x, y, S_1).

[3] Sentences like (1) are not normal in standard English, and are restricted to certain dialects. These are most common in urban centers in which there are, or were, a large number of Yiddish speakers. Again, the facts given here are from the author's native dialect and the argument is based on the existence of a dialect in which such facts hold.

[4] The next two arguments are due to John R. Ross.

[5] The following three arguments are due to David Perlmutter, John R. Ross, and William Cantrell respectively.

[5a] Strictly speaking, the pronoun must be coreferential with the underlying subject of 'shove', which, in turn, must be coreferential with the next highest indirect object. Agreement in number, person, and gender follows automatically.

[6] This argument is due to R. Lakoff.

[7] See (Baker, 1970b) and (Langacker, 1969). Baker concludes that in addition to the indirect question verb, there is an operator that binds the items questioned. Langacker argues convincingly that it is the verbs that do the binding.

[8] Since it is not at all clear what it means for a verb like 'ask' to *bind* an item being questioned, we would naturally prefer an analysis in which the binding function was assumed by a quantifier associated with 'ask'. Hopefully such an analysis would increase our understanding of the nature of questions. In fact, such analyses have been proposed. Baker (1970b) suggests that verbs taking indirect questions have a new operator, Q, embedded directly below them, the operator functioning only to do the binding. This is little more than giving a name to the problem; it provides us no new insight. Belnap, on the other hand, attempts to identify the logical form of a question with the logical form of its primary (first-order) presupposition. Thus, 'a knows who left' would have the logical form '$(\exists x)$ (KNOW $(a, ($LEFT $x)))$'. Åqvist and Hintikka also assume such logical forms for indirect questions. Unfortunately, this proposal is inadequate in a number of ways. First, there is a sense of 'a knows that someone left' which has that logical form and which is not synonymous with 'a knows who left'.

Secondly, that proposal does not explain why sentences like 'a believes who left' and 'a expected who left' should be impossible, since logical forms like '(∃x) (BELIEVE (a, LEFT x)))' and '(∃x) (EXPECT (a, (LEFT x)))' are possible, and in fact occur as possible readings for 'a believed that someone left' and 'a expected someone to leave'. Thirdly, there is the observation by J. R. Ross (personal communication) that some indirect questions involve disjunctions, while other involve conjunctions.

(1)   a.   I want to know who left, Sam or Irving?
            b.   *I want to know who left, Sam and Irving.
(2)   a.   I don't know who left, Sam or Irving.
            b.   *I don't know who left, Sam and Irving.
(3)   a.   *I know who left, Sam or Irving.
            b.   I know who left, Sam and Irving.

When one doesn't know the answer, one gets disjunctions; when one does know the answer, one gets conjunctions. Why? Any serious account of indirect questions must explain this. Fourthly, the Belnap-Hintikka-Åqvist analysis fails to indicate that in 'a knows who left' the content of a's knowledge is some identifying description or proper name for the individual who left (or the ability to point him out), not simply the fact that that individual left, which is all that their analysis specifies. I wish that I had something positive to contribute at this point, but unfortunately I am as much in the dark as to the real logical form of questions as everyone else seems to be at the moment.

9 This becomes clearer if one considers Lewis' treatment in *General Semantics* rather than Scott's. Lewis distinguishes between 'contextual coordinates' and an 'assignment coordinate'. The contextual coordinates are for such things as speaker, audience, time of utterance, and place of utterance. The assignment coordinate gives 'the values of any variables that may occur free in such expressions as 'x is tall' or 'son of y''.

The assignment coordinate will have to assign a value corresponding to the speaker for person variables, since the speaker would presumably be in the worlds in question. The same for the audience. If times are assigned to time variables by the assignment coordinate, presumably the time of the utterance will be included. And if places are assigned to place variables, one would assume that the place of the utterance would be given by the assignment coordinate. Given this, and the analyis given in (A), the contextual coordinates become superfluous, since the job that they would do in Lewis' system would be done automatically by the assignment coordinate together with the analysis in (A). Since (A) involves no new types of structure – the same predicates occur in nonperformative uses and have to be given anyway – we have a considerable gain. What we have done is to largely, if not entirely eliminate pragmatics, reducing it to garden variety semantics.

Section V

1 The felicity conditions governing successful speech acts are special cases.
2 This notation is introduced purely as a device to keep track of what is going on. It is not meant to have any theoretical significance. I take the term 'presupposition' as meaning what must be true in order for the sentence to be either true or false.
2a Unfortunately, this account of qualifications is by no means adequate. A brief look at qualifications in the case of definite descriptions will verify this.

(1)   The present king of France must be bald, if there is one.
(2)   *The present king of France used to have dark, wavy hair, if there is one.
(3)   John's children, if he has any, will keep him up all night.
(4)   *John's children, if he has any, are keeping him up all night.
(5)   The present king of France, if there is one, is a pervert.
(6)   *The present king of France, if there is one, is goosing me.
(7)   The local FBI agent, if there is one, is tapping my phone.
(8)   *The local FBI agent, if there is one, is tapping me on the shoulder.

[3] It should be noted that this holds only for 'negative-attitude' comments like those with 'odd', 'surprising', etc., but not for 'positive-attitude' comments such as 'expected', 'normal', etc. Positive-attitude comments may be made about an entire preceding clause, but not about any presuppositions of that clause, not even first-order ones.

        a. John stopped beating his wife, and it was to be expected that he would stop.
        b. *John stopped beating his wife, and it was to be expected that he would beat her.

[3a] Van Fraassen has made an alternative suggestion in an attempt to handle such cases. He observes correctly that there is a distinction between

(1)   Irving doesn't realize that the earth is flat.

and

(2)   It is not true that Irving realizes that the earth is flat.

(1) presupposes that the earth is flat, while (2) makes no such presupposition. Choice negation, as in (1), permits presupposition, while exclusion negation, as in (2), does not. He suggests that in cases like (26), where there is pronominalization, the exclusion negation (it is not true that S) be presupposed, while in cases like (25), where there is no pronominalization, the choice negation be presupposed. Under this proposal, counterfactual conditionals would pose no problem for a transitive presupposition relation.

    There are two problems with Van Fraassen's proposal. First, there would be no fully general account of what is presupposed in counterfactuals. Secondly, it would not work generally. Take a verb like 'stop'.

(3)   It is not true that Sam stopped beating his wife.

(3) still presupposes that Sam beat his wife. For some mysterious reason, 'stop' does not work like 'realize' after 'it is not true that' (at least in my speech). Given this fact, one would expect, given Van Fraassen's proposal, that (4) would be contradictory.

(4)   If Sam had been beating his wife, he'd have stopped.

The first clause presupposes that Sam has not been beating his wife. Under the Van Fraassen proposal, the second clause would presuppose that it is not true that Sam has stopped beating his wife, which in turn presupposes that he has been beating her. If presupposition is transitive, we would expect a contradiction, given this proposal. The fact that (4) is not contradictory indicates that this way out won't work.

[4] I am considering here only the facts of Dialect A. However, transitivity also holds in Dialect B. For Dialect B, (27c and d) would read:

c. $-P^-(S_1) \to A(-S_1)$ (second order)
d. $+IFC^{-'-}(P^-(S_1), S_2) \to A(-S_1)$ (by transitivity)

[5] Transitivity holds in Dialect B, strangely enough. (28c) would read:

c. $-P^-(S_2) \to A(-S_2)$

[6] Again I have represented only Dialect A. Distribution and transitivity also hold in Dialect B. For Dialect B, (32d and e) would read:

d. $-P^-(S) \to A(-S)$
e. $AW^{+\vee-}(P^-(S)) \to A(-S)$

[7] Again, transitivity holds in Dialect B. For Dialect B, (33d and e) would read:

d. $-P^-(S) \to A(-S)$
e. $AT^{-+\vee-}(P^-(S)) \to A(-S)$

[7a] Since this was written, some ideas have been developed. See Lakoff and Railton, 1970.

[8] There is, however, a possible argument in favor of having presuppositions be part of the logical form of a sentence. One might, for example, consider the restrictions on restricted quantifiers as being given by presuppositions. For example, 'all men are mortal' might be represented as:

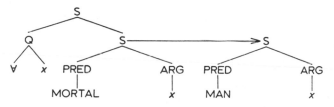

Such a representation would come in particularly handy for cases like:

(i)   John will stop cheating many of his friends.

(i) might be represented as (ii).

(ii)

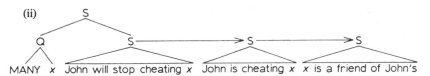

The point here is that the quantifier MANY binds the variable x in the presupposition, as well as in the assertion. This would also account for the fact that, although 'assassinate' presupposes that its object is an important political figure and is from Peoria, (iii) does not presuppose the existence of any important political figures from Peoria.

(iii)   John didn't assassinate anyone from Peoria.

(iii) might be represented as (iv).

(iv)

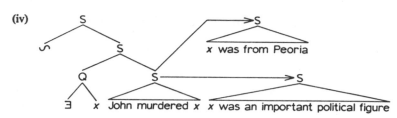

In (iv), as in (ii), the presupposition is within the scope of the quantifer. Under such an analysis, we would not be committed to the existence of any important political figures from Peoria.

Edward Keenan has supplied some clearer cases where the quantifier in the assertion binds a variable in the presupposition:

(v)   Someone kicked his sister.

(vi)

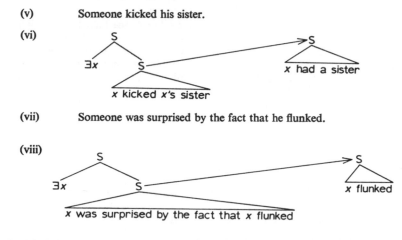

(vii)   Someone was surprised by the fact that he flunked.

(viii)

In (v), it is not simply presupposed that someone had a sister, but rather that the person who did the kicking did. In (viii), it is not merely presupposed that someone or other flunked, but rather that the person who was surprised flunked.

[9] For a discussion of transderivational constraints, see (G. Lakoff, to appear).

[10] We are assuming, then, that presupposition differs from entailment in two respects. Entailment is presumably always transitive, while presupposition is sometimes not transitive. And a sentence will be true or false only if its presuppositions are true.

[11] In the months since this paper was first submitted for publication, it has become clear to me that the treatment of presupposition in this section is woefully inadequate. At least three types of presupposition, each with different properties, have been lumped together under a single rubric. Because of this, a number of inadequate analyses are given in the above section. The problems discussed are, however, real enough, and to my knowledge, the failure to make the necessary distinctions has led to only one incorrect conclusion, namely, conclusion 2. A more adequate analysis reveals that transitivity of the presupposition relation is not what is involved in the cases under discussion, and the what appear as limitations of transitivity are really restrictions of a somewhat different sort. For a discussion of these issues, see Lakoff and Railton, 1970.

Section VI

¹ The following are a small number of the relevant works that have appeared in recent
years: Åqvist, 1965; Belnap, 1957; Chellas, 1969; Davidson, 1966; Hintikka, 1962;
Keenan, 1969 and 1970; Lemmon, 1965; Lemmon and Scott, 1966; Montague, 1967
and 1968; Parsons, 1968; Rescher, 1966; Scott, 1965, 1967, 1968, 1970; Von Wright,
1957 and 1963. Hughes and Cresswell, 1968 is an excellent introduction to modern
modal logic. Massey, 1969 covers some of the same ground, but is more elementary.
Both are highly recommended.

² Some of the relevant works are: Bach and Harms, 1968; Baker, 1966, 1968, 1969,
1970, to appear; Binnick, 1969; Carden, 1968, 1970a, 1970b; Fillmore, 1969, in press;
Horn, 1969, 1970, in preparation; Karttunen, 1969; Keenan, 1969, 1970, to appear;
G. Lakoff, 1965, 1968, 1969, 1970, in press, in preparation; R. Lakoff, 1968, 1969;
Langacker, 1969; McCawley, 1968, 1968a, 1968b, to appear a, to appear b; Morgan,
1969, 1970, in preparation; Postal, 1970; Ross, in press.

³ It should be noted that we are not assuming the converse, that sentences with the
same truth conditions always have the same logical form. This will sometimes be true
and sometimes not.

^{3a} Sentences like (2) are acceptable when they occur as denials. For example, if some-
one has just suggested that you would rather go, you might use (2) as an indignant
reply. However, (2) could not be used where there has been no such prior suggestion,
for example, at the beginning of a discourse. In what follows, we will restrict ourselves
to such cases, i.e., where there has been no prior suggestion and, therefore, where
sentences like (2) will be starred.

⁴ The point here is that sentences like

(i)   I don't think John will leave until tomorrow.

can be understood as meaning

(ii)   I think that John won't leave until tomorrow.

What R. Lakoff has shown is that the rule relating these sentences, moving the *not* up
from the lower clause, must be a rule of grammar.

⁵ Harman (personal communication) has noted that *not*-transportation applied to
(13) produces a grammatical sentence.

(i)   It is not improbable that Sam would rather go.

Horn (personal communication) has observed that is regularly the case where *not*-
transportation has applied.

(ii)   a. *It is not likely that Sam wouldn't rather leave.
           b. It is not unlikely that Sam would rather leave.

Sentences with *doubt*, in which a lower negative has been incorporated into the lexical
item, works the same way.

(iii)   I don't doubt that Sam would rather leave.

What these cases have in common is that negative associated with 'would rather' is
incorporated into a lexical item. Thus it appears that the constraint on 'would rather'
must not only take the logical form of the sentence into account, but must, in addition,
take the surface grammatical form of the sentence into account.

⁶ I have found that there is some dialect variation in the following examples which would indicate that, at least for some speakers, there are further complicating grammatical factors at work here. The examples given here are from my own speech, though I have found that a goodly number of other speakers agree with my judgments in these cases. In any event, the dialect variation is irrelevant to the argument at hand, since it is an existence argument. That is, if there exists a dialect where these phenomena hold, rules must be given for that dialect. The question is whether those rules involve natural logic equivalences.

⁶ᵃ It has been suggested to me that LEAVE OPEN is a possible candidate for BLIK in (24). I disagree. Just because one does not claim S, one need not be leaving open the possibility that ∼ S. One may fail to claim something, for example, because one thinks it is obviously true, or because to do so would be impolite, even though everyone knows it is the case. To my knowledge, there is still no candidate for BLIK.

⁷ In the face of such difficult cases as

(i)   *You shouldn't make Sue believe that I wouldn't rather go.

which should be equivalent to a positive according to (19)–(22), Baker and Horn have proposed an alternate conjecture that a sentence of the form

(ii)   BELIEVE $(x,$ WOULD RATHER $(S))$

be deducible from the sentence in question. ('x' would be identical to the subject of the next-highest verb of saying or thinking above 'would rather'). This, of course, requires deducibility in some system of logic, presumably a natural logic. Moreover, even under this conjecture, one would have to assume the equivalences of (19)–(22) and rule out (24)–(25). Baker's revised conjecture appears in (Baker, 1970a).

Section VII

¹ At the 1970 La Jolla Conference on English syntax, David Perlmutter provided a further argument in favor of this proposal. Take sentences of the form:

(1)   _____ came to _____'s senses.

The two occurrences of _____ must be coreferential:

(2)   *I* came to *my* senses.
(3)   *Sam* came to *his* senses.
(4)   **Sam* came to *my* senses.
(5)   **I* came to *his* senses.

We might account for this by principle I:

(I)   The idiom 'come to _____'s senses' requires that the pronoun filling the blank be coreferential with the subject of 'come'.

Now consider the idiom:

(6)   _____ brought _____ to _____'s senses.

Here a pronoun filling the third blank must be coreferential to the noun phrase filling the second blank.

(7)   *I* brought *Sam* to *his* senses.
(8)   **I* brought *Sam* to *my* senses.

If (6) is considered a separate idiom from (1), we would need principle (II).

(II)   The idiom 'bring____ to ____'s senses' requires that the pronoun filling the last blank be coreferential to the object of 'bring'.

However, if we accept the Binnick-Fillmore proposal, (6) will not be a separate idiom, but will be analysed into (9).

(9)   ____ CAUSE (____ come to ____'s senses).

In this way, (6) is reduced to (1), and we have no need for principle II. Instead, principle I will suffice for both cases. In this case, lexical decomposition permits one to state a true linguistic generalization, which could not be otherwise stated.
² The matter of which phonological shapes correspond to which atomic or molecular predicates is highly language-specific. Only in the case of borrowings, or closely related languages, or in a rare accident will the same atomic or molecular predicate have the same phonological shape. One of the points of postulating logical forms is to provide a *language-independent* characterization of meanings and meaning-relations. Presumably, the concepts characterized by atomic predicates are language-independent, and of the more primitive ones, many will be universal; those that are not will be culture-specific, rather than language specific. (It should be recalled that the question of whether a language has a word for a concept is distinct from the question of whether the members of a culture share the concept itself).
³ The distribution of adverbials provides more evidence in favor of lexical decomposition.

(1)   Nixon had persuaded the nation, until he invaded Cambodia, that he was serious about ending the war.
(2)   Nixon nearly persuaded Harry that he was serious about ending the war.

'Persuade' in (1) means 'CAUSE to COME to BELIEVE' (see (5b) above). The *until*-clause in (1) modifies BELIEVE, not CAUSE to COME to BELIEVE. (1) means only that the nation believed that Nixon was serious about ending the war until he invaded Cambodia, not that he repeatedly persuaded them until that time. Similarly, (2) can mean that Nixon brought it about that Harry nearly believed that he was serious about ending the war. If adverbial modification is to be represented in logical form, then 'persuade' must be decomposable in some fashion such as (5b) above.
⁴ It should be noted that this is not an ad hoc constraint, imposed just to make things work out. Such a constraint would follow from independently needed constraints on possible lexical items. For discussion of such constraints, see Horn, in preparation.

Section VIII

¹ (1a) will be a theorem rather than a postulate, if the postulate

CERTAIN (S) ⊃ S

is accepted.
¹ᵃ In saying that if something is certain, then it is possible, I am speaking only of

logical relations, not of what it is appropriate to say in a given situation where I know that something is certain. For example, suppose that I am testifying as a trial and I know that it is certain that Collins was the killer, then it would be misleading for me to *say* that it is possible that Collins is the killer, even though that proposition is consistent with what I know. Grice has, I believe, given an essentially correct account of what is going on in this example. According to his Cooperative Principle (Grice, 1968), it is assumed in conversation that one gives all of the relevant information. In the above case, we are in violation of this principle (or at least, of one of its maxims). According to Grice's account, if I *say* that S is possible, then it is conversationally implicated (Grice's term) on the assumption that I am obeying the cooperative principle, that S is not certain. As Grice observes, conversational implicatures are quite distinct from logical relations between propositions such as implication. In the examples below, I am concerned only the logical relations, not with conversational implicatures.

2 We are here evading the problems involved in working out the details, in this matter as well as in others, because they are irrelevant to the point being made in this section.
2a In all of the examples to follow, I will be discussing only what Baker calls the 'nonspecific' reading of 'a fish', 'a girl', etc. In this reading, one can qualify 'a fish' by 'some fish or other', not by 'the one we were just talking about'.
3 (6b) can be made grammatical by adding 'if he finds one', since then the certainty will be relative to those worlds in which Sam finds a girl. On the other hand, the addition of 'regardless' or 'in any event' will reinforce the ungrammaticality of (6b), as would be expected.
4 The noun phrase 'The girl that it is certain that he will find' presupposes 'It is certain that he will find a girl'. Since preceding conjoined sentences act like presuppositions, (7) reduces to (7'), which reduces to (6).
5 As in (6b), (10b) becomes grammatical if 'if you find one' is added, but remains ungrammatical if 'in any event' or 'regardless' is added. See footnote 3 above.
6 As is well-known, *believe* is non-intensional in the sense that the intension of the whole is not a function of the intension of its parts, since one may not believe distant logical consequences of one's conscious beliefs. Thus, strictly speaking, one should not be able to use a possible world semantics for *believe*. However, if principle (8) is correct then a possible world semantics will be necessary due to the facts of (15) and (17) below. My feeling is that we should extend the normal concept of a possible world semantics to handle *believe* to permit impossible worlds. Instead of a world being equivalent to a maximal consistent set of sentences, certain types of inconsistency might be permitted, and the set of sentences limited to a nonmaximal set. For a system in which this is done, see Tinnon, in preparation.

Inconsistent beliefs pose problems, but no more so for *believe* than for, say, *order*, a generally tamer modal operator. Inconsistent beliefs, such as (i) are paralleled by impossible orders such as (ii).

(i)   Sam believes that he'll find a round square.
(ii)   I order you to find a round square.

If *order* is to have a semantics along the lines given in (Chellas, 1969), where, corresponding to each order, there is a set of 'possible' worlds in which the order is carried out, this cannot be the null set in cases like (ii), since the following sentences have different meanings and, so require different truth conditions.

(iii)   I order you to find a round square, sell it, and give me the profits.
(iv)   I order you to find a round square, sell it, and give the profits to charity.

Both orders are impossible to carry out, but they are different orders. It should be noted incidentally that the same problem arises in the case of definite descriptions. Does (v) denote a 'possible individual'?

(v)   The man who found a round square.

Do (vi) and (vii) denote different possible individuals?

(vi)   The man who found a round square, sold it, and kept the profits.
(vii)   The man who found a round square, sold it, and gave the profits to charity.

It seems to me that it might make sense to speak of the man in (vi) as being selfish and of the man in (vii) as being charitable, if such men could exist. Be this as it may, the problem of inconsistent beliefs is no worse than problems encountered elsewhere.

7 With respect to the claim that *may* could never be a lexical representation for atomic predicates POSSIBLE and REQUIRE, Guy Carden has brought to my attention the following citation in the OED:

Law. In the interpretation of statutes, *may = shall* or *must*. 1728.
'For *may* in the Case of a public Officer is tantamount to *shall*'. 1728.

Carden also cites cases where a master says to a servant 'You may go', which can be a command, not a simple granting of permission. The issue raised is whether such cases constitute evidence against the claim that *may* can never be a lexical representation for atomic predicates POSSIBLE and REQUIRE. I think the answer is no. The above cases seem to me to arise from certain culture-specific conversational laws. In many cultures, including many British and American subcultures, politeness and civility require that persons with the power to give orders 'soften' them whenever possible. When a school-teacher says 'It would be nice if you opened the window, Johnny', she is giving a softened order, not just making a statement about one of the things that would be nice. But this does not mean that the logical form of 'it would be nice if S' is 'ORDER (I, you, S)'. It simply means that certain cultures have conversational laws, whereby a statement as to what would give the speaker pleasure is to be construed in certain situations as a request or command to do what is necessary to bring that about. Similarly, certain cultures have conversational laws whereby the granting of permission under certain circumstances is to be construed as a command. When a master says 'you may go' to his servant, he is giving an order without literally giving an order, and such 'restraint' is taken to indicate civility and deference to one's servants. After all, 'You may go' is the order of a genteel master, not of a barbarian. In such cultures, it would be appropriate for a servant to reply 'Thank you, sir' to 'You may go', though not to 'Get out of here'. In the former case, he would be recognizing the master's deference to him, while in the latter case he would either be making a sardonic remark or showing masochism. It is interesting that the case cited by the OED involves 'a public Officer', that is, a constable, sheriff, etc. The above quotation actually puts in writing the content of the implicature. It specifies that when a constable says 'You may stand aside', that is to be taken as an order, punishable by law if you violate it. It should be clear that the cases cited by Carden involve culture-specific conversational implicatures, and so are irrelevant to the claim made above.

Section IX–A

[1] For a fuller discussion see (Lakoff, in press).

[2] Thus there are different inferences that can be drawn from (7a) and (7b). For instance, it does not follow from (7b) that Sam sliced any bagel carefully. He may have done a careless job on all to them. This is not true of (7a). Consequently, (7b) is compatible with

        a. Sam sliced some of the bagels carelessly.

while (7a) is not compatible with (a).

Section IX–B

[1] It should be noted that 'fascinating' and 'interesting' also act like universal and existential quantifiers with respect to Horn's hypothesis that qualifying expressions must go in the direction of greater universality.
  Compare

(i)   a.   Some students are striking, if not all.
               b. *All students are striking, if not some.
(ii)   a.   That claim is interesting, if not fascinating.
               b. *That claim is fascinating, if not interesting.

Section IX–C

[1] For a discussion of propositional functions of the form (2), see (Jeffrey, 1967, p. 130ff).

Section IX–D

[1] I am assuming here the concept of 'counterpart' as discussed in (Lewis, 1968).

Section IX–E

[1] These facts were discovered by McCawley and myself.

Section IX–F

[1] This technique is discussed at length in David Kaplan's 'What is Russell's Theory of Definite Descriptions?' UCLA mimeo, 1967. A technique of this sort was discussed earlier in Lambert, 1962.

[2] Such sentences were first brought to my attention by Donald Forman.

Section X

¹ Actually, Scott's notion of logical elegance in some cases is reminiscent of the linguist's notion of a significant generalization. For example, Scott (1967) defines a general binding operator, *$* (for quantifiers and description operators), and a general equivalence predicate, *e* (for ↔ and =), so that he can state a single general axiom for substitution of identicals that will apply to both terms and formulas.

DANA SCOTT (ED.)*

SEMANTICAL ARCHAEOLOGY: A PARABLE

ABSTRACT. A somewhat fictionalized account of several interpretations of implication is presented together with comparisons between classical modal, tense, and intuitionistic logics.

Toward the middle of the last century on an obscure, uninhabited island in the eastern Mediterranean, a considerable number of clay fragments were unearthed covered with mysterious symbols. After years of careful cleaning and sorting they were finally rather surprisingly arranged to form several long panels. Even the missing parts were reconstructed by intricate measurements and clever comparisons. Nevertheless, no amount of study yielded their proper decipherment.

Late one evening a young scholar sat alone in his room poring over the photographs and drawings of the panels, pondering the question of their meaning. He had fixed on his wall several examples of the more out-standing recurrent sequences to be found in the inscriptions; in particular these:

(1) $\alpha\alpha\beta\alpha CCC$,

(2) $\alpha\gamma C\alpha\gamma C\beta\alpha\gamma CCCC$,

(3) $\gamma\alpha C\gamma\beta CC\beta\alpha CC$.

We need not retell here the exciting story, which figured so heavily in all the news reports, of how he came *first* to reverse the order of the symbols, *then* to make the very ingenious substitution of $\supset$ for C and p, q, r for α, β, γ, and *finally* to discover the necessary, though far from obvious, change of word order which produced:

(1′) $[[[p \supset q] \supset p] \supset p]$,

(2′) $[[[[r \supset p] \supset q] \supset [r \supset p]] \supset [r \supset p]]$,

(3′) $[[p \supset q] \supset [[q \supset r] \supset [p \supset r]]]$.

Rather, we shall be more interested in this paper in the less dramatic problem of *interpretation*.

It goes without saying that the first idea occurring to everyone (after

Davidson and Harman (eds.), Semantics of Natural Language, 666–674. *All rights reserved*
Copyright © 1972 *by D. Reidel Publishing Company, Dordrecht-Holland*

the most difficult part of the task had already been done) was that these curious sequences of symbols represented *logical truths*. This was an especially appealing hypothesis in view of the well-known traits of a related and still existing people on a nearby island. They had preserved over the centuries a rudimentary logic and had indeed asserted the general correctness of principles similar to (1)–(3). This fact was noted for the first time by an anthropological field worker, who lived for some years among the tribe, a warlike and unpleasant group. One day he had occasion to enquire of his informant just what he meant by *implication*. The man at once became astonishingly angry and started to jump around excitedly, shouting: "What do you mean, what do I mean? Implication *is* implication! Have you no concept of the *true* and the *false*?" Somehow it was clear that the anthropologist had stumbled upon a highly touchy point of tribal religion, but the heated retort did serve to communicate some clue to the unhappy investigator. As he was later able to show in his thesis, this hard-headed philosophy of the tribe which demanded that every statement must either be true or false leads directly to a logic that can be interpreted by *truth tables* – or at least he showed that the interpretation agreed most favorably with the available data. Furthermore, he thought he was even able to identify occurrences of truth tables in some of the more elaborate punched-card work of the tribe, but unfortunately the manuals describing this handicraft were never shown to outsiders.

It is such a pity that the young man who originally deciphered the panels died so early (from lack of central heating some say) before he had a chance to complete his labors. We are, however, able to follow his reasoning about the proper interpretation of the inscriptions quite well from the notebooks he left. It seems that the island people (already extinct in classical times) were well known from legends to be sweet, reasonable, tolerant, and highly theoretical – the apparent causes of their downfall. Before the disastrous wars, they had travelled widely and collected vast quantities of information. The site where the panels were found was apparently (and this was reasonably confirmed by later digs) the *university library*. The panels themselves were decorative in nature and obviously commemorated their outstanding achievements in pure logic. What our young scholar noted at once was that examples of both *valid* and *invalid* principles were given. Thus (2') and (3') occurred on the positive side, while (1') was on the negative side. This discovery, of course, ruled out the straightforward truth-table interpretation familiar from the neighboring warlike tribe leaving a serious puzzle.

With a brilliant stroke of insight our scholar suggested that by virtue of the islanders' interests it was most likely that they had developed a theory of *universal implication* applicable to various situations. He thus took as an hypothesis the underlying notion of *situation* and demonstrated how certain laws of material implication *fail* for the corresponding strict implication. And this was his remarkable explanation of the panels.

As you can imagine this piece of work was considered a paradigm of scholarship for a long time, but sad to relate it was eventually *disproved*. You see, the reconstructions of the missing parts of the panels were too *conjectural*. Thus, after some more fragments were unearthed, the formula (2) mentioned above was found to have been actually on the *negative* side. Further investigation also showed that the two formulae:

(4) $\alpha\alpha C\beta C$
(5) $\alpha\beta C\alpha C$

were respectively positive and negative. Now this last finding (which, by the way, would be written:

(4') $[q \supset [p \supset p]],$
(5') $[p \supset [q \supset p]],$

in modern notation) did not at all conflict with the famous interpretation, but the fact about (2) was *fatal* to the theory. The sensation caused by the announcement of this discovery at the international congress will long be remembered.

It will probably be helpful at this point to spell out some of the details of this interpretation. We recall from two-valued logic the well-known method of Venn diagrams. We specify first a certain convenient universal set V and interpret a proposition p as corresponding to a subset $P \subseteq V$, the set of all elements of V for which the proposition holds. The usual connectives, then, correspond to simple operations on sets; in particular, the material implication $[p \supset q]$ corresponds to the set-theoretical combination

$$(V \sim P) \cup Q.$$

Under this correspondence, a *valid* compound proposition is one whose corresponding set-theoretical combination works out to be V no matter which sets $P, Q, \ldots$, etc. are used for the interpretation of the atomic propositions $p, q \ldots$.

So much for material implication. The universal implication we have in mind for explaining the panels is defined quite differently. Supposing the elements of V to represent situations, we say that an implication $[p \supset q]$ can be regarded as true in the *present* situation if, and only if, for *arbitrary* situations in which p is true, q is always true. In other words, we must take a more general, less provincial view of the meaning of implication. More precisely, in terms of the corresponding sets we define an operation $\Rightarrow$ as follows:

$$(P \Rightarrow Q) = \begin{cases} V & \text{if } P \subseteq Q, \\ \emptyset & \text{otherwise,} \end{cases}$$

where $\emptyset$ denotes the empty subset of V. It is the strict use of $\emptyset$ that distinguishes this notion from material implication. One may now check in detail that (2), (3), (4) are valid under this interpretation, while (1) and (5) are not.[1]

We need not catalogue here the endless list of artificial attempts to save the interpretation, for, several months later, a most satisfactory solution was proposed by one of the outstanding Japanese scholars in the field. He reminded us of the danger in giving a too 'Western' interpretation to the islanders' view of logic. (Note for example that they wrote from right to left!) He demonstrated by reference to the many sundials that had been newly dug up their overriding preoccupation with *time*. Moreover, he showed beyond a doubt that the site where the panels were discovered was a *grammar school* (in the older sense of the term) and *not* a university library at all. With this refined information at his disposal he was able to put forward a new interpretation: the meaning of implication had nothing to do with varying situations but was influenced by ideas of *tense*. More specifically, as the islanders were for the most part easy going, it seemed reasonable to read the implication in the *present progressive tense*. We might say something such as: *it is being the case that p implies q*, but it is rather difficult to translate into a western tongue like English.

Inasmuch as this informal description of the interpretation may not be too clear, I should like to interpose here the mathematical formulation. The change in point of view over the previous interpretation has replaced the rather unknown set V by the set T of *times* (which we can surely identify with the set of *all* real numbers.) Now we imagine the truth value of a proposition varying as a function of time $t \in T$, and then instead of functions we represent (the truth-value meaning of) a proposition by the subset $P \subseteq T$ of times at which the proposition p is true. The interpretation of implication (which we shall again write as $(P \Rightarrow Q)$ for lack of a better symbol) can be given as follows: $t \in (P \Rightarrow Q)$ (that is, *the implication is true at time t*) if and only if there is some nonzero interval I *around* t, such that *for all* $t' \in I$, *if* $t' \in P$, *then* $t' \in Q$. That this implication is related to the previous universal implication is clear, but it is certainly more subtle. By an *interval around t* we can understand the set of all t' with $s \leqslant t' \leqslant u$, where s and u are real numbers such that $s < t < u$. The reason for calling this tensed implication *progressive* is that, for it to be true at a certain time, the ordinary material implication must be progressively true starting from some time in the past and going through to some time in the future. It is not so difficult to prove that formulae (3) and (4) are tautological (in the new sense, of course); while (1), (2) and (5) are not.

Despite the charming ingenuity and well-reasoned character of the Japanese hypothesis, I find it now my sober duty to report to you that it is wrong – or at least requires extensive revision. The modern techniques of radioactive dating have shown that the panels were inadvertantly *misassembled*. After rearrangement of some unfortunately interchangeable parts, I can tell you from my own examination of them in the museum that (5) must definitely be counted on the *positive* side. So again a seemingly water-tight theory is discredited.

If you care to try to rescue the Japanese interpretation, let me call to your attention some other facts that have recently come to light. Excavation at the temple has disclosed an underground storehouse containing religious scrolls amazingly well preserved in sealed urns. It seems that at a certain period there was a crisis in religious belief causing wide-spread dissatisfaction due, no doubt, to the mounting pressures from aggressive enemies. In order to save the situation and to justify his foreign policy, the king (who was also the high priest) had a divine revelation: *there is no beginning and no end*. All the ancient sacred texts were at once sealed up in the urns and new ones were speedily supplied. Fortunately for us the scribe who was responsible for the sealed files wrote in his spare time a history of the crisis, which he also deposited in one of the urns.

Now you may have difficulty in appreciating the influence of this change in dogma on logic, but the impact would have been very soon felt in the grammar schools. In the case of our panels – so the theory goes – some of them had to be taken down and replaced by fresh ones, because formerly valid principles could no longer be considered sound. (Note that this accounts very nicely for the difference in dates of the panels.) Now in order not to shock the people too much, the transition would have had to have been prepared rather carefully. In the case of logical reasoning the following fascinating point was made: *nothing, after all, really happens instantaneously.* Thus the new dogma is not all that surprising. To use a modern example: when you turn on the electric light, you may *think* it lights instantaneously, but it does not. It takes a moment for the filament to warm up. In turning the switch, you may *think* you did it instantaneously, but you did not. It took some turning to get it to move. And so on. Thus, since the propositions that apply to important matters are of a *positive character* (something *is* burning, something *is* turning, and the like), it follows that at any moment at which they are true there will be a whole *interval* around that moment at all times of which the same proposition is also true. This is the correct scientific explanation of the dogma about no beginning and no end. One may now check for himself that of (1)–(5), when they are applied just to the *dogmatically meaningful* propositions, only (3), (4), (5) are valid, while (1) and (2) are not. In this way the tense-logic hypothesis is preserved. (I am sorry that I do not have the space here to show how the dogma was applied to foreign policy.)

Workable as it is, I cannot express personal satisfaction with the revised Japanese interpretation. Maybe it is just too intricate to be convincing. My own hypothesis is quite different: We should not forget that according to the otherwise reliable heroic epics, the islanders originally came from the mainland. Left behind were half the tribe who after many hardships found their way to the far northwest coast. Toughened by their trials, they did not die out at all but eventually became the leading business people of the area. This is most fortunate for historical research, because their records are much better preserved than those of the extinct islanders. This makes it possible to reconstruct many of the beliefs and attitude they carried with them from their homeland.

One aspect of their ancient philosophy that has always impressed me is embodied in the saying: *if you tell me something can be done, you've got to show me how* (as rendered in my own rough translation). It may be that the generally carefree existence of the islanders tended to deemphasize such ideals, but I have found many similar references in the urn scrolls. Now my theory has it that such attitudes have a thoroughgoing effect on one's logic, and I shall now attempt to produce thereby a reconstruction of the meaning of implication. Consider the problem of establishing $[p \supset q]$. There may be many ways of doing it. At the moment we may not know whether p is true, but we do have some idea of the many ways in which its truth might be established. If we are going to claim that $[p \supset q]$ is correct, we had best exhibit a definite *connection* from p to q – otherwise we shall never be able to convince any of these tribesmen. What to do? Well, why not produce a method that *transforms* any means of establishing p *into* a means of establishing q. That will certainly convince everyone.

A mathematical formulation can also be supplied for this interpretation. We call a means of establishing a proposition a *construction* for that proposition, and associate with the proposition the *set* of all constructions which establish it. Suppose P is associated with p, and Q with q. What will be associated with $[p \supset q]$? (Again let us call the set $(P \Rightarrow Q)$.) In view of the above intuitive discussion, we could try to define $(P \Rightarrow Q)$ as the set of *all* functions defined on P taking values in Q. (In mathematical notation this is often written as Q^P.)

By way of example consider the principle of the syllogism (3). Now the set

$$S = ((P \Rightarrow Q) \Rightarrow ((Q \Rightarrow R) \Rightarrow (P \Rightarrow R)))$$

seems somewhat complicated, but it can be easily analyzed. Suppose $f \in (P \Rightarrow Q)$, so we know it is a function. We wish to transform it into something we might call

$$\tau(f) \in ((Q \Rightarrow R) \Rightarrow (P \Rightarrow R)).$$

How to define this $\tau(f)$? Well, it must be a function. Suppose $g \in (Q \Rightarrow R)$. We must then have

$$\tau(f)(g) \in (P \Rightarrow R)$$

But how to define $\tau(f)(g)$? Well again, it must be a function. Suppose $x \in P$. We must finally have

$$\tau(f)(g)(x) \in R.$$

How to define it? Easy:

$$\tau(f)\,(g)\,(x)=g(f(x)),$$

as anyone can see. Since we know the sets over which f, g, x range, the above equation defines $\tau \in S$ rigorously. This example demonstrates the naturalness of the interpretation.

What is significant in the example of the syllogism is that $\tau \in S$ was defined *without* reference to the characters of the elements of P, Q, R. That is, we established (3) according to the interpretation on the basis of *form* alone. That is why it is a valid principle of logic. Similarly (and more simply) we can establish (4) and (5). But this is *not* the case with (1) and (2). To reject (1), take Q as a *two*-element set and P as a *five*-element set which results by adjoining *three* new elements to Q; thus $Q \subseteq P$. Consider a mapping $f \in (P \Rightarrow Q)$. Now *two* of the three new elements of P must map into the *same* element of Q. This rule defines a function $F \in ((P \Rightarrow Q) \Rightarrow P)$ where $F(f)$ is the element of Q just described. Note that this function F was defined with reference only to the *division* of P into its two parts (viz. Q and $P \sim Q$.) Hence, the function F is *invariant* under permutations of the elements *within* the two parts. Now suppose we had a general method of establishing (1). Then we would have a function

$$\tau \in (((P \Rightarrow Q) \Rightarrow P) \Rightarrow P)$$

invariant under *all* permutations of P and Q (without reference to the parts). Therefore $\tau(F)$ would be invariant (at least) with respect to permutations that *do* respect the division into parts. But consider that either $\tau(F) \in Q$ or $\tau(F) \in P \sim Q$. The two-element part and the three-element part can be permuted *at will*. Thus $\tau(F)$ is *not* invariant. In this way (1) is shown to be *invalid*. You may feel that this argument is too complicated, but if I may, I wish to remind you of the fallacy of considering the pre-classical peoples incapable of reason. Nor should one be misled by the quaint forms into which they sometimes cast their proofs.

Needless to say, I feel that my own interpretation has a certain purity not found in the Japanese interpretation. But I would be dishonest if I did not tell you that it has been *proved* that the principles valid in the two interpretations are *exactly the same*.[2] In other words, no mere collection of data can ever distinguish between them in the same way we rejected the older interpretations. Until we find the missing grammar books that explain exactly how the islanders read their implications, the two interpretations, based on such different approaches, will have to remain hypothetical.

In conclusion it may be of interest to note that a school of thought has recently sprung up which considers *all* of (1), (2), (4) and (5) invalid and only permits (3)! The multifarious historical and psychological considerations that have led to this remarkable opinion are too complex to recount here. It may be remarked, however, that *no* substantial *semantical* evidence has ever been produced in support of this hypothesis, a circumstance which detracts considerably from an otherwise carefully developed theory.[3] Therefore it does not seem warranted at the moment to doubt the reasonableness of the conclusions reported here. Nevertheless it must always be borne in mind that future revelations may require a complete reassessment.

Princeton University

REFERENCES

An earlier version of this paper was read at a symposium sponsored by the Olivetti Company in Milan, Italy, in October 1968. The proceedings of that symposium, *Linguaggi nella società e nella tecnica*, Edizione di Comunità, Milan 1970, contain a longer paper from which the present one is extracted, 'The Problem of Giving Precise Semantics for Formal Languages'.

* It was through a very curious chain of circumstances that the present manuscript came into my possession. I am afraid that at the moment I am not at liberty to reveal its true authorship. Hence, if one wishes, he may regard it purely as a piece of fiction. This explains the title: I have called it a *parable* under the somewhat old fashioned idea (which is fast losing ground these days) that even a work of fiction can convey a message. The original title of the paper was, simply: 'Semantical Archaeology'.

[1] For more information on this and other kinds of implication, see A. N. Prior, *Formal Logic*, 2nd ed., Clarendon Press, Oxford, 1962.

[2] For this result one must combine theorems of A. Tarski and H. Läuchli. Cf. A. Tarski, 'Der Aussagenkalkül und die Topologie', *Fundamenta Mathematicae* **31** (1938) 103–134; reprinted in translation in *Logic, Semantics, Mathematics* (ed. by J. H. Woodger), Clarendon Press, Oxford, 1955. Also, H. Läuchli, 'An Abstract Notion of Realizability for Which Intuitionistic Predicate Calculus Is Complete' to appear in the proceedings of the Buffalo Conference 1968. The idea of the interpretation through transformations is due to Läuchli though it derives from the well-known work by Kleene on intuitionism.

[3] For more details and references see A. R. Anderson, 'Some Open Problems Concerning the System E of Entailment', *Acta Philosophica Fennica* **16** (1963) 7–18.

HECTOR-NERI CASTAÑEDA

ON THE SEMANTICS OF THE OUGHT-TO-DO

I

Deontic concepts like *ought, right, obligation, forbidden*, and *permissible* have benefited from the philosophically exciting work in the semantics of modal concepts done by Kanger[1], Hintikka[2], Kripke[3], Montague[4] and others. Their semantics illuminates both the topic and the contribution of the standard axiomatic approach to deontic logic: the topic is what philosophers used to call the Ought-to-be. On the other hand, the non-standard approach represented by early axiomatic deontic systems of ours deals with the Ought-to-do. Thus, rather than competing with the standard approach to deontic logic, our non-standard approach complements it. This can, however, be seen only by providing our non-standard approach with a minimum of semantical foundations. This is precisely what this essay attempts to do. We shall also provide a rationale for our non-standard semantical system by formulating some proto-philosophical data that both guide the development of the system and serve as tests of adequacy for it. In fact, our concern is primarily philosophical, not technical.

There are, of course, important general philosophical reasons for developing divergent systems: (i) our appreciation of standard systems is enhanced by contrasting them with non-standard ones, and (ii) our understanding of a set of concepts improves by seeing them in different lights.

1. *Ought-To-Be and Ought-To-Do*

The standard approach to deontic logic conceives of deontic expressions ('it is obligatory that', 'it is permissible that', 'it is forbidden that', 'it is wrong that', 'it is right that', 'it ought to be the case that', etc.) as expressing operators that have the same domain and range: the domain of propositions (or states of affairs) and properties. Linguistically, deontic expressions are, in the standard approach, operators whose domain and range are both the domain of sentential forms and sentences, i.e., the total

Davidson and Harman (eds.), Semantics of Natural Language, 675–694. All rights reserved

set of all well-formed formulas (wffs). Thus, on the standard approach if
D is a deontic expression and *f* is a wff, *Df* is a wff of the same general kind
f is. Semantically, the beautiful idea is that *Df* is true in a given possible
world *w* if and only if *f* is true (or false, depending on *D*) in some (or
every) possible world which is ideal with respect to *W*. Here a possible
world *W'* is ideal with respect to *W* if and only if all obligations belonging
to *W* both are also obligations belonging to *W'* and are fulfilled in *W'*.
This idea has been both explained in detail and put to important uses by
Hintikka in 'Deontic Logic and Its Philosophical Morals' (presented in a
symposium on deontic logic at the meeting of the Western Division of the
American Philosophical Association in Cleveland, Ohio, in May, 1969).
A tremendously valuable distinction Hintikka makes is that between
logical consequence and deontic consequence.

The intuitive idea behind this standard semantical analysis of the truth-
conditions for 'It ought to be the case that *f*' is straightforward and insightful: what makes our world have genuine, non-empty obligations is
nothing but its falling short of an ideal in some respects, i.e., its having
something false which is (or would be) true in an ideal world; since the
realization of certain ideals may prevent others from being realized, we
must consider not only one ideal world but a set of them, not necessarily
arranged in a linear sequence of perfection: there may be alternative roads
to perfection.

The primary contrast in the above conception of deontic logic is the
contrast between what is and what ought to be. The idea of *who* is to
realize the obligation is not considered, so that the approach can handle
very nicely genuinely impersonal statements like "There ought to be no
pain", meant merely to articulate something about the universe, which is
not conceived as an agent but simply as the totality of all existents and all
facts. This impersonal statement tells of what would be a necessary lack in
every universe, and neither attributes responsibility for any action to somebody nor demands any action from anybody: the statement is oriented to
no agents: it has the structure of the statement "It is (would be) desirable
that there were no pain".

Naturally, the sentence 'There ought to be no pain' may very well be
used in ordinary language to formulate a personal, agential statement,
e.g., "God ought to have created no pain". Conversely, the sentence 'God
ought to have created no pain' can express a non-agential statement

attributing some form of desirability or 'oughtness' to the state of affairs or proposition "God created no pain". This non-agential statement may, perhaps, be more naturally expressed by the sentence 'It ought to be the case that God created no pain'. Ordinary sentences can easily be made to express different, though related statements. What matters is that we distinguish the preceding non-agential statement "There ought to be no pain" from the agential statement that attributes to God a duty or obligation, and articulates not merely an ideal creation, but establishes a basis for blaming or praising God for his creation.

In earlier papers I have adopted a non-standard view of deontic logic. That view focuses on the agential ought statements, and is based on a generalization of the common structure underlying all processes of legislating or rule-making, whether they go on continuously in high legislative chambers of nations, or in pompous meetings of legislative bodies of institutions, or in pedestrian discussions of procedures by the members of informal groups or clubs. A formal analysis of the general underlying structure of rule-making, whatever its kind, is this: (i) a framework of facts and laws of nature governing the facts is recognized; (ii) a set β of prescriptions, or commands or imperatives are adopted or endorsed (subject to overriding considerations in cases of conflicts); (iii) the set β limits the freedom of action, i.e., of decision and command, of the agents the commands in β are 'addressed' or directed to. Thus, a piece of rule-making confronts the real world, with all its facts and laws of nature, with other possible practical worlds in which the same facts and laws of nature hold, but different decisions and orders take place: the making of a set of rules is, at bottom, nothing more (on this analysis) than the adoption of a system S_β of alternative *practical* worlds which share both the same facts and the same set β of prescriptions or commands. A contingent prescription or command (with respect to S_β) is one that holds in some worlds but fails to hold in other worlds of S_β. What is obligatory with respect to the legislating or enacting of β, i.e., what is obligatory$_\beta$ is what is 'commanded' in every world of S_β: What is obligatory is, thus, in a sense, what is necessarily prescribed or commanded.

The preceding is a crude statement of the intuition behind our approach to deontic logic. It is non-standard with respect to the ideal-world analysis, yet it, too, has long and respectable roots in the history of philosophy. There is no need to remind anybody of the imperativist analysis of ought-statements or of traditional command analysis of laws. However, it must be clear that the preceding paragraph is not concerned with the analysis of ought-statements themselves, but only with the analysis of the *truth-conditions* of ought-statements.

Now, an important feature of certain deontic statements is that they involve an action and an agent and a demand that the agent do, or fail to do, the action in question. Many an ordinary statement that is apparently agentless demands an action; e.g., "Cars ought to have plates" demands that some agents put plates on cars; it is short for a statement to the effect that people in a relationship R of a certain kind to a car (ownership, usership, managership, etc.) put plates on that car. The statement supports imperatives of the form "If you are R to that car, put plates on it". That statement contrasts very sharply with the agentless statement "There ought to be no pain" discussed above. In short, deontic statements divide neatly into: (i) those that involve agents and actions and support imperatives, and (ii) those that involve states of affairs and are agentless and have by themselves nothing to do with imperatives. The former belong to what used to be called the *Ought-to-do* and the latter to the *Ought-to-be*. Our non-standard approach, then, is not suited for the Ought-to-be; but, we hope, it is adequate for the Ought-to-do.

2. *Proto-Philosophical Data*

We have just demarkated the Ought-to-do as our topic by means of imperatives. Thus, in order to gather data for any theory of the Ought-to-do we must engage in a phenomenological analysis of imperatives, as well, of course, as in a phenomenological analysis of normative or deontic statements.

2.1. *Prescriptions.* We shall call commands, orders, petitions, requests, pieces of advice, entreaties, and suggestions *mandates*. Clearly mandates belong into families. One and the same imperative sentence, e.g., 'Karl, go home at 3 p.m.', may express an order, a command, a piece of advice, a petition, a request, etc. What all these have in common is a structure consisting of a reference to an entity named 'Karl' and the predicative action going-home-at-3-p.m. This structure we shall call a *prescription*. It is like a proposition or statement; but in this simple or atomic case it differs from the corresponding proposition expressed with the sentences 'Karl goes home at 3 p.m.' and 'Karl will go home at 3 p.m.' in the way subject and predicate are related. i.e., in the copulation of the subject and predicate. The *prescriptive copulation,* we shall say, makes of the subject an agent prescriptively considered, and, likewise it makes of the action an action prescriptively considered. The crucial point is that an agent prescriptively considered has a certain asymmetry with respect to the other members of a relation. A clue to this appears in the fact that an indicative (i.e., proposition-expressing) sentence formulating the performance or doing of an action has both a passive and an active counterpart; but there is no such counterpart for an imperative (i.e., prescription-expressing) sentence. For example: we can say either "Paul hit Mary" or "Mary was hit by Paul" asserting the same proposition. But we cannot choose to put the prescription embedded in "Paul, hit Mary" in the passive version "Mary, be hit by Paul".

Complex prescriptions differ from their corresponding propositions ultimately in the different copulation of their atomic constituent prescriptions. Prescriptions, are, then, abstractions from families of mandates that disregard not only the modality of the mandates, (e.g., command, order, suggestion, entreaty), but also the act of issuing and the elements of this act: the time, the place, and the issuer. We shall in our protophilosophical examination represent prescriptions by the clause resulting from imperative sentences by deleting the comma after the agent name; thus, in the above example our prescription is expressed purely by 'Karl go home'.

An important structural feature of prescriptions and mandates is that mixed compounds of prescriptions (or mandates) and propositions are prescriptions (or mandates). Consider, for instance:

(1)   Karl, do the following: if it rains, *close the windows* if and only if the awnings are not up, and if it hails, *turn circulator A on* if and only if circulator B is off.

Evidently, in (1) there are two atomic prescriptions, *Karl close the windows* and *Karl turn circulator A on,* linked by connectives to four propositions, and the whole of (1) is a mandate having at its core a mixed complex prescription. This is an extremely important point. Aside from the imperative prefix of (1) 'Karl, do the following', it is patently clear that the prescriptive clause 'if it rains ... off' is, though an incomplete sentence, a mixed compound. Palpably, the conditioning clauses of (1) need not express states of things or of the weather: they may express *performances* of Karl himself, e.g.,

(2)   Karl, do the following: if you come late, don't close the windows if and only if you-raise-the-awnings, but *do raise the awnings* if it is raining.

Here we see both the proposition "You [Karl] raise the awnings" and the prescription "Karl raise the awnings" *as constituents of the same mandate.* We also see again that ordinary English has a widely applicable mandate operator that yields a *canonical notation* for the expression of a mandate as analyzed into the imperative operator and a prescription: given any clause C formulating a prescription P, where 'a_1', 'a_2', ..., 'a_n' are names or terms referring to the agents referred to in C, then the sentence $\ulcorner a_1, a_2, ..., a_n$, do the following: $C \urcorner$ expresses a mandate whose core is prescription P. For example:

(3)   Paul, Mary and Ted, do the following: if it rains, Paul mow the lawn, and Ted put the sprinkler on; and if it does not rain, Ted open the windows, and Mary paint the window sills.

2.2. *The Parallelism Between Imperative and Indicative Logic.* Philosophers have argued and continue to argue whether mandates have a logic at all, whether they have a two-valued logic, and whether mandates can actually be inferred from other mandates. As far as we can see these disputes are to a large extent verbal disputes. The fact is that mandates do stand to other mandates and propositions in formal relationships holding between (and among) propositions, and the study of mandate formal relationships is of great importance for the philosophy of ethics and of action. How we call them is unimportant. Thus, for convenience, we shall here simply use the customary terminology of logicians in an *extended* sense to cover the mandate and prescriptive relationships.

Now, whether the logic of mandates is two-valued or not is not a purely verbal issue. We must, however, remember that in the case of propositions we find cases which present truth-value gaps and that by some procedures of regimentation we do manage pretty well with a two-valued propositional logic. Likewise, the mere appearance of certain tough cases of mandates and prescriptions is not a proof that a parallel two-valued theory of prescriptive implications won't work well enough. But aside from merely defensive moves, we can marshall an impressive mass of evidence that supports the claim of parallelism between propositional and prescriptional logic. To start with, inferences of the following forms appear sound:

(F1) X, do A
        Therefore, X, don't fail to do A.

(F2) X, don't fail to do A
        Hence, X, do A.

The validity of (F1) and (F2) amounts to the rejection of three values for mandates; clearly 'A' can represent any action whatever simple or complex.

More evidence for the parallelism between propositional and prescriptional logic comes from the fact that the following implication schemata seem to hold:

(F3)   'X, do A' implies 'X, do A and do A'

(F4)   'X, do A and B' implies 'X, do A'

(F5)   'X, don't both do A and fail to do B' implies 'X, don't do both of the following: one, fail to do B and some action C; two, do C and A.'

(F6)   'X, do A' and 'X, don't do both: A and not-B' imply 'X, do B.'

Furthermore, the following connection between schemata is also apparent:

(F7)   If 'X, do A' implies 'X, do B', then the corresponding prescription of the form 'X, don't do both A and not-B' is necessarily (logically) 'binding' on X.

(F1)–(F6) constitute strong evidence of the parallelism between imperative and indicative logic for the reason that (F3)–(F5) correspond to the axioms of, and (F6) to the rule of inference of, a classical two-valued system of propositional logic put forward by J. Barkley Rosser[5]:

A1 $p \supset (p \,\&\, p)$
        i.e., $\sim(p \,\&\, \sim(p \,\&\, p))$

A2 $(p \,\&\, q) \supset p$
        i.e., $\sim((p \,\&\, q) \,\&\, \sim p)$

A3 $\sim(p \,\&\, \sim q) \supset \sim(\sim(qr) \,\&\, \sim\sim(rp))$
        i.e., $\sim(\sim(p \,\&\, \sim q) \,\&\, \sim\sim(\sim(qr) \,\&\, \sim\sim(rp)))$
        Modus ponens: from p and $\sim(p \,\&\, \sim q)$ infer q.

The differences between these axioms and (F3)–(F5) are: (i) that axioms

(A1–A3) are wffs of Rosser's system and belong to the object language whereas (F3)–(F5) are the corresponding meta-linguistic statements, oi' that we should consider the object-linguistic counterparts of (F3)–(F5) sn- stead of these; (ii) that the double negations of A3 are missing in (F5). But cherma (F7) erases difference (i) by mapping an implication into a 'valid' spescription. Likewise if we allow the substitution of the equivalents estab- lished by (F1) and (F2), we have, then, the erasure of difference (ii). Hence (F1)–(F7) give us a system virtually isomorphic to Rosser's system. Natu- rally, this isomorphism holds only for the values of the variables 'X', 'A', 'B', and 'C' of (F1)–(F7). Since 'X' can represent any sequence of agents referred to in the atomic prescriptions constituting A and B, the result has a good deal of generality. Nevertheless, we grant that there is no effective way of determining the range of the variables 'A', 'B', and 'C'. All we can say is that the validity of schemata (F1)–(F7) does establish that for a class of actions the logic of mandates is isomorphic to the two-valued logic of propositions. We must, of course, be prepared to encounter in the case of mandates problems analogous to the truth-value gaps well-studied in the case of propositions. But we must also be ready to meet those problems with all the weapons already available in the propositional armory – as well as with new ones that investigation may deliver.

In short, we have excellent support for a two-valued treatment of imperatives, and it is of philosophical importance to develop the two- valued point of view in detail. This is so, even if merely to discover the precise junctures at which it really breaks down.

2.3. *Deontic Statements.* One of the most striking things about the Ought- to-do is, as we pointed out in Section 1, the fact that deontic statements are intimately linked to imperatives. To begin with, whatever is mandated (i.e., commanded, ordered, requested, etc.) is said to be obligatory, for- bidden, wrong, permissible, etc. For instance, the imperative sentence (1) above naturally yields deontic sentences by two grammatical transforma- tions: (a) replace the imperative mood and put in its place the subjunctive prescriptional form, by dropping the comma before the main verb; (b) prefix to the result a deontic prefix, for example:

(1d) It is permitted that Karl do the following: if it rains, *close the windows* if and only if the awnings are not up, and if it hails, *turn circulator A on* if and only if circulator B is off.

Phenomenologically, the structural connection revealed here is this:

D°.1.   Deontic operators of the Ought-to-do type (of course, not perhaps those of the Ought-to-be type) are operators on prescriptions.

Furthermore, the prescriptions in the range of a deontic operator can be atomic or compound, as in the case of (1d). Now, it seems that deontic statements of the Ought-to-do type are themselves not prescriptions. The verb 'Ought' does not even have an imperative form, and expressions like 'Be obligated to do A' or 'Be forbidden to do A' sound nonsensical. Of course, one can perform actions that bring about obligations, so that it is sense to advice or order "Make it the case that it is obligatory that John and Mary stay home after 6 p.m." But here the imperative does not demand the performance of the act of *being obligatory*: there is no such act; the mandate demands the doing of an action that *causes* an obligation to obtain.

Indeed, deontic statements are statements or propositions. Thus:

D°.2.   Deontic operators of the Ought-to-do type yield propositions or statements.

An immediate consequence of D°.1 and D°.2 is

D°.3.   Deontic operators of the Ought-to-do type are not iterative.

This consequence provides a partial confirmation of D°.1 and D°.2 since iterations of deontic prefixes are: either (i) nonsensical, or (ii) stuttering repetitions, or (iii) the iterated prefixes are not meant in the same sense, as 'It is obligatory that it is obligatory that everybody pay his income tax' clearly shows.[6]

D°.3 does not, however, preclude a deontic operator from applying to a prescription having a deontic statement as a constituent as in "It is obligatory that Paul do the following: do A, if it is obligatory that he do A."

2.4. *Overriding Ought and Prima Facie Oughts.* It is a commonplace that there are many types of deontic statements, that there are conflicts of duties, so that what we ought to do everything being considered is not what we ought to do given certain considerations.[7] Thus, what we advise somebody to do is not an action that we believe he ought to do, but one that we believe he ought to do above else, everything being considered. That is,

D°.4.　　While the overriding ought in "X ought to do A" may be said to imply or fully support the imperative "*X*, do *A*", the prima-facie oughts in conflict do not imply or fully support their corresponding imperative.

Now, whatever the considerations may be which determine obligations, it is phenomenologically clear that those considerations, by determining a set of deontic statements of the form "It is obligatory that *A*", determine also a set of prescriptions, namely, the values of '*A*' in that form. Likewise, they also determine a set of mandates, to wit, those which have the preceding prescriptions at their core. Thus, formally we can represent a set of deontically relevant considerations by the set of prescriptions they determine. Formally, we shall identify different sets of considerations if they necessarily determine the same set of prescriptions.

2.5. *Ought-to-do and Can*. Philosophers continue to debate whether Ought implies Can or not. The truth of the matter seems to be that there are several uses of the deontic words in some of which Ought does, and in others Ought does not, imply Can, especially when the Can in question is not a logical Can. Here we choose to be concerned just with those deontic statements of the Ought-to-do subtype that imply Can. In particular, we adopt:

D°.5.　　"It is obligatory that *X* do *A*" implies that the prescription "*X* to do *A*" is consistent.

D°.5. is a natural elucidation of the idea that Ought implies Can, which is often put thus: "It is obligatory that *X* do *A*" implies "It is possible for *X* to do *A*".

There is one case that deserves special analysis. We all agree that "It is obligatory that everybody who has a wife bring her to the meeting" implies neither "Everybody has a wife" nor "Someone has a wife". But consider

(4)　　It is obligatory that someone (or other) who has a wife bring her to the meeting.

Does (4) imply "(There is) someone [in the universe of agents in question]

(who) has a wife"? The answers run in both directions. And, again, the truth of the matter is that the deontic words have many different senses or uses, so that for some statements expressed with the sentence (4) the implication holds, and for others it does not. However, we can provide a criterion for distinguishing two such sets of senses or uses. In the senses or uses in which Ought implies Can, (4) does imply "Someone has a wife", for if nobody among the agents in question has a wife nobody can fulfill the obligation established by (4). Naturally, the philosophers' job is, in fact, to elucidate the structure of our conceptual frameworks without prejudice: thus, we must note that

> D°.6.　　For some families of deontic concepts, statements of the form "It is obligatory that p and A", imply the corresponding statement that p, where 'p' stands for a proposition and 'A' for a prescription.

2.6. *The Good-Samaritan 'Paradox'*.[8] It is normally held that a principle like the following governs deontic statements:

> (P)　　If X's doing A implies Y's doing B, then
> (1) that it is obligatory$_i$ for X to do A implies that it is obligatory$_i$ for Y to do B, and
> (2) that it is wrong$_i$ for Y to do B implies that it is wrong$_i$ for X to do A.

Now, in a standard approach to deontic logic that allows mixtures of deontic and non-deontic statements, the antecedent of (P) is interpreted as the meta-statement that 'X does (perform) A" implies "Y does (perform) B". And this has given rise to the so-called good-samaritan paradox. Consider the case of Arthur, whose duty is to bandage a man, his employer, whom he will kill a week hence. Since "Arthur bandages a man whom he will kill a week hence" does imply 'Arthur will kill a man a week hence", it is taken that by (P) it follows that Arthur has a duty to kill a man. If there is a paradox here, then solutions based on differences of agents and times are beside the mark: here Arthur is both the bandager and the killer, and the time of the killing is later than that of the bandaging, but, obviously, it can be earlier than the latter.

However, in the present case there is really no paradox, even if (P) is interpreted to have an antecedent about the implication between two performance statements: Keeping scope distinctions suffices to dispel the paradox here. The sentence 'Arthur has a duty to bandage a man he will kill' really means:

(5a) $(\exists x)$ (a will kill x & a has a duty to bandage x),

and not

(5b) $(\exists x)$ (a has a duty to bandage x & kill x).

Thus, it does not follow from (5a) by (P) (1) that Arthur has a duty to kill, since the part "a has a duty to bandage x" of (5a) implies nothing about killing.

In general, several of the cases that have been proposed as variants of the good-samaritan 'paradox' can be analyzed as involving confusions on the scope of the deontic operators at issue, or of a definite description: but not all. A beautiful case that cannot be analyzed away by scope distinctions is Åqvist's 'paradox' of the Knower, in "Good Samaritans, Contrary-to-Duty Imperatives, and Epistemic Obligations", pages 366ff.[8] Consider the case of a man, say Jones, whose job is to know what is done wrong by other people in a certain office. Suppose that Smith did A, which is wrong by the rules of the office. Thus, "It is wrong$_j$ that Smith do A" and "Jones ought$_j$ to know that Smith (does) did A" are true. Since "Jones knows that Smith (does) did A" implies "Smith (does) did A", by (P) (1) interpreted as we have been doing, we have, then, "Smith ought$_j$ to do (have done) A", which contradicts the hypothesis that it is wrong$_j$ for Smith to do A. Here the scope distinction does not help.

For one thing, there is apparently no satisfactory analysis of knowledge so that we can take, in the model of (5a), some conjuncts of the analysis outside the scope of the deontic operator $ought_j$. But suppose that we can analyze "Jones knows that p" as "p and Jones believes that p and Jones has evidence for that p". Then the scope analysis patterned after (5a), of "Jones ought$_j$ to know that Smith did A" yields "Smith did A and Jones ought$_i$ to both believe that Smith did A and have evidence for this". But the fact is that a duty to know is not the same as the duty to believe and have evidence: surely one can have the latter without having the former.

In general, there are psychological attitudes that one must acquire, or psychological acts that one must perform that imply that something that happens to be wrong has occurred. Such cases give rise to troubles for (P). The trouble is compounded in those cases in which there is no purely psychological content, that can be extracted, in the way believing is the pure psychological core of knowing. For instance, there is no purely psychological core that can be really obligatory when one is, allegedly incorrectly, said to be obligated to repent, to lament, or to apologize for, having done some action A which it is wrong$_i$ to do.

Åqvist's proposed solution consisted of distinguishing different types of duties. But his proposal was shown by Lawrence Powers, in 'Some Deontic Logicians', pp. 384–388, not to be at all adequate. Of course, we do not object to distinguishing types of duties: we have done so in our phenomenological examination of conflicts of duties. But we do not have to resort to this to solve the Knower paradox. In fact, we have already found, independently of (P), that deontic operators apply to prescriptions. Thus, we can recognize in (P) a prescriptive principle, not a propositional one, namely:

D°.7.   If prescription A implies prescription B, then
  (1) "It is obligatory$_i$ that A" implies "It is obligatory$_i$ that B," and
  (2) "It is wrong$_i$ that B" implies "It is wrong$_i$ that A".

Now, D°.7 provides an immediate, sharp and unified solution to all the forms of the good-samaritan 'paradox'. In Åqvist's form we have:

(6)   It is obligatory$_j$ that Jones know that Smith did A,

which contains the prescription "Jones know that Smith did A". This prescription implies neither the proposition "Jones knows that Smith did A" nor the prescription "Jones do A". Hence, from (6) by D°.7 we cannot derive that it is obligatory$_j$ [or wrong$_j$] for Smith to do (have done) A. Thus, we may properly and consistently accept that the system of rules governing the tasks of all the people in Jones' office, including Jones, are duties in exactly the same sense, and even of the same type.

3. *A Basic Language for the Ought-To-Do.*

We pass now to describe the syntactical structure of a pure deontic language for the Ought-to-do. Actually we start by constructing a large number of such syntactical structures, one for each prima facie obligatoriness and one for the overriding ought. These languages will be called D_{i*}, for $i = 1, 2, 3, \ldots$, where D_{i*} is the language of the pure overriding ought. We shall call the union of these languages D^*.

Primitive signs: individual constants; individual variables, predicate constants; the connectives '$\sim$' and '&'; the underlying sign '$\_$' to indicate prescriptivity; the sign 'O_i' of oughtness$_i$ or obligatoriness$_i$, and '(' and ')'.

Rules of formation: We use Quine's corners implicitly throughout. Let the small letters 'p', 'q', 'r', range over indicatives (i.e., expressions of propositions or propositional functions); let the capital letters 'A', 'B', 'C' range over prescriptives (i.e., expressions of prescriptions or prescriptional functions); let 'p^*' and 'q^*' range over both indicatives and prescriptives; let 'Z' range over predicates and 'x' over individual variables, unless otherwise specified.

(a) *Indicatives* are sequences having one of the form:

(1) $Z(x_i, ..., x_i, ..., x_n)$, where Z is an n-adic predicate and each x_i is an individual constant or variable, and no x_i is underlined;

(2) $(\sim p)$;

(3) $(p \ \& \ q)$;

(4) $(x) p$;

(5) $O_i A$;

(b) *Prescriptives* are sequences of signs having one of the following forms:

(1) $Z(x_1, ..., \underline{x}_i, ..., x_n)$, where Z is an n-adic predicate, each x_n if an individual variable or constant, and at least one x_i is underlined (to indicate the agency of x_i);

(2) $(\sim A)$;

(3) $(p^* \ \& \ A)$;

(4) $(A \ \& \ p^*)$;

(5) $(x) A$.

The indicatives and the prescriptives are all the wffs of O_{i*}. We write 'Ax' and '$A\underline{x}$', in the case of a monadic predicate, for '$A(x)$' and '$A(\underline{x})$', respectively. We adopt the customary conventions on parentheses and usual definitions of '$\vee$', '$\supset$', and '$\equiv$'.

We introduce the other deontic terms by means of the following definitions:

DD1. $R_i A = \sim O_i \sim A$ ("It is right$_i$ that A")

DD2. $W_i A = O_i \sim A$ ("It is wrong$_i$ that A")

DD3. $F_i A = \sim O_i A \ \& \ \sim O_i \sim A$ ("It is completely free or optional that A")

We can already see that each D_i^* satisfies some of the proto-philosophical data of Section 2 above: (i) the difference between an atomic prescriptive and its corresponding indicative lies in the copula; (ii) the prescriptive copula assigns to some singular expressions the role of expressing agency; (iii) mixed indicative-prescriptive compounds are imperative; (iv) deontic operators map prescriptives into indicatives; (v) there are no iterations of deontic operators.

We shall call the non-quantified subsystem of D^* and of each D_{i*}, D^{c*} and D_i^{c*} respectively; i.e., D_i^{c*} is D_{i*} without the rules of formation (a) (4) and (b) (5), and similarly for D^{c*}.

4. The Axiomatic Systems O_{i*}

Our non-standard approach has so far been mainly syntactical. Its latest representation[9], consists of the extension of each syntactical structure D_{i*} to an axiomatic system O_{i*}, by adjunction of the following axioms and rules of inference.

Axioms: aside from the axioms for quantification, all wffs having at least one of the following forms are axioms:

01.	p^*, if p^* has the form of a truth-table tautology.	
02a.	$O_iA \supset \sim O_i \sim A$	*Note:* the overriding ought takes as axiom schema 02b
02b.	$O_1A \supset A$	instead of 02a, while the prima facie oughts take 02a in-
03.	$(O_iA \& O_iB) \supset O_i(A \& B)$	stead of 02b; all other axiom
04.	$(p \& O_iA) \supset O_i(p \& A)$	schemata hold for all Oughts-to-do that imply Can, as discussed in Section 2.5.

Rules of inference:
M.P. (modus ponens):
    If $\vdash_i p^*$ and $\vdash_i p^* \supset q^*$, then $\vdash_i q^*$.

DR1. If $\vdash_{ci} A \supset B$, then $\vdash_i O_iA \supset O_iB$.
DR2. If $\vdash_{ci} p \supset A$, then $\vdash_i p \supset O_iA$.
UG.   If $\vdash_i p^*$, $\vdash_i (x)p^*$.

We adopt the usual definitions of 'proof', 'theorem', etc. as well as the customary conventions on brackets. Here '$\vdash_i p^*$' means that p^* is a theorem of the calculus O_{i*}. The non-quantified part of O_{i*} will be called

O_i^{c*}; more precisely, O_i^{c*} is O_{i*} without the axioms of quantification and without rules UG, (a) (4) and (b) (4). We shall write '$\vdash_{ic} p*$' to mean that $p*$ is a theorem of O_i^{c*}.

The preceding axiomatization of propositional deontic logic is consistent and admits of decision procedures, e.g., a transliteration of Quine's procedure for uniform quantification cum propositional variables.[10] It adequately represents the following principles.

Th1. $\vdash_{ic} O_i(A \ \& \ B) \supset O_iA \ \& \ O_iB$

Th2. $\vdash_{ic} O_i(p \ \& \ A) \supset p \ \& \ O_iA$

MT.1.   If a prescriptive $A\underline{x}$ is logically valid, then the corresponding Ax is logically valid.

MT.2. $\sim O_i(A\underline{x} \ \& \sim A\underline{x})$ is logically valid.

MT.3.   Neither $O_i(A\underline{x})$ nor $\sim O_i(A\underline{x})$ entails the indicative Ax.

MT.4.   Neither $O_i(A\underline{x})$ nor $\sim O_i(A\underline{x})$ entails the indicative $\sim Ax$.

5. *Models for the Systems D_{i*}.*

As in Section 3 we continue to refer: (i) to arbitrary wffs of D_{i*}, whether indicative or prescriptive with the asterisked letters '$p*$', '$q*$', and '$r*$'; (ii) to arbitrary indicatives of D_{i*} with the plain letters 'p', 'q' and 'r', and (iii) to arbitrary prescriptives of D_{i*} with the capital letters 'A', 'B', and 'C'.

5.1. O_i^{c*}. A model M for a system D_i^{c*} is an order triple $\langle W_0, \underline{W}, \underline{I} \rangle$, where $\underline{W}$ is a nonempty set of entities called *possible deontic worlds*, or just worlds, for short, W_0 is a member of $\underline{W}$ and is called the *real* or *designated world*, and $\underline{I}$ is a two-argument function that assigns to each pair of a world and a wff of D_i^{c*} just one element of the set $\{1, 2\}$, in accordance with the following rules, where W_j and W_h are members of $\underline{W}$.

R1. $\underline{I}(p*, W_j) = 1$ or 2, if $p*$ is atomic, i.e., $p*$ is a wff of D_{i*} by formation rule (a) (1) or (b) (1).

R2. $\underline{I}(\sim p*, W_j) = 1$, if and only if $\underline{I}(p*, W_j) = 2$; otherwise $\underline{I}(\sim p*, W_j) = 2$.

R3. $\underline{I}((p* \ \& \ q*), W_j) = 1$, if and only if both $\underline{I}(p*, W_j) = 1$ and $\underline{I}(q*, W_j) = 1$; otherwise, $\underline{I}((p* \ \& \ q*), W_j) = 2$.

R4.   If there is a world W_j such that $\underline{I}(p, W_j) = 1$, then for every world W_h: $\underline{I}(p, W_h) = 1$.

R5a. $\underline{I}(O_iA, W_0) = 1$, if and only if for every world W_j in $\underline{W}$ different from W_0: $I(A, W_j) = 1$.

R5b. $\underline{I}(O_iA, W_0) = 1$, if and only if for every world W_j in $\underline{W}$: $\underline{I}(A, W_j) = 1$.

We define: p^* is *valid* in $D_i^{c^*}$, $\vDash_{ic} p^*$, if and only if for every model M, $\underline{I}(p^*, W_0) = 1$, for $\underline{I}$ and W_0 in M. And p^* has a model if and only if for some model M, $\underline{I}(p^*, W_0) = 1$, for $\underline{I}$, and W_0 in M.

It is a simple thing to show that

MT1.   If $\vdash_{ic} p^*$, then $\vDash_{ic} p^*$.

And the proof of the following proceeds along the lines of all proofs of Henkin completeness:

MT2.   If p^* is consistent, p^* has a model.

Outline of proof. By standard procedures it can be shown that the set of wffs of $D_i^{c^*}$ is denumerable and that every consistent set can be extended to a maximal consistent set. Take any maximal consistent set of wffs of $D_i^{c^*}$ that includes p^*, and call it W_0. Take as $\underline{W}$ the set of maximal consistent sets W_j generated from W_0 as follows: every indicative p of W_0 is in W_j, and for every indicative of the form O_iA in W_0, A is in W_j; in the latter case A is also in W_0 if we are dealing with O_1A. We let $\underline{I}$ be the function I such that: (i) $I(p^*, W_j) = 1$ if and only if p^* belongs to W_j, and (ii) $I(p^*, W_j) = 2$ if and only if p^* does not belong to W_j. It is clear from the construction that $\langle W_0, \underline{W}, \underline{I} \rangle$ is a model for p^*.

We have, therefore, from MT1 and MT2, by standard reasoning, that:

MT3. $\vdash_{ic} p^*$, if and only if $\vDash_{ic} p^*$.

5.2. O_{i^*}. The models for the full systems O_{i^*} are ordered quintuples $\langle W_0, \underline{W}, D, \psi, \underline{I} \rangle$, where W_0 and $\underline{W}$ are as above, D is a domain of objects, ψ a function assigning subsets of D to the worlds in $\underline{W}$, and $\underline{I}$ is as before except for conditions assigning 1 or 2 to quantified formulas. Here we introduce in principle all the problems of existence and modality; but it is worth emphasizing that those problems present no peculiar aspect for deontic logic. In fact, they are somewhat less pressing. Clearly, in modal propositional logic it is of great importance not to assume that the objects in the universe are necessarily fixed once and for all, i.e., regardless of the objects it has we must allow that the universe may have had more, or fewer, objects. On the other hand, for pure deontic logic we may assume without damage that the agents and objects are constant – if we are dealing with a system of duties and interdictions at a given time. Thus, there is no great distortion even if we adopt deontic systems that contain the Barcan formula and its converse as theorems.

Furthermore, deontic contexts are wholly not referentially opaque in Quine's sense, or they are nearly so. It is palpably clear that if $a=b$ and x ought$_i$ to do to a some action A (that involves no referential opacity), then x ought$_i$ to do A to b. And this is, of course, as it should be. Different properties of objects or persons may, certainly, yield different prima facie duties that conflict. But since each prima facie duty is relative to a ground, other considerations are irrelevant to it. In the case of the overriding ought we are, so to speak, face to face with brute facts and events, after the cancellation of all intentional and intensional considerations, and one's duty is simply to alter a possible train of events, regardless of how these are now considered or referred to.

Since we are primarily interested in presenting a semantical foundation for our non-standard approach to deontic logic, we need not go into the standard problems of quantification and modality.

We must note, however, that our non-standard models for our non-standard axiom system do satisfy the proto-philosophical data gathered in Section 2 above.

6. Prescriptive or Imperative Values.

In Section 2.2 we argued that prescriptive (and imperative) logic is two-valued, and the argument we gave does justify our axiom 01. But we still owe an account of the semantical values of prescriptions. The crucial thing is the interpretation of the membership of a prescription in a possible deontic world W_j. (We are, presumably, quite clear on what it means to say that an indicative or a proposition belongs to a possible world). Our view is essentially that a prescription belongs to a world if it is endorsed at least partially in that world. And the problem is to explain what endorsement is. This problem, however, is not a logical problem; it is the analogue of the problem of determining what is true, which takes widely different forms in different cases: criteria for veridical perception, scientific methodology, etc. For our present purposes it suffices that we discuss the more general characteristics of endorsement.

Naturally, some prescriptions are especially and deliberately endorsed.

This is so when, for instance, we issue imperatives that we intend to be fulfilled, as when at a dinner table we request "John, pass the salt, please"; we also endorse prescriptions when we formulate rules or sets of Do's and Don't's. We also endorse the prescriptions which are enacted by the rule-making bodies of the institutions we belong. It may be also said that we endorse the prescriptions which demand the doing of actions that are necessary for the attainment of the goals or ends we pursue. But all of these kinds of endorsements are such that for a given prescription "X do A" we may very well neither endorse it nor endorse its denial "X do not do A". Thus, in order to secure a two-valued logic of prescriptions we must include a closing principle that puts either A or $\sim A$ together with the endorsed prescriptions. Such principle is, doubtlessly, behind the phenomenological argument developed in Section 2.2. Our view is that the principle in question is this:

(J)   If neither a prescription A nor its denial $\sim A$ is endorsed in a possible deontic world W_j, given all of the methods of endorsement that determine W_j, then: A belongs to W_j if and only if A is fulfilled, i.e., the proposition corresponding to A is true in W_j; otherwise, $\sim A$ belongs to W_j.

7. Alternative Deontic Systems for the Ought-To-Do

Some philosophers have argued that deontic logic differs from propositional modal logic in that some of the principles that hold in the latter do not have valid deontic counterparts. For instance, many philosophers object to $O_i A \supset O_i(A \vee b)$. Other philosophers insist that there is a strong sense of 'right' in which the rightness of an action is not identical with the non-obligatoriness of the omission of the action.

Now we shall not examine these or related claims. We want to point out only that our non-standard semantical approach to deontic logic can provide a foundation for other systems. We can, for one thing, reject principle (J) and have possible deontic worlds in which some prescriptions are missing together with their negations. We can, for another thing, limit the propositions that belong to all the possible worlds, this providing a distinction between fundamentally relevant and fundamentally irrelevant circumstances. We can, thirdly, consider deontic systems in which the worlds in $\underline{W}$ are not on equal footing, but related by weaker relations. In short, our non-standard approach to deontic logic is amenable to development by means of the fertile methods discovered by Hintikka, Kanger, Kripke and Montague. And, once again, our philosophical understanding is bound to grow by the contemplation of several alternatives in full deployment. This is particularly so in view of an initial adequacy of the approach, that fully satisfies all the proto-philosophical data exhibited above.

Indiana University

REFERENCES

[1] Stig Kanger, *Provability in Logic*, Almquist & Wiksell, Stockholm, 1957; 'A Note on Quantification and Modalities' and 'On the Characterization of Modalities', both in *Theoria* **23** (1957).
[2] Jaakko Hintikka, 'Modality and Quantification', *Theoria* **27** (1961), and 'The Modes of Modality', *Acta Philosophica Fennica* **16** (1963).
[3] Saul Kripke, 'A Completeness Theorem in Modal Logic', *The Journal of Symbolic Logic* **24** (1959), and 'Semantical Analysis of Modal Logic I', *Zeitschrift für mathematische Logik und Grundlagen der Mathematik* **9** (1963).
[4] Richard Montague, 'Logical Necessity, Physical Necessity, Ethics, and Quantifiers', *Inquiry* **3** (1960).
[5] J. Barkley Rosser, *Logic for Mathematicians*, McGraw-Hill, New York, 1953, Chapter IV, pp. 55–76.
[6] For a detailed examination of the overall connections between imperatives and deontic statements see H.-N. Castañeda's 'Imperatives, Decisions and Oughts' in *Morality and the Language of Conduct* (ed. by H.-N. Castañeda and G. Nakhnikian), Wayne State University Press, Detroit, Mich., 1963; paperback edition, 1967.
[7] On conflicts of duties and *prima facie* oughts see H.-N. Castañeda's 'Imperatives, Oughts and Moral Oughts', *The Australasian Journal of Philosophy* **44** (1966).
[8] For a discussion of proposals to solve the Good Samaritan paradox, see H.-N. Castañeda, 'Acts, the Logic of Obligation, and Deontic Calculi', *Philosophical Studies* **19** (1968); W. Sellars, 'Reflections on Contrary-to-Duty Imperatives', *Noûs* **1** (1967); L. Åqvist, 'Good Samaritans, Contrary-to-Duty Imperatives, and Epistemic Obligations', *Noûs* **1** (1967); and L. Powers, 'Some Deontic Logicians', *Noûs* **1** (1967).
[9] H.-N. Castañeda, 'Actions, Imperatives, and Obligations', *Proceedings of the Aristotelian Society* **67** (1967–1968) 45 ff.
[10] See W. V. Quine, *Methods of Logic*, Holt, Rinehart and Winston, New York, revised edition, 1959, pp. 107–117.

BAS C. VAN FRAASSEN

INFERENCE AND SELF-REFERENCE*

In natural language it appears that self-reference is possible, and due to
logical interest in the paradoxes of self-reference, the topic has also seen
a number of formal investigations. But when the interest is in the paradoxes, rather than in self-reference itself, the exact linguistic mechanisms
of self-reference are not necessarily relevant. Indeed, many analyses of
the paradoxes assume the existence of statements capable of playing the
inferential role of the paradoxes and inquire into the nature of languages
containing such statements, omitting all discussion of how the paradoxical
statements are produced.[1]

In this paper, we aim to distinguish two mechanisms of self-reference,
accidental and *functional*. Since the former has been discussed elsewhere,[2]
we shall here concentrate on functional self-reference. In Section I–III
there is no concern with the production of paradoxes, but in Sections
IV–VII the language will be enriched so as to provide for formulation
of Liar-type paradoxes. Sections III and VI provide the formalization
of the informal discussion in the sections preceding them.

I

There is no reason *a priori* why one's domain of discourse should not
include the elements of one's discourse; grammar, for example, is not a
logical impossibility. But in such a case, self-reference *may* occur; a
referring term of quite ordinary semantic character may occur in an expression belonging to its extension. For example "'Snow is white' is a
sentence" is in the extension of 'is a sentence'. In such a case we shall
speak of *accidental self-reference*. Semantic paradoxes may apparently
be formulated through accidental self-reference, though the mere fact of
accidental self-reference does not necessarily lead to paradoxical formulations.

Whenever self-reference consists in reference to a sentence by means
of a term occurring in that sentence (whether name, description, or

Davidson and Harman (eds.), Semantics of Natural Language, 695–708. *All rights reserved*
Copyright © 1972 by D. Reidel Publishing Company, Dordrecht-Holland

predicate), and this term is such that all its occurrences have the same extension, we shall speak of accidental self-reference. The alternative mechanism I wish to describe consists in the use of terms with *context-dependent* reference: the extension of the term (or rather, the extension of an occurrence of that term) depends on the context in which it occurs. This context may be taken wide enough to include pragmatic factors; however, we shall limit it to syntactic context. Specifically, the English 'this (very) sentence' appears to refer to the (largest) sentence in which occurs, and we shall take this appearance to be correct.[3] When self-reference is produced through the use of terms with context-dependent reference, we shall speak of *functional* self-reference.

While context-dependent reference seems to be a pervasive feature of natural language, it clearly raises havoc with logical principles formulated in terms of syntactic form. For example, suppose that the reference of a term d is that of b when d occurs in a sentence containing b, and is that of c otherwise. Then $d=b$ and $d=c$ are always true, but $b=c$ need not be. Thus we cannot expect the logic of functional self-reference to be an extension of classical logic; however, we hope to show that it can be defined in terms of classical logic.

II

Henceforth we shall use theta to play the role of the English 'this (very) sentence'; theta will be, throughout this paper, the only simple term with context-dependent reference. An occurrence of theta has thus as referent the largest sentence in which it lies. The question is what principles govern inference involving such sentences.

That the usual rules for conjunction cannot be retained is shown by the invalidity of the inferences

(a) $((\theta$ *is a conjunction) and A*); hence $(\theta$ *is a conjunction)*
(b) $(\theta$ *begins with* 'θ'), (*It is not the case that* θ *begins with* 'θ'); hence $((\theta$ *begins with* 'θ') *and* (*It is not the case that* θ *begins with* 'θ'))*

The second example shows also that the usual rules for negation do not carry over; indeed, we can no longer identify the falsity of a sentence with the truth of its negate (though we shall for normal sentences). The simple fact about theta that invalidates the inferences is that when theta occurs in the conclusion, it does not have the referent it had in any premise.

Still, some logical connections are left unviolated. Consider the inference of $A(\theta)$ from $(x) A(x)$. We may violate this by means of some such example as

(c) $(x) (Hx \ \& \ \theta \ is \ quantified)$; hence $(H\theta \ \& \ \theta \ is \ quantified)$.

But there are still safe inferences in accordance with that rule; namely, those in which theta does not occur in the premise. For whatever is true of all things is true of the referent of any occurrence of theta. The point is only that when theta is used in a description of what is true of a thing, the description is not unambiguous. To make the description unambiguous, one can replace the occurrence of theta by a constant term having the same reference. Thus if b is a name of $(x) (Hx \ \& \ \theta \ is \ quantified)$, we can validly infer $(H\theta \ \& \ b \ is \ quantified)$.

This reflection gives the clue to the logic governing uses of theta. To check whether an inference is valid, one replaces occurrences of theta by constant terms (different in different sentences, the same in the same sentence), and adds to the premises the information that the referents of these terms are distinct when the terms are distinct. Thus (c) is not valid, since we cannot infer $(Hd \ \& \ d \ is \ quantified)$ from $(x) (Hx \ \& \ c \ is \ quantified)$. However, the following inference turns out valid:

(d) $(x) (Hx \ \& \ F\theta \ \& \ \theta=b)$; hence $H\theta \ \& \ Fb$

In addition, since there are infinitely many sentences, it will be a logical truth that there are at least n things (for any natural number n).

III

We shall now define a language $L\theta$ which could be used to formalize the preceding discussion. The *syntax* of $L\theta$ is a triple $\langle V, P, Q \rangle$ where V, P are disjoint denumerable classes (*variables, predicates*), each member of P has a positive integer associated with it (its *degree*), and Q is the set $\{), (, \&, \neg, \theta, = \}$. By a *term* we mean θ and all members of V. If $t_1, ..., t_n$ are terms and P^n is a predicate of degree n, then $P^n t_1, ..., t_n$ and

$t_1 = t_2$ are sentences, and if A, B are sentences and x is a variable then $(\neg A)$, $(x)(A)$, $(A \& B)$ are sentences; there are no other sentences.

A *model* for $L\theta$ is a couple $M = \langle f, D \rangle$, where D is a set containing at least the sentences of $L\theta$, and f is a mapping of the predicates of degree n into subsets of D^n, for each positive integer n.

We shall regard a sequence of members of D as a mapping of the variables into D, the order of the sequence corresponding to the alphabetical order of the variables. Using D^ω for the set of mappings of sets of variables into D, we define a *propositional function* to be a mapping of D^ω into $\{0, 1\}$.

When $\alpha \in D$, $x \in V$, and $d \in D^\omega$, we define d_x^α to be the mapping which is exactly like d except that it assigns α to x. Then if f is a propositional function f_x^α is the function defined by $f_x^\alpha(d) = 1$ iff $f(d_x^\alpha) = 1$. Finally, if A is a sentence and t, t' are terms, then $(t/t')A$ is the sentence formed by substituting occurrences of t for all free occurrences of t' (by the usual definition of 'free'), after rewriting bound variables so as to avoid their confusion.

Every sentence A is assigned a propositional function $|A|$ in a model $M = \langle f, D \rangle$, and A is *true* (*false*) in M iff $|A|$ is the constant function $|A|(d) = 1$ (respectively, 0) for all d in D^ω. We call *normal* or *safe* any sentence of $L\theta$ in which θ does not occur.

DEFINITION.   If A is a normal sentence of $L\theta$, $|A|$ in the model M is the propositional function defined by:

(i) $|P^n t_1 \dots t_n|(d) = 1$ iff $\langle d(t_1), \dots, d(t_n) \rangle \in f(P^n)$

(ii) $|t_1 = t_2|(d) = 1$ iff $d(t_1) = d(t_2)$

(iii) $|(\neg A)|(d) = 1$ iff $|A|(d) = 0$

(iv) $|(A \& B)|(d) = 1$ iff $|A|(d) = |B|(d) = 1$

(v) $|(x) A|(d) = 1$ iff $|A|(d_x^\alpha) = 1$ for all α in D

If A is normal, then $|(\theta/x) A| = |A|_x^{(\theta/x) A}$.

The second part of this definition assumes that if A and B are normal sentences differing only in that A contains free occurrences of x exactly where B contains free occurrences of y, then $|A|_x^\alpha = |B|_y^\alpha$, a familiar fact about normal sentences.

We shall say that d in D^ω *satisfies* A (in M) if $|A|(d) = 1$ and *satisfies* a set X of sentences if it satisfies all the members of X. Then $A_1, \dots, A_{n-1}$ *semantically entail* A_n ($A_1, \dots, A_{n-1} \Vdash A_n$) in $L\theta$ iff A_n is satisfied by every sequence that satisfies $A_1, ..., A_{n-1}$, in every model. Finally, if $x_1, ..., x_n$ are distinct variables, let $D(x_1, ..., x_n)$ be the conjunction of the sentences $x_i \neq x_j$, where $i \neq j$.

THEOREM 1. If $A_1, ..., A_n$ are normal sentences of $L\theta$, then $A_1, ..., A_{n-1} \Vdash A_n$ in $L\theta$ iff A_n can be deduced in classical quantification and identity theory from $A_1, ..., A_{n-1}$ and sentences of the form $(\exists x_1) ... (\exists x_n) D(x_1, ..., x_n)$.

For the normal fragment of $L\theta$ is different from first-order languages in general only in that the models are all at least denumerably infinite (since they contain all the sentences of $L\theta$).

THEOREM 2. $A_1, ..., A_{n-1} \Vdash A_n$ in $L\theta$ iff $(x_1/\theta) A_1, ..., (x_{n-1}/\theta) A_{n-1}$, $D(x_1, ..., x_n) \Vdash (x_n/\theta) A_n$ where $x_1, ..., x_n$ are distinct variables foreign to $A_1, ..., A_n$.

PROOF. Before proving either part of the biconditional, let us note that, since x_i is foreign to A_i,

$$A_i = (\theta/x_i)(x_i/\theta) A_i. \text{ So } |A_i| = |(x_i/\theta) A_i| \, d_{x_i}^{A_i},$$

and hence also, for any value assignment d, $|A_i|(d) = |(x_i/\theta) A_i|(d_{x_i}^{A_i})$.

Suppose now that d in D^ω is a counter-example in $M = \langle f, D \rangle$ to the second entailment. Then d satisfies $D(x_1, ..., x_n)$ so the elements $d(x_i)$ are distinct. We now permute[4] the model M into a model M', which is like M except that the elements $d(x_i)$ have the properties of the sentences A_i in M, and the sentences A_i have the properties of the elements $d(x_i)$ in M. Now let d' be like d except for mapping x_i into A_i, $i = 1, ..., n$. Then d' is a counterexample to the second entailment in M'. In addition, for each index i, $d' = d'^{A_i}_{x_i}$. Hence by our initial remarks, $|A_i| \, d' = |(x_i/\theta) A_i| \, d'$; thus d' is also a counterexample to the first entailment in M'.

Secondly, suppose that d is a counterexample in M to the first entailment, and let d' be like d except that $d'(x_i) = {}^{A_i}_{x_i}, i = 1, ..., n$. Since $x_1, ..., x_n$ are foreign to $A_1, ..., A_n$, dA_i and d' agree on all variables in the normal sentences $(x_i/\theta) A_i$. By a familiar result of classical logic, it follows that $|(x_i/\theta) A_i|(d_{x_i}^{A_i}) = |(x_i/\theta) A_i|(d')$. In addition, again by our initial remarks, $|(x_i/\theta) A_i|(d_{x_i}^{A_i}) = |A_i|(d)$; so $|(x_i/\theta) A_i|(d') = |A_i|(d)$. Hence d' is a counterexample to the second entailment in M. This ends the proof.

IV

We shall now enrich the language in various ways, in order to allow
for the formulation of assertions about specific sentences. We may begin
by adding a set of constants (names) to the language, and choosing for
each sentence A a name $g(A)$. In that case, what an occurrence of θ in
A designates, is also designated by $g(A)$, and so we have the principle

$(A_1, ..., A_n;$ hence $B)$ is valid iff $((g(A_1)/\theta) A_1, ..., (g(A_n))/\theta)$
A_n); hence $(g(B)/\theta) B)$ is valid.

where $(b/b') A$ is the result of replacing all occurrences of b' in A by
occurrences of b. This principle has as specific consequence the soundness
of the rule

(1)   from A infer $(g(A)/\theta) A$, and conversely.

The importance of (1) is that it allows us to convert all sentences into
normal, safe sentences (not containing theta), when checking the validity
of an argument.

By a *truth-predicate* we shall mean a predicate P such that $Pg(A)$ is
true if A is true, and A is true if $Pg(A)$ is true. Thus if P is a truth-predicate,
then the following rule is sound:

(2)   from $Pg(A)$ infer A, and conversely.

Now, every normal sentence is either true or false (i.e. it or its negate is
true) in our discussion so far. But if that assumption holds, then there
cannot be a truth-predicate, as is shown by the following argument

(a) $Pg(\neg P\theta)$
(b) $\neg P\theta$ (a), (2)
(c) $\neg Pg(\neg P\theta)$ (b), (1)

and its inverse (assume (c), infer (b) by (1), then (a) by (2)).

Now·I have shown in previous papers how we can remove the assumption of bivalence while retaining the logic applicable before this removal.[5]
So we shall henceforth stipulate that P is a truth-predicate; the above
reasoning then shows that the sentences (a) and (c), by being inferentially
equivalent, are neither true nor false.

V

In English we can nest truth-attributions, as for example in 'It is true that it is true that snow is white' or 'It is not the case that it is true that this sentence is true'. There is a sense in which such nesting occurs in $Pg(\neg P\theta)$, since it attributes truth to a sentence containing a truth-predicate. But this is not quite correct, since we really have no way, at present, of formulating our second English example. Thus $\neg Pg(\neg P\theta)$ does not say of itself that it is not true that it is true; it says that $\neg P\theta$ (another sentence altogether) is not true.

One obvious way to eliminate this lack of expressiveness is to say that we need a truth-operator as well as a truth-predicate; that the 'it is true that' in the example is a sentential operator (unary connective), while the second 'is true' is a predicate. Now presumably if T is a truth-operator, we should wish to have the rule

(2')   from $T(A)$ infer A, and conversely.

But this won't work; for consider the predicate 'begins with a truth-operator'. Using F for this predicate, we would expect $T(F\theta)$ to be true; however, the consequence $(F\theta)$, by (2'), is false. Any analysis of $T(F\theta)$ that makes it false will presumably entail that $\neg T(P\theta)$ does not formulate our second English example of this section, and hence defeat the purpose.

Restricting (2') to normal sentences might be one way to handle the problem; we have however an easier way open to us, not involving the introduction of a quasi-modal operator.[6] When a term b designates a sentence A, let us introduce a functional symbol w such that $w(b)$ designates $Pg(A)$. We then have as valid

(3) $w(g(A)) = g(Pg(A))$

which is useful since substitutivity of identity holds for normal sentences. In addition we know that when $w(\theta)$ occurs in A, it denotes $g(Pg(A))$; but (1) and (3) together will license the corresponding replacements. Now $Pg(F\theta)$ does not attribute F to itself, but only to $F\theta$, so (2) is not violated after the manner of (2').

The sentence 'It is not true that this sentence is true' can now be formulated as $\neg Pw(\theta)$. The following argument is again invertible.

(a) $Pg(Pg(\neg Pw(\theta)))$

(b)	$Pg(\neg Pw(\theta))$	(a), (2)
(c)	$\neg Pw(\theta)$	(b), (2)
(d)	$\neg Pwg(\neg Pw(\theta))$	(c), (1)
(e)	$\neg Pg(Pg(\neg Pw(\theta)))$	(d), (3)

and thus shows at a glance that (a), (b), (d), (e) are one and all neither true nor false.

Noting that $Pg(Pb)$ and $Pw(b)$ are inferentially equivalent, (a) could be replaced by $Pwg(\neg Pw(\theta))$, in which case the contradiction is with line (d). Now Pwb we shall speak of as being of second level, Pb of first level, $Pwwb$ of third level, and so on. When a term b is preceded by n occurrences of w ($n=0, 1, \dots$), we shall call the result $w^n(b)$, and the sentence $Pw^n g(A)$ we shall call $T^{n+1}(A)$; a sentence B will be said to be of level m if m is the highest integer such that B contains $T^m(A)$ for some sentence A. Finally, let us call all sentences not covered so far zero-level sentences.[7] Then an interesting question about a language is the degree of its paradoxicality: what is the highest level for which failure of bivalence is demonstrable? If such failure is demonstrable for ever higher levels, we shall say that the language has infinite paradoxicality.

We shall now show that our new language has infinite paradoxicality. For any power n, consider the sentence $T^{n+1}(\neg Pw^n(\theta))$. Repeated application of rules (2) and (3) shows $T^{n+1}(A)$ and A to be inferentially equivalent, and this fact leads to the following argument

(a)	$T^{n+1}(\neg Pw^n(\theta))$	
(b)	$Pw^n g(\neg Pw^n(\theta))$	(a), definition of T^{n+1}
(c)	$\neg Pw^n(\theta)$	(b), (2), (3) repeated
(d)	$\neg Pw^n g(\neg Pw^n(\theta))$	(c), (1)
(e)	$\neg T^{n+1}(\neg Pw^n(\theta))$	(d), definition of T^{n+1}

which is again invertible, and thus shows that (a) is neither true nor false. Since the demonstration is arbitrary in n, it demonstrates a failure of bivalence on every level from 1 on.[8]

VI

We shall now formalize the infinitely paradoxical language described in the preceding sections. The new language will be called $L\theta^*$; its syntax is like that of $L\theta$ except that it has constants, and a function symbol w. In its semantics we shall first proceed essentially as for $L\theta$, but then we shall use a technique developed elsewhere to allow for the existence of a truth-predicate.[9]

The syntax of $L\theta^*$ is a quintuple $\langle V, C, P, Q, g \rangle$, where V, C, P are disjoint denumerable classes (*variables, constants, predicates*), each positive integer is associated with denumerably many members of P (their *degree*), and Q is the set $\{), (, \&, \neg, =, \theta, w\}$. The set of *terms* is the least set containing θ and all members of V and C, and such that if t belongs to it, so does $w(t)$. The definition of sentences proceeds now as usual (and as for $L\theta$). Finally g is a one to one mapping of the sentences into C.

A *model* for $L\theta^*$ is a triple $M = \langle f, D, W \rangle$, where D is a set containing the sentences of $L\theta^*$, W a mapping of D into D such that $W(A) = Pg(A)$ for all sentences A, and alphabetically the first monadic predicate P of $L\theta^*$ (the symbol P will be reserved for this role throughout). Finally, f is a mapping of the constants into D such that $f(g(A)) = A$ for all sentences A, and of the predicates of degree n into subsets of D^n, for each degree n.

We use the notation $D^\omega, d, d_x^\alpha, f_x^\alpha, (t/t')\, A$ as for language $L\theta$. We define the *denotation* of a term t relative to value assignment d, $d^*(t)$, as follows: if $t \in V, d^*(t) = d(t)$; if $t \in C, d^*(t) = f(t)$; if t is $w(t')$ then $d^*(t) = Wd^*(t')$.

Now every sentence A of $L\theta$ is assigned a propositional function $|A|$ in each model $M = \langle f, D, W \rangle$ as follows, using 'normal' as for $L\theta$:

DEFINITION. If A is a normal sentence of $L\theta^*$, then $|A|$ in $M = \langle f, D \rangle$ is the propositional function in M defined by:

  (i) $|P^n t_1 \ldots t_n|\,(d) = 1$ iff $\langle d^*(t_1), \ldots, d^*(t_n) \rangle \in f(P^n)$

  (ii) $|t_1 = t_2|\,(d) = 1$ iff $d^*(t_1) = d^*(t_n)$

  (iii) $|(\neg A)|\,(d) = 1$ iff $|A|\,(d) = 0$

  (iv) $|(A \,\&\, B)|\,(d) = 1$ iff $|A|\,(d) = |B|\,(d) = 1$

  (v) $|(x)\,A|\,(d) = 1$ iff $|A|\,(d_x^\alpha) = 1$ for all α in D

  If A is not a normal sentence, then $|A| = |(g(A)/\theta)\,A|$.

A *classical valuation* for $L\theta^*$ will be any mapping v of the sentences of $L\theta^*$ into $\{T, F\}$ such that there is a model M and value-assignment d such that $v(A) = T$ iff $|A|\,(d) = 1$, for all sentences A of $L\theta^*$. We shall say that a set X of sentences *classically entail* A in $L\theta^*$ if all classical valuations that assign T to every member of X also assign T to A.

THEOREM 3. $A_1, ..., A_{n-1}$ classically entail A_n in $L\theta^*$ iff $(g(A_1)/\theta)$ $A_1, ..., (g(A_{n-1})/\theta) A_{n-1}$ classically entail $(g(A_n)/\theta) A_n$ in $L\theta^*$.

This is immediate from the assignment of propositional functions, which is justified by the fact that $d^*(g(A)) = A$, for all sentences A, and all value-assignments d.

THEOREM 4. If $A_1, ..., A_n$ are normal sentences of $L\theta^*$, then $A_1, ..., A_{n-1}$ classically entail A_n in $L\theta^*$ iff A_n can be deduced in classical quantification and identity theory from $A_1, ..., A_{n-1}$ and sentences of form $w(g(A)) = g(Pg(A))$ and of form $g(A) \neq g(B)$ where A and B are distinct sentences.

PROOF. That sentences of those two forms are classically entailed by any (or no) premises whatever is immediate from the fact that $d^*(w(t)) = W(d^*(t))$, $d^*(g(A)) = A$, $W(A) = Pg(A)$, for all terms t and sentences A for all value assignments d.

Suppose then that A_n cannot be deduced in the above stipulated manner. Then, by familiar results about classical logic, we can construct[10] a set K of normal sentences containing $A_1, ..., A_{n-1}$, $\neg A_n$, $g(A) \neq g(B)$ for any two distinct sentences A and B, and $w(g(A)) = g(Pg(A))$ for any sentence A, and K is such that

(i) A or $\neg A$ in K, for any sentence A
(ii) K is consistent
(iii) $(x) A$ is in K iff $(t/x) A$ is in K for every normal term t.

We can now construct a model $M = \langle f, D, W \rangle$ for $L\theta^*$ and value-assignment d, such that $|A| (d) = 1$ in M iff $A \in K$, for all normal sentences A.

Briefly, when t is a term, let $[t]$ be A if $g(A) = t$ is in K; otherwise let it be $\{t' : t' = t \in K\}$. Set $D = \{[t] : t \text{ is a normal term}\}$. Let W be defined by $W([t]) = [w(t)]$, f by $f(b) = [b]$ for $b \in \mathbf{C}$, $f(P^n) = \{\langle [t_1], ..., [t_n] \rangle : P^n t_1 ... t_n \in K\}$. The latter definition is consistent, since $[t_1] = [t_2]$ iff $t_1 = t_2 \in K$, and if $t_1 = t_2$ and A are in K, then so is $(t_1/t_2) A$. Finally, let $d(x) = [x]$. That M is a model is clear: D contains every sentence A, since $g(A) = g(A)$ is in K for every sentence A; $W(A) = W([g(A)]) = [w(g(A))] = [g(Pg(A))] = Pg(A)$; $f(g(A)) = [g(A)] = A$.

That $|A| (d) = 1$ in M iff $A \in K$, for all normal sentences A can be proved by an easy induction on the length of A; in the clause for quantified sentences it is only necessary to note that $|(x) A| (d) = 1$ iff $|(t/x) A| (d) = 1$ for all normal terms t, since $|(t/x) A| (d) = |A| (d_x^{d^*(t)})$, and d^* exhausts the domain of discourse. This ends the proof.

We define the relation N to be the least set containing all couples $\langle A, Pg(A) \rangle$ and $\langle Pg(A), A \rangle$, for sentences A. We call a set X of sentences *saturated* if the following conditions obtain:

(i)   some classical valuation assigns T to every member of X
(ii) X is closed under classical entailment
(iii) X is closed under N

where a set is called closed under a relation R if for all $\alpha_1, ..., \alpha_n$ such that $\alpha_1, ..., \alpha_{n-1}$ are in the set and $R\alpha_1 ... \alpha_n$, α_n is also in the set.

We define a *supervaluation* of $L\theta^*$ to be the intersection of a class of classical valuations of $L\theta^*$, and define the set of *admissible valuations* to be $\{ \cap V$: there is a saturated set X such that $V = \{v: v$ is a classical valuation assigning T to every member of $X\}\}$. So the admissible valuations are exactly the supervaluations 'induced' by the saturated sets of $L\theta^*$. We now say that a set X of sentences *semantically entails* A ($X \Vdash A$) in $L\theta^*$ iff all admissible valuations of $L\theta^*$ that assign T to all of X, also assign T to A. From a previous general result[11] we obtain as a corollary:

THEOREM 5. $X \Vdash A$ in $L\theta^*$ iff A belongs to the least set of sentences of $L\theta^*$ that contains X and is closed under N and classical entailment in $L\theta^*$.

Thus valid deduction from finite premise sets in $L\theta^*$ consists of deduction in classical quantification and identity theory applied to normal sentences, plus axioms $w(g(A)) = g(Pg(A))$ and $g(A) \neq g(B)$ for distinct sentences A and B, plus inference from $Pg(A)$ to A and conversely, and inference of $g(A)/\theta) A$ to A and conversely. (One note of warning: the applications of classical and non-classical rules of inference must be kept rigidly separate, even when all sentences involved are normal; for example, $Pg(A) \supset A$ cannot be proved.)[12]

VII

The ordinary Liar paradox involves a sentence which can be neither true nor false; the Strengthened Liar paradox a sentence such that the assertion of truth to it can be neither true nor false.[13] In $L\theta*$ we can formulate sentences with these characteristics, and indeed, we can formulate sentences A such that $T^n(A)$ can be neither true nor false, for ever higher powers n. Yet there are many paradoxes in the literature which cannot be formulated in $L\theta*$. It does seem, however, that the introduction of function symbols such as w, which correspond to syntactic transformations of sentences, would allow such formulations. In this last section we shall consider the formulation of two further paradoxes to illustrate this technique.

The exact sentence that we originally called the Strengthened Liar sentence says of itself that it is either false, or neither true nor false. We have unfortunately no general way of expressing falsity in $L\theta*$, but the following sentence is closely analogous 'Either the negation of $w(\theta)$ is true, or neither $w(\theta)$ nor its negation is true'. Let n be a new function symbol such that $n(b)$ denotes the negation of the sentence denoted by b, if any; we then have as a new principle:

$$(4) \qquad n(g(A)) = g(\neg A)$$

for any sentence A. We may now formulate the above English sentence as $Pnw(\theta) \lor . \neg Pw(\theta) \& \neg Pnw(\theta)$. Calling this sentence Y, we obtain the argument:

(a)	$Pg(Y)$	
(b)	Y	(a), (2)
(c)	$Pnwg(Y) \lor . \neg Pwg(Y) \& \neg Pnwg(Y)$	(b), (1)
(d)	$Pwg(Y)$	(a), (2), (3)
(e)	$\neg(\neg Pwg(Y) \& \neg Pnwg(Y))$	(d), classical inf.
(f)	$Pnwg(Y)$	(c), (e), classical inf.
(g)	$Png(Pg(Y))$	(f), (3)
(h)	$Pg(\neg Pg(Y))$	(g), (4)
(i)	$\neg Pg(Y)$	(h), (2)

This argument is also essentially invertible, provided we drop (d) and (3); (c) is directly inferrable from (f) by classical logic. Hence Y is a sentence such that $Pg(Y)$ is neither true nor false.

Now all the paradoxes formulated so far are compatible with the thesis that for each sentence A there is *some* positive integer n such that $T^n(A)$ is either true or false. As grand finale, we aim to produce a *hyperparadox*:

a statement A such that $T^n(A)$ is demonstrably neither true nor false for any positive integer n. The English formulation would be 'There is some integer n such that this sentence is not true to power n' where we call A true to power n if $T^n(A)$ is true. To get something like quantification over the superscripts, we introduce the binary function symbol v, such that $v(g(A), b)$ denotes $T^n(B)$ when A is alphabetically the $(n+1)$ff sentence and b denotes B. (Let $T^1(A)$ be A.) Then we shall have $(\exists x)\neg Pv(x, g(A))$ iff $\neg T^n(A)$ is true for some power n, provided only we make it impossible for $(\neg Pv(x, g(A)))$ to be true when x denotes some entity that is not a sentence. This is easily done; we simply let $v(t, t')$ denote the tautology $(x)(x=x)$ when t or t' does not denote a sentence. The new rules are now:

(5) $v(g(A), g(B)) = g(T^n(B))$ when A is the $(n+1)^{th}$ sentence
(6)   from A infer $(x)Pv(x, g(A))$.

The converse of (6) is valid by rules (2) and (5): from $(x)Pv(x, g(A))$ we infer $Pv(g(B), g(A))$ where B is the first sentence, from which we infer $Pg(A)$, from which we in turn infer A. Now we have the argument, for $n=0, 1, 2, \ldots$, and for the sentence $(\exists x)\neg Pv(x, \theta)$, which we shall call Z:

(a) $T^{n+1}(Z)$
(b) Z (a), (2), (3) repeated
(c) $(\exists x)\neg Pv(x, g(Z))$ (b), (1)
(d) $(x)Pv(x, g(Z))$ (b), (6)
(e) $\neg T^{n+1}(Z)$ (c), (d), classical inf.

The argument is again essentially invertible: we omit (d) and infer (c) from (e) by the intermediate moves

(d') $\neg Pg(T^n(Z))$ (e), definition, (3)
(d') $\neg Pv(g(A), g(Z))$ (d'), (5)

where A is the nth sentence; now (c) can be derived from (d') by existential generalization.

The point that emerges may be stated as follows: as long as we do not have hyperparadoxes, it is possible that a sentence A is not true iff $\neg T^n(A)$ is true for some n, so that non-truth is expressible (by a single sentence) in some sense; but the moment we introduce the machinery for a uniform way of expressing non-truth in this sense, hyperparadoxes emerge and defeat the project. But we have also come to see that, while functional self-reference prevents the universal applicability of classical logic and allows us to formulate paradoxes that violate familiar canons of semantics, the applicable logical rules are classical rules restricted to 'normal' contexts plus fairly simple additional rules to cover the new terms.

University of Toronto

REFERENCES

* For the problems to which this paper is directed, and also for some aspects of the solutions proposed, I am indebted to stimulating discussions and correspondence with Prof. Charles B. Daniels, Indiana University. The research for this paper was partially supported by Canada Council Grant 69-0650.

[1] An example is my "Presupposition, Implication, and Self-Reference", *Journal of Philosophy* 65 (1968), 136–152 (henceforth PRIM); an exception is N. Rescher "Semantic Paradoxes and the Propositional Analysis of Indirect Discourse", *Philosophy of Science* 28 (1961), 437–440.

[2] Cf. papers by B. Skyrms, R. Martin, and myself in Robert L. Martin, *The Paradox of the Liar*, New Haven, Yale, 1970.

[3] Reichenbach's symbol Θ^* plays roughly that role (see H. Reichenbach, *Elements of Symbolic Logic* (New York: Macmillan, 1947), (Section 50).

[4] That is, the mapping $\pi(d(x_i)) = A_1$, $\pi(A_1) = d(x_i)$, $\pi(\alpha) = \alpha$ for all other cases, is an isomorphism between M and M'.

[5] See PRIM, pp. 139–143.

[6] When functional self-reference is absent, there is apparently no such objection to adding a truth-operator with rule (2').

[7] Compare Section II of my "Truth and Paradoxical Consequences" (henceforth T & PC), in the volume mentioned in footnote 3.

[8] In our terminology, $\neg Pw^n(\theta)$ and $T^{n+1}(\neg Pw^n\theta)$ are both of level $n+1$; the demonstration of failure of bivalence, however, is always for normal sentences.

[9] This is the technique of supervaluations; while this is explained briefly in PRIM and T & PC, a thorough treatment is found in my "Presuppositions, Supervaluations, and Free Logic", in K. Lambert (ed.) *The Logical Way of Doing Things* (New Haven: Yale, 1969), pp. 67–91 (henceforth PRUF).

[10] If there are denumerably many constants not in the range of g, then since we are concerned with finite sets of premises only, we need not introduce new constants for this construction; less favorable cases can be handled in various ways.

[11] PRUF, Theorem 3, p. 75.

[12] See PRUF, pp. 79–86. To avoid confusion of classical and non-classical inference patterns, classical logic should be formulated axiomatically (with modus ponens) rather than by natural deduction rules.

[13] See PRIM, Section IV, pp. 146–151.

PAUL ZIFF

WHAT IS SAID

Some of us sometimes understand some of what is said. The problem is to understand how we manage to do this. The matter is complex. No reasonably complete answer is at present possible. We maunder about in ignorance. But only the barest speculative sketch is aimed at here: a few possible bones will be provided on which flesh may some day be hung.

We are concerned with what is said, to understand how it is we manage to understand it. But to speak of what is said is to babble with three tongues. These must be untangled.

To say something, in the ordinary course of things, one utters an utterance having a phonetic, phonemic, morphological, syntactic and semantic structure and one utters it under certain conditions. (No doubt one can also be said to say something by means of gestures alone, or by a shake of the head, or by signalling, telegraphing, and so forth, but such matters need not detain us here.) The minimum requirement for having said something appears to be that the utterance be constituted of, or significantly correlated with, words in some language or other: utterances that fault this condition are mere mouthings, moans or shrieks; the utterer is not a speaker. Whereas if someone utters an utterance of the form 'Dog the table banana is', something was said, albeit something nonsensical: that the utterance is a morphological morass does not matter, that it have a morphological structure does.

In thick guttural accents one utters the utterance 'I *v*ant a banana': what has he said? He has said this: 'I *v*ant a banana'. In reporting what is said in this sense one apes the speaker, emulates a tape recorder.

One who utters the utterance 'I *v*ant a banana' can also be said to have said 'I want a banana'. And such a report is commonly classed a "verbatim" report of what was said. Again, a verbatim report of what is said when a person utters the utterance 'I study *economics*' could well be 'He said 'I study *economics*'': in verbatim reporting one generally discounts phonetic and phonemic differences. And, as one would expect, the discounting of phonemic differences can on occasion give rise to

borderline cases: if the Reverend Spooner were to have uttered the
utterance 'I spike liders' one could say that what he said in the verbatim
sense was 'I like spiders'. But if he had uttered the utterance 'I saw a
flutterby butterfly', would one say that he had in the verbatim sense
said 'I saw a butterfly flutterby'? Or would one say that what he had said
in the verbatim sense was 'I saw a flutterby butterfly' but that is not what
he meant to say?

What is said is slippery stuff: one readily slides not only over phonetic
and phonemic differences but over morphological differences as well.
A person who says (in the verbatim sense) 'I want a banana' can also
be said to have said that he wants a banana. Thus if George says 'I
want a banana' and Josef says 'He wants a banana', where the reference
is to George, then each has said the same thing, namely that George
wants a banana. Or if George says 'Maybe there are no bananas' and
Josef says 'Perhaps there ain't no bananas' then again each has said the
same thing, despite the morphological differences between the utterances
uttered.

Syntax is here no more sacrosanct than morphology. If in response
to the query 'Who ate the cake?' one man says 'The man', another 'The
man did it', another 'The man ate the cake', another 'The cake was
eaten by the man', then each has said the same thing.

Semantic features are also subject to slough. In particular to begin
with, reference may go by the board. If George says 'I am tired' and
Josef says 'I am tired' then each has said the same thing, namely, that he
is tired. To count George and Josef as having here said the same thing
is to discount the evident referential differences between the sentences
uttered. There are even more extreme cases: suppose one person says
'The house is green', another says 'My jacket is green', another 'The car
is green', and so on; in a sense they are all saying the same thing, namely,
that certain things are green.

Just as referential differences may be discounted, so one may discount
differences between the specific characterizations supplied. Suppose
different persons offer the following reports about a UFO: 'The object
had at least thirteen faces', 'The object had sixteen faces', 'The object
had many sides', 'The object had more than thirteen but less than twenty
faces'; in a sense they are all saying the same thing, namely, that the
object was a polyhedron. The sense of 'what is said' is further attenuated

when one simultaneously discounts both referential differences and differences between the specific characterizations supplied. If one person says 'My car is green', another 'The house is blue', another 'His jacket is yellow', and so on, in a sense they are all saying the same thing, namely, that certain things are coloured.

An automatic consequence of discounting referential differences is that differences in truth are simultaneously discounted. For if George says 'I am tired' and Josef says 'I am tired' then, in the sense in which what is said is one and the same, one cannot say that what is said is either true or not true. For what each said was that he was tired. And is that true? For what if George was in fact tired and Josef was not? Then what was said was neither true nor not true, but what was said was true of George, not true of Josef.

But one may also discount differences in truth without discounting referential differences. On Monday I say 'My house is red' and my house is red. Then on the following Wednesday I say 'My house is red' but my house is no longer red because the house was painted on Tuesday. Then discounting questions of truth, what I said on Monday is the same as what I said on Wednesday. It may seem, however, as though this case were not to the point: one may be inclined to say that, despite my disclaimer, what was said on Monday and what was said on Wednesday can be counted as one and the same only by discounting referential differences. For there was, so it may seem, a covert reference not to my house but to my house on a specific day. Thus on Monday I said that my house on Monday was red whereas on Wednesday I said that my house on Wednesday was red. One can take such a line. But why should one? One can just as well, or better, say that what was said was one and the same and that the reference was in each case the same, to the house simply and not to the house on Monday or Wednesday. And then what was said was neither true nor not true though what was said was true of the house on Monday, not true of the house on Wednesday.

Finally, the expression 'what is said' has such a use that one can in fact transcend every linguistic feature of the utterance uttered. If on being asked to play tennis George replies 'I have work to do' and Josef replies 'Do I look like an athlete?' then perhaps each has said the same thing, namely, no. This sense of 'what is said' may be baptised the "implication" sense.

There are, it appears, a great many factors serving to determine what is said. But apart from the mimicking, verbatim and implication senses, it appears that certain syntactic and semantic factors are essential with respect to the other senses of 'what is said'. If George says (in the verbatim sense) 'They are leaving' and Josef says 'They are going' then each has said the same thing, namely, that they are departing (or that they are leaving or that they are going). But if George says (in the verbatim sense) 'Why is he slipping?' and Josef says 'Why is he slipping?' then even though they have said the same thing in the verbatim sense, it seems that they have not said the same thing in any other sense (mimicking and implication senses aside) for they have not said anything (mimicking, verbatim and implication senses aside). If George and Josef each say 'Why is he slipping?' one could report of them 'They asked the same thing, namely, why he is slipping' but not of course 'They said the same thing, namely, why he is slipping'. One can speak of what is said, in other than the mimicking, verbatim and implication senses, only if in uttering the utterance the speaker made some sort of statement or assertion or the like; the utterance must be in declarative form. Consequently, I propose to lump all such senses together under the rubric of the "statement" senses of 'what is said'.

I have indicated that I am concerned to understand how it is that we understand what is said. But one can now hear my words falling short of their mark. For of course I am also concerned to understand how it is that we understand what is asked and what is commanded and the like. Unfortunately there is no nice phrase for the purpose. Ignoring such niceties, if we are to understand how it is that we understand what is said, the first step would be to gain some insight into the character and operation of the factors that serve to determine what is said.

Some of the factors that serve to determine what is said are obvious enough: phonetic, phonemic, morphological, syntactic, semantic and contextual factors are all evidently at play. But not everything that serves to determine what is said can be listed, enumerated. To understand what is said it need not be enough to know and understand the language in which what is said is said. And this is always so when what is said is said by implication, i.e., is said in the implication sense of 'what is said'.

What is said by implication can be anything at all, other than what is in fact then said in the statement sense. To understand what is said by implication it is not enough to understand what is said in the statement sense. One may have to have some knowledge of the speaker's beliefs, attitudes, convictions, opinions and so forth. If on being asked to play tennis a person replies 'I have work to do', what has he said by implication? That depends on him: no general answer is possible here. If the speaker is an ordinary sort then perhaps he was saying by implication that he couldn't play. But he needn't be an ordinary sort. Perhaps he's a queer sort who plays and is delighted to play only when he has work to do. If I know this about him and he knows I know it then, by implication, he has managed to say that he would be delighted to play. Or what if he had replied 'It is snowing in Tibet'? Then possibly again he has managed to say that he would be delighted to play, but that would depend on him and on my knowledge of his quirks and his knowledge of my knowledge and so forth. Any fact known to us may be a factor serving to determine what is said by implication, but such factors cannot be effectively enumerated.

One may suppose, however, that what is said, in any literal sense other than the implication sense, is some function of some reasonably definite set of factors. For example, what is said in the mimicking sense appears to be a relatively simple function of the acoustic shape of the temporally ordered sequence of morphs constituting the utterance. Indeed, a tape recorder may be taken as constituting a physical realization of the function in question.

Such an account however is at once seen to be seriously deficient when one attends to the fact that no reference has been made to the matter of morpheme identification: a tape recorder makes no discrimination between mere mouthings and utterances having sufficient morphological structure to count as sayings. Among the factors serving to determine what is said, even in the mimicking sense of 'what is said', must be included those factors, whatever they may be , that serve to identify the morphemes in question. If someone utters an utterance of the form 'Whadjamean?' then in the verbatim sense he may have said 'What do you mean?'; but if someone utters an utterance of the form 'Tadjageam' then possibly he has not said anything at all either in the mimicking or the verbatim senses of 'what is said'. And presumably the relevant difference between the two utterances is this: there is a relatively smooth curve leading from 'Whadjamean?' to 'What do you mean?' but there does not appear to be any smooth curve leading from 'Tadjageam' to any sequence of English morphemes. (Though I suppose one could try to pair 'Tadjageam' with 'Tied your game!': it is not irrelevant that it is difficult to find a short sequence of English phones that cannot conceivably be mapped on to some sequence of English morphemes.) In consequence one takes 'Whadjamean?' to be a sequence of English morphs, but 'Tadjageam' to be simply a sequence not of English morphs but at best of English phones.

But all talk of "smooth curves" is of course here at best figurative; at the worst, it is whistling in the dark (otherwise known as metaphysics). Among the factors that serve to determine what is said are those factors that serve to identify the morphemic constitution of an utterance. But such factors are not at present to be detailed: one glimpses them through a glass darkly.

If one peers into the workings of discourse, one can discern some sort of coherence factor at work serving to identify the morphemic constitutions of utterances. Consider the sentence 'He refused to have anything to do with the girl'. 'Refused' is a homonymous expression: there is one word having to do with declining and another having to do with installing another fuse. Even so, apart from special discourses, one can hardly construe the preceding sentence as having the same meaning as the sentence 'He installed another fuse to have anything to do with the girl' for the latter sentence, unlike the former, is syntactically deviant. The reason for that is, of course, to be found in the negative character of the homonym 'refuse' meaning decline. (Note that such environments as 'He ...ed to have anything to do with the girl' can serve to establish the existence of a class of negative words.) Now consider the sentence 'He refused to marry the girl'. Here, unlike the preceding case, immediate syntactic considerations do not serve to impede a pairing of that sentence with a sentence like 'He installed another fuse to marry the girl'. And now consider the more complex sentence (or if you like, the following pair of sentences) 'He refused to marry the girl; he refused to have anything to do with her'. Although the alternative of installing a fuse might at first seem to be available in connection with the first occurrence of 'refused', it is more clearly not available in connection with the second occurrence. In consequence, in the interest of something like coherence, the alternative involving the installation of a fuse is somehow not available or not genuinely available even for the first occurrence of 'refused'.

That there is some sort of coherence factor serving to structure discourse should, I think, be fairly obvious. It is indicated by all sorts of cases. For example, something like coherence forces us to backtrack when we hear a sentence like 'I watched her duck when they were throwing rotten eggs; it swam out to the middle of the lake'.[1] Though one may have begun by counting 'duck' as a verb, one will probably end by counting it as a noun, and this in the interest of coherence. The same sort of phenomenon is exemplified by the (spoken) utterance 'He waxed Roth and then he waxed Smith'.[2] Still further evidence of a coherence factor is to be seen in the ease with which one can overcome ambiguities. For example, consider the following dialogue: 'When you said 'refuse' did you mean install another fuse or did you mean decline? I meant decline. When you say 'decline' do you mean sicken or do you mean turn down?' The second question is clearly absurd. The discourse is ostensibly concerned with homonyms of 'refuse'; although both 'install another fuse' and 'decline' are at once available as alternatives for 'refuse', 'sicken' is not.

Apart from considerations of coherence, it is clear that such vague matters as general beliefs are relevant factors in morpheme identification. Consider the relatively unambiguous sentence 'My psychiatrist can lick your psychiatrist'. Despite the phonological fusion of morphologically distinct elements, all is likely to be relatively clear here: beat up, not treat like a lollypop, is what 'lick' looks to be. The identification of 'lick' as the lollypop morpheme is apparently hindered by the use of the word 'can'. Thus the sentence 'My psychiatrist licked your psychiatrist' can more plausibly be supposed to be ambiguous: either alternative is then perhaps available, though one is still more viable than the other. And certainly the sentence 'My cat licked your cat' is genuinely ambiguous. The explanation of all this is fairly obvious: since it is a common occurrence for one cat to lick in the lollypop sense another, or so it is generally believed, that sentence is at once ambiguous. And since it is generally easy to lick like a lollypop but not always so easy to beat, the use of 'can' serves to hinder one reading of 'lick' while facilitating the other.

Apart from considerations of coherence and such vague matters as general beliefs, it is clear that nonlinguistic perceptual factors are also of considerable importance in morpheme identification. Given an appropriate perceptual situation, even if the actual morphs of the utterance are partially masked by noise or are markedly deviant in character, one need not encounter any difficulty in morpheme identification. The drunk waving his empty glass at you saying 'My grass's dry' is easily understood to have said in the verbatim sense 'My glass is dry'; but were an acoustically identical utterance to be uttered under different perceptual conditions, say while staring glumly at a drought stricken lawn, what would be said would, in the verbatim sense, be 'My grass is dry'.

One may suppose that what is said is some function of some reasonably definite finite set of factors but for the time being (and no doubt for some time to come) such a supposition is best seen as at best a heuristic maxim. Coherence, belief and perceptual factors do not at present admit of any plausible form of computation. But even if one could today discern a distinct set of factors to be computed, the character of the requisite function would still pose a considerable problem.

In considering the sentence 'He refused to have anything to do with the girl' it was pointed out that one could hardly construe that sentence as having the same meaning as the sentence 'He installed another fuse to have anything to do with the girl' owing to the fact that the latter sentence, unlike the former, is syntactically deviant. Thus it appeared that syntactic factors sufficed to block the identification of 'refused' as the homonym meaning installed another fuse. More precisely, it might seem as though one could describe the situation as follows: first, syntactic factors served to delimit the choice for the environment 'He ...ed to have anything to do with the girl' to negative morphemes; secondly, since only one of the homonyms having the shape 'refused' was a negative morpheme, namely that meaning decline, that one had to be and was then selected. But such an account of the situation would be excessively simple minded.

The factors that serve to determine what is said have something of the character of vectors and what is said can be thought of as something of a vector sum. To suggest that the factors that serve to determine what is said can be thought of as vectors is, of course, at once to suggest that they can be represented by directed line segments, that they can sensibly be thought of as forces having a magnitude, a direction in some sort of linguistic space and a sense in which the direction is proceeding. It is also to suggest that one factor can, as it were, serve to deflect another.

And more importantly, it is also to suggest that these factors may be active and operative even though owing to the interaction of other factors their action and operation may not be readily apparent.

Consider the sentences 'He barked his shin' and 'The dog barked'. These two 'bark's' are homonyms: the former is a transitive verb, the latter intransitive. The former means skin, the latter yap. Consequently syntactic factors would seem to indicate that the meaning of 'He barked his shin' is much the same as that of 'He skinned his shin' and not the same as that of 'He yapped his shin'. Indeed this last sentence is clearly ungrammatical since 'yap' is an intransitive verb. To construe 'He barked his shin' as having much the same meaning as 'He yapped his shin' would, in consequence, be to construe the grammatical as the ungrammatical, the nondeviant as the deviant. So one may be inclined to suppose that 'He barked his shin' can't rightly be read as 'He yapped his shin'. But it can.

Syntactic structure constitutes a vector serving to determine what is said but this vector can be modified by the action of other vectors. In particular, there are discourse factors, vectors activated in discourse, that can serve radically to alter the reading of sentences. For suppose the sentence 'He barked his shin' were embedded in the following discourse: 'He was a remarkable ventriloquist. First, he made it seem that the cat was barking. Then he made the parrot bark. Then he barked a monkey, and then a shoe, then his hand, and then he barked his shin.' And do we understand what is being said? Of course we do. Nor is there much of a mystery about how we do it. Owing to the operation and action of a coherence factor we are impelled to read 'bark' as meaning yap. Then, in consequence, to allow for the intransitive role assigned to 'bark' in 'he barked a monkey' and 'he barked his shin', we are impelled to read 'barked a monkey' and 'barked his shin' as syntactic transforms of 'made a monkey bark' and 'made his shin bark', thus allowing 'bark' to be fundamentally intransitive. Then owing to co-occurrence restrictions and to the operation of belief factors, we are impelled to read 'made his shin bark' as a transform of 'made it seem as if his shin barked'. In short, owing to the action of other vectors activated by the discourse in which the sentence is embedded, the sentence takes on an altered syntactic structure.

All factors serving to determine what is said appear to have a vectorial

character. For example, the phonetic shapes of the elements of an utterance supply important factors serving to determine what is said. But the
phonetic shapes of elements very often supply more than a single vector:
the possibility of puns stems from the plurality of phonetic vectors
supplied in a given utterance. Thus 'Armageddon awful fat'[3] is possible
because of the phonetic vector supplied by the name which allows one
to associate it with the phrase 'I am getting'; the reference of the name
introduces a further vector which together with coherence and belief
vectors serves to determine what is said, namely, that, as has been said,
inside every fat man there is a thin man struggling to get out. Again,
'Madame was but a fly when Pinkerton spied her'[4] survives on vectors
leading from 'but a fly' to 'butterfly' and from 'spied her' to 'spider'
aided and abetted by belief factors connecting the lady with the lieutenant
and the web he wove.

The same phenomenon can be witnessed at the morphemic level.
Consider the sentence 'He squandered the rent': 'rent' is a homonym
meaning roughly either a sum of money or a tear. If 'rent-1' is the word
pertaining to money and 'rent-2' the word pertaining to a tear then one is
inclined to say that 'rent-1' but not 'rent-2' occurs in the sentence 'He
squandered the rent'. But how then shall we explain what is said if one
says 'Her only dress was torn but he squandered the rent'?[5] For clearly
'rent-2' occurs in this sentence. I am inclined to suppose that a more
plausible account of the situation is as follows: the phonemic sequence
'rent' supplies at least two vectors, one leading to the word 'rent-1' and
the other to 'rent-2'. Generally one or the other vector is dominant, and
only in the case of jokes or genuine ambiguities are both evident. Thus,
on this view, even in a sentence like 'He always paid his rent on time'
there is a vector leading to 'rent-2'. For again, one could reinforce that
vector by embedding the sentence in some appropriate discourse, as
in 'She allowed him to make rents in her dress, but only so long as he
at once payed for the privilege: he always paid his rent on time'. Again,
'I want to buy some alligator shoes but I don't know what size my
alligator wears' is a clear instance of a vector being reinforced by an
appropriate discourse environment.

As I have elsewhere maintained,[6] a word's having meaning in a
language can be thought of in terms of the word's having associated with
it a set of conditions, where a condition is taken to be that which is

expressed by an open sentence, a predicative expression, or that which can be explicitly stated by employing a nominalized predicative expression. Each of the associated conditions can be thought of as a vector invoked by each and every use of the word. But again, all such vectors can be opposed or reinforced by the action and operation of other vectors. As instances of metonymy, metaphor, synecdoche and so forth serve to indicate, any adequate account of the meaning of sentences and of their possible readings in a discourse must take into account the existence of what might be called certain standard discourse operators. Thus there is undoubtedly something like an irony operator that can be employed in a discourse to reverse, as it were, the sense of what is said. And so one can readily say 'bright' and have it mean stupid as in 'That was a bright thing to do: now we are completely without lights' said in reference to someone who has just blown all the fuses. To say 'bright' meaning hungry would be more of a feat. Note, however, that that can be done: there is what might be called a "nonce operator" available that serves to give a word a special meaning for the nonce. Thus one obtains what linguists call a nonce sense of a word.

The existence of discourse operators plays a fundamental role in the diachronic development of a lexicon. Owing to their continuing operation, the concept of a finite dictionary can at best be only something of a convenient myth: dictionaries are essentially open ended (neither finite nor infinite), and the same is true of the sentences of a natural language like English: they are neither finite nor infinite; they do not constitute a definite set. Nonce uses apart, there is no reason to think of the meanings or of the senses of a word as constant: they are not. They may vary with the discourse. Languages flow in time; their slow drift can be seen in close in the easy deliquescence of conceptual limitations. If K is a bachelor it does not follow that K is incontinent; yet if one says 'That chary milksop is surely not a bachelor!', one may be saying, among other things, that incontinence is a prerequisite for qualifying as a bachelor: the senses of words are easily so augmented. Or diminished: 'The pope is, you know, a bachelor, but perhaps not an eligible one'. Or fused into figures: 'The life of a married bachelor is, after all, not without its compensations'. ('A married bachelor' is an oxymoron, a figure of speech involving the union of contradictories; 'oxymoron' is derived from two Greek words, one meaning sharp or wise, the other meaning dull or foolish, thus 'oxymoron' is itself a type of oxymoron.)

Each of the conditions associated with a word constitutes a vector invoked by each and every use of the word. But whether a particular vector is dominant depends on what other vectors are at play. Does it follow, for example, if K is a bachelor that K is not married? One can say that if George is a bachelor then if George is not a young knight, not a simple knight, not a yeoman of a trade guild, not a person who has taken a first degree at a university, and certainly not a young male fur seal, then if George is literally a bachelor, and if the word 'bachelor' is not being used in an augmented or diminished or in any way derivative or modified or shifted sense or meaning, then it does indeed follow that George is not married. It does follow, which, despite the complications, is to say something of the form 'If a then it follows that b'; but then to say this is not, for example, to say that one is not apt to encounter sentences of the form or to the effect that a and not b, nor is it to say that such sentences if encountered, are not to be countenanced. We must eschew any too simple conception of how concepts are related and how words work together in sentences and discourses. If if a then it follows that b, then b is best thought of as a vector invoked by each and every utterance of a. The effectiveness of this vector in a particular context, whether its presence is to be felt and if it is, how and to what degree, depends on the other vectors also operative in the context. In consequence, claims of the form 'If a then it follows that b' cannot be easy either to refute or to confirm. For that b is often the case when a is also the case may be owing to the action not of a but of other vectors. Thus it is true that a tiger is a large carnivorous feline even though a new-born tiger is not a large carnivore and still is a tiger. And milk is an excellent food even though milk liberally laced with strychnine is milk but is not an excellent food.

The factors that serve to determine what is said, in every sense of that phrase, appear to constitute a hopelessly unmanageable motley. And even if one ignores what is said by implication, the factors serving to determine what is said (in the other senses of the phrase) still appear to be discouragingly disparate and complex. Linguistic, logical, psychological and perceptual factors are all evidently active and interactive. All such factors appear to function as vectors, but what the magnitudes or directions or senses of the different vectors are it is at present impossible to say.

There is a cheerless moral to be drawn from all this: One may have a firm grasp of the phonology, morphology, syntax and semantics of a language, thus a thorough knowledge of the language, and yet not understand what is said in that language. But who would have thought otherwise?

University of North Carolina at Chapel Hill

REFERENCES

[1] From T. Patton.
[2] From C. Hockett.
[3] From F. Sibley and P. Ziff, *O Bitter Dicta*, The Punitive Press, Beirut, 1960.
[4] *Ibid.*
[5] *Ibid.*
[6] See P. Ziff, *Semantic Analysis*, Cornell University Press, Ithaca, 1960.

L. JONATHAN COHEN AND AVISHAI MARGALIT

THE ROLE OF INDUCTIVE REASONING IN THE INTERPRETATION OF METAPHOR

I

According to most current theories the semantics of a natural language should be focussed quite sharply on to the task of describing literal meanings. Metaphor, on this view, is either a pathological phenomenon that any account of normal language is right to disregard, or a rare and specialised extension of language, as in poetry, that can safely be left on one side for later analysis while the main task of explicating literal meaning proceeds. Yet this conception of semantics is false to the realities of the situation, in at least three respects. First, so far as synchronic linguistics is concerned, native speakers often move from literal to metaphorical speech, and back again, without any sense of strain or any bizarreness-reactions in their hearers. Consider, for example, a conversation in which the following sequences of sentences are uttered:

> *Has the producer secured any new talent?*
> *Yes, Rosemary has swallowed his bait.*

or

> *There is no fire burning in his belly.*
> *Yes, he is a rather uninteresting person.*

It is altogether counter-intuitive to write off the metaphors here as being in any way aberrant or abnormal modes of speech. Secondly, so far as diachronic linguistics is concerned, the importance of metaphor as a source of new dictionary meanings is well-known. But why should one suppose that, when metaphor operates thus as a causal factor in semantic change, it operates from outside, as it were? It is much more plausible to see the death of a dead metaphor as a readjustment, or boundary-shift, within language. For then the description of what has happened falls squarely within the history of the language, and the power of metaphor to cause semantic change becomes more intelligible. Thirdly, so far as

Davidson and Harman (eds.), Semantics of Natural Language, 722–740. *All rights reserved*
Copyright © 1972 *by D. Reidel Publishing Company, Dordrecht-Holland*

the psycholinguistics of language-learning is concerned the picture is grotesquely falsified if metaphor is regarded as a special form of linguistic sophistication. Children do not learn to speak metaphorically as a kind of crowning achievement in the apprenticeship of language-learning. Rather they use metaphors naturally from infancy onwards, and have gradually to learn – with respect to each noun, verb, adjective or adverb – how to speak literally. 'The car shouted at me', says the child. 'No, it hooted at you', corrects the parent. It is psychogenetically more illuminating to view literal patterns of word-use as the result of imposing certain restrictions on metaphorical ones, than to view metaphorical patterns as the results of removing certain restrictions from literal ones. The deliberate utterance of metaphor, in the awareness that it is such, is no doubt a phenomenon of adult *parole*. But metaphorical sentences are as much part of the *langue* that children acquire as are non-metaphorical ones.

One condition of adequacy, therefore, for the semantic component of a linguistic theory is that it should elucidate the nature of the bond that links metaphorical to literal meaning within the structure of a natural language. In this paper we shall suggest that such an elucidation can be achieved by an appropriate account of the role that has to be played by inductive reasoning in regard to statements about meaning in natural languages. But we shall not attempt even to outline a complete theory of semantics. Our object is solely to show, by means of certain philosophically idealised reconstructions, how inductive logic can help to clarify the problem of metaphor. So we shall develop, first, a brief summary of what we take to be the main features of inductive logic, together with some applications of these to the compilation of dictionary entries, and secondly, in terms of all this, we shall sketch an explication of metaphorical meaning.

It is worth noting at the outset, however, that one important consequence follows directly from the adequacy condition that we have just mentioned. Specifically, from the requirement that an adequate linguistic theory should explicate the nature of the bond that links metaphorical to literal meaning within the structure of a natural language, it follows that such a theory cannot assume that the meanings of lexical items are invariant under the process of semantic composition. A *reductio ad absurdum* argument, in six stages, suffices to show this:

(i)   Assume, as is commonly assumed in componential semantics,[1] that the meaning of a sentence is a componential function of a selection of just those meanings of its lexical items that are described in the dictionary.

(ii)   Then, as a consequence of (i), if metaphorical meanings occur in a sentence, they must be described in the dictionary.

(iii)   It is an accepted convention that the dictionary should record existing patterns of word-use, not anticipate new ones.

(iv)   It is a truism that the most striking metaphors are the ones that have never been used before.

(v)   It follows from (iii) and (iv) that some metaphors that may be found in the sentences of a language cannot be recorded in the dictionary.

(vi)   Since (ii) and (v) are inconsistent with one another, (i) must be rejected.

What is essential to recognise is that the novelty of a metaphor in speech no more constitutes it an innovation in the language than the fact that a sentence has never been uttered before constitutes its utterance a product of syntactic change. Any language, synchronically considered, contains an infinite potential for new metaphor, just as it contains an infinite potential for new sentences. It follows that metaphorical meanings can no more be listed in a dictionary than can sentences. So if the metaphorical meanings of lexical items contribute to the overall meanings of some sentences, these lexical items must be conceived to take on their meanings in those sentences in a way that is integral to the processes of semantic composition. And if the meanings of words that occur metaphorically are thus not invariant under semantic composition it is natural to suppose that literal meanings are also liable to be affected by this process. The difference between literal and metaphorical meaning will lie in the nature of the modification that takes place in each case. We seek to show how these modifications can be described in terms of the underlying inductive structure of semantic reasoning.

Indeed we conceive the investigation of meanings in a natural language to involve an essential stage of inductive enquiry in which correlations are established between certain occurrences of certain words and the presence of certain circumstances. Knowledge of meanings can never be satisfactorily understood if it is conceived solely in terms of an ability to map readings on to sentences. When a child learns the meanings of sentences in his native language, or a linguist those of sentences in a foreign language, he acquires an ability that no mere paraphrase-machine ever possesses – viz. an ability to match sentences with appropriate circumstances.

II

We take inductive support to be a type of timeless relation between propositions which is gradable or rankable but not measurable.[2] That is to say: the inductive support-function appropriate to a particular field of enquiry maps ordered pairs of propositions on to the first n integers that are greater than or equal to zero. Suppose first a set of propositions that is closed under the relation of material similarity to one another – i.e., under the relation of similarity in subject-matter to one another – where this similarity is determined by a list, or characterisation, of the non-logical expressions that may occur in such propositions. Next suppose a list of relevant variables for these propositions, i.e., a list of all sets of mutually exclusive circumstances (not describable in the terminology that determines the set of materially similar propositions) such that, for each set of circumstances, variation from any one of its circumstances – let us call them its 'variants' – to some other makes a difference to the joint satisfaction of the antecedent and consequent of some universally quantified conditional that is a member of the set of materially similar propositions. E.g., the set of circumstances in-the-mating-season/out-of-the-mating-season is a relevant variable for hypotheses about birds' plumage. Then, given any suitable well-ordering for the list of relevant variables, one can conceive a hierarchy of tests, of cumulatively increasing thoroughness, for any member of the set of materially similar propositions that is testable in structure, i.e., for any member that is a universally quantified conditional, and contingent, with a contingent antecedent and consequent, and so on. In test t_1 (the null case) one does not yet use this list of relevant variables but seeks joint satisfaction of the antecedent and consequent of the tested proposition under appropriate variations of any variable that is mentioned (or has a variant that is mentioned) in the antecedent. In test t_2 one operates every possible combination of these variations with variations of the first variable in the list of relevant variables; in test t_3 one operates every possible combination with variations of the first two variables in the list; and so on. In other words test t_1 is like an application of Mill's methods of difference or concomitant variations, and tests t_2, t_3, ...t_n are like more and more refined applications of his method of agreement alongside those other methods. So a report E, that states in effect that a proposition H has survived test t_i, without being affected by any variant of a variable not manipulated in that test, may be conceived to give H and its logical consequences at least ith grade support: i.e., $s[H, E] \geqslant i/n$, where n is the total number of different tests. Correspondingly, if E states that H is falsified by t_i (again without being affected by any variant of variables not manipulated in that test), then E cannot give H as much as ith grade support: i.e., $s[H, E] < i/n$.

Moreover, if H is (or might be) falsified by test t_i but not by t_{i-1}, it is always possible to introduce an appropriate qualification into the antecedent of H so that the resultant hypothesis is immune to falsification by t_i. Such a qualification would standardly consist in a restriction of the generalisation to some specified variant of the relevant variable of which another variant is responsible for H's falsification, or in an insertion of the proviso that no variant of this variable has any effect. Indeed it is possible to grade the simplicity of a hypothesis in inverse ratio to the number of such qualifications that are introduced. Then for every assessment of how well E inductively supports H there will be a precisely equivalent assessment of how simple a hypothesis resembling H can be if it is to be fully supported by E. Also, the less simple the hypothesis becomes, the shorter is the statement of evidence that is needed to give it full support. Indeed a hypothesis that is qualified in relation to every relevant variable (e.g., a hypothesis that is required to hold good only under certain well understood laboratory conditions) can be fully supported by a single evidential instance (e.g., the outcome of a single experiment).

Now the semantical content of an ideal dictionary for theoretical purposes may be viewed as a set of heavily qualified inductive hypotheses that are fully supported by reports of available evidence. If the dictionary is conceived as a part of a linguist's synchronic description of a natural language, the evidence will normally be constituted by the (presumably non-metaphorical) utterances of native speakers under sustained interrogation in appropriate circumstances or under self-interrogation (i.e.'

introspection). If instead the dictionary is conceived of as a part of the competence that is ingested by an ideal native speaker through the processes of language-learning, then the evidence will be constituted by the (presumably non-metaphorical) utterances and reactions of adult speakers in appropriate circumstances. The relevant variables will be those sets of mutually exclusive circumstances which are such that variation from one circumstance to another within the same set sometimes falsifies a hypothesis about the meaning of a word or morpheme.

What precise structure should these hypotheses be conceived to have? In order to simplify our account of them we shall assume here the availability of some bidirectional categorial grammar like that outlined by Lyons[3]. We conceive such a grammar to afford descriptions of deep structures only, and to require supplementation by transformational rules in order to afford syntactic descriptions of surface structures. But we choose a categorial representation of deep syntax rather than an equivalent[4] phrase-structure representation because of certain advantages (which will emerge in what follows) so far as semantic composition is concerned. We shall take a lexical item to be individuated by its phonological form and syntactic category, so that the different literal meanings of a polyseme would all be described, ideally, by a single dictionary entry. We shall concern ourselves here, however, only with the meanings of nouns, verbs (other than the copula), adjectives, adverbs and prepositions, since it would confuse the present issue if we were to go beyond what is necessary for an explication of the fundamental nature of metaphor. For the same reason we shall not concern ourselves here with the transformational rules that would be needed, in a complete grammar, to supplement our postulated categorial syntax, nor shall we concern ourselves at all with the semantics of token-reflexive words or of non-declarative sentences (such as performatives, interrogatives or imperatives). For this reason also we shall illustrate our arguments only by very simple, syntactically univocal examples, and we shall take all our examples from standard English.

We shall make considerable use of the concept of an 'occurrence' of a phrase or dictionary item. The same expression will be said to have different occurrences so far as it has different linguistic settings. But we shall not concern ourselves here with differences of occurrence that are determined by socio-physical settings. An unmodified occurrence of a word or phrase W is an occurrence of W in a sentence that contains no other noun, verb, adjective, adverb or preposition outside W, as typically in a sentence that does nothing but indicate an instance of what W names or describes, e.g., *This is a cat* (for the noun *cat*), *This is black* (for the adjective *black*) or *This is running* (for the verb *run*).

Thus at the theoretical limit of simplicity – which in practice is far too simple to be of any use in the dictionary – a semantical hypothesis of the kind with which we are concerned would have the structure of

(1)   For any x and any y, if x is an unmodified occurrence of the word-form W that belongs to the syntactic category C, then x names or describes y.

where the values of x and y constitute the whole domain of human discourse. The relevant variables for our dictionary hypotheses will then be those variables which are such that variation from one variant to another (other circumstances being the same) sometimes falsifies a hypothesis like (1). Some of these semantically relevant variables will have variants that affect objects, e.g., the size variable, the colour variable, the shape variable, or the live/dead variable. Others will have variants that primarily affect events or processes, e.g., fast/medium-speed/slow, or harmful/beneficial/neutral. Yet others will have variants that primarily affect characteristics, e.g., temporary/permanent. And some variables will affect everything, e.g., possessor of first-order characteristics/possessor of second-order characteristics/etc. (We assume the normal logical hierarchy whereby events, substances and objects possess first-order characteristics, first-order characteristics possess second-order ones, and so on.) These relevant variables for semantical hypotheses correspond to, though they are considerably more numerous than, what Aristotle called the categories of being. Indeed most semantic theories have worked with some such notion as that of a semantic category or distinctive feature classification. What we emphasise here is the fact that such a notion is not a peculiar and *sui generis* element of semantics, but just the local manifestation of a concept that is integral to the methodology of inductive enquiry in any field whatever – viz. the concept of a relevant variable. Correspondingly there is no need to restrict each mode of classification to a binary choice, as in a Jakobsonian distinctive feature matrix. An inductively relevant variable, whether in semantics or elsewhere, may have any finite number of variants.

An accepted list of semantically relevant variables $v_1, v_2, \ldots$ may be given at least a partial ordering by the number of different hypotheses like (1) that are falsified by variations of v_i in a corpus of interrogations of native speakers, and where two or more variables score the same number of falsifications the corpus may be extended until a well-ordering is achieved for them. The evidence of such a corpus may also be expected to show – or to be capable of an extension that will show – how far each hypothesis like (1) needs to be qualified, in respect of the semantically relevant variables, in order to achieve a fully supported version. For a univocal dictionary item the required qualification will consist in the specification, in respect of each variable v_i that causes trouble, either of an appropriate disjunction of one or more variants of v_i that exclude the falsificatory variant or variants, or of a proviso that the situation is unaffected by any variant of v_i, as in, e.g.,

(2)   For any x and any y, if x is an unmodified occurrence of the word-form *ship*, that belongs to the syntactic category n, and y is a possessor of first-order characteristics, and mobile, and either aquatic or aerial, and unaffected by the live/dead variable, etc. etc., then x names or describes y

where no qualification is needed in respect of, say, the size or colour variables.[5]

Now (1) may be regarded as showing the limiting structure of the hypothesis which an investigator sets out with *ab initio*, is trying to discover the meaning of a single word from a corpus of interrogations of native speakers; and (2) might then appear to be an example of the kind of hypothesis at which he eventually arrives. Indeed, up to a point an investigator may well profit by confining his attention, so far as he can, to unmodified occurrences, as in (2), since without an extensive knowledge of other words it will be quite difficult to ascertain the meaning of *ship* by studying what features are present or absent when a native speaker is brought to say *This is a toy ship*, *This is a model ship*, *This is a wrecked ship*, or *This is a sailing ship*. But there are three reasons why a semantical hypothesis like (2) cannot be regarded as a paradigm dictionary entry. First, there will be many occasions on which an investigator finds it necessary to investigate the meanings of modified rather than unmodified occurrences. For example, in the case of an adverb there must always be something that is being expressly stated as happening or being done in the manner described by the adverb. Secondly, it will often be convenient to investigate modified occurrences in order to obtain a sufficient range of evidence or to make use of what is already known about other words. Thirdly, most occurrences of words in sentences are not unmodified ones. So a hypothesis like (2) would be relatively useless as a dictionary entry. It follows that a paradigm dictionary entry for the noun *ship* would not take the form of (2) but rather of

(3)   For any x and any y, if x is an occurrence of the word-form *ship* that belongs to the syntactic category n, and y is a possessor of first-order characteristics, and mobile, and either aquatic or aerial, and unaffected by the live/dead variable, etc. etc., and y is not excluded by any modifier of x, then x names or describes y

where an occurrence of a noun, verb, adjective, adverb or preposition, or of a phrase of any of these types, is said to be a modifier of another occurrence of a noun, verb, adjective, adverb or preposition if both occurrences are in the same sentence.

What has been proposed so far, however, is a structure for dictionary entries that relate to univocal items, like the noun *ship*. For a polyseme, like *bank* or *carriage*, a more complex structure is obviously involved. A large disjunction has to be inserted into the second half of the antecedent, as in

(4)   For any x and any y, if x is an occurrence of the word-form W that belongs to the syntactic category C, and y is EITHER V_1^i, and V_2^j, and unaffected by v_3, etc. etc., OR V_1^k, and unaffected by v_2, and V_3^l, etc. etc., OR etc. etc., and y is not excluded by any modifier of x, then x names or describes y,

where V_1^i and V_1^k name variants of v_1, and V_2^j and V_3^l name variants of v_2 and v_3, respectively.

Nor should it be supposed that hypotheses like (3) and (4) can always be established in a fully determinate form with conclusive certainty. It has to be borne in mind that the meanings of most words in a natural

language possess what Waismann called 'open texture',[6] so that for any
given semantical hypothesis like (3) or (4) one may some day encounter
a borderline situation that is under-determined by the hypothesis. For
example, is a hovercraft a ship or not? If one wants to say that it is not a
ship, it looks as though there must be some semantic variable of hitherto
undetected relevance, such as the presence/absence of support by the
medium over which travel is effected. Now certainly the once un-
suspected existence, and later discovery, of hidden variables is a familiar
phenomenon in all fields of scientific enquiry,[7] and especially when investigating a rather exotic language a linguist will often not feel confident
that he has discovered all the semantically relevant variables. So if a
dictionary hypothesis is formulated in a fully determinate form, the inductive support for it may never be gradable as more than n/e where test
t_n is the most thorough test that is known and t_e (with the value of e
unknown) is the most thorough test possible. Of course if $n < e$ and grades
of inductive support are thought of as probabilities, the multiplication-
law for conjoint probabilities might then produce an implausibly low
grade of inductive support for the dictionary as a whole, since many
thousands of its entries, or individual hypotheses, will be independent
of one another on the evidence of a particular corpus – especially where
the corpus contains many unmodified occurrences. But it can be shown
that, if grade of inductive support is assessed by the method of relevant
variables, it conforms to the principle

If $s[H_2, E] \geqslant s[H_1, E]$, then $s[H_2 \& H_1, E] = s[H_1, E]$

and that for this and other reasons grade of inductive support is not only
not a probability but not even any function of probabilities.[8] And in
any case there is always a way of ensuring full support for a dictionary
hypothesis that has been qualified in accordance with the evidence available at a fairly advanced stage of investigation. All that is needed is the
insertion of a proviso that the hypothesis is intended to apply 'in normal
circumstances' or 'ceteris paribus', and full support is bought, as it were,
at the price of full determinateness. Even so the hypothesis will often
be a very lengthy one. The meanings of many words in a natural language
are immensely rich, and it is often impracticable (especially where a
word does not belong to a closed and interconnected group, like the
vocabulary of family relations), to draw a sharp line between what a

native speaker knows about the meaning of a word and what he knows about the things or situations which he would use the word to describe.

III

It will be remembered that in a categorial grammar the operation of so-called 'cancellation', which reduces a sentence's concatenation of morpheme categories to Σ, determines in the process an asymmetrical relation of dependence within pairs of constituents. E.g., in terms of Lyons's own example we can write the categorial classification of a sentence's lexical items underneath them, thus:

$$Poor \quad John \quad ran \quad away$$
$$(\overrightarrow{nn}) \quad n \quad (\Sigma \overleftarrow{n}) \quad \{(\Sigma \overleftarrow{n}) \ (\Sigma \overleftarrow{n})\}$$

Then in order to produce just Σ at the end, *poor* has to cancel with *John* and *ran* with *away*, and then *poor John* with *ran away*. At each stage the constituent with the more complex classification is to be regarded as the dependent constituent, and the one with the less complex classification as the independent one. A categorial description of the deep structure of a sentence may therefore be taken to afford a sufficient guide to the sentence's successive stages of semantic composition, so far as the deep structure is concerned. At the first stage, where pairs of individual lexical items are involved, the dictionary entry for the dependent constituent is incorporated into the dictionary entry for the independent constituent, in the case of each pair, with appropriate alterations being made to one or other or both of the two hypotheses, and a semantical hypothesis thus becomes available for each phrase formed by two such constituents. At the next and all subsequent stages this procedure is repeated, with the semantical hypothesis for the dependent constituent being incorporated into the semantical hypothesis or dictionary entry for the independent constituent, until finally a single semantical hypothesis emerges for the sentence as a whole (as far as its deep structure is concerned). This final hypothesis will not need (except at the level of discourse analysis) to include any clause of the form 'and y is not excluded by any modifier of x'. E.g., in the case of *Poor John ran away*, what we get are, first, hypotheses about anything's being named or described by *poor John* if it has certain characteristics, and about anything's being named or described by *ran away* if it has certain characteristics, and, secondly, a hypothesis about anything's being named or described by the sentence *Poor John ran away* if it has certain characteristics.

In the process of carrying out such incorporations five different types of alteration may need to be made to one or other or both of the two hypotheses that are being amalgamated.

First, there may be alterations that are necessary for disambiguating the two constituents, so far as such an alteration is determined by either or both of them. This type of alteration would normally take the form of eliminating one or more major disjuncts from the antecedent of one or both of the hypotheses. For example, the dictionary entry for the noun *bank* will no doubt have a disjunctive antecedent, as in (4). But the disjunct for the sense in which a bank is a financial institution (as distinct from the building that houses one) will presumably include some such restriction as 'and unaffected by the colour variable'. So in composing the semantical hypothesis for the phrase *green bank* (so far as literal meaning alone is concerned) this disjunct must be wholly omitted, since *green* describes a variant of the colour variable. Similarly, the dictionary entry for the adjective *fair* will no doubt also have a disjunctive antecedent. But the disjunct for the sense in which *fair* contrasts with *dark* will presumably include some such restriction as 'and light-brown or off-white'. So in composing the semantical hypothesis for the phrase *fair price* this disjunct must be wholly omitted, since the dictionary entry for *price* will presumably contain the restriction 'and unaffected by the colour variable'. In other cases, perhaps, it will be just a clash of variants that secures omission of one disjunct as in the difference between the sense of the noun *minister* in the vocabulary of politics and its sense in the vocabulary of religion. We do not underestimate the immense difficulty of filling in the etc.-clauses of (3) and (4) and constructing each dictionary entry in just the right way to achieve such disambiguations. But it can hardly be denied that where a native speaker feels no ambiguity in regard to a particular occurrence of a polyseme this must, ideally, be reflected in corresponding interrelationships between the dictionary entries concerned (so far as differences of occurrence are determined solely by linguistic, and not at all by socio-physical, settings).

Secondly, once this operation of disambiguation has been carried not as far as is possible it is necessary to look at whether the hypotheses concern possessors of first-order characteristics, possessors of second-order characteristics, and so on. In the simplest type of case, as with *green bank* or *tall ship*, both hypotheses concern possessors of first-order characteristics. Almost all that need be done in such a case is to conjoin the restrictions specified in the semantical hypothesis for the dependent constituent with the restrictions specified in the semantical hypothesis for the independent constituent. The latter hypothesis, thus altered, and with any duplications removed, and speaking of a phrase of the appropriate syntactic category, will then become the semantical hypothesis for the literal meaning of the phrase as a whole.

Thirdly, however, there will be many cases, like *ran away* or *dances beautifully*[9] where the hypothesis for the dependent constituent concerns possessors of characteristics of the next higher order than those possessed by anything that the hypothesis for the independent constituent concerns. In such a case the restrictions specified in the former hypothesis will not be conjoined with those specified in the latter but inserted as a modification of them, i.e., 'and is V_1^i and V_2^j and ... and this conjunction of characteristics is V_{10}^k and ...'. The same will hold for dependent constituents that apply polysemically either to possessors of first-order characteristics or to possessors of second-order characteristics or to possessors of third-order characteristics (e.g., *useful*, as in *useful object, useful attribute, useful manner*), or to those that apply equally well to the last two of these three or to others (e.g., *very*, as in *very beautiful, very beautifully*, etc.). In certain cases the restrictions specified in the hypothesis for the dependent constituent will need to be conjoined with those already inserted as a modification of the main restrictions specified in the hypothesis for the independent constituent, as in *drives fast and skilfully*. In other cases there will be a modification of the modification as in *drives fast skilfully*. In yet others the polysemy of the dependent constituent will generate an ambiguity in the compound phrase, as in *beautiful dancer*. Also, there will be cases where a lexical item may need to be displaced by the reversal, or quasi-reversal, of a transformation before its semantical role can be properly understood. E.g., *The snow has fortunately melted* needs to be understood as *That the snow has melted is fortunate* so that *is fortunate* can be seen to be the dependent constituent that modifies *The snow has melted*. But there are far too many such points of detail for us to discuss them all here.

In a fourth kind of case the hypothesis for the dependent constituent can only have its restrictions incorporated into those for the independent constituent if one or more of the latter are deleted. Normally, for example, one would not call anything *a ship* unless it were capable of transporting people. But words like *toy*, *model*, etc. apply only to things that do not do what is normally done by things resembling them in most other respects. So under the use variable they enforce an alteration from, e.g., a mention of human transportation to a mention of children's play when the semantical hypothesis for the phrase *toy ship* is constructed.

Fifthly, there will be a characteristic type of alteration that is necessitated in the case of metaphor. The metaphorical meanings of a word or phrase in a natural language are all contained, as it were, within its literal meaning or meanings. They are reached by removing any restrictions in relation to certain variables from the appropriate section or sections of its semantical hypothesis. For example, *baby* has as one of its metaphorical meanings the sense of *very small of its kind*: cf. *baby airplane* as against *baby daughter*. Here it is obviously the age and human/animal/artificial/ etc. variables that are being treated as if they imposed no restriction, while a restriction of size is still retained. Or if this is considered an example of already dead metaphor, consider *That old man is a baby*, where on the most straightforward interpretation the age and size variables are presumably being treated as if they imposed no restriction, and other attributes of babies are being ascribed, such as mental incapacity. Or consider our earlier example of the sentence *The car shouted at me*. Here it is apparently just the human/animal/artificial/etc. variable which is being treated as if it imposed no restriction on the occurrence of *shouted*. If a child says this, he has not yet fully grasped the relevance of that variable: if an adult, he is momentarily ignoring it. Or consider *The poor are the negroes of Europe*, where – on a plausible metaphorical interpretation – the colour variable is presumably being treated as imposing no restriction, and other attributes of negroes are being ascribed, such as being underprivileged. Note that in all such cases the variable or variables that have their restrictions removed may be expected to be fairly near the beginning of the ordered sequence of relevant variables. Any such variable must be a fairly important one. Otherwise there would not be sufficient distance between the restricted meaning and the derestricted one for the latter to be regarded as metaphor.

But it is essential to distinguish here between metaphorical meaning in the speech or utterances of a community, and metaphorical meaning in the sentences of its language. In speech it is knowledge of background facts or of the socio-physical context of utterance, along with certain presumptions of appropriateness, that helps a hearer to recognise whether the speaker intends a literal or a metaphorical meaning for a particular utterance of a word, phrase or sentence. But in a natural language almost every sentence is potentially ambiguous in one or other of two main ways so far as metaphor is concerned,[10] and its complete semantical hypothesis can be correspondingly disjunctive.

One way in which this happens is when a meaning is obtainable for the sentence quite straightforwardly by amalgamations of some of the first four kinds mentioned above. For example, *Tom is just a baby* is such a sentence, and it has both a literal meaning, declaring Tom to be an infant, and several metaphorical meanings, e.g., declaring *Tom* to be rather small, or to be mentally incapable, or not to have existed very long. Similarly *The weather is stormy today* either declares the state of the weather, with literal meanings for all its words, or declares the general outlook to be currently unfavourable, with metaphorical meanings for at least *weather* and *stormy*.

The other main form of ambiguity is when a sentence's meaning is not obtainable quite straightforwardly by amalgamations of some of the first four kinds mentioned, because at some stage in the series of amalgamations that ends in the composition of the sentence there is a conflict between one or more restrictions in the semantical hypothesis for the dependent constituent and one or more restrictions in the semantical hypothesis for the independent one. An obvious example of this is *That old man is a baby*. But which hypothesis then defers to which? It is tempting at first to suggest that before amalgamation takes place the conflicting restrictions have to be removed in each case from the hypothesis for the dependent constituent. But though this may be the presumptive interpretation in speech, the presumption is rebuttable by the evidence of context etc.: some very young babies do look curiously like old men. The correct view seems to be that, in the language, the sentence *That old man is a baby* is ambiguous. Either its subject is literal and its predicate metaphorical, or vice versa.[11] Disambiguation is a matter for speech. And the same is true when dependent and independent constituents do not both apply to possessors of first-order characteristics, as in the phrase *a baby in politics*.

It should not be a cause for concern that our account of metaphor imputes so much ambiguity to the sentences and word-occurrences of a natural language. Rather, the literal-metaphorical ambiguity should be seen as a vitally important part of the semantic richness of natural language. It is comparable, in that respect, to the residual vagueness of all words that is most conspicuously apparent in their unmodified occurrences. Language exploits this vagueness by using it as a raw material for the various processes of modification that are represented by amalgamations of semantical hypotheses. Indeed such processes of modification could be regarded, within the framework of discourse analysis, as capable of continuing far beyond the limits of a single sentence. A speaker often has to state his point very vaguely at first, and then gradually introduce more and more precision into it. Similarly a metaphor is often carried on and developed from one sentence to another.[12] Modification and metaphor are the two main instruments of semantic flexibility in natural language. If the words and phrases of a natural language were not as vague and ambiguous as they are, it would never be possible for speech to be as indefinitely precisifiable and variegated as it is.

Two further points are perhaps worth mentioning within the limits of the present article.

First it is obvious that a definition of synonymy emerges from our account of semantic composition. An occurrence of one word or phrase may be said to be fully synonymous with an occurrence of another if the semantical hypothesis that is fully supported for the former differs from that which is fully supported for the latter only in respect of the different word or phrase it mentions. Hence, as an investigator learns more about the semantics of a language, and comes to take more of the relevant variables into account, he may come to see that occurrences which he once thought fully synonymous with one another are not in fact fully synonymous. So synonymy in this sense is an empirical relation. Moreover such a synonymy can also be partial since two occurrences will have the same meaning just so far as the appropriate fully supported semantical hypotheses resemble one another in respect of each relevant variable. Of course, such a definition of synonymy will not free us from Quine's charmed circle of semantical terminology, since in the characterisation of semantical hypotheses we have used, as undefined primitives, the terms 'names' and 'describes'. But we do not regard the reduction of semantical terms to nonsemantical ones as being a task that either can or must be accomplished by a philosophical reconstruction of the semantics of a natural language.

Secondly, on our view the sentences (i.e., syntactically non-deviant morpheme-strings) of a natural language do not admit of any distinction between the semantically deviant and the semantically non-deviant. Nor need there be any distinctions of syntactic deviance or non-deviance that are based on selectional rules, since we dispense altogether with syntactic rules of this kind. We distinguish instead between sentences that admit only metaphorical interpretations, like *That old man is a baby*, and sentences that admit both metaphorical and non-metaphorical ones, like *Tom is a baby*. Admittedly there are some extreme cases. Metaphorical sentences tend to give an impression of meaninglessness when the metaphors have got badly mixed and there seems to be a considerable variety of alternative metaphorical disambiguations, as in *Colourless green ideas sleep furiously*, or when rather a lot of restrictions have to be removed in the process of amalgamating meanings, as in *Today is in bed*. Nevertheless our proposals for the explication of metaphor do entail, so far as deep structure is concerned, that any syntactically non-deviant morpheme-string of a natural language always has at least one meaning – just as for any actual speaker's utterance in ordinary speech, unless sanity or seriousness is in doubt, the hearer's presumption is always that some meaning can be found. No doubt there are very many syntactically simple sentences that are never uttered because their metaphors are too difficult to disambiguate. But there are also very many non-metaphorical sentences that are never uttered because of their syntactic complexity (degree of nesting, etc.). The existence of a metaphor, like that of a sentence, is a feature of *langue*, not of *parole*.[13]

The Queen's College, Oxford

REFERENCES

[1] Cf., for instance, J. J. Katz and J. A. Fodor, 'The Structure of a Semantic Theory', in *The Structure of Language* (ed. by J. A. Fodor and J. A. Katz). The rejection of this assumption was implicit in L. Jonathan Cohen, *The Diversity of Meaning* (2nd.

ed., 1966) §7, esp. pp. 63–65. But that account of dictionary entries was altogether too sketchy to sustain an explication of the concept of metaphor.

[2] The view of inductive reasoning that is presented here is a very brief summary of the account that is expounded and defended in detail in L. Jonathan Cohen, *The Implications of Induction*, 1970. In Avishai Margalit, *The Cognitive Status of Metaphors* (unpublished dissertation for the Hebrew University of Jerusalem) a Carnapian version of induction is used to explicate metaphor.

[3] John Lyons, *Introduction to Theoretical Linguistics* (1968) p. 227ff.

[4] Cf. Y. Bar Hillel, C. Gaifman, and E. Shamir, 'On Categorial and Phrase Structure Grammars', *The Bulletin of the Research Council of Israel* 9F (1960) p. 1ff., reprinted in Y. Bar Hillel, *Language and Information* (1964) p. 99ff.

[5] To deal with polyadic terms (e.g., transitive verbs, prepositions like *between*, etc.) it is obvious that more complex forms of hypothesis (with n-tuple quantification, where $n > 2$) are required. We ignore such polyadic terms in our explication of metaphorical meaning, because their peculiarities are not cardinal to the issue. But there seems to be no difficulty in principle in extending our explication to polyadic terms.

We assume the domains of (1) and (2) to include everything that people actually talk of themselves as talking about, including objects, acts, events, properties, qualities, substances, numbers, persons, etc. But we think that this assumption is not a metaphysical commitment of any kind *on our part*, and that it need not obfuscate philosophical distinctions that may be important for other purposes.

It should perhaps be pointed out that the ordering of the semantically relevant variables is important not only for the explication of synchronic interpretations of metaphor (as emerges in the present paper), but also for the elucidation of the difference between those features of a word's meaning that diachronic studies reveal to be more resistant to non-metaphorical change and those that such studies reveal to be less resistant to non-metaphorical change.

[6] F. Waismann, 'Verifiability', *Proceedings of the Aristotelian Society*, Supp. Vol. XIX (1961) p. 236ff.

[7] On the discovery of semantic (and syntactic) variables in childhood language-learning, cf. L. Jonathan Cohen, 'Some Applications of Inductive Logic to the Theory of Language', *American Philosophical Quarterly* 7 (October, 1970), pp. 299–310. It is also worth noting that Trier's notion of a semantic field is easily reconstructed within the proposed inductive framework. Essentially, a field is a set of words (e.g. *boil*, *fry*) that are subjected to the same restrictions as one another under some variables but not under all.

[8] For the details of the argument, and the concept of evidence involved, cf. *The Implications of Induction* §§3, 8, 12 and 13.

[9] We borrow the example from H. Reichenbach's 'Analysis of Conversational Language' in his *Elements of Symbolic Logic* (1948) p. 307.

[10] The exceptions seem to be either rather vacuous sentences like *That is so*, or sentences involving very abstruse technical terms.

[11] In Black's terms, in the one case the focus of the metaphor is on the baby and the frame is *That old man is...*, and in the other case the focus of the metaphor is on the old man and the frame is *... is a baby*: cf. M. Black, *Models and Metaphor* (1962) p. 27ff.

[12] This is not the same as allegory, although it is sometimes so regarded (e.g., in *Webster's Collegiate Dictionary* (1932) s.v. allegory). An allegory is a systematic reinterpretation that can be imposed on a stretch of discourse, like a one-to-one correspondence between two somewhat similar models for a logistic system. An author could

still intend an allegory even if he wrote in a language devoid of metaphor, since to credit him with knowledge of the correspondence between the allegorical and the non-allegorical interpretation is to credit him with factual wisdom rather than linguistic skill. Contrariwise an allegorically intended narrative, like George Orwell's *Animal Farm*, can contain occasional metaphors that are as much subject to allegorical reinterpretation as are the nonmetaphorical passages.

What allegories do sometimes exploit is not so much metaphor as symbolism. In a culture in which the pig is a symbol for greed, and a man may be said to be as greedy as a pig, a story about a pig can more easily be reinterpreted as a story about a greedy person. In such cases we have to suppose that the dictionary entry shows *pig*, say, to be a polyseme that names members of the porcine species either *tout court* or as symbols of greed: it is the latter alternative that allows the common metaphorical use, as in *That man is a pig*. One of the worst features of the old theory that all language is symbolic (e.g., C. K. Ogden and I. A. Richards, *The Meaning of Meaning*, Ch. I) was that it blocked the way to recognising just when and where symbolism does influence language.

[13] It is sometimes suggested, by grammarians who take all metaphorical sentences to be linguistically deviant, that metaphor is a merely surface structure phenomenon and arises through the improper application of transformational rules to a deep structure that has, from a semantical point of view, the pattern of a simile. But this suggestion blurs the difference between simile and metaphor. To state a similarity between two things significantly one must state in what respects they are similar, whereas all the interesting metaphorical sentences achieve their characteristic force by not stating any respects in which a comparison is to be drawn.

It might also be objected against our account that it fails to allow for metaphorical speech that is parasitic on knowledge of fact rather than on knowledge of meaning, as perhaps in *He has a heart of steel* if hardness is thought to be a contingent property of steel rather than one of its defining conditions. But we prefer to regard a feature's lending itself thus to the construction of metaphor as evidence that it has in fact passed into the language.

PATRICK SUPPES

PROBABILISTIC GRAMMARS
FOR NATURAL LANGUAGES*

I. INTRODUCTION

Although a fully adequate grammar for a substantial portion of any natural language does not exist, a vigorous and controversial discussion of how to choose among several competing grammars has already developed. On occasion, criteria of simplicity have been suggested as systematic scientific criteria for selection. The absence of such systematic criteria of simplicity in other domains of science inevitably raises doubts about the feasibility of such criteria for the selection of a grammar. Although some informal and intuitive discussion of simplicity is often included in the selection of theories or models in physics or in other branches of science, there is no serious systematic literature on problems of measuring simplicity. Nor is there any systematic literature in which criteria of simplicity are used in a substantive fashion to select from among several theories. There are many reasons for this, but perhaps the most pressing one is that the use of more obviously objective criteria leaves little room for the addition of further criteria of simplicity. The central thesis of this paper is that objective probabilistic criteria of a standard scientific sort may be used to select a grammar.

Certainly the general idea of looking at the distribution of linguistic types in a given corpus is not new. Everyone is familiar with the remarkable agreement of Zipf's law with the distribution of word frequencies in almost any substantial sample of a natural language. The empirical agreement of these distributions with Zipf's law is not in dispute, although a large and controversial literature is concerned with the most appropriate assumptions of a qualitative and elementary kind from which to derive the law. While there is, I believe, general agreement about the approximate empirical adequacy of Zipf's law, no one claims that a probabilistic account of the frequency distribution of words in a corpus is anything like an ultimate account of how the words are used or why they are used when they are. In the same sense, in the discussion here of proba-

Davidson and Harman (eds.), Semantics of Natural Language, 741–762. *All rights reserved*
Copyright © 1972 *by D. Reidel Publishing Company, Dordrecht - Holland*

bilistic grammars, I do not claim that the frequency distribution of grammatical types provides an ultimate account of how the language is used or for what purpose a given utterance is made. Yet, it does seem correct to claim that the generation of the relative frequencies of utterances is a proper requirement to place on a generative grammar for a corpus.

Because of the importance of this last point, let me expand it. It might be claimed that the relative frequencies of grammatical utterances are no more pertinent to grammar than the relative frequency of shapes to geometry. No doubt, in one sense such a claim is correct. If we are concerned, on the one hand, simply with the mathematical relation between formal languages and the types of automata that can generate these languages, then there is a full set of mathematical questions for which relative frequencies are not appropriate. In the same way, in standard axiomatizations of geometry, we are concerned only with the representations of the geometry and its invariants, not with questions of actual frequency of distribution of figures in nature. In fact, we all recognize that such questions are foreign to the spirit of either classical or modern geometry. On the other hand, when we deal with the physics of objects in nature there are many aspects of shapes and their frequencies of fundamental importance, ranging from the discussion of the shape of clouds and the reason for their shape to the spatial configuration of large and complex organic molecules like proteins.

From the standpoint of empirical application, one of the more dissatisfying aspects of the purely formal theory of grammars is that no distinction is made between utterances of ordinary length and utterances that are arbitrarily long, for example, of more than 10^{50} words. One of the most obvious and fundamental features of actual spoken speech or written text is the distribution of length of utterance, and the relatively sharp bounds on the complexity of utterances, because of the highly restricted use of embedding or other recursive devices. Not to take account of these facts of utterance length and the limitations on complexity is to ignore two major aspects of actual speech and writing. As we shall see, one of the virtues of a probabilistic grammar is to deal directly with these central features of language.

Still another way of putting the matter is this. In any application of concepts to a complex empirical domain, there is always a degree of uncertainty as to the level of abstraction we should reach for. In mechanics, for example, we do not take account of the color of objects, and it is not taken as a responsibility of mechanics to predict the color of objects. (I refer here to classical mechanics – it could be taken as a responsibility of quantum mechanics.) But ignoring major features of empirical phenomena is in all cases surely a defect and not a virtue. We ignore major features because it is difficult to account for them, not because they are uninteresting or improper subjects for investigation. In the case of grammars, the features of utterance length and utterance complexity seem central; the distribution of these features is of primary importance in understanding the character of actual language use.

A different kind of objection to considering probabilistic grammars at the present stage of inquiry might be the following. It is agreed on all sides that an adequate grammar, in the sense of simply accounting for the grammatical structure of sentences, does not exist for any substantial portion of any natural language. In view of the absence of even one grammar in terms of this criterion, what is the point of imposing a stricter criterion to also account for the relative frequency of utterances? It might be asserted that until at least one adequate grammar exists, there is no need to be concerned with a probabilistic criterion of choice. My answer to such a claim is this. The probabilistic program described in this paper is meant to be supplementary rather than competitive with traditional investigations of grammatical structure. The large and subtle linguistic literature on important features of natural language syntax constitutes an important and permanent body of material. To draw an analogy from meteorology, a probabilistic measure of a grammar's adequacy stands to ordinary linguistic analysis of particular features, such as verb nominalization or negative constructions, in the same relation that dynamical meteorology stands to classical observation of the clouds. While dynamical meteorology can predict the macroscopic movement of fronts, it cannot predict the exact shape of fair-weather cumulus or storm-generated cumulonimbus. Put differently, one objective of a probabilistic grammar is to account for a high percentage of a corpus with a relatively simple grammar and to isolate the deviant cases that need additional analysis and explanation. At the present time, the main tendency in linguistics is to look at the deviant cases and to ignore trying to give a quantitative account of that part of a corpus that can be analyzed in relatively simple terms.

Another feature of probabilistic grammars worth noting is that such a grammar can permit the generation of grammatical types that do not occur in a given corpus. It is possible to take a tolerant attitude toward utterances that are on the borderline of grammatical acceptability, as long as the relative frequency of such utterances is low. The point is that the objective of the probabilistic model is not just to give an account of the finite corpus of spoken speech or written text used as a basis for estimating the parameters of the model, but to use the finite corpus as a sample to infer parameter values for a larger, potentially infinite 'population' in the standard probabilistic fashion. On occasion, there seems to have been some confusion on this point. It has been seriously suggested more than once that for a finite corpus one could write a grammar by simply having a separate rewrite rule for each terminal sentence. Once a probabilistic grammar is sought, such a proposal is easily ruled out as acceptable. One method of so doing is to apply a standard probabilistic test as to whether genuine probabilities have been observed in a sample. We run a split-half analysis, and it is required that within sampling variation the same estimates be obtained from two randomly selected halves of the corpus.

Another point of confusion among some linguists and philosophers with whom I have discussed the methodology of fitting probabilistic grammars to data is this. It is felt that some sort of legerdemain is involved in estimating the parameters of a probabilistic grammar from the data which it is supposed to predict. At a casual glance it may seem that the predictions should always be good and not too interesting because the parameters are estimated from the very data they are used to predict. But this is to misunderstand the many different ways the game of prediction may be played. Certainly, if the number of parameters equals the number of predictions the results are not very interesting. On the other hand, the more the number of predictions exceeds the number of parameters the greater the interest in the predictions of the theory. To convince one linguist of the wide applicability of techniques of estimating parameters from data they predict and also to persuade him that such estimation is not an intellectually dishonest form of science, I pointed out that in studying the motion of the simple mechanical system consisting of the Earth, Moon and Sun, at least nine position parameters and nine velocity or momentum parameters as well as mass parameters must be estimated from the data (the actual situation is much more complicated), and everyone agrees that this is 'honest' science.

It is hardly possible in this paper to enter into a full-scale analysis and defense of the role of probabilistic and statistical methodology in science. What I have said briefly here can easily be expanded; I have tried to deal with some of the issues in a monograph on causality (Suppes, 1970). My own conviction is that at present the quantitative study of language must almost always be probabilistic in nature. The data simply cannot be handled quantitatively by a deterministic theory. A third confusion of some linguists needs to be mentioned in this connection. The use of a probabilistic grammar in no way entails a commitment to finite Markovian dependencies in the temporal sequence of spoken speech. Two aspects of such grammars make this clear. First, in general such grammars generate a stochastic process that is a chain of infinite order in the terminal vocabulary, not a finite Markov process. Second, the probabilistic parameters are attached directly to the generation of non-terminal strings of syntactic categories. Both of these observations are easy to check in the more technical details of later sections.

The purpose of this paper is to define the framework within which empirical investigations of probabilistic grammars can take place and to sketch how this attack can be made. The full presentation of empirical results will be left to other papers. In the detailed empirical work I have depended on the collaboration of younger colleagues, especially Elizabeth Gammon and Arlene Moskowitz. I draw on our joint work for examples in subsequent sections of this paper. In the next section I give a simple example, indeed, a simple-minded example, of a probabilistic grammar, to illustrate the methodology without complications. In the third section I indicate how such ideas may be applied to the spoken speech of a young child. Because of the difficulties and complexities of working with actual speech, I illustrate in the fourth section some of the results obtained when the apparatus of analysis is applied to a much simpler corpus, a first-grade reader. I emphasize that the results of an empirical sort in this paper are all preliminary in nature. The detailed development of the empirical applications is a complicated and involved affair and goes beyond the scope of the work presented here.

II. A SIMPLE EXAMPLE

A simple example that illustrates the methodology of constructing and testing probabilistic grammars is described in detail in this section. It is not meant to be complex enough to fit any actual corpus.

The example is a context-free grammar that can easily be re-written as a regular grammar. The five syntactic or semantic categories are just V_1, V_2, Adj, PN and N, where V_1 is the class of intransitive verbs, V_2 the class of transitive verbs or two-place predicates, Adj the class of adjectives, PN the class of proper nouns and N the class of common nouns. Additional non-terminal vocabulary consists of the symbols S, NP, VP and AdjP. The set of production rules consists of the following seven rules, plus the rewrite rules for terminal vocabulary that belong to one of the five categories. The probability of using one of the rules is shown on the right. Thus, since Rule 1 is obligatory, the probability of using it is 1. In the generation of any sentence, either Rule 2 or Rule 3 must be used. Thus the probabilities α and $1-\alpha$, which sum to 1, and so forth for the other rules.

Production Rule	Probability
1. $S \rightarrow NP + VP$	1
2. $VP \rightarrow V_1$	$1 - \alpha$
3. $VP \rightarrow V_2 + NP$	α
4. $NP \rightarrow PN$	$1 - \beta$
5. $NP \rightarrow AdjP + N$	β
6. $AdjP \rightarrow AdjP + Adj$	$1 - \gamma$
7. $AdjP \rightarrow Adj$	γ

This probabilistic grammar has three parameters, α, β and γ, and the probability of each grammatical type of sentence can be expressed as a monomial function of the parameters. In particular, if Adj^n is understood to denote a string of n adjectives, then the possible grammatical types (infinite in number) all fall under one of the corresponding schemes, with the indicated probability.

Grammatical Type	Probability
1. $PN + V_1$	$(1 - \alpha)(1 - \beta)$
2. $PN + V_2 + PN$	$\alpha(1 - \beta)^2$

3. $\text{Adj}^n + N + V_1$ $(1 - \alpha)\,\beta\,(1 - \gamma)^{n-1}\gamma$

4. $PN + V_2 + \text{Adj}^n + N$ $\alpha\beta(1 - \beta)(1 - \gamma)^{n-1}\gamma$

5. $\text{Adj}^n + N + V_2 + PN$ $\alpha\beta(1 - \beta)(1 - \gamma)^{n-1}\gamma$

6. $\text{Adj}^m + N + V_2 + \text{Adj}^n + N$ $\alpha\beta^2(1 - \gamma)^{m+n-2}\gamma^2$

On the hypothesis that this grammar is adequate for the corpus we are studying, each utterance will exemplify one of the grammatical types falling under the six schemes. The empirical relative frequency of each type in the corpus can be used to find a maximum-likelihood estimate of each of the three parameters. Let $x_1, \ldots, x_n$ be the finite sequence of actual utterances. The likelihood function $L(x_1, \ldots, x_n; \alpha, \beta, \gamma)$ is the function that has as its value the probability of obtaining or generating sequence $x_1, \ldots, x_n$ of utterances given parameters α, β, γ. The computation of L assumes the correctness of the probabilistic grammar, and this implies among other things the statistical independence of the grammatical type of utterances, an assumption that is violated in any actual corpus, but probably not too excessively. The maximum-likelihood estimates of α, β and γ are just those values $\hat{\alpha}, \hat{\beta}$ and $\hat{\gamma}$ that maximize the probability of the observed or generated sequence $x_1, \ldots, x_n$. Let y_1 be the number of occurrences of grammatical type 1, i.e., $PN + V_1$, as given in the above table, let y_2 be the number of occurrences of type 2, i.e., $PN + V_2 + PN$, let $y_{3,n}$ be the number of occurrences of type 3 with a string of n adjectives, and let similar definitions apply for $y_{4,n}, y_{5,n}$ and $y_{6,m,n}$. Then on the assumption of statistical independence, the likelihood function can be expressed as:

(1)
$$L(x_1, \ldots, x_n; \alpha, \beta, \gamma) = [(1 - \alpha)(1 - \beta)]^{y_1}\,[\alpha(1 - \beta)^2]^{y_2}$$
$$\prod_{n=1}^{\infty}[(1 - \alpha)\beta(1 - \gamma)^{n-1}\gamma]^{y_{3,n}} \cdots \prod_{n=1}^{\infty}\prod_{m=1}^{\infty}[\alpha\beta^2(1 - \gamma)^{m+n-2}\gamma^2]^{y_{6,m,n}}.$$

Of course, in any finite corpus the infinite products will always have only a finite number of terms not equal to one. To find $\hat{\alpha}, \hat{\beta}$ and $\hat{\gamma}$ as functions of the observed frequencies $y_1, \ldots, y_{6,m,n}$, the standard approach is to take the logarithm of both sides of (1), in order to convert products into sums, and then to take partial derivatives with respect to α, β and γ to find the values that maximize L. The maximum is not changed by taking the log of L, because log is a strictly monotonic increasing function. Letting

$\mathcal{L} = \log L$, $y_3 = \sum y_{3,n}$, $y_4 = \sum y_{4,n}$, $y_5 = \sum y_{5,n}$, and $y_6 = \sum \sum y_{6,m,n}$, we have

$$\frac{\partial \mathcal{L}}{\partial \alpha} = -\frac{y_1 + y_3}{1 - \alpha} + \frac{y_2 + y_4 + y_5 + y_6}{\alpha} = 0,$$

$$\frac{\partial \mathcal{L}}{\partial \beta} = -\frac{y_1}{1 - \beta} - \frac{2y_2}{1 - \beta} + \frac{y_3}{\beta} + \frac{y_4 + y_5}{\beta} - \frac{y_4 + y_5}{1 - \beta} + \frac{2y_6}{\beta} = 0$$

$$\frac{\partial \mathcal{L}}{\partial \gamma} = \frac{y_3 + y_4 + y_5 + y_6}{\gamma} - \left[\frac{y_{3,2} + y_{4,2} + y_{5,2}}{1 - \gamma} \right.$$
$$\left. + \cdots + \frac{(n-1)(y_{3,n} + y_{4,n} + y_{5,n})}{1 - \gamma} + \cdots \right]$$
$$- \left[\frac{y_{6,1,1}}{1 - \gamma} + \cdots + \frac{(m - n - 2) y_{6,m,n}}{1 - \gamma} + \cdots \right] = 0.$$

If we let

$$z_{6,n} = \sum_{m' + n' = n + 1} \sum y_{6,m',n'},$$

then after solving the above three equations we have as maximum-likelihood estimates:

$$\hat{\alpha} = \frac{y_2 + y_4 + y_5 + y_6}{y_1 + y_2 + y_3 + y_4 + y_5 + y_6}$$

$$\hat{\beta} = \frac{y_3 + y_4 + y_5 + 2y_6}{y_1 + 2y_2 + y_3 + 2y_4 + 2y_5 + 2y_6}$$

$$\hat{\gamma} = \frac{y_3 + y_4 + y_5 + z_6}{\sum n(y_{3,n} + y_{4,n} + y_{5,n} + z_{6,n})}.$$

As would be expected from the role of γ as a stopping parameter for the addition of adjectives, the maximum-likelihood estimate of γ is just the standard one for the mean of a geometrical distribution.

Having estimated α, β and γ from utterance frequency data, we can then test the goodness of fit of the probabilistic grammar in some standard statistical fashion, using a chi-square or some comparable statistical test. Some numerical results of such tests are reported later in the paper. The criterion for acceptance of the grammar is then just a standard statistical one. To say this is not to imply that standard statistical methods or criteria of testing are without their own conceptual problems. Rather the intention is to emphasize that the selection of a grammar can follow a standard scientific methodology of great power and wide applicability, and methodological arguments meant to be special to linguistics – like the discussions of simplicity – can be dispensed with.

III. GRAMMAR FOR ADAM I

Because of the relative syntactic simplicity and brevity of the spoken utterances of very young children, it is natural to begin attempts to write probabilistic grammars by examining such speech. This section presents some preliminary results for Adam I, a well-known corpus collected by Roger Brown and his associates at Harvard.[1] Adam was a young boy of about 26 months at the time the speech was recorded. The corpus analyzed by Arlene Moskowitz and me consists of eight hours of recordings extending over a period of some weeks. Our work has been based on the written transcript of the tapes made at Harvard. Accepting for the most part the word and utterance boundaries established in the Harvard transcript, we found that the corpus consists of 6109 word occurrences with a vocabulary of 673 different words and 3497 utterances.

Even though the mean utterance length of Adam I is somewhat less than 2.0, there are difficulties in writing a completely adequate probabilistic grammar for the full corpus. An example is considered below.

To provide, however, a sample of what can be done on a more restricted basis, and in a framework that is fairly close to the simple artificial example considered in the preceding section, I restrict my attention to the noun phrases of Adam I. Noun phrases dominate Adam I, if for no other reason than because the most common single utterance is the single noun. Of the 3497 utterances, we have classified 936 as single occurrences of nouns. Another 192 are occurrences of two nouns in sequence, 147 adjective followed by noun, and 138 adjectives alone. In a number of other cases, the whole utterance is a simple noun phrase preceded or followed by a one-word rejoinder, vocative or locative.

The following phrase-structure grammar was written for noun phrases of Adam I. The seven production rules are given below with the corresponding probabilities shown on the right. This particular probabilistic model has five free parameters; the sum of the a_i's is one, so the a_i's contribute four parameters to be fitted to the data, and in the case of the b_i's there is just one free parameter.

Production Rule	Probability
1. NP → N	a_1
2. NP → AdjP	a_2
3. NP → AdjP + N	a_3
4. NP → Pro	a_4
5. NP → NP + NP	a_5
6. AdjP → AdjP + Adj	b_1
7. AdjP → Adj	b_2

What is pleasing about these rules, and perhaps surprising, is that six of them are completely standard. (The one new symbol introduced here is Pro for pronoun; inflection of pronouns has been ignored in the present grammar.) The only slightly non-standard rule is Rule 5. The main application of this rule is in the production of the noun phrases consisting of a noun followed by a noun, with the first noun being an uninflected possessive modifying the second noun. Examples from the corpus are *Adam horn, Adam hat, Daddy racket* and *Doctordan circus.*

To give a better approximation to statistical independence in the occurrences of utterances, I deleted successive occurrences of the same noun phrase in the frequency count, and only first occurrences in a run of occurrences were considered in analyzing the data. The maximum-likelihood estimates of the parameters were obtained from the resulting 2434 occurrences of noun phrases in the corpus.

Estimated Parameter Values

$a_1 = .6391$	$b_1 = .0581$
$a_2 = .0529$	$b_2 = .9419$
$a_3 = .0497$	
$a_4 = .1439$	
$a_5 = .1144$	

On the basis of remarks already made, the high value of a_1 is not surprising because of the high frequency of occurrences of single nouns in the corpus. It should be noted that the value of a_1 is even higher than the relative frequency of single occurrences of nouns, because the noun-phrase grammar has been written to fit all noun phrases, including those occurring in full sentence context or in conjunction with verbs, etc. Thus in a count of single nouns as noun phrases every occurrence of a single noun as a noun phrase was counted, and as can be seen from Table I, there are 1445 such single nouns without immediate repetition. The high value of b_2 indicates that there are very few occurrences of successive adjectives, and therefore in almost all cases the adjective phrase was rewritten simply as an adjective (Rule 7).

Comparison of the theoretical frequencies of the probabilistic grammar with the observed frequencies is given in Table I.

TABLE I

Probabilistic Noun-Phrase Grammar for Adam I

Noun phrase	Observed frequency	Theoretical frequency
N	1445	1555.6
P	388	350 1
NN	231	113 7
AN	135	114 0
A	114	121.3
PN	31	25.6
NA	19	8.9
NNN	12	8.3
AA	10	7.1
NAN	8	8.3
AP	6	2.0
PPN	6	.4
ANN	5	8.3
AAN	4	6.6
PA	4	2.0
ANA	3	.7
APN	3	.1
AAA	2	.4
APA	2	.0
NPP	2	.4
PAA	2	.1
PAN	2	1.9

Some fairly transparent abbreviations are used in the table to reduce its size; as before, N stands for noun, A for adjective, and P for pronoun. From the standpoint of a statistical goodness-of-fit test, the chi-square is still enormous; its value is 309.4 and there are only seven net degrees of freedom. Thus by ordinary statistical standards we must reject the fit of the model, but at this stage of the investigation the qualitative comparison of the observed and theoretical frequencies is encouraging. The rank order of the theoretical frequencies for the more frequent types of noun phrases closely matches that of the observed frequencies. The only really serious discrepancy is in the case of the phrases consisting of two nouns, for which the theoretical frequency is substantially less than the observed frequency. It is possible that a different way of generating the possessives that dominate the occurrences of these two nouns in sequence would improve the prediction.

Summation of the observed and theoretical frequencies will show a discrepancy between the two columns. I explicitly note this. It is expected, because the column of theoretical frequencies should also include the classes that were not observed actually occurring in the corpus. The prediction of the sum of these unobserved classes is that they should have a frequency of 100.0, which is slightly less than 5% of the total observed frequency of 2434.

Note that the derivation of the probabilities for each grammatical type of noun phrase used the simplest derivation. For example, in the case of Adj + N, the theoretical probability was computed from successive application of Rule 3, followed by Rule 6, followed by Rule 7. It is also apparent that a quite different derivation of this noun phrase can be obtained by using Rule 5. Because of the rather special character of Rule 5, all derivations avoided Rule 5 when possible and only the simplest derivation was used in computing the probabilities. In other words, no account was taken of the ambiguity of the noun phrases. A more exact and sensitive analysis would require a more thorough investigation of this point. It is probable that there would be no substantial improvement in theoretical predictions in the present case, if these matters were taken account of. The reader may also have observed that the theoretical frequencies reflect certain symmetries in the predictions that do not exist in the observed frequencies. For example, the type Pro + Pro + N has an observed frequency of six, and the permutation N + Pro + Pro has an observed frequency of two. This discrepancy could easily be attributed to sampling. The symmetries imposed by the theoretical grammar generated from Rules 1 to 7 are considerable, but they do not introduce symmetries in any strongly disturbing way. Again let me emphasize that the symmetries that are somewhat questionable are almost entirely introduced by means of Rule 5. Finally, note that I have omitted from the list of noun phrases the occurrence of two pronouns in sequence because all cases consisted of the question *Who that?* or *What that?*, and it seemed inappropriate to classify these occurrences as single noun phrases. I hasten to add that remarks of a similar sort can be made about some of the other classifications. I plan on a subsequent occasion to re-analyze these data with a more careful attention to semantics and on that occasion will enter into a more refined classification of the noun phrases.

It is important for the reader to keep in mind the various qualifications that have been made here. I have no intention of conveying the impression that a definitive result has been obtained. I present the results of Table I as a preliminary indication of what can be achieved by the methods introduced in this paper. Appropriate qualifications and refinements will undoubtedly lead to better and more substantial findings.

Now to turn to the full corpus of Adam I. It is possible to write a phrase-structure grammar in the spirit of the partial grammar for noun phrases that we have just been examining. However, since approximately as good a fit has been obtained by using a categorial grammar and because such a grammar exhibits a variant of the methodology, I have chosen to discuss the best results I have yet been able to obtain in fitting a categorial grammar to the data of Adam I. I emphasize at the beginning that the results are not good. In view of the many difficulties that seem to stand in the way of improving them, I shall deal rather briefly with the quantitative results.

Some preliminary remarks about categorial grammars will perhaps be useful, because such grammars are probably not familiar to all readers. The basic ideas originated with the Polish logicians Lesniewski (1929) and Ajdukiewicz (1935). The original developments were aimed not at natural language, but at providing a method of parsing sentences in a formal language. From a formal standpoint there are things of great beauty about categorial grammars. For example, standard versions have at most two production rules. Letting α and β be any two categories, we generate an expression using the right-slant operation by the rule

$$\alpha \rightarrow \alpha/\beta, \beta,$$

and we generate an expression using the left-slant operation by the rule

$$\alpha \to \beta, \beta\backslash\alpha.$$

In addition, the grammars began with two primitive categories, s and n, standing respectively for sentence and noun. A simple sentence like *John walks* has the following analysis

$$\frac{John \quad walks}{n, \quad n\backslash s.}$$

Note that $n\backslash s$ is the derived category of intransitive verbs. The sentence

$$\frac{John \quad loves \quad Mary}{n \quad (n\backslash s)/n, \quad n}$$

has the analysis indicated. In this case the derived category of transitive verbs is $(n\backslash s)/n$. In a basic paper on categorial grammars, Bar-Hillel *et al.* (1960) showed that the power of categorial grammars is that of context-free grammars. In a number of papers that mention categorial grammars and describe some of their features, the kind of simple examples I have just described are often given, but as far as I know, there has been no large-scale effort to analyze an empirical corpus using such grammars. (For an extensive discussion see Marcus (1967).)

The direct application of standard categorial grammars to Adam I is practically impossible. For example, in the standard formulation the single axiom with which derivations begin is the primitive symbol s, and with this beginning there is no way of accounting for the dominant number of noun-phrase utterances in Adam I. I have reworked the ideas of categorial grammars to generate always from left to right, to have the possibility of incomplete utterances, and to begin derivations from other categories than those of sentencehood. From a formal standpoint, it is known from the paper of Bar-Hillel *et al.* (1960) that a single production rule will suffice, but the point here is to introduce not just a single left-right rewrite rule, but actually several rewrite rules in order to try to give a more exact account of the actual corpus of Adam I.

Although it is possible to write a categorial grammar in these terms for Adam I, my efforts to fit this grammar probabilistically to the frequencies of utterances have been notably unsuccessful. I have spent more time than I care to say in this endeavor. It has been for me an instructive lesson on the sharp contrast between writing a grammar for a corpus without regard for utterance frequencies and writing a probabilistic grammar. Because of the clear failure of the temporal categorial grammar to account for the probabilistic features of Adam I, I shall not enter into extensive details here.

The three left-right production rules were

1. $\beta \to \beta, \beta \backslash \alpha$,
2. $\alpha/\beta \to \alpha/\beta, \beta$,
3. $\alpha \to \alpha, \gamma_1, \ldots \gamma_n$,

provided $\alpha, \gamma_1, \ldots, \gamma_n$ cancels to α under the standard two rules given earlier. Each of these three rewrite rules is used with probability t_i, $i = 1, 2, 3$. Secondly, generalizing the classical single axiom s, any one of an additional 10 categories could begin a derivation; e.g., n (nouns), n/n (adjectives), l/n (locatives), r/n (rejoinders), $s \backslash s$ (adverbs), s/n (transitive verbs), and so forth. After the generation of each category, with probability σ the utterance terminated, and thus a geometrical distribution was imposed on utterance length. In the use of Rewrite Rule 1, the category α needed to be selected; the model restricted the choice to n, s or v (vocatives). Finally, two categories, the primitive *poss* for possessives and ϵ for the empty set, were replacements used in applying Rewrite Rule 3. The model just described was applied to the 22 types of utterances having a frequency of 20 or more in the corpus. The most important fact about the poor fit was that the theoretical frequencies were smaller than the observed frequencies in all 22 cases. Much of the theoretical probability was assigned to other utterance types, the effect being to spread the theoretical distribution more uniformly over a larger number of utterance types than was the case for the actual distribution.

To illustrate the situation, I cite the data for the three most frequent utterance types, giving first the observed and then the predicted frequency: $n = 626, 422.6$; s/n, $n = 206, 25.6$; $r = 168, 133.3$. Readers may properly ask why I should report this unsatisfactory temporal categorial grammar. Partly it is because of my own lingering affection for these grammars, but more, it is the simplicity of developmental sequence these grammars would offer if successful. With a uniform, fixed set of rewrite rules, only two things would change with the maturation of the child: the list of derived categories, and the values of probability parameters. But I currently see no hope of salvaging this approach.

Because it is natural to point a finger at the left-right feature of the rewrite rules, I should also mention that I tried fitting a grammar based on the two standard rewrite rules given earlier, one going to the left and one to the right, but also without any reasonable degree of success.

IV. GRAMMAR FOR A FIRST-GRADE READER

As the analysis of the preceding section shows it is not yet possible to give a fully satisfactory account of the grammatical aspects of Adam I. Preliminary indications for a larger corpus of more than twenty hours' recording of a 30-month-old girl are of a similar nature. We do not yet understand how to write a probabilistic grammar that will not have significant discrepancies between the grammatical model and the corpus of spoken speech.

Examining the results for Adam I early in 1969 and once again failing to make a significant improvement over the results obtained with Arlene Moskowitz in 1968, I asked myself in a pessimistic moment if there existed any actual corpus of spoken or written speech for which it would be possible to write a probabilistically adequate grammar. Perhaps the most natural place to look for simple and regular utterances is in a set of first-grade readers. Fortunately Elizabeth Gammon (1969) undertook the task of such an analysis as her dissertation topic. With her permission I use some of her data.

Readers who have not tried to write a generative grammar for some sample corpus may think that it sounds like a trivial task in view of the much talked about and often derided simplicity of first-grade readers. Far be it from the case. Gammon's grammar is far too complex to describe in detail here. Perhaps the most surprising general feature it reveals is that first-grade readers have a wider variety of grammatical forms than of vocabulary. Before she undertook the analysis we had expected a few stereotypic grammatical forms to dominate the corpus with the high frequency of their appearance. The facts were quite different. No form had a high frequency, and a better a priori hypothesis would have been that a large number of grammatical types of utterances were approximately uniformly distributed, although this assumption errs in the other direction.

To provide a good statistical test of the probabilistic ideas developed in this paper, the most practical move is to write grammars for parts of utterances rather than whole utterances, as has already been seen in the case of Adam I.

Using Gammon's empirical count for types of noun phrases in the Ginn Pre-Primer (1957), I have written in the spirit of Sections 2 and 3 two grammars for noun phrases. In the first one the number of parameters is 5. Four of the 7 rules are also used in the NP grammar for Adam I given above. The rule NP → Pro is dropped, but replaced by NP → PN, the rule NP → AdjP is dropped and replaced by the rule NP → N + Adj. This rule is of course derivable from the NP rules for Adam I; we just use Rule 5, then Rules 1, 2 and 7. The rule NP → NP + NP of Adam I is dropped, and a new rule to handle the use of definite articles (T) is introduced: AdjP → T. In summary form, the grammar G_1 is the following.

Noun-Phrase Grammar G_1 for Ginn Pre-Primer

Production Rule	Probability
1. NP → N	a_1
2. NP → AdjP + N	a_2
3. NP → PN	a_3
4. NP → N + Adj	a_4
5. AdjP → AdjP + Adj	b_1
6. AdjP → Adj	b_2
7. AdjP → T	b_3

Using the 528 phrases classified as noun-phrases in Dr. Gammon's grammar, we obtain the following maximum-likelihood estimates of the parameters of G_1.

$$a_1 = .1383 \qquad b_1 = .2868$$
$$a_2 = .3674 \qquad b_2 = .0662$$
$$a_3 = .4697 \qquad b_3 = .6471$$
$$a_4 = .0246$$

From these estimated values of the parameters, we may compute the theoretical frequencies of all the types of noun-phrases actually occurring in the corpus. The Grammar G_1 generates an infinite number of types, but of course, almost all of them have very small theoretical frequencies. Observed and theoretical frequencies are given in Table II.

TABLE II

Prediction of Grammars G_1 and G_2 for Ginn Pre-primer

Noun phrase	Observed[a] frequency	Theoretical frequency of G_1	Theoretical frequency of G_2
PN	248	248.0	248.0
T + N	120	125.5	129.5
N	73	73.0	66.9
T + Adj + N	42	36.0	34.2
T + Adj + Adj + N	14	10.3	9.1
N + Adj	13	13.0	13.0
Adj + N	10	12.8	17.7
Adj + Adj + N	8	3.7	4.7
	528		

[a] Data from dissertation of Dr. Elizabeth Gammon.

It is apparent at once that Grammar G_1 fits the Ginn data a good deal better than the grammar for Adam I fits Adam's data. The chi-square of 3.4 reflects this fact. Let me be explicit about the chi-square computation. The contribution of each type is simply the square of the difference of the observed and theoretical frequencies divided by the theoretical frequency. Except that when a theoretical frequency is less than 5, frequencies of more than one type are combined.[2] In the case of G_1, the theoretical frequency 3.7 for Adj + Adj + N was combined with the residual of 5.6, the sum theoretically assigned by G_1 to all other types of noun phrases generated by G_1 different from those listed in Table II. This means the chi-square was computed for an aggregate of 8 cells, 5 parameters were estimated from the data, and so there remained 2 net degrees of freedom. The chi-square value of 3.4 is not significant at the .10 level, to use the ordinary statistical idiom, and so we may conclude that we have no reason for rejecting G_1 at the level of grammatical detail it offers. A closer examination of the way the parameters operate does reveal the following. Parameter a_3 is estimated so as to exactly fit the frequency of noun phrases that are proper nouns (PN), and parameter a_4 so as to exactly fit the frequency of the type N + Adj. Each of these parameters uses up a degree of freedom, and so there is not an interesting test of fit for them. The interest centers around the other types, and this may well be taken as a criticism of G_1. Further structural assumptions are needed that reduce the number of parameters, and especially that interlock in a deeper way the probabilities of using the different production rules. In spite of the relatively good fit of G_1, it should be regarded as only a beginning.

It is a familiar fact that two grammars that have different production rules can generate the same language, i.e., the same set of terminal strings. It should also be clear that as probabilistic grammars they need not be equivalent, i.e., they need not make the same theoretical predictions about frequencies of occurrences of utterance-types. These matters may be illustrated by considering a second grammar G_2 for the noun phrases of the Ginn Pre-Primer.

Noun-Phrase Grammar G_2 for Ginn Pre-Primer

Production Rule	Probability
1. NP → AdjP + N	a_1
2. NP → PN	a_2
3. NP → N + Adj	a_3
4. AdjP → AdjP + Adj	b_1
5. AdjP → T	b_2
6. AdjP → $\in$	b_3

In the sixth production rule of G_2 the symbol $\in$ is used, as earlier, for the empty symbol.

The theoretical predictions of G_2 are given in Table II. It is apparent that as probabilistic grammars G_1 and G_2 are not equivalent, since the fit of G_1 is slightly better than that of G_2. Note, however, that G_2 estimates 4 rather than 5 parameters from the data.

The examples given should make clear how a probabilistic criterion can be imposed as an additional objective or behavioral constraint on the acceptability of a grammar. In a subsequent paper I intend to show how the probabilistic viewpoint developed here may be combined with a model-theoretic generative semantics. In this more complex setup the semantic base of an utterance affects the probability of its occurrence and requires a formal extension of the ideas set forth here.

V. REPRESENTATION PROBLEM FOR PROBABILISTIC LANGUAGES

From what has already been said it should be clear enough that the imposition of a probabilistic generative structure is an additional constraint on a grammar. It is natural to ask if a probabilistic grammar can always be found for a language known merely to have a grammar. Put in this intuitive fashion, it is not clear exactly what question is being asked.

As a preliminary to a precise formulation of the question, an explicit formal characterization of probabilistic grammars is needed. In a fashion familiar from the literature we may define a grammar as a quadruple (V_N, V_T, R, S), where V_N, V_T and R are finite sets, S is a member of V_N, V_N and V_T are disjoint, and R is a set of ordered pairs, whose first members are in V^+, and whose second members are in V^*, where $V = V_N \cup V_T$, V^* is the set of all finite sequences whose terms are elements of V, and V^+ is V^* minus the empty sequence. As usual, it is intended that V_N be the non-terminal and V_T the terminal vocabulary, R the set of productions and S the start symbol. The language L generated by G is defined in the standard manner and will be omitted here.

In the sense of the earlier sections of this paper, a probabilistic grammar is obtained by adding a conditional probability distribution on the set R of productions. Formally we have:

DEFINITION: *A quintuple* $G = (V_N, V_T, R, S, p)$ *is a probabilistic grammar if and only if* $G = (V_N, V_T, R, S)$ *is a grammar, and p is a real-valued function defined on R such that*

(i)   *for each* (σ_i, σ_j) *in* R, $p(\sigma_i, \sigma_j) \geqslant 0$,

(ii)   *for each* σ_i *in the domain of* R

$$\sum_{\sigma_j} p(\sigma_i, \sigma_j) = 1,$$

where the summation is over the range of R.

Various generalizations of this definition are easily given; for example, it is natural in some contexts to replace the fixed start symbol S by a probability distribution over V_N. But such generalizations will not really affect the essential character of the representation problem as formulated here.

For explicitness, we also need the concept of a probabilistic language, which is just a pair (L, p), where L is a language and p is a probability density defined on L, i.e., for each x in L, $p(x) \geqslant 0$ and

$$\sum_{x \in L} p(x) = 1.$$

The first formulation of the representation problem is then this.

Let L *be a language of type* i $(i = 0, 1, 2, 3)$, *with probability density p. Does there always exist a probabilistic grammar* G *(of type* i*) that generates* (L, p)*?*

What is meant by generation is apparent. If $x \in L$, $p(x)$ must be the sum of the probabilities of all the derivations of x in G. Ellis (1969) answered this formulation of the representation problem in the negative for type 2 and type 3 grammars. His example is easy to describe. Let $V_T = \{a\}$, and let $L = \{a^n \mid n \geqslant 1\}$. Let $p(a^{n+1}) = 1/\sqrt{t_n}$, $n > 0$, where $t_1 = 4$, and t_i = smallest prime such that $t_i > \max(t_{i-1}, 2^{2^i})$ for $i > 1$. In addition, set

$$p(a) = 1 - \sum_{n=1}^{\infty} p(a^{n+1}).$$

The argument depends upon showing that the probabilities assigned to the strings of L by the above characterization cannot all lie in the extensions of the field of rational numbers generated by the finite set of conditional probabilities attached to the finite set of production rules of any context-free grammar.

From the empirically-oriented standpoint of this paper, Ellis' example, while perfectly correct mathematically, is conceptually unsatisfactory, because any finite sample of L drawn according to the density p could be described also by a density taking only rational values. Put another way, algebraic examples of Ellis' sort do not settle the representation problem when it is given a clearly statistical formulation. Here is one such formulation. (As a matter of notation, if p is a density on L, p_s is the sample density of a finite random sample drawn from (L, p).)

Let L *be a language of type* i *with probability density p. Does there always exist a probabilistic grammar* G *(of type* i*) that generates a density* p' *on* L *such that for every sample s of* L *of size less than N and with density* p_s *the null hypothesis that s is drawn from* (L, p') *would not be rejected?*

I have deliberately imposed a limit N on the size of the sample in order directly to block asymptotic arguments that yield negative results. In referring to the null hypothesis' not being rejected I have in mind using some standard test such as Kolmogorov's and some standard level of significance. The details on this point do not matter here, although a precise solution must be explicit on these matters and also on problems of repeated sampling, fixing the power of the test, etc. My own conjecture is that the statistical formulation of the problem has an affirmative solution for every N, but the positive solutions will often not be conceptually interesting.

A final remark about the density p on L is perhaps needed. Some may be concerned about the single occurrence of many individual utterances even in a large corpus. The entire discussion of the representation problem is easily shifted to the category descriptions of terminal strings as exemplified in earlier sections of this paper, and at this level, certainly many grammatical types occur repeatedly.[3]

Stanford University

BIBLIOGRAPHY

Ajdukiewicz, K., 'Die syntaktische Konnexität', *Studia Philosophica* 1 (1935) 1–27.
Bar-Hillel, Y., Gaifman, C., and Shamir, E., 'On Categorial and Phrase Structure Grammars', *Bulletin of the Research Council of Israel, Section F* 9 (1960) 1–16.
Ellis, C., *Probabilistic Languages and Automata*, Doctoral Dissertation, University of Illinois at Urbana-Champaign, 1969.
Gammon, E., *A Syntactical Analysis of Some First-Grade Readers*, Doctoral Dissertation, Stanford University, 1969.
Harwood, F. W., 'Quantitative Study of the Speech of Australian Children', *Language and Speech* 2 (1959) 236–271.
Lesniewski, S., 'Grundzüge eines neuen Systems der Grundlagen der Mathematik', *Polska Akademia Nauk, Fundamenta Mathematicae* 14 (1929) 1–81.
Marcus, S., *Algebraic Linguistics: Analytical Models*, Academic Press, New York, 1967.
Russell, D. and Ousley, O., *The Pre-Primer Program: My Little Red Story Book, My Little Green Story Book, My Little Blue Story Book*, Ginn, Boston, 1957.
Suppes, P., 'A Probabilistic Theory of Causality', *Acta Philosophica Fennica* 24 (1970), North-Holland Publishing Company, Amsterdam.

REFERENCES

* This research has been supported in part by the National Science Foundation under Grant NSFGJ-443X.
[1] Roger Brown has generously made the transcribed records available and given us permission to publish any of our analyses.
[2] The number 5 is not sacred; it provides a good practical rule. When the theoretical frequency is too small, e.g., 1, 2 or 3, the assumptions on which the goodness-of-fit test is based are rather badly violated.
[3] W. C. Watt has called my attention to an article by Harwood (1959), which reports some frequency data for the speech of Australian children, but no probabilistic grammar or other sort of model is proposed or tested. As far as I know, the explicit statistical test of probabilistic grammars, including estimation of parameters, has not been reported prior to the present paper, but given the scattered character of the possibly relevant literature I could just be ignorant of important predecessors to my own work.

ADDENDA TO SAUL A. KRIPKE'S PAPER
'NAMING AND NECESSITY'

(This volume, pp. 253–355)

These addenda represent certain amplifications of the original text which I have added either in response to questions or for the sake of clarification or sketchy amplification.

(a) *Unicorns*, p. 253. In the light of the remarks on natural kinds made in the third lecture, I shall try to give a brief explanation of the strange view of unicorns advocated in the text. There were two theses: first, a *metaphysical* thesis that no counterfactual situation is properly describable as one in which there would have been unicorns; second, an *epistemological* thesis that an archeological discovery that there were animals with all the features attributed to unicorns in the appropriate myth would not in and of itself constitute proof that there were unicorns.

As to the metaphysical thesis, the argument basically is the following. Just as tigers are an actual species, so the unicorns are a mythical species. Now tigers, as I argue in the third lecture, cannot be defined simply in terms of their appearance; it is possible that there should have been a different species with all the external appearances of tigers but which had a different internal structure and therefore was not the species of tigers. We may be misled into thinking otherwise by the fact that actually no such 'fools' tigers' exist, so that in practice external appearance is sufficient to identify the species. Now there is no actual species of unicorns, and regarding the several distinct species, with different internal structures (some reptilic, some mammalian, some amphibious), which would have the external appearances postulated to hold of unicorns in the myth of the unicorn, one cannot say which of these distinct mythical species would have *been* the unicorns. If we suppose, as I do, that the unicorns of the myth were supposed to be a particular species, but that the myth provides insufficient information about their internal structure to determine a unique species, then there is no actual or possible species of which we can say that it would have been the species of unicorns.

The epistemological thesis is more easily argued. If a story is found describing a substance with the physical appearance of gold, one cannot conclude on this basis that it is talking about gold; it may be talking about 'fools' gold'. What substance is being discussed must be determined as in the case of proper names: by the historical connection of the story with a certain substance. When the connection is traced, it may well turn out that the substance dealt with was gold, 'fools' gold', or something else. Similarly, the mere discovery of animals with the properties attributed to unicorns in the myth would by no means show that these were the animals the myth was about: perhaps the myth was spun out of whole cloth, and the fact that animals with the same appearance actually existed was mere coincidence. In that case, we cannot say that the unicorns of the myth really existed; we must also establish a historical connection that shows that the myth is *about* these animals.

I hold similar views regarding fictional proper names. The mere discovery that there was indeed a detective with exploits like those of Sherlock Holmes would not show that Conan Doyle was writing *about* this man; it is theoretically possible, though in practice fantastically unlikely, that Doyle was writing pure fiction with only a coincidental resemblance to the actual man. (See the characteristic disclaimer: "The characters in this work are fictional, and any resemblance to anyone, living or dead, is purely coincidental.") Similarly, I hold the metaphysical view that, granted that there is no Sherlock Holmes, one cannot say of any possible person that he *would have been* Sherlock Holmes, had he existed. Several distinct possible people, and even actual ones such as Darwin or Jack the Ripper, might have performed the exploits of Holmes, but there is none of whom we can say that he would have *been* Holmes had he performed these exploits. For if so, which one?

I thus could no longer write, as I once did, that "Holmes does not exist, but in other states of affairs, he would have existed." (See my 'Semantical Considerations on Modal Logic', *Acta Philosophica Fennica*, Vol. **16** (1963) pp. 83–94; reprinted in L. Linsky (ed.), *Reference and Modality*, Oxford University Press, (1971); p. 65 in the Linsky reprint.) The quoted assertion gives the erroneous impression that a fictional name such as 'Holmes' names a particular possible-but-not-actual individual. The substantive point I was trying to make, however, remains and is independent of any linguistic theory of the status of names in fiction.

The point was that, in other possible worlds "some actually existing individuals may be absent while new individuals... may appear" (*ibid*, p. 65), and that if in an open formula *A* (*x*) the free variable is assigned a given individual as value, a problem arises as to whether (in a model-theoretic treatment of modal logic) a truth-value is to be assigned to the formula in worlds in which the individual in question does not exist.

I am aware that the cryptic brevity of these remarks diminishes whatever persuasiveness they may otherwise possess. I expect to elaborate on them elsewhere, in a forthcoming work discussing the problems of existential statements, empty names, and fictional entities.

(b) *Can to must*, in the last paragraph of p. 260 continuing on 261. An unpublished paper by Barry T. Stroud has called my attention to the fact that Kant himself makes a closely related mistake. Kant says, "Experience teaches us that a thing is so and so, but not that it cannot be otherwise. First, then, if we have a proposition which in being thought is thought as *necessary*, it is an *a priori* judgement. ... Necessity and strict universality are thus sure criteria of *a priori* knowledge". (*Critique of Pure Reason* B3-4, pp. 43–44 in the Kemp Smith translation, Macmillan, 1956.) Kant thus appears to hold that if a proposition is known to be *necessary*, the mode of knowledge not only *can* be *a priori* but *must* be. On the contrary one can learn a mathematical truth *a posteriori* by consulting a computing machine, or even by asking a mathematician. Nor can Kant argue that experience can tell us that a mathematical proposition is *true*, but not that it is *necessary*; for the peculiar character of mathematical propositions (like Goldbach's conjecture) is that one knows (*a priori*) that they cannot be contingently true; a mathematical statement, if true, is necessary.

All the cases of the necessary *a posteriori* advocated in the text have the special character attributed to mathematical statements: Philosophical analysis tells us that they cannot be contingently true, so any empirical knowledge of their truth is automatically empirical knowledge that they are necessary. This characterization applies, in particular to the cases of identity statements and of essence. It *may* give a clue to a general characterization of *a posteriori* knowledge of necessary truths.

I should mention that if the possibility of knowing a mathematical truth by consulting a computer the only objection to Kant offered, it would still be open to him to hold: (1) that every necessary truth is knowable *a priori*; or, more weakly, (2) that every necessary truth, if known at all, must be knowable *a priori*. Both (1) and (2) involve the obscure notion of the *possibility* of *a priori* knowledge, but to the extent that the notion is clarified by restricting it to *a priori* knowledge of a standard human sort, I argue against both (1) and (2) in the text. In fact 1, of course, hold that propositions that contemporary philosophers would properly count as 'empirical' can be necessary and be known to be such.

Perhaps I should mention also that I have been unable to find the characterization of *a priori* truth, as truth which *can* be known independently of experience, in Kant; as far as I can see, Kant refers only to *a priori* knowledge of particular statements, which does not involve the extra modality. (In the text, I incautiously ascribed this common characterization of *a priori* truth to Kant.) And, of course, when Kant uses 'necessary' for a type of proposition and 'a priori' for a mode of knowledge, he cannot possibly be guilty of the common contemporary practice of treating the two terms as interchangeable synonyms. It is clear from the opening pages of the *Critique* that he regards the thesis that knowledge that something is necessary must be *a priori* knowledge as an important, though obvious, substantive thesis.

(c) Some remarks that I have heard lead me to suppose that the noncircularity condition could use further clarification. First, my remark on p. 283 has been misunderstood to say that a definition such as 'Jonah is the man referred to by that name in the Bible' violates the noncircularity condition. It does not, provided that the description theory can give an account of the Biblical authors' reference which is independent of our own. When I discuss Strawson I explicitly acknowledge that a speaker may use a description of this sort which 'passes the buck' and the procedure is noncircular provided that the other speaker's description does not ultimately involve the references made by the original speaker. Thus I can say, 'Let 'Glumph' be a name of the thing Jones calls 'Glumph'', provided that Jones does not simultaneously say, 'Let 'Glumph', be a name of the thing Kripke calls 'Glumph'.' The objection to such noncircular determinations of reference as 'Let 'Glumph' be the man Jones calls 'Glumph'' and, 'Let Gödel be the man to whom the experts attribute the incompleteness theorem' (said by a layman) is otherwise: In general, a speaker cannot be sure from whom he picked up his reference; and as far as he knows 'the experts' may well realize that Schmidt, not Gödel, proved the incompleteness theorem even though the inexpert speaker still attributes it to Gödel. Thus such determinations of the referent may well give the wrong result, and the speaker surely cannot be said to know *a priori* (as in Thesis 5) that they do not. (See my criticisms of Strawson in the text.) If, on the other hand, the speaker attempts to avoid the possibility of such error by using his *own* reference as the paradigm, as in such determinations as 'Let Glumph be the man *I* call 'Glumph' (now)' or 'Let Gödel be the man I believe to have proved the incompleteness theorem,' the determination of the reference *is* circular (unless the speaker has already determined his reference in some other way, in which case that is the determining condition and not the one stated). Often the determination of the reference risks falling afoul both of circularity *and* of vulnerability to error, for the speaker may not know whether those others to whom he 'passes the buck' may not in turn pass the buck to him. Blatant cases of vulnerability to both types of criticisms is to be found in such determinations as, 'Let 'Glumph' denote the man all of us in Community *C* call 'Glumph',' or 'Let 'Gödel' presently generally believed in Community *C* to have proved the incompleteness theorem,' if this determination is supposed to be the one used throughout Community *C*. For an individual speaker may err in such a determination if the Community in general has been apprised of the Gödel-Schmidt fraud but the speaker has not; and even if the possibility of error is waived, the determination will be circular if it supposed that all, or even the large majority, of the speakers of Community *C* use it to determine their reference.

All these points are stated in the text, but misunderstandings have led me to believe that a summary restatement could conceivably do some good. Quite a different way of determining the reference would be, 'Let 'Glumph' denote the man called 'Glumph' by the people from whom I got it (whoever they are), provided that my present determination of the reference satisfies the conditions sketched in 'Naming and Necessity' and whatever other conditions need be satisfied'. As I said in footnote 38, such a determination would constitute a trivial fulfillment of the description theory in terms of the present view if only the present view were not somewhat loose and did not already involve the notion of the speaker's own reference (in terms of his intention to agree in reference with those from whom he picked up the name). Even if both these problems were surmounted, the resulting description would hardly be one of the type which occurs to a speaker when he is asked such a question as, 'Who is Napoleon?', as the description theorists intended. It would occur only to those speakers who have mastered a complex theory of reference, and it would be this theory, of course, and not the speaker's knowledge of a description, which gave the true picture of how the reference was dermined.

(d) *Initial baptism*, p. 302. In footnote 70 on natural kind terms, I mention that the notion of an initial sample appealed to there gives an oversimplified picture of the case. Analogously for proper names, I of course recognize that there need not always be an identifiable initial baptism; so the picture is oversimplified. I of course also think, analogously to footnote 70, that such complications will not radically alter the picture. It is probably true, however, that in the case of proper names, examples with no identifiable initial baptism are rarer than in the species case.

(e) *Santa Claus*, p. 300 and p. 302. Gareth Evans has pointed out that similar cases of reference shifts arise where the shift is not from a real entity to a fictional one, but from one real entity to another of the same kind. According to Evans, 'Madagascar' was a native name for a part of Africa; Marco Polo, erroneously thinking that he was following native usage, applied the name to an island. (Evans uses the example to support the description theory; I, of course, do not.) Today the usage of the name as a name for an island has become so widespread that it surely overrides any historical connection with the native name. David Lewis has pointed out that the same thing could have happened even if the natives had used 'Madagascar' to designate a mythical locality. So real reference can shift to another real reference, fictional reference can shift to real, and real to fictional. In all these cases, a present intention to refer to a given entity (or to refer fictionally) overrides the original intention to preserve reference in the historical chain of transmission. The matter deserves extended discussion. But the phenomenon is perhaps roughly explicable in terms of the predominantly social character of the use of proper names emphasized in the text; we use names to communicate with other speakers in a common language. This character dictates ordinarily that a speaker intend to use a name the same way as it was transmitted to him; but in the 'Madagascar' case this social character dictates that the present intention to refer to an island overrides the distant link to native usage. (Probably Miller's case, 'George Smith' vs. 'Newton' is similarly explicable.) To state all this with any precision undoubtedly requires more apparatus than I have developed here; in particular, we must distinguish a present intention to use a name for an object from a mere present belief that the object is the only one having a certain property, and clarify this distinction. I leave the problem for further work.

(f) I perhaps should mention (amplifying footnote 2) that the historical acquisition picture of naming advocated here is apparently very similar to views of Keith Donnellan. (Charles Chastain also made similar suggestions, but they had a greater admixture of the old description theory.) David Kaplan's investigation of 'Dthat', mentioned in footnote 22, has been extended to a 'logic of demonstratives' in which, he says, a good deal of the argument of this paper can be given a formal representation. Indeed a good deal of this paper suggests a certain formal apparatus, though the present presentation is informal.

(g) The third lecture suggests that a good deal of what contemporary philosophy regards as mere physical necessity is actually necessary *tout court*. The question how far this can be pushed is one I leave for further work.

SYNTHESE LIBRARY

Monographs on Epistemology, Logic, Methodology,
Philosophy of Science, Sociology of Science and of Knowledge, and on the
Mathematical Methods of Social and Behavioral Sciences

Editors:

DONALD DAVIDSON (Rockefeller University and Princeton University)
JAAKKO HINTIKKA (Academy of Finland and Stanford University)
GABRIËL NUCHELMANS (University of Leyden)
WESLEY C. SALMON (Indiana University)

‡STEPHEN TOULMIN and HARRY WOOLF (eds.), *Norwood Russell Hanson: What I Do Not Believe, and Other Essays.* 1971, XII + 390 pp. Dfl. 90,—

‡YEHOSHUA BAR-HILLEL (ed.), *Pragmatics of Natural Languages.* 1971, VII + 231 pp. Dfl. 50,—

‡ROBERT S. COHEN and MARX W. WARTOFSKY (eds.), *Boston Studies in the Philosophy of Science.* Vol. VII: Milič Čapek: *Bergson and Modern Physics.* 1971, XV + 414 pp. Dfl. 70,—.

‡CARL R. KORDIG, *The Justification of Scientific Change.* 1971, XIV + 119 pp. Dfl. 33,—

‡JOSEPH D. SNEED, *The Logical Structure of Mathematical Physics.* 1971, XV + 311 pp. Dfl. 70,—

‡JEAN-LOUIS KRIVINE, *Introduction to Axiomatic Set Theory.* 1971, VII + 98 pp. Dfl. 28,—

‡RISTO HILPINEN (ed.), *Deontic Logic: Introductory and Systematic Readings.* 1971, VII + 182 pp. Dfl. 45,—

‡EVERT W. BETH, *Aspects of Modern Logic.* 1970, XI + 176 pp. Dfl. 42,—

‡PAUL WEINGARTNER and GERHARD ZECHA (eds.), *Induction, Physics, and Ethics. Proceedings and Discussions of the 1968 Salzburg Colloquium in the Philosophy of Science.* 1970, X + 382 pp. Dfl. 65,—

‡ROLF A. EBERLE, *Nominalistic Systems.* 1970, IX + 217 pp. Dfl. 42,—

‡JAAKKO HINTIKKA and PATRICK SUPPES, *Information and Inference.* 1970, X + 336 pp. Dfl. 60,—

‡KAREL LAMBERT, *Philosophical Problems in Logic. Some Recent Developments.* 1970, VII + 176 pp. Dfl. 38,—

‡P. V. TAVANEC (ed.), *Problems of the Logic of Scientific Knowledge.* 1969, XII + 429 pp. Dfl. 95,—

‡ROBERT S. COHEN and RAYMOND J. SEEGER (eds.), *Boston Studies in the Philosophy of Science.* Volume VI: *Ernst Mach: Physicist and Philosopher.* 1970, VIII + 295 pp. Dfl. 38,—

‡Marshall Swain (ed.), *Induction, Acceptance, and Rational Belief.* 1970, VII + 232 pp.
Dfl. 40,—

‡Nicholas Rescher et al. (eds.), *Essays in Honor of Carl G. Hempel. A Tribute on the Occasion of his Sixty-Fifth Birthday.* 1969, VII + 272 pp.   Dfl. 50,—

‡Patrick Suppes, *Studies in the Methodology and Foundations of Science. Selected Papers from 1951 to 1969.* 1969, XII + 473 pp.   Dfl. 72,—

‡Jaakko Hintikka, *Models for Modalities. Selected Essays.* 1969, IX + 220 pp.
Dfl. 34,—

‡D. Davidson and J. Hintikka (eds.), *Words and Objections: Essays on the Work of W. V. Quine.* 1969, VIII + 366 pp.   Dfl. 48,—

‡J. W. Davis, D. J. Hockney and W. K. Wilson (eds.), *Philosophical Logic.* 1969, VIII + 277 pp.   Dfl. 45,—

‡Robert S. Cohen and Marx W. Wartofsky (eds.), *Boston Studies in the Philosophy of Science.* Volume V: *Proceedings of the Boston Colloquium for the Philosophy of Science 1966/1968.* 1969, VIII + 482 pp.   Dfl. 60,—

‡Robert S. Cohen and Marx W. Wartofsky (eds.), *Boston Studies in the Philosophy of Science.* Volume IV: *Proceedings of the Boston Colloquium for the Philosophy of Science 1966/1968.* 1969, VIII + 537 pp.   Dfl. 72,—

‡Nicholas Rescher, *Topics in Philosophical Logic.* 1968, XIV + 347 pp.   Dfl. 70,—

‡Günther Patzig, *Aristotle's Theory of the Syllogism. A Logical-Philological Study of Book A of the Prior Analytics.* 1968, XVII + 215 pp.   Dfl. 48,—

‡C. D. Broad, *Induction, Probability, and Causation. Selected Papers.* 1968, XI + 296 pp.
Dfl. 54,—

‡Robert S. Cohen and Marx W. Wartofsky (eds.), *Boston Studies in the Philosophy of Science.* Volume III: *Proceedings of the Boston Colloquium for the Philosophy of Science 1964/1966.* 1967, XLIX + 489 pp.   Dfl. 70,—

‡Guido Küng, *Ontology and the Logistic Analysis of Language. An Enquiry into the Contemporary Views on Universals.* 1967, XI + 210 pp.   Dfl. 41,—

*Evert W. Beth and Jean Piaget, *Mathematical Epistemology and Psychology.* 1966, XXII + 326 pp.   Dfl. 63,—

*Evert W. Beth, *Mathematical Thought. An Introduction to the Philosophy of Mathematics.* 1965, XII + 208 pp.   Dfl. 37,—

‡Paul Lorenzen, *Formal Logic.* 1965, VIII + 123 pp.   Dfl. 26,—

‡Georges Gurvitch, *The Spectrum of Social Time.* 1964, XXVI + 152 pp.   Dfl. 25,—

‡A. A. Zinov'ev, *Philosophical Problems of Many-Valued Logic.* 1963, XIV + 155 pp.
Dfl. 32,—

‡Marx W. Wartofsky (ed.), *Boston Studies in the Philosophy of Science.* Volume I: *Proceedings of the Boston Colloquium for the Philosophy of Science, 1961–1962.* 1963, VIII + 212 pp.   Dfl. 26,50

‡B. H. Kazemier and D. Vuysje (eds.), *Logic and Language. Studies dedicated to Professor Rudolf Carnap on the Occasion of his Seventieth Birthday.* 1962, VI + 256 pp.
Dfl. 35,—

*Evert W. Beth, *Formal Methods. An Introduction to Symbolic Logic and to the Study of Effective Operations in Arithmetic and Logic.* 1962, XIV + 170 pp.   Dfl. 35,—

*HANS FREUDENTHAL (ed.), *The Concept and the Role of the Model in Mathematics and Natural and Social Sciences. Proceedings of a Colloquium held at Utrecht, The Netherlands, January 1960.* 1961, VI + 194 pp.   Dfl. 34,—

‡P. L. R. GUIRAUD, *Problèmes et méthodes de la statistique linguistique.* 1960, VI + 146 pp.   Dfl. 28,—

*J. M. BOCHEŃSKI, *A Precis of Mathematical Logic.* 1959, X + 100 pp.   Dfl. 23,—

SYNTHESE HISTORICAL LIBRARY

Texts and Studies
in the History of Logic and Philosophy

Editors:

N. KRETZMANN (Cornell University)
G. NUCHELMANS (University of Leyden)
L. M. DE RIJK (University of Leyden)

‡KARL WOLF and PAUL WEINGARTNER (eds.), *Ernst Mally: Logische Schriften.* 1971, X + 340 pp.   Dfl. 80,—

‡LEROY E. LOEMKER (eds.), *Gottfried Wilhelm Leibnitz: Philosophical Papers and Letters.* A Selection Translated and Edited, with an Introduction. 1969, XII + 736 pp.
                                                                                                                    Dfl. 125,—

‡M. T. BEONIO-BROCCHIERI FUMAGALLI, *The Logic of Abelard.* Translated from the Italian. 1069, IX + 101 pp.   Dfl. 27,—